Training International Managers

Training International Managers

Designing, Deploying and Delivering Effective Training for Multi-Cultural Groups

ALAN MELKMAN and JOHN TROTMAN

GOWER

Published by
Gower Publishing Limited
Gower House
Croft Road
Aldershot
Hants GU11 3HR
England

Gower Publishing Company
Suite 420
101 Cherry Street
Burlington,
VT 05401-4405
USA

British Library Cataloguing in Publication Data
Melkman, Alan
Training international managers: designing, deploying and delivering effective training for multi-cultural groups
1. Executive – training of 2. International business enterprises – Employees – Training of 3. Multiculturalism
I. Title II. Trotman, John
658.4'071245

ISBN 0 566 08630 1

Library of Congress Cataloging-in-Publication Data
Melkman, Alan.
Training international managers: designing, deploying and delivering effective training for multi-cultural groups / by Alan Melkman and John Trotman.
p. cm.
Includes index.
ISBN 0-566-08630-1
1. Executives--training of. 2. International business enterprises--Employees--Training. 3. International business enterprises--Cross-cultural studies. 4. Multiculturalism--Study and teaching. 5. Multicultural education. I. Trotman, John. II.Title.
HD30.4.M45 2005
658.4'07124--dc22

2004029104

Typeset by Bournemouth Colour Press, Parkstone, Poole.
Printed in Great Britain by MPG Books Ltd, Bodmin.

Contents

List of Figures

List of Tables

Preface

The authors developed the idea for this book in order for others involved in designing, deploying, delivering or studying the training of international managers to capture the experience they have gained during more than 20 years of training multi-cultural groups. The principal purpose of the book is to help those involved and interested in this field to see how to maximize the value from training interventions which are aimed at helping international managers become more effective.

The points made in the book are illustrated by examples taken from training courses which the authors have designed, developed, deployed and delivered in all parts of Europe, the Far East, the Middle East, and America.

During the last ten years the authors have jointly developed a methodology for the training and learning process called SUCCESS. It provides a thorough approach to the whole process of training, and has been used in the book as a structure for training international managers from the first indication that there might be a training need, through the design, development, deployment, delivery and evaluation of the training, to the steps that can be taken to maximize transfer of learning to the workplace and the achievement of effective behaviours and results. This methodology is described in detail, with examples of how it will work, including a series of usable tools and models. The third and final part of the book, in particular, is rich in examples of how to make training events come alive in terms of how trainers need to behave to be truly effective in training multi-cultural groups.

The book makes reference to important work in the area of cultural understanding and learning that has been published in the last 30 years and how each part of that work relates to the principles developed in the SUCCESS process.

The key focus in writing the book has been to help students appreciate what needs to be done to deliver effective learning and to provide training and learning practitioners with practical guidance on how to make training and learning really effective in the context of multi-cultural groups.

The authors recognize that this is a dynamic field in which practitioners are developing new approaches every day. They are interested in having a dialogue with those involved in the field of training and learning, and welcome contact either through the Gower website at www.gowerpub.com or direct by e-mail to either of the addresses given on the author pages at the end of the book.

Alan Melkman and John Trotman
2005

Acknowledgements

We would like to thank our wives Sue and Bridget for all their patience and help with the preparation of this book.

Discussions with colleagues and clients have provided many of the insights that we have been able to develop. Feedback from the carefully selected group of people who have read the book for us in advance of publication has been extremely valuable. We would like to thank everybody involved for their help and advice, particularly Dr Jill Armfield, Roger Smith, John Tew and Colin Webb who commented on the book for us before the manuscript was finalized.

PART I

The Context of International Management Training

The book opens with an introduction to the challenge of training international managers who come together from diverse cultures to participate in learning experiences. It uses work that has been previously carried out on understanding cultural diversity and different learning styles, in order to consider how trainers need to approach the challenges posed in leading learning events for international managers. It also looks at the learning challenge from the point of view of the client who is going to commission a suitably qualified trainer to manage an international training course. It then discusses the considerations for trainers who need to be able to agree the principles and details of training with clients. Finally, the book reviews the economics of international training and how it differs from training that takes place near to the workplaces of participants. This chapter focuses on the need to deliver maximum value from training in terms of helping participants on multi-cultural courses to develop competencies and behaviours that they can use effectively in the workplace. In this way it sets a context for Parts II and III, which consider in detail a process for developing, deploying, implementing and evaluating training for international groups of participants.

CHAPTER

1 Introduction

You are standing in front of a group of international managers at the beginning of a training course. You are the trainer, the course leader. As you look around you see the usual mixture of facial expressions and body language – anticipation, hope, cynicism, boredom, and preoccupation. Some are chatting to their colleagues in German, French and other languages. Others, clearly too busy to socialize, are on their mobiles or deeply absorbed in their e-mails.

How are you going to cope? Will they all be familiar with the English language in which the course will be run? How will you understand them when they speak in their own language in the breakout sessions? Will they understand your jokes and witticisms? How well will they contribute? Will they express their real concerns and opinions? Will they expect you to come up with all the answers or will they want to work them out for themselves? What about sticking to the timetable – will they want it to go like clockwork, or to be flexible in order to reflect the course of the discussion or their daily routine in their own culture with breaks for coffee, prayers and a variety of starting and stopping times? Will they understand you? Above all, what assumptions are you making, based on your own culture and experience, that you do not even think about that may alienate, distract or antagonize your participants and detract from the achievement of the learning objectives? These are some of the many questions that this book attempts to answer.

The global perspective

The increasing speed of communications is enabling organizations to extend their influence across the globe. Electronic communication allows us to send messages across time zones, so that the sender can despatch a message at the end of the day to be opened in another part of the world at the beginning of the next day. Such ease of communication brings peoples from different cultures closer together.

In many fields, certainly in business and academia, English has become the common tongue. Businesspeople and academics are motivated to learn English as a second or third language in the same way that they have been motivated to develop computer skills. This combination of skills has dramatically increased the ability of people from different corners of the globe to share information.

Organizations, which already considered themselves as having an international outlook, are now able to easily and frequently keep in touch with their counterparts on different continents. They are able not only to exchange information but they can also trade ideas and knowledge electronically. Taken together, these developments mean that most managers are exposed to the thinking and approaches of managers from different cultures on an increasingly frequent basis.

These technological developments are being reinforced by the greater volume and lower costs of air travel. This is exposing individuals to an increasing diversity of cultures and encouraging travel to far-flung, as well as nearby, destinations.

Vast trading blocs such as the European Community (EC), North American Free Trade Agreement (NAFTA) and others have been created and trade barriers are reducing, increasingly leading companies to align language and vision and develop a common corporate culture that overlays any stereotypical perceptions of nationalities.

At the same time the different cultures are becoming more similar. Whether it is CNN, McDonald's or Coca-Cola, Sony, Mercedes or Phillips, foreigners find themselves confronted by increasing numbers of offerings they recognize from back home, wherever they are. This is not to say that significant differences do not exist. Indeed, for a trainer to assume that just because the Vodafone logo appears on their mobile phone when they get off the aeroplane and the bar serves Carlsberg that there is little difference between how people operate and respond is a cardinal error.

Cultural challenges for international managers

Organizations of all types need to manage this extension of their global reach. Even in organizations that have operated worldwide for half a century there is a need to equip them to manage larger regions, encompassing more diverse cultures. In many other organizations managers are having to learn how to operate across different cultures and even local managers are finding it necessary to learn how to contribute to multi-national teams. Managers in this environment have new and more effective tools for communication and soon find they are working in a world where there is a common language and common technologies but a great diversity of cultures. The challenge presents itself as soon as communication begins. Even within Europe there will be a difference in perception about establishing a meeting at say, 11.00 am, and this is not because of time zones. As a generalization, people of Northern European origin will understand 11.00 am to be within five minutes of that time and people of Latin origin will have a more elastic concept of 11.00 am.

In large multi-national companies young managers will often find themselves working in virtual teams with colleagues from all over the world, sometimes without ever meeting face to face. They will be expected to agree objectives, develop a project plan, implement agreed actions and review results with colleagues who are from societies with different values, religions, beliefs and priorities. They will have different understandings of the role of a leader, how to measure success and other critical factors that they may never discuss, but which will drive their behaviour in ways which will often surprise and sometimes frustrate their distant colleagues.

Learning events in the early twenty-first century

One opportunity to deepen individual managers' understanding of the cultures of their colleagues, peers and opposite numbers from different regions is to share a learning environment. The need to appreciate cultural differences and the relative speed and lack of expense of modern travel is increasing the frequency with which learning events are arranged that are attended by managers from a number of different countries and sometimes different continents. These events can take place within multi-national organizations or they can be arranged by specialist providers for managers with similar learning requirements, from diverse organizations.

In this book we are concerned about learning events for managers. These events often have objectives that are aimed at increasing knowledge, developing new skills and modifying personal behaviours. If they are very ambitious they may also aim to change attitudes as well. Trainers have long recognized that increasing the knowledge of participants is a reasonably attainable goal, although there are of course more and less effective ways in which it can be done. Developing skills requires practice and is more challenging in the learning environment. Changing personal behaviours of participants on any sort of permanent basis is extremely challenging, and changing attitudes is something trainers will only believe can be achieved as a result of a learning event in their most optimistic moments. This is our mature perception when we are thinking of a group of participants from a single culture. It is many times more challenging when we are considering a group of participants from many and varied cultural backgrounds brought together in a group for the purpose of learning and development.

The main purpose of this book

The reasons for it being so much more challenging to train participants from varied cultural backgrounds will be explored throughout the book. The main purpose of the book is to extend our understanding of what the challenges are and how the trainer can attempt to meet them so that not only is it possible for effective learning to take place within multi-cultural groups of participants, but also that it is possible for learning to be enriched and enhanced by the fact the participants can share the widely different perceptions that are intrinsic to varied cultural backgrounds. This focus is aimed at increasing the value from training by making it one hundred per cent relevant to global enterprises, many of which are operating in increasingly competitive markets with profit margins that are under pressure. The book recognizes that expatriate managers are a very expensive commodity and that they need to maximize the understanding of the cultures in which they will operate so that they can make an immediate impact on taking up assignments that expose them to cultures with which they are not familiar, never having lived in those cultures.

How the book is structured

To achieve its purpose, the first part of this book considers the context within which the training takes place. It is structured to give an insight into the cultural and learning differences the trainer is likely to meet with groups of participants from different regions of the world and the additional economic considerations that need to be incorporated.

The second part of this book looks in depth at the design and development of training processes to maximize the learning. For this part to be as easy as possible to digest and use in designing, developing and delivering training, it will follow a structure, which has been developed from the 'Systematic Training' model based on Douglas Seymour's work (see Further Reading). This was developed by the Industrial Training Boards almost 40 years ago. This model follows the acronym of SUCCESS and it describes principles that are important in developing any training intervention, particular aspects of which become critical when considering the training of multi-cultural groups.

Most importantly this will lead on, in the third part of this book, to detailed consideration of the most effective styles, techniques and behaviours that can be adopted by the trainer when facilitating the learning of participants from different cultures.

Before immersing ourselves in the world of learning it will be helpful, in Chapter 2, to focus on a well-researched model of cultural diversity.

Summary

Towards the end of each chapter readers will be able to identify the most important implication for them from the material they have just covered. From this introductory chapter, the Reading plan shown below performs this task. Subsequent chapters will have similar frameworks to help readers get as much practical value as possible from the materials.

To get the most from this book, readers should explicitly consider these following issues and formalize their responses.

Reading plan

Issues	*Response*
My objectives in reading this book are:	
Issues that I would like to be resolved are:	
Particular difficulties I have experienced in training international managers are:	
I intend to apply the learning in these ways:	
The four main challenges I see in training international managers are:	

CHAPTER

2 A Model of Cultural Diversity

> While we were training a group of experienced managers in a beautiful resort hotel just outside Kuala Lumpur, Malaysia, a senior manager entered the training room and approached one of his subordinates. On seeing his boss, the participant immediately rose and followed him out of the room. The boss did not look at the trainer. His subordinate made brief eye contact, smiled and nodded his head before exiting.
>
> During the same training programme on the first morning, another participant rose without acknowledging the trainer, moved to the side of the room, spread a prayer mat on the floor and began to pray.
>
> We put this behaviour down to cultural differences and moved on. But it concerned us that our authority in the training room, which we felt we had earned, appeared to be being undermined. How should we respond? Should we take the individuals aside at a convenient moment and let them know how we felt? Would others adopt similar behaviours and totally undermine the rest of the training course?

At the end of this chapter and in Part III of this book we will answer these questions, but for now we will look at some of the key dimensions that describe cultures and help us to understand better the behaviour of others.

A model of cultural diversity

Over the last 25 years a number of authors have attempted to develop models to help us understand the key dimensions of cultural difference. Some of the key texts are listed in the Further Reading section at the end of this book.

Dr Geert Hofstede conducted perhaps the most comprehensive study of how values in the workplace are influenced by culture. From 1967 to 1973, while working at IBM as a psychologist, he collected and analysed data from over 100 000 individuals from 40 countries. From those results, and later additions, Hofstede developed a model that identifies four primary dimensions to differentiate cultures. He later added a fifth dimension.

As with any generalized study, the results may or may not be applicable to specific individuals or events. In addition, although Hofstede's results are categorized by country, often there is more than one cultural group within that country. In these cases there may be significant deviation from the study's result. An example is Belgium, where the majority Dutch-speaking population in the Flanders region and the minority French-speaking population in the Walloon region have moderate cultural differences.

Geert Hofstede's dimensions analysis can assist the trainer in better understanding the intercultural differences within regions and between countries.

The five dimensions are:

- power distance
- individualism
- masculinity
- uncertainty avoidance
- long-term orientation.

The extent to which each of these five dimensions is present or absent from a society determines how it operates and the written and tacit rules. Importantly, from the trainer's perspective, the dimensions determine the mindset of individuals belonging to that group. They will perceive their society's behaviours, norms, rules and expectations as normal and often as better than those of other cultures, which will appear alien and confusing.

Looking at each in turn:

POWER DISTANCE

Power distance (PD) focuses on the degree of equality, or inequality, between people in the country's society and indicates the extent to which the less powerful expect and accept that power is distributed unequally. A high power distance ranking indicates that inequalities of power and wealth have been allowed to grow within the society. These societies are more likely to follow a caste system that does not allow significant upward mobility of its citizens. A low power distance ranking indicates the society de-emphasizes the differences between citizens' power and wealth. In these societies equality and opportunity for everyone is stressed.

A country such as India, for example, with its traditional caste system, ranks high on power distance. However, in today's world things can change quickly, creating additional cultural dynamics not part of Hofstede's original work. For India, therefore, with its growth of a sizable, well-educated middle class, it is likely that its power distance rating is declining.

For the trainer it suggests that an authoritative or expert approach will be acceptable to trainees coming from high PD societies, while a more inclusive style will be welcomed by participants from low PD countries. High PD learners expect the trainer to take the initiative, while in low PD cultures the trainer can expect the participants to take initiatives.

INDIVIDUALISM

Individualism (IDV) focuses on the degree to which the society reinforces individual or collective achievement and interpersonal relationships. A high individualism ranking indicates that individuality and individual rights are paramount within the society. The ties between individuals are loose; everyone is expected to look after themselves and their own immediate family. Individuals in these societies may tend to form a large number of loose relationships. A low individualism ranking typifies societies of a more collectivist nature with close ties between individuals. These cultures reinforce extended families and collectives where everyone takes responsibility for fellow members of their group. From birth onwards, individuals are integrated into strong, cohesive in-groups, which throughout people's lifetime continue to protect them in exchange for unquestioning loyalty.

Anglo-Saxon societies tend to value individualism and score highly on this dimension. Arab societies, on the other hand, tend to have a fairly low individualism score, with strong loyalties to family, tribe and sect in that order. When, in Anglo-Saxon societies, for example, individuals come together to protest, then they are in some ways acting counter culturally, driven by a stronger force. On the other hand, in Arab countries, unless banned by the authorities, such protests are just a normal way of expressing loyalty to the local society.

For the trainer it suggests that participants from high IDV countries expect, as of right, to express their viewpoint, while those from low IDV societies will be more consensus oriented. For low IDV participants, trainers must first manage the group, while for high IDV participants, the trainer must first concentrate on the individual. Clearly where there is a mix of participants from high and low IDV cultures the trainer needs to be as aware of the need to manage the group as of the need to pay attention to each individual.

MASCULINITY

Masculinity (MAS) focuses on the degree the society reinforces, or does not reinforce, the traditional masculine work role-model of male achievement, control and power. A high masculinity ranking indicates the country experiences a high degree of gender differentiation. In these cultures, males dominate a significant portion of the society and power structure, with females being controlled by male domination. Money and possessions are indicators of success. A low masculinity ranking indicates the country has a low level of differentiation and discrimination between genders. In these cultures, females are treated equally to males in all aspects of society. Caring for others and quality of life are of great importance.

Scandinavian societies have low masculinity rankings, while countries such as Afghanistan, Japan, Austria and Germany score high.

Clearly, female trainers will have to work hard to overcome participant perceptions in high MAS countries. Here, trainers are expected to be assertive. In low MAS cultures, humility and modesty are perceived as signs of confidence and competence. Also, in high MAS countries, female participants may need to be encouraged and supported to make contributions and actively express their viewpoint.

UNCERTAINTY AVOIDANCE

Uncertainty avoidance (UA) focuses on the level of tolerance for uncertainty and ambiguity within the society, in other words unstructured situations. A high uncertainty avoidance ranking indicates the country has a low tolerance for uncertainty and ambiguity. This creates a rule-oriented society that institutes laws, rules, regulations and controls in order to reduce the amount of uncertainty. South American countries such as Guatemala, Uruguay and Panama, as well as European ones such as Portugal and Belgium, have a high ranking. A low uncertainty avoidance ranking indicates the country has less concern about ambiguity and uncertainty and more tolerance for a variety of opinions. This is reflected in a society that is less rule-oriented, more readily accepts change, and takes more and greater risks such as Singapore, Denmark and the United Kingdom.

For the trainer working with high UA participants it is likely to mean that single, correct answers are being sought by the learners. They prefer tightly structured training and the setting up of rules to govern how the training will be conducted and how the participants will conduct themselves. Low UA participants will feel comfortable with open-ended learning situations where a range of answers are possible, each of which can be correct. They are comfortable with a lack of structure.

LONG-TERM ORIENTATION

Geert Hofstede added a fifth dimension after conducting an additional international study using a survey instrument developed in collaboration with Chinese employees and managers. That survey resulted in the addition of the Confucian dynamism. Subsequently, Hofstede described that dimension as a culture's long-term orientation (LTO). It focuses on the degree to which the society embraces, or does not embrace, long-term devotion to traditional, forward-thinking values. A high long-term orientation ranking indicates the country subscribes to the values of long-term commitments and respect for tradition. This is thought to support a strong work ethic where long-term rewards are expected as a result of today's hard work. However, businesses may take longer to develop in this society, particularly for an 'outsider'. Countries such as China or Japan are good examples. A low long-term orientation ranking indicates the country does not reinforce the concept of long-term, traditional orientation. In this culture, change can occur more rapidly as long-term traditions and commitments do not become impediments to change. The Philippines, United Kingdom and Canada are examples.

Each country can be analysed along these five dimensions and an example is shown in Table 2.1 for the USA. Its profile can be represented in graphical form, as shown in Figure 2.1.

Table 2.1 Scores

	Power distance	*Individualism*	*Uncertainty avoidance*	*Masculinity*	*Long-term orientation*
USA	40	91	46	62	29

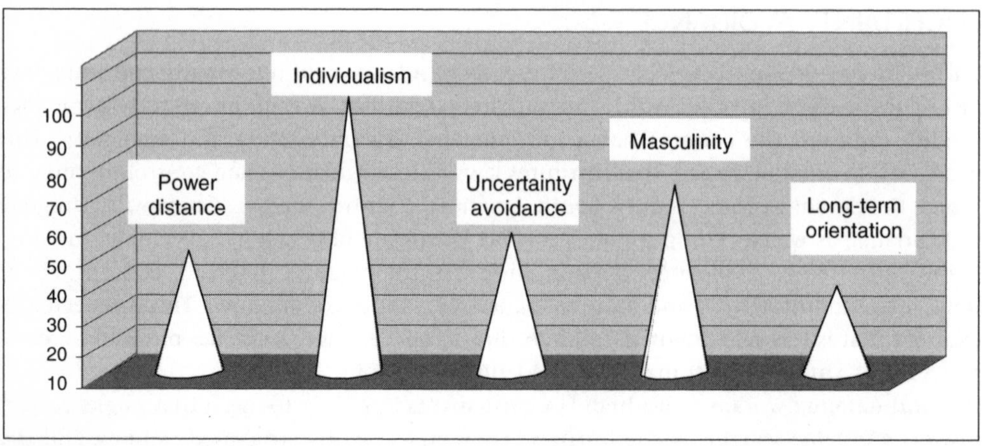

Figure 2.1 Geert Hofstede analysis graph for the USA

In Figures 2.2 and 2.3 the LTO criteria is not plotted because it has only been established for around 20 countries.

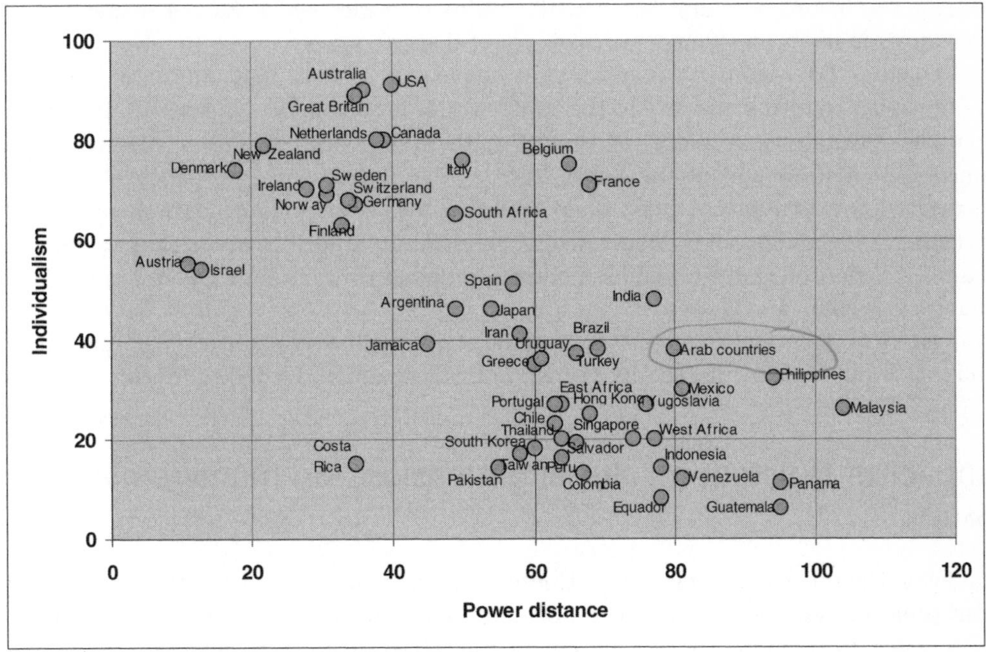

Figure 2.2 Power distance vs. individualism

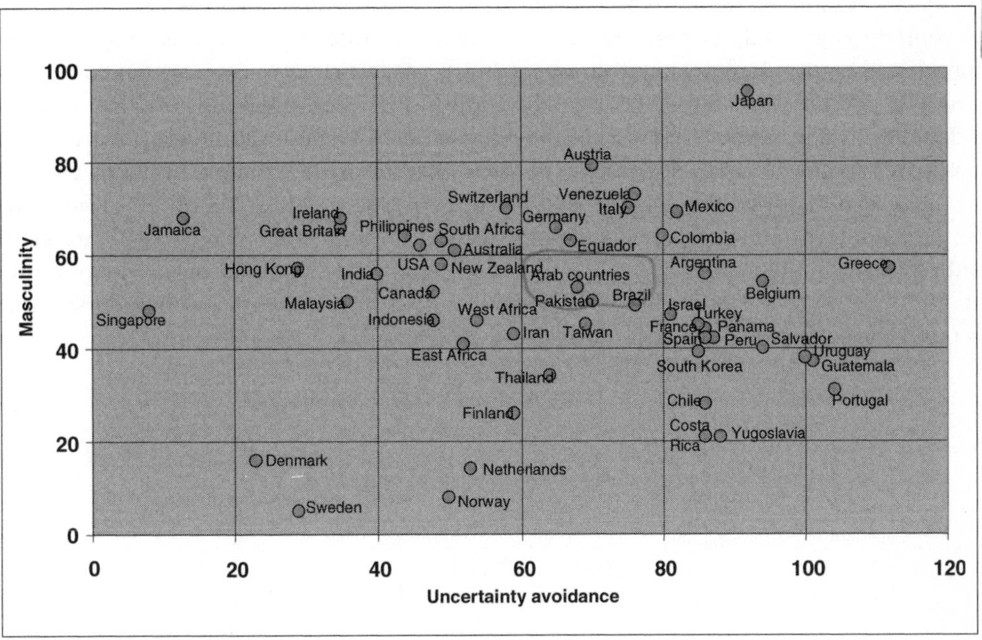

Figure 2.3 Uncertainty avoidance vs. masculinity

In Figure 2.2, power distance is plotted against individualism. Two broad groups are apparent. One group of Anglo-Saxon, northern/central European countries have a relatively high individualism index, with a low power distance index. This contrasts with Central African, South American and Southern European countries which have a moderate/low individualism index and a moderate/high power distance index.

In Figure 2.3, which plots uncertainty avoidance against masculinity, a group of Scandinavian countries and The Netherlands exhibit low/moderate uncertainty avoidance and low masculinity. A group of central/southern European countries, Central/South American countries and South Korea have a high uncertainty avoidance index and moderate/low masculinity. A group where English is the primary or secondary language, and including Switzerland, show moderate/high masculinity and low uncertainty avoidance indices. A variety of countries exhibit moderate to high on both indices: Japan, Austria, Arab countries, Belgium and Greece.

Again it is important to emphasize that the above are the results of a generalized study and that, while valid for the society overall, individuals can and will be different.

Impact of Hofstede's cultural dimensions on management issues

It is helpful, at this stage, to review how Hofstede's cultural dimensions impact on a number of management issues that directly affect the design and implementation of management training.

In Table 2.2 opposite, some management issues relevant to each dimension (excluding long-term orientation) and the implications, in the form of questions, for trainers are listed. Readers should ponder these and, based on the analysis above, develop their own insights.

So, for example, under power distance, particular issues are: the nature of the appropriate organization structure, the use and acceptability of status symbols, the importance of not losing face, the acceptability of participative management and the perceived role of the manager. Taking organization structures, these can be flat, typical of societies with low power distance, or of a hierarchical pyramid nature with many layers typical of high power distance cultures. For the trainer one issue is: should bosses be allowed or encouraged to attend the training sessions of their subordinates? For low PD groups this can be helpful in terms of showing support for the training and helping the manager to understand both the materials and how they can support their staff following the training. For high PD groups it is probably less appropriate as both the manager and subordinate will feel uncomfortable, with the boss dominating and the subordinate obedient.

Table 2.2 Impact of cultural dimensions

Power distance (PD)	*Low*	*High*	*Some training implications*
Appropriate organizational structure	Relatively flat	Hierarchical pyramid	Can bosses and subordinates attend the same training? To what extent should the boss sanction the training content?
Use of status symbols	Relatively unimportant	Very important	How should the trainer demonstrate their status? How will participants broadcast their status in the absence of symbols?
Importance of 'face saving'	Face saving less important	Face saving important	How will trainees be made aware of their mistakes? How will offended parties be dealt with?
Use of participative management	Possible and often encouraged	Not possible or desirable	How will teams work together and achieve a positive result? How will team leaders emerge and how will they behave?
Role of manager towards subordinate	Facilitator	Expert	What is the appropriate role for the trainer? How will bosses be involved?

Individualism (IDV)	*Low – Collectivist*	*High – Individualist*	*Some training implications*
The responsibility for making decisions	Reached by group consensus	Made by individuals	Can both these modes work in one team? How will dominant individuals be contained and conformists brought out?
Basis of the personal reward systems	Based on how the whole group performs	Based on individual performance and on merit	How will softer training topics such as motivation, leadership and performance appraisal be handled?
The basics of ethics and societal values	Particular to the group	Universal across all cultures	How can the trainer show respect for the client's perspective on issues such as confidentiality and the value accorded to 'networking'?
The focus for organizational responsibility	Look after employees	Employees look after themselves	How can/should the overall organizational good/objectives set the context for the training? Should the trainees be encouraged to relate the experience to their own career development plan?

Table 2.2 *continued*

Uncertainty avoidance (UA)	*Weak – tolerate ambiguity*	*Strong – crave certainty*	*Some training implications*
Use of corporate plans	Seen as general, flexible guidelines	Seen as important to follow precisely	Should rules be set up for how the training will be run and how participants are expected to behave; and if so, how? When covering planning issues be explicit on the cultural context
Attitudes towards competition between individuals	Seen as advantageous	Seen as damaging	How should competition between individuals and groups be stimulated?
Application of budgeting systems	Flexible and subject to revision	Inflexible and, if an unavoidable need to change, then perceived as failure	How can the trainer show understanding of the client's approach to setting and managing budgets? (More on budgets in Chapter 5)
Application of control systems	Loose, allowing plenty of scope for individual interpretation	Tight, with unambiguous measures that are regularly monitored	How will the effectiveness of the training be evaluated? How will preparation by participants before the training be communicated and monitored?
Attitude to taking risks	Happy to take risks	Tendency to avoid taking risks	How much time should be given for participants to prepare any presentations during the training?

Masculinity/Femininity (MAS)	*Low – Feminine*	*High – Masculine*	*Some training implications*
The types of rewards that are valued and sought	Desire for quality of life	Striving for money and desire to 'win'	How should the trainees be assessed? Can the programme start/run on a weekend?
Role of networking in achieving business objectives	Contact network seen as the essential basis for productive business	Performance is regarded as the best indicator of achieving business success	Do networking events need to be organized outside the regular training day? Should networking be incorporated as a specific training objective?
Importance of interpersonal relationships	Building and maintaining relationships is fundamental	Getting the task done well determines successful outcomes	How will time issues be dealt with? How will conflict be handled?
Basis for motivation	Service to others	Ambition — getting ahead	How will the benefits of the training be positioned?

Summary

Hofstede's model of cultural diversity identifies four primary dimensions – power distance (PD), individualism (IDV), masculinity (MAS) and uncertainty avoidance (UA). Later, a fifth dimension, long-term orientation (LTO), was added. Each country/culture exhibits a unique combination of these dimensions which has direct implications for the style of training which is likely to be most effective.

It is important to recognize that this is a generalized model and that individuals can and do have different attitudes and behaviours. Therefore, the trainer of international managers needs to be sensitive to these differences and avoid stereotyping participants. In addition, cultures change over time as they evolve and its citizens are increasingly exposed to other cultures.

Nevertheless, Hofstede's model provides a good starting point. Considering the incidents recounted at the beginning of this chapter, Malaysia, from where a number of the participants emanated, is a culture which has a high power distance index and is low in respect of individualism. Managers see themselves benefiting from their position in the organizational hierarchy and the power it bestows, as of right. This means that subordinates accept and respect managers' rights to do what they believe best for the business as the boss is more experienced and has a 'bigger picture' regarding business issues than they do. The subordinate will suppress their view in favour of their manager's.

On the other hand, Malaysia is relatively low regarding uncertainty avoidance. This means that little discomfort is felt by individuals going against the prevailing flow. Hence it is seen as perfectly acceptable to perform prayer rituals in full sight of the rest of the class while the training is proceeding.

How should such situations be handled? More will be said in Part III, but for now the importance of the trainer explicitly developing a set of courtesy rules governing participant behaviour at an early stage of the course is emphasized. While it can also be of value in mono-cultural training situations where acceptable and unacceptable behaviours are implicitly understood, it is vital to agree 'the course rules' in multi-cultural environments. However, the degree to which they will be adhered to is dependent on the level of uncertainty avoidance of the participants. Nevertheless, even in low uncertainty avoidance cultures the rules provide an anchor that the trainer can refer back to.

To help the reader use the contents of this chapter, the questions that follow enable trainers to formalize their perceptions of their own culture and to identify the cultural values that make them feel uncomfortable and with which they may have difficulties in dealing.

Table 2.3 Culture benchmarking

Cultural dimensions	*My culture has the following values …*	*Personally, I feel uncomfortable with this dimension when it …*
Explicit use of status symbols		
Importance of 'face saving'		
Extent of use of participative management		
Role of manager towards subordinate		
Consensus orientation of decision-making		
Extent that reward systems are group or individual based		
Attitudes towards competition between individuals		
Rigidity in the application of control systems		
Attitude to taking risks		
Role of networking in achieving business objectives		
Importance of interpersonal relationships		

CHAPTER 3

Learning Styles and Training Styles in a Multi-Cultural Setting

Much of management training in France tends to be in the form of lectures requiring considerable attention from participants, with questions allowed at the end of the presentation. Participants feel privileged to receive training from respected authorities knowledgeable in the subject and believe that the responsibility for understanding and learning from them is theirs alone. In the USA the process tends to be much more interactive, with trainees feeling they have a right to influence and input into the training they receive. In this situation the learning is largely on the shoulders of the trainer, with attendees feeling a responsibility to help the trainer to help them.

> While conducting a training course in Central Europe we were invited to dinner by the manager of the participants. Naturally we accepted, saying we looked forward to joining them. On arriving at the restaurant we found that only the manager and his boss were waiting for us and that none of the participants were there. As the meal proceeded we became concerned that we would have problems the next day from the participants. They, of course, knew that we were talking with their bosses and that their performance during the training was the focus of the discussion. How should we start the next morning? Should we tell them about our dinner and, if so, how? Should we make light of it or stress the careful thought we had given it, or should we not refer to it at all?

In this chapter we will attempt to answer these questions by looking at some theories of learning and training and relating them to Hofstede's cultural dimensions.

What are 'learning styles'?

How do different cultures learn? Is there any difference in the learning process or styles? The Learning Skills Research Centre (LSRC) has produced an important research paper (available at www.lsda.org.uk) in 2004 which lists 13 different learning styles models, with a critique of each. Of these, the one with which readers are likely to be most familiar is the Honey and Mumford learning styles framework. Although the LSRC report is critical of the apparent lack of empirical research carried out to substantiate this model to date, its wide usage has led us to choose it as a basis for relating learning styles to cultural styles. For those who wish to refresh their knowledge, it is summarized in Table 3.1.

Table 3.1 Honey and Mumford learning styles

The term 'learning styles' is used as a description of the attitudes and behaviours that determine our preferred way of learning.

Most people are unaware of their learning style preferences, they just know vaguely that they feel more comfortable with, and learn more from, some activities than others. When a group of training participants comes together they are likely to have a mixture of learning styles. The trainer, having no control over this, needs to develop a mixture of training methods in the programme so that it is never too long before a method is used which will appeal to each individual.

Knowing about different learning style preferences is the key to becoming more effective at learning from experience.

Readers wishing to find out their learning style can complete the learning styles questionnaire which can be found on the Internet at: www.peterhoney.com/main/

What are 'learning style preferences'?

Learning style preferences determine the things people learn and the ease with which they learn them. They exert a hidden, but powerful, influence on learning effectiveness. Honey and Mumford's model, based on Kolb's learning cycle, identifies four types of learning preference:

Activists – 'I like to have a go and see what happens.'
Reflectors – 'I like to gather information and mull things over.'
Theorists – 'I like to tidy up and reach some conclusions.'
Pragmatists – 'I like tried and tested techniques that are relevant to my problems.'

To assess an individual's learning style, Honey and Mumford developed a simple, self-scoring questionnaire, which shows the style(s) where the learning has strong preference and those with moderate or low preference. Each individual will use each style to a greater or lesser extent.

Activists: are enthusiastic and welcome new challenges and experiences. They like to take direct action and are less interested in what has happened in the past or in putting things into a broader context. They are primarily interested in the here and now. They like to have a go, try things out and participate. Being the centre of attention appeals to them.

A trainer working with activists should bear in mind that they do not like to sit around and have relatively short attention spans. Sessions should therefore be short with plenty of variety and opportunities for them to 'think on their feet', initiate, participate and have fun. The training style adopted by the trainer will be as important as the training content.

Reflectors: like to think about things in detail before taking action. They are thoughtful and take a measured approach. Often they are good listeners and prefer to adopt a low profile. They are prepared to read and reread and welcome the opportunity to repeat a piece of learning.

Working with reflectors, trainers should bear in mind that they should be given time to think before they act, that they like to prepare thoroughly, take time to make decisions, and like to 'stand back' to listen and observe. It is important that they be given sufficient 'space' and not pressurized. Trainers should not jump to the conclusion that they are slow learners.

Theorists: want to see how things fit into an overall pattern or framework. They tend to be logical and objective, keen on systems and prefer a sequential approach to problems. Being analytic, they pay attention to detail and tend to be perfectionists.

The trainer needs to pay particular attention to content when dealing with theorists. They prize logic and want to see sound, intellectually challenging frameworks and models. The trainer's style is relatively unimportant to them unless it detracts from the content. Sessions should be tightly structured with a clear beginning, middle and end, with regular signposts. They love new ideas and concepts but they feel they are wasting their time when covering material they already know.

Pragmatists: are practical, down-to-earth people who like to solve problems. They enjoy experimenting with new ideas and appreciate the opportunity to try out what they have learned.

When dealing with pragmatists lots of practical examples and anecdotes are welcome. Giving them opportunities to apply the learning directly to their work is valued and they like to the security of knowing that the techniques and tools they are learning are proven in other organizations.

Training styles

Although best known for their work on learning styles, Honey and Mumford have also developed a similar classification for training styles: Activist, Reflector, Theorist and Pragmatist. Each of us tends to have one or two dominant training styles which we feel most comfortable in using. Naturally, we perform better with trainees with the same learning styles.

ACTIVISTS

Trainers who are Activists like the limelight and want to be inspirational. They are energetic and enthusiastic, welcoming new challenges and experiences and do not shy away from taking risks. They seek a high degree of audience involvement and use participative exercises. Experimenting with new materials and training methods is a way of maintaining their interest in the training process, particularly in a subject that they have delivered many times. They use humour and give entertaining presentations, pushing participants to try new things and to keep up. Sticking to time is not a strength and they tend to be flexible, happy to go with the flow and react to the participants' requirements. This may mean that they do not adhere rigidly to the agenda and may omit parts of the programme and bring in additional materials. They like to move about, get 'stuck in', try things out and participate. They are less interested in what has happened in the past or in putting things into a broader context. They are primarily interested in the here and now. Detail is not a strong point; they prefer to see the bigger picture.

REFLECTORS

Trainers who are Reflectors prepare carefully and like to think about things in detail before taking action. They take a thoughtful approach and encourage participants to do the same. They are good listeners and do not hog the limelight. They reflect on, and make good use of, their personal experiences. Their feedback to participants is objective and non-judgemental and their facilitation unobtrusive. Helping trainees explore options rather than provide answers comes naturally to them. They prepare in detail and often build in pre-course work for the participant. Sometimes they can appear to be a little slow, indecisive and lacking authority.

THEORISTS

Trainers who are theorists like to see how things fit into an overall pattern. They are logical, analytical and objective. They prefer a sequential approach to problems and frequently use flow charts, boxes and arrows to illustrate points. Models and theories attract them. They are analytical, pay great attention to detail, spell things out precisely and tend to be perfectionists. Usually they believe that there tends to be one correct answer and it can be arrived at by analysing the facts and data. Unlike Activists, they respect the timetable and will stick to it. They dislike uncertainty and prepare thoroughly. Trainers who are theorists thrive when working with participants who are challenging and questioning and of whom they will ask insightful and probing questions. On the negative side they can appear to be distant from reality, adopting an 'ivory tower' approach, and can be pedantic.

PRAGMATISTS

Trainers who are Pragmatists relate the application of the training directly to the issues faced by participants in their daily roles, offering guidelines and implementation tips. As practical and down-to-earth people they like to use case studies and share concrete techniques. They offer themselves as role-models and do not ask the trainees to do anything that they cannot do. Developing skills is seen as being important so that new knowledge can be applied. At the end of a course they will encourage the participants to develop an action plan to implement their learning.

Learning styles, training styles and culture

Hofstede's cultural classification provides a generalized framework which gives a good overall picture but may not apply to any particular individual. The same is therefore true in drawing some generalized conclusions on the preferred learning styles of different cultures as shown in Table 3.1. Indeed, in practice, a trainer should structure the learning process to appeal to all four different learning styles. However, in deciding which to emphasize the following framework may be useful.

Table 3.2 would suggest that Activists are well represented amongst low power distance and high individualism cultures such as the USA and other Anglo-Saxon countries and in Central and Northern Europe, although not France or Belgium. Reflectors can frequently occur in low masculinity and low uncertainty avoidance cultures such as Denmark and Sweden. Theorists are well represented in cultures with high power distance and high uncertainty avoidance such as some Central and South American countries. Finally, Pragmatists are prevalent in low individuality and high masculinity cultures such as Central America, and Asian countries such as Hong Kong, Japan and Pakistan.

Table 3.2 Relating Hofstede's cultural dimensions to preferred learning styles

	Power distance (PD)		*Individualism (IDV)*		*Masculinity (MAS)*		*Uncertainty avoidance (UA)*	
	High	*Low*	*High*	*Low*	*High*	*Low*	*High*	*Low*
Activists		✓	✓					
Reflectors						✓		✓
Theorists	✓						✓	
Pragmatists				✓	✓			

Increasing the sensitivity of participants to cultural differences

Where training events are more than three or four days in length then it is often useful in order to improve the learning process to sensitize multi-cultural participants to each other's differences. Indeed, there will be occasions when one of the client's key objectives for a training event will be to sensitize managers to the particular challenges of working with colleagues from different national and cultural backgrounds. This can be the case where young managers enter their first job, where they will either be expected to manage a project across national boundaries or be part of a virtual team, which is spread across a region of the world or indeed the whole world. To work effectively in these circumstances managers need to understand many important aspects of cultural difference, including:

- different perceptions of the role of the leader
- different approaches to sharing information
- different degrees of 'directness' in giving instructions
- challenges of working in a second language.

Clients who have a long experience of international working will recognize that this type of learning is more likely to be achieved through structured exercises and case studies where small groups of mixed nationalities work together to solve a problem, than it is by the trainer talking with the group about the different approaches of different nationalities. The trainer would be relying on generalizations, whereas in group work participants learn to appreciate the differences that are due to national and cultural background and those that are due to differences between individual personalities.

If the client does not have any depth of international experience, this is an area where the trainer needs to influence the client to see that this is where time spent on theory should be minimal and where group work to solve simulated business problems is likely to be very productive in enhancing participants' appreciation of the different approaches of people from different cultures. The trainer needs to brief, facilitate and debrief these training sessions with a fairly light touch in order for the learning to be maximized.

Summary

The Honey and Mumford learning styles and training styles models with their four classifications – Activist, Reflector, Theorist, Pragmatist – are helpful in helping trainers realize that they need to cater for all four learning styles in delivering their materials and that they will probably feel more comfortable with one or two training styles than with the others. In Part III of this book we look at a number of training techniques that can help trainers broaden their delivery range.

Within any group of delegates from any country one would anticipate that a variety of learning styles would be represented. Relating the training/learning styles to Hofstede's model of cultural diversity, however, suggests that there may be a heavier representation of certain styles in certain countries.

Central Europe has more than a fair representation of Activist learners and, coming back to the incident recounted at the beginning of this chapter, as Activist trainers we felt very comfortable in this environment. However, we felt very uncomfortable discussing each participant in great detail with their bosses. Not only were we disappointed that what we had hoped would be a relaxing social evening with the participants had turned into a business meeting, but we also felt uncomfortable with the large number of hypothetical questions regarding the participants on which we were being asked to proffer an opinion.

However, our resulting concern that the trainees would be more guarded and regard us with suspicion the following day, wondering what we had told their bosses, proved groundless. They knew before they embarked on this training, as with any training, that the trainers would be asked for their views by their bosses. It was standard practice with which they had learned to deal.

Finally, we have highlighted the value of sensitizing multi-cultural participants to their different cultural approaches at first hand through the trainer facilitating, with a light touch, group work on simulated business problems.

By considering the issues in Table 3.3, trainers will be able to respond to the issues and adapt their training to enhance its effectiveness with international managers.

Table 3.3 Learning and training style issues

Issue	*Implications*
What are the advantages of the trainer understanding their own training style and the participants' learning styles?	
Under what circumstances can the trainer realistically collect information about the participants' learning styles?	
Where it is not practical to collect information about the participants learning styles, how does knowledge of Honey and Mumford learning styles theory help in the design and delivery of training?	
How can multicultural participants be helped to increase their sensitivity to other cultures as a means to improve the effectiveness of the overall training?	

CHAPTER 4 *The Client Perspective*

> An established international client called us in to discuss a new training programme that was required for a group of recently recruited Western European managers. They had joined the company in their thirties and had been specially selected for their ability to bring new ideas to the organization. An element of familiarization training was clearly in the client's mind, but other than that the training needs of the group had not been well defined. We suggested that a sample of the intended participant group and their immediate managers were interviewed to gain a better understanding of the common training needs. This revealed the needs from the perspective of the potential participants and their bosses. These perspectives were different but valid and were reported to the client with some ideas on how the programme could be developed to attempt to meet all the perceived needs.
>
> As the development of the programme progressed, it became clear that the client saw the main purpose of the course as being to introduce the participants to the strategy and main business processes of the company. Although this requirement did emerge from the discussions with the participants and their bosses, it did not feature as so important as the need to allow the participants, as might be expected from the cultures they came from, to input on management approaches that they had learned with their previous employers. This conflict of priorities was only partially resolved during the development of the programme. As a consequence there was some disappointment on the part of the participants when the course ran, because they had hoped for more opportunity to express their own views about how the company was managed.

Although such situations do occur in mono-cultural environments, this mismatch of expectations is more likely to occur with an international group of participants. How could this have been handled to achieve a more positive outcome? In this chapter we will analyse the client perspective in more detail and suggest how this and similar situations could be handled to produce effective training interventions which are positioned to satisfy client expectations without disappointing the participants.

This is as important if the training is being organized internally, as it is if a trainer is being paid a fee to develop and deliver the training.

Client expectations from training

The client, by whom we mean the holder of the training budget, usually expects to see participants doing something differently following a training event. The challenge for the trainer is to be able to identify just what the client wants to observe being done differently. It is often a challenge because the client can find it difficult to articulate what they want to see that is different. The client will probably know what it is when it is observed, but it may prove very problematic to explain beforehand. Herein lays one of the biggest challenges faced by trainers of managers. What will be certain is that the client needs to see value from the training investment. This may be perceived in terms of specialist skills and knowledge developed, but could equally well be perceived as the ability of participants to deploy more appropriate interpersonal behaviours when operating in previously unfamiliar cultural environments.

Very often it will be a participant's direct manager who will evaluate whether the participant is doing something differently after the training, rather than the client who contracts for the training. This makes it even more difficult for the trainer to judge what change is really required. The client commissioning the training and the participant's manager may have different perceptions of the requirement, and their perceptions of the observed change after the training could also vary. In the face of these difficulties the trainer has to make the best possible judgement about the change required and attempt to develop learning experiences to bring about this change.

The desired change, in increasing order of difficulty for the trainer, is likely to be in one or more of the following areas:

- more knowledge
- more skill
- greater competence
- different behaviours
- different attitudes.

Whichever of these appears to be required, there will also be an expectation that the training will contribute to the participant producing better results for the organization after completion of the programme.

Increasing knowledge may be possible through distance learning alone. Changing a person's attitudes through training is many times more difficult to achieve. Some might say it is impossible!

To deliver successful training, it is important to understand the client's perspective on which category of change is perceived as being necessary. It is always worth exploring this with the client. A good place to start is to ask the broad question 'What would you want to see the participants doing differently as a result of the training?' and to follow up with questions about the client's perception of whether this will require developments in knowledge, skill, competence, behaviour or attitude. It is even worth exploring at this point whether the client has some preconceived ideas about the best training methods to achieve the change sought. Whatever the trainer's own judgement about the validity of these ideas, they certainly need to be discussed and taken into account. Clients will judge the training according to their own perceptions, not those that the trainer feels are most valid in the light of what is known about the theory of learning. If the client feels the room should be wallpapered and the supplier uses paint, there is little hope that the job will be seen as successful! In other words, if the client wants the participants to understand why certain things, such as working with other departments, need to be done, while the trainer focuses on how to do this, then there is clearly a mismatch of expectations.

As a broad generalization, clients from industrialized countries, particularly where the training ethos is embedded in the organizations, will place a heavier emphasis on some of the more difficult (for the trainer) changes relating to competences, behaviours and attitudes. Developing countries will focus more strongly on the development of knowledge and skills.

Clients from different cultural backgrounds

Clients from different cultural backgrounds are likely to take a different view about the types of outcome they see as most important from training interventions. Also, due to different experiences, they may also have different views on how that outcome can best be achieved.

For example:

- UK clients often tend to put a very heavy emphasis on developing positive interpersonal behaviours.
- German clients frequently tend to focus on increasing competence levels in important job-related tasks.
- French clients commonly tend to want participants to develop depth of knowledge and understanding of principles and processes.
- Clients in developing countries often want participants to gain knowledge of approaches and situations in the more developed countries.

Clearly these are generalizations and the client focus will depend on the particular training need that is being addressed. However, training needs have to be interpreted and clients from different cultural backgrounds are likely to interpret them in different ways.

> A good example of this is dealing with customer complaints. Imagine that a customer complains to her sales contact that a piece of equipment has not been installed to her satisfaction. After making her complaint the supplier's sales manager rather curtly says that the installation is, in his opinion, OK but agrees to see that the changes are made to meet the customer's requirements. The supplier then adds the task to the to-do list of the team responsible for making-good new installations. A week later the job has not been done and the customer makes an angry call to the supplier's contract manager. In this real-life example, when it was discussed in the context of identifying the training needs of the supplier's sales managers, there were two different views on the training needed to correct this type of situation. The product manager from the German parent company immediately identified the need for the sales managers to make proper use of the 'make-good priority system' to ensure that such complaints are dealt with quickly. The English sales director equally quickly identified the need to improve the interpersonal skills of sales managers so that they could deal with this type of issue more courteously in future. The German and English perceptions were both valid in terms of identifying improvements that needed to be made. Both could be dealt with by training and so constituted real training needs.

The trainer needs to be ready for the fact that the client may well interpret situations as requiring different training solutions than the one the trainer has in mind. Indeed, as demonstrated in the example above, different managers within the client organization may have their own perceptions of the training need due to their cultural perspectives. The trainer needs to be able to accept this too and resist the temptation to feel that their own interpretation is the correct one. After all, the trainer is subject to the influence of cultural background just as much as is the client.

To put this in perspective, it is similar to the different emphasis the clients from the public and private sectors are likely to place on an 'organization development' programme in their respective organizations. Public-sector clients are likely to be much more concerned with systems and documentation, whereas private-sector clients are likely to focus more on communications and relationships. Again this is a generalization. The key point is that the trainer needs to appreciate that a client's background and experience will influence the way that problems and the types of solution required are perceived.

Trainers need to be very flexible in accepting these differences. There is very rarely just one effective solution to any business problem, and the trainer certainly does not necessarily have all the best answers. It is vitally important to take the client's perceptions on board and be seen to work with them, introducing the trainer's own approaches within a framework that is acceptable to the client.

A good example of this would be designing a 'presentation skills' programme for a worldwide group of participants, where the client is European. The client is likely to emphasize the need for opportunity to be given to all participants to practise presentation skills. The trainer should be aware that where there are Australians and Koreans, for example, amongst the participants, the Australians are going to have far fewer reservations than the Koreans about practising in front of an audience of fellow participants. So it is the trainer's responsibility to respect the client's requirement for the opportunity to practise, while organizing the event to minimize the potential discomfort of the Koreans when it comes to be their turn in front of an audience.

Client perceptions on training evaluation

When we come to look at training evaluation (Chapter 11) we will recognize how important it is to discuss evaluation methods and criteria with the client at the very outset of the development of a training programme. In evaluating training, clients will also be influenced by their experience and cultural background when deciding how they are going to measure the success of the training. UK clients traditionally put a great deal of emphasis on participants' initial reaction to the training, spoken and written. Clients from cultures with a longer time horizon (Chapter 2) may well study participant behaviour after the event and measure the results of the training over several months, often with pre- and post-training tests. This is more difficult to do but, for example, Chinese organizations are likely to attempt to do it. Naturally the trainer must respect these differences and not present obstacles to the longer-term evaluation of the effect of training inputs.

Client involvement with the development of training materials

Clients will vary greatly in the degree to which they want to review the development of training materials as they are written. This is more likely to depend on their individual personality than their cultural background. However, where the organization has had relatively little experience of implementing management training, as can be the case in developing economies, then they are more likely to want to see the training materials prior to the training event.

Trainers should see a client's request to review training materials as an opportunity to increase the commitment from the client. It is also a chance to refine the materials so that the client feels they fit the organization's requirements more closely. It may take time, and it may be uncomfortable when a client suggests omitting one's favourite exercise, but it will pay off in terms of the acceptability of the training event. Clients want some subjects presented in a particular way for political reasons and it is a foolish trainer who ignores this! It is the client who controls the training budget and it is the same person who can influence whether a training programme is repeated or whether this trainer or another one will be asked to develop the next programme.

To return to the anecdote in the introduction to this chapter: the conflict between the client's and the participants' priorities could have been resolved by the major part of the trainer's delivery focusing on the client company's strategy and business processes, while the focus of the exercises could have been mainly on the participants identifying and evaluating the differences in approach between their new company and the approaches of their previous employers.

Summary

Clients' perceptions of what type of training is likely to be effective, the training methods to be used, the points of emphasis and the method of evaluation is likely to be influenced by cultural background, experience and personality. It is important that trainers accept these perceptions and work within them if they are to gain the client's commitment to the training that is going to be developed and delivered.

Clients usually want to see participants do something differently as a result of a training intervention. It is very important that the trainer asks questions to identify just what the client wants to see in terms of improved skills, competences, behaviours or attitudes.

Clients from different cultural backgrounds are likely to have a variety of views on the best way to evaluate the effectiveness of training inputs. European clients often favour a quick measurement of participant reaction, spoken and written, whereas clients from China and the Far East may be inclined towards an evaluation that takes into account longer-term evidence of changes in performance.

Trainers should take every opportunity to share draft training materials with the client during the development phase. This can only increase the client's commitment to the training so long as the trainer is flexible in allowing the client to influence the content and style of the training.

Action plan

The action plan below should be completed by the trainer.

Issues	*Actions trainers consider*
What do I need to do if my client, from a different cultural background, has a perception of a group's training needs, which is different from my own, even though it is based on the same data?	
How should I react if my client, from a different culture, begins to prescribe training methods, which are quite different from the ones I had in mind, for a group of participants from the client's culture?	
What do I particularly need to look out for where a client with little international experience begins to describe a scenario where participants are to be trained in the culture and customs of people from the other side of the world?	
How should I react if a client from the Far East suggests that the results of a particular training event are evaluated over a one-year time span, when I had intended a quick end-of-course evaluation process?	
How should I react to the client who asks to see all my training materials before a particular event is delivered?	

CHAPTER

5 The Economics of Training International Managers

> We were regularly running a five-day programme for managers from across Europe, most often with participants travelling from nine or ten countries. The course was always held in Brussels, near to the headquarters (HQ) of the organization which the managers were working for. The course required that all the participants were in the same place at the same time and so travel costs were unavoidable. Brussels was reasonably accessible and so the cost and time for travel probably could not be reduced significantly by changing the location. But what about accommodation costs? Brussels is less expensive than London, but by no means the least expensive venue in Europe.
>
> Some alternatives were considered. Splendid venues were available much more cheaply in Portugal, for instance. However, there were downsides to Lisbon as a location. It is not so accessible from other major cities in Europe. Moreover, the programme required that several managers from the HQ in Brussels make an input to the programme in person. How would these additional travel costs and the opportunity cost of the time required for travel balance against the savings to be made from accommodation in Portugal? The question was never answered in fine detail because the opportunity cost of the time spent in HQ staff travelling from Brussels to Lisbon was considered too great.

These are some of the issues involved in considering alternative locations for training international managers, and location is just one issue where there are costs and benefits. In this chapter we will examine the main costs and benefits of training international managers in a group.

Benefits of training managers from different cultures as a group

As already discussed in Chapter 3, it is widely understood that where managers need to work in teams with colleagues from other cultures there are enormous advantages in them attending training sessions together. This helps to get first-hand experience of interacting with colleagues who will work in a particular and different way purely because it is the norm for their country of origin. It is extremely difficult to say what is the value, in financial terms, of an enhanced understanding of the different approach of colleagues. Most managers would, however, agree that projects can easily be delayed and sub-optimal solutions produced if managers from different cultures are asked to work together, without any attempt being made to give them an understanding of cultural differences and how they affect ways of working. This is especially the case if the team-leader is not experienced in managing a multi-cultural team. The experience does not necessarily have to be gained through training, but this is usually faster than a series of working secondments in nine or ten countries.

A more easily identifiable payoff is one where the training is specifically aimed at developing managers to understand unfamiliar cultures prior to taking management responsibilities that will involve them managing people within these cultures. The fact that it will cost three times as much to use an expatriate manager from Europe in another European country, five times as much to introduce a manager from Latin America and 30 times as much to transfer a European to China as it would to use local managers is evidence enough that training which is effective in sensitizing managers to unfamiliar cultures will enable companies to see a handsome return on their training investment.

Attempts have been made to train managers in their own country in the customs of people from different cultures, and some knowledge can be gained from this type of training. However, as discussed earlier in this book, for this knowledge to be turned into sufficient understanding to enable managers from different cultures to work effectively together it really does require that they interact face to face as a group, while undertaking some type of problem-solving, case study or business simulation activity.

Within a large multi-national company there is also the benefit of forming a network of colleagues in different countries, which can be achieved very effectively at residential training events. This can be extremely effective in integrating the process of management across national boundaries and moving all parts of the organization in the same direction at the same time. This is even the case where there are integrated systems and business processes that have been developed to integrate the strategic and operational management of the company. Again it is difficult to convert the benefit of effective management integration into financial terms, but the costs of fragmentation and inconsistency can be seen in terms of delays and ineffective service to customers.

One of the major driving forces towards integrated management of large businesses across the world has been customer pressure to supply products and services consistently in all geographic regions. Take the example of a capital goods supplier to the motor industry. This supplier is not only expected to negotiate worldwide supply contracts centrally in Detroit or in Stuttgart, but is expected to deliver a consistent service in countries as far apart as the USA, the UK, Mexico and the Czech Republic. The degree of co-ordination required to do this can only be achieved by managers who are fully conversant with approaches that work in all the countries where they have operations and also where their customers need the products and services to be delivered. The benefit of training and developing managers to achieve this is the ability to compete with other companies who are achieving it now. The price of second-rate service due to lack of co-ordination is failure to compete and ultimately business failure.

For organizations that are truly global, English is normally the common language. Where the company is determined to run totally integrated operations it is now usual for managers, who will be expected to interact with colleagues in other countries, to have a working knowledge of English. Language facility increases only with usage and so a by-product of training held in English is increased fluency in the language. This will have a benefit outside the training room, in the everyday management of the company's operations. Again it is difficult to evaluate this benefit financially, but mistakes made due to the inability to communicate effectively can be extremely expensive.

Another benefit of taking managers away from their home country for training is that it presents the opportunity to visit the company's operations in the country where the training takes place, thus exposing managers to a different environment and some new practices that could be of value in their home country. Likewise, it may be possible to visit

A young Italian manager was interested in a position in his company's UK corporate office but had not applied for it because of his concern about his aptitude in English. After spending a week on a training course where only English was spoken he realized that working in England was a real possibility, as the English participants were not at all critical of his use of English and were quite prepared to take time to explain things carefully when it would help him to understand. He subsequently transferred to the UK and worked there very successfully for three years before accepting another transfer to the USA.

customers in the training location and appreciate how business is developing in another part of the world.

Costs of training managers from different countries as a group

Clearly the unavoidable additional cost, when compared with training managers in their home country near to their workplace, is that of travel to the chosen location. Travel also involves time, so there is potentially an opportunity cost too. However, if we are looking at a region like Europe, where the distances are not too great and transport is fairly easily available to and from a large variety of destinations, the time involved should not be prohibitive and currently there are good opportunities for economical travel by air.

Clearly the trainer will also have to travel, unless the most convenient venue happens to be in the trainer's locality. The same applies to any additional contributors to the course. Thus arise some other unavoidable additional costs.

Although accommodation is of course a cost, this would be likely to arise anyway with residential training. Only if training is conducted near to each manager's place of work can this cost be avoided. However, with many types of training it is recognized that there is a benefit in it being conducted on a residential basis, as business discussions rarely end when the trainer turns off the projector.

Again, hiring a training facility is a cost, but this is as likely to arise in a manager's home country as it is in another country. It can only be avoided if the organization has a facility of its own, which is convenient, but even then it is of course a fixed cost.

One factor that has to be considered is making arrangements with a venue, which could involve the need to visit in order to put everything in place before the training event takes place. This should be a contained cost in that it should not be necessary for more than one person to visit, usually an administrator who understands the requirements in detail.

So there are identifiable additional costs and benefits of training international managers together in one place. The costs are clear. The benefits are less easy to identify in strict financial terms.

Summary

Table 5.1 Summarize the costs and benefits

Costs	*Benefits*
Participant and trainer travel to the location	Learning about different cultures
Travel for any speakers and other contributors	Learning about management practices in different countries
Accommodation	Forming an international network
Training facility (may not be an additional cost)	Meeting virtual team members
Visiting to make arrangements	Improving second-language facility
The opportunity cost of travel and training time	Visiting locations that are 'business relevant'

Action plan

Consider a training event for international managers and describe the benefits and costs in the table below, assessing the financial impact where you are able to do so.

Benefits	*£000s*
Describe	Assess
	Total
Costs	*£000s*
Describe	Assess
	Total

PART II

Training Design, Development and Learning Processes

In Part II of this book we look primarily at processes and systems to implement effectively the training of managers, and in particular the training of international managers.

Chapter 6 sets up the basic framework SUCCESS, a new and complete process for planning the development, deployment, evaluation and reinforcement of training. The acronym stands for:

- **S**urvey
- **U**nderstand
- **C**reate
- **C**onduct
- **E**valuate
- **S**trengthen
- **S**ustain.

Each element is explained in the next seven chapters. Importantly, Part II provides a model to help readers benchmark their own and client organizations in order to identify which parts of the framework they should apply in individual situations. This tool, in common with the whole SUCCESS model, is applicable to any training intervention, but the authors feel it is particularly relevant to delivering value in training multi-cultural groups. Chapter 6 contains a new model to help trainers and others using learning interventions to recognize the level of training commitment within individual organizations. This model has been identified as extremely useful in matching the trainer's approach to the stage of development of the organization in terms of its commitment to training.

Chapters 7 and 8 focus on ensuring that the training is relevant to the organization and the individuals, and is capable of achieving meaningful objectives for both. Most trainers spend much of their time constructing learning architectures, developing materials and conducting training programmes. How this needs to be adapted for multi-cultural groups is covered in Chapters 9 and 10.

Assessing how the training has been appreciated is reviewed in Chapter 11, while ensuring that both the individual international manager and their organization obtain long-term benefit from what they have learned is covered in Chapters 12 and 13.

CHAPTER

6 *The SUCCESS Structure for Designing, Deploying, Delivering and Evaluating the Learning Process*

In a discussion with the HR director of a large multi-national in the environmental control market, a problem became apparent. Although centrally organized management training was very popular, attendances fluctuated dramatically. When the business was doing well, courses were full. When there was pressure on budgets, filling courses proved to be difficult and many courses were cancelled. 'Although they all say training is important, I can't get managers to take a long-term view,' he complained. 'They're driven by short-term cost savings and they ask me what impact the training has on the bottom line; and I can't tell them.'

It would be unrealistic to assume that investment in training will not be influenced by the same economic factors as other parts of the business. However, it could be argued that international management training is more affected than most other investments that a company makes, particularly as it is often seen as a bit of a luxury and positioned partly as a reward. 'How can we justify sending busy managers away for a week to a nice location, when everyone is working 12 hours a day?' is the refrain.

In this chapter we review a structure that helps to develop training in a way that builds value for the budget holder, enhances benefit to the participants and gives the central training management the business case to support the investment needed. This is more than merely trying to evaluate what additional revenues have been generated, or costs saved, or efficiencies improved as a result of a particular piece of training. It means that we need to look at the total process.

The training process

The planning, deployment, implementation, evaluation and reinforcement of training are complex even when working in a single culture. Line management, ideally assisted by the central training function, has to bring together resources from both inside and outside the organization, work across functions, fitting in with performance appraisal and talent recognition systems to plan and deliver the training and to ensure it produces results. For international management training the process is even more difficult and fraught with pitfalls.

The very challenge of this total process is often of such enormity that many organizations remain content to just deliver training activity on the assumption that some training must be better than none. However, the return on the investment will be considerably multiplied by using a structured, proven methodology to plan, manage, control and reinforce the training activity. The simple outline of this structure is shown in Figure 6.1.

Training must be relevant to the business. This relevance is determined by the business objectives and strategy, which identify how the business relates to its environment. The knowledge, skills, competences, behaviours and attitude needed to implement the strategy are identified. Relating these to the existing situation enables the competences gap that training needs to fill to be scoped. The training is then planned, implemented and evaluated and its impact should be manifest in improved individual, group and company performance. In turn this impacts on training needs and the training cycle continues.

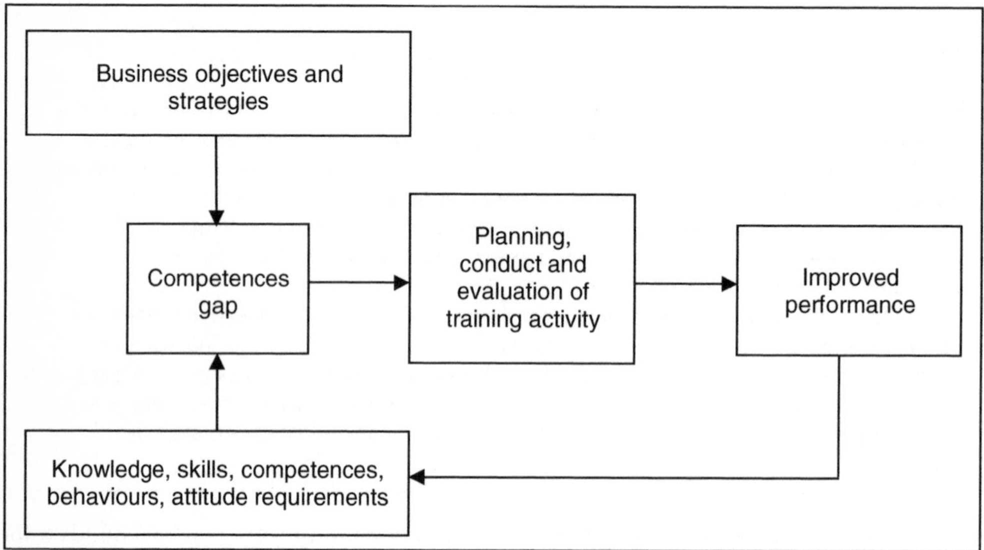

Figure 6.1 The training cycle

It is important to highlight a number of issues:

- Training is not an altruistic endeavour to improve people. Its primary function is to improve company performance.
- Training occurs within the framework of company strategy and is one of the tasks involved in the implementation of that strategy and the achievement of company objectives.
- The identification of the impact of training on results achieved is fundamentally important. Sometimes this can be straightforward as, for example, with production line workers learning particular assembly procedures. Sometimes it is more difficult, for example assessing a course on enhancing cultural sensitivity. A distinction frequently made is between hard and soft skills training with the impact of the former being easier to assess than the latter.
- The training process is cyclical, not a one-off or a series of individual events. It only works if the process continues after and between training events.

The outline process shown in Figure 6.1 can be developed at a number of levels. For example, Figure 6.2 expands the 'planning, conduct and evaluate' part of the process by one level.

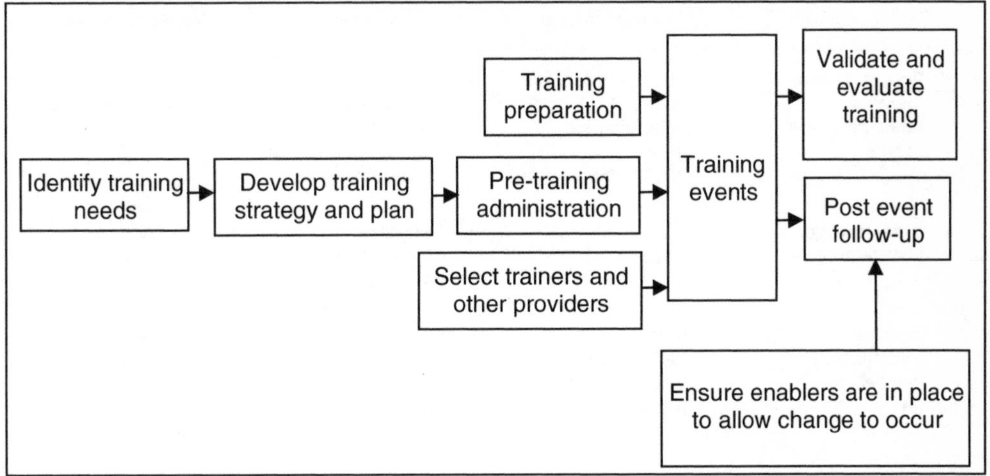

Figure 6.2 Planning, conduct and evaluation of the training process

Each part can be expanded several more levels. The resulting model is quite complex. To make it easier to understand we have developed and synthesized the total training process in one acronym.

SUCCESS is the name of this process and its application will lead to it.

But before explaining each part of SUCCESS, we will sketch out a model of the different phases through which the training function evolves against which it is helpful to relate the training process.

Levels of organization training commitment

Each organization is different in terms of its commitment to training. Some will see it as a key strategy for achieving and maintaining competitive advantage in the market. Others may view it as a necessary expense that should be kept to a minimum. From our work with many organizations we have observed that there are broadly four different training phases or levels, through which organizations tend to evolve over time. These are shown in Table 6.1 with a summary of the characteristics of each level.

The most basic form we call 'trainee driven'. At this level, all or nearly all training is induction training for new recruits at operator level and possibly first line management. Beyond this it is in response to individual managers asking to receive training usually by attending outside courses.

The second level, 'manager driven', places more emphasis on managers identifying the training needs, mostly by observation, of their subordinates and agreeing it with them. Training usually takes the form of attendance at outside courses with occasional in-house programmes.

Level three, 'TNA driven', is characterized by a more systematic attempt to identify training needs through some form of training needs analysis (TNA). A view is taken of the

Table 6.1 Levels of organization training commitment

Level 1 *Trainee driven*	*Level 2* *Manager driven*	*Level 3* *TNA driven*	*Level 4* *Strategy driven*
• People develop themselves; trainee is prime mover	• Manager identifies needs of subordinates through observation	• Process established for identifying training needs in relation to job requirements	• Company strategy drives the training requirement
• Little manager involvement	• Mostly external courses	• Central co-ordination of all training activity	• Training is a boardroom issue
• Training responsibility diffused	• Manager expects training to be the total answer to the problem	• Central approval for organization and provision of training	• Training seen as a major strategy to gain and maintain competitive advantage
• Small training budget held at departmental level	• Training occurs spasmodically	• Manager expected to give support	• System of coaching and mentoring in place
• Managers go to external courses	• Small training budget held at departmental level	• Larger training budget	• All training is controlled and co-ordinated centrally
• Only operative and induction training held internally		• Each person has a personal development plan (PDP)	• Training is organized locally and centrally

job requirements and competence gaps identified. This process is usually co-ordinated through a central training/HR manager who will also be responsible for organizing the provision of training to meet the identified needs.

During the fourth level, 'strategy driven', the training is explicitly related to company strategy and both the short- and long-term impact of the training on results are assessed. It is seen as a key driver in achieving competitive advantage. Basically, the philosophy is that people are the limiting resource within the business. That is, human capital is the main inhibiter to the achievement of corporate abjectives. Therefore its value needs to be increased. Sustainable competitive advantage is subsequently created through having people consistently perform better than those in competitor companies. Training is the strategy that leads to superior performance. It is seen as an investment rather than a cost.

The model is applicable to companies operating in a single country and to multinational/global companies. As the latter tend to be larger and generally more sophisticated they will tend to be in level three or four, but not necessarily.

The attitude of operating management to training varies across the four levels. Management in organizations in level one tend to regard training as an unfortunate necessity that removes people from the workplace and negatively impacts on their productivity. They almost welcome negative reports about the training that their subordinates have attended as it means the likelihood of anyone else wanting to attend is reduced.

Level two manager attitudes are more neutral. However, of prime importance is that the training is directly related to the workplace and to the particular practical situation faced by trainees.

Managers in organizations at level three will be more positive about training but still tend to regard it as a cost. Some may feel a little resentful that thinking about and working on their subordinates' training now takes up a significant proportion of their time. The increasing power of the HR/training function within the company can also give rise to negative reactions.

At level four, training is embedded in the organization and perceived as a core activity. It is an investment that will pay back over a number of years just as an equivalent investment in a new factory would be expected to do. Indeed, training could be thought of as a 'virtual people factory'. These types of organization generally have a strong reputation for developing their people and are well respected. Managers will take pride in this reputation and seek to maintain and develop it further.

Although presented above as four distinct levels of training evolution, there is naturally some overlap between them in practice. However, the model is useful, and we will return to it later in this and future chapters, in order to identify the extent to which the training process described below is applicable.

The SUCCESS training methodology

All too often the implementation of training is perceived in terms of the solution rather than the business problem that the training will contribute to solving. For example, an individual may be prescribed a course on 'effective communications' because it is felt that they do not currently have strong skills in this area. Whether the training will make any difference to the results achieved by the individual for the business relates to whether it addresses the issues that will lead to improved results.

It therefore makes more sense to consider the business issues first and then the role of training in resolving them. For example, the business issue may be that the company has an unprofessional image in the market. Several activities including training may be required to resolve this issue, of which communications skills training could be one. Further, if the problem is a significant one it is probable that a number of people will need to be trained across a number of knowledge and skill areas, not just those who feel their communication skills are inadequate.

A well-structured approach will ensure that organizations both deliver the correct training – 'Do the right things' - and also conduct and maintain the activity to produce maximum value – 'Do things right'. This approach is summarized in the SUCCESS model – a comprehensive description of the total training process. It provides a step-by-step guide to each element that the trainer should consider when designing, implementing, deploying and evaluating training. This powerful framework enables the trainer to develop and apply training that is relevant to both the organization and the trainees as well as facilitating the management of the whole process.

Each letter of SUCCESS represents one step in the training management process – Survey, Understand, Create, Conduct, Evaluate, Strengthen, Sustain. Each uses a specific set of tools and produces prescribed hard and soft outputs – the training context frame, training strategy, SOCMAT, action plans, participant records, learning and training evaluation reviews, implementation dashboard, training portfolio analyser. An overview of the process is shown in Figure 6.3. The stages are:

- **S**urvey: to establish the context for the training activity and the business issues it will address, thereby ensuring it fits into the overall corporate priorities. This involves developing an insightful appreciation of the organization's priorities and strategies.
- **U**nderstand: to establish the training strategy, identifying the various forms of training that are appropriate to contributing to the resolution of the business issues. Key requirements are that training is a relevant input, that it addresses and contributes to the solution of the relevant business issues and that it is congruent with the culture of the organization.
- **C**reate: to develop the course architecture and a detailed plan of training actions including courses, mentoring and so on, and the associated time-scales.
- **C**onduct: to put in place the training to deliver the learning. This stage includes developing a detailed plan for the implementation of the training. All the required information should now have been gathered. The training materials are prepared and the training implemented.
- **E**valuate: to put in place procedures to monitor the business impact of the training and to measure the changes. This stage looks to establish the short- and long-term changes that the training has on the participants' attitudes, behaviours and the results they achieve.

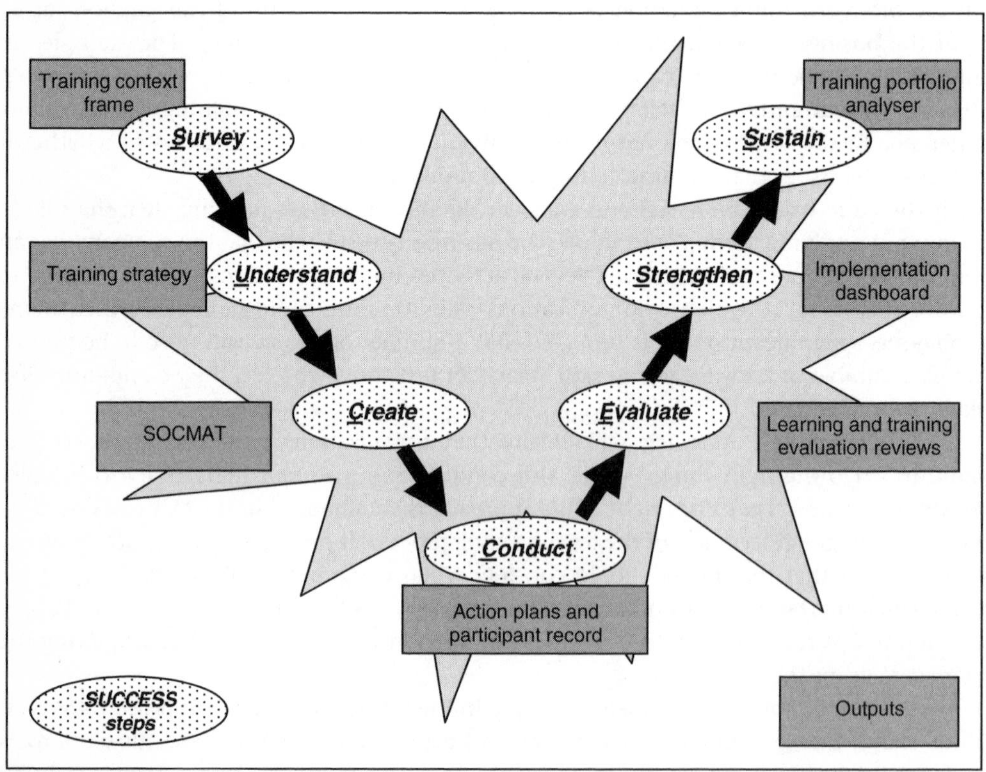

Figure 6.3 The SUCCESS training process

- **S**trengthen: to implement methods that reinforce the training messages. This stage is concerned with the provision of support and assistance to the trainees to implement the learning in their daily work and change their behaviours. Importantly the operational and organizational enablers must be in place to allow the learning to be put into practice.
- **S**ustain: giving management the tools to ensure the learning becomes a part of the normal way the organization does business, providing the platform for further training and development. This stage covers the use of training events to build an organizational learning culture.

Each step of the SUCCESS process generates a number of tangible outputs, which are the inputs into the next step. These outputs are:

- *Training context frame*: in the 'survey' stage, business issues to be addressed and the role of training therein are identified.
- *Training strategy*: in the 'understand' stage, the training methods that are applicable, their links to the management processes operating in the organization and the time-scale for implementation are specified.
- *SOCMAT*: In the 'create' stage, the objectives and main learning points from each session are detailed (see page 68 for further details).
- *Action plans and participant records*: in the 'conduct' stage, the actions that participants intend to implement following the training course and a record of participants' performance on the course are delivered.
- *Learning and training evaluation reviews*: in the 'evaluate' stage, the extent that each individual has achieved their learning objectives following the course and the overall impact of the training are assessed.
- *Implementation dashboard*: in the 'strengthen' stage, the extent of implementation and the extent to which the enablers have been put into place are monitored.
- *Training portfolio analyser*: in the 'sustain' stage, all the training made available is analysed to assess its impact on the implementation of the organization's strategy.

In turn this then feeds into the 'survey' stage, for the next cycle of training.

Applying the SUCCESS model to particular organizations

Readers will, while reading the previous section, have related the applicability of the SUCCESS training process to particular organizations with which they are familiar, and probably concluded that not all parts are applicable or even feasible in particular instances. Clearly the conditions that are present in unsophisticated training organizations, described as 'level one – trainee driven' in our model of organizational training commitment, are not conducive to the implementation of all but a small part of the 'conduct' stage of SUCCESS. On the other hand, organizations at 'level four – strategy driven' will be able to implement all of the elements of SUCCESS.

As a guide, Table 6.2 gives an indication of the parts of SUCCESS that are applicable in whole or in part to each level of organizational commitment to training.

The dilemma facing the HR director described at the beginning of this chapter becomes

Table 6.2 Application of SUCCESS to each level of organizational training commitment

	Level 1 Trainee driven	*Level 2 Management driven*	*Level 3 TNA driven*	*Level 4 Strategy driven*
Survey				✓
Understand			✓	✓
Create		✓	✓	✓
Conduct	✓	✓	✓	✓
Evaluate			✓	✓
Strengthen				✓
Sustain				✓

clearer when put into the context of Table 6.2. The level of organizational commitment to training was at level two – management driven. In fact the role of the central HR function in training had only recently emerged and was still regarded with suspicion by many operational managers. It would therefore appear that there is little that could be done to get stronger buy-in from line managers to the training until the organization has developed further to level three and even level four. This would not be true. It should still be possible to show some link, albeit at an anecdotal rather than scientific level, between training, changed behaviour and results achieved. However, for reasons that are now apparent, the HR director would be unwise to expect this to have a major impact on the attitudes of the line managers, although it would probably be of more than passing interest to the finance director.

Through the remainder of Part II of this book we will look at each stage of the SUCCESS process and identify a number of tools and techniques for the trainer to use in developing and implementing training across varying cultures. Here, we are essentially concerned with structures and processes. In Part III we will address the very specific steps that trainers need to take to deliver exceptionally successful training in an international context.

Summary

Unless training of international managers is perceived to be generating good returns to the business, the holding of training events will tend to be an on-off activity mirroring the economic performance of the company. Four levels of organizational commitment to training have been identified – trainee driven, management driven, TNA driven and strategy driven. Companies evolve through these levels. Generally, multi-national companies will be more sophisticated and are likely to be at levels three or four although there are many exceptions.

Relating the training process to the company's strategy ensures a holistic approach and enhances the likelihood that it will deliver business results. Further, it will increase the buy-in from line management to the training and generate greater support, which the HR director referred to at the beginning of this chapter perceived as a problem.

The acronym SUCCESS neatly sums up the seven steps to implementing the training process – Survey, Understand, Create, Conduct, Evaluate, Strengthen, Sustain. Each step has a number of specific outputs. The extent to which each part of SUCCESS can be applied is dependent on the level of commitment to training that the organization has reached.

Although SUCCESS is equally appropriate when managing local training processes, the need to apply it for international training, for reasons discussed in this chapter, is even more important.

Benchmark your organization

Readers will have subjectively positioned organizations they are acquainted with at one of the four levels of organizational commitment to training. To make a more objective judgement, answer the benchmarking questions in Table 6.1.

Tick the response to each statement that is nearest to your perception of the actual current situation.

For each tick in column A, score 1 point; B, 2 points; C, 3 points; and D, 4 points. Add up the number of points.

Action plan

If the score is between 7 and 12, the organization is at level one – trainee driven.
If the score is between 13 and 18, the organization is at level two – management driven.
If the score is between 19 and 23, the organization is at level three – TNA driven.
If the score is between 24 and 28, the organization is at level four – strategy driven.

	A	*B*	*C*	*D*
The primary responsibility for identifying training requirements lies with ...	the trainee	the trainee's manager	the HR function	the Board
Managers' involvement with the training of their subordinates ...	is very limited	identifies training requirements and obtains post-course feedback	agrees PDP and monitors implementation	agrees PDP, monitors implementation and provides coaching and mentoring
The size of the training budget is ...	small	quite small	moderate	large
The role of the central training/HR function is ...	negligible	to monitor training	to co-ordinate training	to drive training
The status/power of the central HR/training function is ...	low	quite low	medium	high
The attitude of management to training is ...	avoidable cost	unavoidable cost	cost that should generate some benefit	investment
The amount of management time devoted to training and related issues is ...	low	quite low	significant	high

CHAPTER **7**

Surveying the Background and the Context

A Swiss manufacturer of personal care products, distributed through supermarkets and specialist retailers, was concerned about the time it took for new products, conceived and tested in its laboratories, to be launched on the local market. The company's marketing director was convinced that most of the delay was due to the conflicts between managers from the supply chain, finance, marketing, customer development and the innovation centre when they met to plan the launch of a new product. This was the 'training trigger'.

The company is part of a global, fast-moving consumer goods company, the local chief executive being German, the marketing director being Dutch and the remainder of the board being Swiss.

As so often happens, we were invited to discuss the issue with the marketing director alone initially. Clearly this was an important business issue. The company had in the past developed some significant innovations, but had not always achieved first-mover advantage. One contributory reason might be that the launches had been under discussion for so long that the competitors had often received intelligence about the intended launches, giving them time to develop effective strategies in the market either to pre-empt the launch or react very effectively to it.

On leaving the initial meeting we had gathered some useful information about the issue itself, but very many questions were forming in our heads about all the possible reasons for the tardiness of recent launches, including:

- How easy is it for a German-born chief executive to co-ordinate a largely Swiss board?
- Was the very direct and clearly stressed Dutch marketing director pushing too hard in the launch meetings and causing a natural resistance?
- Were there problems in persuading the retailers to list another innovation from this company when the recent history of new product launches was not very positive?
- How realistic were the marketing director's demands for the supply chain to source and fill a new shaped bottle for the most recent new product?

We were being asked to train the heads of the different functions and their immediate reports to work more effectively together as a team so as to reduce the time it took to launch the next new product.

This chapter explores how the consultant can survey the background and context of this type of issue in order to be able to fulfil the brief with greater insight and relevance. The process is shown in Figure 7.1.

Before interviewing relevant managers in the client company, preliminary research should be carried out regarding both the external environment in which the organization operates and its internal situation. This should prepare the trainer for conducting interviews with the training sponsor and other senior managers who can give their views on why the training is required. At the same time the managers will form their own perceptions of the trainer, which are likely to be more positive if they feel the trainer has a good grasp of their company's external and internal environment. Once all the data is obtained it

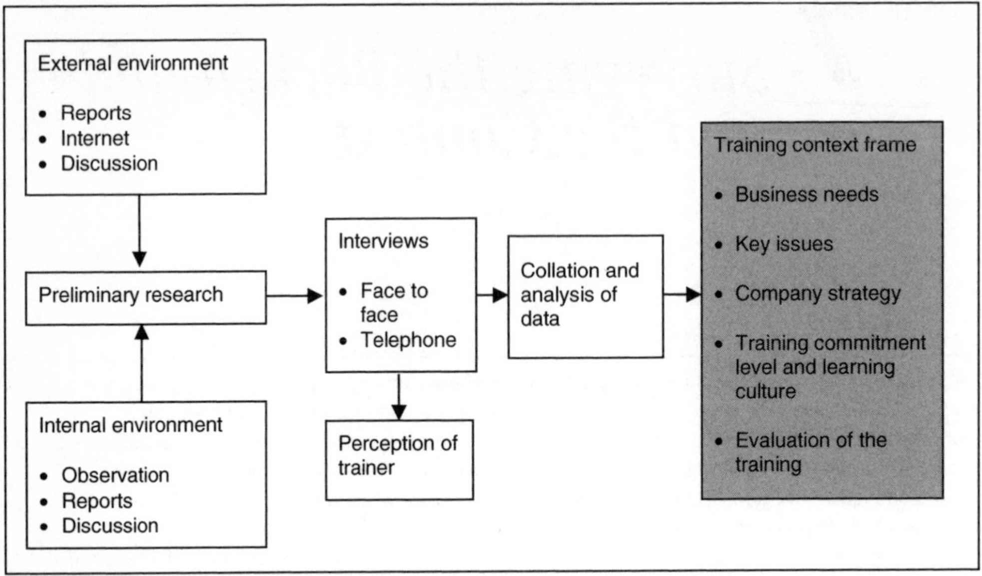

Figure 7.1 The surveying process

should be analysed and a training context frame developed that provides the background and framework for the training.

Breadth before depth

In this type of situation there is a great temptation, particularly when operating in their familiar home culture, for the training consultant to move straight to a series of interviews with the board members and their immediate reports to establish all the perceptions as soon as possible. (The term training consultant is used here rather than 'trainer' as this stage of the process may well be carried out by someone who is a consultant expert in identifying training needs.) Interviewing will of course be an important part of understanding the training needs, and will be discussed in the next chapter, but is there background work to do first? The answer to this question depends on how well informed the training consultant is about the company, its sector, its markets, its customers and its competitors.

If the consultant has only a general understanding of fast-moving consumer goods, but little specific knowledge about the personal products sector, the Swiss market, the local customers and the competition, it is essential to do some research into the external environment in which the client company is working. At the very least this will give the consultant more credibility when meeting the company's senior team and it will probably also enable the consultant to ask more insightful questions at the interview stage.

A considerable amount of the essential background information is in the public domain. A study of recent articles in the local trade press will soon tell the consultant the names of the key competitors and the customers, even if it does not reveal up-to-date details such as market shares. Competitors' websites are likely to give significant information on their product ranges and recent product introductions. Very soon a picture can be drawn of the environment in which the client company is operating. This picture should go beyond local boundaries to include multi-national competitors and customers as well as local players.

Armed with this valuable information it is now time for the consultant to gather information about the client company itself. Is it a stand-alone Swiss company? Does it operate in other markets? Who owns the company? What can we learn about the shareholders' objectives, short term and longer term? Do the statements of vision, mission and aims of the company, if they exist in written form, tell us anything useful about the issue surrounding new product launches?

Useful additional sources of information

At this stage it is worth investigating whether there are any processes within the client company that will have created similar survey data that would be useful. For instance, if work has been done to create a 'balanced scorecard' as shown in Figure 7.2, there may well be an analysis of the changes that need to take place in internal business processes to balance the financial perspective with planned actions to improve strategic performance and results. When working on the survey stage of an assignment concerned with identifying the training needs of senior customer managers in the European subsidiary of a major multi-national, we asked if there had been any recent work done in the area of identifying the strategic challenges of managing 'Pan-European' customers. We were given the results of a balanced scorecard exercise. This showed very clearly that the company needed to recognize the future challenge posed by the consolidation of their customers across national boundaries in Europe. This in

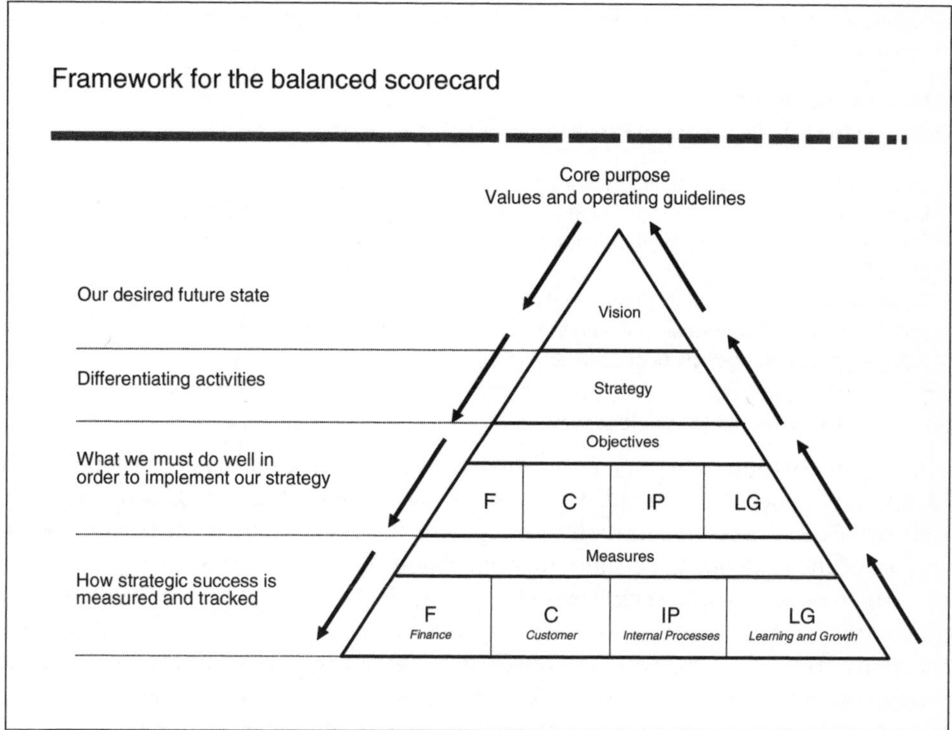

Figure 7.2 The balanced scorecard

turn led to the inclusion of a session, run by an expert in the field, on the consolidation of retailers, not only in Europe, but across the globe, so that participants could appreciate that this trend is only in its infancy but is likely to gather speed over the next few years.

If the assignment was being carried out in the UK it would be worth finding out if the client company had been assessed for the Investors in People award as this could give valuable information about existing plans and actions for training in this and any associated areas, as well as including useful information on the company's business plan and its HR development strategy. An Investors in People diagnostic report could reveal very useful information about the 'training literacy' of the organization, giving a greater insight into the level of organizational training commitment discussed in Chapter 6. It could even give the extent of its annual training budget, as well as information about training policies and plans. Figure 7.3 below gives information about the scope of the Investors in People process.

The Investors in People Standard is based on four key principles

Commitment
Commitment to invest in people to achieve business goals.

Planning
Planning how skills, individuals and teams are to be developed to achieve these goals.

Action
Taking action to develop and use necessary skills in a well-defined and continuing programme directly tied to business objectives.

Evaluating
Evaluating outcomes of training and development for individuals' progress towards goals, value achieved and future needs.

Achieving the Standard
Being recognized as an 'Investor in People' involves a number of steps:

- Understanding the Standard and its strategic implications for your organization.
- Undertaking a review against the Standard to identify any gaps in current practice.
- Making the commitment to meet the Standard and communicating that commitment to all members of staff.
- Planning and taking action, to bring about change.
- Bringing together the evidence for assessment against the Standard.
- Achievement or recognition as an Investor in People.

Figure 7.3 The Investors in People process

During an assignment to design some management training for the professional staff of an Employers' Association in the UK, mention was made of the diagnostic report for Investors in People. The organization was happy to share the report, as the training would form part of the evidence to be submitted in support of achieving the Investors in People award. The report, based on interviews with professional and support staff, painted a clear picture of the need for managers to learn the skills of delegation in order to improve office productivity. This coincided with our observations about the need for a more supportive approach towards working together, between professional and support staff. As a result delegation skills became an important part of the programme which eventually enabled the association to extend its services to members without any addition to staff numbers.

The likelihood of the company sharing this type of confidential information with an external or internal consultant is not just dependent on the nature of the organizational culture but also the social culture. Those organizations with relatively high power distance ratings such as in India or Belgium where knowledge reinforces power are likely to feel more uncomfortable compared with those in the USA or Sweden in allowing access by outsiders or lower-status internal staff to this type of information.

Armed with as much of the above information as possible, plus a chart showing organizational structure and whatever documents exist to describe the new product launch process (in the case of the Swiss company described at the beginning of this chapter), now is the time to prepare for a structured interview with all the senior managers involved in the product launch process.

Preparation for interactions within the client company

In preparation for these interviews, in common with any assignment of this type the consultant needs to think through the following and frame the questions to be asked:

- What is the essential information to be collected about each manager's perceptions of the issue?
- What needs to be recorded about each manager's feelings about recent material events, namely, new product launches in the case of the Swiss company described earlier?
- Where do conflicts about the issue arise?
- How does this issue relate to other business issues that are current?

With these thoughts in mind, a set of questions needs to be established prior to the individual interviews.

Once the framework of questions is in place, the training consultant needs to arrange appointments with each of the senior managers. It is important that each manager is given approximately the same length of time to be interviewed, so that it is clear that the intention is to give similar weight to the views of each interviewee. There is usually a benefit in carrying out the interviews at the place of work of each of the senior managers. It is an opportunity to become more closely aligned with the culture of the organization.

Gaining an understanding of the culture of an organization is very helpful in planning the delivery of training and considering how the new learning is likely to be transferred to the workplace. Organizational culture can be appreciated by observing symbols and noticing the rituals that take place within the company. For instance, the type of building, office layout, the way that people defer to those in authority all provide useful clues when developing the training. Training is much more likely to be accepted if a conscious effort is made to tailor it to the existing culture. If all the signs are that the company is pragmatic rather than sophisticated, the approach to the training needs to be pragmatic. If the atmosphere and dress code is very informal, the training consultant's dress code and approach needs to fit in. Scandinavia, Benelux, France and Germany tend to be fairly informal. Italy, Spain, Portugal, Eastern Europe and the Middle and Far East are more formal. However, even within individual cultures there are likely to be differences between dress codes in organizations. 'Dress down Friday' has been adopted by many non-US organizations.

When conducting the interviews there will be differences in perception due to individual personality and experience as well as differences in national characteristics. In the Swiss example, all the senior managers were Western European in origin and there were clear differences between individuals due to personality and experience as well as nationality. The fact that a person has a supply chain background will impact on that individual's perception about new product launch issues as well as the fact that the person originates within Western Europe. These cultural differences have an important part to play. For example, both in phrasing questions and interpreting the answers the consultant should be sensitive to such issues as:

- saving face, particularly with Eastern and African cultures;
- respect for hierarchy in high power distance cultures;
- importance of respecting the family and social context in low masculinity cultures.

At the same time it is extremely valuable to keep the antennae tuned to pick up clues about the true level of management commitment to training. It is helpful to have the model describing the level of organizational commitment as shown in Figure 6.3 in Chapter 6 in mind when doing this in order to position the client organization at the appropriate level. For instance, client organizations at level four and even level three will want to see any proposed training fitting into the present or likely future market, competitive, general economic and social context, while those at levels one and two will be content that the training is relevant to the individual's job role. Likewise, clues will be obtained regarding later parts of the training process such as the approach to designing and delivering training. In an organization at level two it will be quite different from the approach towards the task in an organization that is a leader in level four. A client at level four will be open to suggestions of involvement of managers and specialist support staff in the follow-up to any traditional off-the-job training, whereas the organization at level two may see the suggestion of follow-up coaching as being an unwelcome diversion of management resources.

Another important consideration is that, even at the survey stage, it is well worth making an assessment about how the training is likely to be evaluated. Certainly it is worth asking 'what is the normal evaluation process?' It may also be possible to learn something from existing documentation. Whatever is written down, it is likely that verbal feedback on the quality and value of the training inputs will be of importance, and some of this feedback will be related to how well the trainer managed to fit in with the cultural norms of the client organization. The reality is that the training consultant needs to be aware that there is likely to be open discussion within any organization about all of the face-to-face interactions, and there are a multitude of opportunities to say the wrong thing or be seen to behave inappropriately within the cultural norms of a particular organization.

Equally important at the survey stage is the need to consider how the learning from the training is likely to be transferred to the workplace. This will give further clues about the level of training commitment in the organization. What is the evidence for successful transfer of previous training? What are the barriers likely to be? How much one-to-one coaching is going on in the daily running of the business? Observation and a few casual questions about previous experience can reveal much information in terms of existing processes and, even more importantly, prevailing attitudes. For instance, if a very positive customer service attitude prevails amongst front-line staff alongside regular training and coaching, it will suggest that where the organization buys-in to people development it is capable of translating the learning into effective behaviour within the business.

Outputs from the survey stage

The outputs from the survey stage can be summarized in the training context frame. This comprises several sections, as shown in Table 7.1.

The left-hand column should be regarded as a checklist. Other issues may crop up during this stage which can be added at the bottom of the context frame.

The training context frame is useful in a number of ways:

- It can be used as part of an interim report specifying the proposed training.
- It ensures all the important issues have been covered in the survey stage.
- It makes explicit the link between the issues and the training, ensuring that none are overlooked.

Table 7.1 Training context frame

	Description	*Implication for training*
External issues • Markets • Customers • Competitors • Suppliers • Technology • Legal • Economic		
Internal issues • Vision/mission/goals • Rhythm of business • Main processes • Core competences/ strengths • Competences gap • Organization culture • Organization structure • Company strategy		
Summary of business needs		
Training issues • Training trigger • Facilitators • Barriers • Approach to training (level of commitment) • Local cultural issues		
Evaluation of training		
Other relevant matters • •		

Summary

Whatever the training assignment, it is important to survey the background and the context of the business issue. First of all, it is appropriate to assess that there should be a training solution to the problem and then to collect as much information as is practical in order to understand the organizational context of the particular issue and the type of training solution that could be possible.

The survey should encompass understanding the factors external to the company that could impact on the issue and the client's preferred approach to organizing the training. Then it is important to collect information about the internal factors, through data collection and interviews where necessary. Importantly for the trainer, senior managers are likely to be drawing their own conclusions about the trainer's suitability for the task based partly on how well he or she understands and relates to the company, its environment and the issues triggering the training.

This process will provide not only the necessary factual information, but also give an important insight into the company culture and the management's approach to the resolution of business problems and the role of training. It can be anticipated that the behaviour of individual managers within this culture will vary according to their personality and experience as well as to their national background.

Even at this early stage it is important to try to find out how training is likely to be evaluated and also what support mechanisms are likely to be practicable in helping participants apply their learning in the work situation.

The training context frame is a useful device to bring together the key outputs from the survey stage and draw out the implications for the proposed training.

For a training event for international managers that you are planning, consider which of the areas in the Action plan need to be investigated at the survey stage, making notes on how you would intend to obtain the information on each one.

Action plan

Areas to be investigated	*How to obtain the information*
Business sector, market environment and customers	
Competitors' strengths and characteristics	
Suppliers, technology, legal	
Vision, mission, aims of the shareholders and directors, strategy	
Organization structure	
Predominant characteristics of the organization's culture	
Core competences and competence gap	
Training trigger	
Company approach towards the resolution of similar problems and the role of training	
Level of organization training commitment	
Features of the organization's rhythm (seasonal, cyclical features)	
Nationalities and background of the 'key influencers' and local cultural issues	
The organization's training policy, plan and budget	
Support mechanisms used to enhance the transfer of learning to the workplace	
How training is normally evaluated	

CHAPTER 8 Understanding the Training Needs, Real and Perceived

An international law firm based in the City of London was finding it difficult to complete documents for clients on time and this sometimes caused delay to major transactions. In common with many lawyers the partners dictated most of their documents for transcription using a secretary. (Dictation is fast for those who have used it for many years and the lawyers are reticent to move to typing their own documents, although some of them were experimenting with voice recognition systems.)

In this case, the partners blamed their secretaries for the delays, because of the length of time it took secretaries to transcribe their tapes and the number of mistakes that were being made in the transcription. They contacted the firm's training manager to organize some training for the secretaries.

The firm had a system of secretarial co-ordinators in each department and the training manager called a meeting of these co-ordinators to discuss the issue with them. They were well aware of the productivity issue and the consequences of the backlog of work. However, they had serious doubts whether training the secretaries would improve the situation. After the meeting they produced a selection of tapes for the training manager to hear. He was surprised how difficult the tapes were to understand, how inconsistently instructions were given on punctuation, and how lawyers mixed the words intended for inclusion in the text with those that were meant to be instructions to the typist.

Certainly a training need had been discovered, but even if some of the secretaries could benefit from a refresher course on transcribing dictation, there were at least an equal number of lawyers who needed to learn the basic skills of dictation. This was not a problem caused by the English language skills of the many overseas lawyers working in the partnership, but a result of the failure to train some of the lawyers properly in how to use a dictation machine effectively.

Following the previous chapter which advocated the need for breadth in surveying the environment in which a training need has arisen, this chapter will focus on the depth of investigation and analysis that is required to identify training needs precisely so that the training is prepared for the right people, with the most appropriate content and the most effective methods of delivery. This 'understanding' process is shown in Figure 8.1. The training needs can be assessed at three levels – at the organizational, the group and the individual level. They are then related to the outputs of the previous stage – the 'training context frame' – and the areas where knowledge and skills are deficient (the competence gap) are identified. This then reveals the learning gap and thereby the training needs. These are then brought together in the form of a training strategy.

Understanding organizational training needs

While the very particular type of issue, described above, is typical of the challenge that training managers and consultants regularly face, we should consider, before moving on to

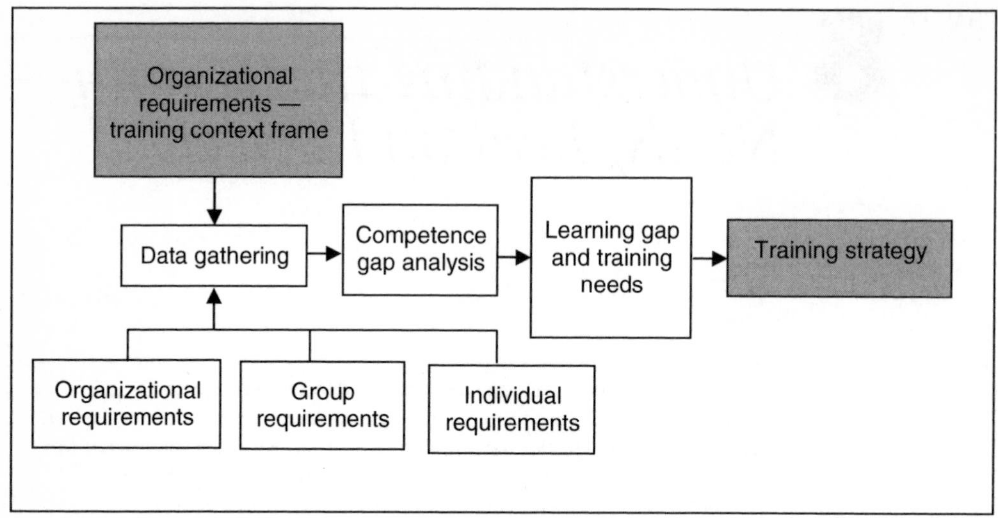

Figure 8.1 Understanding the training needs process

look at group and individual requirements, the possibility that an organization may wish to carry out a complete analysis of the gaps that exist between current levels of competence and the current and future competences required of all or a number of its management groups.

By a competence we simply mean the ability of people to apply a relevant element of skill or knowledge in a business situation. This can be a 'hard' business skill, such as interpreting financial data, or a 'soft' skill, such as motivating a team. It must be pointed out that this is a slightly different use of the word compared with the previous chapter, where it was used more generally in the context of organizational competences to refer to the things that the organization was or needed to be particularly good at in order to succeed in implementing its strategy.

This all-encompassing approach to training needs analysis is not a frequent occurrence but it may be required from time to time when the organization wishes to fundamentally review its training approach and philosophy. This can occur as organizations move between levels two and three or three and four of the 'levels of training commitment model' described in Chapter 6. It can also arise from foreseen changes in market conditions, or from a deliberate change in direction of the business, or from the implementation of an initiative such as Investors in People. It requires a total review of business strategy to identify those management competences required in the future which are different from those required in the past.

When such a fundamental review is required it will usually include, as a first step, the redefinition of the skills, knowledge and competences needed in each function and job. Then a process would need to be established to measure each manager's current level of skills, knowledge and competence against the new requirement to identify the gaps that need to be addressed. There are broadly two approaches that are used: competence gap analysis and benchmarking.

COMPETENCE GAP ANALYSIS

In short, the major challenge in assessing levels of competence in this way for groups of international managers is one of language and context. As an example, using the standards published by the Management Charter Initiative, take Unit 12, Element 1, Performance Criteria 6 of Management NVQ Level 5 in the section dealing with competences needed during a downsizing exercise – 'Your plans for redeployment take account of the personal qualities, situation and preferences of those involved.' Imagine a scenario where there is a plan for significant restructuring of a multi-national organization in many countries across the world. It is necessary to make a judgement about the competence levels of many managers in many different countries on this particular performance criterion, amongst others. Imagine how differently people from a range of cultures would be likely to interpret the phrases 'personal qualities, situation and preferences'. Even where we share a common tongue and live in a homogeneous culture, so much individual judgement is involved that it is extremely difficult to determine objectively what this standard means. Attempting to do it worldwide, whether by translating the standard into local languages, or relying on a person with English as a second or third language to interpret, the challenge is significant.

Consequently most organizations will, within general guidelines, leave the development of performance criteria within competency systems to HR specialists at the local level except possibly for the most senior jobs.

Competence gap analysis is widely used in the USA, Germany and the UK, less in other parts of the world. A development of the last two years in these countries has been to recognize that we should not only be determining current gaps in competence, but should also look forward to probable changes in the business environment and identify those competences which are likely to be required in the future.

BENCHMARKING

Another method used to assess where organizational training needs exist is to measure the performance of particular parts of the organization against the performance of other parts of its own organization or against similar organizations, sometimes competitors. This is usually known as 'benchmarking', and is a valid method of identifying differences in levels of performance, although it will often require a process such as competence gap analysis to determine the reasons for the differences in the levels of performance and to pinpoint the precise area of the training need. Benchmarking is more widely applied than competence gap analysis, with developing countries regularly using it to compare improvements in their performance with more developed areas of the world. For instance, manufacturing performance in some Brazilian businesses has been improved dramatically by investigating areas of 'people performance' in the factories compared with Europe and the USA. Usually the training improvements that are made are part of a Total Quality Management initiative and they do involve a detailed analysis of skill and knowledge gaps as the basis for developing programmes of training.

Defining training needs at the organizational level, as described above, is not a frequent occurrence in organizations, but at the level of the functional group, or the project team, it is much more common.

Understanding group training needs

In the Swiss example in Chapter 7, the group was perceived to have a common need to learn to work together more effectively, managing the conflicts that arose from different personal and cultural experiences.

> Here is another example of group training needs analysis that we were involved in. A number of individual managers, from diverse backgrounds, joined a multi-national company at a similar time in many different countries, all of whom shared the common need to learn about their new organization's business strategy and common business processes.
>
> Detailed understanding of the training needs of this group involved the completion of questionnaires or interviews with the potential participants and their bosses to identify common areas where their functions require them to be able to interpret the current business strategy and use the existing business processes. The questionnaire covered their understanding of their job requirements, its objectives and context; their interactions within the company, and their understanding of the company's strategy and their role within it. The views of their bosses were also obtained on their perceptions of the appointee's job and progress so far; their interactions and relationships within the company; the challenges with and for new appointees and the context and length of the proposed training. The information obtained was not only of a factual nature but also included the perceptions and feeling of the appointees and their bosses about this new form of recruitment and the challenges posed by it. This information was very useful in the design of the training programme because it would potentially identify areas of frustration and misunderstanding which needed to be dealt with.

Clearly the administration of questionnaires requires great sensitivity in some cultures as they are probing areas of knowledge where inadequacies almost certainly exist. The answers may also imply some inadequacy in training that has already been received. In both respects there will be some reticence in giving forthright answers in many parts of the Far East, both for fear of loss of face and criticism from the local management. The interviewer needs to be someone who has gained high levels of trust with both managers and employees. Even in Europe and the USA, answers are more likely to be honest if the interviewer is known to be discreet and trustworthy. The issue for the interviewer in these parts of the world is likely to be the level of validity of the answers, rather than the lack of answers.

Another practical implication is the cost of face-to-face interviews when conducted in places distant from where the project is centred. Local interviewers will be cheaper to use in this sense and may be better in terms of phrasing questions sensitively and respecting the desire to avoid some sensitive issues. They will, however, need to be carefully briefed to use the questionnaires so that important responses are properly recorded.

Sometimes, for both cost and speed reasons, it may be appropriate to administer the questionnaire via the company's intranet or even mail it to recipients. While this has much to commend it, there can be a feeling that the responses will not be treated confidentially and that line managers may be able to access them. This is obviously as much an organizational, as it is an international, culture issue. In addition, with any form of self-completion questionnaire, the amount of thought that has gone into its completion will vary. Was it completed quickly as just one item of the manager's 'to do' list, or was each question answered in detail and were there additional comments over and above the minimum asked for? Further, different cultures react differently to deadlines so the responses may not all be returned by the time they are needed. As a Frenchman once said to us on a training course, the problem of being late is only a problem to those who are punctual.

When information is collected as a result of using a questionnaire or interviewing a number of individuals, great care needs to be taken to ensure that the subsequent analysis is carried out objectively. Clearly, if the same or a similar answer is given by a large proportion of the respondents, significant weight should be attached to it. If only a small minority make a particular point, the training consultant needs to take care not to give this point such weight, even if it is a point with which the training consultant agrees wholeheartedly! The analysis should stand up to inspection. In fact, the client should be invited to review the analysis.

Understanding individual training needs

THE PERFORMANCE APPRAISAL

Most organizations employing international managers derive individual training needs from an appraisal or development review system conducted at least annually. The quality of the training needs assessment carried out by individual managers in this way is typically very mixed. As a result, the needs are satisfied with varying levels of commitment. There is a trend, as organizations move towards levels three and four of organizational training commitment, at least in the USA and Europe for managers to be increasingly responsible for their own development and to take the initiative in arranging their own learning. This trend also includes involving their direct boss to give them coaching in at least the task-related needs, although it has to be said that many bosses find it difficult to give sufficient time to this particular responsibility.

Performance appraisal is surprisingly widely used. In a group of 18 MBA students in their late twenties, with work experience on every continent between them, every one had received an appraisal with a discussion on development needs within the last year. Experiences were extremely varied and there was a cultural flavour depending on the level of power distance in that society. However, even in the USA and Europe where performance appraisal has been common practice for over 30 years, its value in defining genuine training needs varies tremendously depending on the culture of the organization, the relationship of appraiser and appraisee, and the skill of the appraiser in relating levels of performance in particular aspects of a job to a training need.

For this reason it is good practice to check out the validity of the training needs identified at the appraisal by holding discussions with the appraisee, appraiser and possibly peers and more senior managers who are in a position to comment objectively on the appraisee's work.

A review of the 'development needs' section of the appraisal form across the whole range of managers in an organization, checked out with these supplementary conversations, can reveal a considerable volume of similar training needs amongst managers working for the same organization in a range of different countries. Typically the common training needs will include a number of interpersonal and leadership skills, which can be dealt with in groups, followed up by individual coaching from the direct boss or a senior colleague. Other training needs, for instance in areas of specific professional or technical knowledge, are likely to exist amongst far smaller numbers of managers in a single organization, making the training of managers in groups a project on a more limited scale.

THE ASSESSMENT CENTRE AND PSYCHOMETRIC QUESTIONNAIRES

Another fruitful source of training needs is the assessment centre, whether this plays a part in initial recruitment, consideration for promotion, or the derivation of development needs. Assessment centres tend to reveal a very similar range of training needs to the appraisal form. Assessment centres are also a worldwide phenomenon, and discussions with those who have taken part in them in a wide range of different societies reveal a common feeling that they give a more objective view of personal development needs than do the boss/subordinate performance appraisal discussions.

The most commonly identified training needs for managers arising from either assessment centres or performance appraisal are still in the area of interpersonal skills as they were when the very first surveys were commissioned by personnel management associations in the 1970s. Consequently, it is valuable to consider briefly another useful tool in defining these needs for individuals.

There are types of personality questionnaire that are helpful in pinpointing individual needs for interpersonal skills development. It is advisable to use questionnaires that identify dimensions of personality where skills can be developed, rather than those which define a personality type. A good example are the questionnaires which measure dominance, influence, steadiness and compliance, particularly those systems which make an assessment of the requirements of the job on each of the four dimensions as well as an assessment of the individual. These systems, which all derive from Marston's work in the 1920s, have been used to assess working strengths and areas for development since the 1950s. It is, of course, extremely important to be sensitive to local cultural beliefs in administering these instruments. For instance, in France it would still be true at this time that managers give graphology (handwriting analysis) more credence than they do psychometric instruments. The opposite would be true in most other parts of the world!

JOB ANALYSIS

It is also appropriate to mention here the most traditional method for identifying individual training needs, although it is now recognized as being rather static in the context of today's fast-moving workplace. Traditionally the job would be analysed in terms of the skills and knowledge required, and then the current levels of skill and knowledge of the individual would be matched against the results of this analysis to identify the gaps. In addition to this, the common errors made in the job would be analysed to identify the skills and knowledge required to avoid repetition of these errors. This aspect of the analysis certainly has a value in trying to prevent the same mistakes being made time and again by generations of managers during their tenure in a particular job.

Underlying the process of job analysis is the premise that a job can be broken down into discrete tasks that can be tackled and improved individually. It is a very logical approach which will have greater resonance in cultures such as Germany and Switzerland than in Brazil or South Africa.

OBSERVATION

We should recognize that, although all these objective techniques of identifying managers' training needs are reasonably well known, the majority of training requirements are probably identified by observation. Senior managers in all cultures observe and discuss the behaviour of their subordinates and jointly decide that some specific training should improve their performance. When determining how the training budget should be spent, they may even include in their assessment observations made to them by customers and other outside contacts. Although perhaps less objective than the other methods we have discussed, this method will continue to have real value, if only because it carries with it an implied management commitment to use training to bring about an improvement.

Outputs from the understand stage

The analysis of organization, group and individual competences in relationship to those required will lead to the identification of the gap that learning needs to fill and, from there, the training requirement. For example, in the case of the law firm referred to at the beginning of this chapter, the organizational imperative was to improve client service, one element of which was the group requirement for solicitors to dispatch legal documents more speedily. The skill that needed to be enhanced was that of improving the quality of their dictation. The training strategy, which is the output from the understand stage, identifies the main ways in which this will be brought about.

Clearly there are usually a number of alternatives available, from self-study, distance learning and Internet-based learning through to in-house tailor-made training programmes and on-the-job coaching. These alternatives are not necessarily mutually exclusive and indeed a blended solution may be most appropriate. Each alternative has its advantages and disadvantages which are well known and we do not intend to go over them again in this book. Our objective is to add some additional dimensions that need to be borne in mind when training international managers.

Costs generally tend to be higher. International managers need to travel to training locations and generally expect a higher standard of accommodation and facilities than in a local situation. Because of these higher overhead costs, training is often of longer duration. Obviously these considerations do not apply to distance or self-learning where the main issue is one of time-zone differences.

The logistics of conducting international training courses tend to be more complex than holding local events. Organizing flights, finding locations that provide reasonably easy access for all participants takes time. Finding trainers with in-depth experience in dealing with multi-cultural participants may prove more difficult.

In training, as with much else in life, you get what you pay for. Hence more costly forms of training tend to be, though not always, more effective. With international managers, their fluency in the language of the training will have a significant impact. With less personal forms of training there is less opportunity for trainees to ask for help on the meaning of words, although they will be more able to proceed at their own pace and try to find out themselves. Another added benefit of bringing international managers together is that it provides opportunities for networking, which can prove valuable.

Travelling to and spending a few days in a foreign location can be attractive and motivating to participants as compared to more distant forms of learning.

A general framework for evaluating alternatives is shown in Table 8.1. For a particular competence (dictation skills in the above case), each alternative can be judged on a qualitative basis against a number of dimensions. If it is assessed as good then it can be given

Table 8.1 Training methodology evaluation grid

Competence(s) to be trained in						
Score: Poor = 1 Average = 2 Good = 3	*Cost*	*Ease of implement-ation*	*Likely effectiveness*	*Cultural fit*	*Appeal to trainees*	***Total***
Internal tailor-made course						
Internal standard course						
External course						
Distance learning						
E-learning						
On the job and mentoring						
Self-study						

a score of three, average = two and poor = one. Thus a training method that is low cost, easy to implement, very effective, a good cultural fit and will be attractive to the trainees would score three on each of these dimensions and have a total score of 15. If needed, more particular training solutions can be added such as, for example, distinguishing between an internal course led by internal or external trainers, or combining some e-learning with mentoring and so on.

The training strategy can now be developed and a suitable format is shown in Table 8.2. Each training intervention is given a title and the competences it aims to improve are listed. Key is specifying the level that learners need to achieve – from merely gaining an appreciation, to understanding, to having the ability to do or gaining mastery of the materials. The type or mode of training is then described. For example, one training event bringing together groups of no more than 20 managers combined on-line learning of the basic principles with a post-course project activity. The implementation time-scale for each element needs to be identified, and the way the learning is to be incorporated into the organization detailed. The latter might include project work, briefing of the participants' managers on what they need to follow up on, and so on.

If there are different training solutions planned to address different competences, then a training strategy is required for each.

The situation is made even more complex when a company wishes to deploy a particular training structure across a number of countries. This is often driven by a desire

Table 8.2 The training strategy

Course title	
Competences addressed (learning gap to be filled)	
Achievement level	
Training mode	
Time-scale	
How will learning be incorporated into the business?	

for uniform implementation of a centrally driven initiative such as Process Re-engineering or Total Quality Management. Local language skills are frequently needed, and a process needs to be put in place to train local trainers and coaches to meet centrally driven training standards.

Summary

Within the training context framework derived from 'survey', the previous SUCCESS stage, training needs can be identified for the whole organization, a group of employees, or for individuals.

Training needs analysis for the whole organization at one time is rare, and when it does happen it would usually be closely related either to changes in the level of training commitment in the organization or to a particular trend in business results. The main formal methods used, particularly in Europe and the USA, are:

- competence gap analysis
- benchmarking.

It is more usual for needs to be identified for individuals or groups and then aggregated to form a training plan for the organization.

The following methods are the most common for individuals and groups:

- observation of managers' behaviours
- job analysis by skills and knowledge
- development review reports from performance appraisal
- assessment centres
- psychometric questionnaires.

Based on the outputs from the training needs assessment, alternative mechanisms for delivering the training can be evaluated and a training strategy determined.

Think of the changes that are likely to take place in your own or a client's organization over the next two years. Typically there will be changes due to new technology, new systems, customer requirements for new products or services, combining or splitting of functions, geographic expansion or contraction, requirements for more effective performance, and so on. Use the Action plan to help you think through which jobs are likely to change and the most appropriate process to use to identify the training needs precisely.

Action plan

Business changes	*New competences required*
1.	
2.	
3.	
4.	
5.	
6.	

CHAPTER 9

Creating the Training Intervention and Preparing the Groundwork

We were commissioned by a global client who was seeking to create a case study covering the innovation and brand development aspects of marketing in a fast-moving consumer goods company. This was a central part of a five-day training event to introduce newly appointed managers from all functions to the key business processes of the company. There were to be 24 participants, all with a good facility in the English language, from ten different European countries, coming from six different functions.

Our brief was to work with a nominated technical specialist and a marketer to write a case study around the very successful launch of a new product to provide learning on the application of the company's innovation and brand development processes. It was envisaged that the consultant and the two specialists would be available to conduct the training.

The challenge in this assignment was to make the content sufficiently basic for the non-marketing participants to learn about the fundamentals of these processes, while making the methods of training delivery sufficiently challenging for the marketing and technical specialists to feel that they had increased their understanding of how the processes can be applied successfully in the marketplace.

The starting point was the output from the understand stage, the training strategy which answered 'What is the key learning for the participants?' and 'Which are likely to be the most successful methods to achieve that learning with such a wide variety of different functions and cultures?'

Having understood the processes and the main factors involved in this particular launch, we very quickly focused on how to deliver the learning. The participants were to be a relatively young, high-ability group, including a significant number of 'Activists' who would prefer to be doing rather than listening in order to learn effectively. Hence it was important to create some exercises where the participants were using the information in the case study to simulate the decision-making processes which are central to a product launch within this client company.

It was decided that the most effective approach from a learning point of view would be to have a short opening presentation to acquaint the participants with the market background and the proposed product specification. This would be followed by exercises carried out by four breakout groups with six participants in each, carefully mixing nationalities and functional expertise. There would be one exercise that all groups would attempt and four other different exercises, one of the four being specific to each group. The breakout groups would present their findings from each of the exercises to a technical specialist and a marketing specialist who were involved in the actual launch. These specialists would make comments on the feedback from the breakout groups, commenting favourably on the really good ideas and indicating where some piece of information or practical point had been overlooked. Discussion would be encouraged to consolidate the learning. This part of the session would be followed by a short presentation on the decisions that were actually taken and the consequences when the product was introduced on to the market.

The example in the boxed text above of how a particular piece of learning was created took into account the following.

The inputs used in this example were:

- The training strategy to address the identified need to enhance the participant competences in understanding the innovation and brand development processes through a series of centrally held training courses involving both internal and external speakers/trainers.
- The level of learning to be achieved by the participants.
- How the participants are likely to want to learn.
- The national culture and functional background of each participant.
- The materials available.
- The people available to take part in the conduct stage of the training.

The tools to be used in conducting the training course in this example were:

- PowerPoint for presenting facts and processes
- Exercises to challenge participants to use the facts and processes
- Feedback to practise persuasive presentation of ideas
- Breakout groups to encourage participants to learn from one another
- Discussion to consolidate the learning.

The outputs achieved in this example were:

- A set of clear learning objectives
- A schedule to fit the sessions into the overall programme
- Agreement on the roles to be played by each of the facilitators
- A list of equipment and facilities required.

This chapter will now examine a very useful tool that is the output of the create stage of the SUCCESS training framework involved in training international managers. The process is shown in Figure 9.1.

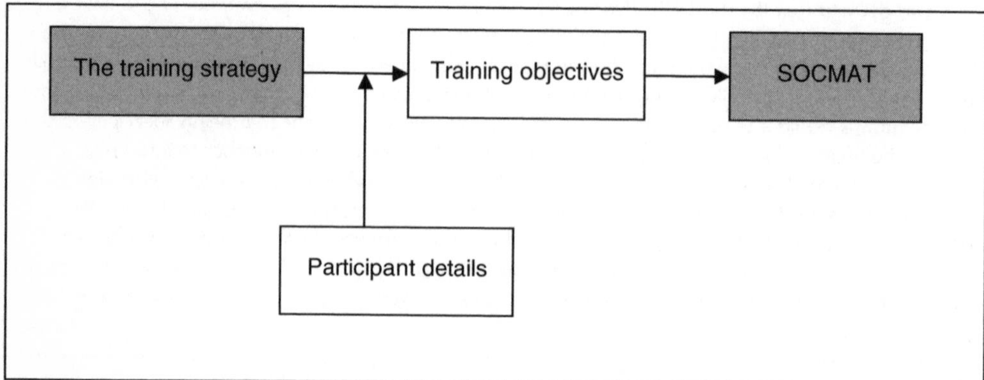

Figure 9.1 Creating the training process

This figure shows the input from the previous stage, plus the participant details leading to the development of the overall learning objectives and the SOCMAT, which is the key tool used in describing the detailed learning objectives and content of the programme (SOCMAT is described in more detail below).

The inputs

Normally the inputs to the create stage of the process will result from one or more of the training needs analysis methods listed in the summary of Chapter 8.

If the training needs analysis has been carried out with care we should have at this stage the training strategy, including:

- course title
- statements about the competences that need to be addressed (the learning gap that needs to be filled)
- information on the levels of learning to be achieved by the participants – appreciation, understanding, ability to do or mastery
- the training mode(s) to be employed
- the time-scales for implementation.

To this, details of the participants in terms of their previous relevant experience, nationality and ability in the course language need to be added.

If great care has been taken we may also have information on the preferred learning styles of each participant. For a small group this can be very useful; for a group as large as 24 given in the example at the beginning of the chapter it will probably be safe to assume that all four preferences – 'Activist', 'Reflector', 'Theorist' and 'Pragmatist' – will be held by the participants as a group.

Overall training/learning objectives

From these inputs, the task is to frame the overall learning objectives of the training and then design each element/module/session.

If the training strategy has been well formulated then the learning objectives will follow quite naturally from the statement of the competences that need to be addressed. In the case of the example described at the beginning of this chapter, the competence gap concerned the understanding and use of an innovation process. The overall objectives could therefore be phrased as follows:

> By the end of this training the participants will have an increased understanding of all the elements of the innovation process and how they impact on their role in the business and in turn how they impact on the innovation process.

Unfortunately, all too often the programme objectives are phrased in terms of the materials that the course covers rather than in terms of what the participants are expected to have achieved by the end of it in terms of appreciation, understanding, ability to do, or mastery of one or more competences. That is why we believe that the objectives should be termed 'learning' rather than 'training' objectives.

The output from the create stage

Having explicitly formulated the overall learning objectives, the next step is to design each element of the training. A fundamental and most useful tool for approaching this process in an orderly and logical way is the SOCMAT. It is so-called as it is an acronym of the first letters of the six aspects of the create process: session title; objectives; content; methods; aids; and timing. It is helpful to consider the training event as made up of a series of learning objects or units that we will call 'sessions'. Figure 9.2 below introduces an example of a SOCMAT for the case study example described at the beginning of this chapter which was part of a five-day training event. The tool is equally applicable to any training intervention including e-learning, coaching and self-study.

Using the SOCMAT format in Figure 9.2, each session should be given a title that describes the content succinctly. Under 'Objectives' should be described what the participants should learn as a result of the session. Initially the content should be outlined as a series of bullet points, so that the training materials for that session can be developed easily using the bullet points as a concise summary of all that is intended to be contained in the session.

At the time that the content is outlined, it is good practice to consider and decide on the learning method[1] to be used to help participants achieve the necessary level of learning as described under 'Methods' in the example in Figure 9.2. It is helpful to regularly review the methods that are available:

- presentation with visuals, videos and DVDs
- question/answer/discussion
- buzz groups
- brainstorming
- quiz
- simulation and role play
- CCTV and feedback
- case study and feedback
- individual and group exercises using participants' previous experience to solve a relevant problem
- practical work related to the content.

Constant reviewing of these methods of learning, along with any tried and tested new ones which are developed, is important if only to limit the proportion of the event which involves a presentation. This is critical in training international managers as it becomes extremely tiring for participants to listen to presentations in their non-native language for lengthy periods of time. In addition, even those participants from cultures that are more in tune with a pedagogical approach to learning often expect, and even hope, that formal international training events will be more enjoyable and insightful than local ones.

---

1 For more details on each of the methods of learning see Leslie Rae, *Effective Planning in Training and Development,* Kogan Page (2000) and Alison Hardingham, *Designing Training,* CIPD (1996).

Day 3: Innovation and brand development

SESSION TITLE	OBJECTIVES	CONTENT	METHODS	AIDS	TIMING
1. Background to the project	To ensure a common understanding of the initial pre-product development conditions	• Market and competitive background • Strengths and weaknesses • Product development process	• Presentation • Q & A	Slides/ projector Two flip charts Post it™ notes	09:00
2. Breakouts	To practise: 1 Anticipating competitive reaction 2 Comparison of competitive brand personalities 3 Ad. agency briefing 4 Defend strategy against competitive attack 5 Next major brand initiative	Exercise briefs	• All groups to do exercise one, and the other four exercises to be given to each of the four groups • Trainer and presenter to facilitate group work	Flip charts	10:00 Break 12:45
3. Feedback presentations	To ensure cross-team learning on: • the innovation and brand development process and the need to assess competitive reaction • the need to anticipate and develop contingency plans for post launch conditions	Key learning points	• Presentations by each group • Observations, discussion and comments by presenters • Each group to identify key learning points	Flip chart, slides/ projector	14:00 Break 15:45
4. The actual situation	• To understand what the real eventuality was • To deepen learning of the practical application of the innovation process	• The successes and required improvement areas in the original innovation and launch process • How the improvement areas were addressed • Relating the outputs from the breakouts to the actual situation and identifying key learning points	• Presentation and discussion • Group work with presentations by each group	Flip chart, slides/ projector	16:00 Break 17:45

Figure 9.2 Example of part of a completed SOCMAT

At the same time that decisions are made on the best training method to be used, it is important to list under 'Aids' any equipment or facilities that are going to be necessary for the delivery of the training and an estimate of the time to be allowed for each session, or part of the session, under 'Timing'. This is useful as an *aide-mémoire*, even if the training designer is also going to be the one to deliver the training. However, it is critical if the designer and deliverer are to be different people.

One of the aids required for each session and/or the course as a whole may be an 'action planning' format for participants to record their key learning and a note of how they are going to implement it after the course. This will be dealt with in more detail in Chapter 10, where a simple action-planning format is shown in Table 10.3.

As well as keeping the formal inputs relatively short, three additional considerations should be borne in mind when training an audience of international managers:

1 More time needs to be allocated to any formal presentational parts of the course to accommodate the need to slow down the pace of delivery and give sufficient time for participants to read any visual materials.
2 Exercises and breakout sessions will take longer as trainees take more time to read and comprehend the written materials.
3 Participants from high uncertainty avoidance, high power distance or low individuality cultures may be uncomfortable with methods such as role playing or brainstorming.

Use of the SOCMAT tool

The division of a training event into sessions is of fundamental importance. It should follow the principles first laid down by Douglas Seymour in his 1968 book *Skills Analysis Training* and called 'the part method' of learning. Seymour and his followers recognized that, where tasks are complex, it is much easier to learn a series of parts of the total task and then learn how to relate them to one another, than it is to attempt to learn the total task all at one time.

Now we will relate this process to creating a training event for international managers.

We should, first of all, create a session that gives an overview of the total task to be learned, along with an indication of how the sessions will approach this as a series of parts. This is following the old teaching adage, 'Tell them what you are going to tell them; tell them; and tell them what you have told them.' The overview session at the beginning is equivalent to the first of these three steps.

The division of the learning into sessions should follow the principle that each session has an identifiable theme and no more than three pieces of significant learning. Ideally it should incorporate at least two methods of learning and should probably not have a duration longer than 90 minutes. If some of the participants are likely to find the use of English challenging, then one and a half hours without a break is probably too long and 45 minutes is more appropriate. So legislating for some sort of different participant-centred activity every 20 to 40 minutes, or calling a five-minute break is appropriate. A participant-centred activity might, for example, include a breakout group working session on an individual situation analysis. Ideally breaks should take place before participants show signs of tiredness or restlessness.

Pre- and post-course activity

The SOCMAT tool provides the basis from which all the training materials can be created in detail. When the SOCMAT is developed, consideration should be given to before and after the training; this is discussed in more detail in the next and subsequent chapters. Especially where there are significant elements of new knowledge involved, thought should be given to providing these knowledge elements prior to the training event, either in hard-copy text or electronically via CD-ROM or the Internet, introducing some interactivity if at all possible. For the training of international managers this can serve an extremely useful purpose in introducing any specific technical terminology with which they may not be familiar.

The possibility of managers learning significant elements of knowledge before a training event depends very much on the culture of the organization where they work. The training designer needs to be totally realistic about what is likely to be done prior to a course and sometimes this will mean discounting the client's view about the international managers' application to this task! In many organizations the norm would be for managers to begin to turn their attention to the pre-course work when travelling to the venue, although they will usually begin earlier if the trainer has asked for questionnaires or other documentation to be returned to course administrators before the event. Where it is expected that participants will familiarize themselves with some knowledge aspects prior to the course, it is good practice to run a light-hearted quiz near to the beginning of the event, where small groups attempt to answer questions related to the pre-course reading material. This will serve to enable those who have absorbed less before the course to catch up a little!

Thought should also be given to how the participants are supported on returning to their place of work, so that arrangements can be made for any necessary coaching or mentoring. We shall return to this in Chapters 12 and 13, which discuss the strengthen and sustain stages of the SUCCESS model.

Summary

Creating the training intervention and preparing the groundwork benefits from a creative and yet disciplined approach. There needs to be a strict adherence to the learning objectives that are constructed from the output of the understand stage, and yet there is considerable room for creativity in the development of training methods that will maintain the interest of the participants.

The SOCMAT tool is invaluable in creating the outline of any training intervention. It requires discipline to use it, but if it is used to its full extent, detailing concisely all the content and associated methods of delivery, it will make the actual creation of materials easier and they should integrate well to ensure a cohesive training intervention.

It is critical to balance presentation and participative elements, especially with international managers. Account also needs to be taken of the fact that most of them will be working in their second language during the training and so do not want to be listening for long periods.

Finally the acceptability of the different methods to varying cultures must be considered.

Action plan

Consider a short piece of training that you are due to design for an international audience. Using the SOCMAT tool in the Action plan, practise breaking the training into parts, with each part having specific learning objectives. Review what you have done to ensure that you

Training event: ....

Session/Unit	*Objectives*	*Content*	*Methods*	*Aids*	*Timing*

have got a good balance of presentation and participation. Try to make realistic estimates of the time it will take to complete each part.

CHAPTER **10**

Conducting the Training of International Managers

This stage deals with the creation and delivery of the training and development activity. We will focus particularly on classroom training, although much of what is discussed will be applicable to other training modes.

Typically, this is the part of the SUCCESS model that takes up most of the trainers' time. However, without considerable attention to the earlier stages, much of the activity during this stage may be wide of the mark and depend to a significant extent on luck and experience for its success.

> Continuing with the example of the innovation and brand development case study discussed in Chapter 9, we were fortunate that a good deal of usable material already existed for the presentation aspects of the case study. Readily available were PowerPoint slides, describing the stages of the decision-making process whereby the project competed with others for the necessary investment, and slides showing the proposed product, its packaging and the type of machines that would be necessary to produce it commercially. In fact, the challenge in the presentation aspects of the case was to select the most relevant information from a mass of materials covering the innovation and brand development processes, the market information, the proposed product and its packaging, the financial justifications, the manpower plan and the proposed launch schedule.

The conduct stage of the SUCCESS model is practically independent of the level of training commitment of the organization. However, the further the company is on its journey from level one to level four, the more training literate the participants are likely to be. This means they will have attended many training courses, good and bad, and will be better judges of quality. They will understand much of the course set-up and structure from earlier training, and therefore the trainer can spend much less time on these issues at the beginning of a course. The downside for the trainer is, having seen it all before, participants are more discerning and perhaps, on occasion, a touch cynical. This makes it even harder for the trainer to score well.

Training and HR managers have often said to us that participants have found the courses we run not only educational but also entertaining. We shall call this 'edutainment'. Most great entertainers appear slick, polished and spontaneous. However, sound systems and processes support them. Great comedians such as Bob Hope have a record on file of every joke they have ever told or heard. The previous chapters suggest it is no less so for the great trainer.

In Part III of this book we will look at numbers of tools and techniques or 'tricks of the trade' for delivering edutainment that will assist the trainer in dealing effectively with a multi-cultural audience. For now we will discuss the processes and systems that are required.

The process in Figure 10.1 shows the various steps involved. Pre-course materials need to be prepared. These may be as simple as joining instructions for the participants or may involve reading or other preparatory work on their behalf as discussed in Chapter 9. Course notes and other support materials need to be developed and the trainers must prepare themselves to deliver the programme. When participants arrive, efforts must be made to ensure they are in the right frame of mind to learn. The training is then delivered and learning takes place. Finally the participants must identify, through their personal action plans, what they will do differently as a result of the training. These action plans, together with a record kept by the trainer of each participant's performance, are the outputs from the conduct stage.

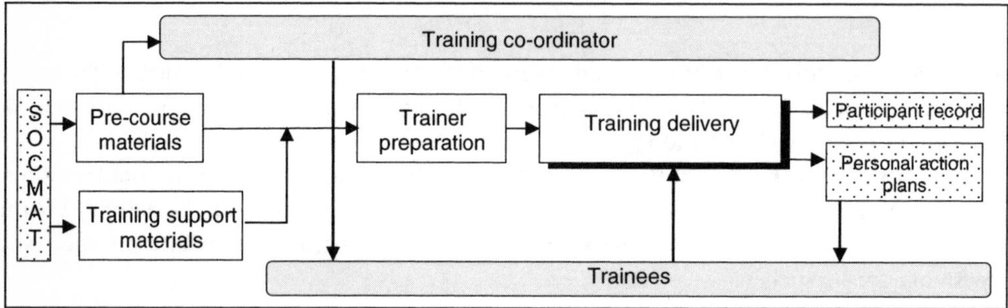

Figure 10.1 Conducting the training process

This process is managed by a training co-ordinator who may be the trainer him/herself. They send out and receive back any pre-course materials and liaise with the trainees throughout the process.

There are four main elements that need to be covered:

- Participants should arrive in the right frame of mind.
- Detailed training materials need to be developed.
- These training materials must be checked against the business objectives and strategy of the enterprise.
- The training must be delivered successfully.

The content of a well-prepared SOCMAT is extremely helpful as an input for the conduct stage. In addition the materials need to reflect all four Honey and Mumford learning styles (see Chapter 3).

The tools

BEFORE THE COURSE

For international management training pre-course preparation is a little more complex. Not only must the normal start/finish times, content and administrative details such as hotels and so on be communicated, but expectations must also be managed. One issue that often arises is that flight times do not fit in with the course schedule. Some delegates will either want to arrive after the course has started or leave before it is due to finish or both. This is not infrequently the case with participants from Southern European countries, for example. Obviously this should be discouraged but it is sometimes unavoidable. Much depends on the company culture. Where processes like SUCCESS are in place to a significant extent, then this is much less of a problem because there is greater line management commitment to the training.

Another key issue is ensuring that participants are in the right frame of mind when arriving at the course. To help bring this about, the trainer/training co-ordinator should communicate to each prospective participant prior to the event. Table 10.1 shows the issues that need to be addressed.

Table 10.1 Managing participant expectation

Issue	*Consideration*
Why are they attending?	The focus here is on the learning objectives. Identify the 'takeaways' from the course and how these will benefit them. Phrases like 'on this course you will learn how ...' are useful.
The training experience	Focus on the importance of interactions between the participants leading to greater understanding of the theory in a practical way. Stress networking, fun and enjoyment. Emphasize that missing even an hour of the course will make it less valuable for their colleagues.
The ground rules	Learning is a serious challenge. Specify, without going into detail, the way the course will be run in terms of timing, use of mobile phones, dealing with e-mails and so on. Try to strike a balance so that it will not seem autocratic to participants coming from cultures with a low power–distance index or too weak for those from high power–distance countries.
Pre-course preparation	This is a good opportunity to reinforce why the trainees need to put aside a little time to do the pre-course work. The joining instructions should have notified them that this is required. It should be pointed out that the work will be referred to in the programme and that it will enable them to get more from the course. It may also help to mention the disadvantage at which they will put themselves during the programme by not completing it.

UNIT/SESSION PREPARATION

When preparing sessions for international managers, a number of additional dimensions need to be borne in mind.

- Non-native language speakers are less likely to understand the subtleties of the language. Colloquialisms and complex sentence structures should be avoided. We shall discuss this more in Part III of this book. Examples which are particular to the home country should be used with care. For instance, television personalities can be very well known in one country but unheard of in another. On the other hand, TV programmes such as *Who Wants To Be a Millionaire* are shown practically everywhere.
- Signposting is very important, as was touched on in Chapter 9. Just to recap, non-native speakers will rely more on the written word. Therefore each session must be structured with a short introduction, clearly divided into logical parts, with a summary at the end.
- Non-native speakers often take more time to respond. They need to think about the words and their meaning, and may need to mentally articulate their response before speaking.
- The response time is further extended when a translator is present to make the materials comprehensive to all or a significant proportion of participants. The trainer must get used to a significant lag in response between asking a question or making a witticism and receiving a response. Where the translation is sequential rather than simultaneous, it will be even longer. In both cases the trainer will need to pause to allow the translator to catch up before asking a question requiring participant response. As a result, less of the material can be covered.

The unit/session preparation template shown in Figure 10.2 helps to structure sessions in a way that is sympathetic to managers from different countries. The link to the previous session is a good starting point that helps participants relate each part to an overall framework.

Based on the SOCMAT tool covered in Chapter 9, the learning objectives for each session are specified.

Each session should then be divided into three parts that will achieve these objectives. This signposting will make it easier for a non-native speaker to grasp, as well as helping to tighten the session. It is also a good idea to think through the visuals that are needed to cover each of the parts. Most management training will involve interaction between trainer and participants. This can be stimulated through thought-provoking questioning which should be planned. Finally, it is likely that exercises and case studies will be used to reinforce the learning.

The visuals need to be prepared. For international managers it may be necessary to expand beyond one-word/phrase bullet points, particularly for those who are not fluent in the course language. They will tend to read the visuals first to try to understand the point being made and then listen to what is being said.

The course notebook will be a valuable aid to understanding for the participants. Sometimes this may simply be copies of the PowerPoint slides. However, more detailed explanation is often appreciated, particularly by participants from high power distance and high uncertainty avoidance cultures. They can read the text at their leisure to deepen their understanding

Additional support materials could include:

- detailed course notes
- exercises
- role-play briefs

- videos and DVDs
- posters and other wall signs
- access to computers.

Unit/Session Preparation Template

Unit/session ....

Link to previous session ....

....

Unit/session learning objectives	*Three-part structure*

Heading for each visual/slide:			
1.	2.	3.	4.
5.	6.	7.	8.
9.	10.	11.	12.
13.	14.	15.	16.
17.	18.	19.	20.
21.	22.	23.	24.

Key questions to encourage trainee participation and thinking:

Case studies	Key learning points	Methodology

Figure 10.2 Unit/session preparation template

TRAINER PREPARATION

We will take it as read that the trainer prepares the delivery of the materials. During the create stage, details about the participants such as their country of origin, education and previous training will have been found out. If there is a large proportion from one culture then they must not be allowed to dominate, to the disadvantage of others. Many participants will have travelled some way to attend the course and may be tired. It is worthwhile to acknowledge the efforts they have made to come to the course. This is a part of managing participants' expectations which will be further discussed in Part III.

Examples used need to be culturally sensitive. Where, for example, a video is used it must not offend. Using World War II anecdotes with German participants may very well create discomfort or worse. Associating the Scots or Dutch with meanness may well cause a negative reaction from some natives of Scotland and the Netherlands.

One further practical issue is that the trainer may be training in an unfamiliar location. It is worthwhile finding out the venue and the contact person who is responsible for the organization of the event. Making contact beforehand and discussing the specific requirements may test the foreign or even English language capabilities of the trainer but could be very worthwhile. Thoroughness in the preparation of materials and the making of arrangements at the training venue will also help to reduce stress.

REHEARSING THE MATERIAL

Having developed the training materials they should be shared with the client who can help correct terminology, express a valuable opinion on how any sensitive content is dealt with, and spot any planned activity that could clash with the culture of the participant group. If possible, it is useful to rehearse at least the most critical parts of the training. Only when someone other than the training designer attempts an exercise or simulation can they be certain that it will work in the way intended and that learning will result. Similarly, only when a presentation is made to an audience can the designer be confident that an accurate estimate has been made of the time required. Where the materials have been developed for use with international managers it is extremely helpful if the audience for the rehearsal can be of mixed nationalities.

Outputs from the conduct stage

PARTICIPANT ACTION PLAN

An example of an action plan format for the delegates to complete after each session is shown in Figure 10.3. At the end of the course these can be reviewed by the participants and the most important points transferred onto the one-page summary action plan shown in Figure 10.4.

These formats are helpful in getting participants to review the learning that has occurred and translate the learning into their own culture. Naturally, the summary action plan provides a mechanism that can assist follow-through of the training after the course. More will be said on this in the next chapter. To this end it is helpful if the trainer receives copies of the action plans.

These action plans appeal particularly to Reflectors and Pragmatists, while Theorists are fairly neutral whereas Activists get frustrated. The latter should focus on the action elements.

Session Action Plan

Session...

The three most important ideas from this session were:

1 ....

2 ....

3 ....

As a result I will take the following action:

1 ....

2 ....

3 ....

Other comments/action:

1 ....

2 ....

3 ....

Figure 10.3 Session action plan

PARTICIPANT RECORD

As any trainer will know, it is often difficult to recall individual participants even a few hours after the course is finished. It is therefore helpful to make a note about each participant's performance during the programme. This is not meant to be a detailed report, merely a record of particular events, responses, attitudes and views expressed that may be helpful in giving support to implementation of the learning. An example is given in Table 10.2. The first column should be completed at the start of the course when the delegates introduce themselves. The rest should be filled out during breaks and when the delegates are involved in exercises as the training proceeds.

Summary

Participants need to arrive at the training in the right frame of mind. Some will have travelled long distances and be tired. With international managers it is important to acknowledge the efforts they have made to come to the training. Managing the delegates' expectations can have a major impact on the outcome of a training event and the pre-course communication can play a vital part in this.

Summary Action Plan

Look back at the action plans completed at the end of each session.

The three most important ideas from this course are:
1 ....
2 ....
3 ....

List the actions you will take to implement these ideas when you return to your workplace

Action	Success criteria	Date	
		Start	Review/end
1.			
2.			
3.			
4.			

Figure 10.4 Summary action plan

Table 10.2 Participant record

Individual details	*Observations*
Name: Company: Position: Background:	
Name: Company: Position: Background:	
Name: Company: Position: Background:	

Even more careful thought needs to be given to the preparation of support materials – visuals, course notebook, exercises and case studies. Generally ideas and concepts need to be spelled out in more detail as non-native speakers tend to derive their initial understanding from reading rather than listening. The unit/session preparation template is a useful tool supporting this activity.

If possible, rehearsing or piloting all or some of the materials will provide feedback on both content and timing.

The use of a summary action plan, a copy of which the trainer may receive, should ensure the smooth transition of new learning into the workplace.

Finally, a participant record should be kept to assist in strengthening the learning; this is discussed in Chapter 12.

Action plan

Think about a course you will be running in the near future. Prepare a pre-course communication to each participant that will incorporate the issues given in the Action plan.

Issue	
Why they are attending	
The training experience they will undergo	
The ground rules the training will follow	
Pre-course preparation the participants need to undertake	

CHAPTER **11**

Evaluating the Training Intervention

On one occasion a client in the UK retail sector said to us that they intended to evaluate the effectiveness of a training intervention by measuring the increase in sales revenue. The brief was to train managers and sales assistants in the in-car-entertainment (ICE) section of a large chain of motor accessory shops in the south of the UK. The training need was to improve meeting/greeting skills and develop abilities to help customers make the most appropriate choice of headsets and speakers for their vehicles.

The company intended to measure the increase in sales for the 12 weeks following the training throughout the 40 southern stores, and compare these results with the 100 stores in other parts of the country where no training was taking place. We discussed the fact that it was inevitable there were other variables that affected sales, apart from the training, but the client was determined to measure success in this way.

The training took place as planned, and reactions were measured at its conclusion in the traditional way with participants completing a course assessment form ('happy sheet'). A lot of positive comments were received this way and then we waited while sales revenue was monitored across the ICE departments of the 40 stores in which the training took place and in the control group of 100 stores. At the end of the 12 weeks it was announced that sales of headsets and speakers were up by 9 per cent in value terms in the south, whereas they had not moved at all in other parts of the country. The training was heralded as a great success!

Previous experience made us raise a lot of mental questions. What other variables could have affected the result? If the result were mainly due to the effects of the training, would the higher level of sales be maintained? Would it be possible to repeat the apparent success in the other stores if the training was rolled out across the remainder of the country? Over the next few weeks the client considered how to move forward and decided it would be beneficial to have in-house staff trained to deliver the training in the remaining stores. We embarked on this next task. While we were doing this work we learned that in the 12 weeks when the monitoring had taken place the company had introduced a new product in some of the southern stores that had helped to drive sales up. No analysis was done, however, to try to isolate the effects of this, but clearly it would have had some impact on the +9 per cent result.

This example demonstrates how difficult it is to measure with confidence the effects of training on business results. There will always be some other variables that are difficult to isolate and it is rarely possible to be certain that training alone has produced an improvement. This is true when all of the population trained are in the same country and the business is subject to a reasonably homogeneous structure and set of economic conditions. Imagine how much more difficult it is when those trained return to businesses in nine or ten countries that are all at different stages of the economic cycle and of economic development. Sales could be increasing in one country at the same time that they are decreasing in another purely through the effect of differing market conditions and regardless of the effectiveness of the training.

For any international organization attempting to deploy a centrally sponsored initiative using training as a leading driver of change, measurement of the results achieved by the training will be further complicated by local variations in its information systems, job titles, reporting structures and operating methods.

However, trainers should always welcome attempts to measure the effectiveness of learning. It would add greatly to the strength of the argument for higher and more consistent investment in training if we could discover how to quantify the results of learning in a way that relates to business results.

In this chapter we look at some ways in which training effectiveness can be evaluated and the challenges of doing this with international managers.

The process is shown in Figure 11.1. The output from the conduct stage is the participant action plans. In the evaluation stage the opportunity exists for the trainees' management to support the implementation and to observe changes in behaviour. It may also be possible to measure the results achieved for the business. During and at the end of the training programme the learning that has occurred can be tested and the participants' reactions can be measured. The learning and training evaluation reviews bring these different elements together and are the output from the evaluation stage of the SUCCESS process.

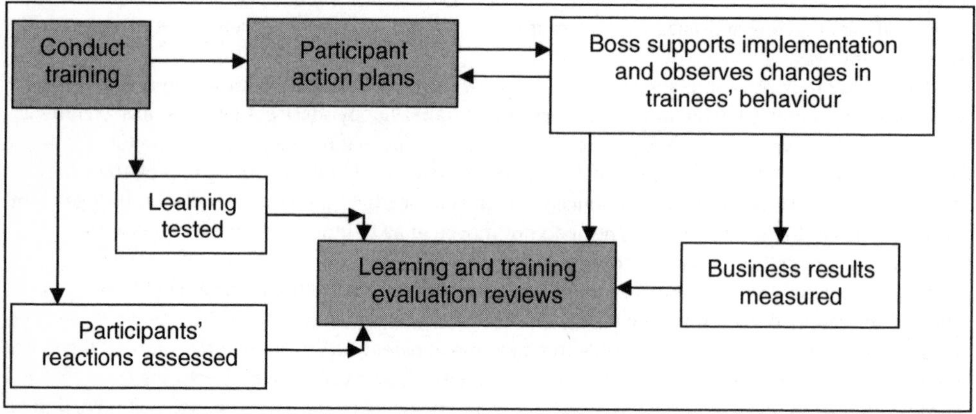

Figure 11.1 Evaluation of training process

Structural framework

Most writers draw a distinction between the validation of training and its evaluation. This is useful in the sense that it is clearly very important to measure success against the original objectives. This is validation. If the training has met its original objectives in full by whatever measures were agreed at the time the objectives were set, then it has been positively validated. For instance, if the objective of a piece of induction training was for trainees to have an awareness of company strategy and after the training the participants reported that they now have a much better appreciation of the background, context and direction being taken by the company then it would be reasonable to say that the training had been validated.

Evaluation of training is a much broader measure of the degree of success of the training. It takes into account effects of the training that are above and beyond those envisaged in the original objectives. Kirkpatrick's model is the best-known and most respected framework for evaluating training.

Kirkpatrick envisaged four possible levels of evaluation that he named as follows:

- Reaction – do participants like the training?
- Learning – do they understand the training?
- Behaviour – do they use the learning in practice?
- Results – does using the training have any impact on results?

Organizations at 'level one – trainee driven' and 'level two – manager driven' of training commitment, described in Chapter 6, are generally content with evaluation of the training based on the trainees' verbal and written reaction to it. This rarely goes beyond the comment of 'it was a good course' or conversely 'what a waste of time and money'. 'Level three – trainee driven' organizations will look also to behavioural changes, while 'level four – strategy driven' ones will also seek to measure the business results achieved.

THE ART OF THE POSSIBLE

While it is clearly desirable to measure the results of the training and hence the return on training investment, this is not generally practical and even if it is it can be costly. So good evaluation is very much the 'art of the possible'. The greater the level of organization training commitment, the more that will be possible.

As mentioned in Chapter 8, it is important to agree on how success is going to be measured at the outset, before the training is created. What are the key performance indicators (KPIs) going to be? For instance, if there is to be a written test of learning at the end of three days' training, the trainer needs to pay a great deal of attention to helping the participants retain the knowledge aspects of the learning. This will probably mean incorporating revision sessions to reinforce the learning. Alternatively or additionally, if the participants' bosses are going to evaluate the training by observing specified changes in their subordinates' interpersonal behaviours, then clearly skills will need to be practised during the training, using methods such as role-playing, possibly with CCTV feedback to identify positive points and behaviours where further improvement is needed during the training.

In reality the vast majority of training organized for international managers, particularly for 'level one – trainee driven' and 'level two – manager driven' organizations (see Chapter 6), is evaluated almost exclusively through session scores and end-of-course written feedback, in addition to the verbal feedback participants will make on returning to their places of work. Recognizing this, most trainers will deliberately stress those interactions that are directly related to the questions included on the course assessment forms, and make the training an enjoyable experience working towards leaving the participants on a high at the end of the course. This will help to achieve positive feedback and, done well, it may even motivate participants to apply the learning on their return to the workplace.

Feedback from participants can be obtained throughout a training programme; this will be further discussed in Part III. Having participants score and register comments on each session is one way of doing this. The trainer can achieve feedback in less formal ways from any of the participative exercises run during a training event. Participants can be asked what they consider they have learned; videos of CCTV feedback can be compared after the training to see if there was any noticeable improvement in behaviours. An exercise can be set which requires participants to recall learning from an earlier part of the course in order to complete the exercise successfully. Feedback of this type is useful in keeping a finger on the pulse as the training proceeds and to enable continuous improvement in the way the learning is delivered. It also provides useful information to feedback to the training sponsor about the aspects of the event that were particularly successful.

If bosses and colleagues (usually those working for level three and four organizations – see Chapter 6) have been involved in the planning of the training they are likely to be supportive when participants return to work and so their motivation will be sustained and newly learned behaviours, knowledge and skills are likely to be evidenced, which, given everything else remains stable, should lead to an improvement in business results.

Another very practical way of evaluating learning and at the same time aiding the transfer of newly acquired skills and knowledge to the workplace is to make really good use of the end-of-session and end-of-course action plans. For instance, it may be possible to arrange, before training takes place, for participants' bosses to review with each participant the key actions that they intend to take as a result of the training and for the boss to do whatever is possible to encourage the successful implementation of these plans. This could involve the boss agreeing to allocate additional resources or to create easy access to senior people in another department to enable some change in procedures to take place. The trainer is then in a position to ask for post-event feedback on the effectiveness of the actions. This feedback can be sought from the boss and from the participant to obtain a good balance of perceptions.

REACTION

By 'reaction', Kirkpatrick meant what participants felt about the value of the training on its completion. This is usually obtained by participants completing a happy sheet as mentioned above. These assessments of reaction usually aim to evaluate the value the participants felt they gained from the training and also provide the trainer and the training sponsor with information that will help them to improve the training ready for the next time it is delivered.

An example of a format for recording participant reactions is given in Figure 11.2. This is the most common form of evaluation applied to the training of international managers today. It is often supplemented by participants being asked to score and make comments on each session of the course. Care needs to be taken that the words used are interpreted in the same way by participants with varying command of the English language. Subtle nuances illustrated by rating scales such as 'very well', 'quite well', 'not very well', 'not at all well' may be lost on many non-native speakers. Care should be taken to use simple words that clearly distinguish each element of the scale such as 'completely', 'mostly', 'partially', 'not at all'.

A second complication is that different cultures will have different perceptions of the rating scales. Northern Europeans regard life as less perfect than it could be and hence any endeavour is capable of improvement. As a result they tend not to give maximum scores to the training. On the other hand, participants from Middle and Far Eastern cultures accepting the implicit authority and greater knowledge of the trainer will out of respect and politeness tend to mark more highly.

Training Assessment

Course title ....

Please mark, with a cross in the box, the answer that most closely reflects your assessment of the course, or write in the space provided after the question.

1. Were the objectives of the module clearly stated?

Yes ☐ No ☐

2. To what extent do you feel the module objectives were met?

Completely ☐ Mostly ☐ Partially ☐ Not at all ☐

3. Which parts of the module were of most value?

4. Which parts of the module were of least value?

5. Should more time have been given to particular issues/subjects and, if so, which ones?

6. Were some issues/subjects covered at excessive length and, if so, which ones?

7. To what extent do you feel that you will be able to use knowledge/skills gained on the course in your everyday work?

Completely ☐ Mostly ☐ Partially ☐ Not at all ☐

8. How well do you think the facilitator understood and responded to the needs and abilities of the course delegates?

Completely ☐ Mostly ☐ Partially ☐ Not at all ☐

9. Which topics do you feel could be covered at a subsequent event that would further develop your skills? Please list topics below.

10. What particular support do you feel you may need from your manager to help you implement the learning from this module successfully?

Figure 11.2 End-of-course participant feedback

LEARNING

By 'learning', Kirkpatrick meant the additional knowledge and skills that had been acquired during training. This is usually measured by a written or practical test. Learning is not often measured in this way following training of international managers. It is felt that adults, particularly in Western cultures, do not expect to be formally tested on their learning.

There are some exceptions and they usually apply to courses that result in a particular qualification, such as the recognition of competence to use a particular type of psychometric questionnaire.

Immediate learning can be tested less formally by asking breakout groups to recall key learning points from a course or by building a quiz into the course to test knowledge retention. These methods are more common to management training than is a formal written test.

BEHAVIOUR

By 'behaviour', Kirkpatrick meant the ways in which participants could be seen to go about aspects of their jobs differently as a direct result of a training intervention. The type of training for international managers where that would typically be evaluated in this way is where the development of interpersonal skills constitutes an important part of the programme. Some evaluation is often part of the programme itself, using feedback from fellow participants or playback of a video recording. Post-course evaluation will often take place when the participants' managers observe changed behaviours back in the workplace.

In some high power distance cultures this may be problematic because there is usually limited opportunity for the boss to observe the subordinate actually performing the job. Also there is a tendency in these cultures for managers to focus on what their subordinate is failing to do rather than what they are successfully implementing

RESULTS

By 'results', Kirkpatrick meant the degree to which a training event directly impacts on the participants' contributions to business results. The case at the beginning of this chapter is a good example of an attempt to evaluate training in terms of its effects on business results.

For many years, accountants and trainers alike have experimented with attempts to carry out cost–benefit analysis on training. In fields such as operator training this has been done quite successfully, by equating the time saved in reaching experienced worker standard to a financial saving and comparing this with the costs of creating and conducting the training. In the case of international managers it is usually possible to assess the costs associated with the training, that is, costs of time spent preparing materials and conducting the training, venue costs, salaries of the participants during training and any other costs directly associated with the training as discussed in Chapter 5. It is, however, much more difficult to assess the benefits in financial terms, because then we are back to the need to measure the effect the training has had on business results.

Nevertheless, some inference can be drawn from changes in behaviour leading to individuals achieving particular results and the impact on the whole organization. Returning to the case discussed at the start of this chapter, it was found that the sales assistants approached customers browsing the audio section of the store with specific questions, rather than the rather general 'May I help you?', more frequently than prior to the training. In turn they converted a higher proportion into purchasers with larger than average order sizes which it was felt was likely to result in increased total sales. However, a word of caution is appropriate: converting more customers at higher sales value does not, on its own, lead to better overall sales results. It was observed that sales assistants were spending longer with each customer and therefore were dealing with fewer customers on average per day. If the higher conversion rate was not more than compensating for the reduction in customers attended to, then overall sales could be negatively impacted. Fortunately this was not the case. In turn, this then led to the identification of the next phase of training to upgrade shop assistants' capability to deal with more numbers while not decreasing their conversion rate or average order size.

Evaluating the results on an international basis is even more challenging, particularly as even in highly centralized companies different regions will operate differently with varying organization structures, systems and operating methods due to historic and cultural reasons. Merely obtaining the metrics can prove very difficult. For example, one of the KPIs for the training of key account managers was the number of projects they organized with customers. However, trying to obtain data on this required setting up a separate reporting process through each country's operating committee to whom this information was to be reported by each account manager once a month. This raised the question whether the value of the information warranted the cost and effort involved.

THE MAIN EVALUATION METHODS

A summary of the main evaluation methods is shown below in Table 11.1, together with the main challenges in using them in an international context.

Output from the evaluate stage

Kirkpatrick recognized that it becomes progressively more difficult to carry out evaluation as one moves through the four levels from 'reaction' to 'results'. This does not mean it should not be attempted at the higher levels of 'behaviour' and 'results' but that the difficulty needs to be recognized.

Within a realistic time period therefore, following the course, the participants' managers and/or the HR department/trainer need to assess the effectiveness of the learning that has occurred, despite the difficulties in so doing. The performance of the participants needs to be evaluated against the learning objectives. Table 11.2 shows a suitable format to achieve this. The results achieved by each individual are reviewed against the learning objectives set and any gaps identified. This in turn leads to the identification of further training needs.

The individual learning reviews can be brought together to systematically evaluate the overall effectiveness of the training using the training evaluation report shown in Table 11.3. The planned objectives for each of Kirkpatrick's four levels of evaluation are compared with that actually achieved and comments made on the variance.

Table 11.1 The main training evaluation methods

	Evaluation methodology	*Measures*	*Challenges to implementation with international managers*
1.	Session and daily feedback	Reaction	Multiple completions of forms are not received well in low uncertainty avoidance cultures
2.	Course evaluation form	Reaction	Words need to be chosen carefully and cultures with low masculinity and low uncertainty avoidance are reluctant to give maximum scores
3.	Pre- and post-testing with same questionnaire	Learning	More acceptable in high power distance cultures
4.	Written tests before, during or at end of course	Learning	More acceptable in high power distance cultures
5.	Verbal test during course	Learning	Those who are fluent in the course language will respond first
6.	Line manager's observation	Behaviour	In high power distance cultures managers often tend to focus on negative rather than positive behaviours
7.	Role plays and exercises	Learning and behaviour	Always more difficult in a second language
8.	Tracking output	Results	The system enablers to measure the outputs need to be in place wherever the trainees are working

Table 11.2 Learning review

Name	*Learning objectives*	*Results achieved*	*Further training needs*
	• • •	• • •	• • •
	• • •	• • •	• • •
	• • •	• • •	• • •

Table 11.3 Training evaluation report

	Anticipated/planned	*When expected*	*When achieved*	*Comments*
Reaction				
Learning				
Behaviour				
Results				

Summary

When there is evidence that the objectives of a training intervention have been met in full, using whatever measure was agreed at the outset, it could be said that the training has been validated positively.

However, Kirkpatrick suggests that training can be further evaluated at different levels. The first level of evaluation is that of 'reaction', which is usually achieved by asking participants to record their reactions and feelings immediately after the training has finished. The trainer needs to be aware of the likely effect of the participants' cultural background on the responses to questionnaires.

The second level of evaluation is that of 'learning', which is usually achieved by asking participants to take a test at the end of the training. This, except for more junior staff, tends to go against accepted norms in Western cultures and is only used in a minority of management training situations.

The third level is that of 'behaviour', which is usually evaluated by bosses and peers observing a participant's behaviour after attendance at a training event. In high power distance cultures there may be a tendency for managers to focus on what their subordinates are failing to implement rather than reinforcing positive behavioural change.

The fourth level of evaluation is that of 'results', when a participant's contribution to business results is measured following a training event. This is particularly challenging in the case of international managers because of the diversity of countries and the situations in which they work.

The learning review form provides a means of assessing the extent that each individual has achieved their learning objectives. This achievement can be brought together in the training evaluation report form to assess the overall impact of the training.

There are particular advantages in focusing participants and their bosses on post-event evaluation through the learning and training evaluation reviews which are the outputs from this stage. These will help to promote the notion that the purpose of training is to achieve lasting change as discussed further in the next two chapters.

Action plan

For the trainer

Consider a training event that is planned to take place in the fairly near future, and consider the type of feedback that it would be useful to receive from participants and their bosses a few months after the participants have returned to workplace. This feedback will be used to evaluate the training.

Construct a format for the feedback, including as many of the following aspects (and others) as you feel are relevant to the training intervention that you have in mind. Bear in mind the culture of your participants and their bosses. Consider attempting to achieve buy-in from the participants and their bosses so that they complete this feedback for you.

For the participant

In which aspects of your job do you feel you have taken a different approach since the training?
Which particular tools or elements of learning from the training have you used since returning to work?
What additional aspect of learning would have been beneficial to you?
Which parts of your action plan do feel you have implemented successfully?
In which parts of your action plan do you feel you need additional support to bring about a successful implementation?
How would you rate the level of support you have received?
Have you had the appropriate information made available to you to enable you to implement your action plan?
What have you told people (colleagues, subordinates, superiors, friends, family) about the training?
What has made it difficult for you to implement what you have learned?
What do you need to overcome these difficulties?
How helpful have your interactions with the trainer been since the course?
How could the training programme be improved?
What further training and development is needed for you to be able to implement all you have learned?

For the participant's boss

In what ways do you see a change in the participant's behaviour following the training?
Which aspects of the job is the participant now approaching differently?
What benefits should this bring to the organization?
What are the key performance indicators?
What changes have been observed in the key performance indicators?
How has the participant shared their end-of-course action plan with you?
Which aspects of the action plan are being implemented successfully?
With which aspects of the action plan are you giving support in implementation?
What have you been told about the course by the participant?
How is the participant using the new knowledge gained?
In what way has the training helped prepare the participant for their likely next job?
How could the training programme be improved?
What further training and development do you feel is needed to fully implement the learning?

CHAPTER **12**

Strengthening the Learning of International Managers

This stage deals with the follow-up of the training and development activity. To maximize the return on the training investment, the training event must be followed up and reinforced. This stage is concerned with ensuring the appropriate systems and materials are in place to ensure that this occurs. This is particularly relevant to level three – TNA-driven and level four – strategy-driven organizations, as detailed in the model of organizational commitment to training in Chapter 6. For most international/multi-national organizations this represents one of the most significant challenges they face.

> For example, one client in the consumer durables industry had developed, over a period of years, an integrated set of training programmes for a particular front-end function to support one of their critical marketing strategies. A number of HQ-based training initiatives had occurred in which around 200 managers had participated from the various regions and countries. For the participants, coming to headquarters was considered to be a reward for good performance and an indication that they were well thought of by the company. It also provided a rare opportunity to network with colleagues from other regions and HQ staff. The overwhelming reaction of the participants was that the training was excellent and that all their colleagues should also participate. Unfortunately, on the ground little changed. The learning had not 'developed roots'; very little had been implemented. Theory and practice in the training room had not been translated into best-practice activity in the workplace.

International managers need to be more motivated and self-disciplined than managers working in the same team at a single geographic location. In the example above, the main reason the training failed was that due to their being located in different geographical locations, the international managers lacked a critical mass of like-minded colleagues and bosses around them when they returned to the workplace. Given time, a critical mass will be created but in today's fast-moving environment waiting for this to happen may be an unaffordable luxury. This was further compounded by the fact that there are local differences in organization, systems, information and processes that impact on how the learning will be implemented.

In anticipation of this, the trainer needs to build in stronger mechanisms during the earlier stages of the process. This means ensuring that the key performance indicators (KPIs), which are the criteria by which local implementation will be judged, are thoroughly understood at the creation stage and incorporated in the training design. For example, if one KPI is the development of a strategic customer plan, as was the case in the situation described above, then the training design and the training 'takeaways' need to be focused to give participants as much process, systems and information to enable them to accomplish this. The next step is to ensure that the appropriate coaching, mentoring and information support is available locally to help the participants develop the plan. This is more likely to be available in level three and four organizations than in those at levels one and two in terms of their training commitment described in Chapter 6.

From time to time, we will receive telephone calls or e-mails from participants on courses we have conducted detailing what they have implemented and how they have adapted the learning to suit their own situation. However, this is the exception rather than the rule, indicating perhaps the proportion of companies at levels three and four in terms of their training commitment compared with those at levels one and two. More usual is the situation where a follow-up workshop is held at which the participants are expected to present what they have put into practice from the previous course and how they have refined it to meet their needs. Only a minority will normally have seriously applied themselves to this, usually those working at the same workplace.

How can this 'strengthen' process be adapted and enhanced to meet the needs of international managers? Figure 12.1 shows the major steps that need to be put in place. The learnings from the training event are implemented by the delegates. Inputs to this activity include the participants' action plans, the participant records kept by the trainer from the course (see Chapter 10) and the learning and training evaluation reviews (discussed in the previous chapter). The participants are given support and coaching by management. The extent of this support will be dependent, at least in part, on the level of commitment of management to the training and managing the changes being sought. (This was discussed in Chapters 8 and 9.) In addition the systems, process and information enablers need to be in place. The new behaviours are reviewed and the extent of learning assessed. The implementation dashboard gives a read-out on how well the 'strengthen' part of the SUCCESS process is working.

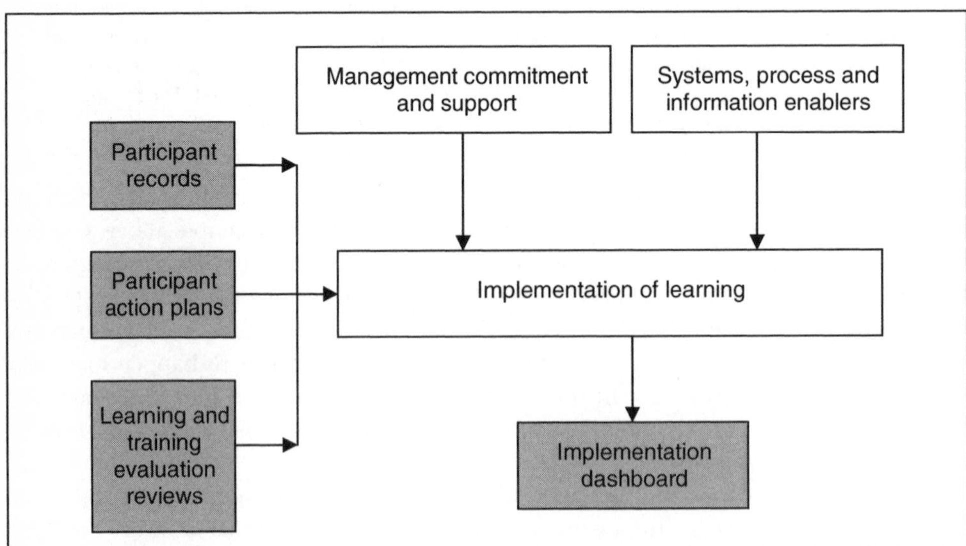

Figure 12.1 Strengthening the learning process

The main issues that need to be covered in the strengthen stage are:

- reinforcement of the learning process;

- ensuring management has the skills to continue training/coaching/mentoring on the job with their staff;
- helping trainees surmount the practical problems faced when implementing their action plans, including ensuring the appropriate information, processes and systems are in place.

The tools

GAINING MANAGEMENT COMMITMENT TO FOLLOW UP THE TRAINING

International managers cannot rely on their locally based colleagues for support since few, if any, will have attended the training event. Critical to the implementation of the learning, therefore, is the attitude, knowledge and skills of the participant's boss. As well as getting buy-in to the objectives and content of the programme, the participant's manager needs to both understand and be committed to implementing the follow-up activity that is required from them. If possible, a session should be held just for the bosses to acquaint themselves with the contents of the course and how it should be followed up. Whether this actually occurs is again a reflection on the level of training commitment of the organization.

In any event, the bosses should be contacted:

- reminding them of the reasons their subordinate attended the course;
- with a summary of the outputs from the course;
- with suggestions for their follow-up with their subordinates.

This follow-up, based on the participant record completed by the trainer during the course, should not be a critical report on the attendee. Rather, it will focus on the positive contributions that they made to the event and the need to build on these to maximize the return on the training investment. A prerequisite is to have a record not just of the participant's contact details, but also of their manager's, for follow-up purposes.

COACHING SKILLS FOR BOSSES

Throughout this strengthen and subsequent sustain stages of the process, the manager needs coaching and mentoring skills to support and help the trainees. These skills, like any other, can be enhanced through training. A typical outline coaching skills programme is shown below:

- skills and aptitudes of an effective coach
- appropriate coaching models and how to use them
- importance of individual learning styles
- importance of setting objectives and KPIs for learning
- importance of rapport and how to establish it
- communication skills for coaching
- listening skills
- how to give and receive constructive feedback.

However, it must be acknowledged that in some cultures, particularly in those exhibiting a high power distance ranking, implementing coaching and mentoring may prove to be particularly problematic. In this situation trainees may have little alternative but to rely on their own resources and any other sources of support that they can link into.

VIRTUAL LEARNING COMMUNITY

Any group of participants coming together from a variety of countries inevitably begin to network and form a community for the duration of the training programme. Following the event this group can be encouraged to keep their identity via the set-up of an intranet-based platform. The virtual community can provide a useful source of support, with members posting their implementation experiences, sharing problems and getting advice. Threaded discussions concerning particular issues enable everyone who so wishes to contribute. The extent to which this resource is used is dependent on:

- how useful members find it;
- the effectiveness with which it is introduced during the course;
- the inputs of the moderator.

The moderator is usually the trainer or training manager. His or her role, unless someone else takes it on, is to kick-start the discussion by requesting feedback on learning implementation. They will also provide help, support and motivation, contributing usefully to the discussions.

Time should be spent during the course highlighting this facility and, as the course proceeds, suggestions made on certain topics could be posted on the platform.

Some companies take this even further. For example, one client in the chemical industry continues the interactions by means of a business simulation for some six weeks after completion of the course. The simulation is introduced during the last part of the course and, working in teams, participants play the first couple of rounds to familiarize themselves with the procedure. On returning to their workplace the now virtual teams continue to compete on a weekly basis, applying what they have learned through the simulation.

REMINDER TO PARTICIPANTS

In most instances, the participant's boss will ask for feedback about the training from the participant when they return to their work. This can range in some cases from a highly structured written report to an informal conversation. To better equip the subordinate for this interaction they should be given a card or sheet summarizing the main takeaways at the end of the course. An example from part of a negotiation course is shown in Figure 12.2. Ideally this should be translated into the native language.

Immediately following the programme each delegate should be contacted by the trainer, in writing. Typically this will include:

- an introduction referring back to the course and the positive outputs thereof;
- individual feedback from course;
- challenge of the personal action plan;
- guidelines to support implementation of the action plan;
- summary.

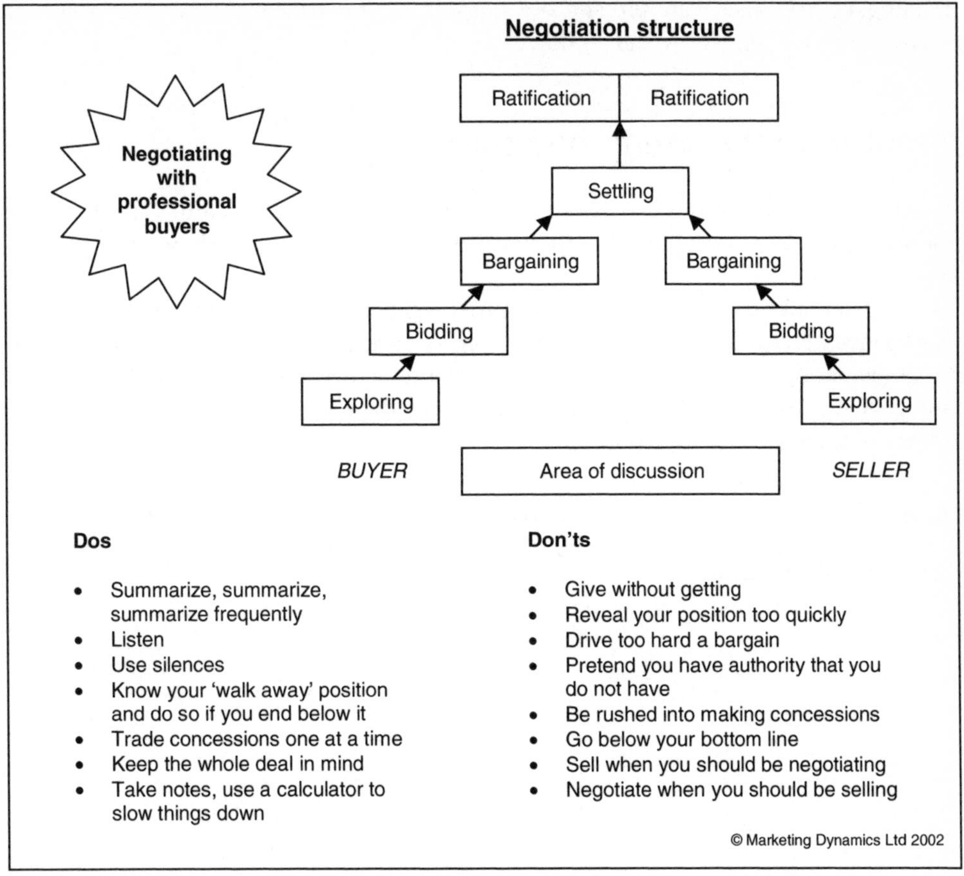

Negotiation structure
Negotiating with professional buyers
Ratification
Ratification
Settling
Bargaining
Bargaining
Bidding
Bidding
Exploring
Exploring
BUYER
Area of discussion
SELLER
Dos
Summarize, summarize, summarize frequently
Listen
Use silences
Know your 'walk away' position and do so if you end below it
Trade concessions one at a time
Keep the whole deal in mind
Take notes, use a calculator to slow things down
Don'ts
Give without getting
Reveal your position too quickly
Drive too hard a bargain
Pretend you have authority that you do not have
Be rushed into making concessions
Go below your bottom line
Sell when you should be negotiating
Negotiate when you should be selling
© Marketing Dynamics Ltd 2002

Figure 12.2 Card summarizing some of the key learning points

To help the trainer recall each participant, the participant record should be used (see Chapter 10).

KEEPING THE LEARNING IMPLEMENTATION GOING

A few months following the training, the trainees should be reminded of the key learning points. Three mechanisms are available:

1 reminder cards/notes from the trainer;
2 discussion with the line manager;
3 follow-up meeting with the trainer.

The first mechanism is the least costly. This should be supplemented with a reminder to the line manager. The third option is likely to have the highest cost, particularly as it normally involves international travel, but it is undoubtedly the most effective. This can take the form of a one-to-one coaching meeting, but more usually it will be a follow-on course; the first part of the course being devoted to the outputs from the previous training event. For example, the participants may be required to conduct a process review as a project following a training course. Each can present the outputs of the review at the next course for discussion and refinement by the group.

Output from the strengthen stage

For each country/region the extent of the implementation of the training and the results achieved should be monitored using the implementation dashboard, shown in Figure 12.3 below.

Each element of the action plan for each participant is detailed and the extent to which it has been achieved is recorded by placing a cross on the scale from 'none' to 'complete'. In a similar fashion, the participant can record the achievement of their KPIs from the training. Next, the support they have received from their manager and the support made available to their manager is assessed.

Date	None ←——→ Complete
Action plan implementation	
–	
–	
–	
–	
–	
–	
Achievement of KPIs	
–	
–	
–	
–	
Boss's support	
Boss's support mechanisms in place	
Systems enablers in place	
Information enablers in place	
Organizational enablers in place	
Process enablers in place	

Figure 12.3 Implementation dashboard

The next part of the dashboard is likely to be appropriate to all participants in the particular region/country and looks at the extent that the system, information, organizational and process enablers been put into place

Summary

The strengthen stage is concerned with supporting the implementation of the learning by the participants when they return from the training. To ensure that it is well implemented with international managers, a stronger process structure is required to overcome the problems of distance, the absence of a work group in a single geographic location, and variable systems, information, organization and processes.

The tools available to support the strengthen stage include:

- gaining management commitment to follow up the training;
- coaching skills for bosses;
- virtual learning community;
- reminder to participants.

The output from this stage is the implementation dashboard which monitors progress.

Action plan

Think about the next training intervention you will be involved with and consider the issues in the Action plan below.

	Implications for action
How is management commitment going to be obtained following the training?	
Are processes in place to coach the participants when they return to their jobs?	
Are mechanisms set up to enable participants to continue learning via a virtual community platform?	
How will the participants be reminded about the key learnings from the training?	

CHAPTER 13 Sustaining International Managers' New Behaviours in the Workplace

Change management within organizations can be viewed as consisting of two elements – fixing the parts, and fixing the people. The former is concerned with the processes and systems that govern and regulate how people work. The latter is about ensuring that the right people are in place who have the knowledge and skill to maximize their contribution to the organization. One important element in getting the people right is training.

Ultimately, therefore, the success of the training will depend upon how the learning is sustained and reinforced by the company's management. This stage is concerned with tools and mechanisms to sustain learning, build skills and achieve better results. It ultimately depends on creating an organizational learning environment that shares best practice and continuously develops knowledge, skills, greater competences, different behaviours and attitudes. This is no small task. Indeed it could be argued that unless the changed behaviours are maintained, no real learning has taken place, despite the many training interventions that may have occurred. Sustaining the learning is highly culturally specific.

> Some time ago we trained and coached a group of English and German product managers from an international agricultural equipment company in developing marketing plans. The training was successful and the format and processes were adopted as standard company practice. Some years later we were asked to conduct the same exercise again with a new set of product managers. We were heartened to find that the processes and systems were still working well within the German operation and indeed had been further developed and improved. Unfortunately this was not the case with the English managers. Their planning system had not developed; it had just vanished and we had to reinvent the wheel. The training, therefore, although successful in the short term, was only partially sustained in the longer term.

During the sustain stage the outputs from the training are integrated in the business in terms of the ways it goes about things, as manifested in its systems and processes and the behaviours of its people (see Figure 13.1). The implementation dashboard will give a read-out on the extent to which the training is being implemented, its objectives are being achieved and the organization, systems, information and organizational enablers are in place. This then leads to activity to close any gaps in the enablers, motivating individuals, their managers and the whole team to continue with their changed behaviours and to share best practice. Further training is implemented to ensure that the changed behaviours are reinforced and extended. In turn the impact of the training on the business is assessed

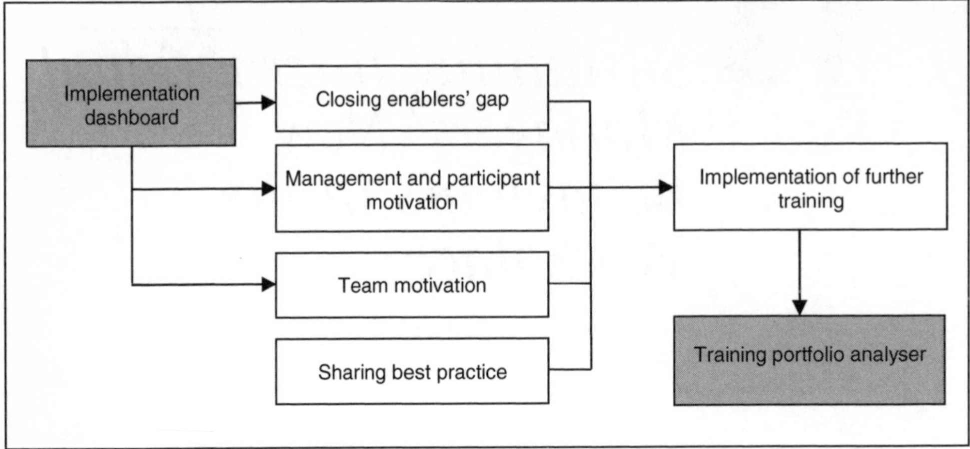

Figure 13.1 Sustaining the training process

using the training portfolio analyser which then feeds back into survey, the first stage of SUCCESS.

Some managers will thrive on change, often creating problems for colleagues who cannot keep up. Others will resist change and the discomfort it brings. This means that change must become the norm and strategic, operational, organizational and individual processes must be implemented to support the change. The methods used tend to be culturally specific. For example, in countries such as the USA which value and respect individual achievement it is not uncommon to put the need for change into an individualistic heroic context. Change is positioned as a life-or-death issue, and individuals who have brought it about successfully are lauded, rewarded and admired. This contrasts with South American countries such as Columbia or Venezuela where the value of group working is more highly prized. Change is positioned as an evolutionary process, which requires a team approach to which each individual contributes.

Objectives of the sustain stage

The main issues that need to be covered are:

- ensuring the enablers are fully in place;
- motivation of management and trainees to maintain changed behaviours;
- processes to cement new practices and share best practice;
- implementation of further training to re-energize participants and build momentum;
- a mechanism that continuously aligns the training strategy with the corporate strategy.

The tools

THE ENABLERS

It is not uncommon for participants at a training course to feel that, while what they are learning is interesting, it does not connect with the practical reality they face in their day-to-day jobs. They see training as theoretical. They would like to implement it, but know that this will be difficult because one or more enablers may be absent. These enablers include:

- time
- priority setting
- information
- systems
- processes
- organization structure
- help and support
- coaching and mentoring.

The read-out from the implementation dashboard will indicate the extent to which the appropriate enablers are in place and what else needs to be done to prevent a disconnect between the learning and its adoption into the organization's change process.

It is not being suggested that it is the trainer's responsibility to ensure that all the enablers are in place. Rather, they need to communicate that, where there is a gap, it is impacting negatively on the return on training investment.

MANAGER AND PARTICIPANT MOTIVATION

Managers are busy people subject to significant pressures that create stress. For international managers this is compounded by travel, operating in unfamiliar environments, cultural misalignments and different time zones. Seeking to do things differently after a training course merely adds to this stress. However successfully this is accomplished in the strengthen stage it is another matter entirely to maintain it in the long run. There is a natural process of attrition, pressures to conform to existing practices and the natural desire for an easy life. A vital element is therefore the motivation of international managers and their bosses to bring about change.

People in business respond to how they are measured and rewarded. Performance and talent appraisals, personal development plans and the training that results need to be integrated with the reward systems. Incentives linked to the implementation of change programmes provide the mechanism to focus the attention of busy managers. Naturally the manager must have an input in setting the targets against which the incentive will be earned. Whether these should be individual or team incentives or a combination of the two is a function of the prevalent culture.

One trigger for the sustain stage is to capitalize further on the debriefing that occurs between the training participant and their manager shortly after the training. As well as discussing the training course and the participant's action plan, attention should be paid to how 'things will be done differently around here' as a result of the workshop. What can be adopted and adapted from the course that will impact on the way the department functions, and how will this increase the effectiveness of the implementation of the company strategy?

For example, a technical support person may attend a course on effective presentation techniques to improve their impact in customer and internal presentations. Takeaways from the course might include a structured planning format for presentations and a methodology to ensure that benefits to the audience rather than features of the product/service are communicated strongly. The strengthen stage is concerned with the way the particular individual implements the learning and measures how effective this is through improved customer relationships, better feedback from internal audiences, reduced customer errors in ordering technical support and so on. The sustain stage is concerned with obtaining these benefits across the department, function, division or even the business unit as a whole, not just for one individual. This may involve adopting the presentation planning procedure and presentation methodologies across the whole technical support function. Targeting the whole department on the measures described above will provide the focus and incentive to sustain the change process.

TEAM MOTIVATION

As well as incentive schemes, team meetings provide a good opportunity to motivate the team and stimulate change. Unfortunately all too often the reverse is the case. With an international team, coming together for a meeting is costly and tends to be relatively infrequent. Virtual team meetings happen more often. A meeting planning checklist is shown below, which can be used as an aide memoir.

It must also be appreciated that the way meetings are held and their purpose varies

- Is the meeting objective clear?
- Is the official agenda relevant?
- What positive results will be highlighted to motivate the team?
- How will negative results be focused on so as to encourage improvement rather than to demotivate?
- How will the hidden agendas be identified and handled?
- How much of the meeting is to be used to reinforce and extend earlier training?
- Is the time allocated appropriate?
- Is the frequency of meeting appropriate?
- Will the relevant people attend?
- Will attendees have the necessary preparatory information?
- What should attendees bring with them to the meeting?
- Who will be chairperson, secretary/recorder and timekeeper?
- What inputs are expected from each attendee?
- How will contributions to the discussion from all attendees be obtained and handled?
- What are the decision-making procedures?
- How will agreed actions be confirmed and tracked?
- Is the venue and its layout appropriate?
- What equipment is required?

between cultures. The Japanese will, for example, hold many informal meetings to consult with colleagues. Their open-plan offices facilitate this process. Anglo-Saxons tend to expect specific outputs from meetings; in particular they expect decisions to be taken and action to be specified. The French tend to have more formal meetings and view them as primarily a communication device to keep all the relevant people informed on a particular issue. Naturally, the meeting checklist needs to be adapted to the culture.

SHARING BEST PRACTICE

With implementation occurring at different geographic locations, sharing information on the practicalities of implementation and learning from successes is problematic. The company intranet provides a good medium for sharing best practice as discussed in Chapter 12. However, merely publishing information in this form does not guarantee that it will be read or acted upon. After an initial flush of enthusiasm many systems lapse. Updating becomes less frequent as do the number of hits on the site. While training participants may be keen to put their successes on the website, they are often less enthusiastic to post their problems and failures, particularly in cultures where saving face is an important dimension.

E-mail is extremely useful in providing another method for communicating and sharing best practice. One client sent a monthly e-mail summarizing progress in each country.

IMPLEMENTATION OF FURTHER TRAINING

The successful management of the sustain part of the SUCCESS process will almost certainly involve further training. Usually the initial training will consist of one or two courses on the fundamentals, designed to build basic knowledge and skills of participants. Then additional, more advanced modules may be undertaken as the initial implementation is successful, in order to build on this success and generate additional momentum.

In this manner the training is an integrated part of the change process within the business. Generally level three and four organizations as discussed in Chapter 6 will be more inclined to view training and change in this manner than level one and two organizations.

Output from the sustain stage

The final step in the sustain stage is to make sure that, in the light of the changes occurring, the balance of training that is taking place does indeed facilitate the implementation of the company strategy. The training portfolio analyser, shown in Figure 13.2, is a good tool to assess this. It provides the means to manage the overall training task and the training and development activities that are taking place within the organization.

The training portfolio analyser assesses each training and development activity in terms of its impact on the business and the total associated investment. The resulting chart shows the balance of different types of training activity and what they should achieve, enabling a judgement to be made as to the most appropriate balance.

Different trainings will have different objectives and their business impact can be assessed. These can be classified into four main categories shown on the horizontal axis:

- *Profit protection* – the training is designed to respond to perceived competitor activity. Without it and possibly other associated activities the business is likely to suffer possible relative or actual decline in profits and/or revenues. This type of training may be the result of benchmarking exercises showing, for instance, that costs or productivity are out of line with competitors. Often this is driven by relatively short-term pressures and is more common in Anglo-Saxon cultures with a relatively short-term focus.
- *Steady change* – the training is focused on improving/strengthening existing activities. Success should result in some improvements to profit, revenue and some aspects of business efficiency; for example fewer complaints, speedier order processing and so on. Quality improvement programmes also fit into this category.
- *Major improvement* – training and development and probably associated activities are

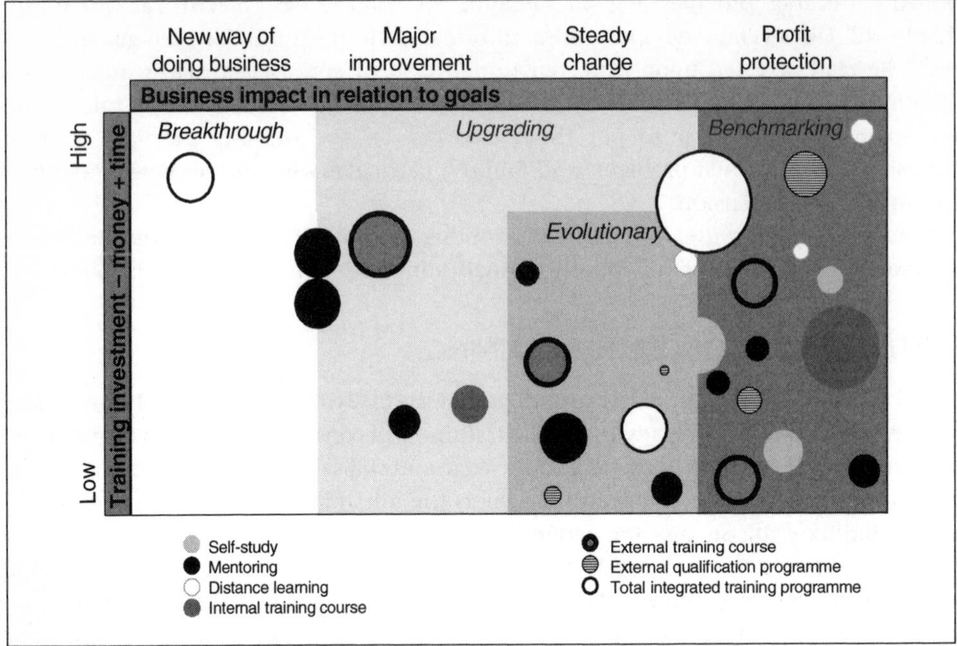

Figure 13.2 The training portfolio analyser

aimed at generating significant enhancement in business performance. Organizational and systems issues are likely to be addressed in a substantive manner and as part of a change programme on which the company is embarked. Typically, this will involve changes in behaviours as well as working methods.

- *New way of doing business* – fundamentals of the business are re-examined, redefined and redeveloped. This is likely to involve adopting new ways of doing things, which have not existed before in the business or the industry. It may mean adopting new technologies, new organizational forms and entering new markets – all of which may demand new attitudes and perceptions.

The vertical axis shows the level of training and development investment for each training activity, assessed both in terms of money and time as discussed in Chapter 5. Care must be taken to include both the direct investment in training and the opportunity costs of the time involved.

To obtain a complete picture of the training and development activity it is necessary to include all forms that the organization undertakes. Typically this will include the following:

- *Self-study* – a process whereby the individual learns on their own by reading, multimedia study, computer-assisted learning and so on. Subsequently some interpersonal exchange/explanation may be involved.
- *Mentoring* – an explicit process whereby trainees can refer to one or more named individuals to give discussion, advice and support in the implementation of specific aspects of their job.
- *Distance learning* – a programme of study, directly related to the business situation,

consisting of a number of units or modules, each of which is reviewed, discussed and assessed on completion.

- *External training course* – participation in a job-related learning event that will involve members of other organizations.
- *Internal training course* – an off-the-job learning event including conferences, seminars and workshops. The event may involve external as well as internal speakers/trainers.
- *External qualification programme* – the trainee will be aiming to obtain a generally recognized qualification. This is likely to involve a structured programme of learning over a period of time. Although it is likely to have some relevance to the present/future job of the trainees it is likely to be of a general, rather than company-specific, nature.
- *Total integrated change programme* – although all training and development activities can be viewed as a part of an integrated approach, this refers to specific, identified initiatives. The programme is likely to involve a large number of different activities. It is likely to be viewed as a project, given a name/brand and take significant time to implement.

Each training and development activity is plotted on the training portfolio analyser and represented by a circle. The size of the circle gives an indication of the total number of managers who should go through the training. The resulting chart classifies the training into four broad categories:

- *Benchmarking* – training aimed at improving current activity. Typically focused on improving knowledge and skills to perform current job.
- *Evolutionary* – training aimed at bringing about change in a controlled manner through enhancing knowledge and skills to carry out new jobs.
- *Upgrading* – enhancing competences to meet the requirements of new job roles which are only broadly defined.
- *Breakthrough* – preparing managers to implement substantive change, fundamentally altering the nature of their roles in situations which are only generally specified.

Naturally there is significant overlap between these categories in practice, and the resulting picture must be interpreted with care. It will show whether the weight of training effort is directed at the right corporate priorities with the appropriate level of cost. For example, if a company is embarked on a major change programme involving reinventing itself, moving into new markets and product areas and adopting new systems and processes then it would be expected that significant numbers of breakthrough training activities would be organized. The pattern shown in Figure 13.2 shows that there is only one such training activity, albeit a totally integrated change programme but only involving relatively few people. On the other hand there are quite a number of maintenance and evolutionary programmes which may be more appropriate to a company seeking to do better what it currently does. Perhaps training resources need to be shifted from benchmarking and evolutionary training to upgrading and breakthrough training.

The training portfolio analyser provides a total training picture that can be reviewed in respect of the investment and the impact of the business. There is no ideal pattern. The balance reflects the training strategy derived from the company's strategy. Ideally low-investment training activities with high business impact are desirable, although rare in practice. Conversely, high-cost initiatives which change the business little or not at all are questionable.

The total number of training activities can be reviewed on a job grade/department level, or any other sub level, as well as for the business as a whole. This will lead to further prioritization of the training effort with the less impactful/higher cost activities being lower priority.

One of the major advantages of the training portfolio analyser is that it produces a pictorial representation of all the training on one piece of paper. This is particularly helpful in discussions with individuals from numbers of different cultures as it avoids possible language ambiguities and the misunderstandings which may occur.

Summary

Sustaining the impact of the training in the long term is probably the most challenging element of SUCCESS. It requires strong support systems and processes, particularly for international managers operating from different geographic locations in virtual teams.

The key to success with SUCCESS is having the enablers in place and having managers and their bosses who are motivated to continue the change process after the immediate positive effects of the training have worn off. One important factor in maintaining this motivation is having a reward scheme linking personal and team rewards to the changes desired. This needs to be supported with good systems that share best practice with those involved with the management of its implementation. Supporting the activities of individuals and the team, the manager needs to have the appropriate knowledge and skills to provide effective coaching/mentoring and to run motivating team meetings.

Finally the training strategy needs to be reviewed regularly to ensure it aligns with the corporate strategy through the application of the training portfolio analyser which shows whether the balance of the training is appropriate.

Action plan

Consider the next training intervention you are planning to make. Identify the extent to which you have legislated for the the considerations outlined in the Action plan below.

	Implication for action
How will the outputs from the training be incorporated within the business?	
What incentives will managers have to implement change?	
How will managers be motivated to maintain the changes in the business?	
Specify the training category – benchmarking, evolutionary, upgrading or breakthrough?	

PART 

Making the Training Sparkle

In this third and final part of our book we look at some of the tricks of the trade – the behaviours that all trainers have in their 'toolkit' – and see how they can be applied and refined to suit international training participants.

First, in Chapter 14, we examine how participants learn from each other and the impacts of language and culture. Next, in Chapter 15, we concern ourselves specifically with the use of language, particularly English, and how it needs to be adapted to facilitate proper communication. Interacting with participants is a key dynamic in training courses, which is discussed in Chapter 16. In Chapter 17 we focus on ourselves, the trainers, and how we should position ourselves and adapt our behaviours when faced with a group of international managers. Finally, in Chapter 18, we return to our SUCCESS methodology and look at some of the essential behaviours to implement before, during and after the training.

CHAPTER

14 Organizing Participants to Learn from Each Other

The trend over the last 30 years in the training of managers is towards increasingly participative forms of learning. The most common training mechanism used is that of getting participants to work together in small groups or teams or, as they are commonly termed, breakout groups. This trend is more marked in the western world than it is in the east, but the progression globally is towards a greater proportion of each training event involving participants in doing rather than listening.

This should be seen as good news for trainers and participants alike. For participants it means that those who have a preference for Activist forms of learning (see Chapter 3), there is a greater part of most training events that suits their preference. For those with the other three learning style preferences it means that, having listened to the trainer explain the theory and having had the opportunity to discuss it, there is also the opportunity to put the new knowledge into practice during the training event to gain confidence in its use.

The general way that participants interact in breakout groups can be viewed as a combination of three factors – the background from which they emanate, the baggage that they bring with them to the training course, and the dynamics of their interpersonal behaviour (see Figure 14.1).

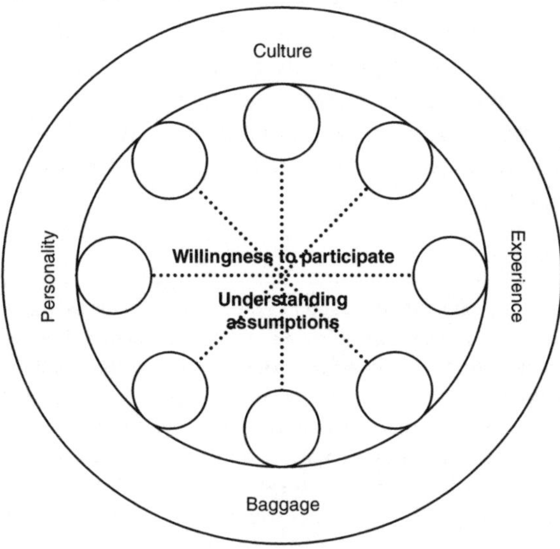

Figure 14.1 Participant interactions

What they bring with them from their workplace and private lives is their culture, experience, personality and any baggage, which may be positive or negative.

During the training they will be influenced by each other's willingness to participate, their ability to understand what is being said and what is being meant, and the tacit assumptions each makes about the other's culture.

The current trend for work carried out in breakout groups has four principal challenges for trainers of international managers. The clearest challenge is whether the participants will be able to understand each other. The majority of training that involves multiple nationalities of participants is carried out in English. Work in breakout groups requires the ability to speak as well as understand English reasonably well. A second challenge is that some participants may be less willing to participate and contribute to group activities than others. This becomes particularly evident when using methods such as role play, where participants are asked to put themselves in a particular and often unfamiliar role to practise a new approach that has been introduced by the trainer. A third challenge is that some breakout work requires participants to organize themselves into teams, with a co-ordinator to allocate tasks and a spokesperson to feedback the group's findings to the plenary group. Depending on the characteristics of the group there can be challenges with its willingness to appoint a co-ordinator to allocate tasks and a spokesperson to feed back to the plenary group in English. A fourth challenge is understanding the cultural assumptions each person is making. For example, a Pakistani delegate at one training programme became extremely angry and upset towards a French participant who, in sheer frustration at the group's lack of progress, shrugged his shoulders, looked up to heaven and turned his back towards him.

Breakout groups in practice

In mono-cultural courses participants generally form breakout groups very readily, although the group dynamic will still impact on the outputs achieved. However, with multi-national participants the trainer cannot assume that participants will as easily begin to work together in breakout groups. With these challenges to address it is good practice, particularly on courses that are to be attended by relatively young or inexperienced managers, for the trainer to deliver a fairly undemanding exercise to the breakout groups initially, making the appointment of a co-ordinator less important and demanding only the simplest of feedback. The objectives of this activity are to allow participants to become used to working with each other in an unsupervised group.

> On a course that we have run regularly with around 20 young international managers from ten different Western and Eastern European countries, a significant element of the five-day event has involved work in groups of around five participants each. As most of them will not have worked with so many different nationalities before, it is useful to arrange a relatively simple and amusing, yet challenging, team-working exercise initially so that they can begin to get used to each other. The exercise we have used most often requires members of the group to share information that they are each given, structure this information and develop a simple methodology to solve a problem that has only one correct answer, thus appealing to cultures with higher uncertainty avoidance ratings.

Another way of accomplishing more effective teamworking involving a mixture of nationalities is to get the breakout groups to discuss the most significant issue each faces in their own organizations regarding the topic of the course and report back on the similarities and differences that are apparent.

Participants regularly give very positive feedback about this initial work that they do together, saying how effective it is in breaking down any potential barriers between them. It also accustoms the participants to completing a task within a pre-determined time-scale, a key discipline with any breakout work.

Important guidance for organizing successful breakout groups

Participants on international courses not only have the opportunity to put new knowledge into practice in breakout groups, but also have the opportunity to learn from each other if the breakout tasks are well conceived and organized.

Some of the imperatives of effective breakout organization for a training event involving a mixture of nationalities are as follows.

IMPERATIVES

Ensure that there is as good a mixture as possible of the nationalities represented in the group as a whole within each breakout group. If possible, it is also beneficial to mix representatives from all the different functions that may be present on the course and to mix genders as well.

While the plenary group is still together, give very clear instructions about the objectives of the task to be completed and the time by which it must be finished. Be specific in terms of the outputs you are looking for. It is important that this is done before the participants go into their breakout groups, so that everyone involved in the training event has an equal opportunity to hear the answers given to any questions that are asked to clarify the task. In the instructions it is important to stress that participants should consider solutions that have a global application (unless a particular local application is specified), if there is to be value in the feedback for participants from many different countries.

Wherever possible, give every participant a written copy of the objectives of the task, the outputs required and the time allowed for completion. These instructions should also include clear guidance on what is expected in terms of feedback from the group, whether a spokesperson should be nominated and how long the feedback should take. It is also extremely useful with groups working in their second language to encourage them to write up the main points of their feedback on flip-chart paper and use illustrations wherever possible so that they use this as a visual aid when the spokesperson is giving feedback. Other participants, in an international event, listening to the feedback will find it much easier to follow if each spokesperson uses this type of visual aid.

Breakout groups need their own space in which to work, whether it is at separate tables within the main training room or in separate breakout rooms. Naturally, each group also needs its own flip chart and other presentation materials.

A well-constructed breakout task for international groups will have the objectives clearly stated on one side of a piece of A4 paper. Any information required to complete the task should also be clearly laid out and should be sufficiently brief that it does not take a person, working in a second or third language, more than 10 per cent of the total time allowed for the exercise to read and absorb it.

Facilitators should circulate around the breakout groups with the objective of clarifying each participant's understanding of the task and of the information provided. Facilitators should *not* get involved in the group's team-working processes except to answer very specific questions, and should *not* help groups solve problems involved in the task unless they are really unable to make a start. There is a particular challenge for the trainer where the breakout group chooses to work in an unfamiliar language. In these circumstances it is probable that the only effective input the trainer can make is to ask the group if there is any need for clarification of the task. Occasionally it may also be beneficial for the trainer to be present when the group is writing feedback points on flip-chart paper if participants need any help in structuring that feedback.

An example of a well-constructed breakout exercise

Figure 14.2 is an example of an exercise used in a course for young international managers from a major consumer goods multi-national. The exercise is part of an introduction to marketing, based around a case study of one of the company's recent product launches.

The objectives of the exercise are concisely expressed; the background information has just been given in a 45-minute presentation, hard copy of which was given to participants on the previous evening, so that those less familiar with this type of marketing challenge could spend more time absorbing the information.

Marketing Case Study 2004

Exercise for the YELLOW group

Imagine you are employed by our main competitor as Market Intelligence Executive for Latin America.

1. By what legitimate means would you expect to get 'early warning' about our company's plans to launch 'Product X'?
2. What plans would you put in place to disrupt the initial stages of the launch?
3. Also describe how you feel our competitor would plan to react in the longer term?
4. How do you believe our company should be prepared to respond?

Working in your groups you have 45 minutes to consider this question and prepare your presentation. Delivery of presentations should be planned to take no longer than five minutes.

Figure 14.2 Breakout exercise

Effective exercises for breakout groups

The very best exercises are up-to-date case studies that require the participants to solve the type of problems they will encounter on returning to their jobs. If the exercise can be designed so that participants have the opportunity to use a model or process that has been introduced by the trainer, the session will score even more highly in terms of its relevance to their needs.

The exercise in Figure 14.2 was produced in conjunction with a case study, which focused on brand activation in a multi-national company where the emphasis was focused on the need to take products that had been successful in one part of the world and launch them effectively in other parts of the world with relevant local support and initiatives. The case was built by giving participants market information about the new part of the world where the product was to be launched, information about the product itself and then setting a number of tasks which replicate the tasks that would have to be carried out by local activation teams. In this case there were four breakout groups of six participants, with each group having one unique exercise to do and one exercise which was common to all four groups. The benefit of the unique exercises is that the feedback session is full of variety, with each group feeding back on a different question.

Clearly there is significant investment in preparing bespoke case studies and exercises such as this. The pay-back on the investment comes from the relevance and currency of the learning. The case can be updated as the actual launch proceeds, building-in new exercises to replicate some of the situations encountered in the real marketplace and comparing the participants' recommendations with the actions that were taken in practice.

Another type of exercise that is more difficult to manage but can be extremely effective is the role-play situation. This is particularly relevant to training events where there is a significant emphasis on participants developing effective personal behaviours such as in managing or selling. Just as with the case study described above, role plays can be constructed to replicate real situations; in this case, situations encountered by the participants themselves at their places of work. A good example would be coaching skills where participants have been introduced to a coaching model by the trainer and now have the opportunity to learn how to use it in a role-play situation. With a mix of nationalities it is important that the trainer takes account of the factors described in Chapter 2 on cultural diversity when dividing the group into pairs for role-play purposes. Asking two participants from countries with very different power distance cultures to practise coaching skills, for instance, is only valid if they are likely to encounter this cultural challenge in the workplace. Role plays of this type can work equally well with CCTV feedback to the participants or with a third participant acting as observer. The trainer needs to take account of any anxieties that either method could cause the participants and, if there is uncertainty about that, to consult the participants on their preference. Where the video feedback is to be reviewed by the whole group, it is important to ask participants to use the 'course language' for the exercise, rather than their local language, which will not be understood by the trainer or, in many cases, by the other participants. Where participants do use a language with which the trainer is not familiar and there is no translator present, any intervention from the trainer is restricted to comments on body language (which again is often culturally specific) and questions of the participants about the learning they have achieved and their feelings during the role play.

The dynamics of breakout groups

Individual personality is an important dimension that affects the way groups behave, irrespective of culture. In addition, with international managers the dynamics of breakout groups will also, as shown in Figure 14.1, depend on the individual's willingness to participate, their ability to understand what is being said and what is being meant, and the tacit assumptions each makes about the other's culture. The possibility for conflict is therefore multiplied with multi-national courses. Such conflict can have many causes. Cultural misunderstandings have already been touched on. Participants also bring along baggage from their private and work lives and even acquire more during the training itself.

> When conducting a residential programme in rural Holland attended by the sales director and his senior and middle managers from around Europe, the participants were encouraged to use the rather splendid sporting facilities to de-stress themselves at the end of the full training days. The sales director saw this as a great team-building opportunity and organized competitions of one sort or another every day in which he also participated and most of which he won. Naturally this caused resentment amongst some participants, and comments such as 'typical of him' and 'he's so busy winning he's no time for living' were muttered in the bar and corridors.

Trainers rarely need to become involved in helping groups resolve these problems, and it is better that groups are allowed to find their own ways of working together effectively. However, sometimes, as in the above case, it can threaten to derail an entire course and the trainer needs to take action. This can be by speaking quietly to the offending individual or, if this is unlikely to work, then calling a time out and, adopting a facilitator role, ask the group including the 'problem' participant, to identify any issues that are inhibiting them getting more out of the learning experience.

Generally it is advisable to change the composition of the groups regularly for events of two days and longer. It is good practice to tell participants in the introduction to the course that the membership of groups will be changed each day or after two days. The reason given should be to give participants a good opportunity to work with different people during the course, while working long enough with one group to develop an effective way of working. This will reduce the likelihood of members of a group becoming embroiled in any sort of serious conflict.

> On one occasion on a programme involving participants from over 20 countries it was apparent that one individual from a Middle Eastern country was particularly forceful and opinionated. Unfortunately, the points that he made rarely had anything to do with the particular subject being discussed. This naturally proved extremely disruptive to the group who did not understand that this was his way of establishing his relative status and that after suitably acknowledging the 'perceptiveness of his comments' that they could then ignore them. By changing the composition of the groups every day the disruption was minimized and each individual got the opportunity to learn a bit more about a particular culture.

It is not our job as trainers to try and explain the particular behaviour of a participant. However, at the end of the day, for example in the evening at the bar or over dinner, if the subject is raised then the participants can be encouraged to discuss it amongst themselves in a constructive manner, including the 'problem' participant, with the trainer adopting a facilitation role.

As the participative elements of training increase, so the management of groups becomes more and more important. As a general rule, trainers should organize international groups to give participants the maximum opportunity for learning from people from different cultures and functions, while keeping their own interaction with the groups to the role of clarifier and adviser unless the whole programme will be derailed, in which case they may need to facilitate a solution.

Summary

The general way that participants interact in breakout groups can be viewed as a combination of what they bring with them to the training course and the dynamics of their interpersonal behaviour. What they bring with them is their culture, experience, personality and any baggage, which may be positive or negative, from their workplace and private lives. During the training they will be influenced by each other's willingness to participate, their ability to understand what is being said and what is being meant, and the tacit assumptions each makes about the other's culture.

In international events, groups should be constructed to mix different nationalities, keeping group sizes, ideally, to no more than six participants. Wherever possible, it is good practice to give the groups an initial task which is straightforward and allows the participants within a group to get to know one another. This and subsequent exercises should be fully explained, with questions taken in the plenary session prior to participants breaking up into groups.

The very best case studies are current, where participants are given the opportunity to address issues similar to those that occur in their jobs and then learn how these issues have been addressed in practice, accompanied by a description of the results. Instructions on the feedback required from groups must be clear, and with groups working in their second language it is essential that feedback is accompanied by the use of visual aids to cover key points, with illustrations wherever possible. The facilitator should visit groups while they are working, but restrict inputs to clarifying the task and giving relevant information.

Action plan

Review an exercise that you have created for a past training course, or one that you have recently created for a future course, and use the checklist in the Action plan to ensure that the way in which the exercise is intended to be used meets all the essential criteria for effective learning, which have been discussed in this chapter.

Essential criteria for effective learning	*Your exercise meets the criteria: Yes/No*	*How you intend to modify the exercise to meet the criteria*
All necessary information for completion of the exercise is given prior to the breakout		
Instructions given to the participants for completion of the exercise: 1. are concisely expressed on one side of A4 paper 2. include a statement of the time allowed for the exercise 3. give guidance on how feedback should be done		
Groups are no more than six participants strong and each one includes a mix of nationalities representative of all the course members		
Time is allowed in the plenary group to answer questions and clarify issues relevant to the exercise		

CHAPTER

15 *Use of English with International Managers*

Language is the biggest potential difficulty in training a group that encompasses a number of nationalities each used to operating in their respective native languages. English is the most commonly used language in training events with multi-national business groups. Within continental Europe the standard of understanding of the English language has increased significantly over the last ten years and is generally at a higher standard amongst managers under the age of 35. In other parts of the world the level of English understanding is variable and depends as much on the client company as it does on the region. Moreover, the motivation to be trained in a language with which participants could have some difficulty understanding differs too. In some Eastern countries, where it is considered an honour to be selected to attend a training course, there is still a danger of meeting participants whose English is barely adequate for comprehension of the most straightforward of training materials. Usually one of the main benefits that these participants will get is an improvement in their English language skills.

Even amongst native English speakers it is challenging to ensure full comprehension on the part of a group of 12–24 participants, just because of different backgrounds and perceptions. Amongst a group working in their second, third or even fourth language the challenge is considerably greater. In all of these circumstances the onus is on the trainer to make the event as comprehensible as possible for speakers of other languages.

Eyes and ears

One method is to support all the main points made verbally with written text and pictures. According to oft-quoted guidance (see Table 15.1), this will increase the probability of understanding the meaning of the spoken word eightfold.

Table 15.1 Impact of various communications modes

Impact	%
Visual	56
Tone	37
Words	7
Total comprehension	100

The same guidance highlights the importance of tone of voice in conveying meaning with the use of words. In training the speaker needs to use very clear diction and speak at a slow pace, as well as modulating the intonation to enhance the meaning and impact of the words. This clarity of diction is not easily achieved and it is instructive for most trainers to tape a piece of their own work and play it back to appreciate how much improvement could be made in making the delivery of the spoken word more comprehensible. Having overcome the shock of hearing one's own voice, it is true of most people that they will recognize the need to slow down the pace of their delivery in order to give speakers of other languages a real opportunity to tune-in and fully understand what is being said. For most of us who speak a foreign language, our first request on failing to catch the meaning of something that is said is for the speaker to slow down the pace of delivery. Unfortunately, those trainers with strong regional accents need to take even more care as the participants will find their pronunciation novel and even more difficult to understand than the traditional BBC English that they have learned.

Moreover, in addition to the support of written text and pictures through slide presentation, the trainer can raise levels of understanding even higher (except in high power distance cultures) by ensuring constant eye contact with all areas of the audience during a piece of presentation. Eye contact raises the level of the audience's focus and it makes it easier for participants to catch the attention of the trainer when a question comes to mind.

Simplicity

When we are delivering training to speakers of other languages, we need to focus deliberately on simplicity. This means using short words and short sentences. Again, the best lesson is to listen to a piece of our own training delivery on tape and analyse it for simplicity. If we speak another language than English we should consider how many of the words we couldn't readily translate into that language and it will give us an appreciation of the difficulty some participants will have in understanding our English. This salutary lesson is one way to be convinced that training delivery would be greatly enhanced if it were restricted to the 500 most commonly used words in English, a list of which can be found on the Internet at www.world-english.org/english500.htm.

Trainers should remember to shorten deliberately the length of sentences used and to leave pauses between each sentence to allow the participants to comprehend fully before starting on the next sentence.

> On one occasion three trainers were operating in Budapest, training a group of 35 participants comprising Russians, Poles, Hungarians and Turks. Two of us rather unkindly competed to note down the less comprehensible words used by our third trainer. Within the first ten minutes these were some of the words and phrases that we recorded which we felt were guaranteed to confuse even the most enthusiastic student of English from those parts of Europe: *head honcho, hiding his light under a bushel, speaking with forked tongue, playing to the gallery*. Imagine how the participants felt at the beginning of a three-day programme!

It has been said elsewhere in this book that it is vitally important to check the understanding of participants by asking questions of members of the group to check how much has been retained of the material that has been delivered in the previous one hour.

This practice gives the measure needed of at least a sample of the members of the group. If the level of understanding is less than complete, it is more likely to be the failure of delivery that is the cause than the lack of intelligence of the audience!

Aids to comprehension

Support documentation is very helpful in enhancing understanding at the moment of delivery and assisting recall if it is referred to later. Copies of slides used as course notes, with space for participants to make their own notes alongside each slide, is effective and widely used. Sometimes notes are translated into a language that all participants will understand such as Russian or Chinese. If the words are accompanied by relevant diagrams and pictures the level of understanding will be even greater. Figure 15.1 is a simple example showing the layout of a SWOT analysis.

A discussion, for example, on the elements of a SWOT analysis accompanied by this chart is going to be much more readily understood than a mere verbal delivery of the concept of strengths, weaknesses, opportunities and threats.

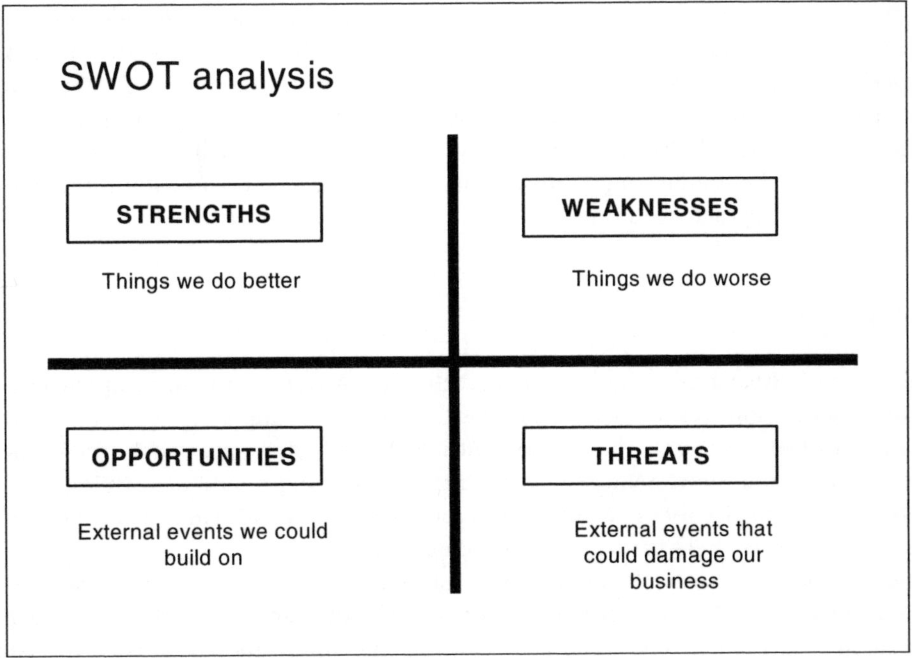

Figure 15.1 Diagram accompanying the words

Understanding the participants' native language

Occasionally we are in a situation where the participants will be fluent in English and yet use their native language in private conversations and breakout groups. It can come as a shock to them to realize that the trainer has understood some, if not all, of these private conversations. Working with a new group in Belgium on a two-day event and delivering the training in English, one of the breakout groups held its own discussions in French, most of which was understood by the trainer. During the discussion at the feedback session the group must have become aware that the trainer understood what was said, as there was a switch to Flemish in the next breakout discussion.

There are options for the trainer where members of the group are reasonably fluent in English:

1 Ask for all discussions to be conducted in English.
2 Tell the group if the trainer is familiar with other language(s), but say that the intention is that the whole event is conducted in English.
3 Operate in English and say nothing of knowledge of other languages.

As a result of the Belgian and similar experiences, our feeling is that the most straightforward course of action is to announce that the intention is that the whole event, including breakout groups, is to be held in English and also to say which other languages are familiar to the trainer. It is preferable that participants realize what the trainer is likely to comprehend!

Where the participants' command of the trainer's language is insufficient, a translator will be used. One aspect that trainers may initially find disconcerting with simultaneous translation when running a highly participative session is hearing their translated words in an earpiece while they are presenting. This distraction soon decreases but does require extra concentration and self-discipline. Naturally group work will take place in the native language and the trainer must make sure the translator accompanies them when visiting/facilitating each syndicate.

Summary

Liberal use of visual aids is the best method the trainer can use to aid comprehension of spoken English. However, along with pictures and charts, it is important to use clear diction, interesting variations in voice intonation and a deliberately slow pace of delivery. Simplicity of vocabulary and short sentences will further assist understanding, while it is very important to minimize (or preferably avoid) the use of idiom and slang. Strong eye contact in most cultures will help participants considerably.

Support documentation, including copies of slides, will help at the time of delivery and subsequently for recall, particularly with participants whose grasp of English is better at the written than at the conversational level. During the conversational parts of the course, particularly in the breakout groups, it is important that all the discussions are held in English so that no one, including the trainer, is excluded from understanding the points being made.

Trainers should ask for all conversations to be held in English and advise the audience of any other languages where the trainer has an understanding. If this is not possible then the trainer must develop good skills in working with a translator.

Action plan

To review your own use of English and reduce the likelihood of participants misunderstanding your meaning on future courses, make arrangements to record a piece of training that you deliver to an international group. Play back the recording privately and make notes under the headings given in the Action plan, along with the actions that you can take to improve your delivery.

Key delivery points	*How delivery could be improved*	*How this can be better expressed*
Clear diction and appropriate pace		
Interesting voice intonation		
Simple vocabulary		
Avoidance of idiom and slang		
Short sentences		

CHAPTER **16**

Seeking and Using Feedback from Individuals and Groups

This chapter has been included as a result of feedback from a client who some years ago asked us to design and run a Train the Trainer course. When we shared the materials with him before the event, he said he felt that we should include a special section on how trainers handle feedback from groups. We were being asked to train a number of technical specialists as trainers and they were said to be concerned about how to handle feedback from their audience.

For most experienced trainers, all feedback is welcomed because it enables the trainer to make a session truly interactive and focus on the needs and interests of the audience. For those only just entering the role of trainer there is often a fear of being asked a difficult question or receiving a critical response to a statement made. The likelihood of both of these eventualities arising is multiplied with the number of different nationalities present in the audience. Different nationalities bring with them a range of cultural perspectives that are going to lead to a variety of questions and a range of perceptions much greater than in a homogeneous, single-nationality group. This chapter will examine the opportunities given to the trainer, along with some advice on how to make the most of these opportunities.

Should the trainer be an expert?

Our advice to trainers would be never to perceive yourself as an expert in the subject of the training event, because then you will avoid giving the impression to the audience that you have all the answers. It is of course important to have knowledge of your subject as this enhances your ability to help others to learn. This is not the same as giving the impression that you are the expert. It enables you to turn a question from one member of the audience into a point of discussion for the whole group. Indeed there are situations when it is essential that the trainer opens up a subject raised by one participant for discussion by the group. An example would be when a participant quotes a writer who has recently taken a different point of view from the one that you are developing at the time. If you had positioned yourself as expert the participants would be expecting you to defend your point of view. As you have merely positioned yourself as a knowledgeable facilitator you are in a very good position to open up the issue for debate. Invariably a balanced discussion will follow with all points of view being given due consideration.

This does not mean that you should open up every issue for discussion. Indeed, in some cultures like Turkey for example, this will be seen as a weakness. Often participants from these high power distance cultures (see Chapter 2) will test speakers early on. Their view is that if the speaker cannot demonstrate that they know a lot more than the participants, then they will not earn respect and have no right to instruct them. However, once this is established, more interactive ways of answering questions become acceptable.

Participants are interested in anecdotes from the trainer where they are used to illustrate a point. This is different from boring your audience with long and detailed descriptions of your experience in the subject. Anecdotes should be short and pithy, with a very clear relevance to the point under discussion. These vignettes can be from the trainer's own experience or an account of an experience that has previously been shared with the trainer. Naturally these stories must be culturally sensitive. US speakers, for example, drawing sporting analogies from baseball or American football risk, not only losing part of their audience, but also of alienating them. Should a trainer wish to use an anecdote which has something specific to say about one country, they should only do so if it is certain that the participants are familiar with the content.

Naturally, if the trainer shares anecdotes with the audience, participants should be encouraged to share their experiences with the group. A good example of how fruitful this can be is when experiences are shared on issues such as leadership styles, coaching experiences and customer interactions: indeed, any area of human interaction is ripe with opportunities for generating interesting anecdotes. The trainer need only relate the stories to the model or principles that are under discussion at the time. Even where the anecdote appears initially to contradict the model it can be useful. In the process of discussion at least one participant will make an attempt to relate it to the model or will come forward with an alternative experience that does relate to the model. All this open discussion is possible and fruitful so long as the trainer has not positioned himself as the expert.

Feedback from breakout groups

In Chapter 14 we looked at some of the principles of creating and managing breakout groups. Receiving their feedback at the end of a group exercise is a very important part of the process and is instrumental in setting the tone of an event.

The first principle is that the trainer needs to look for elements in the feedback that can be praised enthusiastically. This is particularly important with international groups of managers. First it needs to be recognized that giving feedback in a second or third language, on a subject that is also quite unfamiliar and to an unfamiliar audience is in itself a major challenge for many people. Only by making positive comments on what has been delivered will the trainer encourage other participants to come forward as spokespersons from their breakout groups.

The second principle is that if some of the feedback can or should be challenged, it is generally much better that other participants do this rather than the trainer. It is very easy to do this by opening up the feedback points for questions or discussion for the members of other breakout groups. Where the trainer feels a point requires particular discussion it is always possible to ask the audience how they feel about this. It gives people the opportunity to challenge, qualify or simply debate a point that the trainer may feel to be doubtful or suspect in some way.

However, many Middle and Far Eastern cultures do not encourage overt criticism of colleagues in a direct manner as it gives rise to 'loss of face'. Such questions as '...and how could team B's analysis be made even more complete?' are sometimes met with stony silence, not because of lack of knowledge but because the participants do not wish to offend. This raises a particularly difficult problem for the trainer. On the one hand the participants expect the trainer to be critical but on the other hand it must be done in such a manner that there is no loss of face.

A number of approaches can work. At the end of the feedback from all the groups, the trainer can pick up the key learning points from the participants and then add to them without being critical of any one individual or group. Another riskier approach is to use humour to soften the criticism. Alternatively a separate, private conversation can be held with the individual or group where direct feedback is given.

One golden rule on receiving feedback from several groups on the same exercise is to allow each group to give all their feedback before opening up the points made for discussion.

> On one event involving participants from nine countries, we were asked to coach a speaker, who was a senior IT specialist, between sessions, on the delivery of his presentation and the facilitation of the feedback from a straightforward exercise. On the third occasion that this event was run, the presentation went extremely well and participants completed the exercise enthusiastically in their breakout groups. Each group had been asked to complete the same task and, having heard the feedback from the first two groups, our IT specialist gave a lengthy comment on the feedback given by the second group. When he asked for feedback from the third and fourth groups they had very little to say. He had avoided the mistake of being critical about the feedback of the second group, but in making a lengthy comment on it he had inadvertently stolen the points that the third and fourth groups had intended to make. This mistake on the part of the trainer can be very frustrating for groups who have debated a subject in their breakout sessions and come to conclusions of which they are proud, only to be inadvertently upstaged by the trainer who is a little too eager to make his or her own input on the issues under discussion.

Often the best way of avoiding the possibility of upstaging breakout groups is to ask them to give feedback on different aspects of the exercise. This avoids any repetition and resulting boredom by the rest of the group at hearing the same thing being repeated several times.

Dealing with and asking questions

Questions from individual participants are to be welcomed and, if handled effectively, will almost always enhance the understanding of the group on the topic being discussed. It is really important that the trainer repeats the question asked and then answers it for the benefit of the whole group. Repeating the question serves two purposes. First, it is a check that the question has been properly understood. Second, it ensures that the whole group has the benefit of hearing the question clearly before either the trainer or members of the group come up with possible responses to it. This is really important bearing in mind the language issue we have discussed. Participants from Brazil, for example, will have considerable difficulty understanding a question asked in English by a Kenyan or a Russian with their own particular accents. It is extremely frustrating to be a member of a group where the questions are difficult to hear and responses are made without understanding the question in full.

There can be occasions when the questions are detailed and will not serve a purpose in enhancing the understanding of the group on the main topic under discussion. In these instances the trainer has some choices:

- give a short response and then ask if the group wish to debate the question in more detail;
- ask the audience if it is going to be useful to discuss the question in detail in the group session;
- offer to deal with the answer in detail outside of the group session.

In most instances it is good practice to involve the group in deciding whether the issues raised by the question are considered to be of general interest and should be discussed in the group session.

> Very occasionally a participant will ask a question or make a statement that is aimed at testing the trainer's flexibility. A memorable example on a course for international managers was when a participant forcefully stated that he did not feel the subject under discussion was of interest to the group and that the group would like to spend their time doing something more productive. This was one of those occasions when we were present as programme organizers and coaches for the specialist presenters. We did not anticipate the presenter being able to handle this challenging situation very easily. However, she did all the right things, probably better than we as experienced trainers would have done! First, she asked the group if they did in fact feel that the current discussion had little relevance for them, to which she received a rather quiet 'yes'. Then she said that she had an exercise that the group could do which would give them a practical understanding of the issues involved in the subject. She asked if the group would find that more productive, to which she received an overwhelming 'yes'. She introduced the exercise and managed expertly to draw out from it the learning that was her main objective to achieve. This was remarkably skilled. It was also extremely shrewd as she was dealing with a topic that was dear to the heart of the Business Group President and it was not an option to let it go and replace it with a totally different subject.

It would probably be unwise for a trainer to confront the participant who issued a challenge. The challenger will almost always gain the support of the group if that happens. It is also an example of when a trainer needs to be flexible in how learning is achieved. If a group makes it clear that the current activity needs to change, the trainer needs to have the resources to offer another option. In the case above, it was essential that the other option maintained the focus on the subject under discussion. As William James the psychologist is quoted: 'Intelligence is having fixed objectives but being capable of flexibility in how they are achieved.'

There are two very good reasons for asking questions of the group early in a training event or when the trainer switches from one topic to another. First is the need to assess the knowledge level of the group so that the topic is presented to take account of the level of knowledge of the majority of participants. It is likely that the trainer will have attempted to establish this at the point where training needs were being identified, but it is good practice to check it out in a 'live session' to ensure that the training material is being introduced in the most appropriate way. The second reason is to check participants' understanding of the material the trainer is delivering before getting into too much depth. This is particularly important with diverse groups, as it is critically important to check understanding of the language being used by the trainer.

> It was as a result of checking language understanding on an event a few years ago that we found one Turkish participant was giving a running translation from English into Turkish for the benefit of a non-English speaking Turk who had somehow found his way on to a programme which was due to be delivered in English! It is helpful to know such things earlier rather than later, although finding the right solution to that particular problem was not so easy. In this case the Turkish participants saw their selection for the programme as a reward and were keen to remain in attendance even if comprehension was going to be a challenge for some of them.

Another use of questioning to assess how well learning is taking place is to review each day's learning either at the end of the day or, perhaps even better, at the beginning of the subsequent day. This can be done using well-structured questions to test knowledge. Quite often a few prompts are necessary, amongst even the best motivated of groups, to remind participants what was being discussed on the previous day! An alternative is to give a slide-show presentation (accompanied by music to give additional atmosphere if desired) of all the slides shown on the previous day and to ask each participant, working in groups, to come up with a different learning point.

Another way of checking on progress is to ask participants during the breaks how they felt about the previous session. As well as getting an immediate reaction on how it was received, participants will often raise any issues about understanding, which they might not raise when the group is in formal session. This is particularly useful with international groups where individual participants may be hesitant about admitting to a lack of understanding in the formal session. A variant of this is to put up a flip chart at the end of the first day, located near to the exit of the room. The chart is divided into two columns; one headed 'What are we doing right and should continue?' and the other 'What should we do differently tomorrow?' Participants are asked to think about the training they have experienced on the first day and to write down any points on Post-it® notes – one point per Post-it® – and stick them in the appropriate column on the flip chart on their way out. The trainer can then review the points, grouping similar ones together (see Figure 16.1). The next morning the trainer can then give feedback to the whole group using the flip chart as a visual aid on how the course will proceed in response to their comments.

Figure 16.1 Participant feedback flip chart

Summary

Difficult questions and aggressive statements can often be managed effectively by opening them up to the whole group for comment and finding a solution through discussion. However, in some high power distance cultures this can be a way of participants testing speakers early on in the programme and a strong response may be called for. Where participants take an expert stance, the trainer needs to demonstrate knowledge but not enter into a competition on level of expertise. Trainers can manage discussions on detailed points from expert participants more effectively if the trainer is positioned as knowledgeable rather than as the expert.

In responding to questions the trainer must first repeat the question asked slowly and carefully to make sure everyone understands it.

Use of anecdotes and stories is to be encouraged, but they must be culturally sensitive and understandable by the participants. It is also productive to allow participants to relate their own anecdotes where they illustrate a relevant point that can subsequently be discussed by the whole group.

Trainers need to look for the positive aspects of feedback from breakout groups and invite participants to add other comments, some of which can be challenging or critical. With some cultures, face saving is very important, while at the same time criticism is expected if something has been done wrong. If the trainer avoids giving such criticism altogether then participants will feel dissatisfied and learn less.

When receiving feedback from breakout groups it is important to allow the spokesperson of each group to present the group's ideas before the trainer adds any additional viewpoints. Questions from the trainer are essential to check understanding and to assess the knowledge level of participants.

Action plan

Consider the key points in the Action plan in seeking and using feedback from participants. Reflecting on recent international courses that you have run, identify against each item what you could do differently in future to improve interaction with the audience.

Key points in seeking and using feedback	*What I could do differently in future*
Repeating questions from individual participants for the benefit of the whole group	
Opening up participant questions for discussion in low power distance cultures	
Giving a strong response to participants' questions, which are deliberately challenging, in high power distance cultures	
Taking opportunities, outside of formal sessions, to open up one-to-one discussions with participants	

CHAPTER **17**

Effective Trainer Behaviours

All the preparation that is done under the survey, understand and create stages of the training cycle covered in Chapters 7, 8 and 9 is important to the success of a training event for international managers. However, much of this work can be undone by the trainer's behaviour in the first few minutes of an event. This is an important factor that creates the atmosphere for the training. This atmosphere will be critical to how the event progresses over its full duration, whether it is half a day or five days in length. Learning and fun are essential parts of the equation. Having started well, the trainer needs to build and maintain momentum as the course proceeds. In this chapter we look at some of the ways in which trainers can do this with international participants.

Training to entertain

Managers from all cultures will have a more pleasurable learning experience if they are also having some fun and getting some enjoyment from the training. This will colour their perceived value of the learning experience.

In general, with many individual exceptions, North Americans tend to appreciate and evaluate training by focusing on how well it entertains. They love a show. Western Europeans tend to appreciate training for its practical application; Eastern Europeans for the theoretical constructs. Those from the Middle East put a lot of importance on the location and venue, while those from the Far East value the clarity of course structure and the precision of instructions for exercises. South America is similar to North America, as is Africa to Western Europe.

This means that the entertainment aspects need to be adapted to the culture. For American audiences, stories, jokes, exercises, and competitions with winners and losers are generally acceptable. This is much less so with Far Eastern participants. Not only may they have problems understanding the context of many of the stories as well as the language, they will be concerned with losing face. They also will be much more reticent to join in unless the activity is precisely structured.

Visual and oral clues can have a strong influence in creating a fun atmosphere. This is particularly so for cultures such as Japan and France, for example, which have traditionally viewed training as a process where the trainer communicates information and the student absorbs it. Any failure to understand is the responsibility of the student, not the teacher. Typically, trainees in these generally high power distance cultures will perceive training as very much a one-way process from master to student. One advantage of this approach to learning is that the participants will be very sensitive to outside stimuli. On entering the training environment their antennae will be actively scanning what is happening around them. This means that visual and oral stimuli such as music, posters, signs, flip charts, both inside and outside the training room, and indeed the layout of the room itself will be sending signals to them. If these signals differ from their expectations of a training event then they can begin to reorientate themselves to the new situation in their own time, without losing face. They will feel it is their responsibility to adapt to the trainer's style but want to do so in a non-threatening environment. Merely dispensing with classroom-style layout for tables and chairs in favour of a 'U' or even cabaret style can be a powerful dynamic in creating a fun atmosphere.

Thought also needs to be given to how participation can be encouraged. With American participants this is generally not a problem unless they are unhappy with the course. Non-participation is a strong indicator that all is not well, as is the case with Middle Eastern participants. However, with East Europeans or Asians this may be far from the case. They do not expect to make inputs or ask questions, and silence does not mean 'I am unhappy' but 'I am thinking about what I am learning'. This means that participation needs to be encouraged in small steps. Initially the trainer might get participants merely to talk to each other on a relatively straightforward issue with a range of possible outcomes, none of which are wrong. For example, what are the three most important attributes of a strong team? Once the process has started then the extent of two-way interaction can be extended and a competitive element introduced.

Telling stories is a desirable attribute in any trainer. For international audiences this should be done with greater consideration. As has already been mentioned in earlier chapters, cultural and historical sensitivities should be respected. This does not mean that they need to be entirely avoided. On the contrary they can help stimulate openness and active discussion. For example, on many occasions we have used a story about a French defeat in the Napoleonic wars with French participants with considerable effect. On one level the events are far enough in history not to be of personal relevance to any individual. However, more importantly, it provides opportunities to create more empathy and understanding through adding cultural stereotypes.

The all-important opening and dealing with low points

At the beginning of a course, participants will be in varied frames of mind, depending on a range of factors, including their motivation to attend the event, their journey to the venue and their initial feelings about what they first experience at the event. To lead the participants into a positive learning experience, trainers need to bring considerable energy to all the events that they run. With international managers this is even more challenging for the trainer because energy is interpreted differently in different cultures. To a Western European, energy means lots of action and strong body movement, whereas for a participant from the Far East, energy is being inwardly focused and calm. Our general advice here, when faced with participants from varying continents, is to start any programme by standing still, looking over participants' heads until they are silent; and then to begin moving after the first few sentences have been spoken.

This energy will communicate itself to the participants and in turn raise their energy levels. Participants will be reading the trainer's body language and tuning into the trainer's tone of voice in those opening minutes, and the impression formed is likely to be enduring.

Most of all it is important that everything the trainer does in those opening stages fits naturally with the trainer's personality and the culture of the participants for whom the training is being delivered and the participants' organization. A critical aspect of trainers being at ease with the situation and behaving naturally is that they feel satisfied that all the preparation is complete, giving positive feelings of confidence about the value of the event for the participants. This is important because it will be communicated subconsciously through the trainer's body language and tone.

Before we leave these important opening stages of a training event it is worth considering whether trainers should introduce themselves to participants at the pre-course coffee station, which is an almost ubiquitous part of training events. Most trainers see a real benefit in doing this, as it is good to make contact with a few participants prior to the start of the formalities. It is good because it will mean that there are at least some participants to whom the trainer is not a total stranger and when the first question is thrown out to the audience the trainer can anticipate that one of the participants with whom contact was made beforehand will feel at ease in coming forward with a contribution. In fact we always make sure we introduce ourselves to every participant before the course whenever possible and welcome them. Most cultures are more formally polite than Anglo-Saxons and shaking hands is an important sign of showing respect, particularly in mainland Europe.

It should be said that not all trainers share this view. There are those, probably the minority, who like to make an impact with their initial entrance and are confident in their ability to 'play an audience'. They feel their impact will be diluted if they have interacted previously with participants and so prefer not to be seen by course members before the curtain is raised on the formal proceedings. It is for each individual trainer to make a personal choice here. If there is no clear preference it is worth considering one additional benefit of mingling informally with international managers before a training event. It will give the trainer an opportunity to tune in to some of the accents that are going to be encountered during the course and it will give them a chance to hear the pronunciation of some of the names, which even after several decades of training internationally can be a challenge when working from the written word alone! Often it will be difficult to grasp the participant's name on initial introduction and we often will ask the individual to repeat it just to make sure we have got it right. However, it is easily forgotten and, as soon as practical after the course opening, all participants should be asked to write what they wish to be called for the duration of the course on their name card in large bold letters. We make sure that they complete both sides of the card so that we can see their names from all points of the training room. Remembering unusual names can be a major challenge.

When the trainer makes the self-introduction formally to a group of participants it is naturally important that the information given about the trainer's experience fits the subject matter of the event. Most trainers have several areas of expertise but the participants are mainly interested in those areas that are relevant to them. Training conducted for similar organizations and in the countries from which participants have come needs to be highlighted.

Once the formal part is underway there is a case for agreeing on some course rules, so that participants have a common understanding of the etiquette on issues such as taking a break during sessions, asking questions and using mobile phones. Trainers all have their individual concerns on these matters, but one that is particularly relevant to international events is to encourage participants to feel totally comfortable with asking for repetition or further explanation if they feel they are missing a point due to a problem in understanding the speaker's English (assuming that the event is being conducted in English!). Such matters need to be dealt with at the very outset of the training and are part of creating a relaxed and informal atmosphere while maintaining positive behaviours in the group.

Another issue that often arises is one of timekeeping. The differing cultural attitudes to timekeeping have already been covered in earlier chapters. However, one further dimension that can be an issue is starting, finishing and lunch times. For example, Scandinavians generally tend to start work early, lunch around noon or earlier and are likely to finish in advance of Southern Europeans, who start around 09:30, lunch around 13:00 to 14:00+ and finish around 18:00 or later. Generally it is advisable, should this issue arise, to let the group decide the rules it wishes to follow. The reader will observe that time has been referred to in the previous sentence using the 24-hour clock convention. This is used far more widely than the a.m. and p.m. Anglo-Saxon convention and is less likely to cause confusion.

There will be times during the course when the group loses its energy. Some trainers like to use 'energizers' at these points, especially if the low is due to the physical tiredness brought on by an inappropriately large meal or a late night. Gower publishes books of energizers for trainers who need to acquire these types of resources. Interestingly, not all participants appreciate these sudden bursts of mental or physical energy and so other trainers deal with lows by changing the group activity while maintaining the focus on the learning objectives. Moving to an impromptu breakout group or work in pairs can often reinvigorate participants.

Meeting the challenge of diverse cultures and personality types

Instrumental to the success of any international training course is that the trainer enjoys the challenge of being confronted with a mixture of nationalities, personality types, participant expectations and the occasional uncontrollable event. This challenge should be fun to the trainer, as this will communicate itself instantly to the participants. Potential problems will turn out to be interesting challenges if there is an atmosphere of good humour shared by participants and the trainer alike. The unexpected activation of the sprinkler system in the conference room is a problem at a dour event; but it is amusing in the middle of a good-humoured discussion at a course in which everyone is enjoying their participation.

Trainers need to be as aware of the different perceptions and reactions of individual personalities as they do to the more general differences between participants from different cultures. A good example of this is the way in which trainers at international seminars can expect to be challenged by participants having varied approaches to timekeeping. This is not just a matter of Southern European approximation conflicting with Northern precision. There are individual differences too. Some personality types love to see a schedule adhered to precisely and other personality types hate the very idea of a schedule. There are some very clear rules for success in this regard. The trainer needs to respect the schedule that has been published. There is usually a significant proportion of participants who will be unforgiving if a part of the agenda has to be squeezed into an unrealistically short time. Within the schedule there must be allowance for developing subjects in depth where the participants' consensus is that this will be useful. Do not pack the agenda too full!

In terms of managing the punctuality of starting and finishing sessions, the rules must be equally clear. Sessions must finish on time. There is more likelihood of sessions starting on time if the trainer has built some suspense potential for the next session. Participants are more likely to arrive punctually if there is something which they can look forward to. If within a maximum of five minutes of the published starting time some participants are still involved in apparently fascinating calls on their mobiles at the coffee station, the door to the training room should be closed and the session should start. The norms will thus become apparent and timekeeping will improve.

Dealing with challenging behaviour

> During the introduction of a five-day course for young managers we were giving an overview of the programme when one of the Portuguese participants stated that he did not think the group would want to spend 30 minutes at the end of the first day working in breakout groups. The objective of the breakout session was for each group to put together questions to be used as the basis of a session the next day with one of their board members, who had agreed to spend a couple of hours with them answering questions about the business and his role. We opened the issue up for discussion with the group, who expressed a majority view that the idea of preparing questions was a good one, but it would be better if it could be done next morning before the course was due to start. This would conflict only with an individual feedback session for one person on a personality questionnaire and so it was agreed to postpone the breakout session until the following morning, on the basis that the individual feedback session could be done half an hour earlier.

This type of situation, early in a course, is potential dynamite for trainers and can only be resolved satisfactorily, particularly with Western European and American audiences, by opening up the issue raised by one individual for discussion with the whole group. Any attempt by the trainer to resolve such an issue by being dogmatic will almost certainly be met with hostility from the group. Flexibility is critical and the power of the majority has to rule, within the constraints of maintaining the critical aspects of the learning agenda. Basically it means treating participants from all countries as adults.

However, sabotage has many faces. Side conversations between participants from one country in their own language can be disruptive. A participant passing round a private note is disturbing. Bickering about whether the room temperature is too hot or cold between participants from hot and cool climates is annoying. Individuals using their own familiarity with their native culture to weaken a point being made by the trainer by saying 'it won't work in my country' can be undermining.

Sometimes there are dominant participants whose native (or very familiar) language is the language being used to deliver the course. These participants can hinder the ability of the others to learn and enjoy the course. They can be worse than a hindrance, more of an irritation, if they also consider themselves to be blessed with an ability to tell jokes and stories! Such behaviour can consciously or subconsciously sabotage the training. One course of action is to divert the conversation to other members of the group which may be enough to give the message that their dominance is not appreciated. If that fails, the group will usually find a way of quietening them. If that is slow to work it can be productive to channel the saboteur's energies by allocating some challenging task to them that does not leave time for wisecracking!

Dealing with these types of issues is absolutely essential. Left alone they can fester and bring a course to its knees. The trainer needs to bring these matters to the fore and resolve them. In the case of the individual passing around a note, this was resolved on a one-to-one basis and in a fairly direct manner as they came from a high power distance, low individualism culture. Other cases, such as the side conversations, can be dealt with by the group and even added to the list of course ground rules.

Challenging behaviours, such as the refusal to see how something could work in their own culture, can only be dealt with by involving the group. Confronting an individual in front of the group is a risky strategy. Suddenly a supportive group will become hostile and all can be lost. Challenges need to be opened up for discussion to see what the group wants to do, always recognizing that the learning objectives of the group need to remain intact.

Compassion and business building

These must look like unusual bedfellows in a title! First, compassion. When participants are far from home in a foreign environment some may feel particularly vulnerable if they have a pressing personal problem. They will occasionally become ill while attending training courses. They may have deaths in the family, and one of our colleagues actually had a participant drop dead in his seat! Trainers need to be ready for all these eventualities and make a very special effort to be compassionate and helpful to the participant who is dealing with a pressing personal issue. Don't panic but do take effective action to deal with the crisis. Also, keep the client informed. There are more points to be won and lost in how the trainer deals with these situations than there are in raising the course score by 20 per cent.

At this point it is worth saying that those trainers who have been in the business for a number of years will recognize that participants of today can become clients tomorrow. In fact it is almost guaranteed to happen if one-to-one relationships with participants are built effectively and it is made easy for them to find the trainer after the event. Doing something that the individual participant, who is a long way from home, values personally at the time of, or soon after, the training event will register as even more important than the recollection of a truly exceptional training course.

Summary

It is important to consider carefully the most appropriate strategy for meeting participants informally before the training event. Building a one-to-one relationship with a few participants before the formal session begins often results in these people participating in the early stages and makes it easier for the format of the course to be interactive at an early stage. Likewise, being compassionate when dealing with personal issues on behalf of individual participants who are far from home will be remembered perhaps even more positively than an excellent learning experience.

Trainers are responsible for bringing energy to the group and need to consider how best to do it in a way that suits their training style. It is critical to create energy early in the course and there will be low points where it is important to use triggers to re-energize the group. This is best done while creating a relaxed yet focused climate.

Keeping to the programme schedule but leaving space for spending time on a particular area of interest for participants is critical to success. The ability to move fluently through the agenda, while being relaxed about spending time on discussions that are of particular interest to the group, is a key skill of the trainer.

When individual participants are over-dominant or disruptive and thereby sabotage the course, the trainer has to rely both on his or her own personality and on the support of the group as a whole to resolve a difficult situation in the relevant cultural context.

Action plan

Key points in developing effective trainer behaviours	*Planned actions for the next international course*	*Successes and further actions*
Forming one-to-one relationships with some participants before the formal course begins		
Bringing energy to the group, particularly at the beginning of the course		
Keeping to the published schedule		
Being flexible in developing discussions that are of particular interest to the group		
Using the group to deal with dominant or disruptive participants		
Showing compassion in dealing with individual participants who are trying to deal with pressing personal issues during the course		

CHAPTER 18 *Summary of Key Points in Training International Managers*

The purpose of this final chapter is to review the key activities for the trainer in the weeks leading up to the delivery of a training course for international managers, the particular aspects that require the trainer's focus during the course and the actions that need to be taken immediately after the course. It assumes that training needs were identified effectively through the survey and understand stages of the SUCCESS model and that training materials have been created to meet these needs.

Keeping the client and the participants in mind

At this point, in our final chapter, it is worth reminding ourselves that successful implementation of the training of international managers involves satisfying both the client and the participants. Although, during the design and development of the training, we should have been mindful of all we learned about the client's requirements, we should now do a final thorough check that we have remembered to cover every aspect and looked after every detail that the client considered to be important. This should involve looking back at the original proposal to the client that will have specified the objectives and an outline of the content of the training to be delivered. It will also be worthwhile to refer back to the notes that were made during the survey and understand stages of the development of the training.

Delivering pre-course work

When we have reviewed the materials that have been produced against our commitment to the client, we can focus on what needs to be done in detail to produce an enjoyable and satisfying event for the participants. Where we have made an undertaking to the client to produce some pre-course work for the participants to do as part of their orientation towards the learning, we should ensure that this is sent to them in good time for its completion (and return if necessary) before the training event. Pre-course materials can include questionnaires, case-study materials or in some cases a preview of some of the materials to be used on the course. The purpose of pre-course work can be merely to orientate participants to the programme. Alternatively it can be to collect information about the participants' views or experience on particular relevant subjects or produce some specific output such as completed personality questionnaires. Whatever the nature of the pre-course work, it is important that this contact with the participants is carried out professionally as it will give the first impression of how the training event is likely to feel for them. With international managers this step is even more important because it is likely that they will be travelling to a venue far from home to take part in a learning event with unfamiliar people and working in a language that is less familiar than their native tongue. (See Chapter 10 for further details.)

Preparing to deliver the course materials

The next step is usually to ensure that all the materials are made ready for the event. Often this means that course materials need to be prepared and sent to an administrator for reproduction before the course. How much easier this is today than it was even ten years ago before the common use of e-mail! However, great care needs to be taken to ensure that administrators understand fully the trainer's requirements. This usually means time taken to develop an understanding with administrative staff, and even then it needs to be backed up by comprehensive instructions in writing. It is, for example, frustrating to arrive at the venue to find that handouts and exercises have all been bound together when you thought it was agreed that they would be available separately. This is, just another of the challenges of working with a variety of nationalities – thinking everything is understood, when it turns out not to have been understood as well as you had hoped. However, additional care and the use of a combination of telephone and the written word can prevent most of these frustrations if allowance is made for the fact that it is not always easy to understand fine details when working in your second or third language.

Piloting materials for use with international audiences

Should training materials be rehearsed? Certainly, as discussed in Chapter 10, anything that is new or unfamiliar benefits greatly from being piloted, especially if it is to be delivered to an international audience. Ideally the first programme should be with a dummy audience of mixed nationalities but, if that is not possible, it should be with people who are used to working in an international environment. This is probably even more desirable with participative exercises, if only because it is the best way to test how long it will really take for participants working in their second language to absorb case-study materials or understand what the real objectives of an exercise are. Our experience of writing case studies and associated exercises is that two or three hours spent with a small number of people confronted by the materials for the first time in rehearsal will raise and resolve questions which will enable the trainers to fine-tune the way in which the materials are presented.

Having piloted the key sessions and made all the administrative arrangements it is good practice for the trainer to take a long hard look at the programme and mentally run through all of the sessions, recalling all the materials and equipment that will be needed and listing all the items that need to be double checked or indeed need to be ordered for the first time if overlooked. This is also an excellent opportunity to think through and note the key questions that the trainer will want to ask the audience at each stage of each session. It is worth writing down the best way each question can be phrased to maximize the audience's opportunity to understand exactly what the trainer means by each of the questions using the unit/session template discussed in Chapter 10. Precision in the wording of questions, deliberately excluding any use of idiom or slang, will enable the trainer to draw information from the audience much more successfully than the use of questions hurriedly composed on the day. This does not mean that the trainer cannot ask other questions which appear to be appropriate at the time; indeed, being flexible and reading the audience is an essential attribute of a good trainer. However, having prepared a set of well-thought-through and well-phrased questions is a worthwhile insurance policy.

Particular attention needs to be paid to rehearsing the introduction at this stage. It may even be worth writing down and memorizing the opening sentences and questions to ensure that they are capable of being easily understood by people working in their second language. In addition to being easily understood, the opening words need to be delivered with an impact that will begin to raise the energy levels of the group. This will need to be revisited just before the start of the event, but now is a good time to think it through in detail. Some trainers will say that they find this very difficult to do away from the live situation. Unfortunately, the result of lack of preparation often is that the opening sentences carry words and phrases that are almost meaningless to an international audience. It is demanding, but rehearsing will improve the impact of the opening significantly.

Special points for attention during the course

The value of having rehearsed and become really familiar with all of the materials is that the trainer can then spend a large amount of mental energy focusing on the participants and assessing their state of mind at each stage of the programme. This is not just a matter of identifying quiet participants and using the breaks to talk to them to discover what they feel they are learning from the materials, but involves assessing the overall mood of the group. Do they feel the materials are sufficiently relevant and aimed at the right level? Is the trainer meeting their needs in terms of the balance of participation, presentation and discussion? These are questions the trainer needs to be considering through the whole process of delivery. Moreover, if there is any uncertainty about what the audience is really feeling, the trainer should use the opportunity at the end of a morning or the end of a day to ask the audience, 'What is going well that we should spend more time doing?' 'What could be done differently to enhance your attention and learning?' Having gained the information the trainer then needs to be flexible enough to respond. It is quite possible to construct some impromptu exercises if the audience feels that group work is the most productive use of time, or indeed go over some fundamentals again if part of the group failed to understand something the first time around.

At this point it is worth saying that sometime, somewhere, the unexpected will raise its head and the trainer needs to manage the situation. Examples of disruptions within our own experience can be as varied as: total loss of power on a dark afternoon, a quarter of the participants suddenly being affected by food poisoning, a message from base informing three participants that their jobs have been declared redundant, news that the company has been acquired by a competitor, participants announcing that they understood they would be finishing two hours earlier than planned on the final day. It is not possible to foresee these eventualities nor is it possible to have a plan ready for every one, but it is possible to adopt a frame of mind where the unexpected is anticipated. The trainer can usually salvage something from the situation and, by being prepared for the unexpected and handling the consequences by consulting with the group about the best way to move forward, given the new situation, the trainer will earn a great deal of respect from the group and as a result hold their attention even more effectively for the remainder of the programme. The key is to be mentally prepared. You do not know what will cause the disruption, nor when it will happen, but you will meet very few trainers that have never experienced it. So think about the possibilities in advance and decide what is the best way to address the group in order to turn potential confusion into an opportunity to raise the level of attention of the participants.

After completion of delivery of the training

In Chapter 12 we detailed the process of strengthening the learning of international managers. Here we look at the trainer behaviours that are appropriate.

Trainers need to be aware of their own cultural norms and how they can differ from those of the client organization for whom they are working. In Eastern cultures, for instance, it is not an acceptable behaviour for the trainer to disappear after running a course without giving some feedback to the client. Accepting this, there are advantages for the trainer to develop a general approach of reporting. It is advantageous to report back to the client immediately after the training has been completed and if the trainer has completed a participant record form this will be much easier. This is an opportunity to discuss issues that arose during the training that might lead to a requirement for further inputs and also to ask the client about any verbal feedback from participants. Sometimes it is possible to give the client some immediate feedback from the assessment sheets that have probably been completed on the final day of the training. It is also an opportunity to discuss any other planned evaluation processes that need to be activated. Likewise, it may also be possible to talk with the client about any commitments made by participants to post-course actions when they return to their jobs. It is important also to send any materials promised to participants as soon as possible after completion of the course.

Now that the training event is over, the focus needs to be on the transfer of learning from the training environment to the job. This is a major challenge. It may have been possible to make some prior arrangements for follow-up, such as one-to-one coaching of participants or, failing that, a follow-up meeting a few weeks hence for participants to exchange experiences of applying the learning in practice. If this has not been attended to previously it should be raised with the client immediately after the completion of the course.

One-to-one coaching follow-up is probably the most effective way of ensuring that learning is transferred from the training event to the job.

> A good example of one-to-one coaching follow-up was when we were asked to train a group of technical specialists from a range of European countries as trainers so that they could develop and deliver a set of materials to introduce a new logistics process across the European Division of a major multi-national. This involved running a 'train the trainer' course for eight managers, all from different European countries, and then giving each manager one-to-one follow-up coaching on the development of the logistics training materials including a new version of SAP business software. This experience reminded us how powerful it is, from a learning point of view, to train managers in a group and then follow-up individually to address each one's particular needs in the development of training materials and the planning of the delivery. In fact, in this instance, some of the follow-up was done in small groups and some on a one-to-one basis.

Summary

Before delivery of the training it is important to do a final check to ensure that all the client's requirements are going to be covered. Attention to detail in the relationship with administrators who are responsible for producing course materials is essential to the smooth running of the event, especially where the staff are likely to be working in their second language. One particularly important part of this is to see that pre-course work is sent out in a timely and efficient fashion to give participants confidence that the event itself will be an enjoyable and worthwhile experience for them.

When the training materials have been finalized it is important to make arrangements to pilot them. Rehearsal of training materials, particularly participative exercises, is essential in order to estimate timings correctly and give clear instructions on what is expected of the participants.

Special efforts need to be made to ensure that the opening session is very clear to participants, and is free of idiom and slang phrases.

By the time the course is due to start, familiarity with the materials should be at a level where it is possible for the trainer to give total attention to the needs of the participants. He or she should be flexible enough to be able to change activities when necessary to maintain their attention, without losing focus of the main learning objectives.

Trainers need to be prepared for the unexpected and be confident in discussing with the group the best way to resolve any unexpected situations.

Immediately after the course, feedback to the client is essential. This can be really valuable in developing the next piece of similar training. During this conversation with the client it is important to focus on post-training follow-up, as this will increase the success of the transfer of learning considerably and should be arranged wherever the client is willing.

Action plan

The Action plan below provides a checklist that can be used to cover a training course from the time that the preparation of training materials has been completed, to the point where the training has been delivered and participants are returning to their places of work. It can be used as a reminder of the key activities to which attention should be paid before, during and after the delivery of any piece of training for international managers.

Checklist for action	Notes on a specific course
Weeks prior to the training	*Weeks prior to the training*
• Lists of specific admin. issues to be prepared and discussed with administrators four–six weeks before the course • Despatch pre-course work two–three weeks before start of the course • The actual words to be used and questions to be asked in the opening session to be prepared in detail • New or revised materials to be piloted prior to the course	
During the training • Bring energy to the opening session • Be flexible in changing course activities to meet the specific needs of the group • Keep to the schedule and make explanations to the group if this is not possible • Respond positively to any unexpected situations and discuss solutions with the group	
Immediately after completion of the training • Give immediate feedback to the client and discuss follow-up arrangements to strengthen the implementation of the learning • Progress follow-up activities within the agreed time-scales to which you are committed	

Further Reading

HARDINGHAM, A. *Designing Training*, The Chartered Institute of Training and Development, 1996.

HOFSTEDE, G. *Cultures and Organisations*, McGraw Hill, 1991.

HOFSTEDE, G. *Culture's Consequences*, Sage Publications, 2001.

HONEY, P. and MUMFORD, M. *The Manual of Learning Styles*, Peter Honey Publications, 1986.

HONEY, P and MUMFORD, M. *Using your Learning Styles*, Peter Honey Publications, 1986.

KIRKPATRICK, D. *Evaluating Training Programs: The Four Levels*, Berrett-Koehler Publishers Inc., 1994.

RAE, L. *Effective Planning of Training and Development*, Kogan Page Publishing, 2000.

SEYMOUR, D. *Skills Analysis Training*, Pitman Publishing, 1968.

TROMPENAARS, F. *Riding the Waves of Culture*, Nicholas Brealey Publishing, 1993.

Index

About the Authors

Alan Melkman

Alan Melkman MBA, BSc(Eng) is Managing Director of Marketing Dynamics Ltd, a qualified engineer and a graduate of London Business School. He specializes in customer and strategic account management, marketing management and effective selling.

He started his career as a design engineer with construction company, Haden Young, before moving to the USA where he gained interesting experience selling encyclopaedias. Subsequently he worked in retail distribution with Fine Fare Ltd, and then worked as salesman, account manager, brand manager and finally as marketing manager in the European fast-moving consumer-goods market with W R Grace Inc.

He has been a consultant for over 30 years, with substantial experience working for many organizations across a number of markets. He has conducted a wide range of public and in-house training programmes in Europe, North America, Near and Far East and Africa, and has carried out a broad variety of assignments for many substantial companies across varying cultures.

He is the author of *Strategic Customer Planning* published by Thorogood and *How to Manage Major Customers Profitably*, a workbook published by Gower, as well as numbers of articles. He is a highly rated speaker at public seminar and conference organizations such as Management Centre Europe, Frost and Sullivan, and Hawksmere.

His training programmes include:

- Train the trainer
- Facilitating groups
- Strategic account management
- Global account management
- Managing and developing key accounts
- Strategic customer planning
- Introduction to marketing
- The essentials of marketing management
- Product management

- Strategic marketing management
- Customer-focused marketing
- The marketing manager's strategic toolbox
- Developing powerful brands
- Branding in the pharmaceutical industry
- Pricing and profit management
- Finance for marketing and sales staff
- Effective selling
- Advanced selling
- Essential negotiation
- Advanced negotiation
- Effective presentation.

To contact him, e-mail alan.melkman@marketingdynamics.co.uk

John Trotman

John Trotman MA FCIPD is an independent trainer focusing on leadership and teamworking skills through Training and Management Services. He specializes in the training of trainers, the development and delivery of case studies for use in training and using psychometric testing as a basis for advising on the personal development of individual leaders/managers and the development of teams. For over ten years he has worked mainly with multi-cultural groups of participants as a training provider to multi-national companies; designing, delivering and organizing training events. He also teaches at Harrow Business School within the University of Westminster where the majority of his students are from ethnic minorities and from overseas. As a trainer he has worked in Eastern and Western Europe, North America and the Far East.

Prior to being an independent trainer John's career was with two major multi-national companies working at Board level in HR, training and development, business development and finally general management.

He will be pleased to hear from readers either through the Gower website or directly at jtrotman@btinternet.com

The Military in Contemporary Soviet Politics

The Military in Contemporary Soviet Politics

An Institutional Analysis

Edward L. Warner, III

PRAEGER SPECIAL STUDIES • PRAEGER SCIENTIFIC

Library of Congress Cataloging in Publication Data

Warner, Edward L
The military in contemporary Soviet politics.

(Praeger special studies in international politics and government)
Bibliography: p.
Includes index.
1. Russia—Military policy. 2. Russia—Armed Forces.
3. Russia—Politics and government—1953-
I. Title.
UA770.W27 1977 355.03'35'47 77-83476
ISBN 0-03-040346-4

PRAEGER SPECIAL STUDIES
383 Madison Avenue, New York, N.Y. 10017, U.S.A.

Published in the United States of America in 1977
by Praeger Publishers,
A Division of Holt, Rinehart and Winston, CBS, Inc.

9 038 98765432

Printed in the United States of America

CONTENTS

LIST OF ABBREVIATIONS

AAA	antiaircraft artillery
ABM	antiballistic missile
AWACS	airborne warning and control system
BMEWS	ballistic missile early warning system
CCD	Conference of the Committee on Disarmament
CINC	commander-in-chief
CPSU	Communist Party of the Soviet Union
DOSAAF	Voluntary Society for Assistance to the Army, Air Force, and Navy
DICBM	depressed-trajectory intercontinental ballistic missile
EMP	electromagnetic pulse
ENDC	Eighteen Nation Disarmament Conference
FOBS	fractional orbital bombardment system
FRG	Federal Republic of Germany
GAU	Main Artillery Directorate
GRU	Main Intelligence Directorate
ICBM	intercontinental ballistic missile
IMEMO	Institute of World Economics and International Relations
IRBM	intermediate-range ballistic missile
IUSAC	Institute for the Study of the United States and Canada
JCS	Joint Chiefs of Staff (U.S.)
KGB	Committee of State Security
LEFI	Leningrad Electro-Physics Institute
MBFR	Mutual Balanced Force Reductions
MD	Military District
MIRV	multiple independently targetable reentry vehicle
MPA	Main Political Administration
MRBM	medium-range ballistic missile
NATO	North Atlantic Treaty Organization

NTK	Scientific-Technical Committee
OO	special section
PVO-S	National Air Defense Troops
RKKA	Workers' and Peasants' Red Army
RSFSR	Russian Soviet Federated Socialist Republic
SALT	Strategic Arms Limitation Talks
SLBM	submarine-launched ballistic missile
SCC	Standing Consultative Commission
SEATO	Southeast Asia Treaty Organization
SOP	standard operating procedure
SRF	Strategic Rocket Forces
SSBN	ballistic-missile-launching nuclear submarine
TsAGI	Central Aerohydrodynamic Institute
TsIAM	Central Institute of Aviation Materials
TsRL	Central Radio Laboratory
TTB	Threshold Test Ban
VIAM	All-Union Institute of Aviation Materials
VPK	Military-Industrial Committee

The Military in Contemporary Soviet Politics

CHAPTER

1

INTRODUCTION

The Soviet military establishment has been the object of extensive and intensive study in the West. Aspects of its activity, including its organizational structure, weaponry, military doctrine, and apparent role in the determination of Soviet domestic and foreign policy, have been treated in a wide variety of articles, monographs, and books. Yet, despite such a profusion of materials, a comprehensive framework for the orderly integration of these varying concerns has been noticeably lacking. The present study will seek to develop such a framework and attempt to demonstrate its utility through specific applications to a number of Soviet military policy issues.

The central focus of this approach is the institutional setting and internal processes of policy formation of Soviet national security policy. The framework is derived from and builds upon the products of two different bodies of scholarly activity. On one hand, it owes much to Western studies that have applied various interest group conceptions to their examination of the Soviet political scene. In addition, it utilizes a number of assumptions and insights developed and discussed by members of the emerging "bureaucratic politics" school in the study of American foreign and security policy. The salient features of these antecedent approaches are discussed in the succeeding sections of this introductory chapter.

SOVIET POLITICS AND INTEREST GROUP ANALYSIS

The use of interest group concepts for the analysis of Soviet politics has become increasingly frequent over the past two decades. This development has been marked by the appearance of numerous theoretical articles that identify various groupings on the Russian scene and set forth arguments justifying the utility of such an approach.[1] In addition a growing number of writers have adopted this approach in their empirical studies of the Soviet political process.[2]

The fundamental assumptions underlying a group approach to political study are simply stated.[3] (1) Individuals aware of interests held in common with one another are inclined to act in concert to promote these mutual concerns. (2) In any political system, a variety of shared interest collectivities exists whose respective group interests often differ considerably. (3) Conflict among such groups as they seek to promote their distinctive interests is a central factor in the political process.*

Given these assumptions, the standard pattern of group analysis involves the identification of aggregates with shared interests, the study of their internal interaction, often in terms of their organizational form, and the examination of the various influence tactics these groups employ in their self-interested political demand activity. Thus the major concerns for such study are ones of shared attitude, internal interaction, and the varieties of demand behavior.

A number of interest groups have been identified on the Soviet scene. Much of the study of these interest groups has centered upon occupational-functional aggregates, particularly those with an "official" character in that they have formal institutional identity within the extensive bureaucratic hierarchies of the Communist Party of the Soviet Union (CPSU) and the Soviet government. Analysis proceeds from the basic assumptions that "persons engaged in similar activities, particularly of an economic-professional nature, tend to have similar attitudes on key political issues"[4] and that such aggregate constituencies seek to exert influence to secure public actions that favor their particular interests.

Researchers have become increasingly aware that the boundaries of occupational group identification may vary considerably as a function of the degree of specificity of the functional tasks considered. Some group studies have treated such large organizations as the Soviet military or the Party apparatus as monolithic entities with discernible collective attitudes on various policy questions.[5] While this may be useful at a rather high level of generality, more recently attention has been directed toward the need to recognize the importance of further institutional differentiation along functional

---

*In the extreme "group theory" formulations of Bentley and Hagen, groups are the only essential variables for the study of politics. See Eckstein, op. cit., pp. 390-94, for a thorough criticism of this viewpoint.

lines within these large and complex organizations.[6] Thus, at a middle level, one can distinguish between generalists and specialists within the Party apparatus. More specifically, one may focus upon the different functional specializations within the apparatus; for example, examining the different career patterns, departmental organizations, and apparent interests of propaganda-agitation specialists as compared to Party specialists in industrial management.[7] Similarly, the military establishment may be fruitfully disaggregated into its component service branches,[8] and the economic managers divided according to the branches of industry with which they are associated.

The functional group approach, regardless of the specificity of group definition, may utilize either logical or empirical methods in the process of interest identifications. One may talk in terms of the logical concerns of individuals charged with a specific task and then deduce likely policy stands, or, alternatively, empirically examine the statements of prominent individuals or leading newspapers and periodicals connected with a particular group to arrive at its policy preferences. The latter practice involves the crucial assumption that the statements examined are representative articulations of the interests of the occupational or departmental group as a whole.

Some authors have objected to this "spokesman assumption," pointing to the paucity of evidence regarding the processes of internal group interaction. Consequently these authors intentionally reject what they call a reification of groups and limit themselves to the identification of individuals who publicly express similar viewpoints on a particular policy or set of policies. These are called analytic "groupings"[9] or "tendencies of articulation"[10] to denote explicitly the author's inability to demonstrate interaction or mutual dependence among these likeminded persons.

Some scholars choose to ignore questions of institutional affiliation or occupational role and simply identify various "opinion groups"[11] composed of individuals who express similar policy viewpoints. Although in many cases these opinion positions have been explained in terms of underlying occupational interests, such groups are treated as basic units of analysis in and of themselves. Examples of the "pure opinion" approach include the classification and combination of top-level Party figures along a liberal-conservative dimension,[12] the study of policy differences within the Soviet armed forces in terms of modernist, centrist, and radical typology,[13] and the use of liberal and conservative categories to identify schools of thought on the literary scene.[14]

A final kind of group frequently noted and studied in Soviet politics is one defined not by shared issue position but rather identified in terms of interpersonal connections and loyalties. These informal groupings generally develop around particularly dynamic individuals in the form of patron-client or shefstvo* relationships. Such personal followings, which may form within a major institution or may cut across formal organizational lines, develop in the course of career association and collaboration. Western analysts have great difficulty identifying these highly personal alliances, which can be located only by tracing patterns of career affiliation and what appear to be sponsored promotions within the Soviet elite.

Patronage networks identified by Western scholars include a Leningrad-centered group headed by A. A. Zhdanov in the 1940s,[15] a number of industrial managers who were proteges of Malenkov in the 1950s,[16] and a small group associated with Alexander Shelepin, whose members suffered a series of similar setbacks in 1966-67.[17]

The full application of interest group analysis involves not only the identification of the various aggregates on the Soviet scene, but also the examination of their promotional activities and its effect upon the political process. This usually entails some kind of decision-making analysis within a selected issue area. The researcher follows his identification of relevant actors, individual and collective, and the various alliance patterns among them with an analysis of their tactics of influence employed both before and after major policy decisions.[18]

Some U.S. scholars who have utilized a group approach in their studies have emphasized the bureaucratic character of the major groups within the Soviet system. Alfred G. Meyer, for example, draws heavily upon the general characteristics of bureaucratic organizations, as developed by Victor Thompson,[19] to identify several bureaucratic factors in the Soviet political system.[20] Although Meyer speaks of "bureaucratic interest group politics,"[21] he fails to apply his bureaucratic insights to the study of Soviet policy making.

Merle Fainsod also wrote of the existence of "bureaucratic politics" within the Soviet Union:

> The Soviet bureaucratic structure is commonly visualized as a tightly centralized administrative hierarchy in which all initiative and decision-making power are concentrated in the top leadership and in which the lower officials serve as mere automatons to execute the will of the ruling

---

*"Shefstvo," the Russian word for "patronage," is used descriptively in this context by Franz Borkenau in "Getting the Facts Behind the Soviet Facade," *Commentary*, April 1954, pp. 393-400.

> group. While this stereotype performs the useful function of emphasizing the high degree of centralization which characterizes the Soviet system, it also distorts reality by ignoring the fluid play of bureaucratic politics that underlies the monolithic totalitarian facade.[22]

However, like Meyer, Fainsod described the various bureaucratic elements of the Party and government, but largely failed to investigate the contours and processes of political competition within the system.

More recently, Robert V. Daniels has described the Soviet political process as one of "participatory bureaucracy."[23] He apparently uses this designation to emphasize the independent initiative and autonomous policy advocacy roles of the various bureaucratic organizations in the Soviet system. He does not, however, attempt to analyze the processes of interest promotion, conflict resolution, or policy implementation.

Finally, another recent general analysis of Soviet politics, Jerry Hough's "The Soviet System: Petrification or Pluralism?" proposes a composite model of the system that the author calls "institutional pluralism."[24] This model, which is elaborated in considerable detail, describes the political process in terms of pluralistic competition among specialized bureaucratic elites within the "official institutional framework."[25]

All of these studies represent efforts that recognize the bureaucratic and official nature of important interest groups in the Soviet political system. While sometimes offering perceptive insights about how the bureaucratic character of these groups might influence their interests and behavior, none of them develops a systematic framework for the analysis of the Soviet political process from a bureaucratic perspective.

THE BUREAUCRATIC POLITICS APPROACH

In that the applications of group study to Soviet politics have already called attention to group conflict among major institutional actors as a central factor in determining policy, what does the emergent field of bureaucratic politics have to offer? Quite simply, it represents a significant development in the study of official or institutional interest groups and their patterns of activity.

Most of the theorizing about and empirical study of interest groups completed to date has dealt with Western democratic systems. These studies deal almost exclusively in terms of "semipolitical"[26] or "associational"[27] interest groups (pressure groups), such as trade unions, businessmen's organizations, or professional groups, all of which are located within the private sector of society. In contrast, students of bureaucratic politics concern themselves predominantly with the outlooks and actions of self-interested bureaucratic organizations within the governmental structure. It is precisely this kind of official group which is most significant in contemporary Soviet politics.

Under the general rubric of bureaucratic politics, I include a series of concepts drawn from a number of similarly oriented studies. Most prominently this involves the works of a group of scholars who have concentrated their investigations upon the development and execution of American foreign and national security policy. The major figures associated with the elaboration of this approach are Graham T. Allison and Morton H. Halperin, charter members of the so-called "May Group," a continuing seminar operating out of the John F. Kennedy School at Harvard University,[28] and Alexander George, who heads a smaller group at Stanford University. Members of this Stanford group have included David K. Hall, Richard Nehring, William E. Simons, and Richard Smoke.

These students of bureaucratic politics developed their shared perspective on the basis of a variety of sources, including detailed historical case study, direct personal involvement in government, the systematic integration of insights and concepts developed in the fields of organizational theory and public administration, and the examination of previous research on U.S. foreign and security policy. A particularly important group of works of the latter category that were directly consulted by this author is the series of case studies on American defense policy produced under the aegis of the Institute of War and Peace Studies at Columbia University. The works of Samuel Huntington,[29] Warner Schilling,[30] and more recently Michael Armacost[31] in particular represent important empirical investigations which amply demonstrate the bureaucratic nature of military policy formation.

The bureaucratic politics approach is based on a series of fundamental assumptions about the nature of politics in the modern state. This "analytic paradigm,"[32] as Allison has called it, focuses one's attention on various processes associated with the activities of bureaucracies and bureaucrats. First and foremost, it identifies contemporary governments as consisting of a series of important senior figures and a collection of state bureaucracies that have been described as a "loose alliance of semi-independent, quasisovereign organizations."[33] These government bureaucracies are themselves generally composed of several sizable organizational subunits. The approach further assumes that these bureaucracies represent "institutionalized special competences"[34] with their own distinctive tasks, skills, and operations, as well as clearly discernible institutional interests.

The distinctive interests of these bureaucratic entities find expression in an organizational ideology that is largely shared by the members of the organization. This shared viewpoint or "trained outlook"[35] has several aspects including: (1) a consensually shared image of the domestic and international environment; (2) basic policy convictions and preferences reflecting concern about the organization's role, mission, and sphere of responsibility as well as its ability to sustain adequate resource support in terms of budgetary allocations, personnel, and essential materiel; (3) a desire to maintain organizational autonomy in its control over resources and activities; and (4) concern for the morale of its personnel. Graham Allison suggests that these concerns are often viewed as a series of "avoidance imperatives"; that is, the bureaucracies seek to avoid encroachments on functional "territory," reductions in budgetary and manpower allocations, loss of autonomy, and a decline in morale.[36]

Some scholars have concerned themselves with the manner in which members of large organizations come to acquire their bureaucratic world-views. Key factors that have been identified in this process include selective recruitment, common training and indoctrination, shared career experiences that involve recurring exposure to specialized, biased information, group pressures for conformity, self-generated psychological pressures for mutual identification, self-reinforcement as a result of repeated advocacy on behalf of the organization, and calculated adoption of the established viewpoint in response to such inventives provided by the organization as enhanced pay, promotion, and prestige for those who provide loyal support.

Organizational interests are not the only interests with relevance in the development and implementation of policy. Other concerns that frequently come into play are varying conceptions of the "national interest" (a concept that is inherently vague and thus subject to considerable influence from other considerations), personal interests regarding job satisfaction and advancement, and domestic political interests regarding the impact of a particular course of action upon other issues and even continued tenure in office.[37] The latter considerations are apt to be particularly relevant for key senior officials with wider responsibilities and attendant constituencies.

The bureaucratic belief systems that are associated with various organizations play a variety of roles in the political process. They provide their holder with both diagnostic propensities that shape his perceptions and evaluations of the world around him and choice propensities regarding preferable courses of action and policy outcomes.[38] The presence of several organizations with differing bureaucratic outlooks and associated propensities is a crucial ingredient in fostering conflict between these groups.

Several factors influence the degree of political conflict that attends the "partisan mutual adjustments" surrounding the development of public policy. These include (1) issue complexity (the more complex the issue, the more likely it is to inspire differential perceptions among the interested parties and a variety of preferred solutions, thus increasing the likelihood of organizational conflict);[39] (2) issue solution indeterminacy (questions for which there are no ready criteria to compare and evaluate alternative solutions are likely to be accompanied by substantial policy disagreement); and (3) high issue significance (the greater the number of parties that view the favorable resolution of a certain issue as important to their interests, the more intense the level of conflict is likely to be in the policy arena).

The nature of the organizational setting in which key decisions are made also has important impact on the degree of conflict that is likely to arise. Conflict is likely to be more pronounced if several organizations have overlapping jurisdictions, if power is disbursed among the interested parties on a relatively equal basis, and if there are substantial policy disagreements among those concerned.

Whatever the degree of conflict involved, a cornerstone of the bureaucratic politic approach is the belief that almost all government policy can be most profitably viewed as the outcome of political conflict among large government organizations and their various subunits.*

The study of this organizational struggle logically leads one to investigate the sources of bureaucratic advantage that the participants might enjoy. Organizational resources that can prove advantageous in this regard include: a favorable reputation for reliability of information, quality of analysis, and effectiveness of implementation; possession of an administrative charter that confers several distinct spheres of responsibility; control of or at least guaranteed access to information about both the problem at issue and, later, the implementation of the agreed course of action; possession of appropriate analytical resources and expertise; control of implementation activity; access to key decision makers; the presence of personnel with bargaining and persuasive skills; and possession of a favorable "balance of favors" in relation to other interested organizations and their spokesmen.[40]

---

*This is the point emphasized in Allison's Model III, the Governmental (Bureaucratic) Politics paradigm. Allison, op. cit., pp. 144-84.

The process of bureaucratic bargaining has a series of distinctive characteristics. It usually occurs in an organizational setting that is marked by a combination of hierarchical/directive and horizontal/bargaining elements.[41] In most cases, the organizational spokesmen share a perception that some form of policy must be worked out, a characteristic that Warner Schilling has called the "strain toward agreement."[42]

Within this setting, organizational representatives resort to a variety of maneuvers in search of advantage. Their tactics include the manipulation of issue definition, rational persuasion, pragmatic bargaining, mobilization of support, manipulation of the choice of the organizational forums and procedures utilized in policy making so as to maximize one's participation and influence while lessening that of opponents, and various implementation patterns that include faithful compliance, avoidance and delay, and, in some cases, action directly contrary to the agreed policy.[43]

The bureaucratic politics approach also pays special attention to the impact of standard operating procedures (SOPs)--preexisting programs and routines at various stages of the policy process--as an important shaper of policy. In Graham Allison's words, the approach recognizes that governmental policy is, to an important degree, an "organizational output."* Routine activity in accordance with established procedures can have important effects on the initial analyses of a problem, the development, consideration, and selection of a course of action, and the implementation of the chosen policy, even when these processes themselves are not being consciously shaped by the maneuvers of interested parties. Organizational procedures begin to play a role from the very opening of a policy sequence when they influence both the selection of relevant information; that is, what "facts" become "data" and the flow of these data to various organizations in the government.

The development of policy options is also heavily influenced by established programs and routines. As a rule, organizations are prone to define and respond to situations in terms of standard activities or preexisting contingency plans. If a new course of action is deemed necessary, there is a strong tendency simply to make minor incremental adjustments to an established program. The development of more novel responses tends to be done in a "satisficing" manner; that is, the responsible officials will select the first alternative that is judged "acceptable" rather than conducting a more rigorous search for the optimum variant.[44]

---

*Allison treats this as his Model II, the Organizational Process paradigm. Allison, op. cit., pp. 67-100.

The processes of policy choice and implementation also can be significantly shaped by organizational process considerations. Established procedures define the "action channels" with regard to who gets to participate in policy deliberations and what procedures are used in the decisional process. Again, as during the preceding stage of option development, the choice of a course of action from among the options proposed is very likely to be of the satisficing variety. With regard to implementation, barring a major effort to inspire and verify substantial innovation, organizations are strongly inclined simply to set in motion existing capabilities in accordance with long-established routines. In addition, once set in motion, programs tend to develop a self-perpetuating life of their own in what Warner Schilling has described as the "gyroscopic effect."[45]

The bureaucratic politics framework resembles the occupational interest group approach reviewed earlier in many ways. Both emphasize the particularistic interests and loyalties that are formed on the basis of functional specialization. The bureaucratic politics approach offers the additional advantage of explicitly noting the essential elements of a shared organizational outlook, its probable impact upon the holder of such a viewpoint, and the various factors in professional-occupational socialization that contribute to its development and maintenance. Specific applications of these insights will be presented in the analysis of the Soviet military ideology in Chapter 3.

The bureaucratic politics approach also echoes a fundamental interest group assumption in its central proposition that policy decisions represent the resultant of political conflict among self-interested groups.* Again, the benefits offered by the bureaucratic politics framework lie in its further elaboration of the factors which affect the process of policy conflict. This approach directs our attention to the nature of the issue in question as an important determinant of the potential for conflict. It also identifies a variety of bargaining resources that may be utilized by competing organizations and lists a number of tactics of advocacy and kinds of policy outcomes. Once again, application of these concepts to the Soviet military scene will follow.

The organizational process aspects of the bureaucratic politics approach that recognizes the impact of existing operating procedures and standardized routines as factors importantly shaping the policy struggle and the process of policy implementation has no antecedent in the older interest group concept. It represents an insightful

---

*Thus, the second chapter (p. 18) in Robert Conquest's Power and Policy in the U.S.S.R. is entitled "Forces and Resultants."

application of a number of concepts drawn from organizational theory and the study of public administration. The utility of this aspect of the framework in the study of Soviet military policy is most clearly evident in Soviet weapons acquisition practices and the development of Soviet force posture as discussed in Chapter 5.

BUREAUCRATIC POLITICS AND THE SOVIET SYSTEM

The bureaucratic politics framework discussed above has been derived from the works of American scholars who studied almost exclusively the development of foreign and military policy in the United States. As such it has been developed in the context of very abundant research materials, extensive newspaper reportage, memoirs published by key participants in the decision under review, and, in many cases, with the aid of personal interviews with relevant participants.

Unfortunately, the student of Soviet politics is always confronted with a pronounced scarcity of information. This problem is particularly acute with regard to the positions taken and the internal process of policy debate and conflict resolution at the Politburo level. The bureaucratic politics approach cannot alleviate this problem.

However, once our attention is directed to the level immediately below the Politburo, bureaucratic politics appears to offer substantial promise as a tool for understanding Soviet politics. It provides a useful framework for the examination of the roles of various bureaucratic institutions, including the processes of policy option elaboration, advocacy, and eventually implementation following authoritative decision at the top.

Even at this secondary level, data remain difficult to obtain. We lack detailed accounts of the organizational setting and administrative routines within the Party Secretariat and the departments of the Central Committee apparatus or within the higher echelons of the Council of Ministers and individual government ministries. Nevertheless, some information on general organizational patterns is available.

Overt articulations of policy preference by prominent individuals or in the journals or newspapers of particular institutions are relatively abundant. The detailed examination of the Soviet media, particularly with regard to variations in their treatment of a given issue, has been the stuff of Kremlinological research for years. It is on this basis that interest group analyses have been developed, whether in terms of occupational groups or opinion groupings.

The bureaucratic politics approach offers promise not as a replacement for but rather as a supplement to the existing group studies. Like them, it relies upon the well-established practices of careful textual analysis to identify and chart patterns of political conflict. But, in addition, it demands greater attention to the organizational setting, the parochial bases of institutional policy positions, and the impact of administrative routine on the development of policy.

Given the informational deficiencies inherent in the field, no approach to the study of Soviet political affairs can provide a comprehensive description or explanation of a particular event or major policy area. Rather, the test of any approach must be its utility in guiding the researcher in the acquisition of data and in his subsequent efforts to interrelate this information in a plausible and persuasive manner. It is the belief of this author that the bureaucratic politics approach has great merit on these grounds and that the chapters of this study will demonstrate this in their discussions of a variety of Soviet military policy issues.*

NOTES

1. In particular, see H. Gordon Skilling, "Interest Groups and Communist Politics," World Politics 17, no. 3 (April 1966): 435-51, and his chapter, Chapter 2, "Groups in Soviet Politics: Some Hypotheses," and that of Franklyn Griffiths, Chapter 10, "A Tendency Analysis of Soviet Policy-Making," in Interest Groups in Soviet Politics, ed. H. G. Skilling and F. Griffiths (Princeton: Princeton University Press, 1971), pp. 19-46 and 335-78; Michael P. Gehlen, "Group Theory and the Study of Soviet Politics," in The Soviet Political Process, ed. Sidney I. Ploss (Waltham, Mass.: Ginn and Company, 1971), pp. 35-54.

2. Some representative examples include Roger Pethybridge, A Key to Soviet Politics: The Crisis of the "Anti-Party" Group (London: Allen and Unwin, 1962); Philip Stewart, "Soviet Interest Groups and the Policy Process: The Repeal of Production Education," World Politics 12, no. 1 (October 1969): 29-50, and the various case study chapters in Skilling and Griffiths, op. cit.

---

*In recent years one noted expert on Soviet military affairs has embraced a bureaucratic politics approach fundamentally similar to that presented in this chapter in his analyses of Soviet military policy. See Thomas Wolfe, Policymaking in the Soviet Union: A Statement with Supplementary Comments, P-4131 (Santa Monica, Calif.: RAND Corporation, June 1969), and Soviet Interests in SALT: Political, Economic, Bureaucratic and Strategic Contributions and Impediments to Arms Control, P-4702 (Santa Monica, Calif.: RAND Corporation, September 1971).

3. These assumptions are derived from some of the major theoretical works and commentaries on interest group analysis. These include Arthur Bentley, The Process of Government (Evanston, Ill.: Northwestern University Press, 1949); David B. Truman, The Governmental Process: Political Interests and Public Opinion (New York: Alfred A. Knopf, 1951); Harry Eckstein, "Introduction: Group Theory and the Comparative Study of Pressure Groups," in Comparative Politics: A Reader, ed. Harry Eckstein and David E. Apter (New York: The Free Press, 1963), pp. 389-97.

4. Jerry F. Hough, "The Party Apparatchiki," in Skilling and Griffiths, op. cit., p. 48.

5. Such is the approach of Petybridge and Vernon V. Aspaturian, "Soviet Foreign Policy," in Foreign Policy in World Politics, ed. Roy C. Macridis (Englewood Cliffs, N.J.: Prentice-Hall, 1964), pp. 132-210.

6. For a comprehensive inventory of the wide variety of institutional groups identified by various students of Soviet affairs, see Frederic Fleron, "Representation of Career Types in the Soviet Political Leadership," in Political Leadership in Eastern Europe and the Soviet Union, ed. R. Barry Farrell (Chicago: Aldine Publishing Company, 1970), pp. 108-13.

7. Hough, op. cit., pp. 52-92.

8. Roman Kolkowicz, "The Military," in Skilling and Griffiths, op. cit., pp. 146-48; Thomas W. Wolfe, "The Military," in Kassof, op. cit., pp. 136-37.

9. Stewart, op. cit., p. 42.

10. Griffiths, op. cit., pp. 360-77.

11. H. Gordon Skilling, "Groups in Soviet Politics: Some Hypotheses," in Skilling and Griffiths, op. cit., p. 25.

12. See the Kremlinological studies of Michael Tatu, Power in the Kremlin (New York: Viking Press, 1968); and Carl A. Linden, Khrushchev and the Soviet Leadership, 1957-1964 (Baltimore: Johns Hopkins University Press, 1966).

13. Thomas W. Wolfe, Soviet Strategy at the Crossroads (Cambridge: Harvard University Press, 1964), pp. 26-37; Roman Kolkowicz, The Soviet Military and the Communist Party (Princeton: Princeton University Press, 1967), pp. 150-73; and Raymond L. Garthoff, "Khrushchev and the Military," in Politics in the Soviet Union: 7 Cases, ed. Alexander Dallin and Alan F. Westin (New York: Harcourt, Brace and World, 1966), pp. 256-59. A critical examination of these categories is presented in Chapter 4 of this work.

14. Cf. Ernest J. Simmons, "The Writers," in Skilling and Griffiths, op. cit., pp. 269-89.

15. See Robert Conquest, Power and Policy in the USSR (New York: Harper and Row, 1967), pp. 95-111.

16. Jeremy R. Azrael, Managerial Power and Soviet Politics (Cambridge: Harvard University Press, 1966), p. 124.

17. Tatu, op. cit., p. 537.

18. See H. Gordon Skilling, "Group Conflict in Soviet Politics: Some Conclusions," in Skilling and Griffiths, op. cit., pp. 379-416, for a comprehensive review of a variety of applications of interest group analysis to the Soviet scene.

19. Victor Thompson, Modern Organization (New York: Alfred A. Knopf, 1961).

20. Alfred G. Meyer, The Soviet Political System: An Interpretation (New York: Random House, 1965), pp. 198-237.

21. Ibid., p. 235.

22. Merle Fainsod, How Russia Is Ruled, 2d ed. rev. (Cambridge: Harvard University Press, 1967), p. 417.

23. Robert V. Daniels, "Soviet Politics Since Khrushchev," in The Soviet Union Under Brezhnev and Kosygin, ed. John W. Strong (New York: Von Nostrand-Reinhold Co., 1971), p. 22.

24. Jerry Hough, "The Soviet System: Petrification or Pluralism?," Problems of Communism (March-April 1972): 27-29.

25. Ibid., p. 29.

26. Harry Eckstein, in Eckstein and Apter, op. cit., pp. 394-96.

27. Gabriel Almond and G. Bingham Powell, Comparative Politics: A Developmental Approach (Boston: Little, Brown and Co., 1966), p. 78.

28. See Graham T. Allison, Essence of Decision: Explaining the Cuban Missile Crisis (Boston: Little, Brown and Company, 1971), pp. ix-x for an account of this group and its evolution. Allison's summer work in 1967 and 1968 at the RAND Corporation, with Andrew Marshal in particular, provides a bridge to a RAND-centered bureaucratic study group that has concentrated primarily upon the role of organizational factors in the weapons acquisition process and the development of national military postures.

29. Samuel Huntington, The Common Defense: Strategic Programs and Defense Budgets (New York: Columbia University Press, 1961).

30. Warner Schilling, "The Politics of National Defense: Fiscal 1950," in Warner Schilling, Paul Y. Hammond, and Glenn H. Snyder, Strategy, Politics and Defense Budgets (New York: Columbia University Press, 1962), pp. 1-266.

31. Michael Armacost, The Politics of Weapons Innovation: The Thor-Jupiter Controversy (New York: Columbia University Press, 1969).

32. Allison, op. cit., p. 32.

33. Ibid., p. 7; Schilling, op. cit., p. 22.

34. Alexander George, "Stress in Political Decision-Making," paper presented at the Conference on Coping and Adaptation, Stanford University, Palo Alto, California, March 1969, p. 31.

35. Anthony Downs, Inside Bureaucracy (Boston: Little, Brown and Company, 1967), p. 50.

36. Allison, op. cit., p. 82.

37. Morton H. Halperin, Bureaucratic Politics and Foreign Policy (Washington, D.C.: Brookings Institution, 1971), pp. 58-60.

38. George, op. cit., p. 32.

39. Morton H. Halperin, "Why Bureaucrats Play Games," Foreign Policy 2 (Spring 1971): 172.

40. Ibid., pp. 168-69, and Alexander George, "The Case for Multiple Advocacy in Making Foreign Policy," paper delivered at the 1971 annual meeting of the American Political Science Association, Chicago, September 7-11, 1971, p. 15.

41. Armacost, op. cit., p. 13.

42. Schilling, op. cit., p. 23.

43. Halperin, Bureaucratic Politics and Foreign Policy, pp. 107-31.

44. James March and Herbert Simon, Organizations (New York: John Wiley and Sons, 1958), pp. 140ff.

45. Schilling, op. cit., p. 26.

CHAPTER

2

THE INSTITUTIONAL SETTING OF SOVIET DEFENSE POLICY

The description and analysis of the institutional framework and decisional processes of policy formation lie at the very heart of bureaucratic political study. This chapter provides a general overview of the organizational setting for national security policy making in the Soviet Union. More detailed depictions of the policy practices within this organizational milieu on such defense matters as strategy formulation, weapons acquisition, and arms control policy are presented in the succeeding chapters.

Analysis of Soviet defense decision making is a distinctly speculative undertaking. Western knowledge of decision procedures at the upper reaches of the Soviet system in all areas of politics remains extremely limited as a result of a pronounced scarcity of data. This is especially true in the case of military policy where intense security concerns have produced tight censorship. As a result, the framework developed in this chapter is necessarily a tentative construction that draws upon a number of diverse and fragmentary sources.

Especially important among these sources are the discussions of previous Soviet practices in the sensitive national security policy area that are now readily accessible thanks to an abundance of military memoirs. These works are more open concerning the institutional arrangements for defense policy making in the past than any contemporary Soviet accounts regarding defense matters. Western speculations about the general contours of high-level Soviet policy processes are also of considerable use. While one cannot be fully confident about the validity of one's organizational model developed on the basis of historical analogs, secondary analyses, and a scattering of more recent clues, work in this area seems essential if one is to develop a useful construct for policy process analysis.

The Soviet military establishment is simultaneously an important participant within the formal structures of the Soviet government and within the network of organizations that make up the Communist Party of the Soviet Union (CPSU). Both of these institutional frameworks provide important linkages between the Ministry of Defense and other elements of the Soviet political system. The military's connections with the Party are clearly the more important of the two, since it is the higher Party organs--the Central Committee (the Moscow-based apparatus operating under the Secretariat) and the Politburo--that authoritatively control the actions of the Ministry of Defense, as they do all the other important segments of Soviet society. Nevertheless, the position of the Soviet armed forces within the Soviet government merits study, and it is this that is addressed first before moving on to examine the nature of the military's participation in and position vis-a-vis the key bodies of the CPSU.

GOVERNMENTAL INSTITUTIONS

Within the Soviet government there are a number of bodies that play widely varying roles in the development and execution of Soviet military policy. These include the organs of state power--the two popularly elected houses of the Supreme Soviet (the Soviet of the Union and the Soviet of Nationalities) and its Presidium--and a variety of organs of state administration, including the Council of Ministers and several state committees and ministries.

The Supreme Soviet

According to the Constitution of the USSR,* the Supreme Soviet is the "highest organ of state power in the USSR."[1] It is formally charged with a wide range of responsibilities as the primary legislative body within the Soviet state. Its competence within the national security area includes formal responsibility for the "organization of the defense of the USSR, direction of the Armed Forces of the USSR, determination of the directing principles governing the organization

---

*The constitution cited here is the so-called "Stalin Constitution" adopted by the USSR in 1936. The latest Soviet constitution, whose draft contents were made public in June 1977 with adoption expected by fall, assigns all of the powers enumerated below to the same bodies although the numbers of the various articles have been changed.

of the military formations of the Union Republics,"[2] and "safeguarding the security of the state."[3]

The other organs of state power, the Presidium of the Supreme Soviet and the entire ministerial structure, consisting of the Council of Ministers and the numerous ministries and state committees that the Soviets describe as the "organs of state administration," are all elected or approved by and accountable to the Supreme Soviet.[4] This theoretical subordination appears, however, to be of little significance in light of the actual policy activities of these organs.

In its initial session following the direct popular election of its deputies for four-year terms, the chambers of the Supreme Soviet sitting in joint session elect their own Presidium and approve the appointment of the Council of Ministers. The candidates for office within each of these bodies are presented as single slates with the accompanying assurance that the slates have been approved by the Party Central Committee. They routinely receive unanimous confirmation.[5] Thus the Supreme Soviet's right to elect and approve these higher bodies is of little importance.

The participation of the Supreme Soviet in policy making on national security matters is similarly formalistic, with minimal practical impact. Its abbreviated semiannual sessions are largely devoted to the public airing of reports on major domestic and foreign policy questions by various state officials and the passage of legislative decrees that have been drafted and previously approved by other state and Party bodies. Defense policy matters receiving such perfunctory ratification by the Supreme Soviet include the defense appropriation within the annual state budget[6] and the USSR Law on Universal Military Service, passed in October 1967.[7]

Both chambers of the Supreme Soviet elect a number of permanent or standing commissions from among their memberships. These commissions have topical areas of competence with authorization to conduct preliminary review of pending legislation in these areas and the right to investigate the ministerial conduct of policy. There is considerable Western speculation regarding the possible emergence of these commissions as a vehicle for an increased policy role for the Supreme Soviet.[8] However, no such commission exists in the military policy area.

Despite its negligible policy-making role, the internal composition of the Supreme Soviet has sometimes been examined by Western analysts as an indicator of the relative importance of the various institutional and social groups within Soviet society.[9] Such an analysis of military representation within the sixth, seventh, eighth, and ninth convocations of the Supreme Soviet, elected in March 1962, June 1966, June 1970, and June 1974, respectively, yields the following results.

In both absolute numbers and as a percentage of total membership, military representation in the Supreme Soviet of the USSR has been almost constant over the past 15 years. The numbers of military delegates elected were 56 in 1962 and 1966, 58 in 1970, and 56 once again in 1974.* The percentage figures, slightly different due to an increase in the total number of deputies between the sixth and seventh convocations, are 3.9 percent (56 of 1,442) in 1962, 3.7 percent (56 of 1,517) in 1966, 3.8 percent (58 of 1,517) in 1970, and 3.7 percent (56 of 1,517) in 1974.

The military deputies may be grouped into three categories in terms of the apparent reasons for their election. The vast majority appear to merit such distinction as a result of the institutional positions they hold within the military establishment. These ex officio members include leading figures within the central apparatus of the Ministry of Defense, including the minister and all of his first deputies and deputy ministers, as well as the commanders of most of the military districts, groups of Soviet forces in Eastern Europe, and naval fleets. A second smaller and rapidly shrinking group includes those veteran marshals who distinguished themselves in World War II. Finally, a few military deputies appear to be elected to provide visible proof that members of the minority nationalities can attain symbolic recognition within the Soviet state. Lt. Gen. of Aviation N. M. Skomorkhov and Col. Gen. of Aviation A. I. Pokryshkin, both elected to the Soviet of the Union from provinces in the Ukraine in 1966 and 1970 without holding major command positions, appear to fit this category.

The Presidium of the Supreme Soviet of the USSR

The Supreme Soviet's Presidium, like its parent body, is largely involved in symbolic and ratificatory activities. Its formal duties that have an impact on security policy include responsibility

---

*These figures are derived from analyses of the listings of deputies to the first three convocations as given in Pravda on March 21, 1962, June 15, 1966, June 19, 1970, and Deputaty verkhovnogo soveta SSSR [Deputies of the Supreme Soviet of the USSR] (Moscow: Politizdat, 1974) for the ninth convocation in 1974. They differ significantly from those of Clark in Soviet Studies (see note 9). Clark's larger figures, 69 versus 56 for 1966 and 64 versus 56 for 1962, are probably due to his inclusion of KGB officers within his "military" total. The figures for 1966 and 1970 are identical with those of the Radio Free Europe Research paper cited in note 9.

for the appointment and removal of the high command of the armed forces,[10] the power to declare a state of war or fulfill international treaty obligations during intervals between sessions of the Supreme Soviet,[11] the power to declare partial or general mobilization,[12] and its general power to ratify or renounce international treaties of the USSR.[13] In practice, these actions appear to be legitimating exercises for decisions already taken within the highest echelons of the Party.

The Ministerial System

The Council of Ministers of the USSR is the "highest executive and administrative organ" within the Soviet Union.[14] It is a large body composed of the members of its Presidium (the chairman, two first deputy chairmen, and ten deputy chairmen), some 70 heads of the various ministries and state committees, and the 15 chairmen of the Councils of Ministers of the Union Republics.[15] This large council as such is not likely to play any significant role in the development of Soviet defense policy.

Under the Council of Ministers is a vast complex of governmental bureaucracies within which various individuals and ministries have major military policy roles and responsibilities. The most prominent of these is of course the Ministry of Defense. Its internal structure and comprehensive policy activities are reviewed later in this chapter.

In the important area of weapons development and production, several ministries in addition to the Ministry of Defense itself are directly involved. Eight ministries in particular are heavily engaged in armaments production. Although these eight are not the only ministries that produce military goods, they represent the central core of the Soviet "defense-industrial complex." The eight ministries in question and their primary defense products are listed in the following table. Other ministries that contribute to military production include the Ministries of Instrument Manufacture, Tractor and Agricultural Machinery Building, Chemical Industry, and Automobile Industry.*

---

*Thomas W. Wolfe, Soviet Interests in SALT: Political, Economic, Bureaucratic and Strategic Contributions and Impediments to Arms Control, P-4702 (Santa Monica, Calif.: RAND Corporation, 1971), p. 27.

The Defense Industrial Ministries and Their Products

Ministry	Product
Ministry of Defense Industry	Artillery, tanks, armored vehicles, small arms, fuses, primers, propellants, explosives, and possibly tactical guided missiles
Ministry of Aviation Industry	Aircraft, aircraft parts, and probably aerodynamic missiles.
Ministry of Shipbuilding Industry	Naval vessels of all types
Ministry of Electronics Industry	Electronic components and parts (subassemblies, not finished equipment)
Ministry of Radio Industry	Electronic systems including radio and communications equipment, radar, and computers
Ministry of General Machine Building	Strategic ballistic missile and space vehicles
Ministry of Medium Machine Building	Nuclear devices and warheads
Ministry of Machine Building	Possibly some portion of ballistic missiles and space vehicles

Source: Andrew Sheren, "Structure and Organization of Defense-Related Industries," in Economic Performance and the Military Burden in the Soviet Union, Joint Economic Committee, 91st Congress, 2d Session (Washington, D.C.: Government Printing Office, 1970), p. 123. See this article, pp. 124-31, for information on the evolution of the defense-related ministries and brief descriptions of the products of each.

These eight ministries that concentrate on the design and manufacture of military equipment also produce a variety of nonmilitary items. Their production of consumer goods in particular has received increased publicity in recent years, including specific mention by both Brezhnev and Kosygin in their respective major addresses to the Twenty-fourth Party Congress in March-April 1971.*

The internal processes of weapons design, development, and acquisition are discussed in some detail in Chapter 5.

In light of the obvious importance of defense production, a top-level governmental body charged with the coordination of policy in this area probably exists. While we have no positive evidence of this fact, a number of things point to this conclusion.

In the past, the Soviets have developed small governmental councils, commissions, or committees with specific responsibility for the direction of weapons development and procurement. Bodies of this nature specifically identified in both Soviet and Western literature include the Soviet of Workers and Peasants Defense, November 1918-March 1920,[16] and Soviet of Labor and Defense, March 1920-April 1937,[17] the Defense Commission of the Council of People's Commissars, which existed alongside the Soviet of Labor and Defense with unspecified additional functions, March 1934-April 1937,[18] the Defense Committee, April 1937-June 1941,[19] and the State Defense Committee of World War II, June 1941-September 1945.[20] These committees typically included representatives from the defense-industrial production commissariats (now ministries) and the topmost Party-state leadership, with an active consultative role played by the professional military.

In the period since the end of World War II, we lack specific Soviet references to the existence of such a defense development and production committee. Western commentators have nevertheless frequently asserted its existence. Two U.S. government studies of

---

*Brezhnev, while speaking of the need to expand the production of consumer goods, stated: "In this connection I should like to mention the defense industries. Even today, 42 percent of its total output volume goes for civilian purposes." Pravda, March 31, 1971. Kosygin similarly noted, "Excellent consumer goods are produced by many enterprises of light industry and food industry and also by the shipbuilding, electronics, aircraft, instrument manufacturing and radio industries." Pravda, April 7, 1971. See also S. A. Zverev, the Minister of Defense Industries, "The Potentialities of the Sector," Izvestiia, July 7, 1971; P. Dementev, the Minister of Aviation Industry, "More Than Just Airplanes," Izvestiia, May 22, 1971.

the early 1960s provide unattributed discussions of an interagency commission or committee including representatives from the Ministry of Defense, the defense production ministries (then state committees), economic planning organizations, and the Ministry of Finance, which, they report, is charged with monitoring, coordinating, and directing defense-related research, development, and production.[21] Similarly, British and U.S. students of Soviet defense policy wrote in 1971 about a "defense industries committee" in Moscow with the same composition and responsibilities.[22] Most recently, John Newhouse, the author of the definitive work on the first phase of the bilateral Soviet-American Strategic Arms Limitation Talks, has identified a "Military Industrial Commission" within the Soviet government.[23] See Appendix A for a depiction of the evolution of these bodies.

The leading government members of the defense-industrial management team appear to be selected members of the Presidium of the Council of Ministers with long careers in armaments production. Throughout the 1950s and early 1960s the major figure in the governmental structure was Dmitri Ustinov, who appears to have remained active in this area but from a position within the Party apparatus from March 1965 until May 1976, and since then as the minister of defense.[24] Following Ustinov's move to the Party Secretariat, the major defense production supervisor within the state apparatus has been Deputy Chairman of the Council of Ministers L. V. Smirnov. Confirmation of the roles of Ustinov and Smirnov in this area was contained in a Khrushchev speech of April 24, 1963, in which he criticized production inefficiencies in the defense sector and specifically identified the two of them as "answerable for the defense industry."[25] Moreover, Smirnov, identified as the chairman of the Military-Industrial Commission, emerged from the defense-industrial sector to bargain directly with Henry Kissinger regarding the detailed provisions of the SALT I agreements at the Moscow Summit in 1972[26] and later, with Cyrus Vance, during the March 1977 SALT II discussions in Moscow. Other prominent state officials with extensive backgrounds in defense production and thus possible participation on this "team" include V. N. Novikov, chairman of the Commission for Foreign Economic Questions, K. N. Rudnev, minister of Instrument Manufacture, Automation Devices and Control Systems, K. M. Gerasimov, a member of the Collegium of the State Planning Committee (Gosplan), and, prior to his death in 1975, V. M. Ryabikov, a first deputy chairman of Gosplan.[27]

The Ministry of Defense

The leading institution in the development of Soviet military policy is the Ministry of Defense. This ministry includes a massive central apparatus in Moscow, the major components of which are discussed below, and the various strategic missile, air defense, ground, naval, and air forces in the field that are deployed throughout the Soviet Union and several countries in Eastern Europe. The leading positions within this ministry are manned almost entirely by professional soldiers,* a practice in distinct contrast to the mixture of civilian and military leadership elements in the Department of Defense of the United States, and the military establishments of the major Western European nations and Japan. (Fully militarized defense ministries, however, are prevalent throughout most of the world, including the communist states of Eastern Europe and Asia and the developing nations of Africa, Asia, and Latin America.)

The minister of defense, currently Marshal Dmitri F. Ustinov, is the chief administrator of the large military bureaucracy, the commander-in-chief of the various military forces, and the primary military advisor to the Party leadership. The minister is assisted by three first deputy ministers, each with a specific area of responsibility. One, Marshal Viktor G. Kulikov, is commander-in-chief of the Warsaw Pact military forces; another, Marshal Nikolai V. Ogarkov, is chief of the general staff; and the third, Army Gen. Sergei Sokolov, is the first deputy for General Affairs with responsibility for the day-to-day administration of the ministry.

The General Staff

The General Staff of the Soviet armed forces is an organ of immense importance. Modeled in the Prussian tradition of the

---

*An exception is the head of the Main Political Administration (MPA) of the Soviet Army and Navy, General of the Army A. A. Yepishev. The MPA and its role on the Soviet military scene is discussed later in this chapter and in Chapter 3. Yepishev's middle and later career experiences prior to becoming MPA chief in May 1962 included a number of Party secretarial assignments, work in the secret police, and ambassadorial posts in Romania and Yugoslavia. What are sometimes forgotten are his earlier activities as a member of the Red Army (1930-38), his graduation from the Military Academy for Mechanization and Motorization of the Red Army in 1938, his work as a political commissar on the front lines during World War II (1941-43), and work as a deputy people's commissar for Medium Machine Construction (1943), a munitions production commissariat. Thus, while not a career military man, Yepishev had significant experience in national security matters prior to his assumption of the top MPA post. See Robert Slusser's biography of Yepishev in Simmonds, op. cit., pp. 141-45.

German General Staff, the "brain of the army," as Marshal B. M. Shaposhnikov, one of its founding figures, called it,* has wide-ranging responsibilities and enormous power. Its many functional directorates cover a wide spectrum of activities. Some of its more prominent sections include the Main Operations Directorate, which is responsible for the development and possible implementation of military contingency plans for intercontinental and theater warfare, the conduct of major troop exercises, and the maintenance of a military command center within the Kremlin;[28] the Main Intelligence Directorate (often identified in the West by the acronym designation GRU, for its Russian title, glavnoye razvedyvatel'noye upravleniye), which collects and evaluates military intelligence information; the Military Science Administration, whose role in the development of military science and doctrine is examined in Chapter 4; the Main Organization and Mobilization Directorate, which is responsible for developing appropriate organizational forms for combat formations throughout the Soviet armed forces and maintaining Soviet military mobilization plans; and the Main Directorate of Foreign Military Assistance, which coordinates Soviet military aid to its Eastern European allies and other arms recipients throughout the world. During wartime the General Staff is almost certainly slated to become once again the critically important "working organ" of the Supreme High Command, the role it performed so effectively in World War II.[29]

The General Staff has direct controlling links with the main staffs of the various service branches. As a result of its predominant role in the development of strategic plans and the resulting assignment of roles and missions to the different services, it is a focal point for the resolution of interservice rivalries over these vital questions.[30]

The leading role of the General Staff is reinforced by its reputation for highly professional quality and an institutional tradition of excellence.[31] This professionalism has been fostered by the frequent practice of linking duty within the staff with advanced

---

*This expression forms the title of Shaposhnikov's three-volume classic on the historical development of the General Staff published in 1927-29. Portions of this work and autobiographical notes about this former tsarist officer who played such an essential role in the development of the Red Army are found in his Vospominaniya-Voenno-nauchnyye trudy [Remembrances--military scientific works] (Moscow: Voenizdat, 1974).

military education in a series of specialized institutions* and a pronounced stability of assignment tours for a segment of the regular staff officers† and the chief of the General Staff himself.‡

The Services

The major components of the Soviet military establishment are the five services of the armed forces (vidy vooruzhennykh sil): the ground forces, navy, air forces, Strategic Rocket Forces, and the National Air Defense Troops (frequently identified by its acronym, PVO-S, for protivo-vozdushnaia oborona strani, which means "anti-air defense of the country"). Despite the existence of five independent services, Soviet sources frequently speak only of "the Soviet army and navy," as in the title of the political directorate, the Main Political Administration of the Soviet Army and Navy. In these cases, the terminology appears to reflect the organizational structure of an earlier period when the army and the navy were the recognized services while the air and air defense forces were only main administrations within the Workers' and Peasants' Red Army (RKKA) and missiles were found only in the workshops of a handful of far-sighted scientists.

Each of the services is headed by a commander-in-chief (CINC) who by virtue of this command is also designated as a deputy minister of defense. Each service has "its own special organization, recruitment, education, service personnel and supply."[32]

---

*These include special staff courses in the Voroshilov General Staff Academy, founded in 1936, and the military intelligence courses of the Military Diplomatic Academy. Edgar O'Ballance, The Red Army (New York: Praeger, 1964), p. 216.

†General of the Army S. M. Shtemenko notes that some officers served continuously within the General Staff from the war until the mid-1960s. Unfortunately, we have no basis to estimate the numbers of such General Staff professionals in comparison with those serving on the staff as a normal rotation in their more diversified careers. General S. M. Shtemenko, General'nyi shtab v gody voiny [The General Staff in the war years] (Moscow: Voenizdat, 1968), p. 125, cited in Spahr, op. cit., p. 20.

‡Over the past 25 years there have been only five chiefs of the General Staff: Marshal V. D. Sokolovskiy, May 1952-April 1960; Marshal M. V. Zakharov, April 1960-February 1963 and November 1964-September 1971; Marshal S. S. Biriuzov, February 1963-November 1964; General of the Army V. G. Kulikov, September 1971-January 1977, and currently, Marshal N. V. Ogarkov. Of these, the only short-term occupant, Biriuzov, died in a plane crash while in office.

The services are, in most cases, further subdivided into component branches or service arms (rod). In addition, the Soviet armed forces include a series of "special troops" with specific functional competences--the Engineer Troops, Radio-Technical (Signal) Troops, Chemical Troops, and Railroad Troops[33]-- who are apparently directly subordinate to the minister of defense.

The Strategic Rocket Forces. The youngest of the services, the Strategic Rocket Forces (SRF), was created in December 1959, as a significant step in the campaign by Nikita Khrushchev to radically transform Soviet military doctrine and force posture. (Khrushchev's repeated initiatives of this nature and the military's response to them are discussed in Chapter 4.) The establishment of the SRF as an independent service had been foreshadowed by an earlier organizational development, the creation in 1948 of a special section within the Ministry of Defense to oversee the military aspects of the Soviet missile development program.[34]

Soviet missile development was apparently supervised by personnel transferred from the artillery branch within the ground forces. Evidence to this effect includes the affiliations of the commanders of the missile development section noted above, initially Marshal of Artillery M. D. Yakovlev, wartime head of the Main Artillery Directorate, and his successor, Marshal of Artillery M. I. Nedelin, who was subsequently named as the first CINC of the Strategic Rocket Forces.[35] This artillery-to-missile evolution is similarly reflected in the transformation of the Dzerzhinsky Artillery Academy founded in 1918[36] into the Dzerzhinsky Military Engineering Academy, whose curriculum is now reported to be fully devoted to the study of missile systems.[37]

The Strategic Rocket Forces do not have any openly identified combat branches. One basis for such division would appear to be the distinction between the shorter-range intermediate/medium-range ballistic missiles (IRBMs/MRBMs) and the more modern intercontinental-range ballistic missiles (ICBMs). These in turn are likely to be organized into field units--armies, corps, and so forth--in accordance with their widespread geographic deployment. These weapons are certainly under the direct operational control of the minister of defense and, above him, the Party Politburo.

At their central headquarters in Moscow, the Strategic Rocket Forces are organized in accordance with a standard pattern that is followed throughout all of the Soviet services. The commander-in-chief of the SRF is assisted by a first deputy commander and a series of deputy commanders, including the chief of the Main Staff, the chief of the Rear, and the chief of the Political Administration. These commanders are all members of the service's Military Soviet or Council, the collegial body with collective responsibility for the administration and combat readiness of the command, established on June 22, 1960.[38]

National Air Defense Troops (PVO-S). Since the very first signs of an aerial threat to their homeland, the Soviets have undertaken a variety of measures to develop a centralized national air defense system. Following its initial appearance as the Air Defense Administration in the People's Commissariat of Defense in 1932,[39] the national air defense forces attained the status of a fully independent service in 1948,[40] with its commander-in-chief becoming a deputy minister of defense in May 1954.[41]

PVO-S bears the responsibility for antiaircraft, antimissile, and antispace defense.[42] To fulfill these tasks, it possesses three combat branches: interceptor aviation of PVO, surface-to-air missile (SAM) troops, and the radar network manned by radio-technical troops.[43] The 550,000 personnel of the National Air Defense Troops wear the same uniforms and insignia as members of the air forces or ground forces,[44] although as an independent service, PVO-S has developed its own distinctive career patterns.*

The heads of the branches, who are deputy commanders of PVO-S, in combination with the other deputy commanders, the chief of the service's Political Administration, the CINC, and his first deputy are members of the Military Soviet of PVO-S.[45]

Operationally, the National Air Defense units are grouped within two vast air defense districts headquartered in Moscow and Baku. These districts and, almost certainly, a series of other geographically organized air defense zones, control and coordinate the various elements in the air defense system under the overall command of the Ministry of Defense in Moscow.

As is the case in all of the services, PVO-S controls its own network of higher educational and scientific research institutions,

---

*An analysis of the careers of command figures within PVO-S including CINC Marshal P. V. Batitskiy; former First Deputy Commander General A. F. Shcheglov; Col. Gen. V. V. Okunev, former commander, Moscow PVO District; Col. Gen. F. A. Oliferov, former commander, Baku PVO District; and First Deputy CINC Col. Gen. A. I. Koldunov, indicates that all of them have spent at least the last ten years in PVO-S assignments. Biographical information extracted from Prominent Personalities in the USSR, pp. 59, 286, 452, 453, 558. The distinctiveness of officer and enlisted careers in PVO-S was confirmed by a former Soviet naval officer. Interview with Nicholas Shadrin, former Soviet naval officer, Washington, D.C., March 24, 1975.

the most prominent of these being the Air Defense Command Academy in Kalinin.[46]

The Air Forces. Created during the first days of the Soviet regime, the Soviet air forces are a large and diversified organization. Currently manned by just under a half a million personnel and controlling approximately 5,350 aircraft, its three component branches are Long-Range Aviation, Frontal (Tactical) Aviation, and Military Transport Aviation.[47]

The primary responsibilities of the air forces are in the areas of training, maintenance, and aircraft and ordnance development. None of its force components appear likely to be operationally controlled by the air forces in time of war. Military Transport Aviation and Long-Range Aviation appear destined to be placed directly under the control of the minister of defense. Past practices indicate that Frontal Aviation's tactical air armies will almost certainly be controlled by military district, forces group or frontal commanders, all ground force officers. The key figures of the air forces' high command may be slated to supervise major air campaigns in the field on behalf of the supreme CINC, as their predecessors did as Stavka* representatives during World War II.[48]

The air forces' organizational structure includes the familiar Military Soviet composed of the CINC, his first deputy and deputy commanders, and the chief of the Political Administration. Similarly, like the other services, it controls a number of military research and educational institutions, including the renowned Zhukovsky Military Air Engineering Academy, a major center for aeronautical research since the early 1920s, the Air Force Command and Staff School, and the Gagarin Military Air Academy.

The Navy. Since its creation in 1918, the Soviet navy has led a markedly independent existence relative to the other services of the Soviet military establishment. On three separate occasions, February 1918-September 1918,[49] December 1937-February 1946,[50] and February 1950-March 1953,[51] this independence was reflected in the creation of a separate Naval Commissariat or Ministry. Since March 1953, however, the navy has remained a service within the unified Ministry of Defense.

The navy consists of five component branches: the submarine fleet, the surface fleet, naval aviation, the coastal defense troops,

---

*The Stavka was a 10-15 man committee of leading civilian and military figures chaired by Stalin that acted as the "general headquarters" directing the Soviet war effort throughout World War II.

and the naval infantry (<u>morskaia pekhota</u>).[52] Two of these branches, naval aviation and the naval infantry, are main administrations within the central headquarters of the navy.[53]

The navy is directed by its commander-in-chief, his first deputy, a number of deputy chiefs, and the chief of the Political Administration, all of whom combine to form the service's Military Soviet. The Main Staff of the navy and the weapons procurement and shipbuilding administrations actively participate in doctrinal and weapons development.[54] Its higher military educational institutions include the Naval Academy and the Frunze Higher Naval School, both located in Leningrad.

Operationally the navy is divided into four fleets--the Black Sea, Baltic, Northern, and Pacific Fleets[55]--and one flotilla in the Caspian Sea. (Although only the Caspian Flotilla is currently active, the Soviets utilized some 12 lake, sea, and river flotillas during World War II and may well be prepared to create them again in the case of major hostilities.)[56] The fleet commanders control most of the ground, air, and seaborne elements based within their geographic commands, under the general direction of Naval Headquarters in Moscow. The single exception to this pattern appears to be the growing number of strategic ballistic missile (SBM) launching submarines. These submarines, based with and supported by the Northern and Pacific Fleets to facilitate their access to the open ocean,[57] probably fall under the direct operational command of the Ministry of Defense, as do the other strategic strike forces of the Soviet armed forces, the land-based ballistic missiles and Long-Range Aviation. The Caspian Flotilla, a main training center, particularly for submarine crews, appears to be directly controlled by the Navy's Main Training Directorate in Moscow.[58]

<u>The Ground Forces</u>. The ground forces were for many years the premier or "main" service of the Soviet armed forces. Following the development and deployment of nuclear-armed intercontinental missiles and the creation of the Strategic Rocket Forces, however, they encountered considerable difficulty in defending their institutional position through much of the 1960s.

Nikita S. Khrushchev in particular was strongly opposed to the maintenance of massive land forces in the thermonuclear era. His determined efforts to downgrade their significance culminated in the elimination of the ground forces' high command structure in August 1964.[59] This left them as an independent service, but apparently transferred responsibility for their overall direction to a section of the General Staff.[60]

Khrushchev's fall from power less than two months later failed immediately to reverse this important organizational setback. In

December 1967, however, a routine announcement about a seminar for military journalists identified one of the speakers, a recently named deputy minister of defense, Army Gen. I. G. Pavlovskiy, as the "Commander-in-Chief of the Ground Forces."[61] The separate high command structure of ground forces was apparently reestablished in the latter half of 1967, including the familiar military soviet, which includes the first deputy, the various deputy commanders, and the head of the political administration.

The Soviet ground forces are divided into five combat branches: Rocket and Artillery Forces, Troop PVO (Air Defense, not to be confused with the National Air Defense Troops [PVO-S], the independent service discussed above), Motorized Infantry, Tank/Armored Forces, and, according to some accounts, the Airborne Troops. Of these, the armored, infantry, and artillery (now augmented by tactical and operational-tactical missiles) branches have long and distinguished traditions as central elements of Soviet military power.

The operational control of these components of the ground forces is vested in the commanders of the 16 military districts in the Soviet Union (the Baltic, Belorussian, Carpathian, Central Asian, Far East, Kiev, Leningrad, Moscow, North Caucasus, Odessa, Siberian, Transbaikal, Transcaucasus, Turkestan, Ural, and Volga Military Districts). In the case of units deployed in Eastern Europe, control is vested in the commanders of the four "groups of forces," the Northern (headquartered in Poland), Central (in Czechoslovakia), and Southern (in Hungary) Groups, and the large and modern units of the Group of Soviet Forces in Germany [East] (GSFG). These district/force commanders are prominent ground forces officers who exercise operational control over tactical air and sometimes naval units (in the case of flotillas and naval forces engaged in coastal support missions) as well as the land forces stationed within their territorial jurisdictions. During wartime, forces from the military districts would almost certainly be combined into a number of "fronts," as was the case during World War II.[62] The commanders are assisted by military soviets, whose memberships include the chief political workers, the chiefs of staff, the commanders of various combat branches and, in the case of the military districts, prominent local Party secretaries.[63]

Advanced military educational institutions under ground forces control include the renowned Frunze Military Academy, which is simultaneously the command and staff academy for the armed forces as a whole and a higher infantry school,[64] and the branch academies including the Malinovskiy Military Academy of Armored Troops and the Kalinin Military Artillery Academy.

Additional Elements

The Ministry of Defense contains a number of sections aside from those of the General Staff, the services, and the special troops. Among the other elements are the Rear Services, the Main Political Administration, the Civil Defense of the USSR, and the counterintelligence organs.

The Rear Services. The coordination and administration of logistic support activities is a necessary function in any military establishment. While a variety of supply administrations have performed these tasks since the founding of the Red Army, the centralized and modern Rear Services currently responsible for these activities dates from 1953.[65] In recent years, an identifiable "logistics complex" has emerged, manned by its own career officers who have specialized training within the Military Academy of Rear Services and Transport; command representation via the deputy commander for the rear at the military district, formation, and unit levels; and their own internal promotional pattern.[66]

The administrative, service, and supply functions under the broad purview of the Rear Services include the central directorates for personnel, finance, fuel, rations, clothing and equipment, post exchanges (the Main Trade Directorate), and the medical and veterinary services.[67]

The Main Political Administration. Successor to the military commissar system adopted during the Civil War, the Main Political Administration (MPA) has remained an essential element of Soviet military organization. Its dual existence as both a directorate of the Ministry of Defense within the state apparatus and as an organization "which functions with the rights of a department of the [Party's] Central Committee"[68] is unique in the Soviet system. Since its primary functions are related to its Party character, the structure and activities of the MPA are discussed under the portion of this chapter that deals with the Party apparatus.

Civil Defense of the USSR. Soviet efforts to organize the nation for protection and survival in the event of aerial attack predate World War II.[69] Civil defense measures in the nuclear era were initially supervised by the Ministry of the Interior under a decentralized Local Antiair Defense (MPVO) program. In 1961, the civil defense program was fundamentally reorganized, including the establishment of a truly nationwide system headed by a central headquarters within the Ministry of Defense. The increased significance of the new program was indicated by the designation of Marshal V. I. Chuikov as the chief of Civil Defense,[70] although public disclosure of this appointment was not made until July 1964.[71] More recently, Chuikov's successor, Army Gen. A. T. Altunin, was named a deputy minister of defense in October 1972.

A large number of organizations participate in the USSR civil defense program. The military contributions include the central headquarters within the Ministry of Defense in Moscow, heavy military participation in the permanent staffs headed by generals and colonels found at various territorial levels throughout the country, and military civil defense units, which are probably subordinate to the military district commander and bear special responsibility in communications, engineering, radiation, reconnaissance, decontamination, and rescue work.[72]

The Central Civil Defense Staff within the ministry and the various territorial staffs are charged with the development of operational plans for population protection and rescue and recuperation activities, training of the various civil defense formations, and organizing the training of the general populace.[73] The bulk of the implementing activity in these areas is done by civilian groups, including the many operational formations organized on a territorial-production basis and compulsorily manned by collective farmers, workers, and students, and the training activities of several mass organizations that include the Voluntary Society for Assistance to the Army, Air Force, and Navy (DOSAAF), the Red Cross, the Komsomol (Young Communist League), the Znanie (Knowledge) Society, and the trade unions.[74]

Military assignment within the civil defense program does not appear to represent a self-contained career pattern as is the case of the other services and specialties discussed above. It does, nevertheless, include specialized military education but apparently only at the lower levels, for example, the Military Civil Defense School, which offers a three-year technical training program leading to a second lieutenant's commission upon graduation.[75] Additionally, problems of civil defense are continuously publicized in _Sovetskii Patriot_ (Soviet Patriot) and _Voennye znaniia_ (Military Knowledge), the weekly and monthly publications of DOSAAF, various pamphlets and books published by the Military and Atom Publishing Houses, and, at regular intervals, within the central press including _Pravda_, _Izvestiia_, and _Krasnaia zvezda_ (Red Star).[76]

The Military Counterintelligence Organs. A much-feared element within the Soviet defense establishment is the counterintelligence network, the special sections (_osobyi otdel_--OO) of the Third Administration of the Committee of State Security (KGB).[77] These organs are manned by KGB officers who are responsible for monitoring the political reliability of all military and political administration personnel and combating enemy attempts at subversion or espionage. The "osobists" are posted at all levels of the military establishment from the smaller operating units to the central directorates in Moscow.[78]

These KGB officers apparently engender great apprehension among the regular military personnel. They wear the uniform of the military service to which they are assigned, although they have their own independent reporting channels and chains of command extending upward to the KGB rather than to the Ministry of Defense. Most osobists spend their careers associated with a particular service, although movement between services is not unknown.[79] This separation extends to their day-to-day activities as the counterintelligence personnel are isolated from other servicemen in their Party and off-duty activities.[80]

The special sections maintain dossiers on all officers and those enlisted men who come to their attention. They are generally aided in this task by a network of servicemen informers who are recruited voluntarily or pressured into such roles.[81] The KGB men maintain a close liaison with the political officers who share their concern about the political reliability of armed forces personnel.

The Supreme or Main Military Soviets

In discussing the five services of the Soviet armed forces, the military districts, groups of forces, and naval fleets, the presence of a network of collegial leadership organs called "military soviets" within each was noted. Similar collective bodies have existed and apparently continue to exist at the Ministry of Defense level as well.

The ministerial military soviets of the past included the leading military figures (the peoples' commissar or minister of defense and his various deputies) and a few selected members of the Party Politburo in a body of 10-15 members.* These organs generally played an active role in the development of Soviet defense policy. They were variously labeled as "revolutionary," "supreme" (vysshii), and "main" (glavnyi) military soviets.† See Appendix B for a chart depicting the evolution of these bodies.

---

*The single exception to this pattern was the 80-man, purely advisory Military Soviet, staffed fully by military officers in the June 1934 to March 1938 period. Erickson, The Soviet High Command, p. 478.

†In chronological order these were the Supreme Military Soviet, March 4-September 2, 1918; the Revolutionary Military Soviet

Information concerning this type of organization in more recent years has been very sparse. As a result we can only speculate about the current institutional framework in this area on the basis of the past patterns noted above, general administrative practices at the Politburo level, and the scattered bits of recent evidence.

Two sources indicate the presence of a Supreme (vysshii) Military Soviet during the later 1950s and early 1960s.[82] The more detailed of these, The Penkovskiy Papers, allegedly derived from the personal journal of the Soviet spy Col. Oleg Penkovskiy (an operative of the Main Intelligence Directorate [GRU] of the General Staff* describes this body as a joint political-military committee that met at definite intervals with regular attendance by a number of Politburo (then Presidium) members, particularly Khrushchev.[83] Penkovskiy reports that Khrushchev, after having had himself recognized as the supreme commander-in-chief, personally chaired the meetings of the Supreme Military Soviet and skillfully exploited this opportunity to deal directly with the various service chiefs, thus bypassing the formal bureaucratic channels through the minister of defense or his first deputies.[84]

More recent Soviet works speak in terms of a Main (glavnyi) rather than a Supreme Military Soviet. Thus two editions of a book

---

(Revvoensoviet), September 1918-June 1934; the Military Soviet, June 1934-March 1938; the Main Military Soviet and the Main Naval Soviet, March 1938-March 1941; no apparent military soviet as such during the war years, although the Stavka of the Supreme Command, June 23, 1941-September 4, 1945, served as the top directing body that combined the civilian and military leaderships; the Supreme Military Soviet, February 1946-March 1950; the Supreme Military Soviet attached to the Council of Ministers and Main Naval and Main Military Soviets in the Naval and Military Ministries, March 1950-March 1953. Information since 1953 is scanty, as discussed below. Sources: Zakharov, op. cit., pp. 33, 173, 199, 234, 478; Erickson, The Soviet High Command, pp. 26, 36, 369, 476-78, 598; Spahr, op. cit., pp. 7-8, 10-14, 15.

*While there is some question regarding the authenticity of The Penkovskiy Papers, some of the parts appear to offer particularly good grounds for being considered valid. This appears to be the case in the discussions of the Supreme Military Soviet, where Penkovskiy apparently acquired his information from his friend and patron, Marshal S. S. Varentsov, who, as chief of the Rockets and Artillery branch of the ground forces, was a member of that Soviet. See Thomas W. Wolfe, The Soviet Military Scene: Institutional and Defense Policy Considerations, RM-4913-PR (Santa Monica, Calif.: RAND Corporation, 1966), n 9, pp. 142-43, for a similar evaluation.

edited by Col. Gen. A. S. Zheltov (former head of the Main Political Administration, March 1953-December 1957, and later commandant of the Lenin Political-Military Academy) list the Main Military Soviet as first among the "organs of collective leadership."[85] Similarly, Yu. P. Petrov's 1968 work on political work in the armed forces notes a decision of the Main Military Soviet, made in April 1962, concerning Komsomol activity within the military.[86]

The reason for the differing titles attached to the high-level collective organs in the Ministry of Defense may lie in the existence of two separate bodies. The Main Military Soviet may refer to a purely military organ, perhaps embodying a large segment of the top military leadership. Such a body is suggested by John Erickson, who writes of a large collective that numbers among its members the minister of defense, his several deputies, the commanders of the military districts, groups of forces and fleets, and the members of their military soviets.[87] (It should be noted that Erickson clouds the issue by including Politburo members within this organ and calling it the "Supreme Military Soviet," a title he also applies to a much smaller body, similar to the one discussed in the succeeding paragraph.)[88] A council of this size, including so many officers drawn from such farflung field commands, would appear incapable of frequent meetings and the regular consideration of policy matters. Alternatively, the Main Military Soviet may resemble those at the lower levels, that is, simply a collegium with limited membership drawn solely from the important deputies who work close to the Minister of Defense in Moscow.

The designation "Supreme Military Soviet" appears to refer to a small body of the kind described by Penkovskiy, which combines the top military leadership and selected Politburo members. In the early 1970s several Western observers suggested that its name had been changed to "Defense Committee"[89] or "Defense Council."[90] In 1976, Soviet sources revealed the existence of a Defense Council (Soviet Oborony) chaired by Party General Secretary L. I. Brezhnev.[91] This body probably meets regularly and serves as one of the highest policy-making bodies in the area of national security matters.[92] Additional speculations regarding the likely activities of the Defense Council are covered later in this chapter in the discussion of the Politburo's role in the direction of Soviet military policy.

PARTY INSTITUTIONS

Real political power in the USSR rests not with the institutions of the Soviet government but rather with the Communist Party of the

Soviet Union (CPSU). It is the Party, with its some 17 million members, and, in particular, its full-time professional apparatus extending from the Politburo through the secretaries and departments of the Central Committee in Moscow down to the provincial, city, and village organs, that controls and directs virtually all aspects of Soviet life.

In examining the roles of the various Party organs with regard to military policy matters, one may study both their role in the development and implementation of such policy and the degree and nature of military participation within them.

The All-Union Party Congress

Scheduled to be held at least once every five years, the All-Union Party Congress is a major event in the life of the Soviet Communist Party. According to the Party rules, this Congress is "the supreme organ of the CPSU."[93] In practice, however, it serves not as a policy-making body but rather as a highly visible forum for announcement and legitimation of the current Party foreign and domestic policies.

The All-Union Party Congress is attended by thousands of elected delegates from throughout the Soviet Union as well as a large number of foreign Communist delegations. Its ten to fourteen days of deliberation are occupied by public speeches by leading Party figures, a few selected members of the rank and file, and visiting dignitaries; the adoption of a variety of resolutions that have been carefully prepared in advance by the Party leadership; and the unanimous election of a single slate of candidates for two of the higher executive bodies of the Party, the Central Committee and the Central Auditory Commission. While careful textual analysis may reveal significant policy differences among the various speakers,[94] the Congress itself does not provide an arena for the resolution of such differences.

Military policy questions are among those routinely discussed at the Party Congress. The speeches of leading Party figures, including the general secretary and some of the other members of the Politburo with particular interests in these matters, generally include mention of "the need to maintain and strengthen the defense capability of the Soviet Union" as a portion of their discussions of the general international scene. More detailed discussions of defense policy have frequently been presented in the addresses of the minister of defense and the chief of the Main Political Administration of the Soviet army and navy. (Such was the case at the Twentieth, Twenty-second, Twenty-third, and Twenty-fourth Congresses, but neither of these figures spoke at the Twenty-fifth Congress in February-March 1976.) These speeches routinely include a survey of the international scene, a review of the current military posture of the Soviet armed forces and a proud description of the internal nature of the military establishment, with particular emphasis upon the professional skills, ideological commitment, and political reliability of its members. There is no pretense of policy formulation or even critical policy review in these speeches; they serve only as public declarations regarding the existing state of affairs.

A substantial number of military personnel are elected as delegates to the All-Union Party Congresses. Since each delegate represents an officially determined and announced number of Party members, and the Party organizations within the armed forces are composed exclusively of military personnel, the number of military delegates can be easily converted into an estimate of the total Party strength within the military establishment. Soviet awareness of this fact and apparent sensitivity in this regard may explain Soviet alteration of their disclosure practices concerning these matters in 1971.

At the Twenty-fourth Party Congress in the spring of 1971, the Soviets did not publicly announce the level of military participation. Departing from the practices of the two previous congresses, the number of military delegates was not revealed either in the report of Chairman of the Credentials Commission I. V. Kapitonov, who spoke only of "a large group of military representatives"[95] during the Congress, or subsequently in the Stenographic Report of the 24th CPSU Congress published in the fall of 1971.[96] Similarly, in the course of his speech to the Congress, the Minister of Defense, Marshal Grechko, failed to cite even general percentage figures about Party membership within the armed forces,[97] something the Defense Minister had traditionally done in the past. At the Twenty-fifth Congress in 1976, Kapitonov once again returned to the previous practice of listing the number of military delegates in attendance.

Data of this nature were available in April 1967, at the Twenty-third Party Congress. At that time, the minister of defense, R. Ya. Malinovskiy, stated that "more than 80% of the personnel of the Armed Forces" were members of the Party or the Komsomol and that "almost 93%" of the officer corps were thus affiliated.[98] There were 352 delegates identified as military personnel, which, given a representation ratio of one delegate per 2,900 Party members yields an approximate Party strength within the armed forces of 880,000 members.[99] The Twenty-fifth Congress figures of 314 servicemen and a ratio of one delegate for every 3,000 Party members yields a strength of 942,000 Party members in the "Armed Forces."[100]

The Central Committee

Soviet administrative practice with regard to state and Party organizations includes an important two-way relationship between large representative bodies and their smaller executive organs. While the larger bodies are designated as the "highest organs" as in the case of the Supreme Soviet in the governmental structure and the All-Union Congress within the Party, the executive organs they elect have "full directing powers" while the parent bodies are not in session. Given the short periods that the larger bodies in fact remain in session, this amounts to de facto policy formulation and direction roles for the executive organs, the Council of Ministers in the government, and the Central Committee within the Party. The pattern does not end with these organs either, in that the Council of Ministers in turn elects its smaller Presidium and the Central Committee its Politburo, with the same mix of theoretical accountability and practical policy direction. Thus the superior policy-making roles of the smaller executive bodies are not violations of the formal-legal rules in the Soviet system but rather the logical and legitimate outgrowth of them.[101]

The Party's Central Committee is elected, or more accurately, a single list of candidates prepared by the central apparatus under the direction of the Politburo is ratified by the All-Union Congress. The Party rules describe the functions of the Central Committee as follows:

> Between the congresses, the CC CPSU directs the activities of the Party, the local Party bodies, selects and appoints leading functionaries, directs the work of central governmental bodies and social organizations of working people through the Party groups in them, sets up various Party organs, institutions and enterprises and directs their activities, appoints the editors of the central newspapers and journals operating under its control and distributes the funds of the Party budget and controls its execution.
>
> The Central Committee represents the CPSU in its relations with other Parties.[102]

The complete membership of the Central Committee, currently numbering 287 full, voting members and 139 nonvoting candidates, meets regularly in plenary sessions. Although the Party Rules call for at least one plenum within every six months,[103] the number of meetings over the past 15 years have varied between two and six per year.[104]

Plenums of the Central Committee have taken a variety of forms in the post-Stalin period. During the late 1950s and early 1960s these meetings emerged as an important arena for the presentation and review of major policy questions. While both secret and open plenums were held, the significant innovations of that period appeared in the public sessions. Under Khrushchev's personal sponsorship the plenary sessions were greatly expanded in size, including not only the Central Committee members but also scores of other Party members and even non-Party personnel with particular interest in the topic under discussion. The agendas for these sessions were often announced in advance and preceded by extensive press discussion. The plenums themselves appear to have served Khrushchev as a kind of hortatory mass meeting designed to facilitate the direct flow of advice from middle-level officials and administrators to the leadership and to mobilize support for his numerous personal policy initiatives of that period.[105]

Despite the dramatic changes in the style of the Central Committee's plenums during this period, they did not herald significant growth in its role in policy formulation. These meetings were largely used to build support for programs already fully drafted elsewhere and approved from above and as a kind of "checking agency on the fulfillment of Party policy in particular fields."[106]

The only known cases in which the Central Committee appears to have played an important policy-making role over the past two decades occurred during the post-Stalin leadership succession struggle of the mid-1950s. Both of these incidents involved controversy within the highest Party body, the Presidium (now Politburo) of the Central Committee, prior to their referral to the Central Committee. The first case involved V. M. Molotov's adamant opposition to the reconciliation with Yugoslavia in early 1955[107] and the second, the decisive defeat of a majority coalition within the Presidium, the so-called Anti-Party Group, which sought to oust Khrushchev from his post as first secretary of the Party in June 1957.[108] In both these instances Khrushchev was upheld by the Central Committee--results largely attributable to his success in placing supporters within that body from his post as party first secretary.

A somewhat similar case occurred when Khrushchev was successfully opposed by his colleagues within the Party Presidium and removed from office in October 1964. On that occasion an apparently unanimous Presidium was upheld against Khrushchev by a specially convened Central Committee plenum after a lengthy and sometimes fiery debate,[109] an indication that the dominant voice in the selection of its membership was no guarantee of indefinite leadership tenure.

Since the fall of Khrushchev, the Central Committee has convened regularly, averaging three plenums each year. Many of Khrushchev's innovations, including the practice of providing advance publicity concerning its agenda, the inclusion of large numbers of nonmembers within its deliberations, and the open publication of the detailed minutes of the plenary sessions, have been abandoned. The Central Committee plenum appears to continue to serve primarily as an occasion for the announcement, review, and discussion of policy but not as the locus of policy formulation and authoritative decision.

Given the size and qualified importance of the Central Committee, it has often been the focus of elite analysis by Western scholars.[110] In light of the fact that the leading figures in all sectors of Soviet life are generally Party members, the Central Committee appears to provide an ideal body for recognizing such accomplishments by the honor of inclusion within its membership. The Soviet military has been one of those institutional elements that have enjoyed continuous corporate representation within the Central Committee.

The dangers of using such statistical indicators as absolute and percentage representation within the Central Committee as a litmus test of relative political influence should be noted. For example, the lowest level of military representation in the past 20 years, 20 of 255 members or 7.8 percent, occurred within the Central Committee elected at the Twentieth Party Congress in February 1956. Yet it was during the 19 months immediately following that Congress that Marshal Zhukov became directly involved in the highest levels of political decision making, bringing a military man and the institutional interests of the armed forces, at least temporarily, to unparalleled heights.

Military participation within the Central Committee is substantial. While tables listing the military members and their posts upon election to the Central Committee and Central Auditing Commission since 1956 are provided in Appendix C, a few general statements are also in order. The total number of military members within the Central Committee has remained quite constant over the past 16 years with 31, 33, 33, and 30 senior military figures in the Central Committees elected at the Twenty-second, Twenty-third, Twenty-fourth, and Twenty-fifth Congresses respectively. (These totals do not include senior officers who have left military service to work within other sectors of the Party or state, for example, Ministers of Civil Aviation and Communications Col. Generals Loginov and Psurtsev, or Col. Gen. (ret.) Basan B. Gorodovikov, first secretary of the Kalmyk Oblast Committee, all of whom were elected candidate members of the Central Committee at the Twenty-third Congress.) Given increases in size of the Central Committee during this period, the percentage representation figures for the military have dropped on each occasion, from 9.4 percent to 9.2 percent to 8.3 percent and finally to 7.1 percent. The decrease in total representation at the Twenty-fourth and Twenty-fifth Congresses is at least partially offset by a favorable shift in the number of full as opposed to candidate members within the military group. This change was from a 15 full, 18 candidate distribution elected in 1966 to 20 full, 13 candidate figure in 1971 and 20 full, 10 candidates in 1976.

The majority of military members appear to owe their election to the Central Committee to the posts they hold within the armed forces. Thus the minister of defense, his first deputies, the service CINCs, the chief of the Main Political Administration, the chief of the Rear Services, the main inspector, and the commanders of many of the military districts, fleets, and groups of forces appear to gain their membership on an ex officio basis. In addition a number of distinguished veterans, both in service as general-inspectors and in retirement, have been regularly elected.

Departures from these objective bases for selection to serve in the higher Party organs merit special explanation. The failure of Marshal of Aviation V. A. Sudets, head of the PVO-S, to be elected to any higher organ in April 1966, at the time of the Twenty-third Congress, proved to be the harbinger of his removal from that important military post within just two months. On the opposite side of the coin, Marshal N. V. Ogarkov, elected to the Central Auditing Commission in 1966 and as a full member of the Central Committee in 1971, came both times from posts that had not previously merited such distinction. These elections appear to confirm the importance of Ogarkov, at that time a first deputy chief of the General Staff, who played a major role as the chief military representative and number two man in the entire Soviet delegation to the SALT negotiations,[111] and has subsequently become Chief of the General Staff and a first deputy minister of defense. The election of Col. Gen. V. V. Okunev as a candidate member of the Central Committee at the Twenty-fourth Congress, while publicly he was identified only as being engaged in unnamed "important work" within the Ministry of Defense[112] (he was, in fact, on detached duty with Soviet air defense forces in Egypt)[113] represented a similar case of Party recognition for a talented officer on the rise. Okunev lived up to this promise when he was named first deputy commander of National Air Defense in 1974, although he subsequently moved on to the much less important main inspectorate in 1976 at the young age of 56.

Another exceptional case is that of Col. Gen. D. A. Dragunskiy. His election to membership in the Central Auditing Commission at the Twenty-fourth Congress appears directly linked to the prominent role he had recently played as a spokesman on behalf of successful

Jews within the Soviet Union in response to foreign charges of widespread anti-Semitism in the USSR.[114]

Whatever the basis for their election, the sizable military contingent within the higher organs of the Party provides the armed forces with continuous institutional representation in their deliberations. In light of the limited policy formulation role of the Central Committee in normal circumstances, as discussed above, this presence appears to serve primarily as a visible manifestation of the Party's concern for the military establishment. However, it also ensures the Soviet military the opportunity to play an active role should circumstances produce a uniquely important plenary session of the Central Committee, as occurred in the Khrushchev-Anti-Party Group showdown in June 1957--a vital asset for any Soviet institutional interest group.

The Politburo of the Central Committee

The Central Committee elects the most important single political organ in the Soviet Union, its 21-man Politburo. Currently composed of 15 full members and 6 nonvoting candidates, it represents the ultimate decision-making arena for all major domestic and foreign policy issues.

Information concerning the nature of the decisional procedures of this body is fragmentary and incomplete. Nevertheless, the available evidence and informed speculations of Western scholars suggest the general contours of these processes.

The individual members of the Politburo appear to have specific areas of expertise and policy responsibility. On this basis the Politburo itself is apparently divided into a number of topical committees or policy teams. This was the practice in the Stalin period as reported by Khrushchev in his "secret speech" to the Twentieth Party Congress,[115] and it is generally believed to have remained the case throughout the Khrushchev and post-Khrushchev periods.[116] These committees are reported to monitor specific policy areas and prepare general recommendations for consideration by the full body with the aid of key officials who are not members of the Politburo.

The Politburo itself is reported to convene in full session on Thursdays on a weekly basis.[117] Although a majority of its members hold government or Party positions that place them in Moscow, others are engaged in duties that require them to reside elsewhere. (Those posted outside of Moscow are V. V. Shcherbitskiy, first Party secretary of the Ukraine, residing in Kiev; D. A. Kunayev, first Party secretary of Kazakhastan, in Alma Ata; and G. V. Romanov, first secretary of the Leningrad Oblast (Province), in Leningrad among the full members; S. R. Rashidov, first secretary of Uzbekistan, in Tashkent; P. M. Masherov, first secretary of Belorussia, in Minsk; and G. A. Aliyev, first secretary of the Azerbaizhan, in Baku.) Consequently, the nonresidents of Moscow are probably unable to attend the sessions every week and thus are likely to participate on perhaps a monthly basis or as necessitated by the nature of the topic under discussion. Such attendance would be most important, of course, for the full, voting members of the Politburo.

The Politburo, apparently operating on the basis of a majority vote, is responsible for authoritative policy selection and elaboration from among available alternatives. Its deliberations apparently proceed in accordance with a general agenda prepared by the Secretariat and on the basis of staffing papers, memoranda (zapiski), and draft decisions that generally come through the Secretariat from a variety of sources including the Secretariat itself, the various departments of the Central Committee, special topical commissions of a permanent or ad hoc nature, various government agencies, or the personal staffs of the individual Politburo members.[118] When particularly complex matters are under consideration, augmented sessions of the Politburo are held to allow leading Party and governmental figures who are not Politburo members to take part in the discussions.[119]

Politburo consideration of military matters would appear to proceed along these same general lines. It is probable that the Politburo in full session becomes involved in debating and approving such matters as the five-year defense plan that is an almost certain adjunct of the comprehensive national five-year economic plan, the annual military budget, the general outlines of strategic doctrine, the initiation and termination of major weapons acquisitions and deployments, the scheduling of massive training maneuvers, and, of course, the actual applications of military power in domestic or foreign situations. With regard to the last type of situation, it is noteworthy, however, that the direction of Soviet actions during the course of the Cuban missile crisis of 1962 was apparently undertaken by a smaller six-man "inner cabinet" drawn largely from within the ranks of the Politburo of that period.[120] Even today, despite periodic claims about the collective nature of the leadership, an "inner cabinet" from within the Politburo would be likely to be involved in contemporary crisis management.

The Soviet military has been infrequently represented on the Politburo over the past two decades. Marshal Georgi Zhukov served briefly in this capacity in 1956-57 before being summarily removed in October 1957. More recently, however, the institutional fortunes of the military establishment were dramatically improved when the minister of defense, Marshal Andrei A. Grechko, was named a full member of the Politburo along with Foreign Minister

Anatoli Gromyko and KGB chief Yuri Andropov in April 1973.* The joint incorporation of this triumvirate suggests that the move was designed to institutionalize the participation of the leaders of three bureaucracies deeply involved in the formulation and implementation of Soviet foreign policy at a time when the consideration of these matters was probably already involving them frequently in Politburo deliberations. Their selection is also likely to have reflected General Secretary L. I. Brezhnev's assessment that these men had been and would continue to be loyal supporters of his policy of detente with the West.

Whatever the reasons for his selection, Marshal Grechko's rise to full Politburo membership assured the military of unaccustomed opportunities to participate directly in all of the deliberations of this powerful body until his death in April 1976. This represented a significant advance over the previous period when the defense minister, perhaps accompanied by his first deputies and other officers with relevant expertise, were probably invited to attend only those Politburo meetings in which defense issues were under consideration and then only as policy advisors rather than as full-fledged participants. D. F. Ustinov, who was promoted to the rank of marshal of the Soviet Union in the summer of 1976 after succeeding Marshal Grechko as defense minister, has retained his seat as a full member of the Politburo, achieved at the Twenty-fifth Party Congress. His selection as defense minister was a setback for the professional officer corps since it represented a return to a political marshal at the post that the career soldiers had held since Marshal Zhukov replaced N. V. Bulganin in 1956.

The Soviet military establishment was apparently confident of its ability to present its views and have them seriously considered within the highest councils of the Party even prior to its acquiring direct representation on the Politburo, as reflected in a public statement of the late defense minister, Marshal R. Ya. Malinovskiy (1957-67). Writing on the occasion of Khrushchev's seventieth birthday in April 1964, Malinovskiy spoke of the military's advisory access to the Politburo, claiming that Soviet defense policy was made only after "conferences with the representatives of the General Staff."[121]

Military affairs have been traditionally supervised as well by a smaller body with a combined military and civilian composition.

---

*At that time, the first substantial shakeup of the Politburo since the fall of Khrushchev also saw Grigoriy V. Romanov enter that body as a candidate member, while full members Gennady I. Voronov and Petr Ye. Shelest were dropped from its ranks.

In the past, the vehicle for this direction appears to have been variously known as the Main or Supreme Military Soviet. Today it is apparently called the Defense Council (soviet oborony). (See "The Supreme or Main Military Soviets," this chapter).

Careful examination of the obituary notices of leading military and defense production figures and the military-related activities of the various Politburo members suggests that the Defense Council probably includes L. I. Brezhnev, A. N. Kosygin, A. P. Kirilenko, D. F. Ustinov, and perhaps M. A. Suslov. The initial three probably serve in this capacity by virtue of their positions as the leading figures of the collective leadership,* and the fourth due both to his obvious ministerial responsibilities and his prolonged involvement as the Party secretary responsible for supervising weapons development and procurement. In Ustinov, who spent most of his career managing the Soviet defense industries, the military would appear to have a highly placed spokesman who should be very sympathetic to their weapons acquisition aspirations.

We can only speculate about the activities and authority of the Defense Council. Since its probable members are also members of the Politburo, it is very likely to function as a kind of military policy subcommittee for that body. In this capacity it probably reviews and makes recommendations regarding such major defense matters as the defense budget, major weapons programs, and major shifts in military doctrine, which, as previously discussed, would be likely to come before the full Politburo for final decision. The Defense Council may have the authority to approve lesser defense policy

---

*Within this troika Brezhnev had considerable past involvement with the supervision of military matters prior to his emergence as the national Party leader. His previous activities of this kind included assignment as a political commissar at the front during World War II, which eventually earned him the rank of major general, service in 1946 as the chief of the political administration of a military district, and the post of first deputy chief of the Main Political Administration with responsibility for supervision of the navy from March 1953 until February 1954. During his work within the Secretariat in the late 1950s, he was the CC Secretary responsible for supervision of military-political matters. Cf. Yu. P. Petrov, Stroitel'stvo politorganov . . ., 1918-1968, pp. 429, 459; Ploss, The Soviet Leadership Between Cold War and Detente, pp. 3, 49-50; and Sovetskaia voennaia entsiklopediia [The Soviet military encyclopedia], vol. I, s.v. Leonid Ilyich Brezhnev (Moscow: Voenizdat, 1976), p. 587.

questions such as the conduct of major training exercises or non-crisis force deployments and it is very likely to play an important role in monitoring the status of defense programs that were initiated with the approval of the full Politburo.

The Party's Central Apparatus

While the Politburo assisted by the Defense Council and the advisory presence of senior military figures is the highest decisional forum on national security matters, other Party organs are important participants in the development and implementation of military policy as well. The Politburo bases its regular deliberations upon the draft decisions and position papers prepared by the various staffing agencies listed earlier. Following a Politburo decision some of these same bodies are charged with monitoring policy implementation.

The most important body in this respect is the 12-man Secretariat elected by the Central Committee. Operating under the direction of the Secretary General, the Secretariat stands at the pinnacle of a complex network of organs known as the "Party apparatus" and manned by thousands of professional full-time Party functionaries. The secretaries themselves, six of whom are presently also members of the Politburo, * are individually responsible for overseeing specific policy areas. Within the current Secretariat there is currently some confusion about who oversees the defense area. From 1965 until late 1976 Dmitri Ustinov appears to have been charged with the supervision of military affairs, although Brezhnev's marked personal prominence in this area adds credence to the opinion of one author that the national security policy is one area "that the first secretary [now "general secretary"] of the Party Central Committee does not entrust to the official heads or to the corresponding sections of the Central Committee; these he directs personally."[122] In October 1976, Yakov P. Ryabov was added to the Secretariat accompanied by speculations that he would assume at least a portion of Ustinov's defense oversight portfolio, since Ustinov is unlikely to be able to fulfill his responsibilities as defense minister, Politburo member, and Party secretary for defense management simultaneously. Protocol appearances of Ya. P. Ryabov in connection with a

---

*L. I. Brezhnev, M. A. Suslov, A. P. Kirilenko, D. F. Ustinov, and F. D. Kulakov among the full members of the Politburo and B. N. Ponomarev among the candidates.

DOSAAF Congress and the funeral of aircraft designer S. I. Ilyushin in early 1977 appear to confirm his work in this area.

The Secretariat of the Central Committee is assisted in its activities by the sizable central apparatus staff, estimated in 1966 to number between 1,300 and 1,500 personnel.[123] This staff is divided among some 20 functional departments (otdel'), which are overseen by the secretaries of the Central Committee and formally identified as the "departments of the Central Committee." In the aggregate, these specialized departments are concerned with the entire range of economic, cultural, and political matters of Soviet life.

Two of the departments, the General and Administration of Affairs Departments, provide routine staffing support for the Politburo, Secretariat, and Central Committee.[124] Personnel working within the other departments, with their various cultural or economic specializations, maintain regular contact with their counterparts in the appropriate governmental agencies and lower-level Party staffs, which are similarly organized along functional lines.[125] These consultations serve as the basis for the development of policy proposals, which, after approval by the Secretariat or Politburo, are published as resolutions or decrees in the name of the Central Committee.[126]

Four of the departments are directly involved in military policy matters. These are the Departments of Defense Industry, Machine Construction, and Administrative Organs, and the Main Political Administration of the Soviet Army and Navy. The two industrial departments in this group jointly supervise the eight state ministries discussed earlier that are predominantly engaged in defense production.[127]

The Department of Administrative Organs is involved in supervising some aspects of police, judicial, and military affairs,[128] although its precise activities in this regard are difficult to ascertain. Its First Military Section[129] apparently acts as a civilian agency for the "independent outside verification of military fulfillment of Party instructions."[130] Indicative of the involvement of the Administrative Organs Department in Party-military affairs have been the various activities of its current head, N. I. Savinkin.* Savinkin has coedited a book on Party work in the armed forces,[131] attended many military conferences and ceremonies, and appears to be automatically included among the high level Party and state officials who sign the obituaries of leading military and defense production figures.[132]

---

*Savinkin's career assignments include: 1936-50, political posts in the Soviet Army (in the Main Political Administration); 1950, graduation from the Lenin Military-Political Academy; 1950-60, work in the Central Apparatus of the Central Committee; 1960 to present, work in the Department of Administrative Organs.

The Main Political Administration of the Soviet Army and Navy, as was noted earlier, is a unique institution that operates simultaneously as a department of the Central Committee and as a directorate within the Defense Ministry. The MPA is directed by its chief, who is assisted in turn by a collegial bureau. Its central apparatus includes directorates for culture, agitation, and propaganda, military publications, cadres, and the Party and Komsomol organizations within the armed forces.[133] The MPA network extends throughout the Ministry of Defense including political organs in the central apparatus of the Ministry in Moscow, the military educational and research institutions, and all of the services down to such basic military elements (podrazdeleniia) as companies, squadrons, and ships.[134] These organs are involved in designing and administering the massive program of Party-political education* that permeates the armed forces, monitoring and reporting upon the state of morale within the military, and supervising the activities of the many Party and Komsomol organizations in the armed forces. The MPA, acting through its Military Publications Directorate, is also responsible for monitoring the content of the military press.† Its activities in this area and their impact on the institutional politics of the Soviet military establishment are covered in Chapter 3 under "The Study of Soviet Military Ideology."

With the exception of its current head, Gen. A. A. Yepishev, the MPA is manned by career officers. Political administration personnel attend their own training institutions, including its prestigious higher academy, the Lenin Political-Military Academy, and advance within a specialized promotion system.

Institutionalized staffing coordination within the apparatus may also be accomplished by permanent or ad hoc commissions of the Central Committee that include representatives drawn from various Party and state agencies. While these commissions are formally

---

*See Chapter 3 for a discussion of the content of this political education.

†Military publications are also likely to face a final censor's review by a military department of the Central Board for the Safeguarding of State Secrets in the Press, better known as Glavlit, which operates directly under the Department of Agitation and Propaganda of the CPSU Central Committee. Civilian writers who comment on military matters are reported to have to have their material approved by the Military Censorship Section of the General Staff of the USSR armed forces. The relationship of this latter body, called simply "the Military Censor," to the MPA is not known. Leonic Vladimirov, "Glavlit: How the Soviet Censor Works," index 1, no. 3/4 (Autumn/Winter 1972): 31-35.

connected to the Central Committee, they appear to operate under the direction of the Secretariat.

Permanent commissions of this variety include the Ideological Commission and the Commission for Party and Organizational Questions and perhaps, according to one author, foreign policy and defense commissions as well.[135] Such a defense commission is not mentioned within any other sources and this citation may well refer to the same body identified above as the Defense Council.

Ad hoc commissions have been created on a number of occasions to facilitate expert participation in policy formulation. * In military affairs, a special commission was formed in 1957-58 to assist in the drafting of a series of Party statutes and resolutions designed to strengthen the Party's indoctrinational and control activities within the military establishment following the replacement of Marshal Zhukov. The members of this commission were Gen. A. S. Zheltov and Marshal F. I. Golikov, the former and newly appointed heads of the Main Political Administration of that period, Marshal Malinovskiy, the minister of defense, and N. I. Ignatov and M. A. Suslov, secretaries of the Central Committee.[136] More recently, one author has speculated that an interdepartmental commission may have been formed to act as a Moscow-based task force to develop, debate, and monitor Soviet policy positions in the extended Strategic Arms Limitation Talks with the United States.[137]

Leadership Succession

The Party leadership maintains firm control over the selection of personnel to fill the key posts of the CPSU and Soviet government. Ultimate authority in this area resides with the Party Politburo. In the Politburo itself, personnel turnover is routinely determined on the basis of a collective decision by the full membership of that body, with the Central Committee routinely ratifying this decision. On only one dramatic occasion, as noted earlier and discussed further below, has the Central Committee ruled against the majority within the Politburo in this regard.

---

*For example, a special commission on education formed during the debate on production education in 1964, cited by Philip D. Stewart, "Soviet Interest Groups and the Policy Process: The Repeal of Production Education," World Politics, 22, no. 1 (October 1969): 41; a commission on agricultural investment policy in 1959 cited by Jerry Hough, "The Party Apparatchiki," in Skilling and Griffiths, op. cit., p. 83; a livestock commission chaired by Pidgorny established in the spring of 1964, cited by Michel Tatu, <u>Power in the Kremlin</u>, p. 397.

Leadership turnover can occur within the Party or government at any time. This is the case because there are no fixed tenures associated with any of the leading posts in the system. This strengthens the linkage between policy disputes and personal power considerations, since a major policy setback can lead to the loss of one's post as well.

The most dramatic types of leadership turnover are those involving either substantial shifts in the membership of the Politburo or the selection of a new general secretary of the CPSU. During such shifts, the intensity of conflict is likely to be high enough and the maneuvering sufficiently intense to merit calling the process a "succession crisis." In these circumstances, the Soviet military has often played and almost certainly will continue to play a very substantial role.

The bases for the Ministry of Defense's importance in periods of leadership transition are varied. First and foremost, given the stakes involved, recourse to large-scale coercion by one of the leading competitors or factions is a possibility that cannot be discounted. As a result, those institutions that are capable of intervening by force of arms--the police forces (militsia) throughout the nation, the Internal Troops under the Ministry of Internal Affairs, the Border Guards and other armed units of the KGB, and the various regular military formations of the Ministry of Defense--all become the object of serious attention and concern. Since the Soviet military possesses coercive power that is vastly more flexible and powerful than that of the other institutions named, it is bound to be the main focus of attention in this regard.[138]

The significance of the Soviet armed forces during a period of serious leadership conflict is not based solely on their potential as the final arbiter by force of arms. It also derives from the primacy regularly accorded to military concerns within the Soviet system as reflected in its privileged position in the allocations of men, money, and material it receives and in the prominence of military power as a significant instrument of Soviet foreign policy. Consequently, the military leadership is bound to have a major voice in a matter as serious as leadership succession.

The Soviet armed forces have never resolved a leadership conflict by employing their military strength to seize the reins of power. The closest they have ever come to such involvement occurred in June 1953, a few months after the death of Stalin. At that time military units led by Marshals Zhukov and I. Konev were employed to neutralize secret police forces in Moscow while members of the High Command joined with the Politburo (then Presidium) majority to arrest and eventually execute secret police boss Laventri Beria.[139]

Military willingness to support Khrushchev, Malenkov, and the other Party oligarchs against Beria was apparently occasioned by the marshals' fears concerning the dangers a dominant Beria might pose to the survival of the members of the High Command themselves and by their deepseated hatred for Beria as a result of his complicity in the deadly purges of the military between 1937 and 1941.

In June 1957, the Soviet military led by Marshal Zhukov once more played a substantial role in the resolution of a leadership crisis, again on the side of Nikita Khrushchev. On this occasion Khrushchev reaped the benefits for his general support of military resource claims in the immediately preceding years and for his personal support of Marshal Zhukov, who had become defense minister in 1955 and a candidate member of the Party Presidium at the Twentieth Party Congress in February 1956. By June 1957, Khrushchev had lost the support of his fellow full members of the Presidium, who, by an 8 to 4 vote, demanded that he resign. The first secretary refused to do so, claiming that only the Central Committee that had elected him could make such a decision. Supported by Zhukov and other candidate members of the Presidium loyal to him, Khrushchev succeeded in convening an extraordinary plenum of the Central Committee, many of whose members were brought to Moscow for the meeting on short notice by military transport aircraft.[140] These Central Committee members, in many cases, owed their current positions to Khrushchev, who controlled Party appointments as CPSU first secretary, and they generally supported his policies. At the plenum they overwhelmingly rejected the proposals of the Presidium majority, which subsequently became known as the Anti-Party Group, and supported Khrushchev's retention of his Presidium and first secretary posts. Instead it was the leading members of the Anti-Party Group, V. M. Molotov, G. M. Malenkov, L. Kaganovich, and D. T. Shepilov, who lost their Presidium seats. In return for his assistance at this crucial juncture, Marshal Zhukov was promoted to full Presidium membership. However, Zhukov himself soon aroused Khrushchev's displeasure and apprehensions due to his excessive self-confidence and apparent political ambitions. As a result, Zhukov was summarily relieved of his defense minister and Presidium posts in October 1957, apparently without substantial opposition within the Soviet military.[141] Military acquiescence in this shift was probably facilitated by the fact that the defense minister portfolio was passed on to another professional soldier, Marshal R. Ya. Malinovskiy, and perhaps because many of the senior military figures themselves had suffered under Zhukov's often highhanded and abrasive style.

By October 1964, when Leonid Brezhnev led an almost unanimous Party Presidium in the conspiracy that unseated Khrushchev, the ebullient first secretary had strongly alienated his previous supporters within the Ministry of Defense. Although Western observers agree that the military was apparently not an instigator of the anti-Khrushchev move, the leading figures of the Ministry of Defense were most certainly approached and agreed to support the coup prior to its implementation. Their acquiescence is fully understandable in light of Khrushchev's direct personal intervention in the development of Soviet military doctrine and force posture and his determination to impose drastic cuts on the defense budget in the preceding years, as described in Chapter 4. It is noteworthy that after carefully paving the way with a series of special briefings for Central Committee members, Khrushchev's successors convened a special rump session of the Central Committee, which overwhelmingly approved his removal from power.[142]

Since the fall of Khrushchev there have apparently been no major leadership struggles, although several men have been moved in or out of the Politburo, which has been led by Leonid Brezhnev. Soviet dissident historian Roy Medvedev claims that a major challenge to Brezhnev's leadership arose within the Politburo in the spring of 1970. In response to this turn of events, Medvedev asserts, Brezhnev traveled to Minsk where a large military maneuver was being conducted, to meet with Defense Minister A. A. Grechko (at that time not yet a member of the Politburo) in order to solicit military support for his continuation in power. Brezhnev reportedly received such support and the crisis passed.[143] Unfortunately there have been no other reports or even speculations in the West that bear any resemblance to this intriguing vignette, which, if true, says a great deal about the weight of the Ministry of Defense in Soviet leadership politics.

In any case, throughout the Brezhnev period the Soviet military has most certainly been well treated by the political leadership. This is likely to reflect both the military's political strengths, actual and potential, and, equally important, the absence of any serious inclination on the part of Brezhnev and his fellow leaders to support anything less than a massive, diversified defense effort. In this favorable climate, the Ministry of Defense has most likely become accustomed to having a significant voice in defense-related matters without by any means dictating to the once again wholly civilian Politburo leadership. Given this prolonged period of such benefits, the Soviet high command will be very likely to expect at least as much during the post-Brezhnev period, when men aspiring to lead the country collectively or individually will almost certainly be competing for the support of this powerful institution. This consideration strongly suggests that the immediate post-Brezhnev period is unlikely to be one marked by any significant slackening of Soviet military programs.

The Military and Regional Party Organizations

When examining the interrelationship between the Soviet military and the Party apparatus, one cannot ignore the links between the various operational military formations stationed throughout the country and the regional Party organs. Although the basic Party organizations within the military are composed purely of military personnel, the higher Party organs of the oblasts (provinces) and Republics provide a local arena for the joint participation of leading civilian and military figures. A number of senior military officers serve on the Politburos and Central Committees of various union-republics.

Following the republican congresses in the spring of 1966, military men were chosen to serve on the Politburos of the Ukrainian, Belorussian, Uzbek, Georgian, and Latvian Republics (that is within 5 of the 14 republics which elect such bodies). In each case the single military member was the commander of a major military district (MD) located within the area. Thus Army Gen. I. I. Yakubovskiy, commander of the Kiev MD served as a full member of the Politburo in the Ukraine, Col. Gen. S. S. Maryakhin of the Belorussian MD as a candidate in Belorussia, Col. Gen. N. G. Lyashchenko of the Turkestan MD as a full member in Uzbekistan, Gen. A. T. Stuchenko of the Transcaucasus MD as a full member in Georgia, and Gen. G. I. Khetagurov of the Baltic MD as a full member in Latvia.[144] Generals Yakubovskiy and Stuchenko were also elected as full members and Generals Maryakhin and Lyashchenko as candidates to the All-Union Central Committee at the Twenty-third Party Congress that same spring.

Other military district command figures are regularly elected to republican Central Committees and other regional Party organs. For example, the March 1966 elections found six full members and four candidates from the military within the Ukrainian Central Committee and four other military officers on the Belorussian Central Committee.[145] Some 20 or more other general officers and admirals serve on the remaining Republican Central Committees.[146] More recently, a check of the Party "buros," the small leadership organs comparable to the Politburo that are found at the republican level, indicated that as of December 1975, the local military district commanders were full members of these key bodies in four republics (Georgia, Kazakhistan, Latvia, and Uzbekistan) and a candidate member in a fifth (Belorussia).[147] Similar participation by military commanders is found in the various city and oblast Party Committees within the largest of the republics, the Russian Soviet Federated Socialist Republic (RSFSR), which lacks its own Central Committee and Politburo, and operates instead directly under the Party's central apparatus.

The reverse side of this regional civilian-military interchange comes in the inclusion of republican and territorial first secretaries within the military soviets of the military districts and fleets, as was discussed earlier. Their participation would appear to provide a basis for the maintenance of close military-community coordination as well as an independent Party capability to monitor the performance of the military establishment. The direct personal contacts developed due to this arrangement might serve as the basis for cross-institutional patronage ties of the shefstvo variety noted in Chapter 1.

CONCLUSION

The material presented in this chapter clearly indicates that the Soviet military is represented in virtually all of the significant organs of the Soviet government and CPSU. This is especially true in the case of those specialized bodies like the Military-Industrial Commission (VPK) and Defense Council, which play crucial roles in the development of Soviet national security policy. However, the predominant organ of the entire system, the Party Politburo, remains essentially civilian despite the high military ranks carried by "marshals" Brezhnev and Ustinov and KGB "general" Andropov. Nevertheless, even in this body, it is highly probable that when serious deliberations on defense-related matters take place, the professional soldiers have ample opportunity to register their views. This probably occurs via Defense Minister Ustinov, a man likely to be sympathetic to many of their concerns, or through the presence of key military figures such as General Staff Chief Marshal Ogarkov or Warsaw Pact CINC Marshal Kulikov, as specially invited participants in relevant Politburo sessions.

In sum, the Ministry of Defense appears to enjoy regular access to the most important Soviet policy-making forums, thus allowing it to present its case and, in some cases, directly participate in those decisions which have substantial impact on its institutional fortunes. Since this high degree of access and participation is combined with the Ministry of Defense's strong predominance with regard to both information and expertise in the defense field as discussed in succeeding chapters, the Soviet military is in an excellent position to wield enormous influence in those matters that concern it most--budgetary allocations for defense, weapons development and production, military doctrine, arms control, and the exercise of military capabilities in support of Soviet foreign policy.

NOTES

1. Article 30, Constitution of the USSR, in A. Denisov and M. Kirichenko, Soviet State Law (Moscow: Foreign Languages Publishing House, 1960), p. 380.

2. Ibid., Article 14, Section g, p. 376.

3. Ibid., Article 14, Section i, p. 376.

4. Ibid., Article 65, p. 389.

5. Jan F. Triska and David D. Finley, Soviet Foreign Policy (New York: Macmillan Co., 1968), pp. 29, 31.

6. For a discussion of the composition of the Soviet state budget with regard to military expenditures, see Timothy Sosnovy, "The Soviet Military Budget," Foreign Affairs (April 1964): 448-93.

7. Izvestiia, October 13, 1967.

8. Cf. Triska and Finley, op. cit., pp. 27-30, and Henry Krisch, "The Changing Role of the Standing Commissions of the USSR Supreme Soviet," paper delivered at the 1971 annual meeting of the American Political Science Association, Chicago, September 7-11, 1971.

9. Cf. Roger A. Clark, "The Composition of the USSR Supreme Soviet: 1958-1966," Soviet Studies (July 1967): 53-65, and "The New Supreme Soviet," Radio Free Europe Research, July 1, 1970, pp. 1-8.

10. The Constitution of the USSR, Article 49, Section l, in Denisov and Kirichenko, op. cit., p. 384.

11. Ibid., Article 49, Section m.

12. Ibid., Article 49, Section n.

13. Ibid., Article 49, Section o.

14. Ibid., Article 64, p. 386.

15. Ibid., Article 70, pp. 390-92.

16. Marshal M. V. Zakharov, chairman of Editorial Commission, 50 let vooruzhennykh sil SSSR [50 years of the armed forces of the USSR] (Moscow: Voenizdat, 1968), pp. 33, 56; and Marshal V. D. Sokolovskiy, ed., Voennaia strategiia [Military strategy], 3d ed. rev. (Moscow: Voenizdat, 1968), pp. 420-21.

17. Zakharov, op. cit., pp. 11, 198; Sokolovskiy, op. cit., p. 421; William J. Spahr, "The Soviet Military Decision-Making Process," paper delivered at the fifth national convention, American Association for the Advancement of Slavic Studies, Dallas, Texas, March 15, 1972, pp. 8-10.

18. Zakharov, op. cit., p. 198.

19. Ibid., pp. 199, 234; K. Ye. Cherenko and N. I. Savinkin, eds., KPSS o vooruzhennykh silakh Sovetskogo Soyuza [CPSU on the armed forces of the Soviet Union] (Moscow: Voenizdat, 1969), pp. 277, 278.

20. Zakharov, op. cit., p. 264; Sokolovskiy, op. cit., pp. 426-31.

21. National Policy Machinery in the Soviet Union, U.S. Senate, Committee on Government Operations (Washington, D.C.: Government Printing Office, 1960), p. 399, and Staffing Procedures and Problems in the Soviet Union, U.S. Senate, Committee on Government Operations (Washington, D.C.: Government Printing Office, 1963), p. 46. This body probably includes defense industry specialists from the Party's central apparatus as well. This would involve the head of the Defense Industries Department of the Central Committee and the secretary supervising such matters. See the discussion of the central apparatus in this chapter under "The Politburo of the Central Committee."

22. John Erickson, Soviet Military Power (London: Royal United Services Institute for Defense Studies, 1971), p. 27; David Holloway, Technology, Management and the Soviet Military Establishment, Adelphi Papers no. 76 (London: Institute for Strategic Studies, 1971), p. 38; Matthew P. Gallagher and Karl F. Spielmann, Jr., The Politics of Power: Soviet Decisionmaking for Defense (Washington, D.C.: Institute of Defense Analysis, 1971), pp. 88, 128.

23. John Newhouse, Cold Dawn: The Story of SALT (New York: Holt, Rinehart and Winston, 1973), p. 251. A Soviet collection of major speeches and Party documents includes a Central Committee resolution, dated January 31, 1938, which announces the creation of a "Military Industrial Commission" within the Defense Committee and describes it as responsible for the mobilization of industry in defense of the country. Cherenko and Savinkin, op. cit., p. 278.

24. Erickson, op. cit., p. 27. For a description of Ustinov's career in defense production management, see Grey Hodnett's biographical article in Soviet Leaders, ed. George W. Simmonds (New York: Crowell, 1967), pp. 200-12).

25. Pravda, April 26, 1963, cited in Michel Tatu, Power in the Kremlin: From Khrushchev to Kosygin (New York: Viking Press, 1969), pp. 343-44.

26. Newhouse, op. cit., pp. 251-52.

27. These men were identified through an extensive survey of the career patterns of all major officeholders in the Soviet government using Edward L. Crowley, Andrew I. Lebed, and Heinrich Schulz, eds., Prominent Personalities in the USSR (Metuchen, N.J.: Scarecrow Press, 1969).

28. Johan J. Holst, Some Notes on the Soviet Command System, HI-1152-P (Croton-on-Hudson, N.Y.: Hudson Institute, 1969), p. 4.

29. The most illuminating discussions of the activities of the General Staff during World War II are formed in Marshal A. Vasilevskiy's Delo vsei zhizni [Work of a lifetime] (Moscow: Politizdat,

1975) and General of the Army S. M. Shtemenko's two volumes entitled General'nyi shtab v gody voiny [The General Staff in the war years] (Moscow: Voenizdat, 1968 and 1973). These works indicate that after considerable difficulties during 1941 and early 1942, the General Staff played a substantial role in the formulation and implementation of strategic plans under the direction of the State Defense Committee and the Supreme High Command, both of which were dominated by Joseph Stalin.

30. Interview with V. M. Kulish, colonel (ret.), Soviet Army, chief of the Military Affairs Section of the Institute of World Economy and International Affairs in Moscow, Princeton, N.J., March 24, 1970.

31. Thus Marshal A. A. Grechko referred to the General Staff as the "holy of holies" in A. A. Grechko, "25 Years Ago," Voenno-Istoricheskii Zhurnal [Military history journal] (hereafter cited as V.I.Zh.): 6 (June 1966): 12. See also Spahr, op. cit., pp. 14-22.

32. Col. Gen. A. I. Radzievskiy, ed., Slovar' osnovnykh voennykh terminov [Dictionary of basic military terms] (Moscow: Voenizhat, 1965), p. 39.

33. Directory of USSR Ministry of Defense and Armed Forces Officials (Washington, D.C.: 1976), p. 24. Hereafter cited as Directory.

34. J. Malcolm Mackintosh, "The Role of Institutional Factors in Soviet Decisions on Weapons Procurement," unpublished ms., p. 10.

35. Ibid.; Oleg Penkovskiy, The Penkovskiy Papers, trans. Peter Deriabin (New York: Avon Books, 1966), p. 309.

36. John Erickson, The Soviet High Command: A Military-Political History, 1918-1941 (New York: St. Martin's Press, 1962), pp. 79, 410.

37. Penkovskiy, op. cit., pp. 327, 334.

38. Cherenko and Savinkin, op. cit., p. 362.

39. Zakhanov, op. cit., p. 205.

40. Ibid., p. 488; Mackintosh, op. cit., pp. 11-12.

41. Zakhanov, op. cit., p. 511; Mackintosh, op. cit., p. 12.

42. Radzievskiy, op. cit., p. 181.

43. Directory, p. 15; Radzievskiy, op. cit., pp. 9, 86, 189, 200.

44. Erickson, Soviet Military Power, p. 47; The Military Balance: 1976-1977 (London: The Institute of Strategic Studies, 1976), p. 8.

45. See Directory, pp. 15-16, for a listing of these posts and their present occupants.

46. Ibid., p. 28; Penkovskiy, op. cit., p. 334.

47. The Military Balance: 1976-1977, p. 10.

48. For an excellent description of the World War II system, see Major General of Aviation M. Kozhevnikov, "Coordination of Air Force Operations by Aviation Representatives of the Stavka," V.I.Zh. 2 (February 1974): 31-38.

49. Sokolovskiy, op. cit., 3d ed., pp. 416, 418; Zakharov, op. cit., p. 26.

50. Raymond L. Garthoff, Soviet Military Doctrine (Glencoe, Ill.: Free Press, 1953), pp. 361, 411; Zakharov, op. cit., pp. 199, 478.

51. Zakharov, op. cit., p. 478.

52. Radzievskiy, op. cit., p. 201; Siegfried Breyer, Guide to the Soviet Navy (Annapolis, Md.: United States Naval Institute, 1970), pp. 12-13.

53. Breyer, op. cit., p. 12.

54. Ibid., p. 5; Michael MccGwire, "Soviet Naval Procurement," in The Soviet Union in Europe and the Near East: Her Capabilities and Intentions (London: Royal United Service Institution, 1970), p. 74; M. A. Peltier, "Organization, Personnel and Training in the Soviet Navy," in The Soviet Navy, ed. M. G. Saunders (New York: Praeger, 1958), p. 122.

55. For a detailed discussion of the composition of the fleets, see Breyer, op. cit., pp. 6-10.

56. See A. V. Basov et al., Boyevoi put' sovetskogo Voenno-Movskogo Flota [The combat path of the Soviet navy] (Moscow: Voenizdat, 1973), pp. 521-29.

57. Erickson, Soviet Military Power, p. 56.

58. Breyer, op. cit., p. 6.

59. Zakharov, op. cit., p. 510. Penkovskiy claims that Marshal V. I. Chuikov, the commander-in-chief of the ground forces of the early 1960s, was relieved of those duties on August 17, 1961, upon becoming the chief of Civil Defense of the USSR. Penkovskiy, p. 245. Although Chuikov did assume the civil defense post, at that time, he apparently did not lose the ground forces command until August 1964.

60. Erickson, Soviet Military Power, p. 18; R. T. Rockingham Gill, "A Structural Change in the Red Army," Radio Free Europe Research Paper, January 19, 1968, p. 1.

61. Krasnaia Zvezda [Red Star], December 24, 1967.

62. Erickson, Soviet Military Power, p. 65.

63. Yu. P. Petrov, Stroitel'stvo politorganov partiinykh i komsomol'skikh organizatsia armii i flota, 1918-1968 [The construction of political organs, party and Komsomol organizations of the army and navy, 1918-1968] (Moscow: Voenizdat, 1968), pp. 442, 444.

64. Seweryn Bialer, ed., Stalin and His Generals: Soviet Military Memoirs of World War II (New York: Pegasus, 1969), n. 20, p. 567.

65. Erickson, Soviet Military Power, p. 27.

66. Ibid., p. 28.

67. Directory, pp. 19-20; USSR: Strategic Survey, Department of the Army Pamphlet 550-6 (Washington, D.C.: Government Printing Office, 1969), appendix F.

68. Lt. Gen. A. E. Khmel', ed., Partiino-politicheskiia rabota v sovetskikh vooruzhennykk silakh [Party-political work in the Soviet armed forces] (Moscow: Voenizdat, 1968), p. 45; Sokolovskiy, op. cit., 3d ed., p. 450. The MPA came under the direct control of the Central Committee in September 1925. Erickson, The Soviet High Command, p. 191.

69. Leon Gouré, Civil Defense in the Soviet Union (Berkeley, Calif.: University of California Press, 1962), pp. 3-5.

70. See note 59, this chapter.

71. Raymond L. Garthoff, Soviet Military Power: A Historical Analysis (New York: Praeger, 1966), p. 55.

72. Leon Gouré, Soviet Civil Defense Revisited, 1966-1969, RM-6113-PR (Santa Monica, Calif.: RAND Corporation, 1969), p. 12.

73. Ibid.

74. Ibid.

75. Ibid.

76. The most comprehensive recent book on Soviet civil defense activities and one that takes a decidedly alarmist view of their significance in the U.S.-Soviet strategic balance is Leon Gouré's War Survival in Soviet Strategy: USSR Civil Defense (Miami: Center for Advanced International Studies, 1976).

77. "Russian Spy Agencies' Scope Is Described," Denver Post, November 12, 1967; Abdurakhman Avtorkhanov, The Communist Party Apparatus (New York: Meridian Books, 1966), pp. 301-02.

78. Shadrin interview, Washington, D.C., March 24, 1975.

79. Ibid.

80. Boris Kuban, "Politics in the Soviet Air Force," in The Soviet Air and Rocket Forces, ed. Asher Lee (New York: Praeger, 1959), p. 212; Zbigniew Brzezinski, ed., Political Controls in the Soviet Army (New York: Research Program on the USSR, 1954), p. 55.

81. Garthoff, Soviet Military Doctrine, p. 244; Shadrin interview, Washington, D.C., March 24, 1975.

82. Yu. P. Petrov, Partiinoe stroitel'stvo v Sovetskoi Armii i Flote, 1918-1961 [Party construction in the Soviet army and navy, 1918-1961] (Moscow: Voenizdat, 1964), p. 462; Penkovskiy, op. cit.

83. Penkovskiy, op. cit., pp. 210-11, 233, 238.

84. Ibid., pp. 238-39.

85. Col. Gen. A. S. Zheltov, ed., V. I. Lenin i Sovetskie Vooruzhennye Sily [V. I. Lenin and the Soviet armed forces] (Moscow: Voenizdat, 1967), p. 148; 2d ed., p. 131.

86. Petrov, op. cit., p. 507.

87. Erickson, Soviet Military Power, p. 14.

88. John Erickson, "The Army, The Party and the People," in The Soviet Union in Europe and the Near East, p. 18.

89. Gallagher and Spielmann, op. cit., p. 20; David Mark, "Statement of the Deputy Director for Research, Bureau of Intelligence and Research, Department of State," U.S. Congress, Subcommittee on Economy in Government of the Joint Economic Committee, The Military Budget and National Priorities (part 3), 91st Congress, 1st session, June 1969, p. 956.

90. Malcolm Mackintosh, "The Soviet Military: Influence on Foreign Policy," Problems of Communism (September-October 1973): 2.

91. The first such Soviet reference appeared in a review of the first volume of the newly published Soviet Military Encyclopedia in Krasnaia Zvezda on April 7, 1976. The review identified General Secretary Brezhnev as the chairman of the Defense Council, an identification that has subsequently been repeated in several Soviet publications. The 1977 draft Soviet constitution states that the Defense Council is formed and its composition approved by the Supreme Soviet of the USSR.

92. Wolfe, Soviet Interests in SALT, p. 23; Wolfe, The Soviet Military Scene, pp. 11-12; David C. Miller, "The Soviet Armed Forces and Political Pressure," Military Review 49, no. 12 (December 1969): 65; Richard F. Staar, "Current Soviet Military Strategy," Naval War College Review 18, no. 5 (January 1966): 21; Avtorkhanov, op. cit., p. 300; Leonard Shapiro, "Keynote-Compromise," Problems of Communism 20, no. 4 (July-August 1971): 6; Spahr, op. cit., pp. 28, 34.

93. "Rules of the Communist Party of the Soviet Union," in Soviet Communism: Program and Rules, ed. Jan F. Triska (San Francisco: Chandler, 1962), Article 31, p. 173, hereafter cited as Party Rules.

94. Cf. Tatu, op. cit., pp. 127-207, and Linden, op. cit., pp. 117-41 for such analysis of the Twenty-second Congress; Sidney Ploss, "A Cautious Verdict in Moscow: The 24th Party Congress," Orbis (Summer 1971): 561-75, for an examination of the Twenty-fourth Congress.

95. Moscow Domestic Radio, 0830 GMT, April 2, 1971.

96. Cited in Christian Deuvel, "An Armed Skeleton in the Politburo's Closet?" Radio Liberty Dispatch, November 10, 1971, p. 1.

97. Pravda, April 3, 1966.

98. Ibid.

99. Deuvel, op. cit., p. 3. The "armed forces" in this case and in 1976 include the Border Guards of the KGB and Internal Troops of the Ministry of Internal Affairs.

100. Pravda, February 28, 1976.

101. This point is superbly made by L. G. Churchward in Policy-Making in the USSR, 1953-1961: Two Views, ed. T. H. Rigby and L. G. Churchward (Melbourne: Lanadowne Press, 1962), p. 35.

102. Party Rules, Article 35.

103. Party Rules, Article 38.

104. Data on Central Committee plenums from Tatu, op. cit., passim; Frederick C. Barghoorn, "Trends in Top Political Leadership in USSR," in Political Leadership in Eastern Europe and the Soviet Union, ed. R. Barry Farrell (Chicago: Aldine, 1970), pp. 69-73.

105. For descriptions of these practices see Sidney Ploss, "Interest Groups," in Kassof, op. cit., pp. 77-98; Avtorkhanov, op. cit., p. 196; Tatu, op. cit., pp. 369, 395-96; Barghoorn, Politics in the USSR, p. 378; Jeremy R. Azrael, "The Legislative Process in the USSR," in Lawmakers in a Changing World, ed. Elke Trank (Englewood Cliffs, N.J.: Prentice-Hall, 1966), p. 93.

106. Churchward in Rigby and Churchward, op. cit., p. 36.

107. Robert Conquest, Power and Policy in the USSR (New York: Harper and Row, 1967), pp. 264-66; Wolfgang Leonhard, The Kremlin Since Stalin (New York: Praeger, 1962), pp. 100-09.

108. Leonhard, op. cit., pp. 243-48; Conquest, op. cit., pp. 309-21; Roger Pethybridge, A Key to Soviet Politics: The Crisis of the Anti-Party Group (London: Allen and Unwin, 1962), passim.

109. Cf. Tatu, op. cit., pp. 415-17; Martin Page, The Day Khrushchev Fell (New York: Hawthorne Books, 1965); William Hyland and Richard Shryoch, The Fall of Khrushchev (New York: Funk and Wagnalls, 1968).

110. Frederick Fleron, "Representation of Career Types in the Soviet Political Leadership," in Political Leadership in Eastern Europe and the Soviet Union, pp. 108-39; Michael P. Gehlen and Michael McBride, "The Soviet Central Committee An Elite Analysis," American Political Science Review 62 (December 1968): 1232-41; Robert H. Donaldson, "The 1971 Soviet Central Committee: An Assessment of the New Elite," World Politics 24, no. 3 (April 1972): 382-409.

111. Further discussion of the role of the Soviet military in the SALT talks is presented in Chapter 6.

112. "Military Men in the Higher Organs of the CPSU," Radio Liberty Dispatch, April 20, 1971, p. 3.

113. Erickson, Soviet Military Power, p. 34.

114. Radio Liberty Dispatch, April 20, 1971, p. 3.

115. N. S. Khrushchev, The Crimes of the Stalin Era: Special Report to the 20th Congress of the CPSU (published as Section 2 of The New Leader, July 16, 1956), p. S62.

116. Staffing Procedures and Problems in the Soviet Union, U.S. Senate, Committee on Government Operations (Washington, D.C.: Government Printing Office, 1963), pp. 24-25, hereafter cited as Staffing Procedures; Gallagher, p. 35.

117. Khrushchev revealed this in an interview with Turner Catledge on May 10, 1957, cited in Soviet Institutions and Policies, ed. W. G. Andrews (Princeton, N.J.: Van Nostrand, 1966), p. 116. It was more recently confirmed by L. I. Brezhnev in his address to the Twenty-fourth Party Congress, Pravda, March 31, 1971.

118. Avtorkhanov, op. cit., p. 216; Staffing Procedures, pp. 14-16; Gallagher, op. cit., pp. 33-35; National Policy Machinery in the Soviet Union, U.S. Senate, Committee on Government Operations (Washington, D.C.: Government Printing Office, 1960), p. 357.

119. Ploss, in Kassof, op. cit., p. 97; Avtorkhanov, op. cit., p. 99.

120. Staffing Procedures, p. 25.

121. Pravda and Krasnaia Zvezda, April 17, 1964. Sidney Ploss notes a difference in the two newspaper versions, with Pravda omitting the sentence, "Only after all this, is a concrete decision made," which appeared in the Krasnaia Zvezda article, thus seeming to weaken the nature of military participation. Sidney Ploss, The Soviet Leadership Between Cold War and Detente (Philadelphia: Foreign Policy Research Institute, 1964), p. 28. A similar reference regarding political consultation with General Staff concerning military policy was made by Khrushchev in his important troop cut speech to the Supreme Soviet in January 1960. See N. S. Khrushchev, O vneshnei politiki Sovetskogo Soiuza: 1960 [Concerning the foreign policy of the Soviet Union], vol. 1 (Moscow: Gosizdat, 1961), p. 34.

122. Avtorkhanov, op. cit., p. 345.

123. Ibid., p. 209.

124. Gallagher and Spielmann, op. cit., p. 33; National Policy Machinery in the Soviet Union, pp. 23, 27; Leonard Shapiro, The Communist Party of the Soviet Union, 2d ed. (New York: Random House, 1971), p. 654; Avtorkhanov, op. cit., p. 205.

125. Cf. Jerry Hough, The Soviet Prefects: The Local Party Organs in Industrial Decision-making (Cambridge, Mass.: Harvard University Press, 1969), pp. 16-34.

126. Shapiro, The Communist Party of the Soviet Union, 2d ed., p. 590.

127. Avtorkhanov, op. cit., p. 203.

128. Kolkowicz, The Soviet Military and the Communist Party, p. 360.

129. Penkovskiy, op. cit., p. 232.

130. Thomas W. Wolfe, The Soviet Military Scene: Institutional and Defense Policy Considerations, n. 15, p. 144.

131. N. I. Savinkin and K. U. Chernenko, KPSS o Vooruzhennykh Silakh Sovetskogo Soiuza [CPSU on the armed forces of the Soviet Union].

132. Cf. the obituaries of Marshal K. K. Rokossovskiy, Krasnaia Zvezda, August 4, 1968; Marshal V. D. Sokolovskiy, Pravda, May 11, 1968; Marshal A. I. Yeremenko, Pravda, November 20, 1970; Col. Gen., Engineering Technical Services, A. I. Mikoyan (famous aircraft designer), Pravda, December 10, 1970.

133. Directory, p. 3; Petrov, Stroitel'stvo politorganov, 1918-1968, p. 441.

134. General A. A. Yepishev, "Work of the Military Political Organs Described," Kommunist Vooruzhennykh Sil [Communist of the armed forces], no. 7 (April, 1969): 13.

135. Avtorkhanov, op. cit., p. 217.

136. Petrov, Stroitel'stvo politorganov 1918-1968, p. 446. Similarly, another special commission had previously revised MPA instructions in early 1957. Its members included Party Presidium members A. B. Aristov, N. I. Belyaev, L. I. Brezhnev, P. N. Pospelov, N. A. Suslov, and E. A. Furtseva. Ibid., p. 429.

137. Gallagher in Gallagher and Spielmann, op. cit., pp. 35-36.

138. Interview with Roy A. Medvedev, dissident Soviet historian, Moscow, December 4, 1976.

139. Roy A. Medvedev and Zhores A. Medvedev, Khrushchev: The Years in Power (New York: Columbia University Press, 1976), pp. 10-11. Khrushchev himself provides a dramatic account of the arrest of Beria in Khrushchev Remembers, trans. and ed. Strobe Talbott (New York: Bantam Books, 1971), pp. 364-66.

140. Carl Linden, Khrushchev and the Soviet Leadership, 1957-1964 (Baltimore: Johns Hopkins Press, 1966), pp. 40-44; Medvedev and Medvedev, op. cit., pp. 76-78.

141. Zbigniew Brzezinski and Samuel P. Huntington, Political Power: USA/USSR (New York: Viking Press, 1965), pp. 331-65; Paul M. Cocks, "The Purge of Marshal Zhukov," Slavic Review 22, no. 3 (September 3, 1963): 483-98.

142. Tatu, op. cit., pp. 399-421; Medvedev and Medvedev, op. cit., pp. 172-75.

143. Medvedev interview, December 4, 1976.

144. Harriet Fast Scott, "The Soviet Marshals and the Communist Party," unpublished ms., pp. 8-10; Prominent Personalities in the USSR, pp. 754, 757, 762, 765, 775.

145. Scott, op. cit., pp. 8-9.

146. Ibid.

147. Directory of Soviet Officials, Vol. III: Union Republics (Washington, D.C.: Government Post Office, 1975), pp. 43, 83, 103, 145, 271.

CHAPTER

3

THE INSTITUTIONAL IDEOLOGY OF THE SOVIET MILITARY

BASIC THEORETICAL ASSUMPTIONS

One of the fundamental assumptions underlying bureaucratic political study is that within each of the large bureaucracies that together constitute a major portion of any modern government, there exists a distinctive institutional ideology largely shared by its many members. These "trained outlooks,"[1] "subjective rationalities,"[2] or "bureaucratic philosophies,"[3] as they have been variously labeled, are significant factors in the political process. While differing greatly in their degree of explicit elaboration, they play an essential role in shaping their holder's perceptions of events as well as the policy positions adopted and promoted by the leading spokesmen and activists of the bureaucratic organizations.

Study of these parochial weltanschauungs and their political impact may be undertaken from a variety of perspectives. One may focus upon the process of belief transmission, that is, the manner in which members of an organization acquire the complex of values and attitudes prevailing within that organization. Research on this question has led authors to examine patterns of organizational recruitment (and particularly the "entering ideology" of the recruits) and a variety of professional socialization experiences including formal education and training, indoctrination, and impact of various career experiences as noted in Chapter 1.

In terms of policy impact, one must be concerned with the substantive content of these institutional outlooks as well as the processes of attitudinal acquisition. A well-developed institutional ideology provides its holder with a comprehensive value framework. It includes a series of preferred goals directly related to the continued survival and prosperity of the organization and attendant perceptual biases that shape the holder's view of events in a manner supportive of the interests of the organization. Fundamental interests shared by all bureaucratic organizations that commonly find direct expression in an institutional ideology include concerns about the maintenance or expansion of its sphere of assigned policy responsibility, about the acquisition of adequate budgetary and logistic support to perform organizational roles and missions, about the maintenance of high morale among its personnel, and about the protection of institutional autonomy vis-a-vis other organizations and individuals.[4] These common concerns acquire specific character within a particular institutional ideology on the basis of the organization's specialized responsibilities and distinctive kinds of activity.

Within large organizations, the overall institutional ideology is generally supplemented by a number of more narrowly based departmental outlooks derived from the specialized mission responsibilities of its various suborganizations. These differentiated departmental viewpoints introduce elements of intrainstitutional competition and conflict to the body of shared interests embodied in the broader ideology of the organization as a whole.

THE IDEOLOGY OF THE PROFESSIONAL SOLDIER

The belief systems of professional military establishments in general and some specific national officer corps in particular have been the subject of considerable speculation and study. Much of the analysis in this field is of a logical-deductive character, being derived from the obvious functional responsibilities of the military, in particular its assigned task of providing for national security through the maintenance and occasional exercise of coercive military force. Studies of this type seldom utilize direct empirical data, relying instead upon "common-sense" assertions about the military's interests and the occasional citation of a confirmatory quotation by a prominent military figure.

One of the most heralded analyses of this kind is Samuel Huntington's "The Military Mind: Conservative Realism of the Professional Military Ethic," Chapter 3 of his The Soldier and the State.[5] Huntington straightforwardly states that his construct of the "military mind" or "professional military ethic," a term he prefers to use, is an ideal model that "consists of the values, attitudes, and perspectives which inhere in the performance of the professional military function and which are deducible from this function. . . . A value or attitude is part of the professional military ethic if it is implied or derived from the particular expertise, responsibility and organization of the military profession."[6] His theorizing in this regard concerns a military ethic common to all professional armies, thus making his work relevant for our investigation of the Soviet military establishment.

Huntington asserts that the "continuing professional weltanschauung"[7] of his archetypal career military officer in any modern state includes a philosophical view of the nature of man (man is selfish, evil, weak, and irrational),[8] a view of social relations (the individual man should be submerged within the disciplined, traditional group),[9] and a series of national policy views. The latter group consists of a set of beliefs that have frequently been described in a similar fashion by other authors as the logical, self-serving beliefs of the military profession.[10]

The standard military views on national policy identified by Huntington include beliefs that (1) the nation-state is the most important actor in international politics; (2) competition between states is inevitable and continuous, constantly endangering the security of the state with the pervasive threat of war; (3) these direct military threats to national security are urgent and extremely grave, compelling the state to monitor carefully the military capabilities of its enemies rather than paying heed to the largely unknowable and inevitably fickle state of their political interactions; (4) strong, diverse, and combat-ready military forces must be maintained to meet the grave and growing threats posed by the enemy; and (5) while a high state of military preparedness is required, the state should seek to avoid reckless, aggressive, and belligerent courses of action.[11]

Huntington also notes the tendency of the military's institutional outlook to be further differentiated along specific suborganizational lines. In discussing the emergence of interservice rivalries he states:

> Of course, he [the military man] tends to stress those military needs and forces with which he is particularly familiar. To the extent that he acts in this manner he becomes a spokesman for a particular service or branch interest rather than for the military viewpoint as a whole.[12]

A somewhat more picturesque expression of the impact of career and institutional commitments on the service-oriented outlook of senior military figures is provided by Alain C. Enthoven and K. Wayne Smith, both of whom had extensive experience in the development and implementation of U.S. security policy as analysts and managers in the Department of Defense and, in Smith's case, on the National Security Council staff. They speak of the so-called "bomber general":

> Picture if you will a man who has spent his entire adult life in the Air Force, flying bombers and leading bomber forces. Bombers are his professional commitment and his expertise. His chances for promotion, public recognition and success, and those of the officers serving under him, are largely tied to the continued importance of bombers. He believes strongly in what he is doing and that is the reason he does it well. . . . It is no reflection on the honor, patriotism or dedication of such a man to say that it is unreasonable to expect him to be objective about the (possible) shift of the strategic mission from bombers to missiles or from the Air Force to the Navy.[13]

Returning to Huntington, his first major work, The Soldie and the State, largely fails to provide empirical evidence of the various policy preferences he attributes to the professional military ethic. However, his subsequent survey of American defense policy between 1945 and 1960, The Common Defense: Strategic Programs in National Politics, includes a wealth of historical cases revealing the institutional outlooks of the various U.S. military services that generally support his ideal-type model, as well as many of their tactics of institutional advocacy.[14]

A similar exposition of the "functional" or "generic" institutional interests said to be common to the military establishments of all large, modern industrialized states is of particular interest since it is presented within one of the major works on Soviet military affairs. This listing of institutional objectives common to all military establishments developed by Roman Kolkowicz includes:

> 1. Maintenance of a high level of investment in heavy industry since this sector of the economy is the foundation of defense industry.
> 2. Maintenance of a certain level of international tension (by depicting the opponent as dangerous, aggressive and unpredictable), sufficient to provide a rationale for large military budgets and allocations.
> 3. Continuously high levels of military budgets and expenditures necessary to an effective military establishment, as significant reductions of military budgets would destroy or cripple existing military programs and weaken institutional empires.[15]

Kolkowicz also identifies three additional institutional interests, which he claims are peculiar to the Soviet sociopolitical context, although he asserts that they also represent "an extension of the traditional interests of all military institutions."[16] These three objectives of the Soviet military are clearly related to the common bureaucratic concerns noted earlier regarding the protection of assigned spheres of responsibility, the maintenance of institutional autonomy, and the desire to project a favorable collective image. These interests concern:

1. The degree of professional authority and institutional independence that will enable military leaders to formulate strategic doctrine, conduct military planning at the highest level, and execute established military policy.
2. Retention of commanding authority at all levels of the military hierarchy, instead of a system under which the political control organs bestow and withdraw such authority and thus wield a powerful instrument for keeping the commanders malleable and preventing elitism.*
3. Cultivation of a positive, even noble, image of the military as the defender of state and people; as the main contributor to past victories over external enemies; and as the bulwark of the Party in its pursuit of foreign policy.[17]

While Kolkowicz follows his enumeration of these universal professional military interests with substantiating materials from Soviet sources, he fails to link them with the military establishments of other industrialized states. These functional interests appear to be either generalizations derived from the study of the Soviet military or logical formulations of what, in light of its national defense functions, a military establishment's interests ought to be.

Another writer who has analyzed the interests of the Soviet military in a logical, deductive manner is Vernon V. Aspaturian. In the process of identifying various Soviet elite elements in terms

---

*Problems involving the relationship between regular military officers and specialized political organs that monitor the military establishment are largely confined to the military establishments of communist states where these two organizational elements are always present.

of their orientation toward the international environment, Aspaturian includes the military among those groups with a vested interest in the maintenance of international tensions. His logical basis for this evaluation runs as follows:

> War and international tensions maximize the threat to the state and hence almost simultaneously enhance the role, status, prestige and power of the Armed Forces as an institution and its individual members. It guarantees a very high priority in the allocation of money, resources and personnel. High military officials assume greater influence in the formulation and execution of policy because of their indispensable expertise; this results in a significant spillover into nonmilitary areas and retains a high residual political force even as war and external danger recede.[18]

Thus, according to Aspaturian, the Soviet military's parochial interests in acquiring favorable resource allocation, high institutional status, and an effective voice in government policy making lead it to adopt an outlook that emphasizes the external threats to Soviet security and opposes measures that might produce detente and a general relaxation of international tensions.

More systematically empirical investigations of the professional soldier's general outlook than those reviewed above have also been undertaken. Beginning with the attitudinal profile of the American military developed by Morris Janowitz on the basis of a questionnaire survey of senior officers in the army, navy, and air force, completed in the late 1950s,[19] a limited number of direct survey research studies has been completed on segments of other national military establishments.[20]

These empirical studies have dealt with a few elements of the professional military outlook. They have provided substantiating data concerning the political conservatism of career officers with regard to domestic and foreign policy issues as well as the similar conservative beliefs of most cadet officer candidates. The studies of the latter group include limited longitudinal data that fail to show an increase in conservatism during the four years of military education and intense indoctrination.[21] The finding points to the importance of career self-selection rather than professional socialization as the key variable in the initial production of the conservative attitudes that prevail within the military profession. Longer-term studies on the development of the political attitudes of military personnel are not currently available.

It is interesting to note that the Soviets themselves have strongly criticized Western studies that attribute common characteristics to capitalist and communist military establishments. Specifically citing the works of Feld, Kolkowicz, and Abrahamsson noted above, a leading Soviet military writer has denied their validity, describing them as the distortions of imperialist ideologists that ignore the essential differences of the opposing social systems.[22] Nevertheless, despite some systemic differences, the concept of a shared professional outlook within communist military organizations is a valid one that can be applied usefully in the study of the Soviet Ministry of Defense.

THE STUDY OF SOVIET MILITARY IDEOLOGY

Some Methodological Questions

An analysis of the various beliefs prevailing within the Soviet military establishment obviously cannot be based upon direct survey research data. Such information is unavailable and there is no prospect that it can be obtained.* In order to produce an empirically based study one must rely upon materials published under the auspices of the Soviet military and the public statements of its leading figures.

In utilizing such materials, one must confront a serious problem that arises from the organization of the Soviet military establishment. All of the publications of the Soviet Ministry of Defense fall under the editorial control of the Main Political Administration of the Soviet Army and Navy. As noted earlier, the MPA is responsible for controlling the content and ideological direction of the vast amounts of literature published by the Military Publishing House (Voenizdat) in Moscow as well as the central military newspapers.[23] In fact, the editor of the Ministry's daily newspaper, Krasnaia Zvezda (Red Star) is a member of the small executive buro of the

---

*Over the past decade, Soviet authorities have shown increasing interest in gathering survey research data from various elements of the society. For commentary on the growth of Soviet sociological research, see Zev Katz, "Sociology in the Soviet Union," Problems of Communism 20 (May-June 1971): 22-40. Within the Soviet military, the results of a questionnaire circulated among 1,000 junior officers were reported in 1969 but its content apparently did not include data on political attitudes. "1000 Lieutenants," Krasnaia Zvezda, April 5, 1969.

MPA.[24] Moreover, the leading military periodical for the discussion of domestic and foreign policy matters, the bimonthly Kommunist Vooruzhennykh Sil (Communist of the Armed Forces), is published by the MPA's highest school, the Lenin Political Military Academy, and largely composed of articles written by its faculty members and other political administration personnel. In light of the emphasis that Western analysts have placed upon the Party nature of the MPA and its role as the Party's agent for the control of the Soviet military, major reservations could be raised concerning the validity of identifying views set forth within publications under its direction as the policy preferences of the Soviet military establishment.

Yet a more careful examination of the role and nature of the MPA largely serves to dispel such apprehensions. The original network of political commissars, the forerunner of the MPA, was most certainly created at the outset of the Soviet regime as a means to control closely the professional officer corps, which included a large number of former tsarist officers. However, the history of this body suggests a gradual but significant shift in its functions. Some insightful observations of Anthony Downs regarding bureaucracies and their workings appear useful in analyzing this evolution.

Downs notes that checking agencies are often employed by higher authorities as a device to monitor the performance of operating bureaus. When faced by such a body, the operating organization is likely to react in a number of predictable ways. The operators may seek to convince or pressure the higher authorities to limit these intrusions on the grounds that the checker is interfering excessively with the operating bureau's mission performance. Alternatively, the operators may attempt to convince the checkers to shift their allegiance from the higher authorities to the operating organization. Finally, the operators may choose either to conform closely with the directives issued by their superiors (and enforced by the checkers) or to engage in deliberate deception in order to continue their illicit practices while avoiding detection and punishment.[25]

Most studies of the relations between the Soviet officer corps and the members of the Main Political Administration have focused almost solely upon the military's responses of the first type. Protesting excessive interferences, the military on various occasions has sought to restrict the activities of the political officers, an action that often has produced a vigorous counterresponse from the Party.[26] However, Western observers have generally failed to examine the more subtle cooptation process in the MPA-military relationship.

While the MPA remains true to its original task of preventing the military's blatant disregard of Party directives, it appears at the same time to have come largely to embrace the values and preferences of the professional military establishment, the very group it is supposed to control. As a matter of fact, the academic researchers and indoctrinational specialists of the MPA are among the leading articulators and most visible proponents of the institutional ideology of the Soviet military establishment.

The reasons why the officers of the Main Political Administration have adopted a generally military viewpoint are numerous. Many of the political officers were recruited in the past from the ranks of promising young regular officers;[27] more recently they have been recruited from the enlisted ranks and secondary school graduates and trained within a network of specialized service-linked MPA academies that were established in 1967.[28] Although assigned to the Main Political Administration, they are very much a part of the professional military establishment, fully sharing its heroic traditions, privileges, prestige, and responsibilities. Soviet writings clearly indicate that the political officer is expected to assist the "line" officers in the maintenance of military discipline, high levels of professional competence, and the combat readiness of the unit to which he is assigned, as well as directing the inculcation of the proper moral-political outlook.[29] With the prominent exception of its current chief, personnel of the MPA are largely career political officers. Finally, in recent years, they have received an increasing amount of formal professional military education* and, in some cases, direct command experience.[30]

In light of these factors one is led to concur with Fritz Ermarth's observation that "the political officer has been assimilated into the military establishment so thoroughly that the question of his loyalty, whether it is first to the Armed Forces or first to the Party apparatus now stands open."[31]

This development does not mean, however, that significant friction between the political officers and the other military personnel does not persist. Rather it is to suggest that this tension is most appropriately viewed as a predictable internal conflict largely

---

*The commander of the Lenin Political-Military Academy wrote in 1969 that within that Academy "one-third of the total study time is devoted to military subjects and to operational and tactical training as well as technical training." Col. Gen. A. Zheltov, "The Lenin Military Political Academy," Soviet Military Review no. 3 (March 1967): 8. See also Brzezinski, op. cit., p. 31, and Alf Edeen, "The Administrative Intelligentsia," in The Soviet Political System: A Book of Readings, ed. Richard Cornell (Englewood Cliffs, N.J.: Prentice Hall, 1971), p. 299.

centering upon the question of the amount of the officers' and enlisted men's time that should be controlled by MPA operatives and devoted to their Party activities and political study programs as opposed to that spent in routine military duties, operational training, or even individual leisure. This fully natural conflict takes place within the context of a widely shared set of basic beliefs about such matters as the nature of the world environment, the threats it poses for Soviet security, and the proper national priorities required in response to these threats.

In light of these considerations, materials drawn from Krasnaia Zvezda, Kommunist Vooruzhennykh Sil, and the books published by Voenizdat have been utilized extensively in the elaboration of the Soviet military's institutional ideology that follows. This composite viewpoint represents the general "line" taken by military writers regarding a number of different questions. It should be clearly understood that this broad institutional outlook is not attributed uniformly to each individual member of the Soviet armed forces. Additionally, since a major source for this analysis has been those articles carried in KVS that are expressly designed as instructional materials for the compulsory political study programs for officers and troops, this depiction represents the ideal viewpoint the higher military authorities would like their men to embrace rather than the views that they actually hold.

Military commentary on the different subjects that comprise its institutional ideology takes a variety of forms. Much of the material used in this study was derived from the speeches and articles of leading military commanders. Other information was drawn from the editorials or feature-length articles carried in the military press. These included articles published in Kommunist Vooruzhennykh Sil that are expressly designed to guide the political officers in conducting their study programs. Such articles often combine substantive discussions of the issue at hand with detailed instructions to guide the teaching efforts of the MPA, including a list of study questions, a discussion agenda for lectures and seminars, and a selected bibliography. These articles are variously found within the "Featured Articles," "Political Studies," or "On International Themes" sections of Kommunist Vooruzhennykh Sil.

The contents of the articles carried by the military press exhibit a striking continuity in their substance, tone, and composition over the 17-year period investigated for this study. Much of the variation encountered was minor and appears to have been occasioned by efforts to have these articles reflect the most recent foreign and domestic events. There have been a few cases of significant shifts in the policy line expressed by military spokesmen, for example, in the military treatments of West Germany's political intentions and regarding the question of appropriate national economic priorities, both of which are discussed below. These changes almost certainly required major policy direction by the military leadership and probably the Party leadership as well.

The military discussions of international issues include the daily reporting of world events that appears in the pages of Krasnaia Zvezda. This is done by a sizable staff of veteran correspondents, many of whom hold military ranks. They include a few featured generalists* and a large number of specialists with specific topical and geographical reporting responsibilities.† Krasnaia Zvezda's international reportage appears designed to provide the military reader with the most current information on the intrigues of imperialism and the accomplishments of international socialism.

A final group of materials that plays an important role in the development and perpetuation of the Soviet military's institutional ideology is the books and brochures of the Military Publishing House. These range from lengthy volumes on various military topics‡ to short brochures designed for agitational work concerning such matters as the most recent Party decisions or the threatening international situation.[32]

The Substantive Content of Soviet Military Ideology

The Nature of World Politics

The Threat: Enemy Intentions. The most familiar refrain heard within Soviet military statements describing the nature of the international environment is the identification of the main enemy, capitalist imperialism, as a criminal, reactionary, and aggressive force that threatens the very existence of socialism. Virtually every article appearing in the military press or statement by a leading

---

*The premier military commentator on foreign affairs is Colonel Aleksei Leontyev who writes on many topical areas and frequently serves as a commentator on international affairs for Radio Moscow.

†These specialists include A. Malyshkin on Asian affairs, Col. V. V. Mochalov on Southeast Asia, V. Berezin on U.S. military affairs, and Col. M. Ponomarev on Western Europe and NATO.

‡For example, the "Officer's Library" series, which is composed of individually and collectively authored volumes on many topics ranging from military strategy and tactics to Marxist-Leninist teachings on war, military pedagogy, and military law.

military figure includes, at the very least, a perfunctory condemnation of imperialism's aggressive essence. Examples of this malevolent depiction of capitalist intentions are manifest:

> <u>Military Strategy 1962</u>: Contemporary state monopoly capitalism is advancing a clearly stated militaristic program and is intensifying the basic aggressive tendencies of world imperialism.[33]
>
> Marshal R. Ya. Malinovskiy, November 1963: The aggressive circles of the imperialist states stubbornly oppose the relaxation of international tensions, they do not want to disarm, they maintain the positions of the "cold war" and nurture plans for a military attack upon the Soviet Union and other socialist countries.[34]
>
> Maj. Gen. K. Bochkarev and Col. I. Sidel'nikov, January 1965: At present there is no fatal inevitability of a world war. However, this does not mean that its danger is absent. One must always remember that the predatory nature of imperialism has not changed. As long as imperialism exists, there remains the danger of aggressive wars and the danger of a military attack on the USSR and other socialist countries.[35]
>
> Marshall R. Ya. Malinovskiy, address to the Twenty-third Party Congress, April 1966: The imperialists can in no way be reconciled with the triumphant procession of the Soviet Union to communism. . . . They have not abandoned the mad idea of destroying socialist countries by force. . . . the party cannot fail to take into account the growing aggressiveness of the imperialist powers headed by the USA.[36]
>
> Marshal A. A. Grechko, February 1968: The imperialist circles of the Western powers, hiding behind talks about peace, are expanding their military preparations against the USSR and other countries of socialism and are creating dangerous hotbeds or war in various areas of the world. . . . Imperialism has not changed its aggressive aspect.[37]

Editorial, Krasnaia Zvezda, September 1969: The dangers engendered by imperialism and its aggressive policies are ever increasing. While organizing hotbeds of military conflict in one place on the globe, then in another, resorting to armed provocations and inflaming the international situation, imperialism remains the source of the continual threat to the cause of peace and social progress. Despite the fact that imperialism has not grown stronger as a world system, it is still a serious and dangerous enemy. The aggressiveness of the chief imperialist power, the United States, is intensifying.[38]

Marshal A. A. Grechko, address to the Twenty-fourth Party Congress, April 1971: Imperialism's growing aggressiveness, whose spearhead is aimed against the Soviet Union, is creating tension in the modern international situation. . . . The U.S. imperialists' preparations for aggression have never ceased and they continue today at an unflagging pace. . . . the U.S. ruling circles are doing all they can to force-pump the poisonous fumes of militarism and are seeking a way out of the crisis of imperialism's political and military doctrines by stepping up preparations for war against the Soviet Union and against the forces of peace and progress.[39]

Maj. Gen. Ye. Sulimov, June 1971: The firm rebuff to aggression is evoking ferocious malice in the reactionary imperialist circles. . . . the reactionary aggressive essence of imperialism remains unchanged. . . . The general crisis of capitalism continues to deepen and its contradictions are growing more aggravated, a fact which intensifies imperialism's adventurism and its aggressiveness. . . . While losing one position after another, capitalism in the form of its most militant imperialist circles, is making the struggle against socialism and all progressive movements more embittered and is setting in motion all kinds of means. . . .[40]

> Marshal A. A. Grechko, March 1972: Reactionary aggressive forces which have an interest in exacerbating the situation and intensifying the arms race are still active in the world of imperialism. They strive to maintain and if necessary to exacerbate tension in the world. . . . Although they have been pressed, the forces of aggression and militarism have not been rendered harmless. The aggressive policy of imperialism conceals the threat of war.[41]

> Marshal D. F. Ustinov, July 1976: The successes of detente, which have lessened the direct threat of a nuclear clash, are not yet sufficiently strong to guarantee peace against the possible provocations by the most aggressive, reactionary imperialist circles. The nature of imperialism has not changed. It has not lost its aggressive essence and is not surrendering its positions voluntarily.[42]

Given the regularity of such assertions, the quotations presented above could be multiplied many times over.

While the general content of these indictments of imperialism has remained strikingly constant over the period covered by this study (1960-76), some differences were detectable in the portions of these discussions devoted to more specific condemnations of individual imperialist states. The one country most consistently singled out for harsh criticism has been the United States. The only detectable changes with respect to the United States were the variations in the specific American actions coming under attack. These have included the military interventions in Cuba (1961) and the Dominican Republic (1965), and, of course, the war in Southeast Asia, as well as charges of sponsoring the intrigues of other aggressive imperialist powers, most notably the Federal Republic of Germany (FRG) and Israel.[43]

Condemnations of West Germany and Israel have exhibited considerable variation. The West Germans were routinely vilified for their "revanchist desires to replay the Second World War" from 1960 until mid-1970.[44] Since that time a definite muting of such criticism has been evident. Although this has not eliminated all attacks upon reactionary forces within West Germany,[45] the notable change in tone appears to reflect high-level Party instructions generally to eschew hostile references to the FRG during a period of improved Soviet-West German relations, dating from the signing of their Moscow Treaty of August 1970. The Israelis were not included in the military listings of aggressive imperialists prior to the June War of 1967. Since that time, however, they have consistently enjoyed this distinction and Israel has become a prime target for frequent articles condemning Zionist imperialism.[46]

Military writers and speakers have criticized many other Western countries, especially those participating in the major Western alliance systems. Greece in particular became a favorite target following the seizure of power by the Greek colonels in 1967. The anticommunist military blocs themselves--like NATO and earlier SEATO--and the U.S. overseas military bases they legitimize have been the objects of regular and harsh condemnation.[47]

A supposedly "fraternal" socialist country has been among those states most virulently attacked. Hostile discussions of the Peoples' Republic of China's internal policies, ideology, and international conduct have appeared in Soviet military publications, generally in parallel with campaigns of a similar nature throughout the Soviet media. These military articles have taken specific issue with Chinese strategic concepts, particularly regarding the alleged Maoist underestimation of the consequences of nuclear war,[48] and more recently followed the prevailing line throughout the Soviet media in condemning the militaristic and antisocialist clique ruling in Peking.[49] This line remained in effect until attacks on the Chinese were halted at least temporarily throughout the Soviet media following Mao Tse-tung's death in September 1976.

An important aspect of the Soviet military's view of the enemies of the USSR and their intentions is the military's analysis of the internal nature of contemporary capitalism and particularly its major representative, the United States. The picture of U.S. politics presented by military commentators was markedly different from the view that emerged and became firmly established in most nonmilitary Soviet analyses during the mid- to late 1960s.

Under what appears to have been the direct personal sponsorship of Nikita Khrushchev,* the Soviet view of the political elite in

---

*Khrushchev himself frequently utilized the "two tendencies" approach discussed below in his own discussions of American politics (Cf. Pravda, January 25, 1971) and was closely associated with its adoption in journalistic and scholarly discussions. See Robert C. Tucker, The Soviet Political Mind (New York: Praeger, 1963), pp. 201-22; William Zimmerman, Soviet Perspectives on International Relations, 1956-1967 (Princeton, N.J.: Princeton University Press, 1969), pp. 211-31; Vernon V. Aspaturian, "Foreign Policy Perspectives in the Sixties," in Soviet Politics Since Khrushchev, ed. Alexander Dallin and Thomas B. Larson (Englewood Cliffs, N.J.: Prentice-Hall, Inc., 1968), pp. 129-45.

the United States presented in most Soviet commentaries underwent a fundamental transformation in the late 1950s and early 1960s. Where the traditional Soviet characterization of the U.S. ruling class had emphasized the hostile and aggressive nature of the monolithic capitalist ruling elite, the new perspective embraced a more differentiated view. It identified two opposing policy factions within the U.S. ruling circles, one "sober," "reasonable," and "realistic," the other "belligerent," "aggressive," and even "mad." Soviet writers distinguished the realistic forces from their belligerent compatriots on the basis of their recognition of the dangers of nuclear war and attendant commitment to its avoidance.[50]

The fact that some Soviet leaders and observers had come to believe that there were "realistic" elements within the American elite had significant foreign policy implications. Despite their capitalist-imperialist nature, these "sober forces" could be expected to push Washington toward behaving more "reasonably" in the international arena. This, the Soviet authors argued, would make possible an era of "peaceful coexistence" between the Soviet Union and the United States, which would be marked both by the continuation of political, economic, and particularly ideological struggle between the superpowers and by elements of mutually beneficial cooperation, especially in their joint efforts to avoid thermonuclear war.*

Although estimates of the relative influence of the two conflicting groups upon U.S. policy varied considerably between 1964 and 1970 (the military escalations in Vietnam had apparently shaken earlier Soviet optimism about the strength of the sober, moderate group), the more pluralized view of the U.S. political process has been largely accepted by most Soviet writers and politicians since the early 1960s. This outlook has been elaborated further by Soviet academic specialists on U.S. affairs, many of whom were originally affiliated with the Institute of World Economics and International Affairs and now are often connected with the newer Institute for the Study of the United States and Canada, founded in 1969.[51]

Not surprisingly, the spokesmen of the Soviet military establishment strongly resisted the "two tendencies" interpretation of the

---

*This characterization of U.S.-Soviet relations coincides with what Thomas Schelling has called a "mixed motive, limited adversary relationship." Thomas C. Schelling, The Strategy of Conflict (New York: Oxford University Press, 1963), pp. 83-118. Discussions of the mixture of cooperative and competitive elements in the U.S.-Soviet relationship have become commonplace in Western commentary. A pioneering analysis of this type was Robert C. Tucker's "Dialectics of Coexistence" in The Soviet Political Mind, pp. 201-22.

U.S. ruling class, and failed to adopt this perspective throughout the 1960s and early 1970s. Their reluctance to modify the strongly hostile image of the United States that they had traditionally espoused was consistent with the military's generally conservative outlook and supportive of their vested institutional interests in the maximization of the malevolence of their potential enemies. By 1973, however, with the Brezhnev detente policy in full bloom, the military writers, too, began to discover reasonable voices in Washington, although they were quick to locate the aggressive forces as well.[52]

Whatever their motivations, Soviet military writers have frequently discussed the U.S. domestic political scene. Their analyses emphasize the directing role played by big business, particularly those corporations engaged in international trade and defense production. They regularly explain U.S. foreign policy in terms of the economic interests of monopoly capital and the plotting of the "military-industrial complex."[53] While such basic Marxian analysis is also abundantly evident in nonmilitary sources,* these sources frequently balance their discussions with references to the "reasonable" elements noted above. Despite joining in the general chorus of praise for East-West detente, the military writers remain much more prone to dwell upon the evils of U.S. imperialism rather than U.S. inclinations toward "reasonable" behavior.

The Threat: Enemy Capabilities. In contrast to their strongly biased depictions of Western intentions, Soviet military commentary on the coercive capabilities of their Western enemies is straightforward and generally accurate. On the basis of information extracted from "the open foreign press" (a phrase that is almost always included in the introduction to articles discussing Western capabilities), coverage of the force postures and strategies of the imperialist states is extensive throughout the various organs of the Soviet military press. While the capabilities information in these articles is very objective, the accompanying interpretations of Western military doctrines and the political aims they serve are predictably presented in the blackest possible terms.

---

*Brezhnev himself has spoken about the unhealthy impact of military-industrial interests on Western policy. His references include the following comments in 1969: "The influence of the so-called military industrial complex, i.e., the alliance of the major monopolies and the military clique of the state apparatus, is growing rapidly in the most developed capitalist countries. This sinister alliance is exerting a growing influence on the policy of many imperialist states and is making their policy still more reactionary and aggressive." Pravda, June 8, 1969.

Some of the books produced by the Military Publishing House deal with the quantitative and qualitative dimensions of the Western military establishments. The most prominent of these is the collectively authored volume, Organizatsiia i vooruzhenie armii i flotov kapitalisticheskikh gosudarstv (The Organization and Armaments of the Armies and Fleets of the Capitalist States).[54] This book provides extremely detailed information about the size, equipment, and tactical doctrines of the conventional military establishments of the United States, Great Britain, France, and the Federal Republic of Germany. Its footnotes indicate that the specialized military journals of these countries were closely monitored and provided the basis for its comprehensive survey of Western general purpose land, air, and sea forces.

The most detailed discussion of Western strategic forces and the doctrines of their use is found in the important Soviet work on military policy, Voennaia strategiia (Military Strategy) edited by Marshal V. D. Sokolovskiy. This volume has appeared in three different editions since 1962, with each succeeding edition providing the most up-to-date information about the military forces and policies in the West.[55] Its exhaustive coverage of these matters reflects a great familiarity with Western writings on nuclear doctrine and capabilities, in particular the annual Military Balance published in London by the International Institute of Strategic Studies.

Krasnaia Zvezda and the various periodicals published by the Ministry of Defense include articles on the newest weapons developments in the West, particularly the United States. Appearing under such headings as "News From Abroad," "In Foreign Armies," or "Materials from the Foreign Press,"[56] these articles follow the standard pattern of combining largely accurate descriptions of the military equipment with political interpretations that link these innovations to the latest machinations of the imperialist enemy.

War in the Modern Era. Another important element of the Soviet military's institutional outlook is its views regarding the likelihood, probable nature, and anticipated utility of war in the nuclear age. This is an issue with obvious and important implications for the Soviet military establishment and one that has occasioned a variety of treatments by its members.

Contemporary Soviet discussions of international conflict, including those by military writers, feater a number of rather standard themes. In accordance with the basic Marxist-Leninist perspective, war is viewed primarily as a phenomenon whose causes are rooted in the economic interests of its participants. Lenin's adaptation of the classical Clausewitzian dictum that "war is the continuation of politics by other (namely violent) means" is repeatedly cited, although the Soviets hasten to differentiate between Clausewitz's erroneous idealistic conception of politics and Lenin's correct scientific view.[57]

Communist writers have classified wars in a variety of manners. Emphasis is placed upon the sociopolitical nature of the conflict, particularly with regard to the character and objectives of the belligerents. Wars are normatively evaluated on the basis of their impact upon the rise of the proletariat and the historical triumph of socialism. A war is deemed "just" if it contributes to the march toward communism and "unjust" if it impedes this movement. A single conflict is often viewed as simultaneously just and unjust depending on the differing motives of the belligerents. Thus in the so-called "wars of national liberation" the struggle is a "just" one for the native movement fighting for its independence and "unjust" for the colonial power that seeks to maintain its imperial control.

More empirically, wars are distinguished according to the geographic scope of the conflict. Global conflicts are designated "world wars" while less extensive clashes are called "local wars."* Armed conflicts within a particular state without external participation are identified as "civil wars." On the weapons dimension the major distinction drawn is between nuclear and nonnuclear/conventional conflict.[58]

These general points are common to Soviet discussions of war written by military officers and civilians. However, the Soviet military has upon occasion developed somewhat more distinctive policy viewpoints. Military commentary was especially prominent in two separate periods. In one case the military appears to have been mobilized by the Party leadership to discredit Maoist strategic pretensions in the early 1960s, and in the other, the military

---

*The most prominent classification effort emphasizing the "world" and "local" distinction was Khrushchev's report to the 1960 Conference of Communist Parties, published as an article, "Toward New Victories of the World Communist Movement," Kommunist no. 1, January 1961, pp. 17-19. Khrushchev also listed "wars of national liberation" as a third category. This refinement was subsequently criticized by one military writer on the grounds that liberation wars were of limited geographic character and should be grouped with local wars rather than treated separately. This same writer also emphasized the importance of classifying wars according to sociopolitical character (just/unjust) as opposed to the scope of conflict. Col. N. A. Lomov, Sovetskaia voennaia doktrina [Soviet military doctrine] (Moscow: Izdatel'stvo "Znanie," 1963), p. 21.

writers themselves seem to have initiated an attack on the views that were being voiced by other Soviet writers concerned with these questions.

Soviet military participation in the campaign against the Chinese emerged in the fall of 1963. At that time military figures lent their support to a concerted refutation of a series of Chinese accusations regarding errors in Soviet theoretical discussions of war and improprieties in the Soviet Union's international conduct. The disputed Chinese views included their evaluation of the strength of contemporary imperialism, their apparent willingness to accept readily the possibility of nuclear war, and their charges that the Soviets had abandoned Marxist-Leninist teaching on the nature of war and had deserted the world revolutionary struggle as a result of their excessive fear of becoming involved in nuclear conflict. The Soviet military writers responded to these accusations with resolute claims of the continuing Soviet commitment to Marxist-Leninist theory and a reminder that while the forces of imperialism were dangerously aggressive and very powerful, the military might of the Soviet Union represented a reliable guarantee of the defense of socialism. The Chinese were themselves accused of deliberately distorting Marxism-Leninism, of grossly underestimating the destructiveness of nuclear conflict, and of foolishly inviting war.[59]

While the military contributions to the Soviet rebuttal of Chinese positions on the nature of modern war during the early 1960s conformed with general Party declarations on these matters at that time, in 1965-66, signs of disagreement among Soviet commentators became clearly visible. At that time a number of military authors took issue with their civilian contemporaries concerning the probabilities and consequences of war and its possible utility as a political instrument.

The contemporary Soviet ideological position on the likelihood of war between the capitalist and socialist camps is based primarily upon Khrushchev's landmark pronouncement on the subject at the Twentieth Party Congress in February 1956. At that time Khrushchev revised the previous Party line based upon the personal pronouncements of Lenin and Stalin that had viewed such a clash as historically inevitable.* Khrushchev asserted that as a result of the growth of

---

*Lenin's most famous disquisition on this matter, made in 1919, stated: "The existence of the Soviet Republic side by side with imperialist states for a long time is unthinkable. One or the other must triumph in the end. And before that end occurs, a series of frightful collisions between the Soviet Republic and the bourgeois states will be inevitable." Lenin, <u>Sochineniia V. I. Lenina</u> [Works

the strength of socialism, a major war between the opposing social systems was no longer "fatalistically inevitable."[60] While all Soviet writers including those in the military have subsequently embraced this fundamental peaceful coexistence assumption, some, including Khrushchev himself, were inclined to carry this line of reasoning quite a bit further. Their more "extreme" views included a significant transition from the noninevitability of world war to its total undesirability. Emphasizing the destructive character of thermonuclear weapons, Soviet writers of this persuasion declared that any major nuclear war would be mutually disastrous for all participants. This viewpoint appeared to reject the possibility of victory in nuclear warfare and thus the very notion that world war could be a viable political instrument. In its most extreme formulation, one writer stated: "War can be a continuation only of folly."[61] It was precisely this mutual-annihilation aspect of Soviet writings on warfare that the Chinese had attacked and the Soviet military had vigorously denied in the 1963 exchanges referred to previously.

Despite its loyal defense of these positions against Maoist attack, signs of Soviet military disagreement with this interpretation of nuclear age realities became evident in 1965. The ideological dispute that ensued was complicated by the presence of military writers on both sides of the question.

Curiously, a major figure in the elaboration of the rejection-of-victory thesis was Maj. Gen. Nikolai A. Talenskiy, a distinguished career military officer who had played an instrumental role in the accelerated development of Soviet military strategy following the death of Stalin.* Beginning in 1958, Talenskiy emerged as a highly visible spokesman for the Khrushchevian line. He dramatized

---

of V. I. Lenin], 4th ed., vol. 29 (Moscow: Izdatel'stvo politicheskoi literatury, 1941-66), p. 133. For a comprehensive analysis of Soviet writings on the likelihood of war, including evidence that Khrushchev's noninevitability thesis was preceded by previous discussions concerning the "avoidability" of war with the imperialists, see Frederic S. Burin, "The Communist Doctrine of the Inevitability of War," American Political Science Review (June 1963): 334-54.

*During the mid-1950s, Talenskiy occupied the vital post of chief editor of the classified military science periodical Voennaia mysl' [Military thought] published by the General Staff and personally wrote a groundbreaking article in the post-Stalin surge of military thinking. See Herbert S. Dinerstein, War and the Soviet Union (New York: Praeger, 1962), pp. 37-47, 227-28; and Raymond L. Garthoff, Soviet Strategy in the Nuclear Age, pp. 66, 67.

the potential destructiveness of a nuclear conflict and praised the existence of a stable deterrence relationship between the Soviet Union and the United States. Writing frequently in the periodical International Affairs* and participating in the Pugwash meetings,† Talenskiy appeared to lend the endorsement of the Soviet military establishment to this point of view.‡

This, however, was not the case. Talenskiy had retired from active military service in the late 1950s and affiliated himself with the Institute of Marxist-Leninist History of the Academy of Sciences.[62] His enthusiasm for stable deterrence and endorsement of the Khrushchevian line on the destructiveness of war are more properly interpreted as the views of an individual commentator with possible ties to Khrushchev himself rather than those of an institutional representative of the Soviet military.

The views of the keepers of the orthodox military point of view on the nature and utility of nuclear warfare in general and on

---

*This periodical appears in both Russian and English, perhaps explaining Western familiarity with Talenskiy's work. He published some 18 articles in this journal between 1958 and 1966.

†The Pugwash movement, named for the Nova Scotia estate of American millionnaire Cyrus Eaton, is the name given to a number of regular conferences between prominent international scientists and academics in which they discuss various scientific problems. An important Study Group on Arms Control and Disarmament was created in 1964 and involves heavy American and Soviet participation. The movement is formally titled the Conference on Science and World Affairs but has become known as Pugwash in honor of the site of its first meeting in July 1957. Cf. J. Rotblat, Pugwash--The First Ten Years (London: Heinemann, 1967) and Duane Thorin, The Pugwash Movement and U.S. Arms Policy (New York: Monte Cristo Press, 1965).

‡Prominent Western scholars, including experts on Soviet military policy, frequently took note of Talenskiy's "liberal" views but often linked them to a moderate faction within the military, failing to note his departure from active duty within the military establishment discussed below. See Wolfe, Soviet Strategy at the Crossroads, pp. 72, 73; Dinerstein, op. cit., pp. 227, 228; Garthoff, Soviet Strategy in the Nuclear Age, pp. 258, 259; William Zimmerman, Soviet Perspectives on International Relations, 1956-1967 (Princeton, N.J.: Princeton University Press, 1969), p. 189; Marshal V. D. Sokolovskiy, ed., Soviet Military Strategy (Santa Monica, Calif.: RAND Corporation, 1963), U.S. editor's analytical introduction, p. 22; Kolkowicz, The Soviet Military and the Communist Party, p. 304.

Talenskiy's writings in particular became evident in a number of articles published in the military press after Khrushchev's political demise.[63] These articles emphasized the dangers of an imperialist-initiated world war and directly attacked the notion that victory in a nuclear war was no longer possible and thus that war could not serve as an instrument of politics.

Two of these military articles included explicit attacks upon the views of General Talenskiy. Lt. Col. E. Rybkin quoted Talenskiy directly regarding his view that it was a "dangerous illusion" to think that thermonuclear war could serve as an instrument to achieve political aims[64] and then proceeded to repudiate this viewpoint:

> To assert that victory is not at all possible in a nuclear war would not only be untrue on theoretical grounds but dangerous as well from the political point of view. . . . Any a priori rejection of the possibility of victory is harmful because it lends to moral disarmament, to a disbelief in victory and to fatalism and passivity. It is necessary to wage a struggle against such views and attitudes.[65]

Rybkin also strongly presented the case for maximum Soviet military preparedness in the face of imperialist aggressiveness and reiterated the judgment that while the presence of nuclear arms had "circumscribed nuclear war as an instrument of politics, this fact does not negate either the possibility of the aggressors unleashing war or the possibility of victory in the war."[66]

Nine months after its publication, Rybkin's article was carefully reviewed in Krasnaia Zvezda by another major Soviet military writer, Col. I. Grudinin.[67] Grudinin criticized Rybkin on a number of points including the charge that he underestimated the complexity of achieving victory in nuclear war. He also criticized Rybkin in a rather obscure manner for failing to differentiate between the "essence" and the "forms and methods" of war. However, with regard to the possibility of victory in a nuclear conflict, Grudinin had no reservations: "The lecturer's criticism is very much to the point when he takes to task those who deny any possibility of victory in world rocket-nuclear war. Such views are propounded not only by foreign figures but also by some Soviet authors of articles on war."[68] This endorsement was followed by another direct attack upon Talenskiy which echoed that of Rybkin. He accused Talenskiy of holding views on nuclear conflict that were "not only erroneous but also harmful."[69]

This military discussion of the essence of contemporary war was brought to a close with an unsigned editorial in Krasnaia Zvezda in January 1967.[70] This editorial had all the appearances of an authoritative Party-directed response to the preceding military discussions of the feasibility of victory in nuclear war and the attendant demands for the military preparations necessary to make this triumph possible. Expressly criticizing the writings of Rybkin and Grudinin, it emphasized instead the stability of the superpower deterrent standoff and the desirability and possibility of preventing a world war.

The editorial specifically repudiated the Rybkin-Grudinin position on the viability of nuclear war as a political instrument: "All peaceloving and antiimperialist forces oppose a world nuclear war as a means of the continuation of politics. 'A war cannot and must not serve as a means of the solution of nuclear conflict,' says the CPSU Program."[71]

Following the appearance of this exchange of views concerning the essence of war in the mid-1960s, no significant differences regarding this question were evident until 1973-74, when the dispute between military and civilian writers flared up once again. The details of this "debate," which had strong implications for U.S.-Soviet arms limitation negotiations, are discussed in Chapter 6 under "The Interim Agreement Limiting Strategic Offensive Arms." The recent exchange indicates that the Soviet military viewpoint continues to include the elements expressed in the 1965-66 articles by Rybkin and Grudinin. This outlook includes: (1) an emphasis upon the dangers that the imperialists might unleash nuclear war; (2) a belief that maximum military preparedness is necessary for the possible prevention of such a war; and (3) the assertion that with the proper armament measures, should the imperialists initiate a nuclear war, it could be won by the Sovier armed forces for the cause of socialism, despite the unprecedented destruction it would entail. These publicly stated beliefs clearly serve military institutional interests in terms of both their demands for "adequate" resource support from the Party and government and the internal requirements for maintaining the morale and confidence of their servicemen.[72] This point of view represents a decidedly conservative position within the framework of the established Party line on peaceful coexistence and war.

Policy Preferences of the Soviet Military

The institutional ideology of the Soviet military includes a number of regularly articulated preferences regarding Soviet national policies. These preferences are directly related to the military's view of the international environment and their institutional responsibilities. These preferred positions are greatly influenced by such common organizational concerns as the protection and, often, expansion of assigned responsibilities, the acquisition of adequate resources to fulfill assigned roles and missions, the protection of organizational autonomy, and the maintenance of good morale among its personnel.

Assigned Roles and Missions: The Responsibility for Defense. The Ministry of Defense has no significant competitor with regard to its primary role, the protection of Soviet national security. While the conventional military formations of the Internal Troops and Border Troops under the direction of the Ministry of Internal Security and the Committee for State Security, respectively, are reported to have a strength of approximately 430,000,[73] they do not seriously rival the position of the Ministry of Defense as the primary military instrument of the Soviet regime.[74]

The Soviet military establishment is consistently singled out in major Party pronouncements as the essential institution for the defense of socialism. Thus the Party program adopted in 1961,[75] as well as the Resolutions of the Twenty-third,[76] Twenty-fourth,[77] and Twenty-fifth[78] Party Congresses repeat the standardized formulations that maintaining the might of the Soviet armed forces is the "sacred duty of the Communist Party and the Soviet people" and that Soviet military power is "the reliable defender of the accomplishments of socialism." Military writers frequently quote these and similar declarations by members of the Party leadership in an effort to reinforce the military's claim to be the institution charged with this important responsibility.

Conflict over the assignment of roles and missions in the defense posture of the Soviet Union does occur. It is confined, for the most part, however, to competition among the major components of the Ministry of Defense. A variety of incidents indicates that lively interservice rivalries have flourished within the military over roles and missions in the past and almost certainly continue to occur today, although much less visibly than before. These organizational conflicts are treated in some detail in the discussion of Soviet military strategy and doctrine presented in Chapter 4.

Resource Acquisition: Investment Priorities. The Soviet military establishment has exhibited an abiding interest in the patterns of national budgetary allocation. Military figures have consistently emphasized the importance of developing and maintaining the economic base of the country as the foundation of the reliable defense of the Soviet state and the entire socialist camp. This concern has manifested itself in the repeated expression of a number of specific policy recommendations regarding Soviet investment priorities.

Soviet military spokesmen have regularly proclaimed the importance of maintaining priority investment in the heavy industrial sector of the Soviet economy. The eight defense production ministries identified in Chapter 2 (under "The Ministerial System") are part of the large, heavy industrial sector (the "Group A" industries in Soviet parlance) of the economy. On numerous occasions military writers have identified heavy industry as the foundation of Soviet military might.[79] Two typical expressions of the military view on the importance of heavy industry run as follows:

> Strengthening the defense might of our state is accomplished on the basis of the preferential development of the important branches of heavy industry. . . . the production of military equipment is connected with all the branches of industry and above all heavy industry.[80]

> Thus heavy industry constitutes the material-technical base of the entire national economy; it is the material foundation of the entire economy. It makes it possible to maintain the military-economic and scientific-technical potential of the country as a whole at the proper level. It is only possible on the basis of the comprehensive development of heavy industry dependably to guarantee the security of the Soviet state against the plots of the imperialist aggressor.
>
> It is necessary at the present stage of development to regard all heavy industry as the basis of the military power of the state, and not just those branches of a purely military nature which manufacture tanks, airplanes, rockets, ammunition and so forth.[81]

The military preference for the development of heavy industry has often been noted by Western scholars. Roman Kolkowicz listed it among the fundamental institutional interests of the Soviet military cited earlier in this chapter under "The Ideology of the Professional Soldier." It was empirically documented in the comparative content analyses of the periodicals associated with various Soviet elite groups by Milton Lodge. Surveying elite expressions between 1952 and 1965, Lodge found that the military exhibited a uniquely single-minded commitment to priority investment in the traditional combination of defense spending and heavy industry.[82] Over this same period, Lodge discovered that the four other Soviet elite groups studied exhibited a conspicuous shift toward increased concern for what he calls the "instrumental priorities," investment in agriculture, light industry, and the living standard.[83]

In more recent years the military has not remained as resistant to the emergence of these competitive priorities as Lodge discovered. Faced with mounting pressures on behalf of the alternative resource claimants, military calls for defense and heavy industrial spending have been increasingly combined with the explicit recognition of the validity of popular welfare demands. Thus N. Lagutin, writing in Krasnaia Zvezda in January 1970, cited Lenin on the correctness of an economic course designed to bring about "an upsurge in the people's prosperity and culture."[84] Similarly he concluded that "thanks to the successes achieved by us, the undeviating development of the economy and the strengthening of the country's defense capability are implemented simultaneously with a considerable acceleration in the rates of growth of the working people's well-being."[85]

In 1971, an article in Kommunist Vooruzhennykh Sil commented in a similar vein:

> Socialist production is carried out primarily in the interests of more completely satisfying the material and cultural needs of the workers. The interests of society require that reliable security be maintained with a minimum disruption of the national economy. The planned administration of our socialist economy on a scientific basis enables us to develop a military technical policy that will not disrupt the balanced and harmonious nature of our national economy.[86]

Moreover, the military has sometimes exhibited some defensiveness about its claims for resources. While indicating a desire to see improvement of the lot of the consumer, they have cited the continuing threat of imperialist aggression to justify large allocations for defense.

> The necessity of strengthening the defense might of the Soviet state and of its army and navy is dictated exclusively by external conditions and

> by the aggressive strivings of international imperialism. And although the maintenance and arming of a modern army is very costly in terms of resources and efforts, the Soviet people are obliged to resort to this since it is a question of the destiny of the socialist revolution's gains and of peace for hundreds of millions of people.[87]

This rather apologetic line of argument has been heard from both Brezhnev and Kosygin as well in recent years. Thus Brezhnev in an election speech in Moscow in June 1966 said:

> The Party openly tells the people that expenditures on the army and weaponry constitute a great burden for our budget, for our economy. We would like to accelerate the advance to Communism, casting from our shoulders at least a part of this burden. But the situation does not yet permit us to do that.[88]

To further reassure those concerned about domestic priorities, military spokesmen have called attention to the production of consumer goods within the heavy industrial and defense production sectors of the economy. Echoing Kosygin's remarks at the Twenty-fourth Party Congress,* the authors of the May 1972 article in Kommunist Vooruzhennykh Sil quoted earlier noted that 42 percent of the production of the defense industries "is being used to satisfy civil requirements." Another article that defended the priority development of heavy industry took a similar tack in calling attention to the variety of consumer goods produced throughout the heavy industrial sector.[89]

Finally the contending pressures for capital investment have apparently compelled the military to take steps beyond merely recognizing the demands of agriculture, consumer production, and economic growth. These competing concerns have probably been instrumental in stimulating the greatly heightened concern for economy and increased efficiency within the defense sector which has been evident since the mid-1960s.

A variety of measures have been undertaken within the defense establishment as part of a general campaign to improve economic efficiency. They include organizational innovation with the creation

---

*Footnote, Chapter 2, under "The Ministerial System."

of a new high-level post within the Ministry of Defense for the coordination and management of strategic weapons development* and the appearance of a great number of books and articles calling for improved efficiency and discussing various measures to accomplish it.

Two military economists stressed the importance of training military economic cadres in new scientific methods and proposed the introduction of new courses on the economics of defense within the curriculums of professional military schools.[90] Other writers demonstrated an interest in and familiarity with such modern analytical techniques as cost-effectiveness study and systems of planning, programming, and budgeting.[91] While these references reflect a mastery of such methods by a few selected officers, we lack the evidence to evaluate the extent to which these methods are being applied in the routine operation of the Soviet defense establishment.[92]

Whatever their efforts to economize, the Soviet defense effort remains a prime consumer of the nation's resources. One Soviet economist estimated in 1965 that an astounding 30 to 40 percent of the national work force was engaged in defense production activity.[93] In addition to substantial direct budgetary support, the defense sector has consistently enjoyed the highest priority in terms of favorable prices for the purchase of raw materials, the recruitment of the most skilled personnel, and the availability of the most advanced technological equipment in such areas as computers, laboratory equipment, and precision machine tools.[94] The repeated statements of Soviet military spokesmen and the leaders of the defense production ministries indicate that despite their recognition of consumer investment needs and increased commitment to efficiency, the Soviet military-industrial combinant is determined to retain its preferred position in the Soviet economic effort. They are certain to be applying all the political leverage they can muster in order to promote this viewpoint within the highest Soviet policy-making councils.

<u>Resource Acquisition: Manpower</u>. The Soviet military leadership has been consistently concerned about the quantitative levels and qualitative characteristics of its personnel. In the early 1960s the military weathered a determined effort by Nikita Khrushchev to reduce drastically their manpower, particularly within the ground forces. Khrushchev argued that modern technology permitted the

---

*This post involved the 1971 appointment of a new Deputy Minister of Defense for Armaments, Col. Gen. N. N. Alekseyev, who is apparently in charge of research and development management. See John Erickson, <u>Soviet Military Power</u>, pp. 16, 21.

reduction of the number of troops in exchange for increases in firepower.[95] The military reversed this proposition by insisting that the greater destructiveness of nuclear weapons actually increased the need for a mass million-man army as a necessary hedge against the large losses that such a war would inevitably produce.[96] Buttressed by this doctrinal justification, the Soviet military successfully avoided the drastic reductions sought by Khrushchev in the 1960s and their institutional outlook continues routinely to include calls for a numerically large military establishment.

With respect to quality, military spokesmen have regularly emphasized the absolute essentiality of maintaining a highly skilled body of personnel. The importance of having well-trained soldiers who can effectively utilize increasingly complex modern weaponry is a standard theme of military authors and speakers, who frequently cite the educational and training accomplishments of the Soviet servicemen.[97]

Military interest in the attitudes and skills of their troops has been reflected as well in their concern about the interests and abilities of the men entering the armed forces. Soviet military leaders have often praised and actively supported the efforts of DOSAAF and more recently the nationwide "military-patriotic education" campaign that mobilizes several governmental and Party agencies and a variety of public organizations in an extensive program of preinduction training designed to teach Soviet youth a variety of military skills and a patriotic appreciation of their national past.[98] The Ministry of Defense was almost certainly a major architect of this massive effort and annually contributes large numbers of personnel and facilities to it.[99] The high level of military involvement in these activities tangibly demonstrates their commitment to maintaining a supply of well-trained and motivated manpower for military service.

Resource Acquisition: Weaponry Superiority. Soviet military leaders and writers have left no doubt concerning their primary objective in terms of their own military capability. Their spokesmen have undeviatingly called for the attainment of clear military-technological superiority over their imperialist adversary, in particular the main enemy, the United States.

The Soviet military's commitment to "the doctrine of military superiority"[100] has been forcefully articulated on numerous occasions. A classic exposition of this element of Soviet military ideology was presented by Lt. Col. V. M. Bondarenko in 1966.[101] Bondarenko stated his basic thesis at the very outset, asserting that "under contemporary conditions, the significance of strictly military factors . . . and especially of military-technological superiority over the enemy is greater than ever before."[102] He then proceeded to detail the various aspects of such superiority, discussing the necessity of maintaining a broad economic base and describing three component elements of military-technological prowess: (1) the quantity and quality of military equipment; (2) the technical skills and training of troops (once again reflecting military concern with the qualitative nature of their personnel); and (3) the organizational structure of the armed forces. The achievement of superiority along all these dimensions, he stated, would make the possessor capable of defeating the enemy.

Lest one be overly sanguine about the ease of gaining such an advantage, Bondarenko addressed this question directly:

> The achievement of quantitative and qualitative superiority over the enemy usually demands long industrial efforts. . . . although streamlining and perfecting existing machines is a necessary business, it is also important to break away more boldly from accepted schemes, to combine the development of old forms of equipment with a really revolutionary break with former views and ideas.[103]

He was equally concerned about the maintenance of superiority:

> The achievement of military-technological superiority of one side over another is no guarantee of its preservation in the future. The stern dialectics of development are that the struggle for superiority must be waged <u>continually</u>. Any weakening of attention in this field, excessive admiration of success achieved, might lead to a loss of superiority.[104]

While noting the difficulties involved in acquiring and maintaining such superiority, the article closed on an optimistic note, reassuring its military audience of the Party's complete commitment to the successful fulfillment of this considerable task.

> And our Party, while giving great attention to the development of the Soviet Army and Navy, constantly takes into account this circumstance [the difficulties of attaining superiority]. It proceeds from the fact that at the contemporary level of development of military affairs, the solution of the problem of maintaining military-technological

> superiority is only possible with the mobilization of all economic, technical-scientific and moral-political forces of the country.
>
> The Communist Party and its Central Committee are doing everything necessary for the constant strengthening of the defense potential of our country, for securing superiority both in military-technological and also in other areas of military affairs.[105]

Another lucid presentation of the military call for superiority was especially explicit regarding the anticipatory aspects of the problem in an era of rapid scientific advance and in the face of a resourceful and dangerous antagonist. Maj. Gen. (ret.) A. Lagovskiy,* writing just prior to the opening the bilateral Strategic Arms Limitation Talks between the Soviet Union and the United States in the fall of 1969, sounded a forceful reminder of the Soviet military's concern about military preparedness.[106] After a rather routine discussion concerning the importance of the material-technical base of the economy, Lagovskiy unearthed an appropriate quotation from Lenin to advance a strong demand for the continuing pursuit of military superiority.

> The technical equipment of an army is a highly important element of its combat capability and is the material basis of the art of war. V. I. Lenin pointed out that in contemporary wars, victory goes to those who have the greatest technology, the greatest level of organization, discipline, and the best equipment.
>
> At the same time Vladmir Ilyich taught us to pay the closest attention to the enemy's possibilities, study his strong and weak points and take the balance of forces into careful consideration. "Everyone will agree," V. I. Lenin wrote, "that the army that does not prepare itself to master all types of weapons and all means and methods of fighting that the enemy has or might have is behaving senselessly or even criminally."

---

*Maj. Gen. Lagovskiy is a veteran military economist whose major work was Strategiia i ekonomika [Strategy and economics] (Moscow: Voenizdat, 1961).

> Here special attention should be paid to the words "might have." They signify that it is essential to make an assessment of the military, economic, and scientific potential of a possible enemy on the basis of a careful study of both the existing situation and of future prospects. Only with such a sober and scientific approach to the matter is it possible to outline the correct way leading to the achievement of superiority over the enemy in the balance of forces.[107]

This article is particularly candid about the anticipatory nature of the quest for superiority. Its emphasis upon the "might have" aspect of enemy capabilities makes explicit the desire of the Soviet military to receive adequate budgetary support to permit the pursuit of military-technological superiority along a variety of lines of possible weapons development.

In addition to feature articles on the subject such as those quoted above, the call for superiority is regularly included within the speeches of military leaders and routine military science discussions.[108] An entry entitled "Military-Technological Superiority," which appeared in the second volume of the Soviet Military Encyclopedia in 1976, clearly reaffirmed the military's commitment to attain such superiority for the Soviet Union and its socialist allies over the "probable opponents," the imperialist blocs.[109] Once again, these public declarations are almost certainly accompanied by determined Soviet military efforts to convince the civilian Party leadership to embrace their point of view and provide the resources required to support a drive for clear-cut military superiority.

Organizational Autonomy. The primary institutional challenges to the autonomy of the Soviet military establishment have come from the Main Political Administration of the Soviet Army and Navy and the "special sections" of the KGB. Friction between the political officers of the MPA and the professional military has been very visible in the past. However, as argued in an earlier section of this chapter, this conflict appears to have abated considerably over the past two decades to the point that it has been largely transformed from confrontation over the direction of the military units into a largely cooperative relationship, albeit one that includes inevitable differences and recurrent friction over the time to be devoted to political study as opposed to that spent on operational work and training within the military establishment.

The KGB's counterintelligence sections implanted throughout the Soviet armed forces have not similarly assimilated. However, their activities appear to be largely restricted to guarding against subversion and espionage within the defense establishment. The "osobists" are very unlikely to concern themselves with the routine participation of military figures in the development of Soviet resource allocation, defense, and foreign policies,[110] where substantial room for policy contention appears to exist. Consequently, the special sections are likely to have little impact upon the parochial lobbying activities of the Ministry of Defense.

The most significant potential threat to military independence and autonomy lies in the top Party leadership. While routinely deferring to the guiding authority of the Central Committee and, tacitly, its Politburo, military spokesmen have clearly expressed their distaste for overactive involvement in military affairs by even the highest Party figures and the marshals have vigorously opposed such interference.

Nikita Khrushchev in particular earned himself the hearty dislike of many of the Soviet military leaders for his frequent interventions in their affairs. Khrushchev had himself formally designated as the "supreme commander-in-chief" of the armed forces* and reportedly established a personal office within the Ministry of Defense.[111] He repeatedly took a direct part in the shaping of military policy and personally challenged the marshals on such sensitive matters as military doctrine, the defense budget, and the size of the armed forces. In a classic expression of his attitude toward the military, Khrushchev stated in 1959, "I do not trust the appraisal of generals on questions of strategic importance."[112]

While intense military opposition to Khrushchev's defense policies was evident while he was in power,[113] the clearest indications of the depth of military dissatisfaction with his behavior surfaced after his fall. Marshal M. V. Zakharov, who had been fired by Khrushchev from the post of chief of the General Staff in March 1963, apparently as a result of disagreements with the first secretary

---

*Penkovskiy dates Khrushchev's assumption of this post from 1960. Oleg Penkovskiy, The Penkovskiy Papers, trans. Peter Deriabin (New York: Avon Books, 1966), p. 238. It was acknowledged by military figures on various occasions including Marshal Malinovskiy, in his address to the Twenty-second Party Congress, Pravda; October 25, 1961; Krasnaia Zvezda's greetings to Khrushchev on the occasion of his seventieth birthday, Krasnaia Zvezda, April 18, 1964; and Marshal Grechko in a similar birthday article in Izvestiia, April 17, 1964. Khrushchev himself claims he was granted this post by his colleagues in 1955. N. S. Khrushchev, Khrushchev Remembers: The Last Testament (Boston: Little, Brown, 1974), p. 12.

in the wake of the Cuban crisis of 1962, delivered a biting attack on unnamed "subjectivist" and "hare-brained" leaders.[114]

Zakharov perfunctorily acknowledged the leadership of the Party in military affairs, but at the same time he strongly presented the case for the independent military development of strategy and forces. He left no doubt about the major evil to be avoided when he sarcastically attacked "the so-called strategic farsightedness" of "persons who lack even a remote relationship to military strategy."[115] He continued, "With the emergence of rocket-nuclear arms, cybernetics, electronics and computers, any subjective approach to military problems, hare-brained plans, and superficiality can cause irreparable damage."[116]

Zakharov devoted the remainder of his article to the further development of the case for the avoidance of subjectivism and the wisdom of heeding the advice of Soviet military science.* His straightforward advocacy of the importance of maintaining an autonomous professional military establishment remains unparalleled to this day. Exchanges between military and Party spokesmen on the demarcation of Party and military responsibilities in the formulation of security policy have, however, continued to appear and have been discussed by various Western scholars.[117]

None of the oligarchs of the Brezhnev-Kosygin period have evidenced any desire to emulate Khrushchev's interventionary style regarding defense matters. While the Party leaders are by no means inclined to surrender complete control of military affairs to the marshals, they appear equally disinclined to personally dominate this area. Symbolic of this change, no individual has assumed the title of "supreme commander-in-chief" since Khrushchev's fall, although a 1967 article by Marshal Grechko was interpreted by some Western observers as a tentative endorsement of Brezhnev for the post.[118] The Soviet military remains jealously aware of its prerogatives and while fully accepting its ultimate subordination to the Party leadership, apparently seeks to maintain and probably to expand its sphere of independent and relatively autonomous activity.

<u>A Domestic Concern: Popular Attitudes toward the Military</u>. The major impact of the military establishment upon the Soviet domestic

---

*A similar attack on Khrushchev, which nevertheless stressed the continuing validity of Party leadership in military affairs, was presented by Col. I. P. Prusanov, "Improving the Organizing and Directing Influence of the Party in the Armed Forces, 1956-1964," <u>Voprosy Istorii KPSS</u> no. 2 (February 1965): 3-13.

political scene derives from its consumption of scarce resources and the consequent denial of these inputs to other potential consumers. In recent years, however, another form of military domestic involvement has become increasingly prominent. Faced with what may well be the inevitable growth of "amilitary" if not "antimilitary" sentiment among youth in a modern industrial state, the Soviet military has become deeply involved in an extensive campaign to encourage patriotism among its younger citizens.

Military leaders have frequently displayed a pronounced sensitivity concerning general societal attitudes toward the Soviet armed forces. In the wake of World War II, they came to enjoy a distinctly honored position in Soviet society as a result of their heroic efforts in defense of the country. This national esteem has been particularly evident with respect to the Soviet officer corps. They have traditionally enjoyed a variety of privileges, including high pay scales, special housing, stores, and clubs, abundant national honors, and considerable popular respect. Thus some Western observers have noted the "respectful attitudes" toward the military traditionally displayed by the crowds observing the traditional Red Square parades and of "the deference customarily paid high-ranking officers in trains, hotels, and other public places."[119]

However, over the past decade, the military has also been faced with the emergence of considerably less favorable sentiments among the general populace and particularly Soviet youth. Military spokesmen have unhappily noted the appearance of "pacifistic," "antiheroic," and downright "anti-military" sentiments in Soviet literature and films and among the nation's young people.[120]

In response to this turn of events, the Soviet military has become directly involved in a number of activities to counter this trend. These measures include frequent demands that writers and artists present "positive" portrayals of military life[121] and extensive military involvement in the creation and continuation of the national military-patriotic education campaign referred to earlier.

The current military-patriotic education campaign was initiated in the summer of 1964, with the establishment of some 49 military sports camps for youth.[122] The campaign was subsequently extended with the commitment of the Komsomol to year-round military indoctrination activities beginning in late 1965[123] and most importantly with the adoption of the revised Law on Universal Military Service in October 1967.[124]

The new Soviet conscription law lowered the draft age from 19 to 18 and shortened the terms of compulsory military service throughout the armed forces. At the same time it established an extensive preinduction military training program designed to compensate for the reduction in the period of active service. The leadership of this training is assigned to the Ministry of Defense, with DOSAAF, various educational ministries, the economic production ministries and the local Soviets and Party organizations all directly involved as well.[125] Responsibility for the supervision of this massive undertaking led to the creation of a Directorate for Civilian Military Training within the Ministry of Defense. In addition, large numbers of military reservists have been hired as instructors for the classroom instruction on military subjects that are conducted in schools, on farms, and in economic enterprises.[126]

The preinduction training measures are combined with the efforts of the national trade union organization, military veterans organizations, DOSAAF, the Komsomol, and the Young Pioneers in a broad movement known as the military-patriotic-education campaign. In an attempt to accomplish the task of "educating the whole population especially the younger generation, in the spirit of constant readiness for the defense of the Motherland,"[127] the Party and the Soviet military have sponsored such activities as youthful pilgrimages to historic battle sites, visits with veteran military heroes and active-duty servicemen, and annual military sports contests known as _tsarnitsa_ ("summer lightning").[128]

The entire military-patriotic education program represents a fortuitous convergence of interests between the Soviet military with its institutional concern for maintaining favorable popular attitudes toward the armed forces, and the Party, which is similarly motivated regarding the need to inculcate both national loyalty and a sense of discipline within Soviet youth. In light of this overlap, the Party has chosen to allow the military to expand significantly its visible involvement in Soviet domestic affairs. This program is also but a part of the continuous effort within the Soviet Union to perpetuate popular awareness concerning the enormous accomplishments and sacrifices of the nation during the Great Fatherland War (World War II). The regime's campaign in this regard manifests itself in the ceremonies surrounding anniversaries of various major victories during the war, the continued awarding of "hero city" designations over 30 years after the defeat of Nazi Germany, and the central place still accorded the war in Soviet art and literature.*

---

*For an excellent discussion of Soviet patriotism and the many facets of their fixation on World War II, see Hedrick Smith, _The Russians_ (New York: Quadrangle Books, 1976), pp. 302-25.

CONCLUSION

In sum, the Soviet military establishment appears to be a significant institutional entity within the Soviet political system that possesses a set of identifiable viewpoints on several foreign policy and domestic issues. Senior military figures and other military publicists regularly express similar opinions about the aggressive nature of imperialism and the military threat it poses, the possibility of victory in a nuclear war, the crucial importance of continued priority investment in heavy industry and defense, and the desirability of achieving military-technological superiority over all possible adversaries. Moreover, the Ministry of Defense takes an active interest in and strongly supports all efforts to propagate these views, national patriotism, and a general awareness and appreciation of things military among the populace in general and Soviet youth in particular.

In addition, as outlined above, the Soviet military appears to have been very successful not only in enhancing its own corporate self-awareness and popular appreciation of its role but also in strongly attenuating the significance of the Main Political Administration as an external checking agency under Party auspices. Over the years the MPA appears to have been gradually coopted by the military professionals so that its members, while specializing in a variety of ideological indoctrination, training, and morale functions, have come to view themselves as fellow career officers with pride in and shared responsibility for the military proficiency and combat readiness of the Soviet armed forces. Several of the senior indoctrinational specialists of the MPA have become prominent spokesmen for the Soviet military world view as identified in this chapter.

The officers and men of the Soviet military remain under the watchful scrutiny of the informers and career members of the Special Sections of the KGB. However, the business of the "osobists" appears to be that of combating crime and disloyalty or outright opposition to the CPSU and Soviet government. As a result, this network almost certainly has no impact upon the activities undertaken by military figures to promote the legitimate institutional interests of the Ministry of Defense or its various suborganizations within proper government or Party channels.

NOTES

1. Anthony Downs, Inside Bureaucracy (Boston: Little, Brown, 1967), p. 50.

2. Louis C. Gawthrop, Bureaucratic Behavior in the Executive Branch (New York: Free Press, 1969), p. 119.

3. Samuel P. Huntington, The Common Defense: Strategic Programs in National Politics (New York: Columbia University Press, 1961), p. 402.

4. Morton H. Halperin, "Why Bureaucrats Play Games," Foreign Policy 2 (Spring 1971): 76-88; Graham T. Allison, Essence of Decision: Explaining the Cuban Missile Crisis (Boston: Little, Brown, 1966), pp. 82, 167.

5. Samuel P. Huntington, The Soldier and the State: The Theory of Civil-Military Relations (New York: Vintage Books, 1964), pp. 59-79.

6. Ibid., p. 61.

7. Ibid.

8. Ibid., pp. 62-63.

9. Ibid., pp. 63-64.

10. Such analyses include M. D. Feld, "A Typology of Military Organization," in Public Policy: 1958, ed. C. J. Friedrick and S. E. Harris (Cambridge, Mass.: Graduate School of Public Administration, 1958), pp. 3-40; and Kurt Lang, "Military Organizations," in Handbook of Organizations, ed. James G. March (Chicago: Rand McNally & Co., 1965), pp. 838-74.

11. Huntington, The Soldier and the State, pp. 64-70.

12. Ibid., p. 67.

13. Alain C. Enthoven and K. Wayne Smith, How Much is Enough? (New York: Harper and Row, 1971), p. 5.

14. Huntington, The Common Defense, pp. 298-312, 369-85.

15. Roman Kolkowicz, The Soviet Military and the Communist Party (Princeton, N.J.: Princeton University Press, 1967), p. 107. Kolkowicz repeats this listing with only minor modifications in his "The Military," in Interest Groups in Soviet Politics, ed. H. Gordon Skilling and Franklyn Griffiths (Princeton, N.J.: Princeton University Press, 1971), p. 141.

16. Kolkowicz, The Soviet Military and the Communist Party, p. 107.

17. Ibid., pp. 107-08. In his later article in Skilling and Griffiths, op. cit., Kolkowicz includes only the first point (p. 141).

18. Vernon V. Aspaturian, "Internal Politics and Foreign Policy in the Soviet System," in Approaches to Comparative and International Politics, ed. R. Barry Farrell (Evanston, Ill.: Northwestern University Press, 1966), p. 266. Also reprinted in Vernon V. Aspaturian, ed., Process and Power in Soviet Foreign Policy (Boston: Little, Brown, 1971), pp. 534, 535.

19. Morris Janowitz, The Professional Soldier: A Social and Political Portrait (Glencoe, Ill.: The Free Press, 1960), pp. 233-56.

20. Bengt Abrahamsson, "The Ideology of an Elite: Conservatism and National Insecurity: Some Notes on the Swedish Military," in Armed Forces and Society: Sociological Essays, ed. Jacques Van Doorn (The Hague: Mouton, 1968), pp. 71-83; B. Abrahamsson, "Military Professionalization and Estimates on the Probability of War," in Military Profession and Military Regimes: Commitments and Conflicts, ed. Jacques Van Doorn (The Hague: Mouton, 1969), pp. 35-51.

21. John Lovell, "The Professional Socialization of the West Point Cadet," in The New Military, ed. Morris Janowitz (New York: Russell Sage Foundation, 1964), pp. 119-57; Charles L. Cochran, "Midshipmen Political Characterization and Academy Socialization," in Associates of the Department of Political Science, U.S. Naval Academy, Civil-Military Relations: Changing Concepts in the Seventies (New York: Free Press, 1974); Peter Karsten et al., "'Professional' and 'Citizen' Officers: A Comparison of Service Academy and ROTC Officer Candidates," in Public Opinion and the Military Establishment, ed. Charles C. Moskos (Beverly Hills, Calif.: Sage Publications, 1971), pp. 37-61.

22. Col. V. Serebryannikov, "The 'Convergence' Theory in Military Uniform," Krasnaia Zvezda, July 8, 1971.

23. Lt. Gen. A. E. Khmel', Partino-politicheskaia rabota v sovetskikh vooruzhennykh silakh [Party-Political work in the Soviet armed forces] (Moscow: Voenizdat, 1968), pp. 46, 47.

24. M. Kh. Kalashnik, Politorgany i partiinyye organizatskii Sovetskoi Armii i Voenno--Morskovo Flota [Political organs and Party organizations of the Soviet army and navy] (Moscow: Izdatelstvo VPSh i AON pri TsK KPSS, 1963), p. 16.

25. Downs, op. cit., pp. 148-53.

26. Kolkowicz, The Soviet Military and the Communist Party, pp. 15-35, 101-73; Louis Nemzer, Conflicting Patterns of Civil-Military Relations in the USSR, RAC-TP-142 (McLean, Virginia: Research Analysis Corporation, 1964), passim.

27. Raymond A. Bauer, Alex Inkeles, and Clyde Kluckhohn, How the Soviet System Works (New York: Vintage Books, 1956), p. 64; Zbigniew Brzezinski, ed., Political Controls in the Soviet Army (New York: Research Program on the USSR, 1954), p. 32; Derek J. R. Scott, Russian Political Institutions (New York: Praeger, 1961), p. 155.

28. Christopher D. Jones, "The 'Revolution in Military Affairs' and Politico-Military Relations, 1965-70," Survey 20, no. 1 (Winter 1974): 91, 99.

29. See Col. Gen. M. Kalashnik, "Ideological Work Among the Troops Must be Brought to the Level of the Demands of the 24th CPSU Congress," Krasnaia Zvezda, November 16, 1971;

Maj. Gen. S. Ilin, "Certain Questions of Educating Servicemen," Krasnaia Zvezda, February 17, 1972; Gen. A. Yepishev, "Leninism --The Basis of the Education of Soviet Soldiers," Kommunist 6 (June 1969): 60-71; and Maj. Gen. S. Ilin, "The Contemporary Development of the Armed Forces and Some Questions of Troop Indoctrination," Kommunist Vooruzhennykh Sil (hereafter cited as KVS) no. 18 (September 1976): 33-41. John Erickson argues that this increased emphasis upon political officer involvement in combat tasks has been prompted by the MPA's desire to maintain a viable role in the face of rapid technological change within the military establishment. John Erickson, Soviet Military Power (London: Royal United Services Institute, 1971), p. 89.

30. Commander Richard W. Bates, "Communist Party Control in the Soviet Navy," U.S. Naval Institute Proceedings 20, no. 3 (October 1967): 27; Col. V. Kommissarov and Col. G. Murusov, "Political Worker--High Professional Training," KVS no. 13 (July 1966): 41-47.

31. Fritz Ermarth, "Soviet Military Politics," Military Review 63, no. 1 (January 1968): 34. Victor Zorza, a leading British Kremlinologist, similarly observed with respect to General Yepishev, head of the MPA: "General Yepishev, a civilian Party official who was put among the marshals by Mr. Khrushchev to ensure their political loyalty has over the years acquired more and more the coloring of the military milieu. His speeches suggest that he is now the representative of the military in the political leadership rather than the other way around as Mr. Khrushchev intended." "The Marshals Get the Message," Manchester Guardian Weekly, November 7, 1970.

32. See Col. M. Lisenkov, "The Party Congress Decisions for the Soldiers," Krasnaia Zvezda, July 11, 1971, for a summary of the diverse publications of the Military Publishing House in the wake of the Twentieth-fourth Party Congress.

33. Marshal V. D. Sokolovskiy, ed., Voennaia strategiia [Military strategy] (Moscow: Voenizdat, 1962), p. 2.

34. Pravda, November 8, 1963.

35. Maj. Gen. K. Bochkarev and Col. I. Sidel'nikov, "New Age, New Conclusions: On the Development of the Party of V. I. Lenin's Ideas on War, Peace and on Safeguarding the Conquests of Socialism and Communism," Krasnaia Zvezda, January 21, 1965.

36. Pravda, April 3, 1966.

37. "The Fiftieth Anniversary of the Soviet Armed Forces," Voenno-Istoricheskii Zhurnal [Military history journal] no. 2 (February 1968): 12.

38. "Imperialism is Aggression and Brigandage," editorial, Krasnaia Zvezda, September 27, 1969.

39. Pravda, April 3, 1971.

40. Maj. Gen. Ye. Sulimov, "A Policy of Active Counteraction to Aggression," Krasnaia Zvezda, June 1, 1971.

41. Krasnaia Zvezda, March 24, 1972.

42. Krasnaia Zvezda, July 1, 1976.

43. Examples include Col. G. Gorelov, "The Aggressive Preparations of the Imperialism of the USA in the Far East," KVS no. 3 (February 1964): 82-86; Lt. Col. T. Kondratkov, "Imperialism--Source of War: Imperialist Aggressors Headed by the USA Are the Worst Enemy of Peace and Security of Peoples," KVS no. 18 (September 1968): 68-73; V. Vinogradov, "They Are Encouraging the Aggressor," Krasnaia Zvezda, March 12, 1972.

44. See D. Melnikov, "West German Imperialism--Threat to Peace in Europe," KVS no. 8 (April 1961): 74-77; Col. S. Malyanchikov, "Bonn Strategy of Revanchism," KVS no. 8 (April 1967): 80-84; V. Levin, "In Revanchist Gear," KVS no. 22 (November 1969): 75-79.

45. References to the aggressiveness of West German revanchism continue to appear occasionally in major speeches or editorials; see editorial, Krasnaia Zvezda, April 27, 1972. Recent feature articles in the Soviet military press on West German affairs concentrate on the reactionary elements within the country rather than the wholesale condemnation of the West German state. Cf. D. Imanskiy, "The Preachers of Dangerous Tradition," Krasnaia Zvezda, May 5, 1972, discussing the survival of the revanchist outlook in certain Bundeswehr military circles. See also Col. O. Rubtsov, "Captive of Old Illusions," KVS no. 17 (August 1972): 81-85; Col. A. Markov, B kazarmakh Bundesvera [In the barracks of the bundeswehr] (Moscow: Voenizdat, 1971); Col. O. Rubtsov, "What Attitudes Are Being Created in the Bundeswehr?" Krasnaia Zvezda, March 8, 1974; and D. Umanskiy, "Dangerous Aspirations," Krasnaia Zvezda, January 31, 1975.

46. Cf. Col. M. Petrov, "Aggression in the Near East," KVS no. 13 (July 1967): 77-80; G. Nikitina, "The Poisonous Sting of Zionism," Krasnaia Zvezda, July 3, 1971; R. Vasilyev, "Tel Aviv's Impudent Provocations," Krasnaia Zvezda, March 1, 1972; Col. N. Pokormyak, "In the Service of Internationalism and Zionism," KVS no. 9 (May 1972): 78-82; A. Zakharov, "The Near East: A Time of Changes," Krasnaia Zvezda, January 3, 1974; N. V. Pokormyak, Armiia Izraela--instrument imperialisticheskoi aggressii [The Army of Israel--instrument of imperialist aggression] (Moscow: Voenizdat, 1977).

47. Cf. Col. E. Ivanov, "CENTO--Arm of Aggression of the Imperialists in the Near and Middle East," KVS no. 3 (February 1967): 75-79; Col. V. Mochalov, "The Criminal Course of NATO

Strategy," KVS no. 17 (September 1962): 86-90; Maj. Gen. R. Simoyan, "Imperialism's Bloc Strategy: A Survival of the 'Cold War,'" Krasnaia Zvezda, March 30, 1972; Col. Yu. Yerashov, "NATO: In the Trenches of the 'Cold War,'" KVS no. 8 (April 1973): 81-85; Col. Yu. Yerashov, "NATO Against Detente," KVS no. 5 (March 1977): 87-92.

48. Cf. Col. P. Trifonenkov, "War and Politics," Krasnaia Zvezda, October 30, 1963; D. Volskiy and V. Kudriavtsev, "Practical Reality and the Fantasies of the Splitters," Krasnaia Zvezda, October 10, 1963; Col. P. Trifonenkov, "The Most Vital Problem of the Present Day and the Adventurism of the Chinese Dogmatists," KVS no. 21 (November 1963): 23-29; Maj. Gen. N. Ya. Sushko and Maj. T. Kondratkov, "War and Politics in the Nuclear Age," KVS no. 2 (January 1964): 16-23. Vice Adm. V. Shelyag and Lt. Col. T. Kondratkov, "Leninist Analysis of the Essence of War and Shortcomings of Its Critics," KVS no. 12 (June 1970): 15.

49. Cf. Yu. Andreev, "Militaristic Fumes in Peking," Krasnaia Zvezda, January 21, 1970; I. Yelenin and A. Pamor, "The Militarization of Social Life in China," Krasnaia Zvezda, February 25, 1972; N. Konstantinov, "The Antisocialist Essence of the Ideology of Maoism," KVS no. 5 (March 1972): 17-24; Lt. Col. Buturlinov, "The Ideology and Policy of Maoism," Krasnaia Zvezda, December 13, 1974; Col. V. N. Alekseyev, Antimarkisistskaia sushnost' voennoy politiki Maoistov [The anti-Marxist essence of Maoist military policy] (Moscow: Voenizdat, 1973); B. Gorbachev, "The Army in the Service of the Maoist Dictatorship, Krasnaia Zvezda, September 11, 1975; B. Pospelov, "The World Revolutionary Movement and the Schemes of the Maoists," KVS no. 15 (August 1976): 78-82.

50. Zimmerman, p. 223.

51. Ibid., pp. 215-41. For a discussion of the Institute for the Study of the USA and its monthly journal SShA: Ekonomika, Politika, Ideologiia [USA: economics, politics, and ideology] see Merle Fainsod, "Through Soviet Eyes," Problems of Communism 19 (November-December 1970): 59-64.

52. Cf. Col. I. Sidel'nikov, "Peaceful Coexistence and the People's Security," Krasnaia Zvezda, August 14, 1973; V. Berezin, "America's All Pervading Complex," Krasnaia Zvezda, May 17, 1974; Col. V. Larionov, "The Relation of Tension and the Principle of Equal Security," Krasnaia Zvezda, July 18, 1974; V. Vinograd, "A Rise for the Pentagon," Krasnaia Zvezda, August 28, 1974.

53. Cf. Col. V. Vasin, "The Antipopular Essence of the Capitalist Controlled Economy," KVS no. 15 (1964): 49-54; B. Sashin, "In the Power of the Military Industrial Octopus," KVS no. 17 (September 1967): 78-83; Capt. First Rank I. Shtukaturov, "Mili-

tarization of the U.S. Economy and Crises," KVS no. 13 (July 1974): 77-82; B. D. Pyadyshev, Voenno-promyshlennyy kompleks SShA [The military-industrial complex of the USA] (Moscow: Voenizdat, 1974).

54. Col. V. T. Emel'ianov, ed., Organizatsiia i vooruzhenie armii i flotov kapitalisticheskikh gosudarstv [Organization and armaments of the armies and fleets of the capitalist states] (Moscow: Voenizdat, 1965). An updated second edition was published in 1968.

55. See Chapter 2, "The Military Strategy of the Imperialist States and Their Preparation of New Wars," in all three editions of Marshal V. D. Sokolovskiy's Voennaia strategiia [Military strategy].

56. The topical headings used for these articles in Aviatsiia i Kosmonavtika [Aviation and cosmonautics], the monthly journal of the Soviet air forces: Vestnik Protivo-Vozdushnoi Oborony [Herald of the air defense forces]; and Voennyi Vestnik [Military herald], the monthly of the ground forces; and in Krasnaia Zvezda and Kommunist Vooruzhennykh Sil, respectively.

57. See Maj. T. Kondratkov, "Advocates of Aggression," Krasnaia Zvezda, August 24, 1966; and Marksizm-Leninizm o voine i armii [Marxism-Leninish on war and the army], 4th ed., ed. Maj. Gen. N. Ya. Shushko and Col. S. A. Tyushkevich (Moscow: Voenizdat, 1965), pp. 12-15.

58. For an historical review of Soviet warfare typologies, see Thomas W. Wolfe, Communist Outlook on War, P-3640 (Santa Monica, Calif.: RAND Corporation, 1967), pp. 18-28.

59. Military articles making these points included Col. P. Trifonenkov, "War and Politics," Krasnaia Zvezda, October 30, 1963, as well as his "The Most Pressing Problem of the Present Day and the Adventurism of the Chinese Dogmatists," KVS no. 21 (November 1963): 23-28; and Marshal S. Biriuzov, "Politics and Nuclear Weapons," Izvestiia, December 11, 1963. For more detailed descriptions of the Sino-Soviet exchanges on these matters, see Wolfe, Communist Outlook on War, pp. 33-37.

60. Pravda, February 15, 1956.

61. Boris Dimitriev, "Brass Hats: Peking and Clausewitz," Izvestiia, September 24, 1963.

62. Interview, Col. V. Kulish (Soviet Army, ret.), chief of Military Affairs Section of the Institute of World Economics and International Affairs of the Soviet Academy of Sciences, Princeton, New Jersey, March 24, 1970.

63. These include Col. I. Sidel'nikov, "V. I. Lenin on the Class Approach in Determining the Nature of Wars," Krasnaia Zvezda, September 22, 1965; and Lt. Col. G. Teliatnikov, "Capability and Reality in Combat," KVS no. 24 (December 1965): 38-43;

in addition to the important articles by Lt. Col. E. Rybkin and Col. I. Grudinin, which are covered in some detail below. See Benjamin S. Lambeth, "The Politics of the Soviet Military Under Brezhnev and Kosygin," master's thesis, George Washington University, Washington, D.C., 1968, pp. 49-79, 85-91, for a comprehensive and penetrating analysis of the exchange of military-Party opinion on the likelihood and nature of war during 1965-67.

64. Rybkin was expressly criticizing Talenskiy's views as put forward in "Reflections on the Last War," International Affairs no. 5 (May 1965): 23. However, this viewpoint suffused Talenskiy's prolific writings throughout the 1958-65 period. Rybkin also attacked the similar views on the political uselessness of nuclear war expressed by historian N. Nikol'skiy in Osnovnoi vopros sovremennosti [The basic problem of our time] (Moscow: Izdatel'stvo IMO, 1964), p. 381.

65. Lt. Col. E. Rybkin, "On the Essence of World Rocket-Nuclear War," KVS no. 17 (September 1965): 50-56. For an analysis of this article and an English translation, see Roman Kolkowicz, The Red "Hawks" on the Rationality of Nuclear War, RM-4899-PR (Santa Monica, Calif.: RAND Corporation, 1966).

66. Ibid., p. 55.

67. Col. I. Grudinin, "On the Question of the Essence of War: The Merits and Shortcomings of a Certain Lecture," Krasnaia Zvezda, July 21, 1966.

68. Ibid.

69. Ibid.

70. "Theory, Politics, Ideology: On the Essence of War," Krasnaia Zvezda, January 24, 1967.

71. Ibid.

72. Fritz Ermarth, Soviet Military Politics Under Brezhnev and Kosygin (Munich: Radio Free Europe, May 16, 1967), p. 39.

73. The Military Balance: 1976-1977 (London: International Institute of Strategic Studies, 1976), p. 10.

74. For a comprehensive discussion of these security formations and their functions, see James T. Reitz, "Soviet Defense-Associated Activities Outside the Ministry of Defense," in Economic Performance and the Military Burden in the Soviet Union, Joint Economic Committee, Congress of the United States (Washington, D.C.: Government Printing Office, 1970), pp. 133-41.

75. Jan Triska, ed., Soviet Communism: Programs and Rules (San Francisco: Chandler Publishing Co., 1962), p. 105.

76. Pravda, April 9, 1966.

77. Pravda, April 11, 1971.

78. Pravda, March 8, 1976.

79. Cf. Gen. V. Kurasov, "Problems of Soviet Military Science in the Works of V. I. Lenin," Voenno-Istoricheskii Zhurnal no. 3 (March 1961): 3-14; Col. I. Koleshov and Lt. Col. B. Duzenko, "Leninist General Line of the CPSU--The Firm Basis of Communist Construction," KVS no. 23 (December 1965): 47-53; Col. Yu. Vlasevich, "Modern War and the Economy," KVS no. 12 (June 1967): 27-33.

80. V. Sinyagin, "The Creation of the Material-Technical Base of Communism and Strengthening the Defense Capability of the USSR," KVS no. 14 (July 1962): 10.

81. B. Volchkov, "Problems of Defending the Achievements of Socialism: The Foundation of the Country's Defense Might," Krasnaia Zvezda, November 17, 1971.

82. Milton C. Lodge, Soviet Elite Attitudes Since Stalin (Columbus, Ohio: Charles E. Merrill, 1969), pp. 79, 80.

83. Ibid., pp. 80-82.

84. N. Lagutin, "The Building of Communism, Theory and Practice: The Well-Being of the People is Our Supreme Task," Krasnaia Zvezda, January 22, 1970.

85. Ibid. For additional references in the military press on the need to combine defense spending with investment to improve the well-being of the masses, see Gen. A. A. Yepishev, "Important Landmark on the Path to Communism," Krasnaia Zvezda, April 16, 1971; editorial, "The Economic Foundation of the Motherland's Defense," Krasnaia Zvezda, February 13, 1971; F. Kotov, "Structural Changes in the Country's Economy," Krasnaia Zvezda, November 30, 1971; and Col. M. Khitrenko, "The Economic Strategy of the Party in the Contemporary Stage," KVS no. 8 (April 1976): 19-32.

86. Col. M. Gladkov and B. Ivanov, "The Economy and Military-Technical Policy," KVS no. 9 (May 1972): 15.

87. Col. S. Baranov, "The Material Foundation of the Might of the USSR Armed Forces," Krasnaia Zvezda, March 5, 1971.

88. Pravda, June 11, 1966. For similar comments by Kosygin see Pravda, August 4, 1966 and his interview in Life, February 2,, 1968, p. 32.

89. Volchokov, Krasnaia Zvezda, November 17, 1971. See also Maj. Gen. M. Cherednichenko, "Modern War and the Economy," KVS no. 18 (September 1971): 27.

90. Col. I. Prokhorenko, "Economic Training of Military Engineers," KVS no. 5 (March 1966): 47-51; Col. Gen. A. Tsirlin, "Problems of the Economic Training of Military Engineering Cadres," KVS no. 22 (November 1966): 17-21.

91. Cf. P. V. Sokolov, ed., Voenno-ekonomicheskie voprosy v kurse politekonomii [Military-economic questions in a course on political economy] (Moscow: Voenizdat, 1968), pp. 279-98; Yu. S. Solnyshkov, Optimizatsiia vybora vooruzhenii [Optimization of the selection of armaments] (Moscow: Voenizdat, 1968); Maj. Gen. M. I. Cherednichenko, "Economics and Military-Technological Policy," KVS no. 15 (August 1968): 15; Col. Yu. Vlas'evich, "On the Dynamic Tendencies of Military-Economic Expenditure," KVS no. 16 (August 1970): 21; Maj. Gen. N. Ya. Sushko and Lt. Col. I. Kondratkov, eds., Metodologicheskie problemy voennoi teorii i praktaki [Methodological problems of military theory and practice] (Moscow: Voenizdat, 1966), pp. 243-65.

92. For a comprehensive discussion of the military economy campaign see David Holloway, Technology, Management and the Soviet Military Establishment, Adelphi Papers no. 76 (London: Institute of Strategic Studies, April 1971), pp. 32-38.

93. Speech by Dr. Abel Aganbegian, director of Novosibirsk Economics Institute; unpublished within the Soviet Union, appeared as an unsigned article in Bandiera Rossa [Red banner], Rome, July 1965, p. 6.

94. John P. Hardt, The Future Role of the Soviet Central Planner (McLean, Va.: Research Analysis Corporation, July 1964), pp. 5-10; Stanley H. Cohn, "The Economic Burden of Soviet Defense Outlays," in Economic Performance and the Military Burden in the Soviet Union, 1970, pp. 166-81; Richard Armstrong, "Military-Industrial Complex: Russian Style," Fortune, August 1, 1969, pp. 84-87, 124-26.

95. N. S. Khrushchev, "Address before Supreme Soviet," Pravda, January 15, 1960.

96. Cf. Maj. Gen. V. Kruchinin, "Why Mass Armies?" Krasnaia Zvezda, January 11, 1963; Gen. A. A. Yepishev, "The Growing Role of the CPSU in the Leadership of the Armed Forces," Voprosy Istorii KPSS [Problems of history of the CPSU] no. 2 (February 1963): 10; Lt. Col. G. Miftiev, "The Revolution in Military Affairs: Its Significance and Consequences," Krasnaia Zvezda, June 4, 1965; Marshal V. D. Sokolovskiy, ed., Voennaia strategiia [Military strategy], 3d ed. rev. (Moscow: Voenizdat, 1968), p. 295.

97. Cf. Marshal A. A. Grechko, Address to Twenty-fourth Party Congress, Pravda, April 3, 1971; Gen. A. A. Yepishev, "Soviet Armed Forces Prepare for the Party Congress," Kommunist no. 3 (February 1971): 68.

98. Cf. editorial, "Prepare Young People to Defend the Motherland," Krasnaia Zvezda, February 11, 1971; Marshal I. Konev, "Relay the Baton of Heroic Deeds," Izvestiia, November 15, 1969.

The military-patriotic education campaign is examined in greater detail later in this chapter under "Organizational Autonomy."

99. Leon Gouré, The Military Indoctrination of Soviet Youth (New York: National Strategy Information Center, 1973), passim; William E. Odom, "The Militarization of Soviet Society," Problems of Communism (September-October 1976): 34-51.

100. This is the title of Thomas W. Wolfe's chapter on this subject in Soviet Strategy at the Crossroads, pp. 79-90, which contains a detailed discussion of Soviet military pronouncements about superiority 1960-64.

101. Lt. Col. V. M. Bondarenko, "Military-Technological Superiority--The Most Important Factor in the Reliable Defense of the Country," KVS no. 17 (September 1966): 7-14. For a detailed analysis of this article see Benjamin S. Lambeth, The Argument for Superiority: A New Voice in the Soviet Strategic Debate, N-419R (Arlington, Va.: Institute for Defense Analysis, January 1967).

102. Bondarenko, op. cit., p. 8.

103. Ibid., p. 11.

104. Ibid., p. 12.

105. Ibid., p. 14.

106. Maj. Gen. (ret.) A. Lagovskiy, "Lenin and the Defense of the Gains of Socialism: The State's Economy and its Military Might," Krasnaia Zvezda, September 25, 1959.

107. Ibid.

108. Cf. Marshal A. A. Grechko, "On Guard of Peace and Socialism," Kommunist no. 3 (March 1970): 57; Col. S. Vovk, "A Powerful Factor of Defense Capability," Krasnaia Zvezda, June 25, 1970; Maj. Gen. M. Cherednickhenko, "Economics and Military-Technological Policy," KVS no. 15 (August 1968): 11-13.

109. Sovetskaya voennaia entsiklopediia [Soviet military encyclopedia], vol. 2 (Moscow: Voenizdat, 1976), p. 253.

110. Interview, Nicholas Shadrin, former Soviet naval officer, Washington, D.C., March 24, 1975.

111. Penkovskiy, op. cit., p. 238.

112. Khrushchev to a Kremlin Press Conference, November 8, 1959, cited in Raymond D. Senter, "Khrushchev, the Generals and Goldwater," The New Republic, November 21, 1964, p. 8.

113. Cf. Wolfe, Soviet Strategy at the Crossroads, passim, and Raymond L. Garthoff, "Khrushchev and the Military," in Politics in the Soviet Union, ed. A. Dallin and A. F. Westin (New York: Harcourt, Brace, and World, 1966), pp. 243-73.

114. Marshal M. V. Zakharov, "The Imperative Demand of Our Time," Krasnaia Zvezda, February 4, 1965.

115. Ibid.

116. Ibid.

117. See Lambeth, "The Politics of the Soviet Military Under Brezhnev and Kosygin," pp. 94-135; Ermarth, pp. 5-19.

118. Marshal A. Grechko, "The Triumph of Leninist Ideas about the Defense of Socialist Society," KVS no. 20 (October 1967): 37. Some confusion exists regarding who should occupy the post of supreme commander-in-chief even during wartime. This was evidenced in the elimination of a sentence in the third edition of Sokolovskiy's _Voennaia strategiia_ that had appeared in the previous two. The missing sentence had stated that in wartime the highest agency of command, the Stavka, would be headed by the first secretary of the Party and the head of government, who would assume the title of supreme commander-in-chief. See Sokolovskiy, ed., _Voennaia strategiia_, 2d ed., p. 474; 3d ed., p. 434. For a discussion of this shift, see Holloway, op. cit., pp. 9, 10.

119. Thomas W. Wolfe, "The Military," in _Prospects for Soviet Society_, ed. Allan Kassof (New York: Praeger, 1968), p. 125.

120. Ibid., p. 133-35; Kolkowicz, _The Soviet Military and the Communist Party_, pp. 318-19.

121. These demands have been made in numerous articles, for example, Lt. Gen. V. Ya. Golovin, "The Writer and the Army," _Krasnaia Zvezda_, September 6, 1969, and Col. B. Sapunov, "Literature and Art: The Ideological Front of Struggle," _KVS_ no. 2 (January 1971): 16-22, in the direct appeals of major military figures as in the addresses of Marshal Malinovskiy and General Yepishev to a group of Soviet writers and artists in February 1964, _Krasnaia Zvezda_, February 9, 1964, and in the joint message of Marshal Grechko and General Yepishev on the fiftieth anniversary of Soviet cinema, _Krasnaia Zvezda_, August 29, 1969; Col. B. Sapunov, "Literature, Art: The Ideological Front of the Struggle," _KVS_ no. 2 (January 1971): 16-22.

122. Marshal I. Konev, "Relay the Baton of Heroic Deeds," _Izvestiia_, November 15, 1969.

123. Ibid.

124. "USSR Law on Universal Military Service," _Izvestiia_, October 13, 1967.

125. Ibid. See also "Council on Military and Patriotic Education," _Krasnaia Zvezda_, December 15, 1970, and Gouré, op. cit., pp. 14-60.

126. The most comprehensive discussion of this program and the military-patriotic education campaign in general is found in Herbert Goldhammer, _The Soviet Soldier: Soviet Military Management at the Troop Level_ (New York: Crane, Russak, 1975), pp. 39-88.

127. General A. A. Yepishev, "Faithful to Lenin's Behests," Izvestiia, February 23, 1969.

128. Lt. Gen. A. I. Odintsov, "The Basic Training of Youth," Krasnaia Zvezda, July 9, 1968; Lt. Gen. N. Demin, "Leninist Universal Military Training and DOSAAF's Tasks," Krasnaia Zvezda, September 24, 1969; editorial, "Preparing Young People to Defend the Motherland," Krasnaia Zvezda, February 11, 1971.

CHAPTER

4

SOVIET STRATEGIC THOUGHT

The defense policy of any state includes two fundamental and interrelated elements, force posture and military doctrine. Force posture refers to the aggregate of military capabilities available to the state measured in terms of the quantitative levels of its military manpower and various weapons systems, the qualitative characteristics of these elements of military strength, and the pattern of their geographic deployment. Military doctrine encompasses the body of officially adopted concepts that guide a state in the procurement, deployment, and exercise of its military capabilities.

A state's defense policy is importantly influenced by a number of factors. These include the foreign policy objectives of the nation; its geographic characteristics; the international environment in which it finds itself, in terms of both the attitudes and capabilities of other states; the scientific, technological, and industrial resources at its disposal; its historical traditions; and the availability of resource support for defense programs from within the domestic arena.

Defense policies have often been examined according to what Graham Allison has called the unitary, "rational actor" form of analysis.[1] According to this model, the state is treated as if it were a single, value-maximizing individual who possesses a clearly defined hierarchy of foreign policy objectives. This personified state is credited with examining the international environment, its own objectives, and its available technological and monetary resources and then proceeding to elaborate a comprehensive and integrated military doctrine that most rationally links these considerations. This military doctrine in turn is purported to serve as the authoritative blueprint that guides the development of the nation's force posture and its deployment and application of military capabilities in the pursuit of the state's security objectives.

While doctrine and force posture are clearly interrelated and mutually influenced by external circumstances and internal considerations, the idealized rational actor model fails to take note of two essential aspects of this complex interdependence. For one thing, all estimates of foreign and domestic priorities are inherently uncertain and thus are subject to widely varying interpretations and preferences. Additionally, the selection of the most appropriate policies and programs to promote even an agreed-upon objective is similarly an indeterminant problem with a myriad of possible solutions.[2]

In light of these circumstances the defense policies of nations are generally produced not by the elaboration of a sweeping master plan that provides specific guidance for the numerous subordinate policy areas but rather are the result of an ongoing and intensely competitive political process. The potential for differing interpretations and preferences in the complex area of national security policy is generally realized in that conflicting policy recommendations are often championed by specific individuals and groups. These participants, with their differing perceptions, purposes, and preferences, frequently become involved in recurrent pulling and hauling over the basic direction and substantive content of the state's military policy.

The process is further complicated by the extended time period over which military policies typically develop. Force postures and military doctrines generally emerge as the product of a series of disjointed and incremental decisions rather than as the result of a single cardinal choice by a nation's leadership. Moreover, the assignment of a particular mission responsibility or the development and deployment of a single weapons system are likely to emerge from a number of separate decisions, many of which are accompanied by political bargaining and frequently involve significant compromise.

The operation of normal bureaucratic routines also affects the shape of a nation's policy. The variety of incremental decisions noted above is likely to be shaped importantly by such organizational factors as the routine action channels that define the participants within particular types of decisions as well as influencing the information and expertise available to these participants.

Within this study, emphasis is placed upon the political processes that underlie the development of Soviet force posture and military doctrine. Both the Soviet doctrinal guidelines for the application of its military power and the panoply of weapons possessed by the Soviet armed forces appear to represent the outcomes of extended bargaining and political maneuvering among a variety of interested institutions--the military services, sections of the General Staff, the major military academies, the weapons design teams, and assembly plants of the industrial ministries engaged in defense production--and several key individuals including those Politburo members and Party secretaries directly responsible for defense matters, the minister of defense, the chief of the General Staff, and the leaders of the defense-industrial production effort.

Soviet military doctrine that provides the authoritative assignment of roles and missions within the military establishment and guidelines for the employment of military power is importantly related to the size, composition, and armament of the Soviet Armed Forces. However, this relationship appears to be as much a shaping of doctrine to accommodate and rationalize particular weapons systems as a result of the lobbying efforts of the various services, branches, and weapon designers, as it does the programmatic shaping of the services and weapons procurements in accordance with a single doctrinal design.*

MILITARY DOCTRINE AND MILITARY SCIENCE

Soviet writers draw an important distinction between military doctrine and military science. The two are differentiated both in terms of their relative authoritativeness as expressions of Soviet military policy, and with regard to the persons involved in their elaboration.

The scope and content of Soviet military doctrine have been discussed within military publications on numerous occasions. In The Dictionary of Basic Military Terms[3] compiled by the Voroshilov Academy of the General Staff, military doctrine is defined as:

> the system of scientifically based views officially accepted by the government on the character of modern war and the utilization within it of the

---

*Commenting on the interrelationship between Soviet force posture and military doctrine, Thomas W. Wolfe has observed: "This is not the case of having a well constructed doctrinal edifice and then adapting military forces to it. Rather for many reasons these forces develop in a certain way, whereupon one begins to fashion the doctrine to fit the already developed forces" and that "the doctrine is improvised to fit the circumstances which oblige it to accept a particular pattern of forces at a given time." Quoted in The Soviet Union, Arms Control and Disarmament: Background Materials on Soviet Attitudes, ed. George Fischer (New York: School of International Affairs, Columbia University, 1965), p. 318.

> armed forces and also the requirements for preparing the country and the armed forces for war that flow from these views.
>
> Military doctrine has two sides: political and military-technical. The basic contents of military doctrine are determined by the political and military leadership of the state in conformity with the social-political order and the level of development of the economy, science and technology and the military-technological armament of the armed forces of the country and also in light of the conclusions of military science and the views of the probable enemy.[4]

This definition highlights the important fact that military doctrine represents the authoritative military policy concepts adopted by the Soviet state. As such it must be approved by the highest political leadership, the members of the Communist Party's Politburo.[5] Its consideration within this arena makes possible the participation of a number of individuals and institutions from outside the military establishment. These civilian participants are identified and discussed in the institutional section of this chapter.

Within the Soviet scheme of things, military science is clearly subordinate to military doctrine. The _Dictionary of Basic Military Terms_ defines military science as "the system of knowledge about the nature, essence and content of armed struggle, about the forces, means and manners of conducting combat activities by the armed forces and about their comprehensive maintenance."[6] While concerned with the same problems covered by military doctrine, military science deals more flexibly with these issues, permitting and even encouraging a variety of contending viewpoints on various issues. In contrast, Soviet military doctrine represents a single officially sanctioned set of military policy guidelines.[7]

Military science includes a number of constituent elements. The most central of these is military art which embodies "the theory and practice of conducting battle, operations and armed struggle as a whole."[8] Military art is in turn divided into three parts according to the scope and complexity of the military operations being studied. These divisions are _strategy_, the most comprehensive of the three, dealing with the overall planning, preparation, and conduct of war; _operational art_, which is concerned with the theory and practice of warfare at the "front" level, that is involving the largest of the Soviet combat formations; and _tactics_, the preparation for and handling of smaller combat elements in actual battle.[9] Among these, military strategy is frequently singled out as the most important field of military scientific study.

The relationship between strategy and doctrine has been frequently discussed. The authors of Military Strategy, the major text on Soviet military thought that was published in three editions during the 1960s, described it as follows:

> Military strategy occupies a subordinate position in regard to military doctrine. Military doctrine determines the overall policy in principle, while military strategy, starting from this overall policy develops and investigates concrete problems dealing with the nature of future war, the preparation of the country for war, the organization of the armed forces and the methods of warfare.[10]

From a somewhat different perspective, a military historian, Colonel A. A. Strokov, wrote this about the relationships between military doctrine, military science, and strategy:

> Military doctrine is based on military scientific researches and it is inseparably linked with military science. Military doctrine must not be considered as a part of military science. Military science lies at the basis of military doctrine; however not solely.
>
> Military doctrine in these questions is based on the achievements of military strategy (the theory and practice of strategy). The positions of military strategy which are adopted become overall government positions, that is, they go into military doctrine.[11]

In another collective military volume, the entire group of concepts is interconnected in this manner: "In its character military doctrine is the link connecting military science with political practice and through the practice of military affairs with military art, primarily military strategy."[12]

Institutionally, the development of military science and its various components falls almost fully under the purview of the military establishment. It involves such disparate elements as the study of Marxist-Leninist writings on war and society, military historical research, and the examination of the contemporary political and military situation. These tasks are accomplished almost exclusively by officers working within various parts of the Ministry of Defense. The products of their efforts serve as the bases for the military recommendations to the Party leadership for inclusion within the state's official military doctrine.

The military would most certainly like to have its recommendations largely determine the doctrine approved by the political leadership. In this vein, it is interesting to note the self-interested assertion of one military author who flatly claimed that military doctrine is "better" and "less subjective" when it is closely linked to the conclusions of military science.[13]

PARTICIPANTS IN THE DEVELOPMENT OF SOVIET MILITARY THOUGHT

A variety of individuals and institutions are involved in the various aspects of the development of Soviet military thought. The vast majority of these are located within the Ministry of Defense. The only civilian participation in the process apparently occurs at the Politburo level where its members periodically are likely to be involved in approving key doctrinal materials such as field regulations or guidelines for military contingency plans that have been prepared by the military theoreticians, war planners, and leading commanders of the Ministry of Defense.

Historically, three Soviet leaders--V. I. Lenin, Joseph Stalin, and Nikita Khrushchev--have been identified within the Soviet Union as major contributors to Soviet military science. The praise of Lenin in this regard is linked to his leadership of the Bolshevik forces during the Revolution and the Civil War and is consistent with the Soviet practice of lionizing Lenin's accomplishments in virtually all fields of endeavor. Stalin had himself enshrined as a brilliant military theorist during and after World War II. His claims appear at least partially justified since they rest upon his personal direction of the victorious Soviet war effort, a role that has been for the most part upheld in the body of Soviet military memoirs.* Ironically, however, the basic military doctrine that guided the actual employment of Soviet military power had been largely elaborated during the 1930s by a group of officers led by Marshal M. N. Tukhachevskiy.

---

*Although Stalin has often been criticized for mistakes in judgment in his direction of Soviet military operations during the war, the net assessment of his efforts as the supreme commander-in-chief presented by such leading military figures as Marshals Zhukov and Vasilevskiy is overwhelmingly positive. See Marshal G. K. Zhukov, The Memoirs of Marshal Zhukov, trans. Novosti Press Agency (New York: Delacorte Press, 1971), pp. 234-699, and Marshal A. M. Vasilevskiy, "Excerpts from 'The Cause of a Lifetime,'" Novyy Mir [The new world] no. 4 (April 1973): 188-217.

The members of this group were liquidated in Stalin's massive purge of the Red Army officer corps during 1937-38.* Khrushchev's military policy preferences and pretensions which were directly connected with his desire to enhance Soviet military power while cutting defense expenditures, and their impact upon Soviet military doctrine and force posture are discussed in considerable detail in this and the succeeding chapter of this study. Finally, it is noteworthy that none of the members of the current Soviet political leadership, including General Secretary L. I. Brezhnev, have advanced any claims for recognition as a major military thinker, although Brezhnev has increasingly dramatized his wartime accomplishments as a political commisar and had himself promoted to the rank of marshal of the Soviet Union in May 1976.

Within the Ministry of Defense

Military personnel engaged in the development of Soviet military thought can be usefully divided according to their fields of specialization. The major areas of military scientific research and discussion are military history, contemporary military art, and the Marxist-Leninist study of the nature of war and general military affairs. Specific organizations within the Defense Ministry house the various officers who engage in these types of work.

Military Historical Research

The members of the Soviet military establishment have consistently demonstrated an intense interest in the study of their own past and military history in general. Their efforts have included the careful examination of previous Soviet doctrines as embodied in the various field regulations and the study of Soviet combat experiences from the Civil War through the many battles of World War II as well as campaigns of their tsarist predecessors. Such attention to the past has been an important factor in establishing and maintaining the noticeable continuity of Soviet strategic thought that is discussed later in this chapter.

The study of military history has been carried out within the military's higher educational institutions, the General Staff's

---

*For a discussion of this group and their role in the development of Soviet military thinking, see John Erickson, The Soviet High Command: A Military-Political History, 1914-1941 (New York: St. Martin's Press, 1962), pp. 350-56, 381-411.

military-historical element, and more recently the Academy of Science's Institute of Military History. In the first two decades of the Soviet regime, the military-historical department and the military history faculties of the higher military schools were largely staffed by senior officers who had served with the Imperial Russian Army. Although these "military specialists" were eventually replaced by a new generation of Soviet military historians, their teaching activities provided a significant bridge between the tsarist and Bolshevik periods. Throughout the 1940s and 1950s the members of the new generation concentrated most of their attention on the study of Soviet operations during World War II. They did this work in the General Staff's Military Historical Administration and the specially created Administration for the Utilization of the Experience of the War,[14] as well as the historical faculties of the military academies.

During the late 1950s and 1960s the institutional framework for military historical research was importantly modified. The Historical Administration of the General Staff became a department within the newly formed Military Science Administration in 1959. This change was probably occasioned by a shift in emphasis within the General Staff from historical to more contemporary military scientific research as the Soviets sought to develop their concepts for conducting nuclear war. Perhaps as a compensatory measure, the Institute of Military History was created within the Ministry of Defense in 1966. At present it appears to be the major center for military historical research.

The staff of the Institute of Military History commanded by Lt. Gen. P. A. Zhilin includes many prominent military officer-historians. Others are found in the military history faculties of the Voroshilov Academy of the General Staff, the Frunze Military Academy, the Lenin Military-Political Academy, and other higher military schools. These officers generally possess advanced degrees in military or historical science earned from these same academies or from civilian institutions.

Military historical research is published within the monthly editions of Voenno-Istoricheskii Zhurnal, in occasional articles appearing in Krasnaia Zvezda, and in a wide variety of books and brochures published by the Military Publishing House. Conferences hosted by the academies noted above provide another means for scholarly exchange among the military historians.

Contemporary Military Art

The central role in the development of Soviet military science is played by the "defense intellectuals" of the Soviet military establishment. These men are assigned within the military staffs of the services and branches, the Operations and Military Science Administrations of the General Staff, and as researchers or teachers with the faculties of the higher military academies. They include both a cadre of professional military scientists, most of whom hold advanced degrees in military science, and a number of other officers who are generalists serving temporarily in posts that involve them in theoretical research or routine operational planning.

A particularly important group from within the generalist category is composed of the high-level command personnel. Senior military figures ranging from the Minister of Defense to the commanders of the services and branches of the Soviet Armed Forces and the military districts, appear to have an ex officio responsibility to participate in the discussion of strategic concepts and in the planning activities that assign roles and missions among the elements of the armed forces.

It is likely that the speeches and articles on military science publicly attributed to these commanders are frequently written by staff officers with either specialist or generalist backgrounds. This procedure may well work in reverse as well. Particularly outspoken articles by relatively junior military defense intellectuals are likely to reflect the opinions of much higher ranking but unnamed military sponsors.*

Among the military science specialists, one finds a broad rank spectrum. A number of general officers fit within this category. In the past two decades, they have included Maj. Gen. N. A. Talenskiy, who went on after retirement to a controversial civilian-based career in the same field, Col. Generals A. I. Gastilovich and N. A. Lomov, Lt. Generals N. A. Sbytov, I. G. Zavyalov, S. N. Krasilnikov, and Maj. Generals M. M. Kiryan, A. A. Prokhorov, M. I. Cherednichenko, V. Reznichenko, and V. V. Larionov. These men published many books and articles on military art from prestigious posts within the General Staff and the Voroshilov and Frunze Academies.

Two additional senior officers, Marshals V. D. Sokolovskiy and P. A. Rotmistrov, have unique credentials as both first-rate military commanders and bona fide strategic thinkers. Sokolovskiy's military command role ended with his removal from the post of chief of the General Staff in 1960. He went on, however, to occupy a

---

*John Erickson, a leading British student of Soviet military affairs who over the past decade has had the opportunity to interview a number of senior Soviet commanders, suggests that this sponsor-spokesman relationship exists within the Soviet military establishment. Cited in Benjamin S. Lambeth, "Moscow's Defense Intellectuals," unpublished ms., 1970, p. 58.

leading position among writers on contemporary military policy, editing the landmark volume, Military Strategy, the first Soviet book to appear on this subject since the 1920s, and coauthoring with Maj. Gen. M. E. Cherednichenko a number of important articles for military periodicals.[15] Rotmistrov, a leading tank commander during World War II, rose to high-level posts within the ground forces in the 1950s and 1960s, including the command of armored forces and commandant of the Higher Academy of Armored Forces. He holds the rank of professor and of doctor of military science and has been a prolific writer on contemporary military affairs.[16]

The corps of military scientists includes a number of field-grade officers as well. Some of the most prominent of these over the past decade have been Colonels A. A. Sidorenko, I. Sidel'nikov, V. V. Glazov, V. V. Mochalov, S. V. Malyanchikov, and V. K. Denisenko. Like their more senior counterparts they have researched, taught, and written on military scientific questions from assignments within the General Staff and the most prestigious higher military academies. These writers are joined in their endeavors by several less visible colleagues assigned to the same organizations as well as the higher academies of the various service branches.

Discussions of military strategy, operational art, and tactics are presented in a variety of military publications. The most important of these is the classified organ of the General Staff, Voennaia Mysl' (Military Thought). This monthly journal is reportedly restricted to circulation among the senior members of Soviet military establishment as indicated by the instruction printed on each issue which reads, "For Generals, Admirals and Officers of the Soviet Army and Navy Only." Unfortunately, although this periodical was available to Western scholars in the 1950s,* it has not been similarly accessible since that period. The continuing role of Military Thought was attested to by Penkovskiy, who wrote of a special top secret "Special Collection" produced under its auspices that played an important part in the belated but dynamic adaptation of Soviet strategy to the nuclear age in 1960 and 1961.[17]

Denied access to Military Thought over the past several years, American students of Soviet military policy have been forced to rely upon the many open publications of the Ministry of Defense. These include Krasnaia Zvezda, Kommunist Vooruzhennykh Sil, and

---

*Raymond L. Garthoff used Military Thought extensively in preparing his major works Soviet Military Doctrine and Soviet Strategy in the Nuclear Age (New York: Praeger, 1958). Herbert S. Dinerstein had similar access to it in preparing his War and the Soviet Union (New York: Praeger, 1959).

Voenno-Istoricheskii Zhurnal, as well as the service-produced periodicals Morskoi Sbornik (Naval Collection), Aviatsiia i Kosmonavtika (Aviation and Cosmonautics), which serves both the air forces and strategic rocket troops, Voennii Vestnik (Military Herald), published by the ground forces, and Tyl i Snabzhenie (Rear and Supply), published by the Rear Services Administration. Another important group of source materials are the books and brochures printed by the Military Publishing House.

The use of these public materials raises an important question regarding their accuracy as expressions of Soviet military thought. Raymond L. Garthoff, a leading American student of Soviet military affairs, who exhaustively surveyed both classified and open sources on Soviet strategy between 1945 and 1960, has offered this judgment: "These [classified] sources go further into some sensitive matters but in no case did the open materials display any discrepancy or divergence from the secret ones. This confirms and underlines the conclusion that open sources are, to the extent that they do treat strategic matters, a generally reliable source."[18]

Soviet military science discussions follow a rather standard pattern. Those covering the broadest aspects of military strategy are typically authored by officers associated with the General Staff or its academy, the Voroshilov Military Academy of the General Staff. (For example, the important Voennaia strategiia volumes in all three editions were prepared by a collective body headed by Marshal V. D. Sokolovskiy and composed of colonels and generals associated with the General Staff and its academy.) The narrower works on operational art and tactics or the strategic aspects of a particular weapons system, combat branch, or service are generally prepared by men affiliated with the service-linked academies or leading figures of the individual branches and services. (Members of the faculty of the Frunze Military Academy led by Maj. Gen. V. G. Reznichenko authored Taktika [Tactics];[19] Col. A. A. Sidorenko, Nastuplenie [Offensive].)[20] These patterns of Soviet strategy during the Khrushchev period are presented in the latter portion of this chapter.

Ideological Commentary on Military Affairs

All Soviet military writings on military policy include an appreciable Marxist-Leninist content. Even the most technical discussions are routinely interspersed with claims of special insight that inhere in the author's application of Marxism-Leninism's scientific methodology and frequent references to the hostile nature of modern imperialism of the type discussed in Chapter 3.

Some works produced within the military establishment are primarily devoted to Marxist-Leninist analysis and the presentation of the military's institutional viewpoint. These should be clearly differentiated from the materials on military art produced by the military science specialists. While the ideological articles sometimes include descriptions of the broad contours of Soviet strategic thought, they largely serve as vehicles to promulgate existing doctrine rather than important contributions to its development. In most instances, the ideological works are devoted to the discussion of Marxist-Leninist teachings on warfare and the promotion of the military world view on such matters as the nature of the imperialist threat, the demand for Soviet military superiority, and the priority needs for investment in heavy industry and defense. (See Chapter 3 under "The Threat: Enemy Intentions," for a detailed examination of the elements of the military's institutional outlook.) In recent years the ideological specialists have also become increasingly active in the study of military pedagogy and psychology, two fields which they study with the goal of improving Soviet training and discipline.[21] Although these discussions fall within the broad Soviet definition of military science, they are not a significant part of Soviet military thought in terms of its important role in assigning roles and missions among the elements of the Soviet armed forces and establishing the guidelines for the conduct of war.

The military's Marxist-Leninist analyses and statements of parochial preference are produced by the political officers of the Main Political Administration. The officers serving on the faculty of Marxist-Leninist Philosophy of the Lenin Military-Political Academy are the most prolific authors in this area. This cadre of professional teachers and writers range in rank from major to major general, with many holding degrees as candidates or doctors of philosophical science. The most prominent of these are Maj. Generals N. Ya. Sushko, K. Bochkarev, and S. N. Kozlov and Colonels V. M. Bondarenko, G. A. Fedorov, I. A. Grudinin, I. P. Prusanov, I. M. Butskiy, Ye. I. Rybkin, S. A. Tyushkevich, and T. Kondratkov. The writings of these men and their colleagues appear regularly in the MPA's bimonthly Kommunist Vooruzhennykh Sil and other military periodicals, and in a wide variety of books and pamphlets such as the frequently revised Marxism-Leninism on War and the Army. *

---

*Published by the Faculty of Marxist-Leninist Philosophy of the Lenin Political Military Academy, Marksizm-Leninizm o voine i armii (Marxism-Leninism on war and the army) has been issued and reissued regularly since the first edition appeared in 1957 (2d ed., 1961; 3d ed., 1963; 4th ed., 1965; 5th ed., 1968).

"Civilian" Commentators on Defense Matters

While the preponderance of research and writing on military science is conducted within the Ministry of Defense, there has been a small number of civilians active in the study of defense policy matters. These individuals are potentially of great significance in that they represent a source of expert commentary on defense matters from outside the professional military establishment. Their participation in the defense policy process is likely to occur in the role of advisers preparing staff memorandums for members of the Politburo prior to its authoritative deliberations on Soviet military policy questions.

In the early 1960s two analysts of military affairs outside the Ministry of Defense emerged on the Soviet scene. The more prominent of these was a retired senior officer, Maj. Gen. N. A. Talenskiy, who had been a leading member of the General Staff community of military scientists and had served as editor of _Military Thought_. Talenskiy joined the Marxist-Leninist Institute of History in 1958 and rapidly established himself as a prolific writer and active participant in international conferences on questions of contemporary military policy. His writings on these matters departed significantly from the positions taken in standard military analysis. Talenskiy supported instead the deterrence and arms control perspectives of Khrushchev, which are treated later in this chapter. Talenskiy's deviation from the military's institutional viewpoint earned him harsh condemnation from the military after Khrushchev, his apparent patron, had fallen from power (as noted in Chapter 3 under "War in the Modern Era").

Talenskiy was joined in the early 1960s by a similarly oriented young journalist, Gennady Gerasimov, a Novosti news correspondent who has remained an active commentator on military affairs.[22] Both men lacked institutional roles that could serve as a formal basis for their participation in the development of Soviet defense policy. The congruence of their views with those of Khrushchev suggests that their visibility as exponents of a deterrence-oriented security posture was a direct result of his personal sponsorship.

The degree to which Talenskiy and Gerasimov departed from the lines prevailing within the Ministry of Defense is evident in statements by each of them. Talenskiy, for example, quoted Bismarck as follows about the role of the politicians vis-a-vis the military leadership:

> It is natural that in the general staff of an army not only the younger aspiring officers but also experienced strategists feel the urge to display

> in action and demonstrate to history the combat efficiency of troops under their command and their ability to direct them. It should be a matter of regret if the influence of this military spirit were not felt in the army: to contain it within the bounds legitimately required by the peaceful prosperity of the peoples is the duty of the political and not the military leaders of the state.[23]

Gerasimov's independent turn of mind was revealed in his explicit rejections of both the utility of military superiority and the concept of victory in nuclear war, two cherished policy goals and convictions of the Soviet military. Gerasimov wrote:

> Superiority has become a concept that has no bearing on war. No superiority can save the aggressor from retribution. Any efforts of an aggressor to achieve relative nuclear superiority are neutralized in advance by the fact that the other side possesses absolute power which guarantees the destruction of the aggressor. . . .
>
> The need to strive for so-called superiority over a potential enemy has been regarded as an axiom. Of course, he who has more sabres has a better chance. The same is true of more tanks, aircraft or infantry divisions. But it is not true that he who has more nuclear weapons has greater chances. . . . These conclusions follow logically from the recognition of the impossibility of victory in nuclear war.[24]

With respect to another well-known military viewpoint, the utility of strategic defense, Gerasimov reaffirmed his inclination to oppose the prevailing wisdom of the Soviet military. Writing in Pravda Ukrainy he sharply criticized the deployment of antiballistic missile defense for cities. Gerasimov pointed out the impossibility of attaining 100 percent interception of enemy offensive vehicles, which, he noted, was necessary if the system was to be useful in population defense, and suggested that ABM defense could be easily offset by additional investment in strategic offensive systems.[25]

The Institutional Academics*

Only a few civilian organizations have responsibilities that involve them in the study and analysis of military policy. These include the Disarmament Section of the Ministry of Foreign Affairs,[26] the Scientific Group for Disarmament of the Institute of World Economics and International Affairs[27] ("IMEMO" according to its Russian acronym), and the Military Affairs sections of both the Institute for the Study of the United States and Canada (known as the IUSAC) and IMEMO.[28] These groups employ a number of specialists on defense policy and disarmament.

Many of the men analyzing military affairs from positions outside the Ministry of Defense are retired military officers. Both IUSAC and IMEMO employ a number of retirees who were prominent writers on military science while on active duty. IMEMO inaugurated this practice with their selection of former Col. V. M. Kulish to head their newly formed Military Affairs Section in 1967. Kulish, who subsequently became a deputy director of the institute, was joined by Maj. Gen. N. S. Solodovnik, Col. D. M. Proektor, and Col. V. V. Glazov.[29] The USA Institute, founded in 1968, created a similar military affairs section initially headed by Col. V. V. Larionov† and including Col. Gen. N. A. Lomov, Maj. Gen. M. A. Mil'shtein, Col. L. S. Semeiko, Capt. Second Rank (Navy) G. I. Sviatov, and Col. Yu. Strel'tsov.[30]

The IMEMO and IUSAC sections working on national security matters include a few genuine civilians as well. G. A. Trofimenko of USA has been particularly visible in this regard while the IMEMO staff has included Yu. Listvinov, S. Fedorenko,‡ Yu. Kostko, and A. G. Arbatov, son of G. A. Arbatov, the director of IUSAC.

---

*This term is borrowed from Benjamin S. Lambeth's "Moscow's Defense Intellectuals," p. 31. This paper presents an insightful analysis of the perspectives and points of access of a variety of individuals and groups active in the formulation of Soviet military policy.

†Larionov left the USA Institute to return to active military duty in the fall of 1973. Interview, Marshall D. Shulman, professor of political science, Columbia University, Halifax, Nova Scotia, October 15, 1973. A brief Krasnaia Zvezda article on a military history conference held in November 1976 noted that Larionov has been promoted to the rank of major general.

‡Fedorenko, who was originally trained as an aeronautical engineer and later worked for V. A. Kirillin's State Committee for Science and Technology, is currently a member of the Soviet U.N. delegation in New York. He apparently retains his affiliation with IMEMO. Wolfe interview, February 8, 1973.

In their various books and articles the institutional academics have generally limited themselves to discussions of the formulation and content of contemporary American military policy. Their failure to discuss Soviet security affairs has been very noticeable.* However, in the wake of the SALT agreements signed in May 1972, the apparent prohibition on discussing Soviet military policy was at least temporarily breached. Trofimenko and Sviatov were among those Soviet writers called upon to explain and justify publicly the ABM treaty and the Interim Offensive Agreement.[31] In doing this, they dealt for the first time with Soviet as well as American military policy. Since that time, however, they have reverted once more to periodic analyses of U.S. defense matters and discussions of Soviet-American detente.[32]

The small disarmament section of IMEMO, headed throughout the 1960s by L. Glagolev, and a similar section within the International Department of the Ministry of Foreign Affairs have been staffed entirely by civilians. Many of these men are veterans of the prolonged multilateral United Nations-sponsored disarmament negotiations in Geneva and more recently the multilateral Mutual Balanced Force Reductions (MBFR) negotiations in Vienna and the bilateral Strategic Arms Limitation Talks. As a result they are familiar with Western security policy concepts.

The existence of this small body of national security expertise within the two social sciences institutes and the Ministry of Foreign Affairs, which are outside the control of the Ministry of Defense, has great potential significance. While the Soviet armed forces have consistently monopolized military strategic research over the years, their dominance may be subject to challenge by individuals from within this group. However, the military backgrounds of the retirees among the institutional academics casts doubt on their potential as an adversary counterweight to the military scientists of the General Staff. Additionally, none of the military retirees appear to have undergone the kind of conversion that Talenskiy exhibited earlier (see Chapter 3, under "War in the Modern Era"). Nevertheless their discussions of American security policy are, as a rule, significantly more balanced than those produced within the Ministry of Defense.[33]

Among the truly civilian defense intellectuals, G. A. Trofimenko has exhibited a substantial commitment to the development of a stable

---

*Colonel Kulish has claimed that the IMEMO/IUSAC military policy analysts have no authority to concern themselves with Soviet strategic policy in their research. Kulish interview, March 24, 1970.

deterrent relationship between the Soviet Union and the United States and has presented a decidedly moderate view of American intentions.[34] In contrast Yu. Listvinov's hostile depiction of American political objectives differs little from the most strident military commentators.[35]

Should the institutional academics seek to participate in substantive discussions of Soviet military policies, they are likely to face a significant problem of information scarcity. The Soviet penchant for secrecy, particularly regarding highly sensitive military matters, is likely to be utilized by the Ministry of Defense to justify the denial of essential information about weapons deployments and characteristics to any potential critics. To overcome this difficulty, the academics are reported to cultivate informal contacts with those who have access to these data--military or perhaps highly placed Foreign Ministry or Central Committee apparatus personnel.

The Ministry of Defense appears to enjoy near-monopoly control over certain types of defense-related information. This allows the military to control closely the internal dissemination of information on the deployments and characteristics of Soviet weapons systems as well as similar data on American military forces collected and evaluated primarily by the Main Intelligence Directorate (GRU) of the General Staff.

The organizational arrangements for the possible involvement of the institutional academics in the development of Soviet defense policy are unknown. They may be called upon to prepare policy memorandums or to consult personally with either the personal staffs of individual Politburo members or the members of the Secretariat or Central Committee apparatus charged with the coordination of policy making in the defense area. (See the discussion of staffing procedures for the Politburo in Chapter 2 under "The Politburo of the Central Committee.") One IMEMO scholar suggested another mode of participation when he noted that "ad hoc bodies are frequently convened to recommend resolution to knotty issues involving foreign policy and defense interests."[36] The civilian defense specialists are likely to have their most direct influence on Soviet foreign and defense policy deliberations via their roles as staffers providing position papers or advising their prestigious bosses--A. A. Gromyko, Politburo member and Minister of Foreign Affairs, N. N. Inozemtsev, the director of IMEMO, and G. A. Arbatov, the head of IUSAC. (All three men hold prestigious positions within the Party hierarchy with Gromyko a full member of the Politburo, and both Inozemtsev and Arbatov candidate members of the Central Committee. Additionally, they have all been conspicuous participants in the foreign policy activities of the current collective leadership.) These men, in turn, appear to have significant influence as advisors to the Soviet leaders and their immediate staffs. Arbatov in particular has become especially visible over the past few years as a major spokesman for the current Soviet leadership.[37]

The Scientific Intelligentsia

There are a few members of the Soviet scientific community who have demonstrated a special interest in defense affairs. Such accomplished scientists as nuclear physicists L. A. Artsimovich, P. L. Kapitsa, I. E. Tamm, and A. D. Sakharov are among this group. The first three of these men have figured prominently in the annual conferences sponsored by the Pugwash movement. These meetings with Western social and natural scientists, many of whom are members of the vigorous U.S. defense intellectual community,* have provided an important set of experiences that have familiarized the Soviet participants with contemporary Western military doctrinal concepts.[38]

As members of the Soviet scientific elite, these men enjoy regular access to Western scientific periodicals, some of which have published commentaries on current defense policy issues. Thus Andrei D. Sakharov, whose outspoken opposition to many Soviet domestic and foreign policies places him in a distinctly different category than his colleagues listed above, has written an attack upon the wisdom of the Soviet antiballistic missile (ABM) deployment which cited an article in Scientific American for confirmation of his criticisms regarding the technological reliability and strategic utility of ABM systems.[39] While we cannot locate other scientists or academic military policy specialists sharing Sakharov's sentiments or lobbying efforts, Soviet ABM deployment restraint in the late 1960s and the signing of a restrictive ABM Treaty at the conclusion of the first round of the Strategic Arms Limitation Talks in May 1972, clearly demonstrate that Sakharov's point of view did come to prevail among the Soviet leadership.

Leading members of the scientific intelligentsia have traditionally enjoyed direct personal access to the Soviet political leadership.[40] Although the primary basis for this access is linked to their contributions to Soviet scientific achievement, this consultative role can provide an opportunity for such scientists to express their opinions on military policy matters.

---

*American participants have included such defense policy researchers as Henry Kissinger, Don Brennan, Carl Kaysen, Jack Ruina, and George Rathjens as well as scientists active in arms control studies such as George Kistiakowsky and Paul Doty.

THE SUBSTANCE OF SOVIET MILITARY STRATEGY AND DOCTRINE

A variety of books and articles have been written by American and British authors on the historical development and contemporary content of Soviet military doctrine.[41] The discussion that follows does not pretend to be exhaustive. Rather it represents an overview of the basic characteristics of Soviet military thought with particular emphasis upon the impact of institutional factors in its development.

Historical Development

Since its crystallization in the mid-1930s, Soviet military strategy has been guided by a number of basic tenets. These guiding principles, which themselves were derived from a variety of sources, have provided a general framework within which Soviet military policy has developed in the past and continues to evolve.

The cardinal elements of Soviet military thought established at that time were: (1) a commitment to a general balance among the various military branches and services and their coordinated application in battle; (2) an attendant rejection of excessive reliance upon any single weapons system or service branch; (3) emphasis upon mass in both the maintenance of large forces-in-being and in the practice of applying large numbers of men and equipment in combat; (4) a strong predisposition to seize the initiative and conduct offensive operations; and (5) a preference for geographically extensive and highly mobile operations.[42]

These strategic precepts represented a complex amalgam of elements derived from a number of diverse sources. These included the Imperial Russian tradition (mass and the offensive),[43] Bolshevik experience during the Russian Civil War (the offensive and extended mobile warfare),* creative innovation in response to

---

*Discussions concerning the proper lessons to be derived from the Civil War occasioned a bitter debate within Soviet military circles. One group led by Frunze sought to enshrine these experiences in a "unified proletarian military doctrine" while another led by Trotsky harshly ridiculed this attempt to construct an entire doctrine on the basis of such limited experience. In the end its influence was felt but not to the extent advocated by Frunze and his colleagues. See Erickson, The Soviet High Command, pp. 126-31; Dmitri Fedotoff White, The Growth of the Red Army (Princeton, N.J.: Princeton University Press, 1944), pp. 158-82.

the emergence of new combat means, in particular the tank and the airplane (the massive, mobile offensive),[44] and an element of ideological preference (the offensive for revolutionary purposes).[45] This military doctrine was largely the product of two different groups, one a small and dynamic collective of innovative military commanders headed by Marshal M. N. Tukhachevskiy and the other a cadre of former tsarist officers led by Marshal B. M. Shaposhnikov.[46]

The early Soviet doctrinal framework found its fullest exposition in the Field Regulations of 1936. Although they paid lip service to the principle of balanced force development, and all of the branches and services were called upon to mutually support one another, the premier role in this period was clearly assigned to the massive ground forces. Large infantry contingents, supported by artillery and armored formations and numerous tactical (frontal) aviation units which were to serve as a kind of airborne artillery, represented the central element of Soviet military striking power. Soviet doctrine called for this combination to launch an offensive at the outset of a war and conduct a series of deep encirclement operations to crush the enemy.[47]

Soviet experience during World War II did little to modify this doctrine. After finding expression in the battle with the Japanese at Khalgin Gol in August 1939, the Soviets were prevented from implementing this strategy in 1941-42 during the first two years of the war with Germany. Those years were dominated by a series of desperate defensive battles and forced retreats in the face of the superior German forces. These operations, however, were the product of absolute necessity rather than Soviet preference and planning. With the shift of the initiative into Soviet hands after the Battle of Stalingrad, which ended in February 1943, massive combined-arms offensives of the kind envisioned in the doctrine of the 1930s became the order of the day. A cumbersome but nonetheless powerful "Russian steamroller" gradually ground down German resistance and moved westward in a series of massive offensive thrusts that culminated in the occupation of Eastern Europe and the defeat of the Nazi regime. In the brief, successful rout of the Japanese Kwantung Army in July-August 1945, the Soviets were more impressive in their implementation of a multifront offensive over vast distances in a relatively short time.[48]

Between 1945 and 1953 Soviet military science was largely devoted to the careful study and codification of the wartime experiences and the glorification of the personal genius of Generalissimo Josef Stalin. The basic tenets guiding Soviet military thought remained fundamentally unchanged, although they were temporarily overshadowed by a concerted campaign to emphasize the "permanently operating factors" of Soviet military science, which were directly attributed to Stalin. These factors, the stability of the rear, the morale of the army, the quantity and quality of divisions, the armaments of the army and the organizing ability of the command personnel,[49] like similar Western lists of "the principles of war," are common-sense propositions with limited potential either to guide the development of military force posture or to provide an outline for the conduct of combat operations. The Stalinist precepts were so frequently and slavishly repeated that they became a rigid stereotype seriously impeding creative thinking in Soviet military science and retarding its adjustment to the emergence of a new political and technological environment. *

Following Stalin's death in 1953, Soviet military thought slowly and belatedly began its adaptation to the nuclear era. In a pair of ground-breaking articles, two prominent military figures called attention to the importance of strategic surprise.[50] Their recognition of surprise was a major departure from the late Stalinist period, when, apparently motivated by a desire to minimize the significance of the German achievement of strategic surprise in their attack on Russia in June 1941, Stalin had decreed that surprise was only a "transitory" consideration rather than a decisive factor in warfare. The military's rediscovery of the importance of surprise represented a return to their doctrinal position of the prewar period.[51]

Despite its rediscovery of surprise, the development of Soviet military science and doctrine between 1954 and 1960 remained basically conservative in its response to the advent of strategic and tactical missiles and the appearance of nuclear weapons. The new weapons and their delivery systems were merely appended to the traditional "Continental" doctrine with its emphasis upon ground forces-dominated, large-scale offensive operations designed to rapidly overrun Western Europe. While Soviet military writers indicated their awareness of the enormous destructive power of nuclear weapons, they nevertheless treated them primarily as more efficient

---

*It should be emphasized that Stalin's rigidification of military thought did not preclude his personal sponsorship of the vital research and development programs which yielded Soviet missile and thermonuclear weapons capabilities in the 1950s. George Quester suggests that the overt denigration of the significance of nuclear weapons may represent a rational and calculated strategy for a power lacking sufficient numbers of such weapons that faces a possessor opponent. George F. Quester, "On the Identification of Real and Pretended Communist Military Doctrine," Journal of Conflict Resolution 10, no. 2 (June 1966): 172-79.

explosives to be employed in conformance with the traditional supplemental role of artillery rather than as a revolutionary new element in military affairs.[52]

The Khrushchev Initiative

This pattern of incremental assimilation was abruptly challenged in 1960. Nikita Khrushchev, first secretary of the Party and leader of the Soviet government, personally spearheaded an effort to drastically transform Soviet military policy. Apparently motivated by a desire to reduce the sizable costs of maintaining the Soviet defense establishment and convinced of the stability of the nuclear deterrence standoff between East and West, he proposed a radically new force posture and military doctrine.

Khrushchev later provided a revealing commentary on his personal desire to economize in defense spending and the contrary desires of the Soviet military leadership. His memoirs, which he dictated while in retirement in the late 1960s, include these enlightening observations about the institutional interests and lobbying efforts of the Soviet High Command in opposition to his moves to reduce military expenditures:

> I've said quite a bit about the internal forces in the West, the militarists and representatives of big monopolistic capital, who have a stake in producing the means of destruction and who put pressure on the government to increase military expenditures. In our country, of course, since we have no private capitalist ownership and no big industrialists, we have no militaristic class as such. But our military puts similar pressure on our government. I'm not saying there's any comparison between our military in the socialist countries and capitalist generals, but soldiers will be soldiers. They always want a bigger and stronger army. They always insist on having the very latest weapons and on attaining quantitative as well as qualitative superiority over the enemy.
>
> Once again, let me say: I'm not denying that our military men have a huge responsibility, and I'm not impugning their moral qualities. But the fact remains that the living standard of the country suffers when the budget is overloaded with allocations to unproductive branches of

> consumption. And today, as yesterday, the most unproductive expenditures of all are those made on the armed forces.[53]

Khrushchev's proclivity to intervene in military matters had been evident for a number of years prior to his far-reaching 1960 assault upon existing plans. Between 1956 and 1960 he had on numerous occasions publicly denigrated the value of strategic aviation and naval surface vessels.* His interventionist tendencies were compounded by his confident and brash leadership style, which inclined him frequently to gamble upon new policy departures whether in the areas of agriculture,† education,‡ or defense, as he sought to speed

---

*Among Khrushchev's public disparagements of long-range aviation were his statement to James Reston of the New York Times in October 1957 that "military specialists believe that both bomber aircraft and fighters are in the twilight of their existence" and a similar judgment expressed to two British members of Parliament that the age of bombers was past and that they could now be destroyed, both cited in "US Editors' Note A: Changing Soviet Attitudes on the role of the Manned Bombers" in the RAND Corporation translation of Sokolovskiy's Voennaia strategiia entitled Soviet Military Strategy, R-416-PR (Santa Monica, Calif.: RAND Corporation, April 1963), p. 351. With regard to the surface navy, Khrushchev's pronouncements included a statement made while visiting England in May 1956 that cruisers were good only for political visits and the firing of ceremonial salutes (New York Times, May 17, 1956) and a similar revelation while visiting San Francisco in September 1959, when he told newsmen: "The Soviet Navy is largely going to concentrate on submarines. We are scrapping 90 percent of our cruisers; in modern times they are too expensive and of too little use." Associated Press Dispatch, September 22, 1959. Further evidence of his strong views on the obsolescence of many naval surface vessels is found in the second volume of his memoirs. Khrushchev, Khrushchev Remembers: The Last Testament, pp. 18-22.

†Among his many agricultural campaigns were the opening of the virgin lands of Central Asia in the mid-1950s and the massive corn planting schemes of the late 1950s and early 1960s. Cf. Roy D. and Betty Laird, Soviet Communism and the Agrarian Revolution (Baltimore: Penguin Books, 1970), pp. 45, 79; Sidney I. Ploss, Conflict and Decision-making in Soviet Russia: A Case Study of Agricultural Policy 1953-1963 (Princeton, N.J.: Princeton University Press, 1965), pp. 78-93.

‡Khrushchev's major educational reform measure was the introduction of compulsory production education in the secondary school

the development of the Soviet economy and society toward the goal of communist plenty and prosperity.

In January 1960, Khrushchev went well past isolated attacks on allegedly obsolete weaponry and publicly endorsed a comprehensive new defense program. Speaking before the Supreme Soviet, he openly embraced a minimum deterrence strategy. This involved committing the Soviet Union to a doctrine that relied very heavily upon the retaliatory capability of nuclear-armed strategic missiles as the keystone of its security rather than relying upon the powerful theater forces and their massed offensive power as was done in the past.

Khrushchev's dramatic announcement of his new defense policy included the following passages:

> The USSR Council of Ministers is submitting for your examination and approval a proposal to reduce our armed forces by another 1,200,000 men. If this proposal is adopted by the Supreme Soviet, our army and navy will number 2,423,000.
>
> Our state has a powerful rocket technology. Given the present development of military technology, military aviation and the navy have lost their former importance. This type of armament is not being reduced but replaced. Military aviation is being almost entirely replaced by missiles. We have now sharply reduced and probably will further reduce and even halt production of bombers and other obsolete equipment. In the navy, the submarine fleet is assuming greater importance and surface ships can no longer play the role they played in the past.
>
> In our time a country's defense capacity is determined not by the number of soldiers it has under arms, the number of men in uniform. Aside from the general political and economic factors about which I have already spoken, a country's defense capacity depends to a decisive extent upon the firepower and means of delivery it has.

---

curriculum. See Joel J. Schwartz and William R. Keech, "Group Influence and the Policy Process in the Soviet Union," in Communist Studies and the Social Sciences, ed. Frederick J. Fleron (Chicago: Rand McNally, 1969), pp. 298-309.

> The proposed reduction will in no way reduce the firepower of our armed forces, and this is the main thing after all. In essence, the reason why states maintain armies is precisely to have firepower that can withstand a possible enemy and either restrain him from attacking or repulse him if he tries to attack.
>
> A reduction in the size of the army does not prevent us from maintaining the country's defense capability at the proper level. We shall continue to have all the means necessary for the country's defense and an opponent will be well aware of this; if he is not, we warn him and openly declare: While reducing the numerical strength of the armed forces, we shall not reduce their firepower; on the contrary, it will increase many times over in terms of quality.[54]

Khrushchev's announcement, which, he claimed, was preceded by "detailed and comprehensive study" as well as consultation with the "military and the General Staff," presented a serious challenge to the Soviet military establishment. It was nothing less than a fundamental revision of strategic policy and gravely threatened the institutional fortunes of selected parts of the Soviet armed forces. More importantly, it represented a direct challenge to the prestige and authority of the Soviet military as the primary shaper of Soviet military policy.

Khrushchev's initiative precipitated a period of considerable controversy and debate within the Soviet defense policy community. During the next few years a variety of views were evident in military books and periodicals regarding the projected nature of global nuclear war and the appropriate strategic policies and force posture required to prepare for it. The diversity of opinions on these issues was clearly evident in the differing treatments that these problems received in Soviet military commentary and was occasionally openly acknowledged by Soviet authors. Thus Maj. Gen. P. Zhilin, then editor of Voenno-Istoricheskii Zhurnal, wrote in 1961, "Now, as never before, it is necessary to have a unity of views on all the important problems of military art and the employment of troops." But after noting that discussions of these matters were taking place "in the pages of the military press and within the walls of the General Staff Academy," he observed: "Unfortunately, in these discussions, no unity of views has been achieved."*

---

*Maj. Gen. P. Zhilin, "Discussion About a Unified Military Doctrine," Voenno-Istoricheskii Zhurnal 5 (May 1960): 73. A useful

A number of American scholars have analyzed this debate with the assistance of a classification scheme that groups the Soviet military participants according to their stated policy preferences. Examining such questions as the writer's stands on the relative importance of the various branches and services of the armed forces, the prospects for a short or a prolonged world war, the decisiveness of the opening strategic nuclear exchange (the "initial period" in Soviet parlance), and the size of the theater forces required in the nuclear age, British and American analysts have identified three separate Soviet schools of thought, the modernists-radicals, the traditionalists, and the centrists.[55]

According to this typology, the modernists, who supported Khrushchev's minimum deterrence preferences, emphasized the primacy of the nuclear-missile strength of the newly created Strategic Rocket Forces, the decisiveness of the initial period of war, and the prospects for a short war. They also supported reductions in the importance and size of the ground forces as well as long-range and tactical aviation. In contrast, the traditionalists, while acknowledging the increasing importance of missiles and nuclear weapons, continued to emphasize the value of the experiences of the past, endorsed a strategic policy which steadfastly maintained balanced and coordinated roles for all services and weapons, in particular the large ground forces, and urged preparation for a war of extended duration. The centrist group or "enlightened traditionalists"[56] included those individuals who embraced a combination of elements endorsed by the other two schools of thought.

Careful examination of Soviet materials of the 1960-64 period and the corresponding analyses of American scholars convinces this

---

Soviet article on the stages of development of contemporary Soviet military thought including this justification for internal differences and debate:

> But since a constant process occurs for renewing weapons and armaments, views on the means and methods of waging war, operations and battles can change. However, these changes are not perceived identically by all. It is a normal phenomenon to have a debate. The scientific truth is engendered in the struggle between various opinions. In science it is proper to offer proof and argument.

Col. I. Korotov, "On the Development of Soviet Military Theory in the Postwar Years," Voenno-Istoricheskii Zhurnal no. 4 (April 1964): 50.

author that this classification scheme has fundamental shortcomings. The vast majority of Soviet military writings defy straightforward identification. Within a given article or series of articles, individual writers usually managed to endorse a variety of contradictory stands associated with all of the different categories. For example, Soviet military writers were prone to hedge their bets by noting the possibilities that modern war could be either long or short and by acknowledging the decisive importance of the war's initial strategic nuclear exchange while at the same time insisting that the coordinated efforts of all branches and services in a massive theater campaign would also be necessary for the achievement of "final" victory. As a result, most writers are best classified as centrists, a fact that considerably reduces the value of the entire approach.

The problems involved in the application of this typology are clearly evident in the difficulties its American creators have encountered in its use. A large number of Soviet military writers have been placed in more than one of the categories. Thus, for example, Roman Kolkowicz has contradictorily labeled Col. Gen. N. A. Lomov as a traditionalist on one occasion and modernist on another.* Classification differences between authors are evident in Kolkowicz's identification of Col. S. Kozlov as a modernist and "well known apologist of Khrushchev"[57] while the RAND team of Thomas Wolfe, Herbert Dinerstein, and Leon Gouré describe the same individual as a traditionalist who attacked the overvaluation of missiles and the one-sided blitzkrieg notions of some of his fellow writers.[58] Similar inconsistencies are encountered with regard to a number of other writers including the distinguished Sokolovskiy-Cherednichenko team,[59] Marshal Chuikov,[60] and General Shtemenko,[61] to name but a few.

Whatever the problems of individual identification and consistency, the Khrushchev initiative did produce differential reactions among the various military commentators. These differences to a very large extent appear to have fallen along lines of institutional affiliation.

Khrushchev's new military policy presented a serious challenge to the essential interests of some of the services and branches of the Soviet armed forces while obviously benefiting others. One

---

*Kolkowicz identifies Lomov as "generally progressive" (modernist) in The Impact of Technology on the Soviet Military: A Challenge to Traditional Military Professionalism, RM-4198-PR (Santa Monica, Calif.: RAND Corporation, August 1964), p. 14, and as a conservative in The Soviet Military and the Communist Party, p. 164.

would logically expect to find those profiting from this initiative inclined to support the new policy and those endangered opposing it. Additionally, Khrushchev could be expected to be more successful in rallying support from the military-ideological cadres of the Lenin Military-Political Academy of the Main Political Administration who are more directly under Party supervision than from the career soldiers connected with the General Staff and the other higher military academies.

The pattern of military reaction to Khrushchev's plan did in fact occur almost totally along such predictable institutional lines. While picking up support from one prominent military scientist within the General Staff, Col. Gen. A. I. Gastilovich, whose modernist bent defies this form of explanation, most of Khrushchev's supporters within the military were found among those services profiting from the new direction, the Strategic Rocket Forces and the National Air Defense Forces. Additional support was found among some of the military philosophers of the MPA.[62] Thus his most enthusiastic supporters included Marshals Biriuzov[63] and Sudets, the commanders of the Strategic Rocket Forces and PVO-S, and such political officers as Colonels P. Sidorov[64] and N. Ya. Sushko,[65] who were assigned to the Lenin Military-Political Academy. Presumably, these institutionally based differences were strongly expressed in the serious internal debates within the General Staff and other parts of the Ministry of Defense in the policy struggles that accompanied the crystallization of Soviet military strategy and doctrine in response to the Khrushchev challenge.

Virtually all of the military figures selectively endorsed portions of the Khrushchev policy. In particular they sensibly recognized that his demand that nuclear-missile weapons be accorded a prominent rather than an auxiliary role in Soviet strategy was valid. They did so, for the most part, however, while firmly rejecting his attendant imperative that the roles and size of the other branches and services be drastically reduced.

Khrushchev's disdain for the guidelines of the past and determination to cut back on the roles of ground, air, and naval forces elicited substantial resistance among those services. Two leading command figures, Marshal V. D. Sokolovskiy, chief of the General Staff, and Marshal I. Konev, commander of the ground forces, were relieved from their posts in the spring of 1960, apparently as a direct result of their opposition to the new defense policy.* Marshal R. Ya.

---

*This causal relationship, speculated upon by many Western scholars, is emphatically upheld by Colonel Penkovskiy in The Penkovskiy Papers, p. 237.

Malinovskiy, minister of defense, managed to retain his office although he staked out a distinctive policy position that acknowledged the new strategic exchange dimension emphasized in the Khrushchev doctrine but also called for the retention of important roles by the traditional branches.*

Some direct rebuttals of Khrushchev's nuclear fire-power-over-manpower thesis were also encountered. Marshal P. A. Rotmistrov emerged as a determined defender of the value of the lessons of the past and as the spokesman for the ground forces in general and in particular the armored forces, whose commander-in-chief he had been and whose higher academy he had commanded.[66] Similarly Marshal Vershinin, commander of the Soviet air forces, defended the continued viability of aviation, both strategic and tactical.[67] Even Marshal V. I. Chuikov, who had proven himself a particularly loyal supporter of Khrushchev by publicly touting the principle of Party primacy in the wake of the Cuban crisis of 1962[68] and by glorifying Khrushchev as a major architect of victory in World War II,[69] spoke out on behalf of the ground forces which he commanded and directly disputed Khrushchev's contention that mass armies would no longer be required in modern war.[70]

These command figures were joined by several military scientists. While adjusting to an increased emphasis upon missiles, most of the writers associated with the General Staff, the Academy of the General Staff, and the Frunze Academy, led by such prominent figures as Lt. Gen. S. N. Krasil'nikov[71] and Gen. P. Kurochkin,[72] strongly defended the classical framework of Soviet military thought. Their writings included reaffirmations of the utility of balanced forces and massive ground operations, as well as a firm rejection of one-sided, single-weapons theories, a description which easily fitted the policy proposed by Khrushchev.

By 1962 the pattern of adjustment of Soviet military thought to the Khrushchev challenge had begun to crystallize. Military Strategy, edited by Marshal Sokolovskiy and authored by a group of writers from the Higher Academy of the General Staff, presented an important

---

*Malinovskiy departed significantly from the Khrushchev position in his own speech to the Supreme Soviet on the very day that Khrushchev announced his deterrence-oriented policy. At that time, Malinovskiy stated that "all arms" of the Soviet Armed Forces would be retained "in relevant and sound proportions." Pravda, January 15, 1960. Malinovskiy's most complete enunciation of his strategic viewpoint was contained in his brochure, Bditel'no stoiat' na strazhe mira [Vigilantly stand guard over the peace] (Moscow: Voenizdat, 1962).

exposition of the new synthesis. The book included a number of conflicting assertions on the various issues that divided the military.[73] The strategy presented in this important work was a "grand compromise" that combined a greatly increased emphasis upon strategic missiles and nuclear weapons with a determined defense of the continuing need to prepare for massive ground-based theater operations which remained absolutely essential for the achievement of final victory. The compromise character of this authoritative treatise almost certainly reflected a unified position hammered out within the Ministry of Defense to protect the interests of all the services against Khrushchev's "radical" initiative.

Although they had successfully defended their major combat role in the theater offensive in the face of Khrushchev's attacks, the ground forces remained a prime target of the ebullient first secretary while he was in power. In the summer of 1961 Khrushchev's initial troop reductions had been halted short of the stated goal as a result of heightened international tensions over Berlin and the stubborn resistance of the Soviet military establishment.* Continuing opposition to Khrushchev within the Ministry of Defense on this score included an unexpected voice, that of Gen. A. A. Yepishev, chief of the Main Political Administration. Yepishev, who appears to have been a political client of Khrushchev's, had been appointed to his post in May 1961, with the apparent task of more closely disciplining the military establishment. Yet in a major article in the Party periodical _Voprosy istorii KPSS_ in 1963, Yepishev echoed the arguments of the most traditional military elements by explicitly endorsing the need for mass armies in the nuclear era, stating specifically, "The role of mass armies has grown with the increased importance of the technology of war."[74]

Nevertheless, in December 1963, Khrushchev returned to the offensive, calling for the resumption of manpower reductions.[75] Faced with continuing military recalcitrance over the next few months, Khrushchev went to the extreme of breaking up the central staff of the ground forces and terminating their status as an independent service in August 1964, placing them directly under the control of the General Staff. In September 1964, just three weeks before his political

---

*The reductions achieved brought the total manpower of the Soviet armed forces down to 3.1 million men rather than the projected goal of 2.4 million. For discussion of the Berlin Crisis of 1961 and its impact on Soviet defense policy, see Raymond L. Garthoff, _Soviet Military Policy: A Historical Analysis_ (New York: Praeger, 1966), pp. 115-19, and Thomas W. Wolfe, _Soviet Power in Europe, 1945-1970_, pp. 93-95, 165.

demise, he once again vented his general antipathy toward the ground forces, this time with a pessimistic evaluation of the viability of their central element, the tank.

> When I went out into the training field and saw the tanks attacking and how the antitank artillery hit these tanks, I became ill. After all, we are spending a lot of money to build tanks. And if--God forbid, as they say--a war breaks out, these tanks will burn before they reach the line indicated by the command.[76]

Long-Range Aviation (LRA) successfully weathered the Khrushchev challenge while the first secretary was still in office. In the face of his assertions that strategic bombers were doomed to be rapidly replaced by missiles, the defenders of the LRA cited the utility of employing strategic bombers as a launch platform for air-to-surface missiles and pointed out the unique advantages of employing manned aircraft against mobile targets on land or sea.[77]

A. N. Tupolev, the leading Soviet designer of strategic aircraft, presented the case for the manned bomber in the following manner:

> A rocket-carrying aircraft can be considered the first stage of a multistage system which has important advantages over multistage missiles. It does not require permanent launch sites or complex and expensive launch equipment. The first stage, the piloted aircraft, is used repeatedly. When necessary, the aircraft can be redirected after a command decision. If the target is relocated, the aircraft crew can make a decision in order to successfully execute the combat mission. Only rocket-carrying aircraft possess these qualities.[78]

By the fall of 1961, Khrushchev himself had retreated regarding the obsolescence of strategic bombers when he acknowledged their strategic attack role and noted, "We are not leaving the air force out of our reckoning; we are continuing to develop and improve it."[79]

Contemporary Soviet Doctrine

The broad outlines of the doctrinal framework presented in the initial edition of Military Strategy in 1962 have remained basically intact since that time. Thus the institutionally balanced compromise with something for each of the Soviet services has been preserved and reinforced, amply justifying the across-the-board modernization of weaponry noted in Chapter 5, which has benefited all of the elements of the Ministry of Defense. Like all military doctrines, Soviet doctrine deals with the assignment of roles and missions among the various military services, preparations for war, and the coordinated applications of military forces in battle.

Soviet military writings deal predominantly with the problems of global thermonuclear war. While individual authors have periodically noted deficiencies in the Soviet examination of lesser contingencies--that is, conflicts limited in terms of weaponry (conventional or tactical nuclear) or geographic scope--the bulk of Soviet writing remains devoted to the examination of massive world war.

The Soviets pay a great deal of attention to the significance of the opening strategic nuclear exchange that is predicted to accompany the outbreak of a global war. The first edition of Military Strategy emphasized the primacy of the missiles of the Strategic Rocket Forces, both intercontinental and intermediate/medium range, in this phase. Apparently responding to internal criticism and continuing technological developments particularly with regard to ballistic-missile launching submarines, subsequent editions of Military Strategy* and the body of Soviet military writings have more clearly recognized the roles played by both missile-carrying aviation and missile-launching submarines in the strategic attack mission.

The assignment of joint mission responsibilities to the Strategic Rocket Forces, the navy's ballistic missile-launching submarines, and Long-Range Aviation has not been without its continuing parochial rivalries. Thus Col. Gen. V. S. Tolubko, then the first deputy commander of the SRF, called attention in 1965 to the superior response characteristics of land-based ICBMs in the following manner:

> Our intercontinental missiles have unlimited range, enormous flight velocity and accuracy in hitting the target. Targets at a distance of 12,000 to 13,000 kilometers can be reached by missiles within 30 to 35 minutes, with an accuracy of plus or minus a kilometer. This is truly sniper accuracy! To hit so distant a target a modern strategic bomber needs about 10 hours and a submarine 10 to 12 days.[80]

---

*The second edition of Voennaia strategiia appeared in 1963, just 13 months after the first. The third edition was issued in 1968.

With similar parochialism the advocates of Long-Range Aviation have been known to tout the flexibility of missile-carrying strategic bombers, and the navy's spokesmen the relative invulnerability of their missile-launching submarines.[81]

In December 1972, Adm. S. G. Gorshkov, commander-in-chief of the Navy, included the following observation in an article that appeared in a unique year-long exposition on the virtues of and need for Russian naval power.*

> In connection with the equipping of the Navy with strategic nuclear weapons, the Navy is acquiring the capability not only of participating in the crushing of an enemy's military-economic potential but also is becoming one of the most important factors in deterring his nuclear attack.
>
> In this connection, missile-carrying submarines, owing to their great survivability in comparison with land-based launch installations, are an even more effective means of deterrence.[82]

Considerable speculation has been heard in the West about the degree to which the Soviets have been influenced by American strategic concepts.[83] There can be no doubt that the leading defense intellectuals of the Soviet military as well as their less numerous civilian counterparts are well acquainted with the concepts and terminology of the American defense community. This is clearly evident in the abundance of Russian translations of leading Western works and in the frequent analyses of such materials appearing in the Soviet press.[84] Yet this awareness has by no means signified adoption.

The Soviet approach to strategic deterrence provides an example of this interaction. Frequent assertions by the Soviet political and military leadership that their military power acts as a restraint upon the ambitions of the imperialists and their threats to

---

*The series entitled "Navies in War and Peace" appeared in Morskoi Sbornik between February 1972 and February 1973. These articles provide an extended, historically based case on behalf of Russian naval activity including a number of claims regarding the peacetime utility of the Navy, which is said to have "inherent qualities which permit it to a greater degree than other branches of the armed forces to exert pressure on potential enemies without the direct employment of weaponry." Adm. S. G. Gorshkov, "Navies in War and Peace," Morskoi Sbornik no. 12 (December 1972): 16.

deal any aggressor a prompt and crushing rebuff reflect a thorough Soviet understanding of the concept of deterrence. Nevertheless, the Soviets have generally avoided the explicit use of the term "deterrence" in discussing their own military doctrine. (Two Russian terms, sderzhivaniye--"restraining" or "checking"--and ustrasheniye--"terrorization" or "intimidation"--are used to express the concept of deterrence.)

Additionally, the Soviet military has shown no inclination to embrace the Western deterrence concept of "assured destruction." Developed in the early 1960s and forcefully articulated by U.S. Secretary of Defense Robert S. McNamara, assured destruction has become a central element of American strategic thinking. It represents an attempt to establish a specific level of retaliatory damage to be inflicted upon an adversary that can be assumed to be adequate to restrain him from starting a war. Having established such a benchmark,* one can evaluate the ability of alternative strategic force postures to meet this objective by pitting them against the maximum attack and defense capabilities of the enemy. Given the Soviet inclination to concentrate upon both offensive and defensive preparations for war-waging, their failure to discuss their security policy in terms of an assured destruction approach to deterrence is not surprising.

With regard to the targeting of their strategic offensive forces, Soviet military writers have shown themselves to be fully conversant with the distinctions drawn by American strategists between military/counterforce and industrial-population/countervalue targets. While understanding the American doctrine of targeting restraint--that is, U.S. suggestions that a nuclear war, should it occur, might be confined to the exchange of strikes upon purely military targets thus

---

*Assured destruction, defined in American government documents as "the ability to inflict at all times and under all foreseeable conditions an unacceptable degree of damage upon any single aggressor, or a combination of aggressors--even after absorbing a surprise attack" has been quantified in terms of a second strike assault on the Soviet Union which could destroy from one-fifth to one-fourth of the Soviet population and from one-half to two-thirds of its industrial capacity. Statement of Secretary of Defense, Robert S. McNamara before a Joint Session of the Senate Subcommittee on Department of Defense Appropriations on the Fiscal Year 1968-1972 Defense Program and 1968 Defense Budget, January 23, 1967 (Washington, D.C.: Government Printing Office, 1967), p. 39.

limiting the losses and damage on both sides*--the Soviets have sharply criticized this approach.† As is the case with their reaction to assured destruction, Soviet military writers have steadfastly refused to embrace the doctrine of counterforce-only targeting for the application of their own strategic forces. Instead they commit themselves to the simultaneous destruction of military, industrial, political, and administrative centers in a doctrine one American analyst has called "counter-center."[85] While this targeting inventory fails explicitly to include the enemy's population, Soviet strikes upon administrative and industrial centers would most certainly result in massive civilian fatalities.

Despite their frequent denials, the Soviets may in fact be prepared to launch deliberately controlled strategic attacks and thus engage in some form of limited strategic warfare as long envisioned by Western military theorists and more recently endorsed as official U.S. policy by then Defense Secretary James R. Schlesinger.[86] Should the Soviets choose to apply nuclear weapons in a highly controlled manner, their nuclear forces could be directed against the full range of enemy counterforce or countervalue targets, at varying tempos, and as either an initial nuclear strike or as a retaliatory response to such an attack by the enemy. The expansion and qualitative improvement of the Soviet strategic arsenal since the mid-1960s has clearly provided the Soviet leadership with the capability to support such a policy. Thus while the Soviet claim of indiscriminate targeting doctrine may have important deterrent advantages, covert planning or on-the-spot improvisation could permit the Soviets to become involved in a series of carefully controlled strategic nuclear exchanges, should deterrence fail and a nuclear war begin.

---

*The first authoritative proclamation of this American policy was presented in the commencement address at the University of Michigan in Ann Arbor, Michigan, by the Secretary of Defense Robert S. McNamara on June 16, 1962.

†McNamara's speech elicited direct Soviet comment and criticism in Marshal V. D. Sokolovskiy, "A Suicidal Strategy," Krasnaia Zvezda, July 16, 1962. This rejoinder charged that the American counterforce strategy represented an attempt to establish "rules of war" that would allow U.S. aggression, yet spare the American homeland from major destruction. This charge, accompanied by suggestions that the geographic proximity of military and population targets and weapons inaccuracies will make collateral value damage extremely difficult to avoid, have become standard Soviet criticisms of the American concept of limited strategic war. See Voennaia strategiia, 3d ed., pp. 75-80.

The Soviet attitude regarding the initiation of thermonuclear hostilities is also of considerable interest. During the mid-1950s, their frank discussions within the pages of Voennaia Mysl' spoke openly of the possibilities of Soviet preemptive attack should the imperialists prepare to unleash nuclear war.[87] Overt discussion of this drastic option disappeared by 1960, although public declarations clearly continue to reflect the logic of preemption. For example, Marshal Malinovskiy, addressing the Twenty-second Party Congress in November 1961, spoke of "the readiness of the Soviet Armed Forces to break up a surprise attack of the imperialists."[88] Similarly, the second edition of Military Strategy included the statement that: "Hence, the main task is to work out methods for reliably repelling a surprise nuclear attack as well as methods of breaking up the opponent's aggressive plans by dealing him a crushing blow in good time."[89]

Such hints of a Soviet interest in strategic preemption continued to appear from time to time throughout the 1960s and early 1970s. One of the most explicit of these was contained in a 1968 article by Lt. Gen. D. I. Shuvyrin, the deputy chief of civil defense:

> One must keep in mind that the aggressors will not be able to make full use for their purposes of their strategic means of attack. A portion of these means of weapons delivery will be destroyed or damaged before their launching while they are still on their launch sites, bases and airfields.[90]

The current Soviet position on this matter remains ambiguous. Strategic preemption, which would require a large and accurate counterforce capability and the timely and reliable detection of enemy offensive preparations, may remain an actively considered Soviet strategic option. However, the enormous difficulties of executing a disarming first strike against the diversified American force posture, that is, one that can almost totally disarm the United States and thus preclude its meaningful retaliation, would appear adequate to discourage a Soviet preemptive strike in anything other than the very direst circumstances.

During the initial period of a nuclear war, the National Air Defense Forces (PVO-S) are assigned a major role--the defense of the Soviet homeland against strategic attack by aircraft, missiles, and space systems. Citing their commitment to a dialectical balance between offense and defense, Soviet military writers have strongly endorsed defensive measures to protect their military forces, industrial might, and citizenry.[91] This position, of course, admirably serves the institutional interests of both PVO-S and the civil defense component of the Ministry of Defense.

While the military appears committed in theory to the principle of strategic defense, significant differences regarding the effectiveness of such measures have sometimes been evident within the Soviet military establishment. Many of these have fallen along institutional lines. For example, in February 1967, the commanders of the Strategic Rocket Forces and the civil defense forces, Marshals N. Krylov and V. I. Chuikov, whose parochial perspectives would logically incline them to be skeptical about the effectiveness of antiballistic missile (ABM) defense, made statements to precisely this effect.[92] During the very same period, the commander of PVO-S, Marshal P. F. Batitskiy, was decidedly optimistic about the ability of an ABM system to protect the Soviet homeland.[93] Other commentators, whose respective stands are not so easily linked to their institutional roles, had also taken positions on this question at that time. General P. A. Kurochkin strongly endorsed the ABM program,[94] while Marshal Grechko indicated that the Soviet ABM system was limited in its intercept capability.[95] These public differences were probably accompanied by a vigorous internal debate within the military leadership over the fate of the "Galosh" ABM deployment around Moscow. Over the next year, the Soviet political leadership chose to halt the deployment of the Galosh system.* That decision was a definite change in the Soviet attitude regarding negotiated limits on ABMs that eventually culminated in Soviet adherence to the ABM treaty negotiated during SALT I.[96]

In an age of intercontinental missiles and antiballistic missile systems, the spokesmen for PVO-S have not abandoned their concern for their older weapon systems, surface-to-air missiles and conventional antiaircraft artillery. Thus Col. D. Miloserdov, writing in Krasnaia Zvezda in 1968, cited American and West German expert opinion to justify the importance of antiaircraft artillery (AAA) against low-flying aircraft and repeated their conclusion that surface-to-air missiles and AAA guns must be used together. He closed the article heartily endorsing an allegedly West German motto, "the more missiles, the more anti-aircraft artillery guns."[97]

Recognizing the importance of the strategic nuclear exchange, Soviet military writers have referred to this initial period as potentially decisive in determining the outcome of war. Yet at the very height of Khrushchev's challenge in the early 1960s, they qualified their acceptance of his policy guidelines by declaring that the

---

*The "Galosh" ABM system deployed around Moscow leveled out at approximately 60 launchers in 1968 and remained at that level until 1972. See Chapter 5 for a more detailed discussion of Soviet strategic defense deployment.

combined efforts of all the branches and services in a modernized version of the traditional ground offensive remained absolutely essential for the achievement of final victory.

The theater campaigns included in the Soviet world war scenario are massive, mobile, and fully adapted to the nuclear era. They are supposed to commence simultaneously with the initiation of the strategic nuclear exchange and feature their own nuclear character provided by the peripheral-range strategic missiles and bombers of the SRF and LRA as well as the operational tactical missile units that are an integral part of the ground forces and the fighter-bombers of Frontal Aviation.

Khrushchev's general commitment to the superiority of missiles over aircraft helped spur a controversy within the military establishment concerning the relative roles of tactical aviation and operational-tactical missiles in the theater offensive. Once again the impact of organizational parochialism upon doctrinal viewpoints was plainly evident. The commander of the artillery and missiles branch of the ground forces, Marshal S. Varentsov, claimed a distinct superiority for tactical missiles over aviation,[98] while Marshal K. A. Vershinin, commander of the air forces,[99] A. N. Tupolev, a distinguished aircraft designer,[100] and Maj. Gen. V. Bolotnikov, an air force officer,[101] defended the flexibility of missile-carrying aircraft in both strategic and tactical operations. Tactical aviation found a variety of other prominent defenders in the early 1960s[102] and by the end of the decade it appeared that fighter-bomber aircraft had successfully maintained a major role in support of the ground force offensive.[103] Their success is clearly reflected in the substantial modernization of Frontal Aviation as evidenced by the acquisition of such aircraft as the Su-17, "Fitter B," Su-19 "Fencer," and MIG-23 "Flogger" in significant numbers over the past several years.

The role of conventional artillery, which had once been called the God of War, was also called severely into question by the appearance of nuclear weapons but similarly managed to survive. Their successful line of defense was well expressed in 1970 by Marshal of Artillery P. N. Kuleshov, former commander of artillery forces:

> With the appearance during the post war period of rocket-nuclear weapons, especially tactical and operational-tactical weapons, military specialists in a number of countries began to consider artillery an antiquated and cumbersome means of conflict. However, such views have not stood the test of time. Further improvement

> of tactical rocket weapons and analysis of their combat capabilities have shown that they cannot be employed to perform all the fire missions previously entrusted to artillery. It has been found for example that the use of rocket-nuclear weapons is practical only against large-sized and strategically important targets. . . .
>
> Foreign specialists believe that in comparison with tactical rocket weapons, artillery possesses considerably greater precision of fire. It can deliver fire on the enemy without exposing advanced friendly troops to danger. In addition, cannon-type artillery is simpler in construction and more reliable in operation, while mastery of artillery technique presents no special difficulty.[104]

Contemporary Soviet doctrine most frequently discusses the conduct of theater operations in an environment which includes the widespread use of thermonuclear, chemical, and perhaps bacteriological weapons. The ground forces, fully motorized and thus exceptionally mobile, are slated to attack rapidly in large but dispersed formations across a broad front. These assaults are to be spearheaded by tank divisions and rapidly followed up by the motorized infantry units, which also include sizable armored forces. The entire attack is to proceed with direct tactical aviation support. The major attack formations are to be assisted by airborne and helioborne assault units, often operating far behind the front lines against key enemy strong points.[105]

Following their frequent difficulties with Khrushchev described above, the ground forces have fared considerably better under the Brezhnev-Kosygin collective leadership. Although there was a three-year delay before the central command staff of the ground forces was reestablished and a new commander-in-chief named,[106] since 1964 they have been the beneficiaries of a sustained weapons modernization program[107] and a pronounced buildup of their forces, particularly along the Sino-Soviet frontier.*

---

*The total number of divisions within the ground forces has expanded from a stable 140 throughout the mid-1960s to 168 reported in September 1976. This buildup has been concentrated in the Far East, which currently contains 43 divisions where only 15 were stationed in 1968. These additional divisions have been newly formed or transferred from the southern or central USSR. They have not

Leading ground forces commanders have continued to praise their forces in the classical, combined arms manner:

> Marshal P. A. Rotmistrov, September 1968: The appearance of nuclear weapons, of course, has introduced great changes in military science. However history teaches us that harm is caused not only by conservatism on military questions but also by excessive enthusiasm for progressiveness, that is, an excessive tendency toward various kinds of utopian utterances and proposals about the absolute nature of new type of weapon. . . . That is why, giving new types of weapons and primarily nuclear weapons their due, our military doctrine proceeds from the fact that victory in war, if the imperialists unleash it, will be won by efforts of all types and categories of troops. . . . The combat experience of the last war convinced everyone that under conditions of waging a maneuverable war, one cannot win an engagement without tanks or reliable aviation.[108]

> Marshal K. P. Kazakov, February 1969: What do the Ground Forces represent today? Haven't they lost their purpose in the era of electronics, supersonic speeds and missile-nuclear weapons? No, they have not. They stand today in a new completely different capacity and do not resemble at all, even outwardly, their predecessors the infantry. Those attending the military parade at Red Square could see this with their own eyes. . . . The modern motorized infantry can rightly be called the queen of battle.[109]

The Soviet navy is assigned a variety of missions in the overall plan for waging global war. With regard to the initial period of strategic exchange, as previously noted, Soviet missile-launching

---

come either from Eastern Europe, where the deployed Soviet forces increased with the stationing of five divisions in Czechoslovakia since August 1968, or from the western USSR where 60 divisions continue to be identified. Data obtained from the annual editions of The Military Balance (London: International Institute of Strategic Studies, 1967 through 1976).

submarines have become a central element of the strategic offensive strike forces. A number of naval units play strategic defensive roles. Highest priority is assigned to antisubmarine operations directed against the American Polaris force. These efforts are scheduled to involve a large number of surface vessels and hunter-killer submarines. Western aircraft carrier task forces whose attack fighter-bombers are capable of striking either targets within the Soviet Union or their advancing theater forces are also to be the object of operations involving the strategic missile-carrying bombers of land-based naval aviation, surface vessels firing the most modern ship-to-ship missiles, and submarines using short-range ballistic missiles, surface-launched cruise missiles, and conventional torpedo attacks.

Naval forces are assigned a decidedly secondary role in the theater offensive. In coastal areas, the Soviet navy is expected to provide seaborne fire support for the ground forces and possibly launch amphibious landing operations using their naval infantry units.* Should the war be a prolonged one, the sizable Soviet submarine forces could have an impact upon the combined-arms campaign in Europe through their disruption of the oceanic supply lines from the United States.[110]

In addition to the assignment of roles and missions to the various services, an important element of Soviet strategic thought concerns its treatment of the possibilities for the limitation of warfare. We have already noted in Chapter 3 Soviet unwillingness to commit themselves to the concept of targeting limitation in strategic nuclear exchange. Regarding the possibilities that theater conflicts might be confined to particular geographic areas or limited to the application of only conventional weapons, the Soviets have been ambiguous. The overwhelming emphasis in Soviet military writing upon the conduct of nuclear war has conveyed the strong impression that the Soviets have little confidence that any armed conflict directly involving the superpowers can be contained short of global and unlimited conflict. Some of their commentaries have described American-Soviet armed encounters, particularly those involving nuclear weapons,

---

*This was the classical role of the Imperial Russian Navy, which was unexcelled as a coastal naval force, particularly along the Baltic Sea. See Robert W. Daly, "Summation of Course in Russian Military and Naval Doctrine," unpublished manuscript, Annapolis, Maryland, 1962, and his "Russia's Maritime Past," in The Soviet Navy, ed. M. G. Saunders (New York: Praeger, 1958), pp. 23-43. It was also the central element of what Robert W. Herrick has called the "Young School Strategy" during the Soviet period. See Herrick's Soviet Naval Strategy, passim.

as subject to near-automatic escalation into the global nuclear realm.[111] Yet other Soviet military writers have qualified this picture of escalation automaticity and, over the past few years, statements about the need to prepare for strictly conventional battle have become commonplace.[112]

Since the mid-1960s, Soviet writings on theater warfare have increasingly discussed the likelihood of an initial conventional phase during an armed conflict with the West. Their descriptions of this contingency take note of the problems associated with the conduct of conventional operations under the constant threat of the sudden introduction of nuclear weapons. In this regard the Soviets have frankly discussed the advantages of beating the adversary to the punch via massive battlefield preemption because the side which succeeds in getting in the first nuclear strike is likely to enjoy a significant and perhaps decisive advantage.[113]

While coming to embrace the possibility of limited conventional conflict, the Soviets have been less willing to endorse the possibility of maintaining any limitations once nuclear weapons are used. Although calls for preparations to wage war with only tactical nuclear means are occasionally heard,[114] the main thrust of Soviet military writing continues to emphasize that the first use of nuclear weapons, particularly in Europe, is likely to result in a general nuclear conflagration engulfing the continent and perhaps the entire world.[115]

In the last analysis, since its resynthesis in the face of the Khrushchev challenge of the early 1960s, Soviet strategic doctrine has taken the form of a grand compromise. It remains clearly committed to the fundamental tenets that have marked Soviet strategic thinking since the 1930s although the balance among the services has been fundamentally altered to favor the more modern, strategic arms. Yet despite the leading role assigned to the Strategic Rocket Forces, the other services have successfully maintained sizable mission responsibilities that ensure their continued organizational prosperity. This generous allocation of roles has provided all the branches and services with adequate rationales that have allowed them to continue to develop their specialized competences and to justify continuous modernization of their distinctive force capabilities.

NOTES

1. Graham T. Allison, The Essence of Decision: Explaining the Cuban Missile Crisis (Boston: Little, Brown, 1971), pp. 10-38.

2. Warner R. Schilling, "The Politics of National Defense: Fiscal 1950," in Warner R. Schilling, Paul Y. Hammond, and Glenn H. Snyder, Strategy, Politics and Defense Budgets (New York: Columbia University Press, 1962), pp. 11-15.

3. Col. Gen. A. I. Radzievskiy, ed., Slovar osnovnykh voennykh terminov [Dictionary of basic military terms] (Moscow: Voenizdat, 1965).

4. Ibid., p. 41.

5. Marshal V. D. Sokolovskiy, ed., Voennaia strategiia [Military strategy], 3d ed. rev. (Moscow: Voenizdat, 1968), p. 55. See also Thomas W. Wolfe's commentary and appropriate Soviet quotations on this issue in Soviet Strategy at the Crossroads (Cambridge: Harvard University Press, 1965), pp. 92-97.

6. Radzievskiy, op. cit., p. 42.

7. Maj. Gen. S. N. Kozlov, "Military Doctrine and Military Science," in Metodologicheskie problemy voennoi teorii i praktiki [Methodological problems of military theory and practice], ed. Maj. Gen. N. Ya. Sushko and Lt. Col. T. R. Kondratkov (Moscow: Voenizdat, 1966), pp. 94-95.

8. Radzievskiy, op. cit., p. 44.

9. Ibid., pp. 150, 220, 221, 224; see also Raymond L. Garthoff, Soviet Military Doctrine (Glencoe, Ill.: The Free Press, 1953), pp. 30, 31.

10. Sokolovskiy, op. cit., p. 57.

11. Col. A. A. Strokov, Istoriia voennogo iskusstva [The history of military art] (Moscow: Voenizdat, 1966), p. 599.

12. Col. S. A. Tyushkevich, Maj. Gen. N. Ya. Sushko, and Col. Ya. S. Dziuba, Marksizm-Leninizm o voine i armii [Marxism-Leninism on war and the army], 5th ed. (Moscow: Voenizdat, 1968), p. 357.

13. Kozlov, in Sushko and Kondratkov, op. cit., p. 91.

14. General S. M. Shtemenko, Generalnyi shtab v gody voiny [The General Staff in the war years], vol. 2 (Moscow: Voenizdat, 1973), pp. 16, 17.

15. Sokolovskiy and Cherednichenko's collaborative efforts included "Some Questions of Soviet Military Construction in the Post War Period," Voenno-Istoricheskii Zhurnal no. 3 (March 1965): 3-16; "The Revolution in Military Affairs, Its Significance and Consequences," Krasnaia Zvezda, August 25 and August 28, 1964; and "On Contemporary Military Science," KVS no. 7 (April 1966): 59-66.

16. Rotmistrov's many writings have appeared over an extended period and include "For the Creative Examination of the Questions of Military Science," Krasnaia Zvezda, March 24, 1955; "The Causes of Modern War and Their Characteristics," KVS no. 2 (January 1963): 24-33; "Military Science and the Academies," Krasnaia Zvezda, April 26, 1964; "Time and Tanks," Izvestiia, September 10, 1967.

17. Oleg Penkovskiy, The Penkovskiy Papers, trans. Peter Deriabin (New York: Avon Books, 1965), pp. 225-27, 248-55.

18. Garthoff, Soviet Strategy and the Nuclear Age, p. 288.

19. Moscow: Voenizdat, 1967.

20. Moscow: Voenizdat, 1970.

21. Major works in this area include Col. Gen. A. S. Zheltov, ed., Soldat i voina [Soldier and war] (Moscow: Voenizdat, 1971); Lt. Col. A. V. Barabanshchikov, ed., Voennaia pedagogika [Military pedagogy] (Moscow: Voenizdat, 1966); Maj. Gen. S. K. Il'in, Moral'nyi faktor v sovremennoi voine [The morale factor in contemporary war], 2d ed. (Moscow: Voenizdat, 1969).

22. Gerasimov's writings exhibit an acute and critical familiarity with Western strategic concepts. They include "Twist of Military Thought," International Affairs (Moscow) no. 3 (March 1963): 105-06; "War Savants Play Games," International Affairs (Moscow) no. 7 (July 1964): 77-84; "Plans for Controlled War," International Affairs (Moscow) no. 12 (December 1964): 88-89; "The First Strike Theory," International Affairs (Moscow) no. 3 (March 1965): 39-45; and an annual review of U.S. military affairs for International Affairs (Moscow) each entitled, "Pentagonia, 19XX" in 1966, 1967, and 1968. By 1969-70, Gerasimov was a member of two separate groups of Soviet journalists and academics touring the United States including a high-powered delegation led by G. A. Arbatov and N. N. Inozemtsev, who are discussed below. Gerasimov's training or experience in defense matters are unknown. He remains in 1977 an astute observer and commentator on Western foreign and national security policies.

23. Maj. Gen. (ret.) N. A. Talenskiy, "'Preventive War'--Nuclear Suicide," International Affairs (Moscow) no. 9 (September 1962): 16.

24. G. Gerasimov, "Pentagonia, 1966," International Affairs (Moscow) no. 5 (May 1966): 26.

25. G. Gerasimov, Pravda Ukrainy, March 23, 1969.

26. Fischer, op. cit., p. 149; Alexander Dallin et al., The Soviet Union, Arms Control and Disarmament (New York: School of International Affairs, Columbia University, 1964), p. 61.

27. Fischer, op. cit., p. 151; Dallin et al., op. cit., p. 62.

28. Interview, Col. (ret.) V. M. Kulish, Soviet Army, director of the Military Affairs Section, IMEMO, Princeton, N.J., March 24, 1970.

29. Interview, Harriet Fast Scott, McLean, Virginia, February 8, 1973. Kulish, Solodovnik, and Proektor are the joint authors of Voennaia sila i mezhnarodnye otnoshenie [Military force and international relations] (Moscow: "Mezhnarodnye Otnoshenie," 1972).

30. Scott interview, February 8, 1973; interview, Thomas W. Wolfe, Washington, D.C., February 8, 1973.

31. G. I. Sviatov, "Strategic Arms Limitation: The Principle of Equal Security," Krasnaia Zvezda, July 28, 1972; G. A. Trofimenko,

"In the Interests of Mankind," Izvestiia, September 5, 1972; and "The Soviet-US SALT Agreements," SShA: Ekonomika, Politika, Ideologiia [USA: Economics, politics, and ideology] (hereafter cited as SShA), no. 9 (September 1972): 3-16.

32. For example, G. I. Sviatov and A. Kokoshin, "Sea Power in the Plans of the American Strategists," International Affairs (Moscow) no. 3 (March 1973): 77-86; G. A. Trofimenko, "Problems of Peace and Security in Soviet-American Relations," SShA no. 9 (September 1974): 7-18.

33. Maj. Gen. V. V. Larionov, who published prolifically while assigned to the General Staff and was the working editor of the three editions of Marshal Sokolovskiy's Military Strategy, has written a number of detailed and largely accurate descriptions of the American security policy scene after joining the USA Institute staff. Cf. V. V. Larionov's "The Strategic Debates," SShA no. 3 (March 1970): 20-31; "The Transformation of 'Strategic Sufficiency,'" SShA no. 11 (November 1971); and "A Dangerous Line," Pravda, January 15, 1972. See also G. I. Sviatov, "The United States Navy," SShA no. 9 (September 1972): 122-27.

34. See Trofimenko's works cited in notes 31 and 32 above, as well as his "Political Realism and the 'Realistic Deterrence' Strategy," SShA no. 12 (December 1971): 3-15; his chapter, "Military-Strategic Aspects of the 'Nixon Doctrine,'" in Yu. P. Davydov, V. V. Zhurkin, and V. S. Rudnev, Doktrina Niksona [The Nixon doctrine] (Moscow: Izdatel'stvo Nauka, 1972), pp. 28-39; "The USSR and the United States: Peaceful Coexistence as the Norm of Mutual Relations," SShA no. 2 (February 1974): 3-17; SShA: voina, politika, ideologiia [USA: war, politics, and ideology] (Moscow: "Mysl'," 1975); "U.S. Foreign Policy in the Seventies: Declarations and Practice," SShA no. 12 (December 1976): 14-28.

35. Yu. N. Listvinov, Pervyy udar [First strike] (Moscow: "Mezhdunarodniye Otnoshenie," 1971).

36. This unnamed source was quoted in Thomas W. Wolfe, Soviet Interests in SALT: Political, Economic, Bureaucratic and Strategic Contributions, P-4702 (Santa Monica, Calif.: RAND Corporation, September 1971), p. 18.

37. Cf. Arbatov's "American Imperialism and New World Realities," Pravda, May 4, 1971; "On the Planned American-Chinese Summit Meetings," Pravda, August 10, 1971; and "The Power of Realistic Policy," Izvestiia, June 22, 1972; "Soviet-U.S. Relations at a New Stage," Pravda, July 22, 1973; "Soviet-U.S. Relations in the Seventies," SShA no. 5 (May 1974): 26-40; "Soviet-American Relations Today," Pravda, December 11, 1976; "The Big Lie of the Enemies of Detente," Pravda, February 5, 1977.

38. Personal interviews with Dr. Raymond L. Garthoff, Department of State, Washington, D.C., September 16, 1969; Dr. Seweryn Bialer, professor of politics, Columbia University, New York, N.Y., April 13, 1970; Dr. Paul Doty, professor of chemistry, Harvard University, Cambridge, May 3, 1970.

39. The Western article in question, Richard L. Garwin and Hans Bethe, "Anti-Ballistic Missile System," Scientific American 218, no. 3 (March 1968): 21-31, is quoted in Sakharov's underground essay, Progress, Coexistence and Intellectual Freedom (New York: Norton, 1968), p. 35. This eloquent plea for the development of a cooperative relationship between the Soviet Union and the United States remains officially unpublished in the USSR although it has apparently been circulated widely through the illegal samizdat (self-edited) network.

40. Fischer, op. cit., p. 150.

41. The most important of these include John Erickson's The Soviet High Command: A Military-Political History, 1918-1941 and Soviet Military Power (London: Royal United Services Institute, 1971); Raymond L. Garthoff's Soviet Military Doctrine and Soviet Strategy in the Nuclear Age (Westport, Conn.: Greenwood, 1974); Thomas W. Wolfe's Soviet Strategy at the Crossroads and Soviet Power in Europe, 1945-1970 (Baltimore: Johns Hopkins Press, 1970); and Robert W. Herrick, Soviet Naval Strategy: Fifty Years of Theory and Practice (Annapolis, Md.: U.S. Naval Institute, 1968).

42. Erickson, The Soviet High Command, pp. 207-11, 292-98, 308-09, 350-56, 381-83.

43. Nicholas N. Golovin, The Russian Campaign of 1914: The Beginning of the War and Operations in Eastern Prussia (Fort Leavenworth, Kans.: The Command and General Staff School Press, 1933), pp. 30-31, 61-63; Garthoff, Soviet Military Doctrine, pp. 43-48.

44. Erickson, The Soviet High Command, pp. 390-91.

45. Dmitri Fedotoff White, "Soviet Philosophy of War," Political Science Quarterly no. 3 (September 1936): 340-53.

46. For accounts of these groups, their views and activities in the development of Soviet military strategy in the 1920s and 1930s, see Erickson, The Soviet High Command, pp. 179, 292-98, 349-50.

47. Ibid., pp. 406-11, 437-45.

48. For an intriguing examination of post-World War II Soviet writing on the Far Eastern campaign as a model for contemporary Soviet blitzkrieg theater warfare, see John Despres, Lilita Dzirkals, and Barton Whaley, Timely Lessons of History: The Manchurian Model for Soviet Strategy (Santa Monica, Calif.: RAND Corporation, 1976).

49. Garthoff, Soviet Military Doctrine, pp. 32-35.

50. Maj. Gen. N. A. Talenskiy, "On the Question of the Laws of Military Science," Voennaia Mysl' [Military thought], no. 9 (September 1954): 20-39; Marshal P. A. Rotmistrov, "On the Role of Surprise in Contemporary War," Voennaia Mysl' no. 2 (February 1955): 17-28.

51. For accounts of this period see Garthoff, Soviet Strategy in the Nuclear Age, pp. 61-96; and Dinerstein, War and the Soviet Union, pp. 28-64.

52. For comprehensive depictions of Soviet military doctrine in the late 1950s, see Garthoff, Soviet Strategy in the Nuclear Age, pp. 149-237; and The Soviet Image of Future War (Washington, D.C.: Public Affairs Press, 1959), pp. 23-85.

53. Nikita S. Khrushchev, Khrushchev Remembers: The Last Testament (trans. and ed. Strobe Talbott) (Boston: Little, Brown, 1974), p. 540.

54. N. S. Khrushchev, "Disarmament in the Path Toward Strengthening Peace and Ensuring Friendship among Peoples," Pravda, January 15, 1960.

55. For definitions and discussions of the three groups, see Wolfe, Soviet Strategy at the Crossroads, pp. 6-10; Kolkowicz, The Soviet Military and the Communist Party, pp. 156-65; Soviet Military Strategy, U.S. editors' analytical introduction to the RAND translation, pp. 20-24.

56. Raymond L. Garthoff, "Khrushchev and the Military," in Politics in the Soviet Union: 7 Cases, ed. Alexander Dallin and Alan F. Westin (New York: Harcourt, Brace and World, 1966), p. 265.

57. Kolkowicz, The Soviet Military and the Communist Party, pp. 161, 162, 164.

58. Soviet Military Strategy, U.S. editors' analytical introduction, p. 63.

59. For comments on the shifting views of Sokolovskiy-Cherednichenko see Thomas W. Wolfe, The Soviet Military Scene: Institutional and Defense Policy Considerations, RM-4913-PR (Santa Monica, Calif.: RAND Corporation, June 1966), pp. 77-78.

60. Chuikov is an "anti-conservative," "blind supporter of Khrushchev" to Kolkowicz, The Impact of Technology on the Soviet Military, p. 12, but a traditionalist in his defense of the mass army to Wolfe, Soviet Strategy at the Crossroads, pp. 7, 46.

61. Shtemenko comes out a modernist exponent of the short future war in Wolfe, Soviet Strategy at the Crossroads, pp. 132-33, and "generally conservative" in Kolkowicz, The Impact of Technology on the Soviet Military, p. 14.

62. This pattern of opinion is also noted by Wolfe, Soviet Strategy at the Crossroads, n. 35, p. 304; and Kolkowicz, The Impact of Technology on the Soviet Military, pp. 10-11.

63. Marshal S. S. Biriuzov, "Missile-Nuclear Weapons and Combat Readiness," Krasnaia Zvezda, December 4, 1962.

64. Colonel P. A. Sidorov, "To Tirelessly Strengthen the Country's Defense Capability," KVS no. 12 (June 1961): 59-66.

65. Maj. Gen. N. Ya. Sushko et al., "The Development of Marxist-Leninist Teaching on War under Modern Conditions," KVS no. 18 (September 1961): 19-29.

66. A sampling of Rotmistrov's many articles is found in note 16 of this chapter.

67. Cf. Marshal K. A. Vershinin, "Aviation in Modern War," Izvestiia, December 23, 1962; "The Might of the Air Force Is Growing," Krasnaia Zvezda, February 1, 1964; and "Present Day Aviation and War," Aviatsiia i Kosmonavtika [Aviation and cosmonautics] no. 6 (June 1963): 6.

68. Krasnaia Zvezda, November 17, 1962.

69. Pravda, January 30, 1963.

70. "Modern Ground Forces," Izvestiia, December 22, 1963.

71. Lt. Gen. S. N. Krasil'nikov, "On the Character of Contemporary War," Krasnaia Zvezda, November 18, 1960.

72. General P. Kurochkin, "Review of Military Strategy," Krasnaia Zvezda, September 22, 1962. This review was critical of the authors of the first edition of Military Strategy for having concentrated their attention on the Strategic Rocket Forces and having "neither assigned sufficient weight to, nor analyzed deeply enough, the role and methods of operation of other types of the armed forces, particularly of the Ground Forces."

73. See Soviet Military Strategy, U.S. editors' analytical introduction to the RAND translation, pp. 12-78.

74. Gen. A. A. Yepishev, "The Growing Role of the CPSU in the Leadership of the Armed Forces," Voprosy istorii KPSS [Problems of history of the CPSU], no. 2 (February 1963): 10.

75. Izvestiia, December 15, 1963.

76. Pravda, September 22, 1964.

77. Cf. Marshal K. A. Vershinin, "Missile-Carriers: Basis of the Combat Might of the Soviet Air Forces," Krasnaia Zvezda, January 5, 1962; Marshal K. A. Vershinin, "Aviation in Modern Warfare," Izvestiia, December 23, 1962; Marshal F. Agal'tsov, "Soviet Air Fleet," KVS no. 14 (July 1963): 51.

78. A. N. Tupolev, "Missile-Carrying Aircraft," Aviatsiia i Kosmonavtika [Aviation and cosmonautics] no. 6 (June 1962): 4.

79. N. S. Khrushchev, "Address to the Twenty-second Party Congress," Pravda, October 18, 1961.

80. Col. Gen. V. S. Tolubko, "Strategic Intercontinental Rockets," Sovetskaia Rossiia, November 19, 1965.

81. Cf. Vice Adm. V. A. Sychev, "The Development of Artillery and Missile Armaments of the Navy," Morskoi Sbornik [Naval collection] no. 7 (July 1967): 41.

82. Adm. S. G. Gorshkov, "Navies in War and Peace," Morskoi Sbornik no. 2 (February 1973): 21.

83. Cf. Norman Moss, "McNamara's ABM Policy: A Failure of Communications," The Reporter, February 23, 1967, pp. 34-37; Benjamin S. Lambeth and Matthew Gallagher, "The Semantics of Arms Control: Soviet Understanding of American Strategic Concepts," unpublished paper, Institute of Defense Analysis, Washington, D.C., 1970.

84. Cf. the works of Maj. Gen. M. Mil'shtein and Col. A. K. Slobodenko including "On the Military Doctrine of the U.S. Imperialists," Krasnaia Zvezda, February 6, 1963, and their brocure, O voennoi doktrine SShA [On the military doctrine of the USA] (Moscow: Izdatelstvo "Znanie," 1963); Col. V. Larionov, "The Doctrine of Aggression in Doses" (a review of Henry Kissinger's Nuclear Weapons and Foreign Policy), Krasnaia Zvezda, July 8, 1959, and the detailed analysis of American strategic concepts in Voennaia strategiia, 3d ed., pp. 66-149. Soviet translations of Western defense policy materials range from Bernard Brodie's Strategy in the Missile Age to Robert Osgood's Limited War. See Zimmerman, Soviet Perspectives on International Relations, 1956-1967, pp. 52-53, for a listing of a few of these translations. This listing notes that these Soviet versions typically include an introduction by prominent Soviet military commentators such as Lt. Gen. S. N. Krasil'nikov, Maj. Gen. N. A. Lomov, and Col. V. M. Mochalov.

85. John R. Thomas, "The Role of Missile Defense in Soviet Strategy and Foreign Policy," in The Military-Technical Revolution: Its Impact on Strategy and Foreign Policy, ed. John Erickson (New York: Praeger, 1966), pp. 198-201.

86. The revised U.S. nuclear targeting policy is well expressed in then Defense Secretary Schlesinger's Annual Defense Department Report, FY 1975 (Washington, D.C.: Government Printing Office, 1974), pp. 4-5. See also Michael Getler, "The Schlesinger Strategy," Washington Post, February 13, 1974.

87. Dinerstein, War and the Soviet Union, pp. 187, 189-211; Garthoff, Soviet Strategy in the Nuclear Age, pp. 85-87.

88. Pravda, October 25, 1971.

89. Sokolovskiy, Voennaia strategiia, 2d ed., p. 260.

90. Lt. Gen. D. I. Shuvyrin, "A Reliable and Effective System," Voenniye Znaniia [Military knowledge] no. 10 (October 1968): 17.

91. Soviet arguments favoring active strategic defense include Lt. Col. Ye. I. Rybkin, "On the Nature of World Nuclear War,"

KVS no. 17 (September 1965): 55; and Lt. Gen. I. G. Zavialov, "On Soviet Military Doctrine," Krasnaia Zvezda, March 31, 1967.

92. Marshal N. Krylov, "The Strategic Rocket Troops," Voenno-Istoricheskii Zhurnal 7 (July 1967): 20; Marshal V. I. Chuikov, television speech, TASS International Service, Moscow, February 22, 1967.

93. Gen. P. F. Batitskiy interview, TASS International Service, Moscow, February 20, 1967.

94. "General Kurochkin's Press Conference," Soviet News, February 24, 1967, p. 98.

95. Marshal A. A. Grechko, "October Army," Izvestiia, February 23, 1967.

96. For additional discussion of Soviet ABM policy see John Erickson, "'The Fly in Outer Space': The Soviet Union and the Anti-Ballistic Missile," The World Today (March 1967): 106-14; and Thomas W. Wolfe, statement, Scope, Magnitude, and Implications of The United States Antiballistic Missile Program, Hearings Before the Subcommittee on Military Applications of the Joint Committee on Atomic Energy, U.S. Congress, Ninetieth Congress, November 6 and 7, 1967, pp. 63-75.

97. Col. D. Miloserdov, "Missiles or Guns?" Krasnaia Zvezda, August 1, 1968.

98. Marshal S. Varentsov, "Rockets: Formidable Weapon of the Ground Forces," Izvestiia, December 2, 1962, and "Maneuver by Fire," Izvestiia, October 20, 1962.

99. Marshal K. A. Vershinin, "Present Day Aviation and War," Aviatsiia i Kosmonavtika no. 6 (June 1963): 4-9, and "The Might of the Air Force Is Growing," Krasnaia Zvezda, February 1, 1964.

100. A. N. Tupolev, "The Missile-Carrying Aircraft," Aviatsiia i Kosmonavtika no. 6 (June 1962): 4.

101. Maj. Gen. V. Bolotnikov, "Man, Altitude and Speed," Krasnaia Zvezda, April 25, 1964.

102. These included Marshal P. A. Rotmistrov, "Military Science and the Academies," Krasnaia Zvezda, April 26, 1964, and Col. Gen. S. Shtemenko, "Scientific-Technical Progress and Its Influence on the Development of Military Affairs," KVS no. 3 (February 1963): 20-30.

103. See Sokolovskiy, Voennaia strategiia, 3d ed., pp. 306-07.

104. Marshal P. N. Kuleshov, "Preface," in A. N. Latukhin, Sovremennaia artilleria [Modern artillery] (Moscow: Voenizdat, 1970), p. 3.

105. For superb discussions of the Soviet combined arms offensive see John Erickson, "The Soviet Concept of Land Battle," in The Soviet Union in Europe and the Near East: Her Capabilities and

Intentions (London: Royal United Service Institution, August 1970), pp. 26-32, and a similar presentation in his Soviet Military Power, pp. 65-74.

106. John Long, Army General I. G. Pavlovsky Becomes Ground Forces Commander-in-Chief (Munich: Radio Liberty, January 24, 1968); Peter Kruzhin, "The Restoration of the High Command of the Soviet Land Forces," Bulletin, Institute for the Study of the USSR, Munich, March 1968, pp. 20-27.

107. For descriptions of this process see Wolfe, Soviet Power and Europe, 1945-1970, pp. 471, 472; Trevor Cliffe, Military Technology and the European Balance, Adelphi Paper no. 89 (London: International Institute of Strategic Studies, August 1972), passim; and John Erickson, Soviet-Warsaw Pact Force Levels, USSI Report 76-2 (Washington, D.C.: United States Strategic Institute, 1976), pp. 32-39.

108. Izvestiia, September 8, 1968.

109. Moscow Radio, February 7, 1969.

110. For Western accounts of Soviet naval strategy see Herrick, Soviet Naval Strategy; Michael MccGwire, "Soviet Naval Capabilities and Intentions," in The Soviet Union in Europe and the Near East: Her Capabilities and Intentions (London: Royal United Service Institution, August 1970), pp. 33-51; and Carl G. Jacobson, "The Soviet Navy: Acquiring Global Capabilities and Perspectives," Naval War College Review 3 (March 1972): 41-52. For a Soviet account see Marshal A. A. Grechko, "The Fleet of Our Homeland," Morskoi Sbornik 7 (July 1971): 3-9.

111. Cf. Sokolovskiy, Voennaia strategiia, 2d ed., pp. 274, 375; Marshal R. Ya. Malinovskiy, Pravda, January 15, 1960. For Western commentary see Leon Gouré, Soviet Limited War Doctrine, P-2744 (Santa Monica, Calif.: RAND Corporation, May 1963); Thomas W. Wolfe, The Soviet Military Scene: Institutional and Defense Policy Considerations, RM-4913-PR (Santa Monica, Calif.: RAND Corporation, June 1966), pp. 105-08; and the comments of Klaus Knorr in Soviet Nuclear Strategy: A Critical Appraisal, ed. Robert Dickson Crane (Washington, D.C.: Center for Strategic Studies, February 1965), pp. 27-28.

112. Cf. Marshal A. A. Grechko, Na strazhe mira i stroitel'stvo Kommunizma [On guard for peace and communism] (Moscow: Voenizdat, 1971), p. 43; Marshal I. Yakobovskiy, "Ground Forces," Krasnaia Zvezda, July 21, 1967; and the curious incident in 1963 when a group of Soviet military writers resorted to the misquotation of their own work to rebut American commentary on the Soviet treatment of escalation within the first edition of Military Strategy. Maj. Generals I. Zav'ialov, V. Kolechitskiy, and M. Cherednichenko and Col. V. Larionov, "Against Slanders

and Falsifications: Concerning the US Editions of the Book Military Strategy," Krasnaia Zvezda, November 2, 1963. For discussion of Soviet commentary on escalation see Wolfe, Soviet Strategy at the Crossroads, pp. 118-29, and Soviet Power and Europe, pp. 209-14, 452-58.

113. Cf. Col. Gen. M. T. Nikitin, "To Develop the Art of Conducting Battle," Voennii Vestnik [Military herald], October 1968, pp. 9-11; Lt. Gen. I. Zavialov, "New Weapons and the Art of War," Krasnaia Zvezda, October 1970; Maj. Gen. Yu. Z. Novikov and Col. F. D. Sverdlov, Manevr v obshchevoyskom boyu [Maneuver in combined arms combat] (Moscow: Voenizdat, 1967), p. 63.

114. Cf. Col. Gen. S. M. Shtemenko, "Infantry is Motor, Armor and Wings," Sovetskaia Rossiia, November 27, 1965; Novikov and Sverdlov, op. cit., p. 12.

115. Sokolovskiy, Voennaia strategiia [Military strategy], 3d ed., pp. 226, 235-36.

CHAPTER

5

SOVIET FORCE POSTURE

INTRODUCTION

A central element of a state's defense policy is its force posture, that is, the aggregate of military capabilities that the nation possesses. Like military doctrine, the numbers, characteristics, and deployment dispositions of a nation's military forces rarely, if ever, reflect the implementation of a coherent master plan. Rather, a nation's military capabilities at any point in time represent the cumulative resultant of numerous past decisions on the development, procurement, and deployment of several individual weapons systems. These decisions typically have been made over an extended period by a variety of political and military leaders, who acted for differing reasons, under a variety of domestic and international conditions.

The composition of a state's force is affected by a myriad of foreign and domestic policy considerations.[1] From the international side, weapons acquisitions and deployments are influenced by the perceptions and judgments of the political leadership regarding the nation's foreign policy objectives, the utility of military power in international politics, the nature of the threats and opportunities that confront the state, and the desirable military relationships that should be maintained with adversaries and allies. Domestically, force posture is likely to reflect the economic and technological capabilities of the state, the relative priority assigned to military preparedness by the political leadership, the self-interested activities undertaken by the military services and the defense industrial producers to promote the development and acquisition of specific weapons systems, and the standardized procedures that shape the processes of defense decision making in this area.

FACTORS IN THE DEVELOPMENT OF SOVIET FORCE POSTURE

Sustained Soviet efforts to develop and maintain extensive military capabilities for both strategic-intercontinental and theater warfare and other political purposes have diverse motivational roots. Foreign policy considerations include the reinforcing effects of traditional Russian imperialist ambitions and Marxist-Leninist ideological impulses that incline the Soviet leadership to seek to dominate its neighbors in Europe and Asia. In addition, the Soviets clearly want to possess in abundance the visible military manifestations of contemporary superpower status and to wield commensurate influence on a global basis.[2] The pursuit of these objectives has led to deep Soviet involvement in the prolonged East-West arms competition over the past 30 years, the dynamics of which in the strategic arena are described in considerable detail within this chapter.

These foreign policy considerations acquire significance only when perceived and acted upon by influential members of the Soviet defense policy-making community. The perceptions and actions of these participants tend to be importantly influenced by their fundamental political persuasions, and, in many cases, the institutional roles they occupy. Conservative elements, like the members of the Soviet military, are prone to emphasize the threats posed by the West and probably China as well and to counsel the pursuit of strategic superiority over these enemies. In contrast, persons viewing these countries less malevolently almost certainly are inclined to endorse lesser military procurements.

The contours of Soviet force posture have also been affected by a number of domestic considerations. The Soviet political leadership has consistently accorded the highest priority to the nation's military preparedness. This precedence has been manifested in the generous allocation of budgetary support, high-quality manpower, and the most advanced technological inputs--computers, high-precision machine tools, and so forth--to the defense sector of the economy.[3] These priorities have tended to strengthen the political importance of those engaged in this effort. Consequently, any attempt to alter this pattern dramatically would be likely to provoke stiff opposition from the more conservative Soviet domestic constituencies and thus entail substantial political risks for the initiator of such a move.

The maintenance of comprehensive weapons development and production programs is strongly promoted by those with a commitment to the continuous modernization of the Soviet force posture. Such a commitment to the "doctrine of quality"[4] is generally prevalent among those weapons designers and defense producers whose institutional and personal prosperity is closely tied to the level of Soviet activity in this area. These constituencies receive additional support from the services and branches of the Soviet armed forces who share their devotion to the acquisition of numerically large and qualitatively advanced weapons inventories. With each service and its attendant designers and producers seeking attention and budgetary support, the distribution of resources among these groups is bound to reflect their relative political power and ability to convince the political leadership of the priority of their demands. In the last analysis, of course, it is the political leadership, whatever its motivations, that must make the ultimate decisions to develop, procure, deploy, and, if necessary, employ Soviet military capabilities.

Not only the promotion of institutional interests but also established traditions and standardized organizational practices in the process of weapons development and force deployment have importantly shaped the evolution of Soviet force posture. Traditions, frequently embedded in explicit military doctrine, can provide an important source of advantage for a particular military service and its associated weapons producers. Thus the Soviet doctrinal commitment to the massive, combined arms theater offensive as an integral part of modern war strengthens the claims of the ground forces and tactical aviation for the maintenance and improvement of their extensive and diversified military capabilities. Similarly, traditional emphasis upon military operations in Europe may help account for the priority accorded to the procurement of the large numbers of medium- and intermediate-range ballistic missiles and medium-range bombers during the past two decades.

With regard to organizational process, weapons acquisitions and deployments can be strongly influenced by the normal operation of regularized bureaucratic routines. Thus the apparent practice of allotting sizable budgetary shares to each of the five independent mili tary services appears to stimulate across-the-board weapons developments and acquisitions.

In the area of force deployment the Soviet movements of men and weapons into distant areas such as Cuba and Egypt appear to have been accomplished in accordance with standard operating procedures originally developed for the employment and use of these forces in the USSR and its contiguous areas. Thus the medium- and intermediate-range missiles and their associated antiaircraft SAM sites clandestinely moved into Cuba in 1962 were erected in precisely the same configuration as similar systems deployed in the Western USSR, a practice that contributed importantly to their identification by U.S. intelligence.[5] In a similar manner, Soviet ground force divisions deployed to Cuba in 1962 and the Soviet equipment provided to the Egyptian Army in the mid-1960s included the complete invento of weapons--tanks, personnel carriers, forest clearing equipment, and so forth--carried within a standard Soviet division designed to fight in central Europe, without apparent concern for local theater requirements.[6]

THE SOVIET-U.S. ARMS RACE

The development of Soviet military capability since World War II, as noted earlier, has occurred within the context of an arms race with the United States. That is, Soviet force posture has developed in an environment characterized by (1) conscious antagonism between the Soviet Union and the United States; (2) a mutual structuring of forces with attention to their deterrent and combat effectiveness against one another; and (3) an ongoing competition in terms of both the quantitative size and the qualitative characteristics of their armed forces.[7] While this armaments competition has produced irregular spurts of deployment activity on both sides, it has been marked by mutually sustained efforts in weapons research and development across a wide spectrum of systems.

Types of Interaction

The Soviet-American arms race has included two basic types of weapons interaction, the emulative and the offsetting patterns.[8] Both countries have displayed an inclination to imitate the weapons development and procurement actions of their adversary. The emulative type of interaction was evident in the much-publicized bomber and missile gap deployment reactions of the United States in the mid-1950s and early 1960s and appears to have been the case in the Soviet ICBM buildup between 1965 and 1977 and in their deployment of Y-class and D-class ballistic-missile launching submarines. While in some cases the emergence of highly similar weapons systems in both inventories may reflect conscious imitation, in others it appears to be merely the product of parallel development efforts by similarly endowed rivals.[9]

More frequently the Soviet-American force posture interaction has been of an offsetting variety in the manner of the classical offence vs. defense competition. Examples of this action-reaction pattern include mutual Soviet and American activities in the procurement of strategic missile launching submarines and antisubmarine warfare systems to counteract this threat, strategic bomber-bomber defense activities on both sides, and, somewhat later, a similar ballistic missile-missile defense competition. The latter case has included three discrete stages: the development of the basic launch vehicle, the ICBM, the offsetting reaction in the antiballistic missile (ABM) development, and the development of a series of tactical and technological measures including the acquisition of various penetration aids and multiple warheads designed to neutralize and overcome the opponent's missile defenses.

While the emulative-offsetting distinctions are straightforward in theory, the actual pattern of Soviet-American weapons interactions has been highly complex. In light of the lengthy lead times involved in the development of modern weaponry, the efforts to acquire sophisticated offensive and defensive systems are often begun simultaneously. Thus, for example, Khrushchev noted that the Soviet ICBM and ABM development programs were both initiated at the same time.[10] Under these circumstances it is difficult to establish who is reacting to whom.

The action-reaction relationship between the Soviet Union and the United States has been complicated by the extreme secrecy that surrounds the major weapons development programs in both countries. Largely denied information about the early stages of the opponent's research and design efforts, the political-military leaderships on both sides are prone to fear the worst. In the name of prudence, they frequently employ worst-case analysis that attributes to the adversary maximal weapons development efforts and optimum operational performance for a wide variety of weapons. Initial development efforts for offsetting systems are often undertaken based upon the anticipated or vaguely perceived rather than the directly observed activities of the opponent. As a practical matter, the efforts attributed to the enemy are likely to be those that one's own weapons researchers have conceived and proposed. As a result, programs undertaken in response to such anticipated development activities are often the product of an "arms race against oneself" in which one's own offense is pitted against one's defense in a manner that fortifies the claims of each. This process can easily produce an action-overreaction pattern in which, although the anticipated threat fails to materialize, the "response" nevertheless results in the procurement of a major weapons system.[11]

The Soviet Objective: Parity or Superiority?

The existence of the postwar superpower arms race, particularly in the field of strategic nuclear capabilities, raises an important question about what balance of strategic forces has been sought by the Soviet Union and the United States vis-a-vis one another throughout the period. Reciprocal efforts to achieve superiority over the adversary have not been required to fuel the strategic arms competition. Given the secrecy and resultant uncertainties surrounding the wide-ranging weapons development efforts on both sides, the differences in technological achievement at any given time, and varying national traditions in force development, a vigorous superpower strategic arms race could logically have been sustained simply by the presence of simultaneous, well-hedged efforts directed at assuring each side a parity position in relation to the other.

This is not to say that neither the United States nor the USSR has ever striven for strategic superiority. Superiority was the openly acknowledged goal of U.S. administrations throughout the 1950s and into the 1960s. This objective was gradually displaced by the assured-destruction, deterrence approach first associated with Defense Secretary R. S. McNamara, and subsequently by the "sufficiency" and "essential equivalence" objectives that have been added during the course of the Strategic Arms Limitation Talks.*

Soviet public declarations about the "correlation of forces" they seek in the strategic military arena have widely varied. As noted in Chapter 3, Soviet military spokesmen have consistently championed efforts to achieve military-technological superiority over their adversaries. Similar sentiments have been expressed by civilian ideologists who frequently cite Lenin on the intrinsic superiority of the socialist system in terms not only of military power but also in political, economic, ideological, and moral terms. In contrast, some political leaders and civilian commentators have asserted that the Soviet Union seeks nothing more or less than a position of strategic parity with the United States.[12] It is highly likely that whatever their longer-range hopes may have been, confronted throughout the 1950s and 1960s by a substantially superior American strategic arsenal, the Soviet leadership during that period approved the many strategic weapons programs described in this chapter largely in terms of an effort to achieve equality with the United States. How-

---

*The "strategic sufficiency" objective, adopted by the Nixon administration in 1969, calls for the United States to maintain an assured destruction capability against the USSR as well as the ability to assure that the United States can match the Soviets in various damage infliction categories. "Essential equivalence" was developed by the Nixon and Ford administrations during the SALT II negotiations to underline American determination to settle for nothing less than full equality in strategic offensive forces in any new SALT agreement. For an excellent discussion of essential equivalence in the SALT context, see the speech of Defense Secretary Harold Brown delivered at the University of Rochester on April 14, 1977.

ever, the continuing momentum of these and subsequent Soviet strategic weapons programs over the past several years has convinced many Western observers that, after pulling even with the United States, the Soviet political leadership has now adopted a goal of acquiring clear-cut strategic superiority. *

In this author's opinion, one cannot with any degree of certainty determine Soviet intentions in terms of their commitment to attaining either comprehensive parity or superiority over the United States. The Soviet declarations of intent, as reviewed above, are ambiguous. While the pace and scope of Soviet strategic military programs have been considerable, the technologically superior United States has been by no means quiescent in this area despite official declarations about stable deterrence and parity. Thus, either a goal of comprehensive parity in the face of a "worst case" image of the United States or a commitment to attain substantial superiority could be the shared objective among the Soviet leaders rationalizing and promoting the myriad of strategic programs currently being undertaken by the Soviet Union. In fact, the true situation is likely to be a combination of these two orientations. The present Soviet leadership undoubtedly approaches this question with a firm resolve to settle for nothing less than comprehensive strategic military parity with the United States. They are also very likely to be inclined to press on opportunistically toward acquiring more margin of visible advantage as long as they are convinced that it can be attained without undue monetary or political cost. Thus Soviet perceptions and evaluations regarding U.S. capabilities, intent, and resolve are crucial factors in their decisions about the shape and direction of key Soviet military programs, which, as discussed below, often have a considerable momentum on the basis of various domestic considerations. United States decisions regarding the composition of its strategic force posture are made in terms of a similar mix of varying intentions, uncertain evaluations of Soviet intentions and capabilities, and diverse domestic political considerations.

---

*Highly publicized warnings about the threat posed by an undeniable massive Soviet drive to attain strategic superiority over the United States were sounded in early 1977 by the so-called "B team" of experts led by Dr. Richard Pipes, who prepared a supplemental national intelligence estimate for the Ford administration in the fall of 1976, and by recently retired chief of U.S. Air Force Intelligence, Maj. Gen. George J. Keegan, Jr. See John L. Frisbee, "Those National Intelligence Estimates," Air Force Magazine (February 1977): 4; and "A New Assessment of the Soviet Threat," Aviation Week and Space Technology (March 28, 1977): 38-48.

MILITARY ECONOMIC PLANNING

The Soviet military force posture is developed, procured, and maintained in accordance with a variety of economic plans. The Ministry of Defense, like all Soviet governmental institutions, operates in accordance with program guidelines established in its annual and five-year plans.[13] The plans for the Ministry of Defense are in turn components of more comprehensive plans of corresponding length which guide the functioning of the entire Soviet economy.

Given the length of time that passes between the initiation of preliminary design work and the operational deployment of a modern weapons system, a series of longer-range weapons development plans extending beyond the familiar five-year period are also likely to exist. Robert Herrick[14] and Michael MccGwire[15] have written of the existence of 10- and 20-year Soviet naval construction plans since World War II. A recent book on planning practices within the Soviet navy notes the existence of "future plans" covering "considerably prolonged segments of time on the order of 5, 10, 15, 20, and more years."[16] Because of the developmental lead times involved, plans on the order of 10 to 15 years in length are likely to guide the design and procurement of Soviet strategic offensive and defensive missiles and modern aircraft as well. The likelihood that long-term plans are employed in these cases is reinforced by the growing use of 15-year plans within other more "visible" sectors of the Soviet economy.[17]

Soviet military authors have published a few articles that discuss Soviet military planning during the five-year plans prior to World War II.[18] Information from these accounts has been combined with the institutional framework for Soviet defense policy making presented in Chapter 2 and available descriptions of Soviet planning practices within the economy as a whole[19] to develop a speculative depiction of the steps involved in the preparation and approval of the various plans that currently guide the activities of the Soviet armed forces.

The plans of the Ministry of Defense appear to be drafted by a section of the General Staff[20] that probably operates with the assistance of the Ministry's Central Financial Directorate.[21] These plans are evidently developed on the basis of requests initially prepared by the main staffs of the independent services and combat branches of the Soviet armed forces.[22] The elaboration of the ministry-wide spending guidance almost certainly requires the resolution of serious interservice conflicts. Most of these conflicts are likely to be settled within the General Staff,[23] although in some cases they might involve higher-level negotiations between the service chiefs and the Minister of Defense. Interservice negotiations at this level might take place within the collegium of the Ministry of Defense, whose membership is likely to include the Minister of Defense, his three first deputies, and the nine deputy ministers of defense.[24]

The weapons development and production aspects of a defense plan must be closely coordinated with the corresponding plans prepared by the industrial ministries engaged in defense production (see Chapter 2). This coordination is likely to be based on the close and mutually supportive working relationships that are maintained between the services and their defense industrial producers. These ties apparently include regular contacts between weapons development directorates of the services* and the design bureaus and series production plants of the industrial ministries[25] as well as direct links between the main staffs of the services and the central apparatus of the defense production ministries. Projected research and development programs and series production runs are likely to be included in the plans of both the Ministry of Defense and the appropriate defense industrial ministries.

Direct informal exchanges between the services and the industrial ministries in the parallel drafting of their individual plans is probably supplemented by a formal coordination of the Ministry of Defense's requirements with the available defense production capacity. This is likely to occur under the auspices of the interministerial Military Industrial Commission, which is apparently chaired by L. V. Smirnov.[26] This coordination is also likely to include the participation of representatives from a defense section of the State Planning Committee (Gosplan), who are responsible for integrating the defense effort within the national economy.†

The establishment of defense spending priorities and thus the final approval of the plans of the Ministry of Defense and the defense industrial ministries almost certainly lies with the Party Politburo. Supervision of the preparation and implementation of these plans prior to and following Politburo consideration probably is accomplished by the Party secretary supervising defense production, now apparently Ya. P. Ryabov, who is likely to rely in turn upon guidance provided by his predecessor, Minister of Defense D. F. Ustinov, and by the General Secretary L. I. Brezhnev. Ryabov probably performs

---

*See this chapter under "Weapons Design" for the identification of these organizations and a discussion of their role in the weapons acquisition process.

†This section, formerly headed by First Deputy Chairman of Gosplan V. M. Ryabikov, a veteran defense industrial manager, apparently includes a number of "alumni" from the defense industrial ministries. John A. McConnell, "Interest Groups and the Cold War: A study of the Soviet Military Industrial Complex," dissertation in progress, Dalhousie University, Halifax, Nova Scotia, January 1974, p. 29.

this task with the assistance of his personal staff and the Defense Industries Department of the Central Committee headed by I. D. Serbin. Having just moved to the center from Sverdlovsk, he is likely to continue to share this responsibility with Ustinov. Ustinov's lengthy involvement in the high-level supervision of defense industrial matters dates from the early 1940s, thus providing him with close associations with L. V. Smirnov and the heads of the defense production ministries and enormous personal power in the direction of Soviet armaments programs.

Prior to their consideration by the full Politburo, the plans of the Ministry of Defense are likely to be closely examined within its military policy subcommittee, the Defense Council.[27] With regard to military-economic planning, the Defense Council is probably responsible both for providing initial guidelines to the appropriate agencies at the beginning of the planning process and for making recommendations to the Politburo regarding final approval of the plans developed by the Ministry of Defense and the defense-industrial ministries. The deliberations of the Defense Council are very likely to be led by Brezhnev and probably will reflect his consensus-building political style. Consequently, the plans forwarded by this committee to the Politburo for its consideration and approval are likely to reflect in advance the composite preferences of its members.

Nikita Khrushchev's memoirs provide us with direct evidence about the Politburo (then called the Presidium) as the final decision maker regarding defense construction plans. More importantly, one account is extremely revealing regarding the proprietary interest and outspoken behavior of at least one senior military figure, Navy CINC Adm. N. G. Kuznetsov, in advocating a major weapons production proposal.

In 1955 Kuznetsov had just attended a Party Presidium meeting that, led by Khrushchev, had decided to postpone a decision on a ten-year plan for surface ship construction. This, Khrushchev asserts, precipitated the following turn of events:

> After the meeting, I left my Kremlin office in a hurry to get somewhere. There was Kuznetsov waiting for me in the corridor. He started walking along beside me. I could tell he was extremely agitated. Suddenly he turned on me very rudely and belligerently. "How long do I have to tolerate such an attitude toward my navy?" he shouted.
>
> "What attitude? What are you talking about? I think our attitude toward the navy is perfectly good."

> "Then why don't you make a decision today about my recommendations?" As a specialist in his field, Kuznetsov felt it was up to him to tell us what to do and up to us to approve his recommendations without any deliberation. However, that wouldn't have been a decision by the government--it would have been a dictate by the navy.
>
> "We want some more time to examine your proposals closely," I said.
>
> He made another harsh remark, to which I replied, "Look, Comrade Kuznetsov, we haven't rejected your memorandum--we've simply put off the decision for a week. Why don't you just be patient? We'll discuss the problem in detail at the next meeting, then we'll make a decision."[28]

The limits of such military advocacy are clear in that after Admiral Kuznetsov's determined and intemperate opposition continued following a subsequent Presidium decision to reject the navy's plan, this resulted in his being both relieved of his post and demoted in rank for what Khrushchev called his "Bonepartist behavior."[29]

Kuznetsov's successor, Adm. S. G. Gorshkov, has proved more adept politically, successfully weathering Khrushchev's personal animosity toward large surface ships and continuing on to preside over the massive expansion of Soviet naval capabilities and deployments in his more than 20 years as commander-in-chief of the Soviet navy.

SOVIET WEAPONS ACQUISITION

The panoply of weapons held by the Soviet armed forces is a central element of Soviet military capability. This diversified arsenal has been designed and procured within the budgetary guidelines established in the various plans developed by the Ministry of Defense as well as the defense industrial ministries and subsequently approved by the political leadership.

The Soviets have developed a distinctive national style for weapons design and acquisition. This pattern appears to be followed for the development of a wide range of armaments ranging from small arms to ballistic missiles. It includes a standardized organizational format and distinctive set of design practices.

Memoir literature on defense matters provides abundant information about Soviet weapons development practices during the 1920s, 1930s, and 1940s. Information on these procedures is much less plentiful over the past 25 years. The available Western and Soviet materials that describe more recent weapons development activity, particularly with regard to aircraft production,[30] suggest that the basic pattern of institutions and procedures established in the earlier period continues to persist.

Nevertheless, the description of the Soviet weapons acquisition process that follows is necessarily speculative, resting heavily on the assumption that current practices continue to resemble those of the past.

Basic Research with Military Applications

Fundamental scientific research in many areas can have military applications. Within the Soviet Union this research is conducted in a variety of institutions. Much of it is carried out in the extensive network of research institutes that are supervised by the USSR Academy of Sciences.[31] Additional work of this nature is conducted in the research facilities of the higher educational institutions of the Ministry of Education and other governmental ministries including the Ministry of Defense.* Finally, basic research with a very direct connection to weapons development is also conducted within scientific research institutes directly controlled by the eight defense production ministries† and by the Ministry of Defense. For example, the Scientific Research Institute of the Red Army Signals Command (NIIS-KA) played an important role in Soviet radar development.[32]

The Soviets have not written about the manner in which they manage their defense-related basic research program. Their recent efforts to improve the coordination of research and development

---

*This research is carried out in the laboratories of the major academies run by the branches of the Soviet Armed Forces. For example, basic research on ballistics has been carried out in the Dzerzhinskii Artillery Engineering Academy and research with aviation applications continues to be performed in the well-known Zhukovskii Military Air Engineering Academy controlled by the Soviet air forces. Maj. Gen. M. Serebryakov, "Scholar-Artilleryist N. F. Drozhdov," Voenno-Istoricheskii Zhurnal no. 7 (July 1968): 116-19; Robert A. Kilmarx, A History of Soviet Airpower (New York: Praeger, 1962), pp. 68, 116.

†For example, the Central Aerohydrodynamic Institute (TsAGI), the Central Institute of Aviation Motors (TsIAM), and the All-Union Institute of Aviation Materials (VIAM) within the Ministry of Aviation Industry. Alexander, R&D in Soviet Aviation, p. 5.

within the civilian sector of the economy* suggests that a system at least as comprehensive is almost certain to exist in the high priority defense area. Management of weapons-related research probably involves regular supervision from the highest levels of the Communist Party, most likely under the auspices of Secretary D. F. Ustinov or his apparent successor Ya. P. Ryabov and perhaps the Defense Industries and Science Departments of the Central Committee. Coordination of these matters in the Soviet government also is likely to engage the efforts of the Military-Industrial Commission headed by L. V. Smirnov. The highest priority weapons projects such as the development of ballistic missiles are likely to be monitored by the General Secretary L. I. Brezhnev and his Politburo colleagues on the Defense Council. These leaders probably rely upon the detailed research plans of the annual, five-year, and longer-term variety developed within the Academy of Sciences and the various government ministries and coordinated with the State Planning Committee (Gosplan).

Military participation in the funding and supervision of defense-related basic research is likely to be varied. Much of the relevant research done within the Academy of Sciences or the ministerial research institutes will have its own scientific significance independent of its weapons systems applications. Other projects may be undertaken and funded specifically for their military dimensions. (For example, the Main Artillery Directorate (GAU) funded the research work of both the Leningrad Electro-Physics Institute (LEFI) and the Central Radio Laboratory (TsRL) in the early development of Soviet radar.)[33] In either case the Ministry of Defense is likely to be a persistent supporter of substantial research efforts in those areas that appear to promise eventual military utility.

Weapons Design

The creation of weapons designs and the applied engineering that must accompany their development is carried out in a smaller and more specialized group of organizations. This activity is conducted by several scientific research institutes and weapons design

---

*This effort has included the formation of the State Committee for Science and Technology in 1965 and measures to identify priority areas for research and to improve the ties between research organizations and production facilities. Robert Adamson, "Mobilizing Soviet Science," Scientific Research 3, no. 2 (January 22, 1968): 25-34.

bureaus within the various defense industrial ministries and to a considerably lesser extent, within these organizations run by the Ministry of Defense. (Design bureaus are often designated as opytno-konstruktorskoe byuro (OKB), experimental design bureaus, or simply as konstruktorskoe byuro (KB). Some, for example, in the aircraft industry, are semiautonomous organizations that possess only limited prototype construction facilities while others, as in the artillery and tank areas, are integral parts of major armament production plants.)

The most prominent of these design entities have traditionally been headed by senior designers who enjoy enormous personal authority and considerable autonomy in their work and frequently receive the highest national honors. While senior Soviet aircraft designers such as A. I. Mikoyan, P. O. Sukhoi, A. N. Tupolev, and A. S. Yakovlev have been the best-known in the West,* this pattern is also visible in other areas including the development of tanks,† small arms,‡ naval vessels,** and strategic ballistic missiles.***

The vast majority of Soviet weapons design organizations are directly controlled by the defense industrial ministries. They must, however, remain in close touch with their customers in the Soviet military establishment. The primary channels for this interaction appear to be the weapons development directorates of the military

---

*Their fame has been aided by the Soviet practice of designating aircraft with the initials of the chief designer. Thus, Mikoyan and his partner M. Gurevich were responsible for the MIG series, Sukhoi for the SUs, Tupolev for the TUs, and Yakovlev for the YAKs.

†The leading tank designers have included M. I. Koshkin, A. A. Morozov, I. L. Dukhov, Zh. Ya. Kotin, and L. S. Troyanov.

‡The most prominent Soviet small arms designers, who, like the aircraft designers, have their products designated with their initials, included F. V. Tokarev, B. Shpital'nyy, V. A. Degtyarev, M. T. Kalashnikov, and S. T. Simonov.

** Although naval designers are not known by name, MccGwire has written: "The Ministry of Shipbuilding Industry has its own specialist design offices and submarine design teams which have stayed together from the earliest postwar diesel programs to the latest nuclear boats and this presumably applies to surface types as well." MccGwire, "Soviet Naval Procurement," p. 74.

***Leading designers in Soviet missile development have included S. P. Korolev, L. A. Voskresenskiy, V. P. Glushko, A. M. Isayev, V. N. Chelomei, and M. K. Yangel. Nicholas Daniloff, The Kremlin and the Cosmos (New York: Knopf, 1972), pp. 67-88.

services. These organizations have been identified in the air forces,[34] the navy,* and the ground forces,† and are almost certain to exist within the National Air Defense Forces and Strategic Rocket Forces as well. A supervisory role may also be played by a weapons development section within the General Staff‡ and, in the strategic weapons area, by an administration headed by Deputy Minister of Defense for Armaments Col. Gen. N. N. Alekseev.

Initial speculation about the creation of a new high-level organization to coordinate strategic weapons development within the Ministry of Defense was sparked by the appointment in October 1970 of Col. Gen. N. N. Alekseev to the post of deputy minister of defense without a publicly identified area of responsibility. Alekseev had been one of the six chief Soviet delegates to the Strategic Arms Limitation Talks with the United States and is reported to have an extensive technical background in missiles and electronic equipment.[35] By 1976, Alekseev was publicly identified as deputy minister of defense for armaments.

Twice in the past special high-level organizations were formed within the Ministry of Defense to manage weapons development. The first, the chief of armaments and his staff, functioned during the late 1920s and early 1930s at the time of the initial five-year plans. The second, headed by the deputy minister of defense for new weapons, operated during the late 1940s and 1950s and apparently played

---

*The naval high command includes the post of deputy commander-in-chief for shipbuilding and armaments, suggesting the existence of a weapons development directorate of that title. Directory of USSR Ministry of Defense and Armed Forces Officials (Washington, D.C.: Government Printing Office, April 1973), p. 10.

†The ground forces apparently possess two weapons development directorates, the Chief Armor Directorate and an updated version of the prestigious Main Artillery Directorate (GAU). In recent years GAU has probably been expanded to include the management of operational-tactical missile development in addition to its traditional direction of artillery and small arms production. John Milsom, Russian Tanks, 1900-1970 (Harrisburg, Pa.: Stackpole, 1971), p. 80.

‡The General Staff has played an important role in weapons development in the past. During the late 1930s it assumed the broad responsibilities in this area which had been exercised by the chief of armaments and his staff. The role of the General Staff with regard to these matters in recent years, however, is unknown. Marshal M. V. Zakharov, "Communist Party and the Technological Rearmament of the Army and Navy in the Years of the Prewar Five-Year Plans," p. 4, n. 4.

a central role in the management of the Soviet strategic missile program.[36]

Design proposals for the creation of new weapons probably originate from three different sources: (1) from the weapons design organization; (2) from the military customer; and (3) from the civilian political leadership. Historical accounts by Soviet military personnel, weapons designers, and defense industrial executives provide many examples of designs inspired by each of these groups.

Weapons designers have a great deal at stake that prompts them to generate new weapons systems proposals. Each time a design bureau succeeds in winning approval to develop and mass produce a new weapon, it stands to gain added prestige as well as substantial financial reward.

An example of the role of entrepreneurial self-promotion within the Soviet weapons development community is found in the memoirs of a leading aircraft designer, Alexander Yakovlev. In 1951, Yakovlev was disturbed about a decision by Stalin to prohibit further design work on fighter aircraft and to concentrate instead upon modernizing the MIG-15 that had been developed by the rival design bureau headed by Artem Mikoyan. Yakovlev describes his concerns about the decision as follows:

> I was very worried about the situation developing in our design bureau. You see behind me stood 100 people, who might lose faith in me as the leader of the design collective. I understood likewise that if all experimental work was limited to the modernization of the existing production model and not to the creation of new, more advanced models, then in a very short time, this would inevitably lead us to obsolescence.[37]

Moved by these considerations, Yakovlev personally approached Stalin and succeeded in gaining permission to proceed with the development of his own aircraft. This appeal eventually led to the design and production of the YAK-25, an all-weather fighter that became a central element in the Soviet tactical aviation inventory in the mid-1950s.[38]

When the military originated a request for a new system it may emanate from the weapons development experts within the General Staff or the services, who are likely to value weapons modernization as an end in itself, or from the operational planners of the Main Staffs and the General Staff who will probably seek a new system in order to improve the chances for the fulfillment of a particular operational mission.

V. G. Grabin, a prominent artillery designer, has written of the mix between designer initiative and the assignment of tasks by the military in the 1930s and 1940s.

> Our design bureau always carried out two parallel assignments: that of meeting the gross production goals and that of creating new types of artillery systems. As a rule, our plant received its tactical-technical requirements* for the development of new guns from the Main Artillery Directorate. But several guns were developed on our own initiative. There was a special section in our design bureau which worked on long-range developments. The Z1S-3 76-mm division gun was an example of such development. And when during the war the need arose for a new and better gun we were already able to present a completed model to the State Defense Committee.[39]

Grabin's account also sheds light on another important dimension of the Soviet weapons development effort. He clearly illustrates the future orientation of the successful designer and the importance attached to closely monitoring the activities and achievements of potential adversaries with these comments:

> Our design bureau constantly followed the achievements of science and technology, including those of foreign countries. It was necessary for us to foresee many things--the possible velocity of moving targets, the maximum weight limits of bridges, the conditions of roads and the long range perspectives for development of materials. The artillery designer was also obliged to know the industrial potential of the enemy. And if we created a gun designed to destroy only the enemy's existing means of attack and defense, then we had not fulfilled our task of always looking ahead.[40]

---

*This phrase, "taktiko-tekhnicheskii trebovanie" in Russian, is used by the Soviets to describe the performance characteristics sought for a new system in Soviet weapons development efforts ranging from tanks to ballistic missiles.

Other historical accounts reiterate Grabin's point that design bureaus frequently develop weapons in response to the requests of their military customers.[41] In fact, this is likely to remain the prevalent mode of weapons development initiation today. The design specifications for these systems, the "technical-tactical characteristics" noted above, are probably established by the weapons development directorates of the services in cooperation with their main staffs and in some cases, in concert with the weapons development section of the General Staff.

The operation of the military demand pattern is also almost certain to be marked by a heavy dose of parochial self-interest. In this case the active lobbyists will be the military organizations charged with the management of weapons acquisition and those elements which plan for and operate these systems once they are deployed. A cardinal concern of the services of the Soviet armed forces is their desire to continuously modernize their weapons inventory.

Members of the Soviet political leadership have often played an active and highly personal role in weapons development. This involvement included direct personal assignments of design responsibilities by Stalin between 1937 and 1953 during the period of his highly personalized rule.[42] There is abundant evidence that Khrushchev was also personally involved in these matters.[43] The businesslike demeanor of the present regime suggests that while Brezhnev and Kosygin are certain to be kept well informed about major weapons development projects, they are unlikely to be the direct inspirers of many of these efforts.

Whatever the source of a design proposal, a standardized format appears to be generally followed for the full-scale development and eventual production of a new weapons system. In many cases, this process includes a direct competition between design bureaus for the right to add their creation to the Soviet military inventory. These competitions may involve several design bureaus* and can be held at different stages of the development process. They may involve the comparison of detailed plans, full-scale mock-ups, or working prototypes. In the latter case, extensive operational tests are frequently conducted to assist in determining the winner.

---

*Yakovlev writes of a fighter design competition in 1939 that included 11 competitors. Yakovlev, "The Aim of a Lifetime," International Affairs (Moscow) no. 2 (February 1973): 94. Soviet memoirs provide accounts of numerous design competitions throughout the armaments effort.

Whether a competition is being held or a single design is being developed, a new weapons system is carefully monitored and evaluated during its development. This task is performed by a specially appointed scientific-technical commission. This body, composed of specialists drawn from the appropriate defense industrial ministry and the customer military service, regularly reviews the progress of a weapons development effort.[44]

The supervisory and evaluative activities of these commissions are likely to be routinely scrutinized by the staff of the Military-Industrial Commission on the government side and by the Defense Industries Department acting for the Party. High-priority and particularly expensive systems such as a new ICBM, nuclear submarine, or aircraft carrier are likely to merit the direct attention of Party Secretary D. F. Ustinov and perhaps even the Defense Council as well. The Soviets may also form commissions whose members include the highest political figures to supervise special military development efforts, a practice they have employed in the past. This approach was frequently applied in the 1930s and 1940s when special commissions were often formed to troubleshoot specific weapons development programs.[45]

Weapon Production

A successfully developed weapon is eventually certified for series production by the appropriate scientific-technical or "state commission."[46] The transition to series production must then be made. The complexity of modern weaponry will almost always require the coordination of production efforts in several different plants and often between ministries. This responsibility for this interministerial coordination is likely to rest with the ministry most responsible for the production of the particular type of weapon.

Frequently the original design organization is not directly affiliated with the plant selected to mass produce the weapon. In these cases, representatives are commonly sent from the design bureau to the production plant to assist in setting up series production.

During the production phase the military customer continues to be directly involved in the process. A small team of officers, probably drawn from the service's weapons development directorate, is stationed at the plant to monitor its output for conformity with the technical specifications agreed upon by the scientific technical commission. These representatives are empowered to refuse to accept delivery or authorize payment for systems that fail to meet these requirements.[47]

THE EVOLUTION OF SOVIET STRATEGIC FORCE POSTURE

Over the past three decades, the weapons development processes described above have been utilized to design and procure a large and diversified Soviet military arsenal. The composition of this force posture has been influenced by several of the domestic and international considerations previously noted. The sections that follow describe and explain the growth of Soviet strategic offensive and strategic defensive capabilities in recent years. They are designed to illustrate the importance of supplementing traditional explanations that rely heavily upon foreign policy motivations attributed to the Soviet leadership with additional hypotheses that focus upon forces internal to the Soviet policy process.

Strategic Offensive Forces

Land-Based Missiles

The Soviet inventory of strategic missiles currently includes some 1,527 intercontinental ballistic missiles and 600 of intermediate and medium range.[48] The ICBM force includes a mix of older systems--159 SS-7s and SS-8s, which were deployed during the early 1960s; 252 SS-9s, 900 SS-11s, and 60 SS-13s, all third-generation weapons developed in the 1960s and deployed from 1964 onward; and the newest fourth-generation missiles--20 SS-17s, 36 SS-18s, and 100 SS-19s whose deployment began in 1975. The more modern ICBMs are emplaced in a series of launch complexes spread throughout the Soviet Union in dispersed underground silos,* while the second-generation systems are deployed in both "soft" aboveground launch positions and hardened silos.[49] The Soviet practice of hardening these launch positions followed American efforts of this type by a couple of years, thus representing an interaction with both emulative and offsetting aspects.

The pace of Soviet missile deployment and the characteristics of their different systems have varied considerably. In an attempt

---

*Press reports indicate that there are six major SS-9 complexes, each containing several flights of six missiles each, and ten large SS-11 complexes that have a number of ten-missile clusters within them. W. Beecher, "U.S. Data Indicate Moscow Is Slowing ICBM Deployment," New York Times, December 17, 1970. Data on the deployment pattern of the fourth-generation ICBMs are not publicly available.

to explain these differences the recent history of Soviet missile development and particularly the major decisional points in its evolution are discussed below.

At the conclusion of World War II, the Soviets possessed two separate resource bases to support their initiation of a major missile research and development program. The last days of the war had brought the Soviet capture of a number of scientists, many of the plans and blueprints, and most of the production and test facilities associated with the extensive German rocket development program.[50] In addition, a substantial cadre of Soviet scientists with lengthy experience in missile research was available. Led by such figures as S. P. Korolev, V. P. Glushko, and F. A. Tsander, this group of Soviet researchers had worked on basic missile design and research under direct government sponsorship since the 1920s. By April 1932, they were organized into specific design teams working on different aspects of the rocket research effort.[51]

The initiation of the major postwar Soviet missile development program was directly authorized by Stalin and the Party's Politburo in 1946.[52] While undertaken as a portion of the emerging Cold War competition with the United States, this effort represented an independent Soviet initiative that preceded the beginning of a major American missile development program.

Building upon the closely supervised efforts of the captured German scientists and the parallel work of their own missile design teams,[53] by the mid-1950s the Soviets had produced their first generation of operational ballistic missiles. Their original MRBM, the SS-3, was test-fired by 1954 and operationally deployed beginning in 1955, while the first ICBM, the SS-6, was tested in August 1957, and its deployment began in 1958.[54]

The SS-6 was a dual-purpose system, employed both as a military weapon and as the primary launch vehicle for early Soviet space efforts. It had a decidedly large booster, which may be explained by the fact that the parameter for launch capacity was established for the anticipated use of bulky and low-yield plutonium fission warheads, prior to a Soviet breakthrough in the area of thermonuclear weapons technology that greatly reduced the size and weight of these warheads.[55] The SS-6 program helped establish a Soviet tradition of powerful boosters which appears to have been sustained by the efforts of a specialized "big-missile" design team.

Deployment of the SS-6 was limited to a single-launch complex in the northwestern USSR.[56] This abbreviated deployment appears to have been necessitated by the logistic problems associated with servicing the unstable, nonstorable liquid fuels used in this system.[57] Its cumbersome nature precluded the emplacement of the SS-6 in protected launch sites and apparently produced significant problems with its soft configuration as well.[58]

Despite Khrushchev's personal enthusiasm for missiles and frequent claims regarding Soviet ICBM strength,[59] only a few SS-6s were operationally deployed. * This fact, coupled with accelerated American ICBM deployments that had been stimulated by fears of an impending missile gap strongly favoring the Soviets, produced a significant strategic missile superiority for the United States in the early 1960s.

Two factors may have influenced the Soviet decision to procure such a small ICBM force. It is most likely that the SS-6 deployment was halted as a result of the technical difficulties noted above. Additionally, since strategic missiles had not been assigned to an independent military service during the 1950s but instead were apparently controlled by the artillery branch of the ground forces, the early stages of the ICBM effort may have suffered from the absence of adequate institutional support within the Soviet defense establishment.[60]

The abbreviated SS-6 procurement was followed by the leisurely acquisition of two second-generation systems, the SS-7 and SS-8. Developed in parallel, perhaps by competitive design teams, some 220 of these missiles were deployed between 1962 and 1965. Still operational at this time, these liquid-fueled ICBMs reflected the Soviet preference for powerful boosters. More manageable than the SS-6, they were deployed in dispersed and hardened launch sites in the latter phases of their acquisition.

During this same period, the Soviets moved more rapidly toward the acquisition of a substantial medium- and intermediate-range ballistic missile capability. They began with the SS-3, a 600-mile range missile acquired in the mid-1950s, followed by the 1,200-mile range SS-4 whose development began in 1959 and the 2,300-mile range SS-5 beginning in 1961.[61] By 1963 they had deployed a force of 750 M/IRBMs in the western USSR, all apparently targeted against strategic and tactical targets in Western Europe.[62]

Factors explaining the pronounced buildup of the I/MRBM force appear to include the absence of the technical difficulties that plagued the early ICBM program, the emphasis on Soviet military doctrine upon a massive theater campaign in Europe, and a rational Soviet strategy of detering hostile American actions by holding Western Europe as a visible "hostage." The doctrinal tradition may have been reinforced by the leading role of artillery officers in the Soviet

---

*Precise numerical estimates are difficult to locate as authors frequently speak in terms of a "handful" of SS-6s. Cf. "Pentagon Bares Figures Showing Atom Arms Lead," New York Times, April 15, 1964; Wolfe, Soviet Power and Europe, p. 182.

missile program, noted previously. These men are likely to have been inclined to integrate the newly developed systems in a kind of extended contiguous support mission similar to the role played traditionally by artillery rather than directing their efforts toward the fulfillment of a completely novel intercontinental mission.

Returning to Soviet ICBM efforts, we should note that a landmark decision appears to have been made sometime in 1963 to commence a general expansion of Soviet strategic capability. Factors bearing upon this crucial decision appear to have included a commitment within the political leadership in the wake of the Cuban crisis of 1962 to attain a position of at least strategic parity and perhaps superiority vis-a-vis the United States, pressures from the Soviet military to acquire a viable war-waging capability at the strategic level, and the parochial lobbying of the Strategic Rocket Forces, created in 1959, and their industrial producers who sought to expand the ICBM inventory at a time when the M/IRBM construction program was nearing completion.

This decision has all the earmarks of an emulative reaction triggered by the overreactive buildup of U.S. strategic power that had begun three years earlier. Upheld and perhaps expanded by the collective leaderships that succeeded Khrushchev in October 1964, it produced a steady expansion of the Soviet strategic missile capability throughout the decade. This sustained effort eventually yielded the 3:2 advantage in land-based ICBMs currently held by the Soviet Union over the United States.

Included within the 1963 force expansion decision was the choice to begin deploying two third-generation ICBMs, the SS-9 and SS-11. The SS-9 is an exceptionally large, storable-liquid-fueled missile. It is currently capable of carrying a single 25-megaton warhead or a three-part multiple warhead, the so-called "MRV triplet," in which each individual warhead has an explosive equivalent of five megatons. The SS-11 is also a storable-liquid missile, but significantly smaller, being comparable to the U.S. Minuteman in overall size and warhead power, which is approximately one megaton.[63] Development work on both the SS-9 and 11 was probably begun in the early 1960s.

The SS-9 appears to be the product of the heavy missile design tradition noted earlier. Approval for its development may have been facilitated by Khrushchev's interest in large-yield "terror weapons," for whose delivery the SS-9 was ideally suited. (Khrushchev boasted publicly about the Soviet possession of such weapons and the atmospheric thermonuclear test series conducted in August-September 1961 included the explosion of a superwarhead with a yield of approximately 50 megatons.) Alternatively, it may have been developed as a counterforce weapon for use against American silo-based

ICBMs in order to improve Soviet war-waging capabilities. The decision to proceed with the deployment of this system may also have been influenced simply by the availability of the system for prompt deployment without reference to its possible employment. Whatever the original Soviet intentions, by the late 1960s it was its potential for carrying hard-target-killing multiple warheads that became the critical element in Western discussions of the SS-9.

Soviet multiple warhead development efforts appear to postdate the original SS-9 deployment decision, with initial design work probably beginning in the mid-1960s and the first flight tests of their MRV triplet initiated in August 1968.[64] Soviet activity in this area could have been motivated by a variety of considerations. They may have sought a MRV capability in order to attain more efficient city destruction in that the reinforcing character of three separated smaller warheads can produce a cumulative effect that is more powerful than a single warhead.[65] While this may be the reason for the development of the MRV for the SS-11 whose testing began in July 1970,[66] there has been disagreement whether the geographic separation of the SS-9's triplet is sufficient to produce greater destruction than the single warhead.* Alternatively, the MRV, still designed for countercity attacks, may have been developed to multiply the number of incoming Soviet attack vehicles as an offsetting measure in anticipation of an American decision to deploy an ABM system. (The United States did announce its intention to proceed with the deployment of the Sentinel ABM system, which provided for a "thin" city defense, in September 1967.) Finally, basing their case upon the reported "footprint" or dispersal pattern of the SS-9's powerful triplet, some American defense spokesmen have stated that this system was expressly designed for counterforce strikes against the American Minuteman ICBM force. These interactive concerns are likely to have been reinforced by the parochial lobbying of the MRV development design teams and the members of the Strategic Rocket Forces, who would press for the acquisition of such a Soviet capability because: (1) it was technologically feasible, and (2) with adequate

---

*Johan Holst asserts that the impact pattern of the SS-9's MRV triplet is too closely clustered to produce the necessary reinforcement effect that improves destructive efficiency, while Ian Smart claims that the triplet's separation is approximately ten miles, which will produce the desired increase in blast overpressure. See Holst, Comparative U.S. and Soviet Deployments, Doctrines and Arms Limitation, p. 16; and Ian Smart, Advanced Strategic Missiles: A Short Guide, Adelphi Papers no. 63 (London: Institute of Strategic Studies, December 1969), p. 24.

accuracies it could further improve Soviet ability to wage nuclear war, a firm doctrinal commitment of the Soviet armed forces.

While the counterforce capabilities of the SS-9 MRV triplet were eventually discounted,* it most certainly became a valid concern with regard to its follow-on, the SS-18, as the Soviets acquired a true MIRV (multiple independently targetable reentry vehicle) capability.† Nevertheless, one should avoid complete reliance upon this line of argument in accounting for the SS-9. The existence of a well-established large booster tradition in Soviet missile development, the timing of the SS-9 development and deployment decisions, and the presence of other plausible explanations for the development of both the large 25-megaton warhead and the MRV triplet all suggest that it is highly questionable to cite the characteristics of the SS-9 as obvious proof of its intended application as a counterforce, first-strike weapon.‡

Whatever Soviet intentions regarding the SS-9, their inventory of these weapons expanded steadily between 1965 and 1970, reaching a strength of approximately 290. The SS-9 force remained basically stable until the deployment of the follow-on "large/heavy ICBM, the SS-18, began in 1975, although an additional 30 large and initially empty missile silos constructed during 1971 may be slated to receive the present or a modified SS-9 or a completely new heavy missile.[67]

---

*Various press reports and statements attributed to Dr. John Foster, the former director of defense research and engineering of the Department of Defense, indicated that the MRV for the SS-9 was not sufficiently accurate to threaten the U.S. Minuteman force. See Michael Getler, "Soviet Missile Faulted," Washington Post, June 17, 1971; and William Beecher, "Soviet Missile Peril Now Found Unlikely by U.S. Til 1980's," New York Times, March 22, 1972. See also Admiral Thomas H. Moorer, United States Military Posture for FY 1974, Statement before the Senate Armed Services Committee (Washington, D.C.: Government Printing Office, March 1973), p. 11.

†In the summer of 1973, the Soviets began to flight-test MIRVs on three of their four new ICBMs, the SS-X-17 (four reentry vehicles), the SS-X-18 (five reentry vehicles), and SS-X-19 (six reentry vehicles) discussed below. Charles W. Corddry, "Schlesinger Shift Relies on NATO for Nuclear Teamwork," Baltimore Sun, March 4, 1974. Deployment of all three of these ICBMs began in 1975.

‡Cf. Senator Henry Jackson's rhetorical question made during Senate debate on the SALT agreements on August 3, 1972: "Mr. President, for what possible purpose would a nation deploy a missile with a 25 megaton payload capability if it was not for some sort of counterforce?" Congressional Record, Senate, August 3, 1972, p. 18.

As SS-18s have been deployed, the SS-9 force has gradually been reduced. Sizable additional Soviet deployments in this area were effectively constrained for five years by the Interim Offensive Agreement signed in May 1972 at the conclusion of the first round of the Strategic Arms Limitation Talks. This agreement includes a provision limiting Soviet "heavy" missile deployment within a ceiling of 313 missiles. A similar or somewhat lower heavy missile subceiling will almost certainly be a part of a SALT II treaty if it is finally achieved. Nevertheless, continued replacement of the SS-9 by the SS-18, with its 8-10 MIRVs, increased throw-weight, and improved accuracy, means that the capability of the Soviet heavy ICBM force will steadily improve within this ceiling.

The SS-9 also serves as the launch vehicle for the Soviet depressed-trajectory ICBM (DICBM) or fractional orbital bombardment system (FOBS). First flight tested extensively in 1967, the Soviet FOBS has prompted Western speculation that it is intended for south polar attack* against U.S. strategic bomber bases. The system appears capable of carrying a one-three-megaton warhead but with only moderate accuracy, thus limiting its probable use to attacks upon "soft" targets.[68] The Soviet decision to develop this system despite its obvious capability limitations suggests that a particularly favorable attitude toward strategic weapons development prevailed within the political leadership in the mid- to late 1960s. Given the fact that the Soviets had already invested in the development and deployment of the SS-9, the FOBS system may have been a relatively inexpensive system.

While deployment information of the FOBS is unavailable, periodic testing of the system suggests its inclusion as an operational system within the Soviet inventory.

The "light" SS-11 was the central element of the sizable Soviet ICBM expansion between 1965 and 1974. Approximately 1,020 of these missiles were emplaced during this period. The SS-11 force began to shrink from 1975 onward as it was replaced by the SS-17 and SS-19. The SS-11's resemblance to the American Minuteman is marked, although it has a storable-liquid booster rather than solid fuel, a difference that may have been caused by a Soviet lag in this technological area. A closer replica of the Minuteman, the solid-fueled SS-13, did make its appearance as an operational weapon in

---

*This mode of attack would avoid approach detection by the American ballistic missile early warning system (BMEWS), which monitors the northern attack routes. It has prompted an American offsetting response in the deployment of an over-the-horizon radar system that now covers the south polar approaches.

1968. To date, however, its procurement has been quite modest, with only 60 deployed by September 1976.[69] This small SS-13 force may reflect the dependability of the SS-11 or merely the tardy arrival of the SS-13 at a time when the momentum of the SS-11 program made it difficult for the newer system to gain adequate deployment support.

An interesting aspect of the SS-11 deployment was the emplacement of approximately 100 of them in launch complexes in the southwestern USSR that had been previously devoted exclusively to M/IRBMs. This practice was initiated in late 1969, at the same time that the Soviets dismantled a force of 70 SS-4s and SS-5s deployed in the Soviet far eastern maritime provinces that were presumably targeted against China and U.S. forces in Asia. This move appears to have been a simple replacement maneuver in which specially configured, variable-range SS-11s, emplaced in hardened silos and far removed from the tense Sino-Soviet border, that can cover targets in the Far East, were substituted for the older and generally soft-sited SS-4s and SS-5s.[70] Some have suggested that the move was undertaken to complicate American verification efforts, possibly in anticipation of a possible SALT agreement.[71] In light of their intercontinental capability, Western sources continue to count these SS-11s within the Soviet ICBM inventory.

In 1973, as noted earlier, the fourth-generation Soviet ICBMs, the SS-16 through SS-19, began their test flights. By 1975, deployment of three of them, the SS-17 through SS-19, all tested with MIRV payloads, had begun. The solid-fueled SS-X-16, the obvious follow-on to the SS-13, appeared in the spring of 1977 to share the modest fate of its predecessor, and has not yet been deployed. Its potential significance remains high, however, as it is reported to be available in a mobile as well as a silo-based configuration.[72] Moreover, a mobile, two-stage, intermediate-range version of this three-stage ICBM, the SS-X-20, has been flight-tested with three MIRVs and was reportedly nearing deployment in the spring of 1977.[73]

The SS-17 and SS-19 appear to be competitive designs destined to become jointly the MIRVed backbone of the Soviet ICBM force as the replacements for the SS-11. Both represent significant improvements over the SS-11 in terms of throw-weight (especially in the case of the SS-19 which can carry a payload some three times greater than that of the SS-11), accuracy, and their capability to carry MIRVs.[74] The SS-17 and SS-19 have been tested in both single warhead and MIRVed modes, with the SS-17 carrying four MIRVs and the SS-19 carrying six. This dual capability creates some difficulties in a SALT II context because it is likely to prove difficult to distinguish readily between the deployed MIRVed and single warhead versions of these missiles using national technical means of verification (i.e., overhead reconnaissance) for accounting against any agreed subceiling for MIRVed ICBMs included in a SALT II treaty.[75]

The size of the Soviet M/IRBM force showed little change between 1964 and the initiation of the variable range SS-11 deployments in late 1969, remaining at roughly 700 missiles throughout the period. The transfer of the 70 SS-4s and SS-5s noted above from the European USSR to the Soviet Far East apparently took place in 1966 or 1967. This move was probably undertaken to cover Western military targets in East Asia and targets in the People's Republic of China. The deactivation of these soft-configuration systems in 1969-70 suggests that this may have been a precautionary move undertaken in response to the pronounced deterioration of Sino-Soviet relations that had included significant border skirmishes in the spring of 1969. Since 1969 the Soviets have retired approximately 100 SS-4s and 5s, although, given the variable-range character of a portion of the SS-11s, the overall size of the peripheral-range ballistic missile strike forces remains at approximately 700.

The Soviets displayed two mobile I/MRBMs in the mid-1960s. The SS-14 system, given the NATO designation "Scamp" and employing a two-stage version of the solid-fuel SS-13 with a 2,500-mile range,[76] was first shown publicly in 1967. The SS-X-Z "Scrooge" system, which has a range of 3,500 miles, was similarly paraded in 1967. While these systems may have been designed as follow-ons to the SS-4 and SS-5, there have been no reports of their operational deployment to date. Should they be deployed, their mobility would present considerable difficulties for the verification of any agreement controlling I/MRBMs that might emerge from SALT II or the Mutual Balanced Force Reductions (MBFR) talks.

In 1975 the Soviets replicated their mid-1960s dual development of a solid fueled ICBM/IRBM that was evident in the SS-13/SS-X-14 combination when they began to flight-test the SS-X-20 noted earlier. This mobile IRBM, which carries 3 MIRVs, appears destined for deployment as the replacement for the SS-4 and SS-5 force. Its appearance has sparked heavy Western criticism since its kinship to the SS-X-16 raises possible SALT-related verification difficulties and because its range, 3,000 km, makes it a "gray-area" weapon with potential for conversion into the incontestably strategic-intercontinental arena by adding a third stage or by offloading its MIRVs in favor of a single warhead.[77]

The tapering off of the numerical expansion of the Soviet ICBM force in the early 1970s followed by Soviet willingness to accept quantitative ceilings in the SALT I Interim Offensive Agreement, requires some attempt at explanation. Whatever the Soviet military's desire for the attainment of a war-winning strategic superiority, the political leadership appears to have been decided upon at least partial restraint. This is likely to have been the result of a collective judgment that continued launch vehicle expansion threatened to elicit major American emulative and offsetting responses in the form of both a substantial ABM defense of the Minuteman force and possibly an unrestrained ICBM or submarine-launched ballistic missile (SLBM) expansion. To offset such American reactions would entail a Soviet effort that, although not financially unbearable, would require a substantial additional investment at a time when alternative resource claimants, including agriculture, consumer goods production, and investment for economic growth were in need of major financial inputs.[78] These budgetary competitors are likely to have found representation among the various political leaders, who in turn could find support for their case from the few Soviet advocates of a mutual deterrence stalemate with the United States* and apparent American interests in the negotiation of joint restraint. Whatever their motivations, given the momentum of the Soviet buildup of strategic power, it must have required a specific decision by the Politburo to curb the continuing numerical expansion of the Soviet land-based missile force.

The very limited nature of the restraints imposed by the Interim Offensive Agreement has been highlighted by Soviet efforts in the development of the fourth generation of ICBMs described above. The concurrent development of these missiles as well as new SLBMs and an intermediate-range strategic bomber, the Backfire, indicate that spending on strategic offensive arms has almost certainly risen over the past few years. This activity has been consistent with General Secretary Brezhnev's reported comment in 1972 that the Soviets fully intended to press ahead with a vigorous research, development, and deployment program during the five-year life of the Interim Agreement.† This effort, which appears destined to include lengthy deployment programs throughout the 1970s to replace the SS-9, SS-11, and SS-13 force, augurs well for the fortunes of the Strategic Rocket Forces and their defense industrial suppliers.

---

*For example, G. Gerasimov, who has written about the folly of war in the nuclear age and the meaninglessness of strategic superiority. Cf. Gerasimov's "Pentagon, 1966," International Affairs (Moscow) no. 5 (May 1966): 26; and Pravda Ukrainy, March 23, 1969.

†Former President Nixon reported this comment by Brezhnev in his remarks at a Congressional briefing on SALT held at the White House on June 15, 1972. Strategic Arms Limitation Agreements, Hearings before the Committee on Foreign Relations, United States Senate, 92d Congress (Washington, D.C.: Government Printing Office, 1972), p. 393.

Submarine-Launched Ballistic Missiles

One of the most dynamic elements of Soviet strategic missile development in recent years has been the ballistic-missile-launching submarine force. By September 1976, the Soviets possessed 845 ballistic missiles carried aboard 78 submarines. The backbone of this force are the nuclear-powered Y-class submarine carrying 16 SS-N-6 missiles that can be fired from a submerged position and have a range of 1,500 miles, and the nuclear-powered D-I and D-II class subs, which carry 12 and 16 SS-N-8 missiles with a submerged launch capability, a range of over 4,600 miles, and a stellar inertial guidance system respectively.[79] In the fall of 1976, the Soviets were reported to have 34 Y-class, 13 D-I class, and 4 D-II class boats in operation.

Soviet interest in the use of the submarine as a launch platform for missiles dates from the immediate post-World War II period when they studied an unsuccessful German program to launch the V-2 rocket from a submarine-towed container.[80] By 1950, the Soviets had begun the development of two separate submarine missile programs.

In the strategic area, the Russians developed the 300-mile-range SS-N-4, "Sark," designed for firing from a surfaced submarine. In the fall of 1955, this system was successfully fired from a specially converted Z-class diesel submarine.[81] It was eventually deployed on ten such Z-V class submarines carrying two missiles each as well as the G-class diesel and the H-class nuclear subs.

Tactically, the Soviets fitted their adapted land-based Shaddock missile to a specially configured W-class submarine. This was part of a broader development program that yielded a substantial cruise missile capability for both surface ships and submarines. These weapons appear to have been designed for an antiship role with their most likely target the American attack carriers. Soviet cruise-missile-firing submarines include the J-class diesel and the E-class nuclear boats.

The Soviet deployment and procurement of missile-launching submarines in the 1950s appeared to reflect a number of factors. At the political level, Nikita Khrushchev, a key figure in defense policy decisions from 1953 onward, was a firm supporter of both missiles and submarines. Khrushchev was also outspoken in his criticism of the utility of large surface vessels.[82] This was important in that it appears to have been an important factor in the post-Stalin decision to cancel an ambitious 20-year naval building program that had included significant expansion in this area.[83] Opposition to this surface ship program was apparently shared by a number of senior figures in the Ministry of Defense, including the minister himself, Marshal Zhukov. This may also reflect ground force resistance to the budgetary and mission expansion of a rival service. The commander-in-chief of the Soviet navy, Adm. S. G. Gorshkov, commented on these interservice rivalries (which included antipathy toward the submarine as well as surface ships) as follows in 1967:

> Unfortunately, we had some quite influential "authorities" who believed that the appearance of nuclear weapons meant that the Navy had completely lost its significance as a branch of the armed forces. In their opinion, all the basic tasks of a future war could be resolved without the participation of the Navy at all. . . . Not infrequently, it was claimed that landbased missiles alone would suffice for the destruction of surface strike forces and even of submarines.[84]

Denied the opportunity to expand their heavy surface forces during this period, the Soviet navy appears to have opted to shift its parochial advocacy into the submarine area where the climate of opinion was more favorable. From a ship construction standpoint, this certainly proved to be the case as some of the ways slated for capital ship construction were transferred instead to the building of submarines.[85]

The development of a submarine strategic strike force found mixed justification in Soviet naval doctrine. Since the 1930s, Soviet naval strategy had been dominated by the so-called "Young School," which emphasized a peripheral maritime defense conducted by light naval forces and land-based aviation rather than a doctrine based upon a oceanic fleet and involving far-flung offensive operations.[86] Consequently, the emergence of a naval force for delivering strategic attacks upon the homeland of the enemy faced significant obstacles in that it represented a major doctrinal innovation. However, the Young School's light-vessel approach included a strong emphasis upon the construction and use of submarines, thus providing a supportive element for an expanded submarine role in the overall Soviet strategy.

Extensive Soviet submarine construction in the past presumably strengthened the case for the development of an SLBM system from a defense production standpoint. Sizable submarine-building facilities were readily available for such a program and well-established submarine design teams, which have remained intact to this day,[87] could be expected to vigorously promote the procurement of new submarine systems.

Finally, American efforts in this area, in particular the Polaris program of the late 1950s, could be expected to strengthen the arguments for those pressing for continued investment in the development and acquisition of a Soviet SLBM capability.

The Soviets continued their efforts in the SLBM field throughout the 1960s and early 1970s. The surface launched SS-N-4 was succeeded by the SS-N-5 Serb, a 650-mile-range, liquid-fueled weapon that could be fired from a submerged position. It was developed in the early 1960s and became operational on converted G-II class (diesel) and H-II class (nuclear) submarines in 1964.[88]

The most important activity in this area centered around the third-generation system, the SS-N-6, a submerged-launch missile with a 1,500-mile range, and its carrier, the nuclear-powered Y-class submarine. The development of this system is likely to have been authorized as a part of the general post-Cuba force expansion discussed earlier. The configuration of the Y-class sub with its 16-missile capacity, identical to that of the U.S. Polaris, which was operational in 1960, suggests a strong imitative element in its development. Since the first operational Y-class was delivered in late 1967, modern SSBNs have come off the construction ways at Severodvinsk in northern Russia[89] and at a yard in the Soviet far east at the rate of six to eight per year. Since mid-1972, these boars have been supplemented by the D-I and D-II class submarines which carry 12 and 16 of the new SS-N-8 Sawfly missiles respectively. In 1976 the Soviets began flight-testing two new SLBMs, the SS-NX-17, their first solid-fueled SLBM, and the SS-NX-18, their first MIRVed SLBM, with two MIRVs on board.[90]

Sustained Soviet ballistic missile submarine activity is explicable on several grounds. The SLBM submarine with its mobility and concealment appears to be the most secure of contemporary strategic strike systems and thus a very rational choice for continued expansion. Additionally, during the comprehensive and sustained military buildup after 1965, when the Soviet leadership appeared to have made a commitment to attaining first numerical parity and then a marginal superiority with respect to the United States, it was only logical that they include a substantial effort in the area where the United States had maintained a distinct qualitative and quantitative advantage. In addition, the generalized force expansion of the mid- and late 1960s is likely to have made additional funds available to all of the services. With the existence of a submarine force-sub construction lobby, buttressed by a firm role assignment within Soviet military doctrine for submarine-launched ballistic missiles as an important element of the strategic exchange[91] and a sizable submarine construction capacity, it is not surprising that the Soviet submarine program has enjoyed such prosperity in recent years.

All of this is not to say, however, that the Soviets appear inclined to expand their SSBN/SLBM force at substantial expense to the land-based ICBMs of the Strategic Rocket Forces in the coming years. As a matter of fact, despite the recent appearance of the MIRVed SS-NX-18, the Soviet decision to develop the new SS-X-16 through SS-19 generation of MIRV-capable ICBMs suggests that the land-based portion of their strategic attack forces is likely to remain dominant for the foreseeable future. The greatly superior MIRV-carrying capacity of these new ICBMs and their likely advantages in accuracy strongly suggest that the Soviet MIRV deployment effort will continue to be dominated by the SRF, thus giving them the overwhelming bulk of deliverable Soviet reentry vehicles.

Strategic Aviation

The Long-Range Aviation Command of the Soviet air forces currently controls 135 long-range bombers consisting of 100 TU-95 "Bears" and 35 MYA-4 "Bisons" (plus an additional 50 Bisons configured as tankers for in-flight refueling), and a medium bomber force of 650 aircraft, including 450 TU-16 "Badgers," 170 TU-22 "Blinders," and 30 TU-VG "Backfire Bs." This force is supplemented by the shore-based bombers of Soviet Naval Aviation. Its inventory included 280 Badgers and 30 Backfire Bs, both armed with air-to-surface missiles apparently slated for an antiship role, 50 specially configured reconnaissance and tanker Badgers, 60 reconnaissance Blinders, and 60 long-range reconnaissance Bears.[92]

The overall size of the Soviet strategic bomber force has declined steadily over the past decade. While the long-range bomber strength has remained fairly constant, the medium bomber force has declined by almost one-third. The internal composition of the medium bomber inventory has been altered as well with the gradual replacement of the older TU-16 Badgers procured between 1955 and 1960, by the newer TU-22 Blinder, which first entered service in 1962, and the Backfire.

A new strategic bomber, the Tupolev-designed, variable-geometry Backfire, first sighted in 1969, began entering the Soviet operational inventory in 1974. Western sources are in conflict regarding the range capabilities of the Backfire. Some have described it as a truly long-range system,[93] while others attribute shorter-range characteristics to the Backfire. The latter school asserts that the Backfire is designed to fulfill a peripheral attack role and thus should not be identified as a truly intercontinental, heavy bomber in the same class with the Bear and the Bison.[94] The "gray area" character of the Backfire has made it a point of serious contention between the Soviet Union and the United States throughout the SALT II negotiations.

Historically, a critical point in the development of contemporary Soviet strategic aviation was the leadership's decision in the mid-1950s not to deploy a large long-range bomber force. While U.S. officials and commentators were anticipating a major Soviet buildup and speaking of an impending bomber gap (an estimate that the Soviets themselves encouraged by their ploy of creating the impression of a sizable Russian bomber force by a cleverly manipulated fly-by of their limited inventory at the 1955 air show*), the Soviets chose instead to build up their medium-range bomber force, while never acquiring more than 150 of the long-range Bisons and Bears.

A variety of explanations can be put forward regarding this choice. The small long-range bomber acquisition may have represented a rational choice to concentrate Soviet efforts on the development of their first ICBM, which was at that time approaching operational capability. In addition, Khrushchev's personal predilections may have been an important factor in that he publicly displayed a strong aversion for strategic aircraft while enthusiastically endorsing the ICBM.†

The decision to procure a substantial medium-range Badger force while eschewing a substantial long-range capability may be traced to the continental perspective prevailing within the Soviet armed forces that was noted in the earlier discussion of the parallel M/IRBM buildup. It also may reflect the limited organizational strength of the air forces in general and long-range aviation in particular within the Soviet military establishment. Despite sporadic attempts to establish a true strategic aviation capability in the past,‡

---

*For an excellent discussion of the American bomber-gap perceptions, the role of intentional Soviet deception in its emergence, and its eventual disappearance, thanks largely to the American U-2 program, see Ervin J. Rokke, "The Politics of Aerial Reconnaissance: The Eisenhower Administration," Ph.D. dissertation, Harvard University, June 1970, pp. 185-204.

†In the late 1950s and early 1960s Khrushchev frequently spoke of the obsolescence of the manned bomber and its impending replacement by missiles. His attacks included this statement before the Supreme Soviet in January 1960: "Military aviation is being almost entirely replaced by missiles. We have now sharply reduced and probably will further reduce and even halt the production of bombers and other obsolete equipment." Pravda, January 15, 1960.

‡During the 1930s, a cadre of Soviet air forces commanders, led by V. V. Khripkin, vigorously pushed for the development of a Russian strategic aviation arm capable of long-range independent operations. This effort languished after the military purges of

the Soviet air forces had been traditionally assigned an auxiliary role as a kind of flying artillery force in Soviet military planning and operations.

Soviet strategic aviation procurements during the 1950s are likely to have been prompted by the design/production ambitions of the major aircraft design bureaus and those in charge of the production facilities of the Ministry of Aviation Industry. The design bureaus are headed by a small number of prominent designers, who often have been educated at the Zhukovsky Air Engineering Academy run by the Soviet air forces and in many cases hold general officer rank within the engineering and technical services. Their sizable staffs appear to enjoy considerable autonomy in the creation of new aircraft designs, maintain strong institutional and personal ties with the Soviet air forces, and are likely to engage frequently in the type of self-promotional activity evident in the Yakovlev case cited earlier.[95]

During the 1950s, the design collectives led by A. N. Tupolev, V. M. Myasishchev, and S. V. Ilyushin were engaged in strategic bomber design competitions. In this period, the Tupolev collective produced the TU-95 Bear and TU-16 Badger while Ilyushin's group failed to gain authorization for the production of a single design in this area* and Myasishchev was successful only once, with his MYA-4 Bison.

Despite the Soviet decision to limit the size of their strategic aviation inventory to the modest level attained by the beginning of the 1960s, these designers were able to sustain their design organizations in this and other areas. Even in this restricted environment, Tupolev continued to find success in the development of strategic aircraft. His group designed the medium-range TU-22 Blinder, the only strategic bomber produced in the 1960s that was procured as a replacement for a portion of the Badger force, as well as the TU-VG Backfire which began entering active service in 1974. The Tupolev collective also designed other military aircraft that were authorized for production including the TU-28 Fiddler fighter-bomber and the rudimentary airborne warning and control system (AWACS), the

---

1936-38, whose victims included Khripkin. See John Erickson, The Soviet High Command, 1918-1941 (New York: Macmillan, 1962), pp. 382-83.

*Ilyushin's IL-46, a scaled-up version of his tactical bomber, the IL-28 Beagle, competed unsuccessfully with the TU-16 Badger in the early 1950s. This information and that which follows on specific aircraft designs is extracted from a comprehensive listing of Soviet aircraft provided the author by Arthur J. Alexander.

TU-114B Moss, as well as a number of civilian transports including the TU-134 and the supersonic transport, the TU-144.

Ilyushin and Myasishchev turned to other design activities. After failing to have his supersonic MYA-Delta, the Boundar, selected for production in the late 1950s, Myasishchev's group became a leading force in Soviet spacecraft design.[96] During the same period, Ilyushin as well appears to have abandoned the military field, devoting his efforts instead to the design of civilian transport aviation. These include the IL-18V Coot, a standard aeroflot passenger aircraft, and the IL-62 Classic, a deluxe passenger liner that has partially replaced the TU-114.

While these design organizations were shifting their attention into related areas, the production facilities of the Ministry of Aviation Industry displayed similar flexibility. Virtually continuous innovation in the development of tactical fighters and civilian and military transport was sufficient to maintain a substantial level of aircraft production. In addition, their manufacturing facilities have been increasingly devoted to the production of a wide variety of consumer goods including refrigerators, vacuum cleaners, and pleasure boats.[97] The availability of these alternative production areas is likely to have been an important factor lessening the pressures from the aviation design-production complex for the procurement of a larger strategic bomber inventory.

Despite its failure to fulfill American expectancies in the procurement of a massive strategic bomber force, Soviet long-range aviation has successfully acquired and maintained a modest intercontinental capability and a substantial medium-range inventory. The capability of this force has been augmented considerably by the development of a variety of air-to-surface missiles. These weapons provide the Soviet strategic air arm with a stand-off capability that permits it to attack many targets without encountering their point defenses. The addition of these weapons has been reflected in the Soviet discussion of their strategic bomber capability, which routinely extols the virtues of their "jet-propelled, missile-carrying aircraft."

The relatively low priority accorded to strategic aviation within the family of Soviet strategic offensive systems was evident in its failure to share in the broad expansion of Soviet military capabilities that occurred in the mid-1960s. While missile-carrying strategic aviation successfully resisted Khrushchev's determined attack upon its very existence, its partisans apparently lacked the strength to capitalize upon the disposition of the Soviet political leadership, which allowed a major expansion of the land- and sea-based ballistic missile forces described above.

However, the appearance of the Backfire in 1969 after a delay of some ten years since the emergence of the previous new Soviet intermediate- to long-range bomber design provides ample proof of the persistence of those who seek to maintain or expand a substantial Soviet strategic aviation capability. Further evidence of sustained Soviet interest in strategic aviation was the official U.S. government acknowledgment that by late 1976 the Soviets "may be working on a follow-on heavy bomber to replace the aging Bears and Bisons."[98]

Strategic Defensive Forces

The Soviets have expended a great deal in the development and maintenance of a large and diversified national air defense system. This mission is assigned to one of the five independent military services of the Soviet armed forces, the National Air Defense Forces, which is frequently identified by its Russian abbreviation PVO-S.

A variety of weapons systems have been procured to defend the Russian homeland from attack by enemy aircraft and missiles. Their vast antiaircraft system includes an extensive radar detection and tracking network, a large fighter-interceptor force of approximately 2,650 aircraft and some 10,000 surface-to-air missiles (SAMs) of a variety of types located at over 1,000 different launch sites. The Soviets have also deployed a modest antiballistic missile (ABM) system centered around Moscow, which currently includes some 64 launchers housed in four separate complexes.[99] Under the terms of the ABM treaty negotiated at SALT I, they were authorized to expand this system to a maximum of 100 launchers and were additionally authorized to construct a second 100-launcher system deployed to defend one of their ICBM launch complexes, although to date no reports about the initiation of the latter system have been heard. At the summer summit in Moscow in 1974 the Soviets agreed to limit themselves to a single 100-launcher system that may be emplaced in defense of Moscow or an ICBM field. They have chosen to retain the Moscow-centered system.

The large and continuing Soviet investment in strategic defense is frequently attributed to a long-standing Russian tradition of defense-mindedness. In light of their bitter experiences at the hands of the invading armies of Charles XII of Sweden, Napoleon, Kaiser Wilhelm, the Western powers during the Russian Civil War, and Adolf Hitler, such a Russian concern is perfectly understandable.

Substantial strategic defense efforts are also justified within Soviet military doctrine. Although throughout the Soviet period their doctrine has been marked by a preference for seizing the initiative and boldly conducting offensive operations, their simultaneous commitment to the "combined arms concept" provides a firm basis for substantial defensive measures as well. In addition, in the adjustment of their military strategy to the nuclear missile revolution, the Soviets, as noted earlier, have not adopted an assured destruction approach to the problems of modern war. The Soviet strategy calls instead for comprehensive preparations to wage and win any thermonuclear conflict, including serious attention to measures designed to limit possible damage to the Soviet Union itself. Consequently, the fundamental thrust of Soviet military doctrine fails to share the judgment that contemporary strategic defense is basically a futile exercise, a conclusion that has predominated in American strategic thought.[100] With the growth of antagonism between the Soviet Union and the People's Republic of China and expanding, albeit still modest, Chinese strategic capabilities, this doctrinal commitment to damage-limiting defense has almost certainly been reinforced.

Whatever the basis of its mandate, in PVO-S the Soviet strategic defense mission has found a vigorous institutional advocate that has been demonstrably successful in acquiring and maintaining substantial budgeting support for that purpose. In the late 1940s and 1950s, their efforts to gain support for the development of an antiaircraft defense capability were probably assisted by the fact that the chief antagonist, the United States, made strategic bomber attack on the Soviet homeland the keystone of its military policy. Moreover, the Soviets continue to face a substantial aviation threat which includes both American long-range strategic bombers and forward-based fighter-bombers as well as the strategic attack aircraft of third countries including France, the United Kingdom, and China. Soviet ABM development and procurement activities could be similarly supported in a straightforward offsetting manner due to the growth and importance of U.S. missile capabilities. While such arms-race interaction, reinforced by the Soviet predisposition to pay close attention to active defense, are adequate to substantiate the sizable Soviet air defense effort, there are some anomalies in the composition of this force that merit further discussion.

In the 1940s and 1950s the Soviets procured a truly massive conventional antiaircraft artillery (AAA) capability. The nationwide emplacement of these weapons ran well beyond what could be rationally justified in the face of the numbers and characteristics of the increasingly jet-powered American bomber force.[101] During the same period they procured a large inventory of fighter-interceptors centered around the MIG-17 and the early MIG-19 with exclusively daylight capabilities. Given the probabilities of night assault by the enemy, this acquisition also confounds the logic of rational interaction.[102] Instead, these decisions appear to reflect the efforts of PVO-S, which had achieved the status of an independent service in 1948, to fully expend its sizable annual budget. Viewed from this organizational perspective, these procurements that expanded the weapons inventory under PVO's control and apparently increased its ability to fulfill its assigned role made great sense despite the deficiencies of these systems.

Apparently following the same bureaucratic logic, the Soviets followed their oversized AAA procurement with a similar saturation acquisition of surface-to-air missiles (SAMs) as soon as these systems became available. Their SAM acquisitions began in the mid-1950s with the SA-1 system, whose deployment revealed another tendency evident in the development of the Soviet air defense system. This weapon system was apparently prematurely deployed in that it was never deployed in any place other than its original Moscow-centered configuration.[103] The practice of moving rapidly from development to an initial operational deployment, which was to appear again in the ABM area in the 1960s, may have been prompted by PVO's budget-spending imperative as well as a standardized Soviet practice of emplacing systems when additional development and testing remained to be done. A similar practice has frequently been followed in the Soviet navy, where new ship designs are routinely deployed as "production prototypes" to undergo continuing sea trials during their initial years of operation.[104]

The limited acquisition of the SA-1 was followed by the large-scale procurement of the second-generation SA-2. This missile, which first appeared in 1958, may have been designed by the design bureau of P. A. Lavochkin, formerly a major aircraft designer who had turned to missile development after failing repeatedly in a number of fighter design competitions in the late 1940s and early 1950s.[105] SA-2 production was voluminous as it became the workhorse of the extensive Soviet SAM network and was regularly included in arms shipments to a variety of nations including Cuba, Egypt, and North Vietnam. Its apparent deficiencies against low-altitude attackers prompted the development and procurement of the complementary SA-3 system beginning in the late 1950s and continuing to the present day.

The early 1960s saw the appearance of the Griffon missile, which was employed in a Leningrad-centered deployment. This surface-to-air missile never became operational and has been generally described as an unsuccessful ABM system.[106] From a characteristics standpoint, the missile was capable of high-altitude interception and thus had a marginal capability against the first-generation Polaris A-1 missile and the medium-range Thor[107] that was emplaced in Europe in the early 1960s.

Following the abortive Leningrad deployment, another high-altitude defensive missile, the SA-5, was deployed, particularly in the so-called Tallinn Line, an arc of launch sites extending northeast from the Baltic city of Tallinn and protecting the northwestern approaches to the European USSR.[108] The Tallinn Line appears to represent an offsetting Soviet response to American attack systems that were not in use by the time it became operational. This system may have been directed against the Polaris A-1 missile, a possibility suggested by the fact that the oceanic launch area for this 1,300-mile-range SLBM was limited to the Barents Sea thus bringing their flight path to the European USSR directly through the area covered by the Tallinn Line.[109] If this was the case, it has proved to be a costly and futile Soviet effort in that the Polaris A-1 has been replaced by the longer range A-2 and A-3 thus extending its potential launch areas and changing its entering trajectory in a manner making it less likely to be vulnerable to the SA-5. Alternatively, the SA-5 may have been designed as an anticipatory measure to combat the American supersonic bomber, the B-70. If this was the case, Soviet planning was once again rather grievously in error as this aircraft, although advancing to the prototype stage, was never procured as an operational system.

Whatever their original intentions, the Soviets have deployed some 1,000 SA-5s[110] both in the Tallinn Line and in the southeastern USSR. Its capabilities against high-flying strategic bombers and perhaps their air-to-surface missiles appears formidable. Western concern about a possible ABM role for the SA-5, particularly if it could be successfully integrated with the sophisticated radar network of the Soviets' unambiguous ABM, the Galosh/Moscow system, persisted into the early 1970s.[111] This possibility has been explicitly prohibited in the ABM treaty signed at the conclusion of SALT I.

In the mid-1960s the Soviets began to deploy an ABM system in a series of launch complexes around Moscow. This system utilizes the Galosh missile, an area defense vehicle capable of intercepting incoming vehicles outside the earth's atmosphere where it can utilize its nuclear warhead to produce a lethal electromagnetic pulse (EMP).[112]

The deployment of the Galosh was probably authorized in the landmark Soviet force expansion decision of 1963. Its construction pattern shows signs of the Soviet premature emplacement syndrome noted earlier in that the construction was temporarily halted in 1968 with only 64 launchers completed. Although construction around Moscow was reportedly resumed in the spring of 1971 perhaps to accommodate an improved missile,[113] Western sources continue through 1976 to report only 64 missiles deployed and any additions would have to be kept within a maximum of 100 launchers as agreed upon in the ABM treaty of 1972.

The limited Soviet ABM deployment may be traced to second thoughts regarding the probable effectiveness of the system.* First their own self-restraint and then their willingness to agree to the explicit numerical limitations embodied in the SALT-negotiated ABM treaty represent a serious setback to PVO-S. Although initially authorized by the 1972 ABM treaty to construct a second 100-launcher system for the protection of an ICBM launch complex, PVO-S has been denied the opportunity to emplace a thick ABM network. At the midsummer Nixon-Brezhnev summit in 1974, the Soviets further agreed to limit themselves to a single 100-launcher ABM system. As a result of these agreements, PVO-S may prove vulnerable to pressures from the other military services for a reduction of its share of the defense budget.

Soviet ABM development, which began in the late 1940s, provides an example of self-generated weapons development with obvious arms race impact. As in the entire air defense area, there were elements of rational offsetting response to American offensive development mixed with the shaping influences of their active defense tradition and internal bureaucratic factors. The Soviet propensity to deploy air defense missile systems at the first possible opportunity has meant that they have often triggered American reactions rather than responding in an emulative manner.†

The 2,650-aircraft inventory of fighter-interceptors assigned to PVO-S has gradually been reduced from a strength of 8,000 a decade ago but has undergone continuous modernization.[114] The predominance of day-fighters noted previously began to disappear

---

*From the scientific community, the voice of the dissident nuclear physicist Andrei Sakharov was raised against the Soviet deployment of an ABM on grounds of its projected ineffectiveness and undesirable political consequences in his underground manifesto, Progress, Coexistence and Intellectual Freedom (New York: Norton, 1968), p. 35. There were also signs of disagreement concerning the effectiveness of their ABM among senior figures within the Ministry of Defense in early 1967. See Wolfe, Soviet Power and Europe, p. 439 and p. 152 above.

†Soviet construction of the Moscow/Galosh system proved to be an important precipitating factor that influenced political calculations within the Johnson administration and prompted the imitative initiation of deployment of the American Sentinel ABM system in 1967-68. For an insightful analysis of this decision, see Morton H. Halperin, "The Decision to Deploy the ABM: Bureaucratic and Domestic Politics in the Johnson Administration," World Politics (October 1972): 62-95.

with acquisition of the all-weather YAK-25 and the MIG-19P in the late 1950s. While sizable numbers of the 1950s aircraft remain in active service, the capabilities of air defense interceptor aviation have been steadily improved with the addition of a new generation of advanced fighters including the SU-9, SU-15, YAK-28P, TU-28P, SU-11, MIG-23, and MIG-25, all of which are equipped with modern avionics and air-to-air missiles.[115]

The maintenance of this large interceptor force is supported by the various components of the Soviet commitment to strategic defense discussed above. It probably benefits as well from the existence of two institutional sponsors within the Soviet armed forces. The aircraft assigned the air defense role are frequently also deployed by the Soviet air forces who will tend to reinforce PVO-S requests for their development and production. The pressures for continuous fighter development and series production are also likely to emanate from the prestigious Mikoyan, Sukhoi, Tupolev, and Yakovlev design bureaus. The appearance of new fighter prototypes at regular three- to four-year intervals suggests the potency of this group. In addition, the manufacturing plants within the Ministry of Aviation Industry are likely to lobby for additional aircraft acquisitions in accordance with their own "production line imperatives."* Blessed with this array of parochial advocates and the continued existence of plausible aviation threats from the West and China, the PVO air arm appears to be in a good position to maintain and improve its substantial capabilities.

From an interaction standpoint, the Soviets are known to monitor carefully Western aircraft development, a practice with obvious emulative and offsetting design implications. Soviet interceptors are most certainly designed with an eye toward their capabilities against probable Western attackers. Thus the supersonic, high-

---

*A provocative discussion of the impact of available production capacity on the awarding of aviation contracts in the United States is found in James Kurth, "Aerospace Production Lines and American Defense Spending," in American Defense Policy, ed. R. Head and E. J. Rokke, 3d ed. (Baltimore: Johns Hopkins Press, 1973), pp. 626-40. For a trenchant critique of Kurth's "production line imperative" hypothesis, see Arnold Kanter and Stuart J. Thorson, "The Logic of American Weapons Procurement: Problems in the Construction and Evaluation of Policy Theories," paper delivered at the 1972 Midwest Regional Meeting of the International Studies Association and Peace Research Society, Toronto, Ontario, May 11-13, 1972. We lack sufficient information on Soviet aircraft production to test the validity of this theory on the Soviet scene.

altitude characteristics of the MIG-25 Foxbat A suggest that it may have been designed as a counter to the anticipated American procurement of the B-70. The convergence of Western and Soviet aircraft design activity in such areas as vertical takeoff and landing and variable-geometry airframes appears largely attributable to the simultaneous advance of the technological state of the art by similarly proficient aviation design complexes rather than an imitative action-reaction sequence on either side. Yet when one side develops and acquires a particular capability it is likely to strengthen the demands for the funding of both imitative and offsetting activity within the decision arena of the other.

CONCLUSION

This review of Soviet military-economic planning and weapons development practices and the evolution of Soviet strategic force posture since World War II indicates that there are many factors at work relevant to these activities. While Soviet force procurements have in many cases been responsive to American weapons developments, they have also exhibited their own distinctive characteristics. These have reflected the impact of key individuals like Nikita Khrushchev and such talented weapons designers as A. N. Tupolev and M. K. Yangel, as well as the shaping influences of Soviet military doctrine, the parochial promotional efforts of the various military services and design bureaus, and well-established habits and practices in Soviet weapons design, production, and deployment such as concurrent development of competitive designs and a tendency to favor conservative incremental change in the development of new systems. As a result of these internal influences, one must agree with the conclusion of one long-time student of Soviet weapons development, Andrew W. Marshall, that while the superpower arms competition has been a continuous one, "the interaction between American and Soviet force postures is muffled, lagged and very complex."[116]

It appears that imaginative analysis utilizing the bureaucratic politics framework combined with careful empirical investigation whenever relevant data can be obtained offer great promise as a method to improve our understanding of the development of Soviet force posture.

NOTES

1. Samuel P. Huntington, The Common Defense: Strategic Programs in National Politics (New York: Columbia University Press, 1961), pp. 1-7.

2. This concern appears most evident with regard to the dramatic increase in Soviet distant area naval deployments since the mid-1960s. See Franklyn Griffiths, "Forward Deployment and Foreign Policy," and Robert Weinland, "The Changing Mission Structure of the Soviet Navy," in Soviet Naval Developments: Context and Capability, ed. Michael MccGwire (New York: Praeger, 1973), pp. 7-12, 293-310.

3. For comments on these priorities, see Vernon V. Aspaturian, "The Soviet Military-Industrial Complex--Does It Exist?" Journal of International Affairs 26, no. 1 (1972): 18-19; Richard Armstrong, "Military-Industrial Complex--Russian Style," Fortune, August 1, 1969, pp. 124, 126.

4. For a discussion of this concern and its impact within the American defense community, see Richard G. Head, "Doctrinal Innovation and the A-7 Attack Aircraft Program," in American Defense Policy: Third Edition, ed. Richard G. Head and Ervin J. Rokke (Baltimore: Johns Hopkins University Press, 1973), pp. 432-35.

5. Graham T. Allison, Essence of Decision: Explaining the Cuban Missile Crisis (Boston: Little, Brown, 1971), pp. 102-13.

6. Ibid., p. 105; lecture by Col. Eliyahu Ze'ira, chief of operations, Israeli Army General Staff, U.S. Air Force Academy, Colorado, November 1967.

7. Colin S. Gray, "The Arms Race Phenomenon," World Politics (October 1971): 41.

8. Ibid., p. 54; Johan J. Holst, "Missile Defense, The Soviet Union and the Arms Race," in Why ABM?: Policy Issues in the Missile Defense Controversy, ed. Johan J. Holst and William Schneider, Jr. (New York: Pergamon Press, 1969), pp. 161-63.

9. Samuel P. Huntington, "Arms Race: Prerequisites and Results," in The Use of Force: International Politics and Foreign Policy, ed. Robert J. Art and Kenneth N. Waltz (Boston: Little, Brown, 1971), pp. 391-92.

10. Arthur Sulzberger, interview with Khrushchev, New York Times, September 8, 1961.

11. George W. Rathjens, "The Dynamics of the Arms Race," in Art and Waltz, op. cit., pp. 488-91.

12. Cf. L. I. Brezhnev's speech at Tula on January 18, 1977, carried in Pravda, January 19, 1977, and G. A. Arbatov's "The Big Lies of the Enemies of Detente," Pravda, February 5, 1977.

13. For references to the existence of annual and five-year plans within the Ministry of Defense, see Maj. Gen. A. Baranenkov, "Financial Support to the Troops, Under Annual Planning Conditions," Tyl i Snabzhenie [Rear services and supply] no. 10 (October 1972): 57-61; Col. Gen. V. Dutov, "Improving Economic Operations in the Army and Navy," Kommunist Vooruzhennykh Sil no. 2 (January 1972):

34; and V. D. Sokolovskiy, ed., Voennaia strategiia [Military strategy], 3d ed. (Moscow: Voenizdat, 1968), p. 378.

14. Herrick quotes a "former Soviet naval officer" regarding the existence of a ten-year Soviet naval shipbuilding plan approved around 1950. Robert W. Herrick, Soviet Naval Strategy: Fifty Years of Theory and Practice (Annapolis, Md.: United States Naval Institute, 1968), pp. 63, 64.

15. Michael MccGwire, "Soviet Naval Procurement," in The Soviet Union in Europe and the Near East: Her Capabilities and Intentions (London: Royal United Services Institution, August 1970), pp. 76-77. MccGwire has written in considerable detail about the classes of ships included within this 20-year program and their scheduled delivery dates. This plan, however, is MccGwire's own analytical construct, developed on the basis of observed Soviet ship construction patterns and a single quote from Admiral Weakley, U.S. Navy, on Soviet submarine construction plans in the 1950s, New York Times, February 4, 1959. Michael MccGwire, "Naval Shipbuilding Practices," unpublished manuscript, n. 8.

16. V. D. Skugarev and L. V. Kudin, Setovoye planirovaniia na flote [Critical path planning method in the navy] (Moscow: Voenizdat, 1973), p. 2.

17. See Gertrude E. Schroeder, "Recent Developments in Soviet Planning and Incentives," in Soviet Economic Prospects for the Seventies, Joint Economic Committee of Congress, 93rd Congress, 1st Session (Washington, D.C.: Government Printing Office, 1973), pp. 13-18; and Theodore Shabad, "Soviet Economists Split on Flexibility Planning," New York Times, October 9, 1973.

18. Marshal M. V. Zakharov, "On the Eve of World War II: May 1938-September 1939," Novaia i Noveyshaia Istoriia [New and newest history] no. 5 (September-October 1970): 3-27, and "The Communist Party and the Technological Rearmament of the Army and Navy in the Years of the Prewar Five Year Plans," Voenno-Istoricheskii Zhurnal no. 2 (February 1971): 3-12; Maj. Gen. Ye. Nikitin and Lt. Col. V. Tret'yakov, "Historical Experience of the Party Leadership of Soviet Military Construction," Voenno-Istoricheskii Zhurnal no. 8 (August 1973): 3-10.

19. Barry Richman, Soviet Management: With Significant American Comparisons (Englewood Cliffs, N.J.: Prentice-Hall, 1965), pp. 94-107; Herbert S. Levine, "Economics," in Science and Ideology in Soviet Society, ed. George Fischer (New York: Atherton Press, 1967), pp. 107-38.

20. Zakharov, "On the Eve of World War II: May 1938-September 1939," p. 14.

21. For an account of the planning activities of the Central Financial Directorate, see Col. Gen. V. Dutov, "Leninist Principles

of Financing the Soviet Armed Forces," Tyl i Snabzhenie [Rear services and supply] no. 3 (March 1970): 8-13.

22. Nikitin and Tret'yakov, op. cit., p. 7.

23. Interview, Col. (ret.) V. M. Kulish, Soviet Army, chief of the Military Affairs Section of the Institute of World Economics and International Affairs (IMEMO), Princeton, New Jersey, May 4, 1970.

24. For a reference to this collegium see "In the Ministry of Defense of the USSR," Krasnaia Zvezda, April 7, 1972.

25. Konstantin K. Krylov, "Soviet Military-Economic Complex," Military Review 51, no. 11 (November 1971): 96.

26. See Chapter 2, "The Ministerial System." Smirnov, who played a major role in the strategic arms negotiations at the Moscow Summit in May 1972, was identified as chairman of the Military-Industrial Commission in John Newhouse, Cold Dawn: The Story of SALT (New York: Holt, Rinehart and Winston, 1973), pp. 251-52.

27. See Chapter 2 under "The Supreme or Main Military Soviets" for a discussion of the evolution of this body. Discussions of its role and composition are found in Malcolm Mackintosh, "The Soviet Military: Influence on Foreign Policy," Problems of Communism (September-October 1973): 1-4; and Harriet Fast Scott, "The Soviet High Command," Air Force Magazine (March 1977): 52-53.

28. Nikita S. Khrushchev, Khrushchev Remembers: The Last Testament (Boston: Little, Brown, 1974), pp. 25-26.

29. Ibid., p. 27.

30. Arthur J. Alexander's R&D in Soviet Aviation, R-589-PR (Santa Monica, Calif.: RAND Corporation, November 1970); and "Weapons Acquisition in the Soviet Union, United States and France," in Comparative Defense Policy, ed. F. B. Horton, A. Rogerson, and E. L. Warner, III (Baltimore: Johns Hopkins Press, 1974), pp. 426-44.

31. E. Zaleski et al., Science Policy in the USSR (Paris: Organization for Economic Cooperation and Development, 1969), pp. 216-92; Alexander G. Korol, Soviet Research and Development: Its Organization, Personnel and Funds (Cambridge, Mass.: MIT Press, 1965), passim.

32. John Erickson, "Radio Location and the Air Defense Problem: The Design and Development of Soviet Radar, 1934-1940," Science Studies no. 2 (1972): 255-59.

33. Ibid., p. 247.

34. The air forces' Chief Administration for Aviation Engineering Service is identified in Robert Kilmarx, op. cit., p. 113, and in Raymond L. Garthoff, "Soviet Air Power: Organization and Staff Work," in The Soviet Air and Rocket Forces, ed. Asher Lee (New York: Praeger, 1959), p. 181.

35. John Erickson, Soviet Military Power (London: Royal United Services Institution, 1971), p. 27; Mackintosh, op. cit., p. 10.

36. Marshal M. V. Zakharov, "The Communist Party and the Technological Rearmament," p. 4; Malcolm Mackintosh, "The Role of Institutional Factors in Soviet Decisions on Weapons Development," unpublished manuscript, 1967, p. 10; Oleg Penkovskiy, The Penkovskiy Papers, trans. Peter Deriabin (New York: Avon, 1966), p. 309.

37. Aleksander S. Yakovlev, Tsel' zhizni: zapiski aviakonstruktora [The goal of life: notes of an aviation designer], 2d ed. (Moscow: Izdatel'stvo Politicheskoi Literatury, 1968), p. 491.

38. Numerous cases of designers' promotion of their own weapons are described in Soviet memoir literature. Noteworthy examples include the creation of the T-34 tank by designers M. Koshkin and A. Morozov as described by Col. V. Mostovenko, "Steps in Tank Construction," Tekhnika i Vooruzhenie [Technology and Armaments] no. 9 (September 1966): 14; S. Ilyushin's initiation of the design of the IL-2 "Stormovik" ground attack fighter-bomber, S. Ilyushin, "A Front Line Weapon," Tekhnika i Vooruzhenie no. 5 (May 1970): 22; A. N. Tupolev's efforts to develop the TU-4 medium bomber, A. N. Tupolev, "TU--The Man and the Aircraft," Znamya no. 9 (September 1973): 41; the development of the 122-mm howitzer, Lt. Gen. F. Petrov, "Search for Design Perfection," Tekhnika i Vooruzhenie no. 11 (November 1968): 2-4; and the self-initiated work on the 85-mm gun for the T-34 tank by Zh. Kotin, P. Murav'yev, "Guns for Tanks," Tekhnika i Vooruzhenie no. 5 (May 1970): 12.

39. V. Grabin, "Contribution to Victory," Tekhnika i Vooruzhenie no. 5 (May 1970): 7-8.

40. Ibid., p. 8.

41. Cf. B. L. Vannikov, "From the Notes of the People's Commissar of Armaments," Voenno-Istoricheskii Zhurnal no. 2 (February 1962): 80; Muravyev, op. cit., p. 12; Marshal N. N. Voronov, Na sluzhbe voennoi [In wartime service] (Moscow: Voenizdat, 1963), p. 235.

42. Numerous memoirs testify to Stalin's pervasive involvement in the weapons development process. Cf. Vannikov, op. cit., on artillery and small arms, pp. 79-83; Yakovlev, op. cit., on aviation, passim; and Adm. N. G. Kuznetsov on naval shipbuilding, "Before the War," Oktyabr' [October] no. 11 (November 1965]: 141-44.

43. Khrushchev's directing role in the Soviet missile program is described in Leonid Vladimorov, The Russian Space Bluff (London: Tom Stacey, 1971), passim. Khrushchev himself provides several accounts of his personal dealings on weapons design matters with such key figures as missile designers S. P.

Korolyev and M. K. Yangel and aircraft constructor, A. N. Tupolev. Khrushchev, op. cit., pp. 40-42, 46, 50.

44. Alexander, "Weapons Acquisition in the Soviet Union, United States and France," p. 430.

45. Cf. B. L. Vannikov, "The Defense Industry of the USSR on the Eve of the War," Voprosy Istorii no. 1 (January 1969): 122-23; "Submachine Guns," Tekhnika i Vooruzhenie no. 6 (June 1971): 12.

46. References to the routine approval activity of these commissions are found in A. Nikitin, "The History of the Creation of an Anti-tank Aviation Bomb," Voenno-Istoricheskii Zhurnal no. 9 (September 1969): 72-73; Vannikov, "The Defense Industry of the USSR on the Eve of the War," p. 120; and Mostovenko, op. cit., p. 13.

47. Krylov, op. cit., p. 96; Vannikov, "From the Notes of the People's Commissar of Armaments," pp. 79, 86; Maj. Gen. N. E. Novovskiy, "Our Arsenal of Armaments," Voprosy Istorii no. 11 (November 1970): 126-27; Andrew Sheren, "Structure and Organization of Defense-Related Industries," Economic Performance and the Military Burden in the Soviet Union, Joint Economics Committee, 91st Congress, 2d Session (Washington, D.C.: Government Printing Office, 1970), p. 126.

48. These and all subsequent figures on the size of Soviet military forces are extracted from The Military Balance: 1976-1977 (London: International Institute of Strategic Studies, September 1976).

49. Thomas Wolfe, Soviet Power and Europe, 1945-1970 (Baltimore: Johns Hopkins Press, 1970), p. 183.

50. Asher Lee and Richard E. Stockwell, "Soviet Missiles," in The Soviet Air and Rocket Forces, ed. A. Lee (New York: Praeger, 1959), pp. 147-59.

51. G. A. Tokaty-Tokaev, "Foundations of Soviet Cosmonautics," Spaceflight (October 1968): 335-46; G. A. Tokaty-Tokaev, "Soviet Space Technology," Spaceflight (February 1963): 58-64; Michael Stoiko, Soviet Rocketry: Past and Present and Future (New York: Holt, Rinehart and Winston, 1970), pp. 42-65.

52. Tokaty-Tokaev, "Foundations of Soviet Cosmonautics," p. 343.

53. Ibid., pp. 343-45; Lee and Stockwell, in Lee, op. cit., pp. 149-57. A Soviet defector, Leonid Vladimirov, identified S. P. Korolev, M. Yangel, and V. Chalomei as leaders of the major Soviet ballistic missile design teams in the 1950s and 1960s. Vladimirov, op. cit., pp. 53, 82. See also Nicholas Daniloff, The Kremlin and the Cosmos (New York: Knopf, 1971), pp. 57-58.

54. Johan J. Holst, Comparative US and Soviet Deployment, Doctrines, and Arms Limitation (Chicago: University of Chicago Press, 1971), p. 10.

55. Henry J. Simmons, "The Soviet Space Program," Space/Aeronautics (December 1965): 54.

56. Desmond Ball, "The Strategic Missile Program of the Kennedy Administration, 1961-1963," Ph.D. dissertation, Australian National University, Canberra, June 1972, p. 102.

57. Charles J. V. Murphy, "Khrushchev's Paper Bear," Fortune (December 1964), p. 228.

58. Penkovskiy, op. cit., pp. 339-43.

59. Arnold L. Horelick and Myron Rush, Strategic Power and Soviet Foreign Policy (Chicago: University of Chicago Press, 1966), passim.

60. Allison, op. cit., p. 116.

61. The Military Balance, 1972-1973 (London: International Institute of Strategic Studies, 1972), p. 65.

62. The Military Balance, 1962-1963 (London: Institute of Strategic Studies, 1962), p. 3.

63. The Military Balance, 1972-1973, p. 65.

64. Holst, Comparative U.S. and Soviet Deployments, Doctrines and Arms Limitation, p. 16.

65. Peter Ognibene, "ABM Pact Is Better Than None," Washington Post, July 4, 1971.

66. Michael Getler, "Soviets Test New Version of Missile," Washington Post, August 2, 1970.

67. See William Beecher, "Soviet Prepares Big New Missiles," New York Times, April 23, 1972; Stewart Alsop, "Good News at Last," Newsweek, June 14, 1971; Michael Getler, "New Soviet Silo Building Seen as Protection for Two Missiles," Washington Post, May 27, 1971.

68. Cecil Brownlow, "Soviets Prepare Space Weapon for 1968," Aviation Week and Space Technology (November 13, 1967).

69. The Military Balance, 1976-1977, p. 8.

70. William Beecher, "Soviet Is Said to Dismantle Some of Its Older Missiles," New York Times, March 3, 1972; "100 Old Missiles Retired by Russia in Five Years," Washington Post, March 4, 1972.

71. William Beecher, "Soviet ICBM Shift Detected by U.S.," New York Times, February 11, 1970.

72. John W. R. Taylor, "Gallery of Soviet Aerospace Weapons," Air Force Magazine (March 1975), p. 73.

73. Donald M. Rumsfeld, Annual Defense Department Report to Congress, FY 1978 (Washington, D.C.: Government Printing Office, January 17, 1977), p. 62.

74. Ibid.

75. Jan Lodal, "Verifying SALT," Foreign Policy no. 24 (Fall 1976): 49-54.

76. Holst, Comparative U.S. and Soviet Deployments, p. 17.

77. Rumsfeld, op. cit., p. 62.

78. See Thomas W. Wolfe, Soviet Interests in SALT: Political, Economic, Bureaucratic and Strategic Contributions and Impediments to Arms Control, P-4702 (Santa Monica, Calif.: RAND Corporation, September 1971), passim.

79. William Beecher, "Soviet Advance on Missile Seen," New York Times, October 1, 1972; and "Russia Tests New Sub Missile," Baltimore Sun, November 29, 1972.

80. Thomas W. Wolfe, Soviet Naval Interaction with the United States and Its Influence on Soviet Naval Development, P-4913 (Santa Monica, Calif.: RAND Corporation, October 1972), p. 16.

81. Ibid., p. 17.

82. For Khrushchev's comments in this regard, see Chapter 4 under "The Khrushchev Initiative," and Khrushchev Remembers: The Last Testament, pp. 30-33.

83. MccGwire, "Soviet Naval Procurement," pp. 76-78.

84. S. G. Gorshkov, "The Development of Soviet Naval Art," Morskoi Sbornik [Naval collection] no. 2 (February 1967): 19. See Robert Waring Herrick, Soviet Naval Strategy: Fifty Years of Theory and Practice (Annapolis, Md.: U.S. Naval Institute, 1968), pp. 67-71.

85. MccGwire, "Soviet Naval Procurement," p. 78.

86. Ibid., p. 82; Herrick, op. cit., pp. 19-27.

87. Status of Naval Ships, Hearings before the Special Subcommittee on Sea Power of the Committee on Armed Services, House of Representatives, 90th Congress, 2d Session, and 91st Congress, 1st Session (Washington, D.C.: Government Printing Office, 1969), pp. 226, 233.

88. MccGwire, "Soviet Naval Procurement," p. 84.

89. "Soviets Stressing Offensive Mix of Strategic Arms for Which the US Has Little Defense," Aviation Week and Space Technology (October 11, 1971): 38.

90. Rumsfeld, op. cit., p. 63.

91. The Soviet navy appears to have been forced to lobby strongly to acquire a substantial cut of the strategic exchange in Soviet military doctrine. See Adm. V. A. Alafuzov's review of the first edition of Sokolovskiy's Military Strategy, which was part of a successful naval effort to gain recognition of the role of SLBMs as important strike weapons. Adm. V. A. Alafuzov, "On the Publication of the Work 'Military Strategy,'" Morskoi Sbornik no. 1 (January 1963): 95.

92. The Military Balance, 1976-1977, p. 9.

93. Edgar Ulsamer, "Backfire: Special Report on the New Soviet Strategic Bomber," Air Force Magazine (October 1971): 35.

94. The Military Balance, 1972-1973, p. 5.

95. For a discussion of Soviet aircraft design and production practices, see Arthur J. Alexander, R&D in Soviet Aviation, and his further comment on this subject in "Weapons Acquisition in the Soviet Union, United States and France."

96. William H. Gregory, "Soviet Union Seeks Balance in Technology Growth," Aviation Week and Space Technology (March 18, 1968): 87.

97. This development has been noted publicly by a number of prominent Soviet figures, including Premier Kosygin in his major address before the Twenty-fourth Party Congress, Pravda, April 7, 1971. See also the article by P. Dementev, Minister of Aviation Industry, "More Than Just Airplanes," Izvestiia, May 22, 1971.

98. Rumsfeld, op. cit., p. 63.

99. The Military Balance, 1976-1977, p. 8.

100. For the most comprehensive recent exposition on Soviet military doctrine and capabilities, see John Erickson, Soviet Military Power (London: Royal United Services Institute of Defense Studies, 1971), pp. 7-12, 41-74. See also Thomas W. Wolfe's excellent discussions in Soviet Power and Europe, pp. 195-216, 427-58, 501-10.

101. Johan J. Holst, "Missile Defense: The Soviet Union and the Arms Race," in Why ABM? Policy Issues in the Missile Defense Controversy, ed. J. J. Holst and W. Schneider, Jr. (New York: Pergamon Press, 1969), p. 147.

102. Ibid., p. 146.

103. Wolfe, Soviet Power and Europe, 1945-1970, p. 185.

104. Michael MccGwire, "Soviet Naval Capabilities and Intentions," in The Soviet Union in Europe and the Near East: Her Capabilities and Intentions (London: Royal United Service Institution, August 1970), p. 43.

105. Robert A. Kilmarx, The History of Soviet Air Power (New York: Praeger, 1962), p. 299.

106. Wolfe, Soviet Power and Europe, p. 188.

107. The Soviet Military Technological Challenge, Special Report Series, no. 6 (Washington, D.C.: Center for Strategic Studies, September 1967), p. 61.

108. Ibid., p. 63.

109. Geoffrey Jukes, The Indian Ocean in Soviet Naval Policy, Adelphi Papers no. 87 (London: International Institute for Strategic Studies, May 1972), p. 5.

110. Erickson, Soviet Military Power, p. 47.

111. Cf. Joseph Alsop, "Soviet Missile Analysis," Washington Post, June 4, 1971.

112. The Soviet Military Technological Challenge, pp. 63-64.

113. William Beecher, "Laird Says Soviet Renews ABM Work," New York Times, April 29, 1971.

114. Cf. Cecil Brownlow, "Soviet Air Force Unveils Advanced Designs for Expanded Limited War Capability," Aviation Week and Space Technology (July 17, 1967): 32-35; "Soviets Push Advances in Fighters," Aviation Week and Space Technology (October 18, 1971): 24-27.

115. "Soviets Closing Gap in Avionics, Computer Science Military Development," Aviation Week and Space Technology (October 25, 1971): 28-30.

116. Quoted in Allison, op. cit., p. 98.

CHAPTER

6

THE SOVIET MILITARY AND ARMS CONTROL

Over the past two decades, arms control and disarmament* negotiations have come to play an increasingly prominent role in Soviet foreign policy. These negotiations have generally sought to develop international agreements on measures to restrain military programs and, in some cases, to improve crisis management

---

*The terms "disarmament" and "arms control" have different meanings in their common Western usage. Disarmament implies a straightforward reduction in or even abolition of national weapons inventories, while arms control is a broader concept, embodying a variety of measures designed to stabilize the international arms competition, reduce the likelihood of war, and limit war's destructiveness should it occur. The Soviets have traditionally preferred the term razoruzhenie--"disarmament" over kontrol' nad vooruzheniami --"arms control" which has strong connotations of intrusive inspection and external supervision associated with the Russian word kontrol. The Soviets have described Western arms control proposals and agreements over the past two decades as "partial disarmament measures" and substantially modified their attitude from strong condemnation in the 1950s and early 1960s to support of these steps in recent years. For discussions of these terms, see Walter C. Clemens, The Superpowers and Arms Control: From Cold War to Interdependence (Lexington, Mass.: Heath, 1973), n. A, p. 87, and Alexander Dallin et al., The Soviet Union, Arms Control, and Disarmament: A Study of Soviet Attitudes (New York: School of International Affairs, Columbia University, 1964), n. 7, p. 200. In spite of these differences, the terms "arms control" and "disarmament" are used interchangeably throughout this chapter.

capabilities in order to reduce the likelihood of war or mitigate its effects should it occur.* The Soviet military establishment has a large and obvious interest in these matters.

Western analysts have consistently portrayed the Ministry of Defense as an active opponent of Soviet adherence to international arms control agreements. Most frequently, they have asserted that this opposition derives from the combined effects of the military's parochial interests in expanding and improving its own weapons inventories and the institutional outlook prevailing among the military leadership that emphasizes the likelihood of war and the grave threat posed by a hostile and powerful imperialist enemy.† This evaluation has often been simply asserted as logically and self-evidently true. Many Western writers have supported this conclusion by citing statements of Soviet officers that confirm the military's desire for a continuous modernization of the Soviet arsenal and their pessimistic view of the international arena.[1]

This chapter seeks to describe and evaluate more fully the role and attitudes of the Soviet military regarding arms control. It discusses the manner in which various Soviet institutions and individuals have participated in disarmament matters, examines Soviet military statements bearing directly and indirectly on the issue, and presents a case study of relevant Soviet military behavior between 1969 and 1975 during the course of the Strategic Arms Limitation negotiations with the United States. It indicates that

---

*The Soviet-American Hotline Agreement signed in 1963 and its subsequent 1971 updating are examples of arms control measures that are designed to improve the chances of avoiding war or or to minimize its consequences should fighting occur, but do not affect regular military programs.

†Logical judgments about overall military opposition have sometimes been qualified in favor of statements about the likely opposition of those branches of the Soviet armed forces most directly affected by a particular arms control measure. Thus the Strategic Rocket Forces and PVO-S (National Air Defense) have been identified as probable opponents of the 1963 nuclear test ban treaty and the SALT I negotiations. Cf. the statements of Herbert Dinerstein and Malcolm Mackintosh in The Soviet Union, Arms Control and Disarmament: Background Materials, ed. George Fischer (New York: School of International Affairs, Columbia University, 1965), pp. 106, 107; and Matthew Gallagher, "The SALT Issue in the Soviet Political Context," in Roman Kolkowicz et al., The Soviet Union and Arms Control: A Superpower Dilemma (Baltimore: Johns Hopkins Press, 1970), p. 13.

over the years the Soviet military has been consistently skeptical about and generally hostile to arms control. It also demonstrates that the Ministry of Defense has come to play a much more prominent role in international arms control negotiations as these talks became increasingly technical and began to focus on questions with increased potential for imposing limits on Soviet weapons developments and deployments. Finally, with regard to the SALT negotiations, it suggests that over the past few years the Soviet military has apparently come to view these deliberations with relative equanimity since they have not yet yielded and appear unlikely to yield agreements that will impose substantial constraints on most of their strategic weapons programs. This is not to say that the Ministry of Defense has become an enthusiastic supporter of Soviet-American political and military detente, but rather that it has apparently found that it can live quite comfortably with detente as long as arms control agreements appear likely to constrain adversary military programs without threatening their own present and projected courses of action.

ORGANIZATIONAL SETTING

Individuals affiliated with several organizations within the Soviet system have been regularly involved in arms control activities. The leading role in these matters has been played by officials of the Ministry of Foreign Affairs. Men drawn from the Ministry of Defense and the eight defense production ministries (see Chapter 1), as well as several commentators on political matters and research scientists affiliated with the network of research institutes controlled by the Academy of Sciences have also published articles on this subject, attended informal arms control conferences, and served on official Soviet delegations engaged in international disarmament negotiations.

Participation in Pugwash and Disarmament Research

For the past two decades participation in the various international conferences and study groups sponsored by the Pugwash Conference on Science and World Affairs* has been a major element

---

*In addition to its large annual conferences, the Pugwash movement has spawned the smaller U.S.-USSR Study Group on Arms Control and Disarmament formed in 1964, which has become a major

of Soviet arms control activity. Over the years, a large number of Soviet scientists, scholars, diplomats, and military personnel have attended these meetings. Their participation, which is supervised by the Commission for Scientific Problems of Disarmament of the Academy of Sciences,[2] has served to familiarize them with Western arms control concepts and concerns.[3]

Soviet Pugwash delegations have traditionally been headed by prominent scientists such as academicians L. A. Artisimovich, M. D. Millionshchikov, and V. S. Emelyanov. On several occasions, Soviet military personnel as well have attended the Pugwash sessions. Generals (ret.) A. A. Blagonravov and N. A. Talenskiy* and Admiral (ret.) I. S. Isakov, who were embarked upon successful academic careers after leaving active military service, were regular attendees in the 1950s and 1960s.[4] These men were occasionally joined by active duty military officers such as Col. Gen. A. A. Gryzlov and then Col. V. V. Larionov, both of whose extensive involvement in other arms control matters is discussed below. Most recently, the Soviet military presence at Pugwash has been provided by a few of the retired officers drawn from the ranks of those who work on defense policy matters for the Institute for the Study of the United States and Canada (IUSAC) or the Institute of World Economics and International Relations (IMEMO), the most prestigious social science "think-tanks" of the Academy of Sciences (see Chapter 4 under "The Institutional Academics").

The Soviets have produced a sizable literature on disarmament questions.[5] Most of these publications have been authored by men associated with IMEMO, IUSAC, or the Institute of International Relations which is operated by the Ministry of Foreign Affairs.[6] The extensive research program underlying these publications is apparently coordinated by the same Disarmament Commission of the Academy of Sciences[7] noted earlier.

---

channel of Soviet-American dialogue. Duane Thorin, The Pugwash Movement and US Arms Policy (New York: Monte Cristo Press, 1965), p. 47.

*Academician/Lt. Gen. of Artillery (ret.) A. A. Blagonravov was a leading researcher in ballistics and educator during his military career. After his retirement in the early 1950s he became one of the most prominent men managing the Soviet space program and served on the Presidium of the Academy of Sciences. Voenno-Istoricheskii Zhurnal [Military history journal] no. 6 (June 1974): 56. For information on Maj. Gen. (ret.) N. A. Talenskiy, see Chapter 3 under "War in the Modern Era."

The work on these problems within IMEMO was done throughout the 1960s by a ten-man disarmament section headed by I. S. Glagolev[8] with the assistance of some members of V. Ya. Aboltin's economics section. The disarmament group was apparently absorbed by a newly formed military affairs section headed by retired Soviet Army Col. (ret.) V. M. Kulish in the late 1960s. The similarly oriented defense policy section of the Institute for the Study of the United States and Canada, whose staff includes Yu. G. Strel'tsov, G. A. Trofimenko, L. S. Semeiko, and M. A. Mil'shtein, has been actively studying arms control matters since the late 1960s as well. While its researchers have not yet produced any books or monographs specifically devoted to disarmament matters, they have written several articles on U.S. policy positions and attitudes regarding these matters.[9] These sections of IUSAC and IMEMO are also reported to prepare policy background papers on arms control issues for the Ministry of Foreign Affairs and the apparatus of the Central Committee.[10]

Reportage on disarmament matters routinely appears in several Soviet foreign affairs periodicals. The most prolific authors in this area include V. Viktorov, V. Shestov, and A. Alekseyev of Mezhdunarodnaia Zhizn' (International affairs) and N. Nikolaev of the New Times. Some of the most prominent foreign affairs analysts in the Soviet media, including Pravda's Yuri Zhukov and Izvestiia's Viktor Matveyev, have periodically weighed in with commentaries on topical disarmament issues as well.

Formal Negotiations

Since the early 1960s the Soviet government has been almost continuously involved in international arms control negotiations. The mainstay of this effort has been the U.N.-sponsored disarmament conference in Geneva long known as the Eighteen Nation Disarmament Conference (ENDC), which met regularly in Geneva between March 1962 and July 1969 and was retitled the Conference of the Committee on Disarmament (CCD) in August 1969. In the past few years the Soviet negotiations activities have expanded dramatically, first with the addition of the bilateral Strategic Arms Limitation Talks between the United States and the USSR which opened in November 1969, and more recently with the convening of the multilateral East-West talks on the Mutual Reduction of Forces in Central Europe begun in October 1973.

The leading role among Soviet institutions in the conduct of these negotiations has been played by the Ministry of Foreign Affairs. Soviet disarmament delegations have been routinely headed by senior foreign ministry officials, some of whom are generalists experienced in international negotiations, while others have long associations with arms control matters. In the first category, the Soviet negotiating team at the SALT negotiations has been continuously headed by Deputy Foreign Minister Vladimir S. Semenov, a versatile career diplomat, and the Soviet MBFR delegation in Vienna was initially led by Oleg N. Khlestov, head of the Legal and Treaty Department of the Ministry of Foreign Affairs and a professor who specializes in international law.[11] The delegation chief most experienced in arms control matters is Ambassador Aleksei A. Roshchin, a former head of the Second European Department of the Foreign Ministry, who has headed the Soviet group at the ENDC/CCD in Geneva since the early 1960s.[12]

The majority of those serving on Soviet disarmament delegations have been drawn from the Ministry of Foreign Affairs. Many of them apparently work within the 10-to-15-man Disarmament Section, which is part of the International Organization Division of the Ministry.[13] Others are leading figures from the regional desks of the geographic areas most directly affected by the negotiations in question. Thus the Soviet SALT delegation has included G. M. Korniyenko, chief, and V. G. Komplektov, deputy chief of the United States Department[14] and the USSR delegation to the MBFR talks includes Yu. A. Kvitsinskiy, a deputy chief of the Third European Department, which is responsible for West German and Austrian affairs.[15] Presumably the other personnel staffing these departments have also served on the delegations and are regularly involved in Moscow-based staff work that supports the development of Soviet policy in these negotiations. Professor Marshall D. Shulman of Columbia University, a veteran observer of Soviet arms control activity, reports that the Policy Planning Division of the Foreign Ministry joined the Disarmament Section and the America desk in the preparations for SALT I.[16]

Next to the Ministry of Foreign Affairs, the most consistent Soviet institutional participant in arms control negotiations has been the Ministry of Defense. Its participation in these deliberations is unsurprising in light of the obvious military content and possible ramifications of any arms control agreement. While the presence of representatives of the Ministry of Defense has been constant, the role of these officials in the various negotiations has differed widely. The single military participant within the 8-to-12-man Soviet delegation to ENDC/CCD,* for example, has been notable

---

*Between 1962 and 1973 this position was held by three men: Col. Gen. A. A. Gryzlov, Lt. Gen. S. G. Kholoptsev, and Maj.

for his minimal participation in the multinational negotiations.[17] In contrast, senior military officers have played a leading role, both numerically and in terms of concrete negotiations, in both the Strategic Arms Limitation Talks* and the Mutual Force Reduction negotiations. (The Soviet MBFR delegation includes delegates Maj. Gen. A. P. Tokum and Col. P. G. Kapitonov and advisers Col. I. T. Altukhov and Lt. Col. V. N. Chernishov.)[18] In each case the military has provided approximately one-third of the Soviet delegation, including the number two negotiator, Col. Gen. N. V. Ogarkov, during the opening phases of SALT I.† This active military role had its precedent in 1958 when the Soviet delegation to the highly technical Surprise Attack Conference in Geneva included three military officers among its six members, Col. Gen. A. A. Gryzlov, Maj. Gen. S. D. Romanov, and Maj. Gen. A. V. Pisarev.[19]

The organizational arrangements for staffing arms control matters within the Ministry of Defense are unknown. The generally low level of military participation in international disarmament negotiations prior to the late 1960s suggests that a small staff was probably all that was required. This group, whose head was probably the ubiquitous Gen. A. A. Gryzlov,‡ may have been located within the

---

Gen. N. V. Pesterev. Data gathered from "Lists of Members of Delegations to the Eighteen Nation Disarmament Conference/Conference of the Committee on Disarmament" (Geneva: United Nations, 1962-73).

*Soviet military participation in SALT is discussed in detail in the latter part of this chapter under "The Institutional Role of the Military."

†Maj. Gen. Royal B. Allison, USAF, JCS representative to SALT I, reports that Ogarkov, now a marshal, who then occupied the post of first deputy chief of the General Staff, acted as the number two man in the Soviet delegation during 1969 and 1970. Ogarkov is currently a first deputy minister of defense and chief of the General Staff. Interview with General Allison, U.S. Air Force Academy, Colorado, October 2, 1970; John Newhouse, Cold Dawn: The Story of SALT (New York: Holt, Rinehart and Winston, 1973), p. 192.

‡Gen. A. A. Gryzlov, who died in August 1974, was a distinguished staff officer who served as a key planner in the Main Operations Directorate of the General Staff during World War II, went on to become chief of staff of the Kiev and Belorussian Military Districts, and later returned to "assignments in the General Staff." His disarmament experience included attendance at the Geneva "surprise attack" conference in 1958 and the Ten Nation Conference

General Staff, perhaps within the Main Operations Directorate, or directly under the minister of defense. Since the opening of the SALT and MBFR negotiations, a much larger arms control staff, again either within the General Staff or reporting directly to the minister, almost certainly has been created within the Soviet military establishment. With Gryzlov's departure, this group is probably led by Col. Gen. Ivan I. Beletskiy, one of the military's "full delegates" in the SALT II deliberations.[20]

Representatives of a new institutional group have appeared on the Soviet arms control negotiating team during the Strategic Arms Limitation Talks. For the first time, men connected with the weapons development and production sector of Soviet science and industry could be positively identified in this capacity. Two men from the Soviet "military-industrial complex," Petr Pleshakov, initially a deputy minister and since 1973 minister of Radio Industry, and Academician Aleksander N. Shchukin, a leading weapons development scientist, have served as full delegates in the five-to-six-man Soviet group throughout much of SALT I and SALT II.[21] Moreover, L. V. Smirnov, a deputy chairman of the Council of Ministers and the chairman of the Military-Industrial Commission, whose role in coordinating defense production was discussed in Chapter 5 under "Defense Plan Development," emerged to play a central part in the final rounds of bargaining at the Moscow summit in May 1972, which culminated in the signing of the ABM Treaty and Interim Offensive Agreement[22] and again during the SALT portions of the Vance mission to Moscow in March 1977. Presumably, these prominent defense production personalities have been supported by a SALT staffing group within the defense industrial sector, perhaps operating under the auspices of the Military-Industrial Commission. This group or the individual defense production ministries are likely to be called upon both to provide technical analyses of adversary weapons capabilities and to assess the possible impact of restraints upon Soviet development and deployment programs.

Having identified three major institutional participants in Soviet arms control negotiations, the foreign, defense, and defense production ministries, and having noted the high probability that each received direct staff support in Moscow, we must address the

---

in 1960, regular participation in ENDC between 1962 and 1966, presentation of a paper at the Pugwash conference in Ronneby, Sweden in 1967, and an active advisory role during SALT I. Gryzlov obituary, Krasnaia Zvezda, August 23, 1974; Gen. S. M. Shtemenko, General'nyi shtab v gody voiny [The General Staff during the war years] (Moscow: Voenizdat, 1968), p. 129.

questions of interagency coordination and the manner in which they relate to the top-level decision-making forums. There is no evidence that a single formal coordinating organization analogous to the U.S. Arms Control and Disarmament Agency exists in the USSR. A major obstacle to the establishment of such an organization is likely to be the extreme sensitivity of the Soviet military to allowing civilians to deal with defense issues or even to have access to information on Soviet weapons characteristics and deployments. Direct evidence of the latter concern surfaced during the SALT I negotiations when General Ogarkov on one occasion privately urged an American delegate to be circumspect in his discussions of Soviet weapons systems because such information was clearly not appropriate for the Soviet civilian delegates to hear.[23]

Lacking a single unified arms control organization, the Soviets are likely to handle their interagency coordination for the various negotiations through working group or task force arrangements.[24] Raymond Garthoff reports that in late 1967 or early 1968 the Ministry of Foreign Affairs and the Ministry of Defense did in fact form a SALT working group to study issues and prepare draft positions for higher-level decision.[25] These bodies probably serve to maintain substantial compartmentalization among the ministries. The overall operation of these working groups could be supervised by either the Ministry of Foreign Affairs, whose leading role within the Soviet negotiating delegations was discussed above, or by elements of the Party Central Committee apparatus. The section of the apparatus most likely to supervise arms control matters is the International Department headed by Boris Ponomarev.[26]

The deliberations of the Soviet leadership on arms control are very likely to take place within the organizational settings and according to the procedures discussed in Chapter 2 under "The Ministry of Defense" and "The Politburo of the Central Committee." Major decisions on negotiating stands almost certainly require strong consensual agreement within the full Politburo. Preliminary examination of these issues and the routine monitoring of arms control matters probably takes place in the smaller Defense Council, which is likely on these occasions to add the Foreign Minister to its normal membership of Brezhnev, Kosygin, Podgorny, Kirilenko, and Ustinov. Given the central place of disarmament matters in the politics of East-West detente, General Secretary Brezhnev and his personal staff undoubtedly keep a careful watch on the handling of these issues throughout the Soviet bureaucratic labyrinth.

MILITARY COMMENTARY ON ARMS CONTROL

The public speeches and writings of Soviet military figures have dealt with arms control issues in a variety of manners. The overall military approach to arms control can be best understood through an examination of the different groups of military spokesmen --the military scientists of the General Staff, the military ideologists/philosophers of the Main Political Administration, the uniformed news correspondents of Krasnaia Zvezda, and the leading military commanders--and their varying discussions of disarmament questions.

The Military Scientists

Despite the considerable volume of their publications, the large fraternity of military scientists who work in the General Staff and the faculties of the higher military academies has largely failed to produce a theoretical literature on arms control and its military-strategic aspects.* The rare exceptions to this silence have come from the pens of the late Col. Gen. A. A. Gryzlov, whose wide-ranging arms control activities are discussed in this chapter under "Formal Negotiations," and Maj. Gen. V. V. Larionov.

General Gryzlov presented an arms control paper, "The Freezing of Defensive Anti-Missile Systems," to the Seventeenth Pugwash Conference on Science and World Affairs in Ronneby, Sweden, in September 1967. The essay is of particular interest in that it repeated the then prevailing Soviet line that antiballistic missile (ABM) systems were purely defensive weapons and thus not the source of the vigorous U.S.-Soviet arms competition. Gryzlov argued that it was the expansion of strategic offensive systems rather than ABM deployment that endangered international stability. This argument had been first asserted authoritatively by arms control activist Maj. Gen. (ret.) N. A. Talenskiy in a much-publicized 1964 article in International Affairs[27] and repeated by Premier Aleksei Kosygin in February 1967.† This Soviet claim that

---

*In 1964, Thomas W. Wolfe wrote, "Soviet military literature itself is distinguished by an almost total indifference to disarmament and arms control as a technical problem of serious professional interest to military theorists and planners." Soviet Strategy at the Crossroads (Cambridge: Harvard University Press, 1965), p. 238. This judgment has remained valid up to the present day.

†Kosygin, in a press conference in London on February 9, 1967 stated, "I believe that defensive systems, which prevent attack, are not the cause of the arms race, but constitute a factor preventing the death of people." Quoted in Why ABM? Policy

"defensive" ABM systems did not destabilize the strategic arms competition had been abandoned by June 1968, when the Soviets responded favorably to U.S. proposals to begin negotiations on the limitation of both offensive and defensive systems.

Gryzlov's 1967 Pugwash paper is also notable in that it includes two lines of argument that were to figure prominently throughout the SALT I negotiations. In criticizing a U.S. proposal for freezing the strategic inventories of the superpowers, Gryzlov noted that the socialist bloc was threatened not only by intercontinental weapons but also middle-range NATO-based systems.[28] This foreshadowed the persistent U.S.-Soviet disagreements over definition of "strategic offensive systems," which largely revolved around the Soviet demand that U.S. "forward-based systems"--carrier and land-based tactical aircraft--be included in the strategic balance. The Gryzlov article also asserted that any successful arms control agreement must be based on "the principle of equal security for both sides."[29] This principle which was first enunciated by the disarmament negotiators in the summer of 1961* was to become the premier public axiom invoked in support of Soviet positions at SALT I and II after its use by Brezhnev at the Twentieth-fourth Party Congress in March 1971. This principle was most heavily utilized in Soviet public commentary during the summer-fall of 1972 following the signing of the ABM Treaty and Interim Offensive Agreement at the Moscow Summit.

Maj. Gen. Larionov's association with arms control matters has been an intriguing one. As one of the most prolific writers on military science throughout the 1960s, Larionov followed the normal Soviet military practice in not discussing disarmament issues. In 1969, however, Larionov apparently retired to head the Military Affairs Section of the newly formed USAC Institute. Thus dissociated from the Ministry of Defense, Larionov wrote on disarmament issues[30] and participated in international arms control conferences including the Twentieth Pugwash Conference at Lake Geneva, Wisconsin, September 9-15, 1970 and the bilateral Soviet-American discussions of the "Committee on International Studies of Arms Control" in Moscow, August 18-20, 1971. In this sense his activities were similar to those of Gen. N. A. Talenskiy after his retirement

---

Issues in the Missile Defense Controversy, ed. Johan J. Holst and William Schneider, Jr. (New York: Pergamon Press, 1969), p. 110.

*It was raised during discussions in Moscow that culminated in agreement on a joint statement on basic principles for a treaty on general and complete disarmament. Interview, Thomas W. Wolfe, Washington, D.C., February 8, 1973.

in 1958. In the fall of 1973, however, Larionov apparently returned to military active duty,[31] most likely with either the Military Science Administration or Arms Control Section of the General Staff. He continued to comment on arms control matters, however, contributing an article in Pravda in April 1974, discussing the SALT II negotiations.[32] Larionov called for the expansion of military detente to support political detente, castigated several American "cold warriors," and strongly criticized U.S. Secretary of Defense James R. Schlesinger for his announcement of a revised nuclear targeting strategy.* Thus, although registering a strong stand in favor of detente and further strategic arms limitation that is unprecedented by a military writer, Larionov provided no evidence concerning what kind of SALT II agreement might be preferred by the Ministry of Defense.

In July 1974, then Colonel Larionov once again discussed the progress of detente and SALT II, this time in the pages of Krasnaia Zvezda. His tone again was strongly positive as he reviewed the accomplishments of the Brezhnev-Nixon summit of two weeks before and the state of Soviet-American relations. Larionov expressed his support for additional "constructive, practical measures in the sphere of military detente."[33] With this article, Larionov confirmed his unusual role as a major military spokesman on detente and disarmament with a uniquely positive view of these matters. The fact that Larionov was allowed to publish these favorable views after returning to active duty suggests that in midsummer 1974 the leaders of the Ministry of Defense were relatively pleased with Soviet-American detente relations and did not feel seriously threatened by the prospects for or likely terms of a comprehensive SALT II agreement.

The Military Ideologists

Like their military-scientific contemporaries, the military ideologists affiliated with the Main Political Administration have

---

*Larionov was the first military commentator to discuss the revised U.S. targeting policy. The most detailed Soviet attacks on Defense Secretary Schlesinger and the new policy were subsequently authored by three of Larionov's former colleagues at the USAC Institute. G. A. Trofimenko, "Problems of Peace and Security in Soviet-American Relations," SShA no. 9 (September 1974): 7-18; and M. A. Mil'shtein and L. S. Semeiko, "The Problem of the Inadmissibility of a Nuclear Conflict," SShA no. 11 (November 1974): 1-13.

seldom examined arms control issues. The comments of the ideological spokesmen of the Ministry of Defense have generally been confined to the inclusion of a few sentences favorably noting the most recent achievements in international disarmament negotiations in their discussions of current events. These laudatory citations have invariably been accompanied by strongly worded reminders that the imperialists continue to be dangerous and powerful adversaries and that only the steady growth of Soviet military might can protect the socialist camp from their intrigues.

The timing of these policy endorsements has sometimes aroused the interest of Western analysts. Several writers noted the failure of Soviet military publicists and leading commanders to join in the chorus of praise in the Soviet media following the August 1963 signing of the treaty banning the testing of nuclear weapons in the atmosphere, in space, and underwater.[34] Matthew Gallagher described this "blackout" as a "conspiracy of silence," designed to convey the displeasure of the Ministry of Defense over the conclusion of the partial test ban.[35] The manner in which the military press deleted favorable references to the treaty from major speeches it published during August and September further suggests military opposition to its conclusion.[36] Whatever their initial reluctance, by the fall of 1963, military commentators were describing the test ban as "a new success of the policy of peaceful coexistence,"[37] "an event of major international significance,"[38] and a "real step toward the relaxation of international tensions."[39] These favorable descriptions were coupled with calls for continued Soviet vigilance and warnings that high levels of military preparedness must be maintained. Nevertheless, the military's initial silence supports the logical conclusion that the Soviet military establishment was displeased by and almost certainly opposed to the conclusion of the partial Test Ban Treaty. Its opposition was probably a major factor in the subsequent Soviet decision to expand substantially its nuclear testing program underground, where the Moscow Treaty had failed to impose any restrictions.[40]

The same initial silence pattern was evident in the behavior of the military press following the conclusion of the ABM Treaty and the Interim Agreement on Offensive Systems at the Moscow Summit in May 1972. While _Pravda_, _Izvestiia_ and the other elements of the Soviet media were extolling the latest achievements of the Peace Program, the press organs of the Ministry of Defense limited themselves simply to publishing the texts of the agreements in _Krasnaia Zvezda_ at the time of their signing[41] and then lapsed into silence. They observed this moratorium for two months before breaking it with a lengthy article in _Krasnaia Zvezda_.[42] While this commentary strongly supported the new agreements, it also included the most outspoken criticism of U.S. strategic arms programs of that period. Moreover, it is interesting to note that the article was not written by an active-duty military officer, but instead was authored by Georgi I. Sviatov, a retired naval captain, second rank,* who works in the military affairs section of the Institute for the Study of the United States and Canada.

After overcoming their initial reluctance, military reviewers of the international scene have regularly included brief but positive references to the SALT I agreements and subsequent Soviet-American arms control advances.[43] Again these positive evaluations have always been combined with warnings about the serious dangers posed by the unrepentant imperialists.

Aside from these obligatory acknowledgments of major Soviet foreign policy accomplishments, the military philosophers have addressed arms control matters on only a couple of occasions. The most explicit of these appeared in a 1968 book review by Col. Ye. I. Rybkin. At a time, when the beginning of SALT I was being negotiated, he questioned the wisdom of disarmament negotiations in the following manner:

> It is impossible to agree with the view that disarmament can be achieved as a result of peaceful negotiations concerning this acute and difficult question by representatives of opposing social systems. Disarmament cannot be the result of any utopian "calming" of the class political struggle in the international arena. Quite to the contrary, it can be achieved only as a result of the most active pressure on their governments by the revolutionary forces in the imperialist countries combined with the flexible and principled policy of the socialist camp. Any other concept about the path to the achievement of disarmament is an illusion.[44]

Rybkin went on to note that "under contemporary conditions the primary task for the socialist countries is to strengthen its armed forces," and to criticize the authors of the book under review for their failure to emphasize this point.[45]

A more recent book written by a collective of Main Political Administration luminaries included an indirect slap at any arms

---

*He was not identified as a retired military officer in the June 28, 1972 <u>Krasnaia Zvezda</u> article.

control agreements designed to prohibit international warfare. The authors unearthed a quotation from Lenin that counseled against Soviet adherence to any agreement that would limit their freedom to initiate military operations. To this effect they noted that Lenin had pointed out "time and time again," that should the Soviets give their "solemn promise" never again to undertake "active, offensive military operations, we would be not only stupid, but criminals as well."[46]

The Leading Military Commanders

For the most part, senior officials within the Ministry of Defense have treated arms control in much the same manner as their military-philosopher subordinates. On those infrequent occasions when they have addressed disarmament issues, the high-ranking commanders have generally confined themselves to a few positive comments about existing agreements and ongoing negotiations.

Again like the military ideologists, the marshals have repeatedly coupled their favorable disarmament citations with assertions that the military might of the Soviet Union must be maintained to protect the socialist camp. Defense Minister Marshal A. A. Grechko provided an excellent example of this line of argument in June 1974 when he followed a positive evaluation of detente and the Brezhnev Peace Program with this warning: "The danger of war remains a grim reality of our times. Under these conditions the party and the Soviet Government still proceed from the inseparability of tasks involved in the strengthening of peace and national defenses."[47]

In late 1974, however, two deputy defense ministers were called upon in an unprecedented manner to comment directly on the provisions of the SALT I agreements and on Soviet compliance with them. First, Army Gen. V. F. Tolubko, commander-in-chief of the Strategic Rocket Forces, utilized a major news weekly to refute directly charges made publicly by U.S. Senator James Buckley that the Soviet government was violating the SALT accords signed in 1972. Buckley had accused the Soviets of engaging in deceptive practices to complicate verification of constructing new ICBM launch silos beyond those authorized by the Interim Agreement and of preparing to deploy a mobile ICBM.[48] In the course of an interview, General Tolubko was directly questioned about these allegations. His reply, which was specifically directed toward Senator Buckley, was explicit:

> All the more, it [the Soviet Union] will not violate its obligation in such a most important political

> issue as the interim agreement between the USSR and the United States on the limitation of strategic arms. We are strictly adhering to the signed documents. Not one single new silo for a surface launching installation has been emplaced since May 1972 and we are not conducting any tests of new mobile intercontinental systems.[49]

A month later, Marshal P. F. Batitskiy, commander-in-chief of PVO-S (National Air Defense), utilized another newspaper interview to reiterate Soviet denials of any violation of the SALT I accords. Batitskiy simply asserted, "We have strictly observed all international agreements signed by our state, particularly the agreements with the United States on the limitation of strategic offensive arms and ABM treaty."[50]

Adm. S. G. Gorshkov, the navy commander-in-chief, has compiled a varied record on arms control. In his unusual 12-part series in Morskoi Sbornik published during 1972-73, Gorshkov discussed the naval disarmament conferences of the 1920s and 1930s in a decidedly skeptical manner. Gorshkov noted that these conferences--the Washington Naval Conferences, 1921-22; the Geneva Naval Conference, 1927; and the London Naval Conferences, 1930 and 1937--not only failed to contain the naval arms competition between the major powers but even seemed to intensify international tension and the military preparations of the major powers.[51] Gorshkov also indicated that another significant development of that period had been the rise of the United States to full parity with the other major naval powers.[52] This observation may have been intended to suggest that Soviet participation in any contemporary arms control negotiations should be conducted with such a parity goal firmly in mind.[53]

Despite these negative remarks on the past efficacy of naval disarmament, in July 1974 Admiral Gorshkov publicly endorsed the recurrent Soviet proposal for designating the Mediterranean Sea as a nuclear-free zone.[54] At that time he utilized his annual Navy Day newspaper interview to repeat General Secretary Brezhnev's most recent suggestion for prohibiting vessels carrying nuclear weapons from being deployed in the Mediterranean.[55]

INDIRECT EVIDENCE OF MILITARY ATTITUDES TOWARD ARMS CONTROL

Faced with the paucity of direct Soviet military commentary on arms control outlined above, Western observers have often inferred attitudes on these issues from public statements by military men on other matters. This approach has been often utilized to identify the existence of strong and active military opposition to arms control. The Soviet military attitudes most frequently cited in this manner were previously discussed as components of the organizational outlook of the Ministry of Defense in Chapter 3. They include an exceedingly hostile depiction of the imperialist enemy; a maximalist view of Western military capabilities; calls for vigorous Soviet research, development, and weapons production efforts designed to secure military-technological superiority for the USSR; demands that the defense effort be accorded the highest allocational priority; and indications that the military should be accorded a major role in Soviet policy making.

This method of identifying military opposition to arms control must be employed with great care. In some cases the timing of the expression of these standard lines of argument by military authors suggests that concern over arms control matters was likely to have prompted their articulation. For example, the strong comments of Marshal N. I. Krylov, commander-in-chief of the Strategic Rocket Forces, made in August 1969 on the dangerous nature of imperialism[56] and the pointed reminder of Maj. Gen. A. Lagovskiy a month later that Soviet weapons development efforts must be based upon an assessment of present and projected enemy capabilities[57] are both likely to have been occasioned by uneasiness and perhaps outright policy opposition within the Ministry of Defense to the Strategic Arms Limitation Talks, which were about to open (Helsinki, November 18, 1969). Similarly, Soviet military apprehension about the wisdom of arms control cooperation with the West appears to be regularly expressed in military statements that consistently couple positive comment on arms control achievements with reminders about the essentially aggressive and adventuristic nature of imperialism and the resultant need to strengthen the Soviet defenses.

In many other instances, however, Western analysts have appeared to be unaware of the frequency with which the themes cited above routinely appear in Soviet Military writings. As a result, these writers have often identified the expression of these standard Soviet military viewpoints as an indication of military opposition to arms control, when such a conclusion seems unwarranted.[58]

BASIC MILITARY CONCERNS ABOUT ARMS CONTROL

The limited military discussions of arms control outlined above certainly fail to reflect the full range of Soviet military views and concerns regarding these matters. The officers of the Ministry of Defense are sure to view any serious contemplation of substantial arms control by the Soviet government with profound concern.

The Soviet high command as a whole and the leaders of the military services potentially most directly affected by a given arms control measure in particular will be very likely to oppose any agreement that would require the Soviet Union to reduce its existing military forces or to forgo a major new weapons program. They might overcome their antipathy toward arms control if an agreement promised to impose serious limits on enemy military capabilities without placing similarly stringent constraints on Soviet programs. Yet, the Soviet military could easily have second thoughts about supporting even such an advantageous agreement. This apprehension would be likely to arise due to military fears that the amelioration of international tensions that would be likely to accompany any major arms control pact could weaken their chances of retaining solid leadership support for their full range of military programs.

THE SOVIET MILITARY AND SALT

The opening of the bilateral strategic arms limitation talks in November 1969 marked a fundamental turning point in Soviet-American arms control relations. For the first time the superpowers entered into serious negotiations that addressed the possibility of imposing significant mutual constraints on their most important strategic weapons systems. Under these circumstances, the military establishments on both sides were bound to increase their interest and involvement in arms control matters. While the visible role played by the Ministry of Defense in the Soviet negotiating team increased perceptibly, the full picture of the views and influence of the Soviet military in these proceedings remains obscure. Nevertheless, the available information can be utilized to develop plausible speculations about these matters.

Military Objectives in SALT

When the SALT negotiations opened in November 1969, the Soviets found themselves trailing the United States in many of the aspects of the strategic arms competition. In strategic offensive delivery capabilities relative to the United States, the Soviets possessed roughly the same number of intercontinental ballistic missiles (ICBMs), about 1,050; fewer long-range submarine-launched ballistic missiles (SLBMs), 96 to 656; and fewer heavy bombers, 150 to 450.[59] The Soviet forces were also qualitatively inferior to those of the United States in such key areas as ICBM accuracy, the relative quietness of ballistic-missile-launching submarines, and the development of multiple independently targetable reentry vehicles (MIRVs).[60] Their disadvantageous position was mitigated considerably, however, by the fact that the Soviets were in the midst of massive ICBM and SLBM deployment programs that promised to alter substantially the quantitative balance in strategic launchers over the next few years.

The Soviets were in a better position in the balance of Soviet-American strategic defensive capabilities. Their combined force of radar systems, surface-to-air missiles, and fighter-interceptor aircraft gave them a defense against manned strategic bombers that was much larger and more capable than that of the United States. The Soviets also appeared to enjoy a slight edge in antimissile defense since they had begun to deploy the Galosh antiballistic missile (ABM) system around Moscow in the mid-1960s. In contrast, the U.S. Congress had only recently approved the funds to begin construction of the Safeguard ABM system designed to defend Minuteman ICBMs. However, the Soviets had halted work on the Galosh system in 1968, with only 67 launchers under construction or completed,[61] suggesting that they were not satisfied with its potential for coping with the U.S. ICBMs. Thus, despite the U.S. delay in initiating its ABM deployment, the U.S. Sprint-Spartan missile combination was likely to have been judged by the Soviets to be considerably more capable than their own Galosh system.*

Faced with this strategic balance, the Soviet military is likely to have entered the SALT era with the fundamental objective of maintaining sufficient freedom of action to be able to continue their vigorous development and deployment programs in pursuit of, at a minimum, a position of comprehensive parity in strategic weaponry vis-a-vis the United States. This minimal goal of full parity, which almost certainly continues to persist today, is likely to have included both a desire for aggregate equality in the numbers of strategic systems on both sides and a determination to achieve qualitative

---

*Thomas W. Wolfe reports that some American participants in SALT I have indicated that their Soviet counterparts expressed concern about the U.S. lead in both ABM and MIRV technology. Thomas W. Wolfe, Worldwide Soviet Military Strategy and Policy, P-5008 (Santa Monica, Calif.: RAND Corporation, April 1973), p. 22, n. 27. For comparison of the Galosh and Spartan/Sprint systems, see Charles J. J. Murphy, "What We Gave Away in the Moscow Arms Agreement," Fortune, September 1972, p. 10.

parity in such key technological areas as MIRV capability and ICBM accuracy where the United States had long enjoyed marked advantages.

It should be noted that the military requirements associated with the comprehensive parity objective would by no means be modest ones. The drive for equality by itself would appear fully capable of protecting and promoting the budgetary interests of the Ministry of Defense and its defense-industrial allies. It would appear sufficient to underwrite with ease a wide variety of weapons development and deployment activities in order to keep pace with the current and projected strategic programs of the United States over the next several years.

It is highly likely that the Soviet military leadership would like to move beyond the attainment of strategic parity with the United States. If it could be achieved, the military high command would be certain to prefer the attainment of the clear-cut Soviet military-technological superiority they have so often extolled in their professional literature. The Soviet military is likely to support pursuit of superiority for various reasons including their desire to possess the political leverage that military superiority might afford, their parochial interest in the sizable armaments programs that such a quest would demand, and their traditional doctrinally based interest in developing as potent a war-waging capability as possible for use should deterrence fail.

In addition to protecting its own weapons programs, the Soviet military almost certainly entered the SALT negotiations with the aim of hindering U.S. strategic force developments as much as possible. The apparently superior U.S. ABM capability is likely to have been the primary target in this regard during SALT I. From the latter stages of SALT I up to the Vladivostok Summit in November 1974, the Soviets consistently sought to impede new American strategic delivery systems including the Trident ballistic missile submarine and the B-1 heavy bomber. Any successes achieved in this area would be equally helpful in pursuing either the parity or superiority objectives.

Institutional Role of the Military

The role of the Soviet military in the SALT negotiations has been dramatically different than in most previous arms control discussions. Officers from the Ministry of Defense have been more heavily represented and more visibly active on the Soviet negotiating delegation than ever before. Presumably this same higher profile has been evident in the Moscow-based interagency staff coordination and support activities as well.

The Soviet delegations throughout SALT I and SALT II have been composed of five or six full delegates, some ten-twelve second-level personnel designated "advisers," and another three-five less prestigious "experts." The Ministry of Defense has maintained a representational share of approximately one-third within each of these categories since the SALT talks opened in November 1969.[62] Military influence appears to be enhanced by virtue of the fact that the leading military delegate, initially Col. Gen. Nikolai V. Ogarkov and later Col. Gen. Konstantin A. Trusov, has apparently been designated as the second-ranking man behind delegation leader Deputy Foreign Minister Vladimir S. Semenov.[63] The military's position might have been considerably more powerful had the Soviets chosen to follow through on their initial plans, as reported by U.S. delegate Raymond L. Garthoff, to name First Deputy Minister of Defense and Chief of the General Staff Marshal Matvei V. Zakharov as head of the original Soviet SALT I delegation.[64] Nevertheless, military interests in protecting their weapons development and deployment opportunities have no doubt been well served by their own sizable part of the Soviet delegation and the reinforcing presence of full delegates Petr Pleshakov, currently minister of radio industry, and Academician Aleksander N. Shchukin, a leading strategic weapons development scientist, from the defense-industrial complex.

The military officers present at SALT apparently represent several different organizations within the Ministry of Defense. All four of the military's full delegates have held key posts with the General Staff during their service with the SALT delegation. The primacy of the General Staff within the military group is further reinforced by the previously cited report that Marshal Zakharov, chief of the General Staff, was originally scheduled to head the Soviet SALT delegation.

The first two General Staff officers to serve as full delegates were Col. Gen. Ogarkov, then first deputy chief of the General Staff, and Col. Gen. of Engineering-Technical Services Nikolai N. Alekseev, long associated with advanced weapons development and apparently head of the Scientific-Technical Committee (NTK) of the General Staff.[65] Following their departure from the delegation in 1971, when both moved up to higher level jobs in the Ministry of Defense,* the sole military full delegate throughout the remainder

---

*Ogarkov, who left the Soviet delegation in December 1970 after the third round of talks, remained actively involved in SALT matters from his Moscow post as first deputy chief of the General Staff until becoming a deputy minister of defense with unidentified responsibilities in the fall of 1973. In January 1977, Ogarkov was

of SALT I was Lt. Gen. Konstantin A. Trusov, another veteran weapons development figure and perhaps Alekseev's successor as head of the General Staff's NTK.[66] Trusov was joined in 1974 by Lt. Gen. Ivan I. Beletskiy, the probable head of the General Staff's Arms Control Section, who was moved up from service as an advisor during the earlier rounds of SALT II. Both Trusov and Beletskiy have been promoted to colonel general during the SALT II negotiations.

The military officers serving as advisors and experts have included additional General Staff personnel as well as men apparently drawn from and representing the concerns of the services with the most important stakes in the strategic weapons area. Over the first five and a half years of negotiations the advisors included Col. Gen. A. A. Gryzlov, probable former head of the General Staff's Arms Control Section, who was discussed above; Vice Adm. Petr V. Sinetskiy, a former submariner with probable expertise in ballistic-missile submarines, although he was reportedly serving in the Arms Control Section headed by Gryzlov; Maj. Gen. Igor A. Afonskiy and Col. Viktor P. Starodubov from the Strategic Rocket Forces; Colonels Aleksandr A. Fedenko and Vladimir V. Budantsev of the air forces' Long-Range Aviation; Maj. Gen. of Aviation Aleksei M. Gorbunov on behalf of fighter aviation, and Engineer-Colonels Boris T. Surikov and Vasily N. Anyutin, air and missile defense experts from PVO-S; and Rear Adm. Mikhail A. Kovaleskiy and Capt. First Rank Anatoloy N. Mazerkin of the navy, both presumably representing the strategic ballistic missile submarine force.[67] These men have been assisted by several field grade officers serving as "experts" during the course of the negotiations.

The agreements concluded at the end of SALT I in May 1972 provided for the formation of a joint Soviet-American Standing Consultative Commission (SCC) to deal with many of the details associated with the implementation of the new accords. The Soviets named Maj. Gen. Georgy I. Ustinov, whose organizational affiliation within the Ministry of Defense is unknown, as their commissioner.[68] He is assisted by a staff that includes a mixture of military officers and civilians primarily drawn from the Ministry of Foreign Affairs.

---

appointed a first deputy minister of defense and chief of the General Staff and promoted to marshal of the Soviet Union. Alekseev left the delegation after the first few weeks of the fourth session in March 1971 to become a deputy minister of defense with the apparent responsibility of overseeing Soviet weapons development.

Only scattered bits of information are available regarding the behavior of the military members of the Soviet delegation during the SALT talks. All available accounts have indicated that the negotiations have been conducted in a serious and businesslike manner on both sides since their inception. Presumably the Soviet military personnel have shared in this demeanor.

The Soviet military delegates are reported to have entered the initial rounds of SALT I under the personal instructions of Defense Minister Marshal Grechko to avoid any disclosure of information on Soviet weapons capabilities. As a result they "were initially very conservative and restrictive, and displayed traditional suspicion of Western intelligence 'fishing.'"[69] Soviet caution and reticence regarding these matters have generally persisted, although there was apparently a striking departure from this policy during the Moscow Summit in midsummer 1974. At that time, a high-ranking Soviet officer is reported to have told a U.S. counterpart some details about Soviet ICBM accuracy including a claim that they are accurate "to within 500 to 800 meters (1/4 to 1/2 mile) of the target."[70]

During the talks, the chief military delegates have joined in the pattern of informal one-on-one relationships that gradually emerged among the full delegates on both sides.[71] Lt. Gen. Trusov, in particular, has had his most frequent contacts with his American counterparts, Generals Royal B. Allison and Edward L. Rowny, the representatives of the Joint Chiefs of Staff at SALT I and SALT II respectively.[72]

Soviet military personnel have enjoyed a substantial advantage over their civilian colleagues because of their monopoly of access to information on Soviet strategic weapons deployments and technological capabilities. The SALT negotiations have provided a few striking examples of the compartmentalization of such information within the Soviet system. The U.S. participants in SALT I have frequently noted that their Soviet civilian counterparts were very interested in gaining information about the deployment and capabilities of their own weapons systems.[73] Similarly, at a point when such information was of crucial relevance to the negotiations, Deputy Foreign Minister Semenov was uninformed about the numbers of Soviet ballistic missile submarines deployed and under construction.[74] On another occasion, Soviet delegate N. S. Kishilov reportedly told U.S. delegate Raymond Garthoff that his knowledge of the number of ICBMs deployed by the Soviet Union was limited to the observation that they were "approximately equal" to those of the United States and that this information had been provided to him by the Soviet military.[75] Finally, as noted earlier, General Ogarkov acknowledged the military's monopoly in this area when on one occasion, he suggested to a U.S. delegate that information on Soviet weapons deployments should not be discussed in the presence of Soviet civilian delegates.[76]

There is little information about the role played by the Ministry of Defense in the various planning and support activities related to SALT that take place in Moscow. Since his departure from the delegation in late 1970, Marshal Ogarkov has apparently continued to play a leading role in SALT matters.[77] His successor as first deputy chief of the General Staff, Col. Gen. M. M. Kozlov, has also participated in these matters as evidenced by his presence as a primary participant on the Soviet side in the midsummer Moscow summit in 1974. Ogarkov was also present, as he had been at the summit in Washington in June 1973.[78] He was likewise present during social events attending the Vance visit to Moscow in March 1977.

The bulk of the military SALT support work has probably been handled by the various components of the General Staff. The Main Intelligence Directorate (GRU) of the General Staff is likely to be the primary source of intelligence collection and analysis on U.S. strategic capabilities. Its efforts are probably supplemented in the collection area by the work of the Committee on State Security (KGB) and in the analytical field, perhaps by the staffs of the weapons production ministries operating under the direction of L. V. Smirnov's Military-Industrial Commission or I. D. Serbin's Defense Industries Department within the apparatus of the Central Committee.

The central nerve center of the General Staff, the Main Operations Directorate, is likely to play multiple roles in SALT. Its Arms Control Section is probably the primary military monitoring agency regarding the progress of the negotiations themselves. The Operations Directorate is also likely to be responsible for providing information on the status of both deployed Soviet strategic forces and the new weapons systems under development. Information of the latter variety has been especially important because, since the SALT negotiations began, the Soviets have engaged in the development and testing of a plethora of new weapons including a new generation of ICBMs, most of which carry MIRVs,* three new SLBMs (the SS-N-8, SS-NX-17, and SS-NX-18), two modified ballistic-missile submarines (the Delta-I and II classes), a new strategic bomber (the Backfire), and a new ABM system.[79] Finally, should the Ministry of Defense be a partner in a joint SALT working group

---

*Three new Soviet ICBMs, the SS-17, SS-18, and SS-19, are being deployed with MIRV payloads ranging from four to ten reentry vehicles. <u>The Military Balance: 1976-1977</u>, p. 3.

with the Ministry of Foreign Affairs, as speculated earlier, the Main Operations Directorate is probably the major source of military participants in this body.

The ultimate presentation of military advice and policy preferences pertaining to SALT is bound to rest with the Minister of Defense, Marshal Ustinov. His primary assistants in this effort are likely to be First Deputy Minister of Defense and Chief of the General Staff Marshal N. V. Ogarkov and General Kozlov, whose activities were discussed above.

Military Views on SALT

The publications and personalities affiliated with the Ministry of Defense have produced only a smattering of commentary that can be construed as indicative of Soviet military attitudes and objectives in the SALT deliberations. The materials available convey the impression that the Soviet military has been continuously concerned about the strategic threat posed by the United States and determined to maintain a substantial modernization effort to strengthen the Soviet armed forces.

Soviet-U.S. diplomatic exchanges on the possibility of direct strategic arms limitation negotiations began as early as 1966.[80] These exchanges reached a serious preparatory stage after Soviet Foreign Minister Andrei Gromyko made a public declaration of Soviet readiness to enter such talks in June 1968.* The opening of the negotiations was delayed until November 1969, first by the cooling of Soviet-U.S. relations following the Soviet invasion of Czechoslovakia in August 1968, and subsequently by the time required to develop a bargaining position within the newly elected Nixon administration.

During this 17-month period, the Soviet military press contained no direct commentary on the subject of strategic arms limitation. Indirect indications of military opposition, however, did appear. The comment by Col. Ye. I. Rybkin cited under "The Military Ideologists" in this chapter, casting doubt on the wisdom of and prospects for success in disarmament negotiations was published in November 1968. Less directly, the harsh depiction of the

---

*Gromyko's signal was conveyed in a speech before the Supreme Soviet in which he stated that the Soviet government was prepared to discuss "mutual limitations and subsequent reduction of strategic means of delivery of nuclear weapons, both offensive and defensive, including antiballistic missiles." Pravda, June 27, 1968.

imperialist threat penned by Marshal N. I. Krylov[81] and Gen. A. Lagovskiy's blunt call for anticipatory weapons development in quest of military superiority[82] both appeared just a few months before the talks opened in November 1969. Finally, the fact that the editors of Krasnaia Zvezda appear to have deleted several favorable references to the upcoming negotiations from various speeches and communiques they published in 1968-69[83] further suggests that the military was wary about the prospect of strategic arms limitation.

After the talks had begun, relevant Soviet military commentary remained sparse and generally negative in tone. Again, there were few direct references to the talks themselves. Throughout 1970, the military correspondents of Krasnaia Zvezda periodically attacked the United States for continuing its latest strategic weapons programs, asserting that these actions were "undermining" the prospects for strategic arms limitation.[84] These news stories singled out the ongoing deployments of the Safeguard ABM system and the Minuteman III and Poseidon missiles with their MIRV capabilities, as well as development work on the B-1 strategic bomber, as American actions that only served to intensify the arms race.[85]

One 1970 article in Krasnaia Zvezda was particularly notable since it clearly registered military support for a key Soviet demand, which was to complicate the SALT discussions on limiting strategic offensive systems from their very outset. At the opening session in Helsinki, the Soviets adopted a position that they were to hold throughout SALT I and the first two years of the SALT II discussions as well. The Soviets insisted that all weapons systems capable of striking the opposing nation's homeland with nuclear weapons should be identified as "strategic" and included in the aggregate of weapons subject to limitation.[86] Acceptance of this definition would have meant that not only the U.S. long-range strategic weapons ("central systems" in U.S. parlance) but also U.S. nuclear-capable fighter-bomber aircraft deployed at overseas bases or on aircraft carriers within range of the Soviet Union would be counted within the strategic category. At the same time, only the Soviet intercontinental range systems would have been subject to limitation, while their fighter-bombers and peripheral range strategic systems--intermediate and medium-range ballistic missiles and medium bombers--would have been excluded because they do not directly threaten the territory of the United States.

Having advanced this self-serving definition, the Soviets demanded that the United States either withdraw its nuclear strike aircraft from the forward bases or grant the Soviets an appropriate advantage in the balance of central systems as compensation for these systems.[87] While the Soviet leadership, including the military, would surely like to achieve both of these goals, it is also distinctly possible that the Soviets fully anticipated U.S. rejection of this demand and that they raised the issue primarily as a delaying tactic designed to preclude the conclusion of any comprehensive agreement limiting strategic delivery systems. This interpretation gains credence in light of Soviet behavior during SALT I, when they proved willing and even eager to conclude a very restrictive ABM accord while showing little enthusiasm for serious discussions on the limitation of strategic offensive systems.* Whatever the Soviet objectives, the U.S. leaders have steadfastly refused to accede to Soviet demands regarding the inclusion of forward-based systems throughout the SALT negotiations.[88] The entire forward-basing issue at least temporarily lost its significance following the Vladivostok summit in November 1974, when the Soviets dropped this demand and agreed instead on a framework for a ten-year treaty that would cover only long range, "central" strategic systems.[89] However, following the Carter administration's introduction of a new "comprehensive" proposal in March 1977 that included substantial reductions in the ceilings agreed at Valdivostok and new qualitative constraints as well, the Soviets responded by both publicly and privately reintroducing their demand for inclusion of U.S. forward-based systems.[90]

On May 13, 1970, when the Soviets were still pressing the forward-based systems issues, Col. V. Aleksandrov published a long article in Krasnaia Zvezda which strongly argued that all nuclear-capable aircraft within range of the Soviet Union should be considered strategic. While acknowledging that the United States itself distinguished between its Tactical and Strategic Air Commands, Aleksandrov asserted that U.S. fighter-bombers were "tactical in name only" since they were clearly designed for and assigned "strategic tasks."[91] Although the article never directly mentioned the SALT negotiations, it so fully mirrors the position being taken by the Soviet SALT negotiators that it provides impressive evidence that the Ministry of Defense was among those supporting the intransigent Soviet stand on the forward-based systems. The

---

*The Soviets surprised the U.S. representatives at Round Two in April 1970 by accepting the American proposal that ABM defenses be mutually limited to a single complex for the defense of each country's national command authority. Throughout the remainder of SALT I, the Soviets proved very willing to engage in serious negotiations on ABM defenses but seriously addressed restraints on strategic offensive arms only after the United States made it clear that some limit on these systems would be required if any agreements were to be achieved. Newhouse, op. cit., pp. 183-249.

military stand in this regard may have reflected their genuine belief in the military utility of these systems or it may have simply reflected their desire to bargain hard in hopes of forcing the United States either to withdraw these aircraft or to grant the USSR an advantage in the balance of long-range systems.

The year 1971 brought continued publication of articles critical of new U.S. weapons programs. The majority of these comments appeared in a Krasnaia Zvezda summer series on "the strategic arms race in the United States,"[92] authored by military scientists and engineers rather than the usual military news correspondents. While briefly voicing support for negotiated arms limitation, these articles concentrated upon detailed descriptions of contemporary U.S. weapons programs and the dangers they posed to the Soviet Union.* The series also included a direct linkage between the forward-based systems issue and SALT.[93] The military authors charged that the exclusion of these systems from SALT would represent an unacceptable unilateral advantage for the United States and noted that these systems were part of "a poorly concealed attempt to divert retaliation from the United States."[94]

During 1972, military commentary relevant to SALT continued to be dominated by criticism of U.S. strategic weapons modernization programs, which were identified as products of the U.S. military-industrial complex's efforts to impede the SALT negotiations.[95]

As discussed earlier, the signing of the ABM Treaty and the Interim Agreement limiting Strategic Offensive Systems at the Moscow Summit in May 1972 occasioned little comment in the military press.[96] The first military article to mention the Moscow Agreements, which appeared on July 21, said little positive about them. It concentrated instead upon attacking U.S. plans to continue the B-1 and Trident programs, and noted that "influential forces" in the United States opposed the ratification of the SALT accords.[97]

A week later, Krasnaia Zvezda published a lengthy commentary on the Moscow Agreements written by Georgy I. Sviatov, which was noted previously in this chapter. Sviatov coupled high praise of the ABM Treaty and the Interim Agreement with the accusation that the U.S. decision to proceed with and even accelerate its B-1 and Trident programs violated the spirit if not the letter of the agree-

---

*For the first time, the Soviets added the American follow-on ballistic missile submarine ULMS (later to be redesignated the Trident) to their list of provocative U.S. strategic programs. Kharich and Koloskov, Krasnaia Zvezda, July 16, 1971.

ments.[98] He also sounded the familiar refrain that despite these positive steps the imperialists remained predatory and aggressive thus requiring the Soviet Union to adopt "all necessary measures" to strengthen its defense capability.[99]

One can only speculate on the various opinions within the Soviet military leadership regarding the SALT I accords, which are summarized below.

MAJOR ELEMENTS OF THE SALT I ACCORDS

The ABM Treaty

1. Both sides are permitted to construct two ABM complexes, each consisting of no more than 100 launchers and no more than 100 interceptor missiles.
2. The ABM complexes are authorized for (a) defense of the national capital and (b) defense of an ICBM launch area located not less than 1,300 kilometers from the national capital.
3. No restrictions are placed on the development or testing of new land-based ABM systems. The development or deployment of a sea-based, air-based, space-based, or mobile land-based system is prohibited.
4. The modernization and replacement of equipment for the authorized ABM complexes are permitted.

The Interim Agreement Limiting Strategic Offensive Arms

Force levels authorized during the five-year life of the agreement:

	U.S.	USSR
ICBMs	1054* or 1000†	1618* or 1408†
SSBNs-SLBMs	41-656 or 44-710†	740 or 62-950†

---

*The agreement provides no numbers for ICBMs. It speaks only in terms of those ICBM sites constructed as of July 1, 1972. These numbers are those provided by the U.S. government.

†These levels are the ceilings that each country is authorized to attain if it chooses to trade in pre-1964 ICBMs (for the United States 54 Titan IIs, for the USSR 210 SS-7s and SS-8s) on a one-for-one basis for additional ballistic-missile submarines and SLBMs.

The leaders of PVO-S are likely to have been quite unhappy with the ABM Treaty because it decisively ruled out the deployment of a nationwide ballistic missile defense system. Even more seriously, they probably feared that having given up on extensive missile defense, the political and military leadership might proceed along the path taken by the United States since the mid-1960s and begin to dismantle their antibomber defenses as well. Their fears were likely to have been somewhat reduced by the fact that the treaty allowed the completion of the full 100-launcher system around Moscow, authorized the deployment of a second ABM complex for the defense of Soviet ICBMs to be located no less than 1,300 kilometers from Moscow, and permitted continued research and development in the ABM field.*

Marshal Grechko appeared to voice their concern on the latter point when, speaking at the ratification of the ABM Treaty on September 29, 1972, he specifically noted that the treaty "imposes no limitation on the performance of research and experimental work aimed at resolving the problem of defending the country against nuclear missile attack."[100]

The rest of the military establishment is very likely to have been solidly in favor of the accords. They probably welcomed the ABM Treaty because it provided for precise parity in the authorized ABM deployments, thus severely circumscribing U.S. opportunities to defend its ICBMs with the technologically more advanced U.S. Safeguard ABM system, while at the same time avoiding a costly deployment of their own less capable Galosh system.

The promoters of strategic delivery systems, whether in the ministerial offices, the General Staff, or the interested services, had little to complain about regarding the terms of the five-year Interim Agreement. The force ratios agreed upon granted significant advantages to the Soviets vis-a-vis the United States in the numbers of both ICBMs (1,618 to 1,054) and SLBMs (62 subs and 950 missiles vs. 44 subs and 710 missiles).[101] While the Soviet ICBM authorization merely reflected the number of missiles deployed and new silos under construction identified by the United States at the time the agreement was signed,† the missile submarine/SLBM

*The 1,300 kilometer separation was the subject of intensive last-minute negotiation at the Moscow summit in May 1972 as the United States sought to ensure that any Soviet ABM-deployment-defending ICBMs would have to be emplaced east of the Ural Mountains. Newhouse, op. cit., pp. 233, 248.

†Since the Soviets steadfastly refused to provide any count of their ICBMs throughout the SALT discussions, these numbers were provided by the United States on the basis of its intelligence resources.

numbers represent a more intriguing case. The numbers, 62 and 950, had been put forward by the Soviets during the hectic negotiations over ballistic-missile submarines just prior to the Moscow summit.* Since these numbers were well beyond U.S. estimates of the submarines and missiles already deployed or under construction,† they are likely to represent the force level already programmed within the Soviet military-economic plans.

In addition to the favorable authorized force ratios vis-a-vis the United States, the military proponents of an expanded Soviet strategic offensive capability must have been pleased that the Interim Agreement failed to restrict their programs to develop and eventually deploy a large family of new ICBMs that were to prove to be MIRV-capable and decidedly more powerful than the preceding generation.‡ Their desire to preserve maximum development flexibility probably prompted the military to support the Soviet government's refusal to include a ban on mobile ICBMs in the Interim Agreement. (This refusal, incidentally, prompted the United States to register an official unilateral statement that the United States will consider any deployment of operational land-mobile ICBM launchers "inconsistent with the objectives of the Interim Agreement.")

Thus the Soviet military leadership as a whole is likely to have viewed the 1972 Moscow Agreements with considerable satisfaction. Direct evidence of this reaction is provided by a recent Soviet emigre, Dmitri Simes. He reports that in the fall of 1972 Gen. Nikolai Ogarkov, then first deputy chief of the General Staff, whose central role in the SALT process was noted earlier, spoke very favorably

---

*These numbers were first introduced by General Secretary Brezhnev in his presummit negotiations with Dr. Henry Kissinger in April 1972. Newhouse, op. cit., pp. 244, 253-55.

†The United States estimated that the Soviets had between 41 and 43 missile-launching submarines with 640 launch tubes deployed or under construction, while the Soviets claimed to have 48 boats and 768 launch tubes. The dispute was finally resolved by the establishment of the 740 "baseline number" which was included in the protocol to the interim agreement. Ibid., pp. 247, 253, 254.

‡By 1974, analysis of the new generation of ICBMs indicated that the payload carrying capacity of a full deployment of the new missiles would be on the order of 10-12 million pounds in comparison to aggregate throw-weight of 6-7 million pounds for the presently deployed systems. Secretary of Defense James R. Schlesinger, Annual Defense Department Report, FY-1975 (Washington, D.C.: Government Printing Office, 1974), p. 5.

about the SALT I agreements in a presentation to staff members of the Institute of World Economics and International Affairs in Moscow.[102]

Nevertheless, the military leaders were almost certainly concerned lest the spirit of detente prove so attractive to the political leaders that they might contemplate agreeing to much more restrictive terms during SALT II and reducing their commitment to a maximal national defense. This worry was evident in the cautionary note sounded by Army Gen. V. G. Kulikov, chief of the General Staff, in his August 23, 1972 speech before the Foreign Affairs Commissions of the Supreme Soviet during their deliberations on the SALT I accords. After priasing the agreements, Kulikov noted that the United States had been compelled to conclude them "primarily by the growth of Soviet military might" and reminded his audience, "We are fully aware that they do not mean a change in the nature of imperialism or denial of its aggressive essence."[103]

Military commentary relating to strategic arms limitation that has appeared since the commencement of SALT II in the fall of 1972 has generally continued to follow the pattern evident during SALT I. Military spokesmen have regularly criticized the B-1 and Trident programs as well as other new U.S. strategic initiatives.* They identify these programs as U.S. efforts to acquire SALT bargaining chips that are directly contrary to the spirit of the Moscow agreements and detente.[104] Perfunctory praise has appeared for the various Soviet-American agreements that have accompanied detente. Military authors have favorably cited, for example, the Agreement on the Prevention of Nuclear War signed at the Washington summit in June 1973, although they have hastened to add that its impact is limited because it fails to include all the nuclear powers and have reminded their readers that it should not be confused with the complete prohibition and liquidation of nuclear weapons.[105]

In addition to this reportage, during 1973-74 some military figures became involved in an interesting dialogue which appeared to reflect serious differences within the Soviet elite about issues

---

*Among the new U.S. initiatives singled out for criticism was the revived U.S. interest in developing a submarine-launched strategic cruise missile. Engineer Capt. 1st Rank V. Shiltov, "The Arms Race is Being Stepped Up--Cruise Missiles Again," Krasnaia Zvezda, March 22, 1974. U.S. development efforts for air, sea, and ground-launched cruise missiles became much more prominent items of Soviet concern and criticism in 1976-77 as the SALT II negotiations were deadlocked largely over differences on how to control this new generation of strategic weapons.

fundamental to Soviet arms policy and detente. This exchange was largely conducted by military philosophers affiliated with the Main Political Administration and men associated with the Institute for the Study of the United States. It appears to reflect basic differences over the utility of military force in the modern era and the probable consequences of nuclear war, and differing preferences regarding national resource allocation.

Maj. Gen. A. Milovidov, head of the Lenin Military-Political Academy, opened the recent dialogue in May 1973, when he attacked unnamed Soviet authors for committing errors in their analysis of "the essence and consequences of missile-nuclear war."[106] He criticized these writers for having "absolutized the quantitative analysis and arithmetical calculations of the destructive power of nuclear weapon" and chided them for not considering the role of qualitative factors in determining the likely victors in war.[107]

The targets of Milovidov's attack became more clear with the repetition of these charges in Fall 1973. This time Col. Ye. I. Rybkin, a major figure in the previous 1966-67 exchange on the proper Marxist-Leninist interpretation of the essence of nuclear war,[108] entered the recent fray with a direct attack on Aleksander Bovin, a prominent Izvestiia commentator who also serves on the editorial board of the journal SSha. After criticizing Bovin for failing to pay adequate attention to the Marxist-Leninist teachings on war and politics, Rybkin revealed the root of his concern about these matters when he stated: "The assertion that nuclear weapons have deprived war of this ability to be an extension of politics . . . can lead to a weakening of class and defensive vigilance and to a reduction in activity in the struggle for peace against the policy of war."[109]

Bovin's writings in the summer and fall of 1973 and the remarks of IUSAC Institute Director Georgy A. Arbatov in the same period provide evidence of the kinds of evaluations that were so discomfiting to the military establishment. In July, Bovin wrote an article in New Times that asserted that any attempt to resolve the clash between capitalism and socialism "in the cataclysm of a world thermonuclear war would be suicidal."[110] A week later, Arbatov, appearing on Hungarian television, similarly stated that a nuclear war between the United States and the USSR "would be suicidal for both."[111] Bovin must have further irritated his military critics in September when he called for furthering American detente and endorsed disarmament measures as a means "to decrease the burden of military expenditures and release assets which . . . can be utilized in the interests of working people (increasing well-being, health and education, environmental conservation and so forth)."[112] Arbatov raised a similar point when he criticized the United States government for allowing large military budgets to prevent the United States from dealing with "growing domestic problems" including "atmospheric pollution, growing urbanization, and others."[113] Even more explicitly Arbatov went on to note that in the modern era, "it has become clear . . . that the sphere of application of this tremendous military strength has started to diminish sharply."[114]

Further evidence of civilian concern about the likely outcome of a nuclear war was voiced in January 1974 by V. G. Dolgin, a deputy chief of an unidentified department of the Central Committee apparatus. Dolgin claimed that modern warfare would be a hopeless event because "one, several or many nuclear devices will wipe from the face of the earth, cities and even entire states, turn our planet into a chaos of chain reactions, global disasters and undermine the conditions of the existence of mankind."[115]

The officers from the Main Political Administration returned to the offensive in February 1974 when Rear Adm. V. Shelyag wrote an article in Krasnaia Zvezda ostensibly directed at erroneous views on nuclear war found within the West. His discussion, however, repeated the same points General Milovidov had directed against errant Soviet authors nine months earlier. Shelyag attacked "arguments about the death of civilization and about there being no victors in nuclear war" as the products of a "one-sided approach" and "over-simplified mathematical calculations."[116] He declared that these judgments were incorrect because they failed to note that the Soviet Union possesses "at least half the world's nuclear potential" and thus any war waged by the Soviet Union, even with modern weapons, would serve as a "means of defending civilization."[117]

A month later, Marshal Grechko lent his authority to the military side of the debate. Although he failed to mention nuclear weapons, the defense minister repeated the traditional military belief that Lenin's tenet on the essence of war as the continuation of politics by violent means continued to be valid. He also declared that "war and aggression will remain the inevitable accompaniment of capitalist society" and called for the continued strengthening of the defense might of the Soviet Union which he identified as the primary factor restraining the imperialists.[118]

The civilian opposition remained unconvinced. In a February 1974 article, Arbatov evaluated the relevance of the Clausewitz-Lenin dictum connecting war and politics as follows: "It can be said that with the emergence of nuclear missiles any correspondence between the political ends and the means was lost, since no policy can have the objective of destroying the enemy at the cost of complete self-annihilation."[119] Bovin responded as well in the pages of the April issue of Molodoi Kommunist. Once again he asserted that modern thermonuclear war would clearly be irrational because any recourse to it would inevitably trigger a retaliatory strike that would result in the aggressor's self-destruction.[120] Bovin also praised detente and called for efforts to reduce the stockpiles of missile-nuclear weapons which, he said, present a real danger of "destroying life on our planet."[121]

With these rebuttals, the latest debate on the essence and consequences of nuclear war halted, at least for the moment. At a minimum, these exchanges demonstrated the sensitivity of the professional military ideologists like Adm. Shelyag and Col. Rybkin about what they view to be serious mistakes in the handling of these somewhat esoteric issues for which they bear a special caretaker responsibility. More importantly, however, the points of view that were the objects of military criticism appear to combine a belief in the decreasing utility of military force in the nuclear era with an interest in diverting resources from defense spending into other investment areas. The Ministry of Defense is bound to feel threatened by such judgments, which, should they come to prevail within the Soviet political leadership, could easily have a detrimental impact upon their military programs. The very appearance of this dialogue may indicate that such differences have already surfaced near the top of the Soviet system, where they would be likely to shape Soviet SALT policy as well.[122]

Other military commentary more explicitly connected to SALT also appeared in 1974. As discussed earlier, Col. V. V. Larionov, recently returned to active duty from the staff of the USAC Institute, wrote articles in April and July that strongly praised the Moscow agreements and Moscow summit of 1974, and called for further steps in expanding the military detente between the superpowers. Later in the year, the commanders-in-chief of the Strategic Rocket Forces and PVO-S were called upon to refute charges being made in the United States that the Soviet Union was violating the terms of the SALT I accords. None of these discussions provided any insights into military preferences concerning the possible shape of a SALT II agreement limiting strategic offensive systems, a goal which was the subject of repeated high level U.S.-Soviet discussions throughout 1974.

During the spring of 1974, Secretary of State Henry Kissinger engaged in a series of intensive negotiations, first with Anatoly Dobrynin, the Soviet Ambassador in Washington, then directly with Brezhnev in Moscow, in pursuit of a SALT II agreement that might be ready for signature by the time of the upcoming summit in Moscow. Despite some initial optimism, it became clear by mid-spring that no major breakthrough had been achieved.* As a result the best that could be attained at the Nixon-Brezhnev summit was a series of peripheral arms control agreements--a draft treaty prohibiting underground nuclear tests above a threshold of 150 kilotons of explosive power,† a protocol to the ABM Treaty in which both sides agreed to limit themselves to a single deployment area of 100 launchers rather than two as originally agreed upon, an agreement to discuss ways to contain the dangers of environmental modification for military purposes, two protocols governing the dismantling and replacement of missiles,[123] and a mutual pledge to abandon attempts to work out a permanent comprehensive agreement on offensive arms in favor of an effort to conclude a ten-year treaty placing comprehensive limits on strategic delivery systems in 1975.‡

The role of the Ministry of Defense in the failure of the Soviets to agree to a permanent SALT II treaty during the first half of 1974

---

*The initial optimism was voiced by Secretary Kissinger when he spoke of the possibility of achieving a "conceptual breakthrough" before leaving to meet with Brezhnev in March 1974. His hopes had apparently been kindled by his "back channel" talks with Soviet Ambassador Dobrynin in Washington prior to the trip to Moscow. Unfortunately, the discussions with Brezhnev and company did not bear fruit as the Soviets proved unwilling to accept any of the U.S. proposals for a comprehensive SALT II agreement with MIRV subceilings. See Leslie H. Gelb, "Kissinger Said to Offer Halt on New Missile," New York Times, March 31, 1974; Joseph Kraft, "Letter From Moscow," The New Yorker, July 29, 1974, p. 70; Bernard Gwertzman, "Kissinger Fails to Sway Moscow on Nuclear Arms," New York Times, March 29, 1974.

†This treaty, known as the Threshold Test Ban (TTB), did not go into effect until March 31, 1976. "A-Tests Until Deadline," Washington Star-News, July 4, 1974.

‡These agreements came out of an intensive series of exchanges between the two sides in which it became clear that neither a permanent agreement nor a short-term extension of the interim agreement could be agreed upon due to basic differences about how to handle MIRV constraints. For accounts of these discussions see Murrey Marder, "A-Pact Product of Stalemate," Washington Post, July 5, 1974; Leslie Gelb, "Summit Talk Foundered Over MIRVs," New York Times, July 9, 1974; Hedrick Smith, "Moscow Sought Parity," New York Times, July 9, 1974.

has been the subject of considerable speculation. While still in Moscow, Secretary Kissinger appeared to lay the blame for the summit's failure in this crucial area squarely on the doorsteps of the military establishments of both sides. He conveyed this impression with his much-quoted statement that "both sides have to convince their military establishments of the benefits of restraint, and this is not a thought that comes naturally to military people on either side."[124]

Kissinger's admonition was probably prompted by his own experience in the U.S. policy arena and his recent contacts with Brezhnev and the other Soviet negotiators. It may also reflect statements by Brezhnev that the Soviet unwillingness to accept the U.S. proposals was largely due to the resistance of the Ministry of Defense. Even if Brezhnev said such a thing, it is still not clear that such an explanation would amount to anything more than an attempt to blame others for the Soviet leadership's own refusal to bargain seriously at a time when the U.S. position was seriously called into question by the Nixon administration's growing problems over the Watergate affair.

Whatever its role in their development, the Soviet military was probably quite satisfied with the agreements signed at the summer summit. Military advice was very likely to have been a major force behind the Soviet insistence that the threshold agreed upon in the partial test ban treaty be set at 150 kilotons rather than the more restrictive level proposed by the United States.* The leaders of PVO-S were probably disappointed with the protocol to the ABM Treaty, which appears certain to foreclose their opportunity to deploy an ABM complex in defense of ICBMs.† The remainder of the Soviet military probably welcomed this step since they are

---

*A high-level U.S. government official told the press that the United States initially proposed a 50-100 KT threshold while the Soviets sought a limit of "several hundred" kilotons. The negotiations led to the 150 KT threshold. Interview, Murrey Marder, Washington Post correspondent, Washington, D.C., March 10, 1975.

†Article II of the protocol permits the Soviet Union to dismantle its complex defending Moscow and construct a complex defending an ICBM site, if it provides notification to the Standing Consultative Commission between October 1977 and October 1978 or at five-year intervals from those dates. "Texts of Nuclear Accords and of Joint Statement," New York Times, July 4, 1974. The Soviets appear unlikely to exercise this option because of their commitment to defense of the national command authority against possible U.S. or other third country attack.

likely to hope that the resources saved by avoiding such a deployment will be made available for their own weapons programs.

Whatever the reasons for the modest accomplishments of midsummer, in November 1974 the Ford-Brezhnev summit at Valdivostok produced the long-sought-after SALT II breakthrough. At that meeting the two leaders reached agreement on the outline for a comprehensive treaty limiting strategic offensive arms which they agreed would be negotiated in detail during 1975. The Vladivostok accord focuses solely upon the intercontinental-range systems of both countries and proposes an overall ceiling of 2,400 delivery vehicles on each side. It also stipulates that no more than 1,320 of these vehicles will be permitted to carry MIRVs. The agreement grants each side the freedom to establish its own force mix of ICBMs, SLBMs, and bombers within these ceilings, with the additional proviso that the Soviets are prohibited from exceeding a force of 313 modern "large" (SS-9 and SS-18 class) ballistic missiles, the same number allowed by the interim agreement. Within these quanatitative restrictions, both sides are allowed unlimited opportunity to modernize their forces.[125]

The opinions within the Ministry of Defense concerning this accord are unknown. The Soviet military leaders, including the commanders responsible for the strategic delivery systems, are unlikely to have been displeased by the high ceilings agreed upon at Vladivostok, which were reportedly set, at Soviet insistence, beyond those sought by the United States.* They almost certainly welcomed the absence of constraints on qualitative modernization for the sake of their own extensive programs, although they would have liked to impose constraints on U.S. improvement programs. The military surely would have preferred, as well, to maintain the numerical superiorities in ICBMs and SLBMs granted to the Soviet Union in the 1972 Interim Agreement. Similarly, they would have liked to compel the United States either to include its forward-based aircraft within the total aggregate of strategic systems (thus securing for themselves an advantage in long-range "central" systems) or to withdraw these weapons beyond range of Soviet territory, thus gravely complicating U.S. relations with its allies and removing a possible threat to the Soviet Union.

---

*The United States reportedly sought an aggregate ceiling of 2,000 central system delivery vehicles and a subceiling of 1,000 MIRVed missiles when Secretary Kissinger visited Moscow in October 1974. Leslie H. Gelb, "How U.S. Made Ready for Talk at Vladivostok," New York Times, December 3, 1974.

Throughout 1975 and 1976 and on into 1977, however, Soviet-U.S. efforts to conclude a SALT II agreement on the basis of Vladivostok proved unsuccessful. Despite the efforts of both sides at the continuing negotiations in Geneva and periodic high-level exchanges, superpower differences over how to handle the Soviet Backfire bomber and the new generation of highly accurate strategic cruise missiles being developed, at least initially largely by the United States, remained unresolved.

The spring of 1977 brought a new flurry of activity as the incoming Carter administration put forth both a dramatically new approach to SALT II in the form of a "comprehensive proposal" that included significant cuts in the ceilings agreed at Vladivostok and added new qualitative restraints for ICBMS,* and a much more modest "deferral proposal" calling for agreement incorporating the Vladivostok ceilings and postponing any treatment of either Backfire or strategic cruise missiles until a subsequent SALT III negotiation. Both proposals were repeatedly and adamantly rejected by the Soviets due to the "one-sided advantage" they allegedly provided to the United States. Nevertheless, at the time of this writing, May 1977, signs remained that some form of agreement which remained fairly close to the numerical limits agreed upon at Vladivostok and provided "satisfactory" coverage of cruise missiles and Backfire might be reached within 1977 as a follow-on to the Interim Agreement, which expires in October 1977.

Thus in spring 1977 the Soviet military, despite its traditional misgivings about arms control, is likely to view the extended SALT negotiations as a generally successful venture. The leaders of the Ministry of Defense probably appreciate the fact that the talks have registered sufficient progress to support the peace program that Brezhnev seems to value so highly, and yet the arms accords they have yielded appear to legitimize the strategic arms competition without interfering significantly with the vast majority of their own

---

*The comprehensive proposal included an aggregate ceiling for strategic delivery vehicles of 1,800-2,000 (vice 2,400 at Vladivostok), a MIRV subceiling of 1,000-1,100 (vice 1,320), and a "heavy" ICBM subceiling of 150 (vice 313). It also proposed a limit of 550 MIRVed ICBMs on both sides and bans on the development of any new generation ICBMs and the deployment of mobile ICBMs. Strategic cruise missiles with ranges greater than 2,500 km were to be prohibited and Backfire was to be constrained not within the overall aggregate but via some unspecified limits in its deployment. Speech of Defense Secretary Harold S. Brown at the University of Rochester, Rochester, N.Y., April 14, 1977.

highly valued weapons programs. Moreover, the combination of the technical nature of the talks and their importance to the military have resulted in strong direct representation of the interests of the Ministry of Defense throughout their duration. If there has been any Politburo sentiment for imposing limits on Soviet strategic arms programs via SALT (and no evidence of such an inclination has come to light), the military appears to have most certainly prevailed against it.

In addition, some Soviet military figures have almost certainly concluded that the infusion of Western capital and technology that will accompany continuing East-West trade in a period of detente could importantly assist the Soviet economy and thus lessen any internal pressures to reduce investment in defense. Nevertheless, any measures that contribute to the relaxation of East-West tensions are bound to be viewed with considerable anxiety by the military leadership. Consequently, the Soviet high command regularly calls for increased vigilance and continued efforts to strengthen Soviet military capability in the hope that they can contain the internal effects of detente and maintain their premier position as the major institutional benefactor of the current set of priorities prevailing within the Soviet system.

NOTES

1. Cf. Gallagher, op. cit., pp. 14-20; Victor Zorza, "The Marshals Get the Message," Manchester Guardian Weekly, November 7, 1970, p. 13; and Lawrence T. Caldwell, Soviet Attitudes to SALT, Adelphi Papers no. 76 (London: Institute for International Studies, 1971). Many of the articles noted by these authors are discussed within the body of this chapter.

2. Marshall D. Shulman, "SALT and the Soviet Union," in SALT, the Moscow Agreements and Beyond, ed. Mason Willrich and John B. Rhinelander (New York: Free Press, 1974), p. 112.

3. Interviews with Raymond L. Garthoff, Department of State, Washington, D.C., September 16, 1969; Severyn Bialer, Columbia University, New York City, April 13, 1970; and Professor Marshall D. Shulman, Columbia University, New York City, October 15, 1973.

4. J. Rotblat, Pugwash--The First Ten Years (London: Heinemann, 1967), pp. 219-20.

5. For bibliographies on Soviet arms control publications see Dallin et al., pp. 185-95, and J. Tim Fennell, "Soviet Views of the Arms Race," unpublished manuscript, October 1973, pp. 22-61.

6. For example, V. Ya. Aboltin et al., Sovremennyye problemy razoruzheniia [Contemporary problems of disarmament] (Moscow: Mysl', 1970); I. S. Glagolev, ed., SSSR, SShA i razoruzhenie [USSR, USA and disarmament] (Moscow: Nauka, 1967); and V. A. Zorin, ed., Bor'ba Sovetskogo Soiuza za razoruzhenie, 1946-1960 gody [The struggle of the Soviet Union for disarmament, 1946-1960] (Moscow: Institute of International Relations, 1961).

7. Thomas B. Larson, Disarmament and Soviet Policy: 1964-1968 (Englewood Cliffs, N.J.: Prentice-Hall, 1969), p. 38; Shulman, op. cit., p. 111.

8. Fischer, op. cit., p. 151.

9. Their commentaries with regard to SALT matters, for example, include M. A. Mil'shtein and L. S. Semieko, "Strategic Arms Limitation Problems and Prospects" SShA: Ekonomika Politika, Ideologiia [USA: economics, politics and ideology] (hereafter cited as SShA) no. 12 (December 1973); 3-12, and G. A. Trofimenko, "Problems of Peace and Security in Soviet-American Relations," SShA no. 9 (September 1974): 7-18.

10. Personal interviews with Yuri A. Shvedkov, the Institute for the Study of the United States and Canada, Princeton, New Jersey, January 14, 1970, and Dr. Alexander Kaliadin, the Institute of World Economics and International Relations, Princeton, New Jersey, February 9, 1970. Shvedkov also noted that foreign affairs analysts often shift between assignments with the academic institutes and posts in the Ministry of Foreign Affairs.

11. Pravda, June 6, 1972. For a public rendition of his views on MBFR, see O. N. Khlestov, "The Negotiations in Vienna: Tasks and Prospects," Mirovaia Ekonomika i Mezhdunarodnye Otnosheniia [World economics and international relations] no. 6 (June 1974): 42-51.

12. Edward L. Crowley, Andrew I. Lebed, Heinrich Schulz, eds., Prominent Personalities in the USSR (Metuchen, N.J.: Scarecrow Press, 1968), p. 524.

13. Shulman, op. cit., p. 111; Dallin et al., op. cit., p. 61; Matthew P. Gallagher and Karl Spielmann, Jr., The Politics of Power: Soviet Decisionmaking for Defense (Washington, D.C.: Institute of Defense Analysis, October 1971), n. 17, p. 113. The current head of this section cannot be positively identified, although it is likely to be O. A. Grinevskiy, a deputy head of the International Organizations Department and a full delegate to the SALT negotiations with long experience in the disarmament field.

14. New York Times, November 21, 1969, 5:1; Directory of Soviet Officials, vol. 1, National Organizations (Washington, D.C.: Government Printing Office, 1973), p. 110.

15. "List of the Delegation for MFR Negotiations, the Union of Soviet Socialist Republics" (Vienna: USSR, October 29, 1973); Directory of Soviet Officials, vol. 1, p. 111.

16. Shulman, op. cit., p. 111.

17. Interviews with Raymond L. Garthoff, Department of State, Washington, D.C., September 16, 1969; and Larry Weiler, Arms Control and Disarmament Agency, Washington, D.C., February 16, 1973.

18. "List of Delegates for MFR Negotiations, the Union of Soviet Socialist Republics," October 29, 1973.

19. "Conference of Experts for the Study of Possible Measures which might be Helpful in Preventing Surprise Attack and for the Preparation of a Report Therein to Governments," verbatim record of meetings, Geneva, December 1958, p. 3.

20. This speculation is made by a leading student of Soviet military affairs and the executive officer of the American negotiating team at SALT I, Raymond L. Garthoff, in "SALT and the Soviet Military," Problems of Communism 24, no. 1 (January-February 1975): 28.

21. Ibid.; Newhouse, op. cit., pp. 53, 212.

22. Shulman, op. cit., p. 113; Newhouse, op. cit., pp. 251-52; Garthoff, "SALT and the Soviet Military," p. 29.

23. Newhouse, op. cit., p. 192.

24. For speculation on the existence of a Soviet SALT task force, see Gallagher and Spielman, op. cit., pp. 35-36. See also Vladimir Petrov, "Formation of Soviet Foreign Policy," Orbis 18, no. 3 (Fall 1973): 826 for a discussion of the role of "ad hoc committees" in policy formulation.

25. Garthoff, "SALT and the Soviet Military," p. 29.

26. Larson, op. cit., n. 53, p. 37; Petrov, op. cit., p. 826.

27. N. A. Talenskiy, "Anti-Missile Systems and Disarmament," International Affairs (Moscow) no. 10 (October 1964): 15-19.

28. A. A. Gryzlov, "The Freezing of Defensive Anti-Missile Systems," Paper presented to the Seventeenth Pugwash Conference Science and World Affairs, Ronneby, Sweden, September 3-8, 1967, p. 10.

29. Ibid., pp. 4, 10.

30. For example, "The Transformation of the 'Strategic Sufficiency' Concept," SShA no. 11 (November 1971): 27-36; "A Game on Beaten Trump Cards--On the Principle of Equal Security and Relapses into the 'Policy of Strength' in Washington," Novoye Vremya [New times] no. 37 (September 8, 1972): 23-27; "Quantitative and Qualitative Aspects of the Arms Race," paper delivered to the Twentieth Pugwash Conference on Science and World Affairs, September 9-15, 1970, pp. 1-8.

31. Interview with Shulman, October 15, 1973. This report appears increasingly plausible with Larionov's absence from the pages of SShA since that time and his identification as "Colonel" V. Larionov in an article published in Pravda on April 7, 1974, and in Krasnaia Zvezda on July 18, 1974. His rank had been omitted from articles written while he was working with the USA Institute. A Krasnaia Zvezda article in November 1976 on a military history conference brought the news that Larionov had been promoted to the rank of major general.

32. Col. V. Larionov, "Arms Limitation and Its Enemies," Pravda, April 7, 1974.

33. Col. V. Larionov, "The Relaxation of Tension and the Principle of Equal Security," Krasnaia Zvezda, July 18, 1974.

34. These include Robert Conquest, Russia After Khrushchev (New York: Praeger, 1965), p. 186; Victor Zorza, "Military Critics of Khrushchev," Manchester Guardian, October 4, 1963; and Gallagher's chapter in Kolkowicz, op. cit., p. 14.

35. Gallagher, op. cit., p. 14.

36. Sidney I. Ploss, "A New Phase of Soviet Policy Debates," Occasional Papers on Soviet Politics, Center of International Studies, Princeton University, October 16, 1963, pp. 14-17.

37. V. Vershinin, "The General Line of Soviet Foreign Policy," Kommunist Vooruzhennykh Sil (hereafter cited as KVS) no. 18 (September 1963): 13.

38. Lt. Col. E. Fedulaev, "The Race of Rocket-Nuclear Arms in the Countries of NATO--A Threat to Peace," KVS no. 17 (September 1963): 81.

39. Col. P. Trifonenkov, "The Most Vital Problem of Modernity and the Adventurism of the Chinese Dogmatists," KVS no. 21 (November 1963): 26.

40. Abram Chayes, "An Inquiry into the Workings of Arms Control Agreements," Harvard Law Review 85, no. 5 (March 1972): 951.

41. Krasnaia Zvezda, May 28, 1972.

42. G. I. Sviatov, "Strategic Arms Limitation: The Principle of Equal Security," Krasnaia Zvezda, July 28, 1972.

43. For example, Col. I. Sidel'nikov, "Peaceful Coexistence and the People's Security," Krasnaia Zvezda, August 14, 1973, and Maj. Ye. Sulimov, "The Scientific Nature of the CPSU's Foreign Policy," Krasnaia Zvezda, December 20, 1973.

44. Col. Ye. I. Rybkin, "Criticism of Bourgeois Concepts of War and Peace," KVS no. 18 (Semptember 1968): 90. The book being reviewed was Problems of War and Peace: Criticism of Modern Bourgeois Socio-Philosophical Concepts (Moscow: Mysl', 1967).

45. Ibid.

46. A. S. Milovidov and V. G. Kozlov, eds., Filosofskoye naslediye V. I. Lenina i problemy sovremennoy voyny [The philosophical heritage of V. I. Lenin and problems of modern war] (Moscow: Voenizdat, 1972), p. 147.

47. Marshal Grechko's election speech as a candidate for the Supreme Soviet, Krasnaia Zvezda, June 5, 1974.

48. Buckley made his accusations in a speech to the Overseas Press Club in New York City on October 31, 1974. For a discussion of them see John W. Finney, "Questions Arise on Soviet Arms," New York Times, November 6, 1974.

49. Interview with Army Gen. V. F. Tolubko, "Masters of Rockets," Nedelya no. 46 (November 11-17, 1974): 4. Buckley's charges were also disputed by U.S. Defense Department spokesman William Beecher, Michael Getler, "Soviet Missile Silos Discounted," Washington Post, November 1, 1974.

50. Interview with Marshal P. F. Batitskiy, "A Clear Sky Over the Motherland," Nedelya no. 51 (December 19-25, 1974): 4.

51. Adm. S. G. Gorshkov, "Navies in War and Peace," Morskoi Sbornik no. 5 (May 1972): 24 and no. 8 (August 1972): 14.

52. Gorshkov, Morskoi Sbornik no. 8 (August 1972): 14.

53. Robert W. Herrick, "Soviet Commander-in-Chief Advocates Construction of a Much Larger Navy," Center for Naval Analysis, working paper, Arlington, Virginia, May 9, 1973, pp. 28-29.

54. Interview with Admiral of the Fleet of the Soviet Union S. G. Gorshkov, "The Maritime Might of the Land of the Soviets," Pravda, July 28, 1974.

55. L. I. Brezhnev, Speech to the Polish Sejm, Pravda, July 22, 1974. Brezhnev first proposed the establishment of a nuclear-free zone in the Mediterranean on June 12, 1971.

56. Marshal N. I. Krylov, "Instructive Lessons of History," Sovetskaia Rossiia, August 30, 1969.

57. Maj. Gen. (ret.) A. Lagovskiy, "The Economy and the Military Might of the State," Krasnaia Zvezda, September 25, 1969. For a discussion of this article, see Chapter 3 under "Resource Acquisition: Weapon Superiority." The Lagovskiy piece has been frequently cited by U.S. analysts as evidence of Soviet military opposition to SALT.

58. Some of the writers who have cited these viewpoints to identify negative attitudes toward disarmament within the Soviet military include Caldwell, Soviet Attitudes to SALT, pp. 9-17; Zorza, "The Marshals Get the Message," p. 13; "Moscow's Rampant Hawks," Christian Science Monitor, September 15, 1972; and Franklyn Griffiths, "Inner Tensions in the Soviet Approach to 'Disarmament,'" International Journal 22, no. 4 (Autumn 1967): 606, 615.

59. The Military Balance: 1969-1970 (London: Institute of Strategic Studies, September 1969), pp. 1, 2, 5, 6, 9.

60. For discussions of U.S. qualitative advantages in strategic weaponry, see "Congressional Briefing by Henry Kissinger, June 15, 1972," in Strategic Arms Limitation Agreements, Hearings before the Committee on Foreign Relations, United States Senate, 92d Congress, 2d Session (Washington, D.C.: U.S. Government Printing Office, 1972), pp. 400-01; the annual reviews of Soviet and American strategic capabilities in The Military Balance (London: Institute of Strategic Studies, 1969 through 1974); Newhouse, op. cit., pp. 21-25; Edgar Ulsamer, "Soviet Objective: Technological Supremacy," Air Force Magazine (June 1974): 23.

61. John Erickson, "Soviet Military Power," Strategic Review 1, no. 1 (Spring 1973): 46. Since 1970 most references have listed 64 launchers in the Galosh system around Moscow. Cf. The Military Balance: 1970-1971 through 1974-1975.

62. Interviews with Col. Charles G. FitzGerald, U.S. Army, adviser on the U.S. SALT delegation, Washington, D.C., April 8, 1970; Raymond L. Garthoff, executive officer of the U.S. SALT I delegation, February 16, 1973; and Lt. Gen. Edward L. Rowny, U.S. Army, Joint Chiefs of Staff (JCS), representative to the SALT negotiations, Geneva, Switzerland, September 28, 1976.

63. Newhouse, op. cit., p. 53.

64. Garthoff, the original manuscript of his article "SALT and the Soviet Military," pp. 15, 16. This observation and the detailed listing of Soviet military delegates at SALT I cited below were deleted from the Problems of Communism article.

65. Ibid., p. 17; Malcolm Mackintosh, "The Soviet Military: Influence on Foreign Policy," Problems of Communism 12, no. 5 (September-October 1973), p. 10.

66. Garthoff, "SALT and the Soviet Military," p. 28; Newhouse, op. cit., p. 53.

67. FitzGerald interview; Garthoff, "SALT and the Soviet Military" (original manuscript), pp. 19-20.

68. Ibid., p. 20.

69. Ibid., p. 40.

70. Michael Getler, "Soviets Reported Stepping Up Flight Testing of New Missile," Washington Post, July 27, 1974.

71. Newhouse, op. cit., pp. 213, 228.

72. Ibid.; interview with Garthoff, February 16, 1973.

73. Interview with Tad Szulc, independent news reporter, U.S. Air Force Academy, April 8, 1971. Szulc obtained his information in interviews with members of the American delegations.

74. Newhouse, op. cit., p. 238. Semenov is also reported to have been confused about comparative sizes of the Soviet large SS-9

ICBM and the much smaller U.S. Minuteman until corrected by Col. Gen. Ogarkov. Newhouse, op. cit., p. 56.

75. Jack Anderson, "Soviets Seem Eager for Arms Pact," Washington Post, December 27, 1971.

76. Newhouse, op. cit., p. 56.

77. Garthoff, "The Soviet Military and SALT" (original manuscript), p. 16.

78. Ibid.

79. Ibid., p. 8.

80. A superb description of these contacts and the bureaucratic maneuvering on the American side that accompanied them is found in Newhouse, op. cit., pp. 83-132.

81. Marshal Krylov also resurrected the traditional Soviet military claim that victory could be attained by the socialist camp in a nuclear war. This contention was to become the subject of an extended military-civilian debate in 1973-74. Marshal N. I. Krylov, "Instructive Lessons of History," Sovetskaia Rossiia, August 30, 1969.

82. See Chapter 3 under "Resource Acquisition: Weaponry Superiority" for a discussion of the Lagovskiy article, "The Economy and the Military Might of the State," Krasnaia Zvezda, September 25, 1969.

83. Krasnaia Zvezda's selective reporting occurred in its coverage of Foreign Minister Gromyko's speech before the United Nations on October 3, 1968, and its report of the Foreign Ministry's statement urging prompt arms negotiations on the eve of President Nixon's inauguration. Roman Kolkowicz et al., The Soviet Union and Arms Control: A Superpower Dilemma (Baltimore: Johns Hopkins Press, 1970), p. 15, n. 15.

84. Col. A. Leont'yev and V. Berezin, "Once Again the Racket About Safeguard," Krasnaia Zvezda, January 9, 1970; V. Berezin, "Spokes in the Wheel," Krasnaia Zvezda, March 14, 1970; A. Leont'yev, "How Much is Baldwin Worth?" Krasnaia Zvezda, March 19, 1970; Col. A. Leont'yev, "Who Needs Safeguard?" Krasnaia Zvezda, August 15, 1970.

85. V. Berezin, "Arms Escalation," Krasnaia Zvezda, November 18, 1970.

86. Newhouse, op. cit., pp. 174-75.

87. Ibid., p. 194.

88. Ibid.; Leslie Gelb, "Summit Talk Foundered Over MIRVs," New York Times, July 9, 1974.

89. Michael Getler and Murrey Marder, "MIRV Limits High," Washington Post, November 26, 1974. The elements of the Vladivostok Accord are discussed later in this chapter.

90. "Press Conference of Foreign Minister A. A. Gromyko," Pravda, April 1, 1977.

91. Col. V. Aleksandrov, "Assault Aviation of the USA: For Conducting an Aggressive Policy," Krasnaia Zvezda, May 13, 1970.

92. The series included three articles: Col. V. Kharich, "The Strategic Arms Race: Aloof From a Realistic Approach," Krasnaia Zvezda, July 13, 1971; Col. V. Kharich and Engineer-Capt. Second Rank G. Koloskov, "Gambling on Nuclear Might," Krasnaia Zvezda, July 16, 1971; Engineer-Col. N. Yeziazarov, "The Pentagon's 'Deterrent Arsenal,'" Krasnaia Zvezda, August 4, 1971.

93. Kharich and Koloskov, Krasnaia Zvezda, July 16, 1971. The first such public linkage had appeared some five months earlier in a detailed presentation of the Soviet case in V. Shestov, "What is Hidden Behind the Propaganda Screen?" Pravda, February 3, 1971.

94. Ibid.

95. Cf. V. Berezin, "The Pentagon's Blackmail," Krasnaia Zvezda, January 21, 1972. One article presented a detailed and accurate account of the MIRV capabilities of the Minuteman-III, Engineer-Maj. L. Petrov, "The 'Strategic Bus' . . . or the Pentagon's Nuclear Missile Arithmetic," Krasnaia Zvezda, March 15, 1972.

96. See p. 232 above.

97. Col. V. Khalipov, "Peaceful Coexistence and the Defense of Socialism," Krasnaia Zvezda, July 21, 1972.

98. Georgy I. Sviatov, "Strategic Arms Limitation: The Principle of Equal Security," Krasnaia Zvezda, July 28, 1972.

99. Ibid.

100. Pravda, September 30, 1972.

101. These maximum ICBM and SLBM ceilings could not be reached simultaneously because each country would be required to retire a designated number of pre-1964 ICBMs (listed in this section) if it should decide to expand to the highest authorized SSBN/SLBM level.

102. Interview, Dmitri Simes, former staff member of the Institute of World Economics and International Relations (IMEMO) in Moscow, Washington, D.C., March 25, 1975.

103. Pravda, August 23, 1972.

104. Cf. V. Berezin, "Pentagon Demands Increases," Krasnaia Zvezda, February 3, 1973; G. Sviatov, "Counting on the 'Trident of Neptune,'" Krasnaia Zvezda, March 23, 1973; Col. A. Markov and V. Berezin, "The Pentagon's Immoderate Appetite," Krasnaia Zvezda, February 10, 1974.

105. Marshal A. A. Grechko, Vooruzhennye sily sovetskogo gosudarstva [The armed forces of the Soviet state] (Moscow:

Voenizdat, 1974), p. 322; Col. I. Sidelnikov, "Peaceful Coexistence and the People's Security," Krasnaia Zvezda, August 14, 1973.

106. Maj. Gen. A. Milovidov, "A Philosophical Analysis of Military Thought," Krasnaia Zvezda, May 17, 1973.

107. Ibid.

108. See Chapter 3 under "War in the Modern Era" for a discussion of that 1966-67 exchange.

109. Col. Ye. Rybkin, "The Leninist Conception of War and the Contemporary Period," Kommunist Vooruzhennykh Sil no. 20 (October 1973): 28.

110. Aleksander Bovin, "Internationalism and Coexistence," New Times no. 30 (July 1973): 19.

111. Interview with Georgy Arbatov, Director of the USAC Institute, Budapest Domestic Television Service, August 5, 1973.

112. Aleksander Bovin, "Peace and Social Progress," Izvestiia, September 11, 1974.

113. G. A. Arbatov, "U.S. Foreign Policy and the Scientific and Technical Revolution," SShA no. 10 (October 1973): 16.

114. Ibid.

115. V. G. Dolgin, "Peaceful Coexistence and the Factors Contributing to its Intensification and Development," Voprosy Filosofii [Problems of philosophy] no. 1 (January 1974): 64.

116. Rear Adm. V. Shelyag, "Two World Outlooks--Two Views of War," Krasnaia Zvezda, February 7, 1974.

117. Ibid.

118. Marshal A. A. Grechko, "V. I. Lenin and the Soviet State's Armed Forces," Kommunist no. 3 (March 1974): 15.

119. Georgy Arbatov, "The Impasses of the Policy of Force," Problemy Mira i Sotsializma [Problems of peace and socialism] no. 2 (February 1974): 42.

120. Aleksander Bovin, "Socialist and Class Policy," Molodoi Kommunist [Young communist] no. 4 (April 1974): 24.

121. Ibid.

122. This is the interpretation of Victor Zorza, "Kremlin Policy Struggle," Washington Post, February 26, 1974.

123. John Herbers, "Nixon, Brezhnev Delay Key Curbs on Arms Till '85," New York Times, July 4, 1974.

124. Dr. Kissinger's July 3, 1974 Press Conference in Moscow, State Department Bulletin, July 29, 1974, p. 210.

125. Bernard Gwertzman, "Ford Says Accord Gives a Basis for Cut in Arms," New York Times, December 3, 1974. There has been a report from an unidentified Washington source that the Soviets have already embarked on the development of some 10 to 12 new strategic missiles or missile modifications beyond the SS-X-16 through SS-19 family of ICBMs. John W. Finney, "Pentagon Aides Say Soviet Is Developing New Missiles for Use in the 1980's," New York Times, July 26, 1974.

CHAPTER

7

CONCLUSION

The issues examined in the course of this study have provided ample evidence that the Soviet military establishment is an active institutional participant in the politics of the Soviet Union. With the assistance of the bureaucratic politics framework, we have identified a series of basic viewpoints and policy preferences that are regularly expressed by members of the Ministry of Defense and appear to be actively promoted and defended by its leadership and major spokesmen. We have also seen that the efforts of the military to advance their parochial interests are enhanced by the virtual monopolies of defense policy information and expertise they enjoy and the policy-making arrangements that permit them to play leading roles in the formation and implementation of Soviet military policy.

As discussed in Chapters 2, 4, and 6, the leading Soviet military commanders and the ideological specialists of the Main Political Administration have regularly articulated a composite military viewpoint that contains distinctive commentary about the dangerous international environment confronting the Soviet Union due to the continuing strength of the "unrealistic," "aggressive" forces in the West that are described as fundamentally hostile to the socialist camp. In the context of this perceived environment, the military spokesmen have repeatedly stated a series of policy preferences whose centerpiece is the assertion that the Soviet Union must continually strengthen its defensive might by maintaining the high priority traditionally assigned to investment in the heavy industrial sector of their economy, which includes the network of defense-production ministries. These same spokesmen have frequently called for vigorous Soviet efforts to attain military-technological superiority over their Western adversaries and often argued that the Ministry of Defense should be allowed to play a leading role in decisions concerning all military matters.

Although the basic weltanshauung that includes the viewpoints reviewed above appears to be shared by most military men whose opinions are reported in the public media, there is also evidence of substantial differences of opinion among members of the Ministry of Defense. In Chapters 4 and 5 we reviewed several instances of publicly aired disagreements among military officers regarding such matters as the proper content of Soviet military doctrine and the proper evaluation of the effectiveness and advantages of specific weapons systems. These disagreements have consistently fallen along service lines.

There are almost certainly a host of other differences of viewpoint and preference among Soviet military personnel concerning defense-related matters and a variety of broader domestic and foreign policy questions as well. The vast majority of these opinion cleavages, which are very likely to reflect differences in age, nationality, education, or job experience, cannot be identified by examining the vast body of openly published Soviet military literature. Opinion groupings of this kind could be located and analyzed only with the benefit of survey research materials based on questionnaires or interviews and this kind of data, unfortunately, is not available. Nevertheless, it is essential to remember that the available evidence clearly supports the conclusion that there have been and almost certainly continue to be important policy differences among groups and individuals in the Ministry of Defense within the context of the broadly shared military ideology discussed in Chapter 3.

The leaders of the Soviet military establishment do not appear to keep their beliefs and preferences to themselves. Their assertive public declarations and the available memoirs of Soviet political and military figures suggest that the leaders of the Ministry of Defense have often sought to have their points of view accepted and acted upon by the political leadership. Military spokesmen have also shown themselves willing openly to attack Soviet writers like Talenskiy and Bovin outside the military establishment who have voiced opinions on the catastrophic nature of nuclear weapons and the impossibility of attaining victory in a modern world war. These attacks were probably motivated by concern within the military that these views clearly threaten the budgetary fortunes of the Ministry of Defense and might serve to undermine the morale and motivation of Soviet servicemen as well. There is also ample evidence that the senior military commanders and their partners in the defense production field have utilized their direct access to the political leadership both to press their requests for the development and series production of new weapons and to resist vigorously any attempts to cut back on the Soviet defense effort.

The ability of the Soviet military to advance its parochial interests is aided importantly by the institutional arrangements that exist within the Soviet Union for the development and implementation of military policy matters. The Ministry of Defense appears to enjoy considerable autonomy and unrivaled expertise in these questions. The Defense Ministry is greatly assisted by the fact that, unlike most Soviet governmental ministries, it does not have to contend with a specialized department within the powerful central apparatus of the Party, which actively monitors the vast majority of its day-to-day activities. Although three of the departments of the Central Committee--Administrative Organs, Defense Industries, and the Main Political Administration--deal with military matters, none of these appears to play a significant role in such key areas as the drafting of the defense budgetary plans, the development of operational military plans and doctrine, or the myriad of activities connected with the routine administration, training, and exercise of the Soviet armed forces.

The Soviet military is not without its monitoring agencies. The osobists of the Counterintelligence Directorate of the KGB who are found throughout the armed forces are constantly on guard against illegal or subversive, "anti-Soviet" activity by military personnel. Similarly, the deputy commanders for political affairs, the _zampolits_, who are affiliated with the Main Political Administration, direct the massive political training efforts and supervise the various Party organizations in all of the major combat units and staffs throughout the military establishment. As outlined in Chapters 1 and 2, over the years the political officers have apparently come to view themselves as military professionals and thus they seem to identify with their fellow officers of the Ministry of Defense rather than with the men of the Central Committee apparatus of which the Main Political Administration is nominally a part. In any case, the activities of these two "external" organs are unlikely to represent significant impediments to the military in the fulfillment of its many defense policy responsibilities or in its efforts to promote parochial military preferences within Party and governmental councils.

By their very nature, the central issues of Soviet defense policy--How much should be spent for defense? What weapons systems should be developed and procured and in what quantities? Which services should be assigned which roles and missions? What force balances should be sought and what limitations should be accepted within the MBFR and SALT negotiations? What are the appropriate strategies for deterrence and possible war-waging in the theaters of military operations facing NATO and China?--are complex and inherently indeterminate in that no policy solution is demonstrably more correct than others. Consequently, disagreements among the leading figures within the military and political leaderships regarding these issues are almost certain to arise. In an era of collective leadership, these differences, whether aired publicly or debated behind the walls of the Kremlin, are likely to be viewed as both natural and fully legitimate. The Soviet military leadership, assisted by its near-monopoly of relevant information and expertise and assured of the opportunity to participate in the highest level deliberations on these questions, would appear to be in an excellent position to strongly influence the course of Soviet defense policy.

I believe that this study demonstrates both the utility and shortcomings involved in the application of the bureaucratic politics approach to the study of Soviet affairs. The institutional perspective has proved useful in calling our attention to the organizational structures and internal processes that appear to shape the contours of Soviet defense policy. Careful examination of these considerations substantially enriches our understanding of the dynamics underlying such ongoing enterprises as the development of Soviet military strategy and the continuous modernization of their force posture. It permits us to develop process-oriented explanations or predictions concerning either past or projected policy outcomes.

On the limitations side, it is readily apparent that in almost all cases, informed speculations about the domestic political interplay associated with these issues are the best we can manage. The student of Soviet politics lacks the abundance of routine reportage, investigative analysis, and opportunity to conduct personal interviews that are so frequently available in the study of Western policy making. Denied such information, the Sovietologist must settle for analysis that points out the visible signs of political conflict in Moscow, suggests the identity of various individuals and institutions involved, and hypothesizes about the likely shape of their political maneuvering. He is seldom able to provide a firmly grounded description of the tactics employed by the contending parties as they seek to promote their particular interests. Thus we are unable to amass a series of cumulative studies that reveal the patterns of interpersonal access, the lines of argument employed, or the kinds of bargains struck during the day-to-day political interchanges within the government and Party bureaucracies or in the deliberations of the Soviet leadership.

Nevertheless, these data deficiencies notwithstanding, the development of explanations about Soviet policies and actions which seek to take into account the combined influences of institutional concerns and standardized routines in the interaction of interest groups and key individuals on the Soviet scene appears worthwhile. Such considerations have most certainly played substantial roles in the political life of the Soviet Union in the past and are almost certain to continue to do so today and in the future.

APPENDIX A

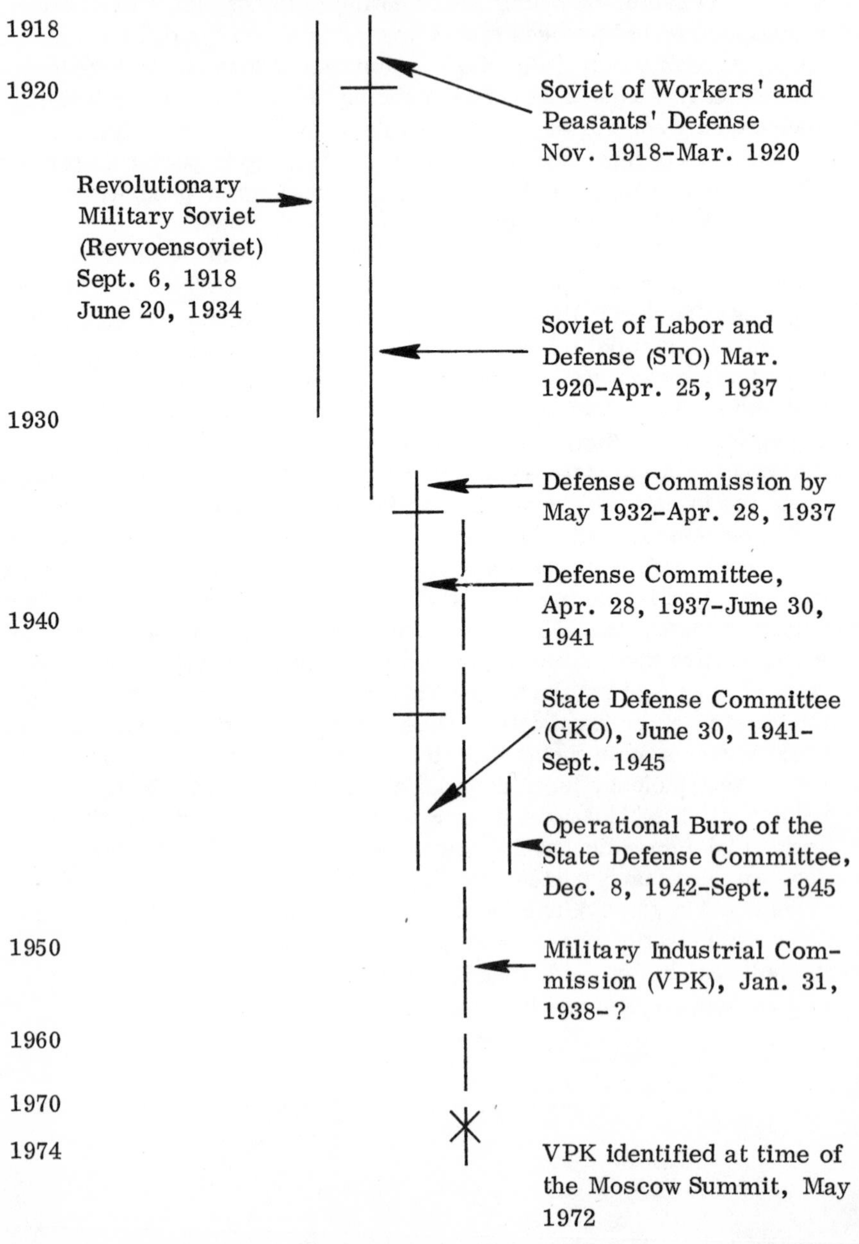
HIGH-LEVEL SOVIET INSTITUTIONS FOR THE SUPERVISION OF DEFENSE PRODUCTION
1918
1920
1930
1940
1950
1960
1970
1974
Soviet of Workers' and Peasants' Defense Nov. 1918-Mar. 1920
Revolutionary Military Soviet (Revvoensoviet) Sept. 6, 1918 June 20, 1934
Soviet of Labor and Defense (STO) Mar. 1920-Apr. 25, 1937
Defense Commission by May 1932-Apr. 28, 1937
Defense Committee, Apr. 28, 1937-June 30, 1941
State Defense Committee (GKO), June 30, 1941-Sept. 1945
Operational Buro of the State Defense Committee, Dec. 8, 1942-Sept. 1945
Military Industrial Commission (VPK), Jan. 31, 1938-?
VPK identified at time of the Moscow Summit, May 1972

Sources: M. V. Zakharov et al., eds., 50 let vooruzhennykh sil SSSR [50 years of the armed forces of the USSR] (Moscow: Voenizdat, 1968).

K. U. Cherenko and N. I. Savinkin, KPSS o vooruzhennykh silakk Sovetskozo Soyuza [The CPSU on the armed forces of the Soviet Union] (Moscow: Voenizdat, 1969).

N. Chervyakov, "Coordination and Control," Red Star, February 10, 1974.

John Newhouse, Cold Dawn: The Story of SALT (New York: Holt, Rinehart and Winston, 1973).

APPENDIX B

HIGH-LEVEL POLITICAL-MILITARY LEADERSHIP INSTITUTIONS

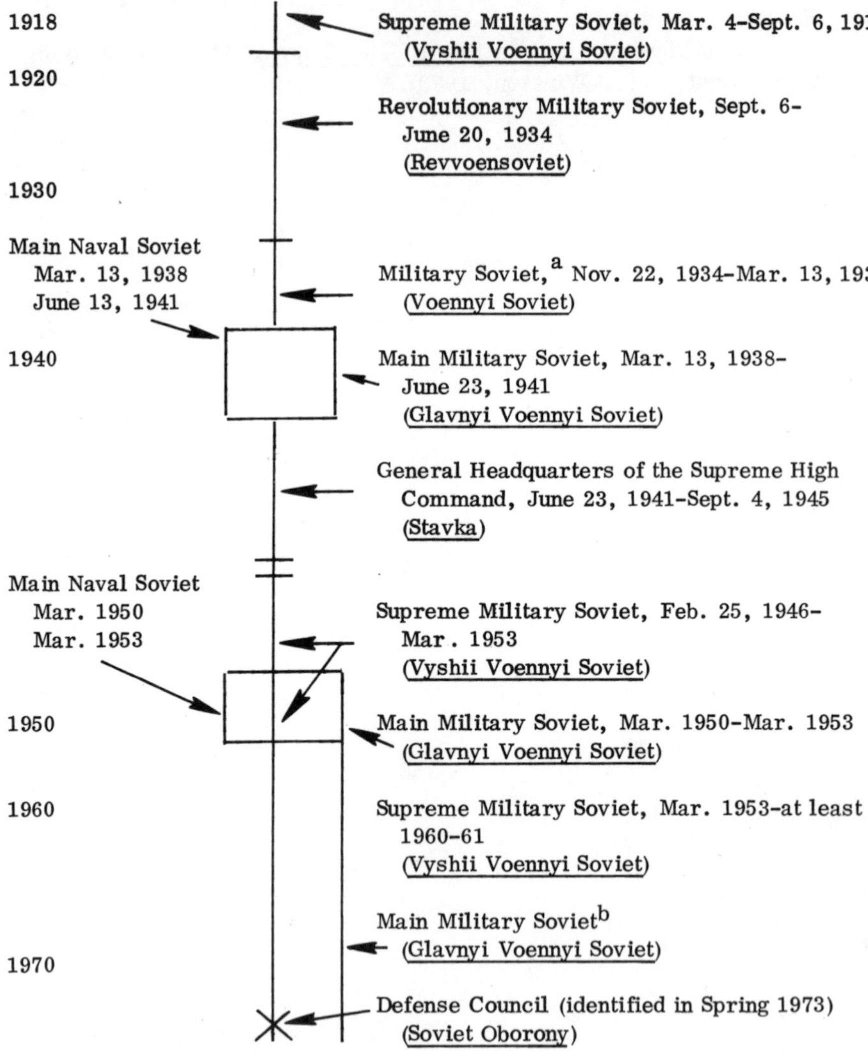

[a]Purely military composition, 90 members, advisory to the People's Commissar of Defense.

[b]Likely to be purely military. It appears to be the highest organ within a network of military soviets that exists within the Ministry of Defense from the military district and fleet levels up through the five military services.

Sources: M. V. Zakharov et al., eds., 50 let vooruzhennykh sil SSSR [50 years of the armed forces of the USSR] (Moscow: Voenizdat, 1968).

Yu. P. Petrov, Partiinoe stroitelstvo v Sovetskoi Armii i Flote [Party structure in the Soviet army and navy] (Moscow: Voenizdat, 1964).

Oleg Penkovskiy, The Penkovskiy Papers, trans. Peter Deriabin (New York: Avon Books, 1965).

A. S. Zheltov, ed., V. I. Lenin i Sovetskie Vooruzhennye Sily [V. I. Lenin and the Soviet armed forces] (Moscow: Voenizdat, 1964).

John Erickson, "The Soviet Naval High Command," US Naval Institute Proceedings Review, May 1973, pp. 68-87.

Malcolm Mackintosh, "The Soviet Military: Influence on Foreign Policy," Problems of Communism (September-October 1973): 1-12.

APPENDIX C

THE MILITARY IN THE HIGHER ORGANS OF THE CPSU

Military Members Elected at the Twentieth Party Congress, February 1956

<u>Full Members of the Central Committee</u> (8 of 133 = 6.0 percent)

Minister of Defense	Marshal G. K. Zhukov
First Deputy Ministers	
General Affairs	Marshal A. M. Vasilevskiy
CINC, WTO	Marshal I. S. Konev
Chief of the General Staff	Marshal V. D. Sokolovskiy
Commanders, Military Districts	
Cdr., Far East MD	Marshal R. Ya. Malinovskiy
Cdr., Moscow MD	Marshal K. S. Moskalenko
Distinguished "Veterans"	Marshal K. E. Voroshilov
(essentially political)	Marshal N. A. Bulganin

<u>Candidate Members of the Central Committee</u> (12 of 122 = 9.9 percent)

Deputy Ministers of Defense	
Main Inspector	Marshal I. Kh. Bagramian
CINC, Navy	Adm. S. G. Gorshkov
CINC, Air Force	Chief Marshal of Aviation P. A. Zhigarev
CINC, Air Defense (PVO-S)	Marshal S. S. Biriuzov
Chief of the Main Artillery Administration	Marshal of Artillery M. Nedelin
Commanders, Group and Military Districts	
Cdr., Group Soviet Forces, Germany	Marshal A. A. Grechko
Cdr. Baltic MD	General A. V. Gorbatov
Cdr., Belorussian MD	Marshal S. K. Timoshenko
Cdr., Kiev MD	Marshal V. I. Chuikov
Cdr., North Caucasus MD	Marshal A. I. Yeremenko
Cdr., Turkestan MD	General Luchinskiy
Distinguished Veteran	Marshal S. M. Budenny

<u>Members of the Central Auditing Commission</u>

Within the Ministry of Defense	
Chief, Higher Military Education	Marshal K. A. Meretskov

Military Members Elected at the Twenty-second Party Congress, October 1961

Full Members of the Central Committee (14 of 175 = 8.0 percent)

Minister of Defense	Marshal R. Ya. Malinovskiy
First Deputy Ministers	
CINC, WTO Forces	Marshal A. A. Grechko
Chief of the General Staff	Marshal M. V. Zakharov
Chief of the Main Political Administration	Marshal F. I. Golikov
Deputy Ministers	
Chief of the Rear	Marshal I. Kh. Bagramyan
CINC, Air Defense (PVO-S)	Marshal S. S. Biriuzov
CINC, Air Force	Marshal of Aviation K. A. Vershinin
CINC, Navy	Admiral S. G. Gorshkov
CINC, Strategic Rocket Forces	Marshal K. S. Moskalenko
CINC, Ground Forces	Marshal V. I. Chuikov
Commanders, Military Districts, Group Forces, Fleets	
Cdr., Group Soviet Forces, Germany	Marshal I. S. Konev
First Deputy Cdr., Group Soviet Forces Germany	Col. Gen. I. I. Yakubovskiy
Cdr., Moscow MD	Gen. N. I. Krylov
Cdr., Pacific Fleet	Adm. V. A. Fokin

Candidate Members of the Central Committee (17 of 155 = 11.0 percent)

Deputy Minister of Defense	
Chief Inspector	Marshal K. K. Rokossovsky
Within the Ministry of Defense	
Cdr., Artillery Forces	Chief Marshal of Artillery S. S. Varentsov
General-Inspector	Marshal A. I. Yeremenko
Chief of Staff, Air Force	Marshal of Aviation S. I. Rudenko
Deputy CINC, Air Force	Marshal of Aviation Ye. Ya. Savitskiy
General-Inspector	Marshal V. D. Sokolovskiy
General-Inspector	Marshal S. K. Timoshenko
Cdr., Long-Range Aviation	Marshal of Aviation V. A. Sudets

Commanders, Military Districts, Fleets	
Cdr., Belorussian MD	Col. Gen. V. A. Penkovskiy
Cdr., Carpathian MD	Col. Gen. A. L. Getman
Cdr., Kiev MD	Col. Gen. P. K. Koshevoi
Cdr., Leningrad MD	Gen. M. I. Kazakov
Cdr., North Caucasian MD	Col. Gen. I. G. Pliev
Cdr., Transcaucasian MD	Col. Gen. A. T. Stuchenko
Cdr., Moscow Air Defense District	Col. Gen. P. F. Batitskiy
Cdr., Northern Fleet	Adm. Chabanenko
Distinguished Veteran	Marshal S. M. Budenny

Members of the Central Auditing Commission

Within the Ministry of Defense	
Cdr., Military Transport Aviation	Marshal of Aviation N. S. Skripko
Commander, Military District	
Far East MD	Col. Gen. Y. G. Kreizer
Head, Mozhaisky Air Academy	Marshal of Aviation S. A. Krasovskiy

Military Members Elected at the Twenty-Third Party Congress, April 1966

Full Members of the Central Committee (15 of 195 = 7.7 percent)

Minister of Defense	Marshal R. Ya. Malinovskiy
First Deputy Ministers	
CINC, WTO	Marshal A. A. Grechko
Chief, General Staff	Marshal M. V. Zakharov
Chief of the Main Political Administration	Gen. A. A. Yepishev
Deputy Ministers	
Chief of the Rear	Marshal I. Kh. Bagramyan
CINC, Air Force	Chief Marshal of Aviation K. A. Vershinin
CINC, Navy	Adm. S. G. Gorshkov
CINC, Strategic Rocket Forces	Marshal N. I. Krylov
Chief Inspector	Marshal K. S. Moskalenko
Within the Ministry of Defense	
First Deputy Chief of the General Staff	Gen. P. F. Batitskiy
General-Inspector	Marshal I. S. Konev
Chief of Civil Defense	Marshal V. I. Chuikov

Commanders, Military Districts	
Cdr., Kiev MD	General I. I. Yakubovskiy
Cdr., Moscow MD	General A. M. Beloborodov
Distinguished Veteran	Marshal K. Ye. Voroshilov

Candidate Members of the Central Committee (18 of 165 = 10.9 percent)

Deputy Minister of Defense	
Chief of Combat Training	Gen. V. A. Penkovskiy
Within the Ministry of Defense	
General-Inspector	Marshal A. I. Yeremenko
First Deputy Chief of the General Staff	Gen. M. I. Kazakov
Chief of Staff, WTO	
Chief, Political Administration of Strategic Rocket Forces	Lt. Gen. I. A. Lavrenov
General-Inspector	Marshal K. K. Rokossovskiy
General-Inspector	Marshal V. D. Sokolovskiy
General-Inspector	Marshal S. K. Timoshenko
Commanders, Groups, Military Districts, Fleets	
Cdr., Group Soviet Forces, Germany	Gen. P. K. Koshevoi
Cdr., Belorussian MD	Col. Gen. S. S. Maryakhin
Cdr., Leningrad MD	Gen. S. L. Sokolov
Cdr., Transcaucasian MD	Gen. A. T. Stuchenko
Cdr., Turkestan MD	Col. Gen. N. G. Lyashchenko
Cdr., Volga MD	Lt. Gen. N. V. Ogarkov
Cdr., Northern Fleet	Adm. S. M. Lobov
Cdr., Pacific Fleet	Adm. N. N. Amelko
Chief, Political Administration, Moscow MD	Lt. Gen. K. S. Grushevoi
Chairman of DOSAAF	Gen. A. L. Getman
Distinguished Veteran	Marshal S. M. Budenny

Members of the Central Auditing Committee

Commanders, Groups, Military Districts	
Cdr., Carpathian MD	Col. Gen. P. N. Lashchenko
Cdr., Far East MD	Gen. I. G. Pavlovskiy
Cdr., Moscow Air Defense District	Col. Gen. V. V. Okunev
Chief, Political Administration Group Soviet Forces, Germany	Col. Gen. S. P. Vasyagin

Military Members Elected at the Twenty-fourth
Party Congress, April 1971

Full Members of the Central Committee (20 of 241 = 8.3 percent)

Minister of Defense	Marshal A. A. Grechko
First Deputy Ministers	
General Affairs	Marshal S. L. Sokolov
Chief, General Staff	Marshal M. V. Zakharov
CINC, WTO	Marshal I. I. Yakubovskiy
Chief of the Main Political Administration	Gen. A. A. Yepishev
Deputy Ministers	
CINC, Air Defense (PVO-S)	Marshal P. F. Batitskiy
CINC, Navy	Fleet Adm. S. G. Gorshkov
CINC, Strategic Rocket Forces	Marshal N. I. Krylov
CINC, Air Force	Marshal of Aviation P. S. Kutakhov
Chief of the Rear	Gen. S. S. Maryakhin
Main Inspector	Marshal K. S. Moskalenko
CINC, Ground Forces	Gen. I. G. Pavlovskiy
Within the Ministry	
General-Inspector	Marshal I. Kh. Bagramyan
General-Inspector	Marshal I. S. Konev
First Deputy Chief of the General Staff	Col. Gen. N. V. Ogarkov
Chief of Civil Defense	Marshal V. I. Chuikov
Commanders of Groups, Military Districts	
Cdr., Group Soviet Forces, Germany	Gen. V. G. Kulikov
Cdr., Central Asian MD	Gen. N. G. Lyashchenko
Cdr., Leningrad MD	Col. Gen. I. Ye. Shavrov
Cdr., Moscow MD	Col. Gen. Ye. F. Ivanovskiy

Candidate Members of the Central Committee (13 of 155 = 8.4 percent)

Within the Ministry of Defense	
Chief of the Political Administration Strategic Rocket Forces	Lt. Gen. P. A. Gorchukov
Detached to Soviet PVO Troops, Egypt	Col. Gen. V. V. Okunev

Commanders, Groups, Military Districts, Fleets	
Cdr., Central Group Forces	Col. Gen. A. M. Mairov
Cdr., Belorussian MD	Col. Gen. I. M. Tret'yak
Cdr., Far Eastern MD	Gen. V. F. Tolubko
Cdr., Kiev MD	Col. Gen. G. I. Salmanov
Cdr., Transcaucasian MD	Col. Gen. S. K. Kurkotkin
Cdr., Northern Fleet	Adm. S. M. Lobov
Cdr., Pacific Fleet	Adm. N. I. Smirnov
Cdr., Moscow Air Defense District	Col. Gen. A. I. Koldunov
Chief, Political Administration, Moscow MD	Col. Gen. K. S. Grushevoi
Chairman of DOSAAF	Gen. A. L. Getman
Distinguished Veteran	Marshal S. M. Budenny

Members of the Central Auditing Commission

Within the Ministry of Defense	
Chief of the Political Administration of Ground Forces	Col. Gen. S. P. Vasyagin
Chief, Higher Officer Courses, "Vystrel"	Col. Gen. D. A. Dragunskiy
Commander, Military District	
Cdr., Transbaikal MD	Gen. P. A. Belik

Military Members Elected at the Twenty-fifth Party Congress, March 1976

Full Members of the Central Committee (20 of 287 = 6.9 percent)

Minister of Defense	Marshal A. A. Grechko
First Deputy Ministers	
CINC, WTO	Marshal I. I. Yakubovskiy
Chief, General Staff	Gen. V. G. Kulikov
General Affairs	Gen. S. L. Sokolov
Chief of the Main Political Administration	Gen. A. A. Yepishev
Deputy Ministers	
CINC, Air Defense (PVO-S)	Marshal P. F. Batitskiy
CINC, Navy	Fleet Adm. of the Soviet Union S. G. Gorshkov
CINC, Strategic Rocket Forces	Gen. V. F. Tolubko

CINC, Air Force	Chief Marshal of Aviation P. S. Kutakhov
CINC, Ground Forces	Gen. I. G. Pavlovskiy
Chief of the Rear	Gen. S. K. Kurkotkin
Main Inspector	Marshal K. S. Moskalenko
Civil Defense	Col. Gen. A. T. Altunin
(portfolio unknown)	Gen. N. V. Ogarkov
Within the Ministry	
General-Inspector	Marshal I. Kh. Bagramyan
General-Inspector	Marshal V. I. Chuikov
Commanders of Groups, Military Districts	
Cdr., Group Soviet Forces, Germany	Gen. Ye. F. Ivanovskiy
Cdr., Central Asian MD	Gen. N. G. Lyashchenko
Cdr., Belorussian MD	Col. Gen. I. M. Tret'yak
Cdr., Far East MD	Gen. V. I. Petrov

<u>Candidate Members of the Central Committee</u> (10 of 139 = 7.2 percent)

Within the Ministry of Defense	
Chief of the MPA, SRF	Gen. P. A. Gorchakov
First Deputy Chief of the General Staff	Gen. M. M. Kozlov
In the Groups, Military Districts, Fleets	
Cdr., Moscow MD	Col. Gen. V. L. Govorov
Cdr., Leningrad MD	Col. Gen. A. I. Gribkov
Cdr., Kiev MD	Col. Gen. I. A. Gerasimov
Cdr., Baltic MD	Col. Gen. A. M. Maiorov
Cdr., Northern Fleet	Adm. G. M. Yegorov
Cdr., Pacific Fleet	Adm. V. P. Maslov
Chief, Political Directorate, Moscow MD	Col. Gen. K. S. Grushevoi
Chairman of DOSAAF	Marshal of Aviation A. I. Pokryshkin

<u>Members of the Central Auditing Commission</u>

Within the Ministry of Defense	
Chief of the Political Administration of the Ground Forces	Gen. S. P. Vasyagin
Chief, Higher Officers' Courses, "Vystrel"	Col. Gen. D. A. Dragunskiy
In the Groups, Military Districts	
Cdr., Transbaikal MD	Gen. P. A. Belik
Cdr., Moscow Air Defense District	Col. Gen. B. V. Bochkov
Chief, Political Directorate, Group Soviet Forces, Germany	Col. Gen. I. S. Mednikov

SELECTED BIBLIOGRAPHY

BOOKS AND ARTICLES--ENGLISH LANGUAGE

Adamson, Robert. "Mobilizing Soviet Science," Scientific Research 3, no. 2 (January 22, 1968): 25-34.

Alexander, Arthur J. R&D in Soviet Aviation, R-589-PR. Santa Monica, Calif.: RAND Corporation, November 1970.

_____. "Weapons Acquisition in the Soviet Union, United States and France." In Comparative Defense Policy, edited by F. B. Horton, A. Rogerson, and E. L. Warner, III, pp. 426-44. Baltimore: Johns Hopkins Press, 1974.

Allison, Graham T. Essence of Decision: Explaining the Cuban Missile Crisis. Boston: Little, Brown, 1966.

_____, and Morton H. Halperin. "Bureaucratic Politics: A Paradigm and Some Foreign Policy Implications." World Politics 24, supplement.

Almond, Gabriel, and Bingham G. Powell. Comparative Politics: A Developmental Approach. Boston: Little, Brown, 1966.

Armacost, Michael. The Politics of Weapon Innovation: The Thor-Jupiter Controversy. New York: Columbia University Press, 1969.

Armstrong, John A. The Soviet Bureaucratic Elite. New York: Praeger, 1959.

Armstrong, Richard. "Military-Industrial Complex: Russian Style." Fortune, August 1, 1969, pp. 84-87, 122-26.

Aspaturian, Vernon V. "Foreign Policy Perspectives in the Sixties." In Soviet Politics Since Khrushchev, edited by Alexander Dallin and Thomas B. Larson, pp. 129-45. Englewood Cliffs, N.J.: Prentice-Hall, 1968.

_____. Process and Power in Soviet Foreign Policy. Boston: Little, Brown, 1971.

_____. "Soviet Foreign Policy." In Foreign Policy in World Politics, edited by Roy C. Macridis, pp. 132-210. Englewood Cliffs, N.J.: Prentice-Hall, 1964.

_____. "The Soviet Military-Industrial Complex--Does it Exist?" Journal of International Affairs 26, no. 1 (1972): 1-28.

Avtorkhanov, Abdurakhman. The Communist Party Apparatus. New York: Meridian Books, 1966.

Azrael, Jeremy R. Managerial Power and Soviet Politics. Cambridge: Harvard University Press, 1966.

Ball, Desmond. "The Strategic Missile Program of the Kennedy Administration, 1961-1963." Ph.D. dissertation, Australian National University, Canberra, June 1972.

Barghoorn, Frederick C. Politics in the USSR: A Country Study. Boston: Little, Brown, 1966.

_____. "Trends in Top Political Leadership in the USSR." In Political Leadership in Eastern Europe and the Soviet Union, edited by R. Barry Farrell, pp. 61-87. Chicago: Aldine, 1970.

Bates, Richard W. "Communist Party Control in the Soviet Navy." Naval War College Review 20, no. 3 (October 1967): 3-44.

Bauer, Raymond A., Alex Inkeles, and Clyde Kluckhohn. How the Soviet System Works. New York: Vintage Books, 1956.

Bentley, Arthur. The Process of Government. Evanston, Ill.: Northwestern University Press, 1949.

Bialer, Seweryn, ed. Stalin and His Generals: Soviet Military Memoirs of World War II. New York: Pegasus, 1969.

Bilinsky, Yaroslav. Changes in the Central Committee: Communist Party of the Soviet Union, 1961-1966. Monograph Series in World Affairs, vol. 4, no. 4. Denver, Colo.: University of Denver, 1967.

Bloomfield, Lincoln, Walter C. Clemens, Jr., and Franklyn Griffiths. Khruschev and the Arms Race: Soviet Interests in Arms Control and Disarmament, 1954-1964. Cambridge, Mass.: MIT Press, 1966.

Borkenau, Franz. "Getting the Facts Behind the Soviet Facade." Commentary 17, no. 4 (April 1954): 393-400.

Breyer, Siegfried. Guide to the Soviet Navy. Annapolis, Md.: U.S. Naval Institute, 1970.

Brownlow, Cecil. "Soviet Air Force Unveils Advanced Designs for Expanded Limited War Capability." Aviation Week and Space Technology (July 17, 1967): 32-35.

_____. "Soviets Prepare Space Weapon for 1968." Aviation Week and Space Technology (November 13, 1967): 30, 31.

Brzezinski, Zbigniew, ed. Dilemmas of Change in Soviet Politics. New York: Columbia University Press, 1969.

_____. Political Controls in the Soviet Army. New York: Research Program on the USSR, 1954.

_____, and Samuel P. Huntington. Political Power: USA/USSR. New York: Viking Press, 1965.

Burin, Frederic S. "The Communist Doctrine of the Inevitability of War." American Political Science Review (June 1963): 334-54.

Caldwell, Lawrence T. Soviet Attitudes to SALT. Adelphi Papers no. 76. London: Institute of Strategic Studies, 1971.

Chapman, William C. "The Soviet Air Forces." In Naval Review, 1965, edited by Frank Uhlig, Jr., pp. 179-89. Annapolis, Md.: U.S. Naval Institute, 1964.

Clark, Roger A. "The Composition of the USSR Supreme Soviet: 1958-1966." Soviet Studies 19, no. 1 (July 1967): 53-65.

Clemens, Walter C. The Superpowers and Arms Control: From Cold War to Interdependence. Lexington, Mass.: D. C. Heath, 1973.

Cliffe, Trevor. Military Technology and the European Balance. Adelphi Paper no. 89. London: International Institute of Strategic Studies, August 1972.

Cocks, Paul M. "The Purge of Marshal Zhukov." Slavic Review 22, no. 3 (September 3, 1963): 483-98.

Cohn, Stanley H. "The Economic Burden of Soviet Defense Outlays." In Economic Performance and the Military Burden in the Soviet Economy. U.S. Congress, Joint Economic Committee, 91st Congress, 2d Session, pp. 166-88. Washington, D.C.: Government Printing Office.

Conquest, Robert. Power and Policy in the USSR. New York: Harper and Row, 1967.

_____. Russia After Khrushchev. New York: Praeger, 1965.

Crane, Robert Dickson, ed. Soviet Nuclear Strategy: A Critical Appraisal. Washington, D.C.: Center for Strategic Studies, February 1965.

Dallin, Alexander. "Soviet Foreign Policy and Domestic Politics: A Framework for Analysis." Journal of International Affairs 23, no. 2 (1969): 212-87.

_____, and Thomas B. Larson, eds. Soviet Politics Since Khrushchev. Englewood Cliffs, N.J.: Prentice-Hall, 1968.

_____, et al. The Soviet Union, Arms Control and Disarmament. New York: School of International Affairs, Columbia University, 1964.

Daly, Robert W. "Russia's Maritime Past." In The Soviet Navy, edited by M. G. Saunders, pp. 23-43. New York: Praeger, 1958.

_____. "Summation of Course in Russian Military and Naval Doctrine." Unpublished manuscript. Annapolis, Md., 1962.

Daniloff, Nicholas. The Kremlin and the Cosmos. New York: Knopf, 1972.

Denisov, A., and M. Kirichenko. Soviet State Law. Moscow: Foreign Language Publishing House, 1960.

Despres, John, Lilita Dzirkals, and Barton Whaley. Timely Lessons of History: The Manchurian Model for Soviet Strategy. Santa Monica, Calif.: RAND Corporation, 1976.

Deuval, Christian. "An Armed Skeleton in the Politburo's Closet." Radio Liberty Dispatch, November 10, 1971.

_____. "The Politburo and Secretariat Elected at the 24th CPSU Congress." Radio Liberty Dispatch, April 13, 1971.

Dinerstein, Herbert S. War and the Soviet Union. New York: Praeger, 1962.

Donaldson, Ronald H. "The 1971 Soviet Central Committee: An Assessment of the New Elite." World Politics 24, no. 3 (April 1972): 382-409.

Downs, Anthony. Inside Bureaucracy. Boston: Little, Brown, 1967.

Eckstein, Harry. "Introduction: Group Theory and the Comparative Study of Pressure Groups." In Comparative Politics: A Reader, edited by Harry Eckstein and David E. Apter, pp. 389-97. New York: The Free Press, 1963.

Edeen, Alf. "The Administrative Intelligentsia." In The Soviet Political System: A Book of Readings, edited by Richard Cornell. Englewood Cliffs, N.J.: Prentice-Hall, 1971.

Enthoven, Alain C., and K. Wayne Smith. How Much is Enough? New York: Harper and Row, 1971.

Erickson, John. "The Army, the Party and the People." In The Soviet Union in Europe and the Near East: Her Capabilities and Intentions, pp. 16-25. London: Royal United Services Institution, 1970.

_____. "The Fly in Outer Space: The Soviet Union and the Anti-Ballistic Missile." The World Today (March 1967): 106-14.

_____. "Radio Location and the Air Defense Problem: The Design and Development of Soviet Radar, 1934-1940." Science Studies no. 2 (1972): 241-68.

_____. "The Soviet Concept of Land Battle." In The Soviet Union in Europe and the Near East: Her Capabilities and Intentions, pp. 26-32. London: Royal United Service Institution, August 1970.

_____. The Soviet High Command: A Military-Political History, 1918-1941. New York: St. Martin's Press, 1962.

_____. "Soviet Military Power." Strategic Review, Special Supplement 1, no. 1 (Spring 1973): 1-127.

_____. Soviet Military Power. London: Royal United Services Institute of Defense Studies, 1971.

Ermarth, Fritz. "Soviet Military Politics." Military Review 63, no. 1 (January 1968): 36-40.

_____. Soviet Military Politics Under Brezhnev and Kosygin. Munich: Radio Free Europe, May 16, 1967.

Fainsod, Merle. How Russia is Ruled. 2d rev. ed. Cambridge: Harvard University Press, 1967.

_____. "Through Soviet Eyes." Problems of Communism 19, no. 6 (November-December 1970): 59-64.

Feld, M. D. "A Typology of Military Organization." In Public Policy: 1958, edited by C. J. Freidrich and S. E. Harris, pp. 3-40. Cambridge, Mass.: Graduate School of Public Administration, 1958.

Fischer, George. The Soviet System and a Modern Society. New York: Atherton Press, 1968.

_____, ed. The Soviet Union, Arms Control and Disarmament: Background Materials on Soviet Attitudes. New York: School of International Affairs, Columbia University, 1965.

Fleron, Frederic J. "Representation of Career Types in the Soviet Political Leadership." In Political Leadership in Eastern Europe and the Soviet Union, edited by R. Barry Farrell, pp. 108-39. Chicago: Aldine, 1970.

_____, ed. Communist Studies and the Social Sciences. Chicago: Rand McNally, 1969.

Gallagher, Matthew P., and Karl F. Spielmann, Jr. The Politics of Power: Soviet Decisionmaking for Defense. Washington, D.C.: Institute for Defense Analysis, 1971.

Garthoff, Raymond L. "Khrushchev and the Military." In Politics in the Soviet Union: 7 Cases, edited by Alexander Dallin and Alan F. Westin, pp. 243-73. New York: Harcourt, Brace and World, 1966.

_____. "SALT and the Soviet Military." Problems of Communism 24, no. 1 (January-February 1975): 21-37.

_____. The Soviet Image of Future War. Washington, D.C.: Public Affairs Press, 1959.

_____. Soviet Military Doctrine. Glencoe, Ill.: The Free Press, 1953.

_____. Soviet Military Policy: A Historical Analysis. New York: Praeger, 1966.

_____. Soviet Strategy in the Nuclear Age. Rev. ed. New York: Praeger, 1962.

Garwin, Richard L., and Hans Bethe. "Anti-Ballistic Missile Systems." Scientific American 218, no. 3 (March 1968): 21-31.

Gawthrop, Louis C. Bureaucratic Behavior in the Executive Branch. New York: Free Press, 1969.

Gehlen, Michael P. "Group Theory and the Study of Soviet Politics.". In The Soviet Political Process, edited by Sidney Ploss, pp. 35-54. Waltham, Mass.: Ginn and Co., 1971.

_____. The Politics of Coexistence. Bloomington, Indiana: Indiana University Press, 1967.

_____, and Michael McBride. "The Soviet Central Committee: An Elite Analysis." American Political Science Review (December 1968): 1232-41.

George, Alexander. "The Case for Multiple Advocacy in Making Foreign Policy." Paper delivered at the 1971 Annual Meeting of the American Political Science Association, Chicago, Ill., September 7-11, 1971.

_____. "Stress in Political Decision-Making." Paper presented at the Conference on Coping and Adaptation, Stanford University, Palo Alto, Calif., March 1969.

Gerasimov, Gennady. "The First Strike Theory." International Affairs (Moscow) no. 7 (July 1964): 39-45.

_____. "Pentagonia, 1966." International Affairs (Moscow) no. 5 (May 1966): 24-26.

_____. "Plans for Controlled War." International Affairs (Moscow) no. 12 (December 1964): 88-89.

_____. "Twist of Military Thought." International Affairs (Moscow) no. 3 (March 1963): 105-06.

_____. "War Savants Play Games." International Affairs (Moscow) no. 7 (July 1964): 77-84.

Goldhammer, Herbert. The Soviet Soldier: Soviet Military Management at the Troop Level. New York: Crane, Russak, 1975.

Golovin, Nicholas N. The Russian Campaign of 1914: The Beginning of War and Operations in Eastern Prussia. Fort Leavenworth, Kansas: Command and General Staff School Press, 1933.

Gouré, Leon. Civil Defense in the Soviet Union. Berkeley, Calif.: University of California Press, 1962.

_____. The Military Indoctrination of Soviet Youth. New York: National Strategy Information Center, Inc., 1973.

_____. Soviet Civil Defense Restricted, 1966-1969. RM-6113-PR. Santa Monica, Calif.: RAND Corporation, 1969.

_____. Soviet Limited War Doctrine. P-2744. Santa Monica, Calif.: RAND Corporation, June 1966.

_____. War Survival in Soviet Strategy: USSR Civil Defense. Miami: Center for Advanced International Studies, 1976.

Gregory, William H. "Soviet Union Seeks Balance in Technology Growth." Aviation Week and Space Technology (March 18, 1968): 87-88.

Griffiths, Franklyn. "Forward Deployment and Foreign Policy." In Soviet Naval Developments: Context and Capability, edited by Michael MccGwire, pp. 7-12. New York: Praeger, 1973.

______. "Inner Tensions in the Soviet Approach to Disarmament." International Journal 22, no. 4 (August 1967): 593-617.

Gryzlov, A. A. "The Freezing of Defensive Anti-Missile Systems." Paper presented at the Seventeenth Pugwash Conference on Science and World Affairs, Ronneby, Sweden, September 1967.

Hagan, Charles. "The Group in Political Science." In Approaches to the Study of Politics, edited by Roland Young, pp. 38-51. Evanston, Ill.: Northwestern University Press, 1958.

Halperin, Morton H. Bureaucratic Politics and Foreign Policy. Washington, D.C.: The Brookings Institution, 1974.

______. "The Decision to Deploy the ABM: Bureaucratic and Domestic Politics in the Johnson Administration." World Politics 25, no. 1 (October 1972): 62-95.

______. "Why Bureaucrats Play Games." Foreign Policy 2 (Spring 1971): 76-88.

Hardt, John P. Economic Insights on Current Soviet Policy and Strategy. RAC-R-92. McLean, Va.: Research Analysis Corporation, September 1969.

______. The Future Role of the Soviet Central Planner. McLean, Va.: Research Analysis Corporation, July 1964.

Head, Richard G. "Doctrinal Innovation and the A-7 Attack Aircraft Program." In American Defense Policy: Third Edition, edited by Richard G. Head and Ervin J. Rokke, pp. 431-45. Baltimore: Johns Hopkins University Press, 1973.

Heimann, Leo. "River Flotillas of the USSR." Military Review 50, no. 8 (August 1970): 45-51.

Herrick, Robert W. Soviet Naval Strategy: Fifty Years of Theory and Practice. Annapolis, Md.: U.S. Naval Institute, 1968.

______. "Soviet Commander-in-Chief Advocates Construction of a Much Larger Navy." Working paper. Arlington, Va.: Center for Naval Analysis, May 9, 1973.

Hilsman, Roger. The Politics of Decision-Making in Defense and Foreign Affairs. New York: Harper and Row, 1971.

_____. To Move a Nation: The Politics of Foreign Policy in the Administration of John F. Kennedy. New York: Doubleday, 1967.

Holloway, David. Technology, Management and the Soviet Military Establishment. Adelphi Papers no. 76. London: Institute of Strategic Studies, April 1971.

Holst, Johan J. Comparative U.S. and Soviet Deployments, Doctrines and Arms Limitation. Chicago: University of Chicago Press, 1971.

_____. "Missile Defense, the Soviet Union and the Arms Race." In Why ABM?: Policy Issues and the Missile Defense Controversy, edited by Johan J. Holst and William J. Schneider, Jr., pp. 145-86. New York: Pergamon Press, 1969.

_____. Some Notes on the Soviet Command System. HI-1152-P. Croton on Hudson, New York: Hudson Institute Inc., 1969.

Horelick, Arnold L., and Myron Rush. Strategic Power and Soviet Foreign Policy. Chicago: University of Chicago Press, 1966.

Hough, Jerry F. "The Party Apparatchiki." In Interest Groups in Soviet Politics, edited by H. Gordon Skilling and Franklyn Griffiths, pp. 47-92. Princeton, N.J.: Princeton University Press, 1971.

_____. The Soviet Prefects: The Local Party Organs in Industrial Decision-making. Cambridge: Harvard University Press, 1969.

_____. "The Soviet System--Petrification or Pluralism?" Problems of Communism 21, no. 2 (March-April 1972): 25-45.

Huntington, Samuel P., and Clement H. Moore, eds. Authoritarian Politics in Modern Society. New York: Basic Books, 1970.

_____. "Arms Race: Prerequisites and Results." In The Use of Force: International Politics and Foreign Policy, edited by Robert J. Art and Kenneth N. Waltz, pp. 365-401. Boston: Little, Brown, 1971.

_____. The Common Defense: Strategic Programs in National Politics. New York: Columbia University Press, 1961.

_____. The Soldier and the State: The Theory of Civil-Military Relations. New York: Vintage Books, 1964.

Hyland, William, and Richard Shryock. The Fall of Khrushchev. New York: Funk and Wagnalls, 1968.

Jacobson, Carl G. "The Soviet Navy: Acquiring Global Capabilities and Perspectives." Naval War College Review no. 3 (March 1972): 41-52.

Janowitz, Morris. The Professional Soldier: A Social and Political Portrait. Glencoe, Ill.: The Free Press, 1960.

_____, and Jacques Van Doorn, eds. On Military Intervention. Rotterdam: Rotterdam University Press, 1971.

Johnson, Chalmers, ed. Change in Communist Systems. Stanford, Calif.: Stanford University Press, 1970.

Jones, Christopher D. "The 'Revolution in Military Affairs' and Party-Military Relations, 1965-70." Survey 20, no. 1 (Winter 1974): 84-100.

Jukes, Geoffrey. The Indian Ocean in Soviet Naval Policy. Adelphi Papers no. 87. London: International Institute of Strategic Studies, May 1972.

Juviler, Peter, and Henry W. Morton, eds. Soviet Policy-Making: Studies of Communism in Transition. New York: Praeger, 1967.

Kanter, Arnold, and Stuart J. Thorson. "The Logic of American Weapons Procurement: Problems in the Construction and Evaluation of Policy Theories." Paper delivered at the 1972 Midwest Regional Meeting of the International Studies Association and Peace Research Society, Toronto, Ontario, May 11-13, 1972.

Karsten, Peter, et al. "'Professional' and 'Citizen' Officers: A Comparison of Service Academy and ROTC Officer Candidates." In Public Opinion and the Military Establishment, edited by Charles C. Moskos, pp. 37-61. Beverly Hills, Calif.: Sage Publications, 1971.

Katz, Zev. "Sociology in the Soviet Union." Problems of Communism 20 (May-June 1971): 22-40.

Khrushchev, Nikita S. The Crimes of the Stalin Era: Special Report to the 20th Congress of the CPSU. Published as Section 2 of The New Leader, July 16, 1956.

_____. Khrushchev Remembers. Translated and edited by Strobe Talbott. New York: Bantam Books, 1971.

_____. Khrushchev Remembers: The Last Testament. Translated and edited by Strobe Talbott. Boston: Little, Brown, 1974.

Kilmarx, Robert. A History of Soviet Air Power. New York: Praeger, 1962.

Kissinger, Henry A. "Congressional Briefing on SALT I," June 15, 1972, in Strategic Arms Limitation Agreements, Hearings Before the Committee on Foreign Relations. United States Senate, 92d Congress, 2d Session, pp. 393-416. Washington, D.C.: Government Printing Office, 1972.

Kolkowicz, Roman. The Dilemma of Superpower: Soviet Policy and Strategy in Transition. Arlington, Va.: Institute for Defense Analysis, 1967.

_____. "Generals and Politicians: Uneasy Truce." Problems of Communism 27 (May-June 1968): 71-76.

_____. The Impact of Technology on the Soviet Military: A Challenge to Traditional Military Professionalism. RM-4198-PR. Santa Monica, Calif.: RAND Corporation, August 1964.

_____. "The Military." In Interest Groups in Soviet Politics, edited by H. Gordon Skilling and Franklyn Griffiths, pp. 131-70. Princeton, N.J.: Princeton University Press, 1971.

_____. The Red "Hawks" on the Rationality of Nuclear War. RM-4899-PR. Santa Monica, Calif.: RAND Corporation, 1966.

_____. The Soviet Military and the Communist Party. Princeton, N.J.: Princeton University Press, 1967.

_____, Matthew P. Gallagher, and Benjamin S. Lambeth. The Soviet Union and Arms Control: A Superpower Dilemma. Baltimore: Johns Hopkins Press, 1970.

Korol, Alexander G. Soviet Research and Development: Its Organization Personnel and Funds. Cambridge, Mass.: MIT Press, 1965.

Krisch, Henry. "The Changing Role of the Standing Commissions of the USSR Supreme Soviet." Paper delivered at the 1971 Annual Meeting of the American Political Science Association, Chicago, September 7-11, 1971.

Krylov, Konstantin K. "Soviet Military-Economic Complex." Military Review 51, no. 11 (November 1971): 89-97.

Kurth, James R. "Aerospace Production Lines and American Defense Policy." In American Defense Policy: Third Edition, edited by Richard G. Head and Ervin J. Rokke, pp. 626-40. Baltimore: Johns Hopkins University Press, 1973.

Lambeth, Benjamin S. The Argument for Superiority: A New Voice in the Soviet Strategic Debate. N-419R. Arlington, Va.: Institute for Defense Analysis, January 1967.

_____. "The Politics of the Soviet Military Under Brezhnev and Kosygin." Master's thesis, George Washington University, Washington, D.C., 1968.

Lang, Kurt. "Military Organizations." In Handbook of Organizations, edited by James G. March, pp. 838-74. Chicago: Rand McNally, 1965.

Larionov, V. V. "Quantitative and Qualitative Aspects of the Arms Race." Paper delivered at the Twentieth Pugwash Conference on Science and World Affairs, September 9-15, 1970.

Larson, Thomas B. Disarmament and Soviet Policy: 1964-1968. Englewood Cliffs, N.J.: Prentice Hall, 1969.

Latham, Earl. The Group Basis of Politics. Ithaca, N.Y.: Cornell University Press, 1952.

Lee, Asher, ed. The Soviet Air and Rocket Forces. New York: Praeger, 1959.

Leonhard, Wolfgang. The Kremlin Since Stalin. New York: Praeger, 1962.

Levine, Herbert S. "Economics." In Science and Ideology in Soviet Society, edited by George Fischer, pp. 107-38. New York: Atherton Press, 1967.

Lindblom, Charles. The Intelligence of Democracy: Decision-Making Through Mutual Adjustment. New York: The Free Press, 1965.

Linden, Carl A. Khrushchev and the Soviet Leadership, 1957-1964. Baltimore: Johns Hopkins University Press, 1966.

Lodge, Milton C. Soviet Elite Attitudes Since Stalin. Columbus, Ohio: Charles E. Merrill, 1969.

Long, John. Army General I. G. Pavlovskiy Becomes Ground Forces Commander-in-Chief. Munich: Radio Liberty, January 24, 1968.

Lovell, John. "The Professional Socialization of the West Point Cadet." In The New Military, edited by Morris Janowitz, pp. 119-57. New York: Russell Sage Foundation, 1964.

McConnell, John A. "Interest Groups in the Cold War: A Study of the Soviet Military Industrial Complex." Unpublished dissertation in progress, Dalhousie University, Halifax, Nova Scotia, January 1974.

MccGwire, Michael. "Soviet Naval Capabilities and Intentions." In The Soviet Union in Europe and the Near East: Her Capabilities and Intentions, pp. 33-51. London: Royal United Services Institution, August 1970.

_____, ed. Soviet Naval Developments: Context and Capability. New York: Praeger, 1973.

_____. "Soviet Naval Procurement." In The Soviet Union in Europe and the Near East: Her Capabilities and Intentions, pp. 74-87. London: Royal United Services Institution, 1970.

McHale, Vincent E., and Joseph P. Mastro. "The Central Committee of the CPSU: Analysis of Composition and Long-Term Trends." Paper delivered at the annual meeting of the American Political Science Association, Los Angeles, September 8-12, 1970.

Mackintosh, J. Malcolm. Juggernaut: The History of the Soviet Armed Forces. New York: Macmillan, 1967.

_____. "The Role of Institutional Factors in Soviet Decisions on Weapons Procurement." Unpublished manuscript, 1967.

_____. "The Soviet Military: Influence on Foreign Policy." Problems of Communism 22, no. 5 (September-October 1973): 1-12.

March, James, and Herbert Simon. Organizations. New York: John Wiley and Sons, Inc., 1958.

Medvedev, Roy, and Zhores Medvedev. Khrushchev: The Years in Power. New York: Columbia University Press, 1976.

Meyer, Alfred G. The Soviet Political System: An Interpretation. New York: Random House, 1965.

Miller, David C. "The Soviet Armed Forces and Political Pressure." Military Review 59, no. 12 (December 1969): 62-68.

Milsom, John. Russian Tanks, 1900-1970. Harrisburg, Pa.: Stackpole Books, 1971.

Moorer, Thomas H. United States Military Posture for FY 1974, Statement before the Senate Armed Services Committee. Washington, D.C.: Government Printing Office, March 1973.

Moss, Norman. "McNamara's ABM Policy: A Failure of Communications." The Reporter 36, no. 4 (February 23, 1967): 34-37.

Murphy, Charles J. V. "Khrushchev's Paper Bear." Fortune, December 1964, pp. 114-15.

_____. "What We Gave Away in the Moscow Arms Agreement." Fortune, September 1972, pp. 110-15, 203-08.

Nemzer, Louis. Conflicting Patterns of Civil-Military Relations in the USSR. RAC-TP-142. McLean, Va.: Research Analysis Corporation, 1964.

Newhouse, John. Cold Dawn: The Story of SALT. New York: Holt, Rinehart and Winston, 1973.

O'Ballance, Edgar. The Red Army. New York: Praeger, 1964.

Odom, William E., "The Militarization of Soviet Society." Problems of Communism (September-October 1976): 34-51.

Page, Martin. The Day Khrushchev Fell. New York: Hawthorne Books, 1965.

Penkovskiy, Oleg. The Penkovskiy Papers. Translated by Peter Deriabin. New York: Avon Books, 1966.

Pethybridge, Roger. A Key to Soviet Politics: The Crisis of the "Anti-Party" Group. London: Allen and Unwin, 1962.

Petrov, Vladimir. "Formation of Soviet Foreign Policy." Orbis 17, no. 3 (Fall 1973): 819-50.

Ploss, Sidney. "A Cautious Verdict in Moscow: The 24th Party Congress." Orbis 15, no. 2 (Summer 1971): 561-75.

_____. Conflict and Decision-making in Soviet Russia: A Case Study of Agricultural Policy, 1953-1963. Princeton, N.J.: Princeton University Press, 1965.

_____. "Interest Groups." In Prospects for Soviet Society, edited by Allen Kassof, pp. 76-103. New York: Praeger, 1968.

_____. "A New Phase of the Soviet Policy Debate." Occasional Paper on Soviet Politics 4. Princeton, N.J.: Center of International Studies, 1963.

_____. The Soviet Leadership Between Cold War and Detente. Philadelphia: Foreign Policy Research Institute, 1964.

Quester, George H. Nuclear Diplomacy. New York: Dunellen, 1970.

_____. "On the Identification of Real and Pretended Communist Military Doctrine." Journal of Conflict Resolution 10, no. 2 (June 1966): 172-79.

Rathjens, George W. The Future of the Strategic Arms Race: Options for the 1970's. New York: Carnegie Endowment for International Peace, 1969.

Reitz, James T. "Soviet Defense-Associated Activities Outside the Ministry of Defense." In Economic Performance and the

Military Burden in the Soviet Union. U.S. Congress, Joint Economic Committee, 91st Congress, 2d Session, pp. 133-65. Washington, D.C.: Government Printing Office, 1970.

Richman, Barry. Soviet Management: With Significant American Comparisons. Englewood Cliffs, N.J.: Prentice Hall, 1965.

Rigby, Thomas H. Communist Party Membership in the USSR: 1917-1967. Princeton, N.J.: Princeton University Press, 1968.

_____, and L. G. Churchward. Policy-Making in the USSR, 1953-1961: Two Views. Melbourne: Lansdowne Press, 1962.

Rokke, Ervin J. "The Politics of Aerial Reconnaissance: The Eisenhower Administration." Ph.D. dissertation, Harvard University, 1970.

Rothblat, J. Pugwash--The First Ten Years. London: Heinemann, 1967.

Sakharov, Andrei. Progress, Coexistence and Intellectual Freedom. New York: W. W. Norton, 1968.

Saunders, M. G., ed. The Soviet Navy. New York: Praeger, 1958.

Schilling, Warner R., Paul Y. Hammond, and Glenn H. Snyder. Strategy, Politics and Defense Budgets. New York: Columbia University Press, 1962.

Schroeder, Gertrude E. "Recent Developments in Soviet Planning and Incentives," in Soviet Economic Prospects for the Seventies. Joint Economic Committee, 93d Congress, 1st Session, pp. 13-18. Washington, D.C.: Government Printing Office, 1973.

Schwartz, Joel J., and William R. Keech. "Group Influence and the Policy Process in the Soviet Union." American Political Science Review 63, no. 3 (September 1968): 840-51.

Scott, Derek J. R. Russian Political Institutions. New York: Praeger, 1961.

Scott, Harriet Fast, and William Kinter, eds. The Nuclear Revolution in Soviet Military Affairs. Norman, Okla.: University of Oklahoma Press, 1968.

_____. "The Soviet View of the Character and Features of Modern War." Technical Note SSC-TN-8260-1. Menlo Park, Calif.: Stanford Research Institute, 1969.

Senter, Raymond D. "Khrushchev, the Generals and Goldwater." The New Republic, November 21, 1964, pp. 8-10.

Shapiro, Leonard. The Communist Party of the Soviet Union. 2d ed. New York: Random House, 1971.

_____. "Keynote--Compromise." Problems of Communism 20, no. 4 (July-August 1971): 2-8.

Sheren, Andrew. "Structure and Organization of Defense-Related Industries." In Economic Performance and the Military Burden in the Soviet Union. U.S. Congress, Joint Economic Committee, pp. 123-31. Washington, D.C.: Government Printing Office, 1970.

Shulman, Marshal D. "SALT and the Soviet Union." In SALT, The Moscow Agreements and Beyond, edited by Mason Willrich and John B. Rhinelander, pp. 101-21. New York: The Free Press, 1974.

Simmonds, George W., ed. Soviet Leaders. New York: Thomas Y. Crowell, 1967.

Skilling, H. Gordon. "Group Conflict in Soviet Politics: Some Conclusions." In Interest Groups in Soviet Politics, edited by H. Gordon Skilling and Franklyn Griffiths, pp. 379-416. Princeton, N.J.: Princeton University Press, 1971.

_____, and Franklyn Griffiths, eds. Interest Groups in Soviet Politics. Princeton, N.J.: Princeton University Press, 1971.

Smart, Ian. Advanced Strategic Missiles: A Short Guide, Adelphi Papers no. 63. London: Institute of Strategic Studies, December 1969.

Smith, Hedrick. The Russians. New York: Quadrangle Books, 1976.

Sokolovskiy, V. D., ed. Soviet Military Strategy. Translated and annotated by Thomas W. Wolfe, Herbert Dinerstein, Arnold Horelick, and Leon Gouré. R-416-PR. Santa Monica, Calif.: RAND Corporation, April 1963.

Sosnovy, Timothy. "The Soviet Military Budget." Foreign Affairs (April 1964): 448-93.

Spahr, William J. "The Soviet Military Decision-Making Process." Paper delivered at the Fifth National Convention, American Association for the Advancement of Slavic Studies, Dallas, Texas, March 15, 1972.

Staar, Richard F. "Current Soviet Military Strategy." Naval War College Review 18, no. 5 (January 1966): 1-23.

Stewart, Philip. "Soviet Interest Groups and the Policy Process: The Repeal of Production Education." World Politics 12, no. 1 (October 1969): 29-50.

Stoiko, Michael. Soviet Rocketry: Past and Present and Future. New York: Holt, Rinehart and Winston, 1970, pp. 42-65.

Stone, Jeremy. Strategic Persuasion: Arms Limitation Through Dialogue. New York: Columbia University Press, 1967.

Tatu, Michael. Power in the Kremlin. New York: Viking Press, 1968.

Thomas, John R. "The Role of Missile Defense Strategy and Foreign Policy." In The Military-Technical Revolution: Its Impact on Strategy and Foreign Policy, edited by John Erickson, pp. 187-218. New York: Praeger, 1966.

_____. Soviet Foreign Policy and Conflict within Political and Military Leadership. RAC-P-61. McLean, Va.: Research Analysis Corporation, 1970.

Thompson, Victor. Modern Organization. New York: Knopf, 1961.

Thorin, Duane. The Pugwash Movement and U.S. Arms Policy. New York: Monte Cristo Press, 1965.

Tokaty-Tokaev, G. A. "Foundations of Soviet Cosmonautics." Spaceflight (October 1968): 335-46.

_____. "Soviet Space Technology." Spaceflight (February 1963): 58-64.

Triska, Jan, ed. Soviet Communism: Programs and Rules. San Francisco: Chandler, 1962.

_____, and David D. Finley. Soviet Foreign Policy. New York: Macmillan Co., 1968.

Truman, David B. The Governmental Process: Political Interests and Public Opinion. New York: Knopf, 1951.

Tucker, Robert C. The Soviet Political Mind. New York: Praeger, 1963.

Ulsamer, Edgar. "Backfire: Special Support on the New Soviet Strategic Bomber." Air Force Magazine (October 1971): 35.

_____. "Soviet Objective: Technological Supremacy." Air Force Magazine (June 1974): 22-25.

Van Doorn, Jacques, ed. Armed Forces and Society: Sociological Essays. Hague: Mouton, 1968.

_____. Military Profession and Military Regimes: Commitments and Conflicts. Hague: Mouton, 1969.

Vladimirov, Leonid. "Glavit, How the Soviet Censor Works." Index 1, no. 3/4 (Autumn/Winter 1972): 31-43.

Weinland, Robert. "The Changing Mission Structure of the Soviet Navy." In Soviet Naval Developments: Context and Capability, edited by Michael MccGwire, pp. 260-74. New York: Praeger, 1973.

White, Dmitri Fedotoff. The Growth of the Red Army. Princeton, N.J.: Princeton University Press, 1944.

_____. "Soviet Philosophy of War." Political Science Quarterly 3 (September 1936): 340-53.

Wildavsky, Aaron. The Politics of the Budgeting Process. Boston: Little, Brown, 1964.

Wolfe, Thomas W. "Are the Generals Taking Over?" Problems of Communism (July-August-September-October 1969): 106-10.

_____. Communist Outlook on War, P-3640. Santa Monica, Calif.: RAND Corporation, 1967.

_____. "The Military." In Prospects for Soviet Society, edited by Allan Kassoff, pp. 112-42. New York: Praeger, 1968.

_____. Policy-Making in the Soviet Union: A Statement with Supplemental Comments, P-4131. Santa Monica, Calif. RAND Corporation, June 1969.

_____. Soviet Interests in SALT: Political, Economic, Bureaucratic and Strategic Contributions and Impediments to Arms Control, P-4702. Santa Monica, Calif.: RAND Corporation, September 1971.

_____. The Soviet Military Scene: Institutional and Defense Policy Considerations, RM-4913-PR. Santa Monica, Calif.: RAND Corporation, 1966.

_____. Soviet Naval Interaction with the United States and Its Influence on Soviet Naval Development, P-4913. Santa Monica, Calif.: RAND Corporation, October 1972.

_____. Soviet Power and Europe, 1945-1970. Baltimore: Johns Hopkins University Press, 1970.

_____. Soviet Strategy at the Crossroads. Cambridge: Harvard University Press, 1964.

_____. Worldwide Soviet Military Strategy and Policy, P-5008. Santa Monica, Calif.: RAND Corporation, April 1973.

Yarmolinsky, Adam. The Military Establishment: Its Impact on American Society. New York: Harper and Row, 1971.

Zaleski, E., et al. Science Policy in the USSR. Paris: Organization for Economic Cooperation and Development, 1969.

Zheltov, A. "The Lenin Military-Political Academy." Soviet Military Review no. 3 (March 1967): 29-32.

Zhukov, G. K. The Memoirs of Marshal Zhukov. Translated by Novosti. New York: Delacorte Press, 1971.

Zimmerman, William. Soviet Perspectives on International Relations, 1956-1967. Princeton, N.J.: Princeton University Press, 1969.

Zorza, Victor. "The Marshals Get the Message." Manchester Guardian Weekly, November 7, 1970.

_____. "Military Critics of Khrushchev." Manchester Guardian, October 4, 1963.

BOOKS--RUSSIAN LANGUAGE

Aboltin, V. Ya. et al. Sovremennye problemy razoruzheniia [Contemporary problems of disarmament]. Moscow: Mysl', 1970.

Cherenko, K. Ye., and N. I. Savinkin, eds. KPSS o Vooruzhennykh Silakh Sovetskogo Soiuza [CPSU on the armed forces of the Soviet Union]. Moscow: Voenizdat, 1969.

Davydov, Yu. P, V. V. Zhurkin, and V. S. Rudnev. Doktrina Niksona [The Nixon doctrine]. Moscow: "Nauka," 1972.

Emel'ianov, V. T., ed. Organizatsiia i vooruzhenie armii i flotov kapitalisticheskikh gosndarstv [Organization and armaments of the armies and fleets of the capitalist states]. Moscow: Voenizdat, 1965.

Glagolev, I. S., ed. SSSR, SShA i razoruzhenie [USSR, USA and disarmament]. Moscow: "Nauka," 1967.

Grechko, A. A. Na strazhe mira i stroitel'stvo Kommunizma [On guard for peace and communism]. Moscow: Voenizdat, 1971.

_____, editor-in-chief. Sovetskaia voennaia entsiklopediia [Soviet military encyclopedia] vols. 1 and 2. Moscow: Voenizdat, 1976.

Khmel', A. E., ed. Partiino-politicheskiia rabota v Sovetskikh Vooruzhennykh Silakh [Party-political work in the Soviet armed forces]. Moscow: Voenizdat, 1968.

Kulish, V. M., N. Solodovnik, and D. Proektor. Voennaia sila i mezhdunarodnye otnoshenie [Military force and international relations]. Moscow: "Mezhdunarodnye Otnoshenie," 1972.

Latukhin, A. N. Sovremennaia artilleriia [Modern artillery]. Moscow: Voenizdat, 1970.

Listvinov, Yu. N. Pervyy udar [First strike]. Moscow: "Mezhdunarodnie Otnoshenie," 1971.

Malinovskiy, R. Ya. Bditel'no stoiat' na strazhe mira [Vigilantly stand guard over the peace]. Moscow: Voenizdat, 1962.

Milovidov, A. S., and V. G. Kozlov, eds. Filosofskoye nislediye V. I. Lenina i problemy sovremmennoy voyny [The philosophical heritage of V. I. Lenin and the problems of modern war]. Moscow: Voenizdat, 1972.

Mil'shtein, M., and A. K. Slobodenko. O voennoi doktrine SShA [On the military doctrine of the USA]. Moscow: "Znanie," 1963.

Novikov, Yu. Z., and F. D. Sverdlov. Manevr v obshchevoyskovom boyu [Maneuver in combined-arms combat]. Moscow: Voenizdat, 1967.

Petrov, Yu. P. Partiinoe stroitel'stvo v Sovetskoi Armii i Flote, 1918-1961 [Party construction in the Soviet army and navy, 1918-1961]. Moscow: Voenizdat, 1964.

_____. Stroitel'stvo politorganov partiinykh i Komsomol'skikh organizatsia armii i flota, 1918-1968 [The construction of the political organs, party and Komsomol organizations of the army and navy, 1918-1968]. Moscow: Voenizdat, 1968.

Radzievskiy, A. I., ed. Slovar' osnovnykh voennykh terminov [Dictionary of basic military terms]. Moscow: Voenizdat, 1965.

Reznichenko, V. G. Taktika [Tactics]. Moscow: Voenizdat, 1967.

Shtemenko, S. M. General'nyi shtab v gody voiny [The General Staff during the war years]. Moscow: Voenizdat, 1968.

_____. Generalnyi shtab v gody voiny, vol. 2 [The General Staff during the war years]. Moscow: Voenizdat, 1973.

Sidorenko, A. A. Nastuplenie [The offensive]. Moscow: Voenizdat, 1970.

Skugarev, V. D., and L. V. Kudin. Setovoye planirovaniia na flote [Critical path planning method in the navy]. Moscow: Voenizdat, 1973.

Sokolov, P. V., ed. Voenno-ekonomicheskie voprosy v kurse politekonomii [Military-economic problems in a political economy course]. Moscow: Voenizdat, 1968.

Sokolovskiy, V. D., ed. Voennaia strategiia [Military strategy]. Moscow: Voenizdat, 1962; 2d ed., 1963; 3rd ed., 1968.

Solnyshkov, Yu. S.. Optimizatsiia vybora vooruzhenii [Optimization of the selection of armaments]. Moscow: Voenizdat, 1968.

Strokov, A. A. Istoriia voennogo iskusstva [The history of military art]. Moscow: Voenizdat, 1966.

Sushko, N. Ya., and T. R. Kondratkov, eds., Metodologicheskie problemy voennoi teorii i praktiki [Methodological problems of military theory and practice]. Moscow: Voenizdat, 1966.

Trofimenko, G. A. SShA: voina, politika, ideologiia [USA: war, politics and ideology]. Moscow: Mysl', 1975.

Tyushkevich, S. A., N. Ya. Sushko, Ya. S. Dziuba. Markisizm-Leninizm o voine i armii [Marxism-Leninism on war and the army]. 5th ed. Moscow: Voenizdat, 1968.

Voronov, N. N. Na sluzhbe voennoi [In wartime service]. Moscow: Voenizdat, 1963.

Yakovlev, Aledsander S. Tsel' zhizni: zapiski aviakonstruktora [The goal of life: notes of an aviation designer]. 2d ed. Moscow: Izdat'elstvo Politicheskoi Literatury, 1968.

Zakharov, M. V., chairman of the editorial board. 50 let Vooruzhennykh Sil SSSR [50 years of the armed forces of the USSR]. Moscow: Voenizdat, 1968.

Zorin, V. A., ed. Borba Sovetskogo Soiuza za razoruzhenie [The struggle of the Soviet Union for disarmament]. Moscow: Institute of International Relations, 1961.

The following periodicals and newspapers were regularly consulted for information on Soviet military affairs for the years indicated:

Daily Newspapers--English Language

New York Times, 1967-74

Washington Post, 1967-74

Daily Newspapers--Russian Language

Izvestiia, 1960-74

Krasnaia Zvezda, 1960-74

Pravda, 1960-74

Periodicals--Russian Language

Political/Historical

Kommunist [Communist] 1960-74

Mezhdunarodny Zhizn' [International affairs] 1960-74

Mirovaia Ekonomika i Mezhdunarodnye Otnosheniye [World economics and international relations] 1967-74

SShA: Ekonomika, Politika, Ideologiia [USA: economics, politics, and ideology] 1969-74

Voprosy Istorii [Questions of history] 1960-74

Voprosy Istorii KPSS [Questions of history of the CPSU] 1960-74

Military

Aviatsiia i Kosmonavtika [Aviation and cosmonautics] 1960-74

Kommunist Vooruzhennykh Sil [Communist of the armed forces] 1960-74

Morskoi Sbornik [Naval collection] 1960-74

Tekhnika i Vooruzheniye [Technology and armaments] 1960-74

Tyl i Snabzheniye Sovetskikh Vooruzhennykh Sil [Rear services and supply of the Soviet armed forces] 1960-74

Vestnik Protivovozdushnoy Oborony [Air defense herald] 1960-74

Voenno-Istoricheskii Zhurnal [Military historical journal] 1960-74

Voennyi Vestnik [Military herald] 1960-74

INTERVIEWS

Allison, Royal B. Major general, USAF, Joint Chiefs of Staff representative at SALT I, U.S. Air Force Academy, Colo. Interview, October 2, 1970.

Bialer, Seweryn. Professor of politics, Columbia University, New York, N.Y. Interview, April 13, 1970.

Doty, Paul. Professor of chemistry, Harvard University, Princeton, N.J. Interview, May 3, 1970.

Fitzgerald, Charles G. Colonel, former U.S. Army attache in the USSR. Washington, D.C. Interview, February 8, 1970.

Garthoff, Raymond L. Department of State, Washington, D.C. Interviews, September 16, 1969 and February 16, 1973.

Kaliadin, Alexander. Staff member of the Institute of World Economies and International Affairs, Princeton, N.J. Interview, February 9, 1970.

Kulish, V. M. Colonel (ret.), Soviet Army, chief of the Military Affairs Section of the Institute of World Economics and International Relations (IMEMO), Princeton, N.J. Interviews, March 24, 1970 and May 4, 1970.

Marder, Murrey. Washington Post correspondent, Washington, D.C. Interview, March 10, 1975.

Medvedev, Roy. Dissident Soviet historian, Moscow, USSR. Interview, December 4, 1976.

Scott, Harriet Fast. Student of Soviet military affairs, McLean, Va. Interview, February 8, 1973.

Shadrin, Nicholas. Former Soviet naval officer, Washington, D.C. Interview, March 24, 1975.

Shulman, Marshall D. Professor of political science, Columbia University, Halifax, Nova Scotia. Interview, October 15, 1973.

Shvedkov, Yuri A. Institute for the Study of the United States in Moscow, Princeton, N.J. Interview, January 14, 1970.

Simes, Dmitri. Former staff member of the Institute of World Economics and International Relatons in Moscow, Washington, D.C. Interview, March 25, 1975.

Szulc, Tad. Independent news reporter, U.S. Air Force Academy, Colo. Interview, April 18, 1971.

Weiler, Larry. Arms Control and Disarmament Agency, Washington, D.C. Interview, February 16, 1970.

Wolfe, Thomas W. Senior RAND analyst on Soviet military affairs, Washington, D.C. Interview, February 8, 1973.

INDEX

ABOUT THE AUTHOR

EDWARD L. WARNER, III is Assistant Air Attache at the United States Embassy in Moscow. A career Air Force officer, he currently holds the rank of Major. Previously he has been an Assistant Professor at the U.S. Air Force Academy, a Visiting Fellow at the Center of International Studies at Princeton, and has graduated from the Armed Forces Staff College and the Defense Language Institute. He is coeditor of Comparative Defense Policy (Johns Hopkins Press, 1973). Major Warner holds a B.S. from the U.S. Naval Academy, and an M.A. and a Ph.D. from Princeton University.